THE POLITICS OF LANGUAGE

The Politics of Language

David Beaver

Jason Stanley

PRINCETON UNIVERSITY PRESS

PRINCETON & OXFORD

Published by Princeton University Press
41 William Street, Princeton, New Jersey 08540
99 Banbury Road, Oxford OX2 6JX

press.princeton.edu

All Rights Reserved

Library of Congress Cataloging-in-Publication Data

Names: Beaver, David I., 1966– author. | Stanley, Jason, author.
Title: The politics of language / David Beaver, Jason Stanley.
Description: Princeton, New Jersey : Princeton University Press, 2023. |
     Includes bibliographical references and index.
Identifiers: LCCN 2022060326 (print) | LCCN 2022060327 (ebook) |
     ISBN 9780691181981 (hardcover ; acid-free paper) | ISBN 9780691242743 (ebook)
Subjects: LCSH: Propaganda. | Language and languages—Political aspects.
Classification: LCC P301.5.P73 B43 2023 (print) | LCC P301.5.P73 (ebook)|
     DDC 303.3/75—dc23/eng/20230320
LC record available at https://lccn.loc.gov/2022060326
LC ebook record available at https://lccn.loc.gov/2022060327

British Library Cataloging-in-Publication Data is available

Editorial: Rob Tempio and Chloe Coy
Production Editorial: Kathleen Cioffi
Jacket Design: Hunter Finch
Production: Erin Suydam
Publicity: William Pagdatoon
Copyeditor: Hank Southgate

This book has been composed in Miller

Printed on acid-free paper. ∞

Printed in the United States of America

10 9 8 7 6 5 4 3 2 1

CONTENTS

ACKNOWLEDGMENTS

WE BEGAN THIS BOOK with conversations in the summer of 2015. Jason had just published *How Propaganda Works*. Drawing on the standard tools and resources of formal semantics, pragmatics, and the philosophy of language, it attempted to analyze propagandistic speech. This project ran into the limitations of these concepts for dealing with the data and processes of political communication. We realized that the issue was general. Slurs, for example, posed similar problems for these orthodox tools and resources. We were particularly disturbed that work on propaganda and work on slurs seemed to use, tacitly or explicitly, an underlying assumption that there could be such a thing as neutral, information-bearing speech.

During the years Jason was developing *How Propaganda Works*, David was in part riding the empirical waves that had driven much of the field of linguistic semantics into increasing use of corpus and experimental methods. But he was also moonlighting from semantics, in projects with scholars from psychology, sociology, communication studies, and computational linguistics. It was clear that these projects centrally involved linguistic meaning, and that both linguistic methodology and linguistic theory were needed. Yet it was both striking and worrying that in these collaborations there was no clear way in which the theoretical constructs and technical innovations of formal semantics could be productively applied. Indeed, some of the computational and experimental results could be interpreted as suggesting that existing formal semantic concepts were not up to the job at all. We both recognized that a new framework was needed, one that used these problematic kinds of speech as core evidence. Almost a decade later, we are finally ready to present it.

We will not even attempt to thank individually the many people who offered us new horizons in the prehistoric phase of the book, before 2015. More generally, we owe more people thanks for this project than we can possibly list exhaustively. However, there are many people who not only helped us see what the project might consist in, but who helped more tangibly with practical support, wise advice, and in some cases hours or days of patient work. We only have space for the lightest dusting of thanks in these acknowledgments, but we hope we can briefly make more apparent the invisible fingerprints on the pages of this book of some of these many friends and colleagues.

Rob Tempio and the team at PUP have been amazing. And patient. Of all those on the PUP team, we must further single out Hank Southgate. If you are considering writing a book, start praying now that Hank will copyedit it for you. We must also thank here David's daughter Anna Beaver, who did superb work on the book, especially the bibliography. She shares some credit with

Hank for turning our efforts into a professional-quality manuscript. We also thank Parris Sammut for his great work on the index.

A number of people helped us with various incarnations of the manuscript. Susan Shol worked on the manuscript as an undergraduate research assistant at UT, when we were about six months from finishing it. That was in 2017. Serena Cho worked on the manuscript as an undergraduate research assistant at Yale, when we were about six months from finishing it. That was in 2020. The fact that our estimates of when the book would be finished were six years and three years off, respectively, is entirely our own fault. Both Susan and Serena provided exceptionally mature and helpful comments on the draft as well as wonderful technical and research assistance. We remain very grateful, and in awe of both of them. Their help was just what should have been needed to get the manuscript into final shape, and yet somehow this was not to be. The book metamorphosed every two years or so, going through various stages of molting and recombination. Whether the result is a butterfly or a beetle, we leave it to the reader to decide.

Susanna Siegel and Lynne Tirrell were Princeton University Press's two referees. Susanna's nineteen-page, single-spaced report created a pivotal moment in our project. Susanna led us, at a rather late stage, to the book's final major metamorphosis, entirely revamping the book's structure. Whatever virtues the final product has, her report can take a large share of the credit. Lynne's report, meanwhile, was the epitome of constructive criticism. Here and in many conversations over the years, she has always been encouraging, and a constant source of inspiration. Our intellectual debt to Lynne, and to her trailblazing work on genocidal and toxic language, will be clear at various points in the book.

When we began this book, Jessica Keiser was writing her dissertation on nonideal semantics at Yale. One of us, Jason, was on her committee. Discussion with her about the ideal/nonideal distinction in the theory of meaning impacted our thinking throughout this project. Anne Quaranto, working on her PhD with David in the UT graduate philosophy program, is at some level a counterpart of Jessica's, and Anne's dissertation work developing a practice-based account of dog whistles and slurs has been an important inspiration for us. But in addition, Anne read many drafts of this book, giving us meticulous and richly insightful feedback each time. Both this regular feedback, as well as intense discussion with her about the issues central to our project, have changed the project immeasurably, and always for the better.

A number of others read and kindly provided crucial feedback on the manuscript. We are especially grateful to Eyal Sagi for passing a psychologist's eye over the first half of the manuscript, and for providing crucial commentary, including references to relevant literatures of which we were unaware. Paul Kiparsky also provided extensive and helpful comments on a near-final version of the complete manuscript, and we further benefited from comments and suggestions on the manuscript from Jack Balkin, Johan van Benthem, Ashwini Deo, Richard Meier, and Tim Williamson.

Hans Kamp does not have a doppelgänger anywhere in the world, and neither does Jack Balkin. But in some ways, Jack has been to Jason at Yale what Hans has been to David at UT. They have cotaught multiple seminars with one or the other of us, and their input and influence have been profound, far beyond their sage commentary on the manuscript itself. We are eternally grateful to both of them.

Other than Jack Balkin, we owe particular thanks at Yale to Robin Dembroff, Roderick Ferguson, Daniel Greco, Elizabeth Hinton, Tracey Meares, Jennifer Richeson, Marci Shore, and Timothy Snyder; all of them have been both important sounding boards for our ideas, and sources of support. And in addition to those already mentioned at UT, we must single out Jamie Pennebaker for many conversations that forced David to look at communication and social meaning, and the relation of both to psychology, in new ways.

Let us here mention three others who have significantly influenced our project. First, Sally Haslanger was, early on, a consistent source of pressure to pivot from the individualist framework of much of classical semantics to one that recognized the importance of social practice. Second, Federico Finchelstein has been an invaluable interlocutor and coauthor for Jason, and has helped us think through key aspects of the workings of fascist language. Third, Elisabeth Camp deserves special mention for the large impact she has had on us, both through her important work on perspective, and from our many conversations with her. She also contributed to a symposium on a draft of the book at the American Philosophical Association in 2022, along with Luvell Anderson and Justin Khoo. All of their contributions helped the final product.

Social and political philosophy of language has exploded in the past few years. We are deeply grateful to the working members of this and abutting intellectual communities in feminist philosophy and political philosophy for their input in multiple forums, formal and informal. More people from these scholarly communities have influenced the work than we can list here, but let us add to those already mentioned some more for whom we are particularly aware of the debt we owe: Elizabeth Anderson, Nikki Ernst, Lori Gruen, Rae Langton, Megan Hyska, Quill Kukla, Samia Hesni, Rae Langton, Mary Kate McGowan, Mihaela Popa-Wyatt, Jennifer Saul, David Livingstone Smith, Eric Swanson, and Olufemi Taiwo.

Parts of three chapters from this volume have appeared in print previously. An antecedent of chapter 9 appeared in a special issue of the *Graduate Philosophy Journal* on Ordinary Language Philosophy, edited and with an introduction by Alice Crary and Joel de Lara. (It appears under the title "Toward a Non-ideal Philosophy of Language," *Graduate Philosophy Journal* 39, no. 2 [2018]: 503–47.) An earlier version of chapter 7, "Neutrality," appeared in *Philosophical Topics* 49, no. 1 (2021): 165–85, in a special issue on "Social Visibility" edited by Alice Crary and Matthew Congdon, with an excellent and challenging commentary by Alice Crary. We are grateful to both of them for pulling the special issue together, and to Matthew for his editorial work on our paper. We are especially grateful to Alice. Her editorship of the two special issues makes clear her important role in our project, and we took her critiques and her suggestions to heart as we worked on the book in the following years. Finally, an extract of chapter 10 appeared as "Raising Hell: On the Hyperprojectivity of Slurs" in the *Proceedings of the 23rd Amsterdam Colloquium*. We thank the editors, Marco Degano, Tom Roberts, Giorgio Sbardolini, and Marieke Schouwstra, and the audience in Amsterdam for comments. But here we note that we cannot reasonably list over a hundred other presentations we have given on aspects of the book over a period of more than seven years, in addition to teaching multiple courses that lent heavily on our ongoing work. So let us just end with two words to all of those audiences: Thank you!

Introduction

The essential business of language is to assert or deny facts.

—BERTRAND RUSSELL[1]

The point of a discourse—at least one central kind of discourse—is the exchange of information.

—ROBERT STALNAKER[2]

Words can be like tiny doses of arsenic: they are swallowed unnoticed, appear to have no effect, and then after a little time the toxic reaction sets in after all.

—VICTOR KLEMPERER[3]

IN BOOK 3 of Thucydides's *The Peloponnesian War*, the Athenian Cleon represents Mytilene's revolt against Athens in the most extreme possible terms, claiming, "Mytilene has done us a greater wrong than any other single city."[4] Cleon claims that were the tables turned, Mytilene would slaughter *every Athenian citizen*—in other words, that the Mytileneans would carry out the very same action toward the Athenians that Cleon urges Athens carry out against Mytilene. Cleon's speech mobilizes the Athenian citizens to genocidal action against Mytilene by employing the accusation that Mytilene is a genocidal threat to Athens. Cleon's speech is political propaganda. It stokes irrational fear and desire for revenge, while simultaneously presenting itself as a reasonable contribution to discourse. It justifies murdering the entire adult population of Mytilene not because of what they did, but because of an imaginary situation that Cleon gives no reason to think would be realized. Cleon uses the savagery he suggests the Mytileneans would do if the tables were turned to justify the exact same course of action against the Mytileneans. Cleon's speech is one of antiquity's classical examples of demagoguery.

In Cleon's speech, he does not represent his own city, Athens, as greater or more exceptional in its value system and history than its enemies. However,

---

1. The quote is from Russell's introduction to Wittgenstein's *Tractatus Logico-Philosophicus*, x.

2. Stalnaker, "On the Representation of Context," 5.

3. Klemperer, *The Language of the Third Reich*, 15–16.

4. Thucydides, *The Peloponnesian War*, 147.

his speech is decidedly also not neutral, as he represents Athens's interests as vastly more important—with a hypothetical future threat to its citizens judged far more serious than the actual threat to the lives of innocent Mytileneans. The speech completely takes the side of Athens while masquerading as some kind of aperspectival reason. Cleon's speech centers the interests of Athens completely. The Mytileneans are visible only as genocidal threats.

Cleon's speech is layered with emotion, values, perspective, and interests. It seeks to mobilize its audience toward action. One way to mobilize an audience is by providing information about the world. This book centers other ways in which language impacts audiences: by emotion, values, perspectives, interests, identity, and shared practices. We build a model of speech that incorporates these aspects as central from the very beginning.

Harmful Speech

One way in which speech impacts a group of people is by harming them. One kind of harmful speech, omnipresent in popular and academic discussions, is *slurs*—terms that target a group with an ideology that derogates its members. But the category of harmful speech is vastly broader than slurs. For example, Victor Klemperer describes a form of the linguistic process he calls "objectification" as follows:

> Why does a palpable and undeniable brutality come to light when a female warder in Belsen concentration camp explains to the war crimes trial that on such and such a day she dealt with sixteen *"Stück"* Gefangenen [prisoner pieces]? . . . *Stück* . . . involves objectification. It is the same objectification expressed by the official term "the utilization of carcasses [*Kadaververwertung*]," especially when widened to refer to human corpses: fertilizer is made out of the dead of the concentration camps.[5]

Linguistic objectification is a characteristic feature of various kinds of harmful speech. In chapter 10, we will return in detail to the topic of harmful speech and give our accounts of slurs, genocidal speech, and bureaucratic speech. To do that, we'll first need to give an account of presupposition, in part II, for we will need to be able to explain, for example, how speaking of prisoners as "pieces" presupposes that they are less than fully human.

To understand Klemperer's second example, we must also understand the connections between practices and "official terms." These are connections that must be understood in terms of how speech attunes people to practices, an analysis of which is a central aim of part I of this book. Here is another illustration, this time from the United States, of how speech attunes people

5. Klemperer, *The Language of the Third Reich*, 154.

to practices. John DiIulio Jr.'s 1996 magazine article "My Black Crime Problem, and Ours" begins by acknowledging that "violent crime is down in New York and many other cities."[6] DiIulio proceeds to predict "270,000 more young predators on the streets . . . [in] the next two decades." He adds, "As many as half of these juvenile super-predators could be young black males." DiIulio's prediction was far off; violent crime continued to plummet.[7] But the introduction of the term "super-predator" into criminal-justice discourse led (in difficult to quantify yet hard to dispute ways) to the adoption of ever-harsher laws concerning juvenile offenders.

Describing juvenile offenders as "super-predators" suggests that the proper practices toward juvenile offenders are the ones that are reasonable to take against enormous threats to humankind: death, or complete permanent isolation. Use of the term "super-predator" to describe juvenile offenders rationalizes treating them with practices that would only be reasonable to use against deadly enemies.

In the 1990s in the United States, criminal-justice policy had become a proving ground for politicians to demonstrate their putative toughness. Debate was dominated by an ethos that frowned on expressions of empathy for perpetrators. Dehumanizing vocabulary targeting those caught up in the criminal-justice system was commonplace, and many of the words were racially coded.[8] Rehabilitation is hard to envisage for those described as "thugs," "super-predators," or "gangsters." During this period where these terms were part of the political discourse, criminal-justice practices became considerably harsher, and sentences longer.[9]

Although the precise mechanisms continue to be a matter of debate, it is widely agreed that the culture surrounding crime policy had an extreme and rapid effect on criminal-justice practices. The incarceration rate in the United States hovered around the norm for liberal democracies of 100 per 100,000 for many decades until the late 1970s.[10] Then it started to rise. The Bureau of Justice Statistics' current rate of 810 for every 100,000 adults (18 years and older)

6. DiIulio, "My Black Crime Problem, and Ours," 14.

7. "Reported Violent Crime Rate in the United States from 1990 to 2017," Statista: The Statistics Portal, October 10, 2022, accessed March 1, 2023, https://www.statista.com /statistics/191219/reported-violent-crime-rate-in-the-usa-since-1990/.

8. For a contemporary report on this phenomenon, see Templeton, "Superscapegoating," 13–14.

9. In 1994, Bill Clinton signed the Violent Crime Control and Law Enforcement Act. This included the "Federal Death Penalty Act of 1994," which created sixty new death-penalty offenses under forty-one federal statutes (Title VI, §§60001–26); the elimination of higher education for inmates (§20411); registration of sex offenders (Title XVII, Subtitle A, §170101); and making gang membership a crime (Title XV, §§150001–9). See: U.S. Congress, *Violent Crime Control and Law Enforcement Act*.

10. Cahalan and Parsons, *Historical Corrections Statistics*, 30.

in prison is by far the highest in the world.[11] The United States has also developed a culture of policing marked by a level of fear and lack of empathy that is without parallel in liberal democracies (a 2015 headline of an article in the *Guardian* states, "By the Numbers: U.S. Police Kill More in Days Than Other Countries Do in Years"[12]). However, the unprecedented two-decade decrease in crime from 1991 until the early 2010s was not strictly due to the intensely punitive criminal-justice path that the United States chose to take in the 1990s. Canada experienced a similarly unprecedented drop in crime during this same time period, without following the United States' path into mass incarceration.[13]

How does one investigate the way in which violent language about a targeted group affects attitudes? As we will argue in part III, focusing on a case like this brings out the limitations of a model of conventional meaning that just theorizes in terms of a connection between words and things. To explain harmful speech, one must recognize conventional connections between words and *practices*, as well as words and *emotions*.

Hustle

The examples of harmful speech we discussed in the last section involved expressions that attune their audiences to harmful practices in ways that are *overt*. Calling young Black American men "super-predators," or, to use an example we will discuss later, calling Rwandan Tutsi "cockroaches" or "snakes," directly attunes audiences to violent practices toward these populations. These examples highlight the need for a theory of meaning that connects speech not just with information, but with practices. But speech does not just impact an audience directly. It can and often does impact audiences *indirectly*.

Why would someone choose to impact an audience indirectly with their words, rather than overtly attempting to attune them in the desired manner? The reason is because the speaker might not wish to be held responsible for their words. The speaker may want to convey something in a way that allows for

11. John Gramlich, "America's Incarceration Rate Falls to Lowest Level since 1995," Pew Research Center, August 16, 2021, accessed March 1, 2023, https://www.pewresearch .org/fact-tank/2021/08/16/americas-incarceration-rate-lowest-since-1995/. Although the title of the article appears to contradict this claim, the article confirms the United States' high incarceration rates.

12. Jamiles Lartey, "By the Numbers: U.S. Police Kill More in Days Than Other Countries Do in Years," *Guardian*, June 9, 2015, accessed March 1, 2023, https://www .theguardian.com/us-news/2015/jun/09/the-counted-police-killings-us-vs-other -countries.

13. Laura Glowacki, "9 Reasons Canada's Crime Rate Is Falling," Canadian Broadcasting Corporation, July 23, 2016, accessed March 1, 2023, https://www.cbc.ca/news/canada /manitoba/9-reasons-crime-rate-1.3692193.

plausible deniability that they intended to convey it. Plausible deniability is a symptom of what we call *hustle—speech that functions nontransparently.* When speech is not transparent, a speaker has latitude to deny that they intended the nontransparent features.

Hustle is a large and diverse category, including insinuation (itself a broad category). One of the goals of the book is to show just how large it is. While chapter 8 will describe hustle in more detail, this type of speech is our focus throughout the book. To illustrate it with an example, we're going to focus in this section on one quite specific mechanism of hustle, the mechanism of the *dog whistle.*

Dog whistling involves employing speech that appears on the surface to be transparent, but, when married to a hearer's background frame and value systems, communicates a message not obvious to those without that background (i.e., it functions nontransparently). Dog whistling is a mechanism specifically designed to allow plausible deniability. Though it is far from the only such method, dog whistling is useful to focus on in this introduction as it is most obviously a kind of hustle with a linguistic trigger.

In 1981, Lee Atwater, later to lead George H. W. Bush's 1988 presidential campaign (featuring the notorious Willie Horton ad, funded allegedly by an independent PAC), had an anonymous interview with a journalist that remains one of the clearest expressions of the strategic value of code words to signal allegiance to ideologies that have been explicitly repudiated. In it, he famously said (although we've censored the original for obvious reasons),

> You start out in 1954 by saying, [N-word, N-word, N-word]. By 1968 you can't say [N-word]—that hurts you, backfires. So, you say stuff like, uh, forced busing, states' rights, and all that stuff, and you're getting so abstract. Now, you're talking about cutting taxes, and all these things you're talking about are totally economic things and a byproduct of them is, blacks get hurt worse than whites. . . . "We want to cut this," is much more abstract than even the busing thing, uh, and a hell of a lot more abstract than [N-word, N-word].[14]

Subsequent research by the Princeton political science professors Martin Gilens and Tali Mendelberg has confirmed the success of the strategy of linking certain discourse to negative racial stereotypes. Their research shows that expressions like "welfare," "the poor," "food stamps," and "homeless" all contribute to priming the thought that Black Americans are lazy.[15] Gilens finds that "the belief that blacks are lazy is the strongest predictor of the perception that

14. Rick Perlstein, "Exclusive: Lee Atwater's Infamous 1981 Interview on the Southern Strategy," *The Nation*, November 13, 2012, accessed March 1, 2023, https://www.thenation.com/article/archive/exclusive-lee-atwaters-infamous-1981-interview-southern-strategy/.

15. See Gilens, *Why Americans Hate Welfare*; and Mendelberg, *The Race Card*, 191–208.

welfare recipients are undeserving."[16] There is a large amount of additional evidence that the word "welfare" has been connected with a flawed ideology of race, in addition to the studies Gilens himself has carried out. Gilens reports similar results from the "welfare mother" experiment from the National Race and Politics Study of 1991:

> Respondents are asked their impressions of a welfare recipient described as either a black or white woman in her early thirties, who has a ten-year-old child and has been on welfare for the past year. Respondents are first asked how likely it is that the woman described will try hard to find a job, and second, how likely it is that she will have more children in order to get a bigger welfare check.[17]

> The largest predictor of opposition to programs described as "welfare" was one's bias against black American mothers receiving various state benefits, where the study found that "nonblack respondents with the most negative views of black welfare recipients are 30 points higher in opposition to welfare than are those with the most positive views of black welfare mothers."[18]

But why, one might ask, are these facts *linguistic*? Perhaps we can explain the political effects of describing a term as "welfare" merely by talking about the social programs that are so described, together with false beliefs, including the ones associated with racist ideology. Why are properties of *language* at issue here?

What fuels Americans' obsession with programs called "welfare"? Is it background commitments to individual responsibility? Is it Americans' supposedly fierce opposition to "big government," in the form of government programs? Is it background racist beliefs and false empirical beliefs about poverty in the United States? Can we explain the political force of describing a program as "welfare" just by discussing the social programs themselves, without discussing the meaning and use of words? Or do we need some explanation that invokes properties of the word "welfare" itself?

Americans are fond of, and committed to, what are by far the United States' largest social welfare programs: Medicare and Social Security.[19] But perhaps the powerful and widespread support for these programs is due to the facts that they "benefit large numbers of Americans of all social classes"[20] and that American opposition to programs described as "welfare" has something

16. Gilens, *Why Americans Hate Welfare*, 95.

17. Gilens, *Why Americans Hate Welfare*, 97–98.

18. Gilens, *Why Americans Hate Welfare*, 99.

19. Gilens, *Why Americans Hate Welfare*, 30.

20. Gilens, *Why Americans Hate Welfare*, 27.

to do with attitudes toward poverty, specifically? Here, too, the explanation would be nonlinguistic.

In surveys from the 1990s that measure public support for government responsibilities, those that do not use the term "welfare," or other terms that evoke paradigmatic programs that Americans think of as instances of welfare, we do not find sentiment against a large government role in providing jobs, housing, and other forms of assistance to needy Americans; in fact, as Martin Gilens writes, quite the opposite is true:

> When asked about spending for the poor, the public again expresses a desire for more, not less, government activity. Over 70 percent of Americans say we are spending too little on "fighting poverty," while a similar number think spending for the homeless needs to be increased. Smaller numbers—but still majorities—think we are spending too little on "poor people," on "assistance to the poor," and on "child care for poor children." And as was true for education, health care, child care, and the elderly, very few Americans believe spending for the poor should be reduced from current levels.[21]

In stark contrast, Gilens observes that in those surveys, between 60 and 70 percent of Americans thought that the government was spending too much on programs described as "welfare," or on programs described as benefiting "people on welfare." It is impossible to describe political communication in the United States—dating back to the 1970s, when Ronald Reagan's campaign introduced the expression "welfare queen" into political discourse[22]—without talking about the connection between such value systems and the linguistic properties of words like "welfare." In a 2018 article, Rachel Wetts and Robb Willer integrate multiple studies providing strong evidence that the connection between White racial resentment toward Black Americans and negative reactions to programs described as "welfare" continues unabated.[23]

If it were a matter simply of Americans rejecting "big government programs," we would find them rejecting large government programs such as Medicare and Social Security, which are designed to help working-class Americans by providing health insurance and support during retirement. Indeed, when programs described as "welfare" are described in other terms, not involving this vocabulary, they receive far more support than when they are described as "welfare," even when they are the *same programs*.

21. Gilens, *Why Americans Hate Welfare*, 29.

22. Gene Demby, "The Truth behind the Lies of the Original 'Welfare Queen,'" NPR, December 20, 2013, accessed March 1, 2023, https://www.npr.org/sections/codeswitch /2013/12/20/255819681/the-truth-behind-the-lies-of-the-original-welfare-queen.

23. Wetts and Willer, "Privilege on the Precipice," 1–30.

A long-term goal of many in the US Republican Party is to cut funding to even very popular government programs that provide support to needy populations, including the elderly. In pursuit of this political goal, the fact that "welfare" and similar expressions such as "public assistance" give rise to negative reactions among certain audiences has proven too tempting to ignore. On March 13, 2017, then president Donald Trump issued an executive order authorizing Mick Mulvaney, the director of the Office of Management and Budget, to oversee a complete reorganization of federal agencies.[24] A draft of Mulvaney's proposals was floated, "Delivering Government Solutions in the 21st Century: Reform Plan and Reorganization Recommendations."[25] The second proposal listed is "Consolidate Non-Commodity Nutrition Assistance Programs into HHS [Health and Human Services], Rename HHS the Department of Health and Public Welfare, and Establish the Council on Public Assistance."[26] The proposal "moves a number of nutrition assistance programs . . . —most notably SNAP and the Special Supplemental Nutrition Program for Women, Infants, and Children (WIC)—to HHS and, acknowledging the addition of these programs to the Agency, renames HHS the Department of Health and Public Welfare."[27] The focus on renaming programs, and bringing more programs that Republicans hope to dismantle under the description "welfare," suggests a clear recognition that it is the label that does damage. This explains why the proposal recommends grouping Health and Human Services and food programs that many Americans use under the heading of "welfare," in an attempt to tie its racial stigma to these programs. "Public assistance" also carries with it racial stigma; appointing a Council on Public Assistance to monitor a vast sweep of government programs connects government spending to the negative racial sentiments that many Americans associate with the words "public assistance."[28] This makes sense as part of a larger mission to dismantle such programs.

The Republican Southern Strategy provides a model for political propaganda, to which we shall return, using the campaign against critical race theory that dominates US politics as of the writing of this book as a contemporary example.

Jennifer Saul's paper "Dogwhistles, Political Manipulation, and Philosophy of Language" is an investigation of the speech act of dog whistling.[29] On Saul's analysis, a dog whistle's message is a function of the ideology of the audience. The function of using a term like "welfare" to describe a program is to make that program less popular in the minds of those with a racist ideology

24. Executive Office, "Comprehensive Plan for Reorganizing the Executive Branch."
25. Executive Office, "Delivering Government Solutions in the 21st Century."
26. Executive Office, "Delivering Government Solutions in the 21st Century," 27–29.
27. Executive Office, "Delivering Government Solutions in the 21st Century," 27.
28. Executive Office, "Delivering Government Solutions in the 21st Century," 27–29.
29. Saul, "Dogwhistles," 360–83.

(such a description will be less pejorative to those who lack a racist ideology). Descriptions of programs as "welfare" or of persons as "on welfare" are paradigm examples of dog whistling in this sense. Describing a program as a "welfare program" gives rise to a strongly negative reaction to that program among one audience (those with at least some racial bias), and considerably less negative reactions among a different audience (composed of members with few indicators of racial bias). Racial bias is a value system; it is a way of valuing things—or, in this case, persons—on a metric of value at least partly determined by race. Describing something as "welfare" signals one very negative message about it to an audience who endorses a racist value system and lacks this negative force with audiences who do not share that value system.

Saul makes an important distinction between different categories of dog whistles. The category of *overt intentional dog whistles* is the most straightforward to define, but perhaps least politically central. Kimberly Witten defines an overt intentional dog whistle as

> a speech act designed, with intent, to allow two plausible interpretations, with one interpretation being a private, coded message targeted for a subset of the general audience, and concealed in such a way that this general audience is unaware of the existence of the second, coded interpretation.[30]

An overt intentional dog whistle is the clearest example—it is one that works, as the label suggests, overtly. Overt dog whistles are meant to be understood as such by their target audiences.

Saul introduces another category of dog whistles, *covert intentional dog whistles*.[31] Overt dog whistles are meant to be understood as such by their target audiences. Covert intentional dog whistles are not meant to be recognized as delivering hidden messages. An example Saul provides is "inner city": this expression is meant to be seen as a race-neutral expression, but hearing it triggers negative responses in those disposed to racial bias; something in the vocabulary triggers value systems that involve degrees of racism.[32] A covert intentional dog whistle triggers a response, perhaps a negative affective one, in those who share the relevant value system. But it does so surreptitiously. Many or most uses of "welfare" in the context of the United States are covert intentional dog whistles, in Saul's sense—those on whom they work most effectively do not realize that the dog whistle is having this effect.

In the 1990s, Bill Clinton appropriated the Republican racial rhetoric with his call to "end welfare as we know it,"[33] thereby attracting White voters who

30. Witten, "Dogwhistle Politics," 2, cited in Saul, "Dogwhistles," 362.
31. Saul, "Dogwhistles," 364–67.
32. Saul, "Dogwhistles," 367.
33. Carcasson, "Ending Welfare as We Know It," 655.

otherwise would have been loath to vote for a party connected to the attempt to lift Black American citizens to equality, which might be seen as helping "the undeserving." Demonizing poor Black Americans has been a successful electoral strategy for both the Democrats and the Republicans in the decades following the Civil Rights Movement, and covert racist dog whistles have been central to this practice. Currently, the Republican campaign against critical race theory continues these strategies.

Covert and overt dog whistles function communicatively by drawing on an ideological background. To understand dog whistles, we must incorporate into our theory of speech the ways in which different ideological backgrounds affect what is communicated by a speech act. The concept we will use to explicate dog whistles, as well as some other kinds of hustle, is *presupposition*. On our analysis, dog whistling functions by *presupposing* certain ideologies. In part II, we will be developing a detailed theory of presupposition and ideology. The example of dog whistles brings out this more general feature of hustle— hustling is characteristically dependent on presupposed narratives, ideology, prejudice, values, and frames. A theory of meaning adequate to explaining hustle must develop and elucidate a novel notion of presupposition that could explain how such notions could be presupposed in a way that enables speakers to hustle their audiences.

The task of explaining dog whistling with presupposition faces an immediate objection, one that will help us elucidate early on some of the ways our project rethinks the terrain. Dog whistling is a paradigm of a speech act that allows for plausible deniability. As Justin Khoo has pointed out, this contrasts starkly with standard examples of presupposition, which cannot be plausibly denied.[34] For example, "I am picking up my sister" presupposes that the speaker has a sister, and so it would be odd for a speaker to say:

(1) I am picking up my sister from the airport, but I do not have a sister.

In contrast, one *can* say:

(2) That program is nothing other than a welfare program, but I don't mean to suggest anything negative about Black Americans.

The worry is this: if the negative racist message associated with "welfare" is *presupposed*, then one cannot explain plausible deniability, the very property that a theory of hustle must explicate.[35] Responding to this objection helps us, from the beginning, elucidate the centrality of speech practices to our model.

---

34. Khoo, "Code Words in Political Discourse."

35. A technical solution to Khoo's problem is available within the presupposition literature. One could say that while the presupposition in (1) is both presupposed and entailed, the presupposition in (2) is only presupposed, and not entailed. Putative cases of nonentailed presuppositions (which can thus be canceled even when not embedded under logical operators like negation) have been discussed at least as far back as the Gazdar's work on

It is familiar from the work of Saul Kripke, among many others, that words are embedded in speech practices, which give those words meaning; according to Kripke, speech practices explain why proper names have the references they do.[36] We agree with Kripke on this point, but we think of speech practices as imbuing significance to words that goes well beyond their referential properties. Every time one uses a word, one presupposes (and manifests) a speech practice, one that is connected to a variety of resonances, emotional and otherwise. The word "welfare" belongs to a racist speech practice that casts a negative shadow on anything so-described. Using the word in this way presupposes this speech practice. But most words belong to multiple speech practices—and to understand what speech practice its use presupposes, one must often know the social location, point, and purpose of the speaker. In a paper that has deeply affected us, Anne Quaranto argues that dog whistles function by exploiting the presence of multiple speech practices governing a single word.[37] In using a dog whistle, one presupposes one speech practice, while taking advantage of the fact that the word can also be used in other ways. If one is challenged, one claims that one was using it in this other way.

What's needed to complete this analysis is an account of presupposition that can make sense of the claim that using a word can presuppose something like a practice. And we need an account of speech practices that explains the resonances of language and the impact language has on us.

The Path Forward

There are clear difficulties in making sense of the multifarious ways in which speech impacts audiences in the terms of the philosophical tradition of semantic analysis that dominate analytic philosophy and linguistic semantics. Let us briefly sketch the problem and where it led us. We start with the tradition that forms the background. It runs through Gottlob Frege at the end of the nineteenth century, the early Ludwig Wittgenstein in the first part of the twentieth century and Richard Montague in the 1960s, and onward into what is now a

---

presupposition (*Pragmatics, Implicature, Presupposition, and Logical Form*). The analysis of presupposition developed in part II of the book allows this type of analysis, and also allows that presuppositions are probabilistic, so that there are tendencies for them to hold in contexts of utterance rather than absolute requirements. However, these facets of our account are not what we take to explain the contrast between (1) and (2). We would submit that while simply analyzing "welfare" as having an unentailed presupposition is possible, this would still leave an explanatory gap, since it is not at all clear why these constructions would be associated with unentailed presuppositions while the bulk of what are standardly taken to be presuppositions are entailed.

36. Kripke, *Naming and Necessity.*

37. Quaranto, "Dog Whistles, Covertly Coded Speech, and the Practices That Enable Them."

rich, well-articulated, and diverse academic enterprise, that of compositional formal semantics. In this enterprise, meanings of words are understood in terms of the bits of the world they refer to and in terms of functions on those bits, and the bits are composed to calculate what the sentence says about the world. Adherents of this approach, ourselves included, see an austere beauty in the smooth way these meanings can be composed, as if they were physical building blocks engineered to slide into place.

We place early Wittgenstein at the heart of the tradition in which we were trained because the approach we are describing can be seen as a realization of what he termed in the *Tractatus*[38] the *picture theory of meaning*. On this view, a sentence functions like a panel in the pictorial instructions accompanying a prefabricated furniture kit: an elongated T-shape with a series of slightly diagonal parallel lines at one end depicts a particular type of bolt, a long rectangle depicts a table leg, and the spatial relationship of these elements together with an arrow depicts an action that the assembler of the furniture must perform. The idea is that the conventions of language determine how arbitrary symbols can be mapped onto real-world objects in the way that pictorial elements are mapped onto real-world objects via iconic similarity. The Frege-Montague line of work makes precise how language can represent in this way, but it creates a quandary (a quandary perhaps not unrelated to the evolution seen in Wittgenstein's own later work): how can a picture theory of meaning like that we have just caricatured possibly help us understand phenomena like harmful speech?

While we will not directly use Wittgenstein's picture metaphor in presenting the account that these worries eventually led us to, it might be said that we still presuppose a depiction theory of meaning. But don't think of a construction manual; think of a picture (from the front page of the October 1936 edition of the Nazi propaganda newspaper *Der Stürmer*) depicting a rich Jew with vampire teeth eating tiny "ordinary" people whole. He has a Star of David on his forehead, in case other aspects of the caricature were insufficient to indicate his identity, and a masonic symbol on his lapel for good measure.[39] Or think of Picasso's *Guernica*, also expressly created and exhibited to support a political cause. There are certainly pictorial elements in the *Guernica* that can be mapped onto things and events in the real world: a bull, a horse, faces and grimaces, a broken sword. Yet what makes the painting so rich is not simply the existence of symbols that stand for things. It is the extraordinary way the elements are chosen, portrayed, and composed so as to immediately evoke powerful emotional reactions, and the way they collectively and holistically

---

38. Wittgenstein, *Tractatus Logico-Philosophicus*, 5–12.

39. Images from *Der Stürmer*, including the one described in the main text, have been collated by Randall Bytwerk. At time of writing, they can be seen at his Calvin University website, https://research.calvin.edu/german-propaganda-archive/sturmer.htm (site verified March 2022).

bring to salience a peculiarly rich web of social and historical associations, of interwoven half-told narratives, and of practices of war and killing.

Although we neither offer nor presume an analysis of artistic representation, what we seek in this book is a theory of how language can evoke similar emotional reactions, social and historical associations, narratives, and practices. Once one begins to look at language in this way, one begins to see even the simpler cases that have been the mainstay of semantic theory in a very different light, such as the relation between "dog" and "cur," which the logician and philosopher Gottlob Frege used to motivate the notion of meaning at the heart of the formal semantic tradition. The view we develop in this book will bring out how even the Ikea instruction manual was never a simple static mapping from 2-D representations to the 3-D furniture of the world, but embodied a complex set of consumer-societal, industrial, and constructional practices. So it is, we will argue, with every piece of language that was ever reduced in a class on semantics or philosophy of language to a sequence of logical symbols. We are not against the practice of performing such formalizations. But we will argue that what must be made precise is not a simple mapping from expressions to things. A conclusion we draw from Wittgenstein's later work is that what must ultimately be made precise, if we are to understand how meaning functions, is rather a set of language practices and the social conditions accompanying their use.[40] We believe that this is as true for the simplest sentence in a learn-to-read storybook as it is for the more complex and subtle ways in which speech mobilizes audiences toward explicitly political action.

The leading ideas of the new framework we develop in this book are as follows. Linguistic actions, such as speaking a word, exemplify social practices, and have *resonances* by virtue of the practices they exemplify. The resonances include things, properties, emotions, practices, and social identities—anything that tends to be around when words are used. The resonances always have ideological significance, and sometimes this is obvious, as when a word like "freedom" is used. The function of speech is to *attune* audiences to each other and to facts of the world, and this attunement occurs via the resonances of what is said. Some resonances concern effects of the linguistic action on the interlocutors, like the gaining of new attunements to the way the world is, or the experience of pain when a slur is hurled at someone. Other resonances are

---

40. There is throughout Wittgenstein's *Philosophical Investigations* a continuous push away from the inner, mental significance of language, and toward the societal practices within which language is used, or, as he would have it, within which language games are played. The view is crystalized in an extraordinary remark with respect to which perhaps we err by merely mentioning it in a footnote; it might be said that the current volume, like much other philosophical work of the last seventy years, is really the footnote: "For a large class of cases—though not for all—in which we employ the word 'meaning' it can be defined thus: the meaning of a word is its use in the language" (20, proposition 43).

presupposed. Presupposed resonances are an especially important way that *hustle* creeps into communication; entire ideologies are presupposed and may be slowly *accommodated,* and yet the presence of ideological presuppositions can escape attention. *Harmonization,* which is a generalization of accommodation, is an adaptive process by which attunements change in the face of mismatches, for example, ideological mismatches between the attunements of different interlocutors. Harmonization does not always repair mismatches, but it can do so, allowing individuals and groups to coordinate; they may coordinate, for example, on ways of speaking, on ways of treating others, or ways of voting. Thus we study the influence of speech on political action, but with a particular interest in covert aspects of this influence.

Here is the plan of our book:

- In part I, we introduce the foundational notions of our model. Words are employed in communicative practices, which lend these words *resonances.* Groups of people form communities of practice, which shape these resonances. This is the topic of chapter 1, which is motivated in terms of political language, but in which the major new development is a general model of meaning as resonance, a model that is not specific as regards its application area. The use of words by a community of practice *attunes* its members to these resonances. The work of chapter 2 is to motivate and explain how attunement functions within such a community. This is where we start to get more explicit about the machinery required for questions of social and political significance, laying the groundwork for a model in which we can make sense of issues like ideological change and transmission. In chapter 3, we analyze the process by which attunement changes at both an individual and group level, or, equivalently, the way people and groups adapt to each other through communicative interactions. We refer to this process as *harmonization.* What we seek is a model of how speech can affect people in the short term, but a model that allows us to make sense of the process by which ideas and ideologies spread and transform over the larger time scales at which political change occurs.
- In part II, we use the notions we develop in part I to redefine the central concepts of formal pragmatics, *presupposition* and *accommodation.* Presuppositions reflect the background of communicative practices, the things that are normally so evident to interlocutors that their significance need not be made explicit. In justification of a tradition of philosophers pioneered chiefly by Rae Langton, we argue that presupposition plays a special role in ideological transfer. In our terms, this is because people tend to harmonize with presuppositions non-deliberatively. This both reflects the positive role of presupposition in helping people coordinate and build common ground, and introduces

a danger, since a propagandist can take advantage of presupposition in order to persuade covertly. In chapter 5, we generalize standard models of presupposition using the notions introduced in part I. We use this to make sense of the idea that a communicative action can presuppose a practice, so that, for example, telling sexist jokes can presuppose sexist ideologies. *Accommodation* refers to the way people adapt to the communicative situation. We suggest in chapter 6 that accommodation be modeled as a special case of harmonization, as introduced in part I. Accommodation is harmonization to a group, especially to a group with which people identify. This move helps us to understand a range of complex phenomena, such as the processes that undergird political polarization and the formation of echo chambers.

- Our model of speech is more realistic than many more standard views in the sense that we aim to avoid certain common idealizations, because we think these idealizations obstruct the analysis of social and political aspects of language. In part III, we step back to look at theoretical issues involving idealization, in particular the issue of how idealizations about speech can serve as ideological distortions. For the sake of perspicuity, we focus on two idealizations standardly made in linguistic and philosophical work on meaning, which we call *neutrality* and *straight talk*. We use these to exhibit two different ways in which idealizations characteristically distort. First, they can distort by being incoherent, as we argue in chapter 7 to be the case with the idealization of neutrality. Words are embedded in practices, and as such are vehicles for ideology. There is no such thing, then, as a neutral word in a human language. The pretense of neutrality functions to mask the way speech transmits ideology. Secondly, idealizations can distort by limiting attention to an unrepresentative subset of language types, as we argue in chapter 8 to be the case with straight talk. In chapter 9, we situate our project within the broader ambit of attempts across philosophy to critique idealizations.

- Finally, in part IV, we turn to the question of the power of speech to harm and liberate. How do we theorize these together? Chapter 10 concerns harmful speech, focusing on several different categories, such as slurs, and bureaucratic speech, which harms by objectifying and masking. In our final chapter, we turn to the question of the liberatory potential of speech. How do we best think of free speech in a democracy, given speech's power to harm? We conclude that arguments against speech restrictions that are based on the democratic ideal of liberty fail. But this does not mean that no at least partial defenses of a free-speech principle are possible—an approach we suggest, cast in terms of maximizing participation in a process of collective harmonization, is to reconfigure the defense of free speech around the other central democratic ideal, that of equality.

PART I

How Words Connect People

CHAPTER ONE

Resonance

You rely on a sentence to say more than the denotation and the connotation; you revel in the smoke that the words send up.

—TONI MORRISON[1]

Gedanken ohne Inhalt sind leer, Anschauungen ohne Begriffe sind blind. (Thoughts without content are empty, intuitions without concepts are blind.)

—IMMANUEL KANT[2]

Although we speak of utterances carrying meaning just as of a pipeline carrying oil, we know perfectly well that the parallel is faulty. The meaning of an utterance is not in the utterance as the oil is in the pipeline; rather, awareness of the meaning is triggered or induced in the hearer BY the utterance.

—CHARLES HOCKETT[3]

1.1. Let Freedom Ring

We will presumably not be thought to be making a controversial claim in saying that the words "equality" and "freedom" have strong resonances. As Martin Luther King Jr. reprised in his most famous speech, freedom can ring. The resonances are highly emotional, and intertwined with group identity, with what it is to be an American, or, for that matter, French. The resonances include ideas, ideals, and broader ideologies. And the resonances also include practices, practices of treating people equally and giving them freedom to live life as they see fit, but also speech practices. These speech practices themselves have many different levels. There are practices of speaking freely and of permitting free speech, and there are practices of treating competing voices equally. More narrowly, there are the very practices of invoking "equality" and "freedom," which have become mantras. Through repetition, the words have

---

1. As quoted by Rosie Blau, *Financial Times* interview, November 7, 2008, accessed March 1, 2023, https://www.ft.com/content/b1c8c954-ac59-11dd-bf71-000077b07658.
2. Kant, *Critique of Pure Reason*, 193 (A51/B75).
3. Hockett, *Refurbishing Our Foundations*, 90.

developed a totemic ability to symbolize ideals without any felt need to state exactly what the ideal is. *Liberté! Egalité! Fraternité!* Such words, in whatever language, are repeated almost ritualistically by sloganeering politicians.

It is a remarkable fact that when the slave states of the American South seceded in 1860–1861, both sides went to war with the same avowed goals: freedom and equality. The position of the North requires no explanation to a modern audience, but the position of the slave states has come to be recognized as anathema. The four published state *declarations of causes*, official state documents drawn up to make the case for secession, are jarring. The Mississippi declaration, for example, says that the hostility to slavery "seeks not to elevate or to support the slave, but to destroy his present condition without providing a better."[4] Looking at this quote now, it makes no more sense than would an attack on a medical charity on the basis that it "seeks not to elevate or to support" cancer patients, "but to destroy [their] present condition without providing a better." Yet we can only assume that in 1861, it was, for many people, an effective framing.

The Georgia declaration, which also includes an explicitly economic argument, invokes both liberty and equality in its conclusion. It ends by saying this of the Republican Party under Lincoln:

> Their avowed purpose is to subvert our society and subject us not only to the loss of our property but the destruction of ourselves, our wives, and our children, and the desolation of our homes, our altars, and our firesides. To avoid these evils we resume the powers which our fathers delegated to the Government of the United States, and henceforth will seek new safeguards for our liberty, equality, security, and tranquility.[5]

This excerpt from the declaration by state of Texas, a call for preservation of inequality if ever there was one, literally emphasizes equality, in the sense that the emphasis below is in the original:

> We hold as undeniable truths that the governments of the various States, and of the confederacy itself, were established exclusively by the white race, for themselves and their posterity; that the African race had no agency in their establishment; that they were rightfully held and regarded as an inferior and dependent race, and in that condition only could their existence in this country be rendered beneficial or tolerable.
>
> That in this free government **all white men are and of right ought to be entitled to equal civil and political rights**; that the servitude

4. "Confederate States of America—Mississippi Secession," Yale Law School, 2008, accessed March 1, 2023, https://avalon.law.yale.edu/19th_century/csa_missec.asp.

5. "Declaration of the Causes of Secession, Georgia," Digital History, 2021, accessed March 1, 2023, https://www.digitalhistory.uh.edu/active_learning/explorations/south _secede/south_secede_georgia.cfm.

of the African race, as existing in these States, is mutually beneficial to both bond and free, and is abundantly authorized and justified by the experience of mankind, and the revealed will of the Almighty Creator, as recognized by all Christian nations; while the destruction of the existing relations between the two races, as advocated by our sectional enemies, would bring inevitable calamities upon both and desolation upon the fifteen slave-holding states.[6]

Alexander Stephens was the vice president of the Confederacy. His most famous speech, the "Cornerstone" Speech, is equally jarring. Toward the beginning, Stephens declares that "all, under our system, stand upon the same broad principles of perfect equality." And yet its most famous (or rather *infamous*) line, only a few paragraphs further, announces that the new government's "cornerstone rests, upon the great truth that the negro is not equal to the white man."[7]

What can explain how such language resonated effectively for many in the antebellum South, persuading them to accept the need for war? Bolstered by the authority of an explicitly racist constitution and by an implicit version of trickle-down economics in which the mass of poor White farmers hoped that the opportunity to enslave others would eventually trickle down to them, the secessionists undermined the ideals of freedom and equality, in the very act of appealing to them.

Secessionist rhetoric relied on a narrow framing, a reinterpretation of the domain of application of undefined terms involved in widely held but imprecisely stated ideals. First, the ideal of universal freedom was undermined by reinterpreting freedom as freedom of "free" states and, almost vacuously, freedom of free people. Given that this notion of "freedom" included the freedom to own another human being, the freedom of some required the enslavement of others. Second is the ideal of equality. The founding of the nation eighty-five years earlier had hinged on a "self-evident" truth expressed with powerful simplicity in the Declaration of Independence: "all men are created equal." But the Constitution pragmatically undermined the ideal of equality, among other ways through its infamously contorted picture of the value of an enslaved person—three-fifths of a free man, for the purposes of congressional representation and taxation. In the Texas declaration of causes, we see a completely

6. "Confederate States of America - A Declaration of the Causes Which Impel the State of Texas to Secede from the Federal Union," Yale Law School, 2008, accessed March 1, 2023, https://avalon.law.yale.edu/19th_century/csa_texsec.asp.

7. Alexander Stephens, "Cornerstone Speech," American Battlefield Trust, 2023, accessed March 1, 2023, https://www.battlefields.org/learn/primary-sources/cornerstone-speech. This sentence continues painfully: "that slavery subordination to the superior race is his natural and normal condition. This, our new government, is the first, in the history of the world, based upon this great physical, philosophical, and moral truth."

unequivocal retrenchment of the ideal that had been expressed in such redolent terms in the Declaration of Independence: "all men are created equal" becomes "all white men are and of right ought to be entitled to equal civil and political rights."

The ritualistic use and totemic quality of "freedom" and "equality" are so strong that the underlying concepts and ideals can often be pushed into the background. Confederate messaging could be seen as persuading people by subverting ideals through the use of conveniently narrow framings. But we should be careful here. While there was clearly an intent on the part of the authors of the declarations to persuade, it is not at all clear whether these authors would have understood their own framings of the notions of freedom and equality as narrow, and it is unclear whether the authors of the four state declarations viewed what they were doing as subversion, or even manipulation.

Some, such as George Fitzhugh, were clear-eyed about endorsing a conception of human freedom that required slavery.[8] For Fitzhugh, freedom for "us" is enslavement for "them." And it is likely that this route to the appeal of "freedom" still resonates with many, in various forms. Toni Morrison writes, "There is quite a lot of juice to be extracted from plummy reminiscences of 'individualism' and 'freedom' if the tree upon which such fruit hangs is a black population forced to serve as freedom's polar opposite."[9] Morrison's suggestion is that talk of freedom sometimes resonates with appreciation of a life that is in contrast to that of Black Americans, one that requires their general subordination in order to be fully appreciated. Talk of freedom might be intended to do one thing, but unintentionally it resonates with a degraded unfreedom, with which it is unconsciously contrasted.

This distinction, between what someone intends a communicative act to achieve and what it actually does, relates to a central theme in this book: hidden meaning. We introduced the term *hustle* to cover the hidden meanings of communicative acts, or, to be a little more precise, the effects of a communicative act that are not mutually identifiable by interlocutors as being intended. Hustle covers many subtle aspects of language that, despite that subtlety, are highly efficacious. It includes choices of framing and optics that politicians and spinmeisters trade in, but it includes equally the way in which a mundane, everyday communicative act drags with it an invisible net of ways of being and doing.

On the political side, the word "freedom" carries much hustle, as does the evocative template "Let freedom ring from," as Martin Luther King rang it out repeatedly in his famous 1963 speech. People are moved by King's words,

8. Fitzhugh, *Cannibals All! Or, Slaves without Masters*.
9. Morrison, *Playing in the Dark*, 64.

and yet most would not be able to say exactly why they are so stirring. Melvin Rogers singles out the power of aspirational democratic rhetoric as a central theme in African-American political thought in his scholarly work on the topic.[10] Rogers draws particular attention to examples in which African-American thinkers not only draw on the language of freedom, but also "appeal, for example, to the Declaration of Independence or the American Founders or they figuratively place themselves into the story of Exodus (not uniquely American)."[11] We can see the terrain of US politics partly in terms of a struggle over the meanings of the word "freedom," that is, over its *resonances*.

A less obviously stirring word, simply because it is so commonplace, is "mom." Yet what word could be more emotionally and socially significant? Just as the word "freedom" carries much hustle, so does "mom," presupposing certain gender roles and family structures, some general to a culture, and some specific to any situation in which it is used.[12] More generally, the resonances of words are often hidden in plain sight: our point is not that the emotional and social significance of the word "mom" is some big secret, but that it is often not brought to awareness in ordinary uses of the word. Our explanation of how a resonance can be hidden (or hidden in plain sight) will be developed gradually. Before we can even begin to explain what it means for a resonance to be hidden, we must motivate and develop our account of what it is for a word to carry resonance at all. This is the job to which we now turn.

1.2. What's in a Word?

Kant famously described thoughts as having "contents," as if thoughts are containers and sitting inside the container there is some sort of objectively real thing waiting to be unpacked.[13] This has been a fruitful metaphor. It is the

---

10. Rogers, *The Darkened Light of Faith*, citation is from unpublished draft.

11. Rogers, *The Darkened Light of Faith*, introduction.

12. Here, as at many points to come in this volume, we are deeply indebted to Sally Haslanger's work on social meaning and practice. For discussion of the ideal of motherhood and the importance of the social meaning of the word "mother" (although not "mom"), see Haslanger, "Social Meaning and Philosophical Method."

13. Although we have not attempted a systematic historical study of the notion of "content" in philosophy of mind and language, it seems likely that Kant's talk of "content" was taken over from Christian Wolff. See Anderson, "The Wolffian Paradigm and Its Discontent," 30–32. The idea of one property or term containing another in the sense that if something is "in" the extension of one then it is also "in" the extension of the other seems to date back at least to Aristotle's *Prior Analytics* (see Ross, *Aristotle's Prior and Posterior Analytics*, 292, notes on 26–28). The idea that a thought might be structured and contain parts is found in Hume, but the structures that Hume is considering are mostly the syntactic Aristotelian subject-predicate structures of sentences used to express thoughts, so

basis for Frege's analysis of meaning, which is now commonly seen as pivotal in the Western analytic tradition of philosophy of language, as well as laying the foundations for the most formally well-developed accounts of meaning in contemporary theoretical linguistics. By now, the idea of words containing meaning or information is standard in philosophy of language, linguistics, and beyond. Let's call the general idea that communication consists of conveying meaning inside container-like vessels consisting of symbols, such that the speaker's job is to wrap the meaning up and the hearer's job is to unwrap it, the *content-delivery model* of meaning. This is a special case of a more general (and much discussed) metaphor for communication, the *conduit* metaphor, to be considered below. In this chapter, we suggest a way to change the focus in theory of communicative meaning, away from the idea of meaning as an object, a lump of special abstract stuff that might be contained inside a word or phrase, and toward the idea of meaning as a process that connects people to the world and to each other.

The idea that the function of words might be to connect people is not new. It was made explicit a century ago by the anthropologist Bronislaw Malinowski in describing a type of discourse he terms "Phatic Communion." Malinowski is completely explicit that the function of this discourse is not to transmit information about the world but (like the gift exchanges he famously described elsewhere) to increase social cohesion:

> Are words in Phatic Communion used primarily to convey meaning, the meaning which is symbolically theirs? Certainly not! They fulfil a social function and that is their principal aim, but they are neither the result of intellectual reflection. . . . We may say that language does not function here as a means of transmission of thought. . . .
>
> Each utterance is an act serving the direct aim of binding hearer to speaker by a tie of some social sentiment or other.[14]

---

that the syntactic expression of a proposition can contain a subject and predicate. He does at one point in the *Treatise of Human Nature* comment (in discussing existential propositions, for which he denies that existence is a predicate), "We can thus form a proposition, which contains only one idea" (Hume, *A Treatise of Human Nature*, 67, fn. 20). However, he does not in that work consistently talk of propositions as containing ideas, and he never refers to the content of a proposition or thought.

14. Malinowski, "The Problem of Meaning in Primitive Languages," 315. If we may be pardoned a historical aside, note that Malinowski is not only explicit about the social function of language, but is also explicit in repeatedly expressing his account in terms of language as *action*. Thus he writes, some ten years before Wittgenstein dictated the notes that eventually became the *Philosophical Investigations*, and over thirty years before Austin gave the William James Lectures that became *How to Do Things with Words*, "In its primitive uses, language functions as a link in concerted human activity, as a piece of human behaviour. It is a mode of action and not an instrument of reflection" (312). Malinowski is explicit in stating that phatic communion also "function[s] not as an instrument of reflection but as a mode of action" (315).

Despite this long history, it remains far from obvious how best to construct a theory in which linguistic meanings can serve the function of connecting people, at least in the strong sense we aim for whereby the connection is sufficiently strong that it can support both collective action and mutual understanding. Further complicating matters, the political interest in language derives in part from the fact that language not only connects, but also divides, setting people apart into groups that lack common understanding. So the task we have set ourselves is a large one. Indeed, to the extent that the essentially Fregean content-delivery model still marks the center of gravity for current work on linguistic meaning, our project is not only large, but also radical. However, it is not without significant antecedents. The development of our positive view will rest heavily on prior work drawn from a range of disciplines, including sociology and psychology, in addition to linguistics and philosophy.[15]

We began the chapter with an example, the resonances of a particular set of words in discourse related to freedom and equality. We now present what we hope is an intuitive picture of why it might be useful to reframe the theory of meaning so that it is not seen as content-delivery, and instead use a metaphor of resonance. To develop the account of resonance, we adapt an idea of David Kaplan's that provides a way of assigning meanings to expressive language in terms of usage conditions. We argue that at base, and leaving aside sociocultural effects to which we turn later, we can gain purchase

---

15. There is, to be sure, much strong work by scholars who share some but not all of our goals, including work that we have, as yet, not attempted to reconcile with our own approach despite the presence of a clearly overlapping agenda. A prime example here is recent work of Jennifer Nagel and Evan Westra on the epistemology of dialogue (Nagel, "Epistemic Territory"; Westra and Nagel, "Mindreading in Conversation"). Like us, these authors seek to analyze not merely individual conversational turns, but also complex interactions taking place over many turns. Indeed, they have gone rather further than us in directly connecting their account to detailed theories of dialogue structure developed in the Conversation Analysis literature. However, there are several respects in which our goals crucially differ. One is that they focus on cooperative conversation, whereas we consider ways in which language can be divisive and drive interlocutors apart. Another is that they focus on recognition of intention, whereas we take a central goal of a theory of political language to account for ways in which what is communicated comes apart from what is intended, or what is intended to be recognized. A third is that they focus on epistemology, how language changes people's knowledge states, whereas we attempt to centralize emotion and social role. Although the focus of the Nagel and Westra work is quite different from that of our work, we should make it clear that we do not deny the importance either of the type of cooperative conversational situation they study or of epistemological aspects of conversation. Indeed, we see no particular reason why the approach Nagel and Westra develop could not, in principle, be reframed in terms of the resonance framework we develop here, a thought we offer not to suggest any shortcoming in their work, but rather to suggest a direction for future development of our own framework.

on expressive meaning by considering the simplest type of conventionalized signaling possible.

The latter part of this chapter analyzes resonance in simple artificial practices, involving a single signal that is associated with a single canonical response. These cases serve as a microcosm of the broader theory of communication we will develop, a seedling of resonance from which to grow a broader model of ideological attunement. The examples are paradigmatic because they are interactional and associative. Meaning is interactional when functional success of a signaling action is measured in terms of patterns of reaction to it, and when the appropriateness of those actions depends on conformity to practice, rather than centering on questions of truth or descriptive adequacy. Meaning is associative in the examples we will develop in the sense that it involves tendencies for certain actions to co-occur with other actions or with states of the world, rather than involving an absolute one-to-one correspondence between signals and things that the signals represent. In the last two sections of the chapter, we develop this idea of simple associative and interactional meaning using standard probabilistic and game-theoretic tools, which allow us to characterize the meaning of expressive acts in terms of their role within a simple practice.

Our broad project requires a move away from the standard content-delivery model of language that focuses on exchange of a single proposition between two individuals, and toward an account that can explain effects seen in mass communication, effects that include mass emotion and mass-coordinated action. The way that the complex resonances of terms like "freedom" develop through the ages must ultimately be set within such an account, but it is far from obvious how this might be achieved. So before launching into the choppy waters of freedom and equality, let us briefly situate the account of resonance we develop in this chapter within the broader framework developed in this first part of the book.

First, anything can have resonances of any sort. A bowl of soup can carry a resonance of comfort, and a boot can have resonances of socks and feet, of a quaint little cobbler's shop, and simultaneously of oppression and authoritarianism; Orwell's "boot stamping on a human face—forever"[16] both adapted and modified the resonances of boots—forever. Of most interest to us in this book are the resonances of words, not boots, but to the extent that a boot is symbolic, we hope that the theory covers boots too. Second, the resonances of things depend on the attunements of people, which include associations and understandings, the emotions that things conjure up, and the ways people tend to interact with or use things. We are particularly interested in the role that the resonances of communicative devices play in shaping the attunements of individuals and groups. We suggest that to understand this process we

---

16. Orwell, *Nineteen Eighty-Four*, 274.

must look not at particular attunements people have to this or that discursive practice or feature of the world, but at systems of attunements. Our thesis is that the way people's attunements change, and the way that propagandists change them, depends on people's need for a type of coherence.

This takes us to a third notion, *harmony*. Here we follow in the footsteps of the social psychologist Leon Festinger, who prefigured our approach sixty-five years ago in his account of cognitive dissonance.[17] We adopt Festinger's hypothesis that change in attunements (or what he termed "cognitions") is often driven by a need to dispel dissonance. We refer to processes of re-attunement that act at the level of complete systems of attunement as *harmonization*. Our thesis is that harmonization is central to the function of political propaganda. But it is not the only type of re-attunement in our model. We also assume a more basic type of re-attunement, a direct and immediate nondeliberative response to a stimulus. For the purposes of this book, the type of stimulus of greatest interest is communicative acts: someone shouts at you, and you get upset, and perhaps you also come to change your beliefs, now being attuned to the world in a way that either is or is not more consonant with the person doing the shouting. It is characteristic of nondeliberative emotional response to speech that it happens without necessarily resulting in increased harmony. For example, we might come to believe something that someone tells us, and only slowly resolve tensions that result because the new belief has left us in a state that is in some way incoherent. Perhaps the update has left us with beliefs that are inconsistent with each other, or with beliefs that are inconsistent with our dispositions. Nondeliberative uptake has produced an incoherent state, and harmonization is then a slower process that, with luck, will pick up the pieces and bring us into a state that is more coherent.

We suggest that thinking in terms of the harmonization of attunements has consequences both at the level of individuals and at every larger level of human organization and activity, from cafe conversation to genocide. Effectiveness of political messaging depends not on logical consistency but on emotional, cognitive, and dispositional resonances, drawing especially on people's need to align their attunements with those of their in-group. Indeed, although the terminology may be unfamiliar, we do not think that the claim should be deeply controversial. What is needed is a proper understanding of the notions of resonance and attunement, so as to found claims like this theoretically. We begin, in this chapter, with resonance, and now turn to some paradigmatic examples of the role that resonance plays in political language and thought.

As Michael Reddy observed,[18] people pervasively frame their talk about language using a metaphor of transfer with a physical container or carrier,

17. Festinger, *A Theory of Cognitive Dissonance*.
18. Reddy, "The Conduit Metaphor."

the *contents* of the container corresponding to the informational *content* of an utterance. Speakers *put* their thoughts *into* words. While insincerity may mean the words are *hollow* or *empty*, speakers may *pack* or *cram* many ideas *into* few words, even *filling* them with more than they can *carry*. They may *give* the hearer an idea of what they mean, or *push* a challenging idea, hoping they will *get* their thoughts *across* to a speaker who will *unpack* them, *extract* meaning *from* them, unless the words are *hard to unpack* or *impenetrable*, in which case the hearer might just *get* the general *drift*, and might not see *where* it's *coming from*. There is always a danger of hearers reading something *into* our words that wasn't there, but then again, perhaps the words were *loaded* intentionally, *freighted* with unseemly *baggage*.

Using this "conduit" metaphor, as Reddy named it, to talk about figurative language itself, we might say that the physical-transfer framing is not merely a way to *package* discussion of communication, but is *baked* into the meaning of the vocabulary itself. Going still further, metaphor theorists, including not only Reddy but also George Lakoff and Mark Johnson and their many followers,[19] suggest that people don't merely talk about words as containers of meaning, but have come to conceive of communication by analogy to the physical transfer of goods.

Theoretical linguists and philosophers of language perhaps use the conduit metaphor in a more limited way than other people, at least when they're theorizing about language rather than talking informally about what someone has said. Probably one reason for that is that prevailing semantic theories suggest that meaning is context dependent in a way that doesn't naturally cohere with that metaphor. An object in a package is shielded from the context around the package: the whole point of packaging is to allow the object to get from one place to another without change. By contrast, contemporary theories suggest that the meaning of particular words is mutable and evanescent. The meaning of a given expression depends on who utters it, and the time and place of the utterance. In cases of so-called *presupposition failure*, the meaning may not be recoverable by someone who does not share the assumptions of the speaker. Yet even semantic theorists cannot easily resist the containment metaphor. Philosophers talk, after all, of words as *meaning-bearing*, and of meaning as *content*. We also use such Kantian phrases as *mental content*, a phrase reminiscent of the more colloquial notion of having an *idea in mind*, as if meanings and ideas could be contained not only inside words, but inside heads.

The word *content* as used in technical talk about meaning has become somewhat divorced from the notion of containment, but it is well to remember that talk of words as something like boxes with *content* or trays that *bear* meaning might easily lead any of us quite unconsciously into a simplistic way of thinking, whereby meanings are treated as fixed entities that can be carried

---

19. Lakoff and Johnson, *Metaphors We Live By*.

in or by an expression. The simplifications invited by the metaphor can be thought of in terms of the idealizations about meaning. On a natural understanding of the metaphor, the speaker's intention is to give the hearer what is in the box, and the hearer recognizes that intention as soon as they open it, so one is inclined to view the exchange as following an idealization of *transparency*.[20] Similarly, while we might imagine that context provides tools that help us in packing or unpacking the container, it does not change what's in there, and if communication is conveying an object in a package, then anyone who has the tools to open the package will find the same thing inside. That suggests an idealization of *shared context*, there being no relevant variation of context across interactants, and an idealization of *language homogeneity*, marginalizing cases where people have different understandings of meaning because of linguistic variation within a speech community. Relatedly, the metaphor draws attention away from who is doing the giving and receiving, thus suggesting an idealization of *social homogeneity* of the linguistic community, whereby we don't have to consider issues like social roles in the study of meaning. (All of these idealizations will be discussed in chapter 9.)

The content-delivery model suggests that conversation can be analyzed in terms of neat exchange of discrete units of information, inviting us to think of individual acts that are complete in themselves, like the act of producing a sentential utterance. It thus defocuses from discourse effects (the idealization we will term *extent*), and suggests that we convey one content at a time with each sentential utterance, and the content is in some sense a complete unit of information within itself (the idealization we call *propositionality*). To be clear, we do think that the notion of content has played a useful role in helping people think about what language does, but we also think that it has helped create an unresolved tension in work on meaning. The very theorists who have recognized the incompleteness of meanings divorced from context have nonetheless strived to isolate those meanings like laboratory samples on a microscope slide. We propose that, instead of treating meanings as objects, albeit with little holes in them where context should plug in, we should focus on meaning as a connection between agents and the processes that lead to it.

---

20. As we will define it, *transparency* means transparency of intentions. One could extend the content-delivery metaphor to allow that a speaker accidentally packaged something they didn't intend to, or that they intended to cover up the true reason they sent the package. We do not claim that the content-delivery metaphor is inconsistent with breakdowns in transparency, i.e., with *hustle*. Rather we claim that the content-delivery metaphor invites focus on something exchanged that is objective and accessible for all parties. Seen in this light, Gricean pragmatics, with its attendant reasoning about speaker intention, is itself a substantial and non-obvious break from a straightforward use of the content-delivery method. However, while Grice recognized that what is intended differs in interesting ways from what might be thought of as literal content, Gricean pragmatics does not offer a general account of unintended meaning, which is central for us.

There is no such thing as an objectively true or correct metaphor (which is not to say that metaphors cannot be used to make true statements). Rather, some metaphors are helpful, some less so, and some lead to productive new ways of thinking. In this latter case, they are, as Donald Schön put it, *generative*,[21] in the sense that they spur creativity and generate new insights. The concept of transfer of packaged goods is so basic to our cultural understanding that it makes for an effective metaphor, redolent with associations. But an alternative, physical analogy is more apt for the view we develop. We will use another classic concept, one that entered the scientific vernacular with Galileo's study of pendulums, and say that meaning is *resonance*. So meaning is not an object but a process, a process of energetic alignment. The resonance metaphor is clearly related to the conduit metaphor in that it involves a type of exchange or transmission. But to the extent that anything is physically transferred, it is, on this view, intrinsically less tangible and discrete than the standard conduit metaphor might suggest. Don't think of information in packets delivered to your door, but as flowing into you like the energy of heavy bass music vibrating your core. And don't think of meaning as an object being transferred, but as a state being shared, so that although resonance requires a physical connection, it may continue even in the absence of energy transfer.[22]

Words *resonate*, interlocutors becoming *attuned* to the world and each other. What you say may *ring true*, or at least *ring a bell*, but it might also *strike a chord*, *tug on heartstrings*, and produce a *ripple* of laughter or applause, or a *groundswell* of enthusiasm. We get with the *vibe*. *Stirred* by tender words, *two hearts* may, for a while, *beat as one*. Amid the *fluxes* and *flows* of conversation, your words may be *pitch perfect* one moment, *striking the right note*, or even *striking a chord*, but *hitting a discordant note* the next, so that *disharmony* reigns. In the fierce *counterpoint* of argument, a *crescendo* of matched voices reaches a *fever pitch*. Then one sharp word may create a *shock wave* that *reverberates* through the community, or through the ages, yielding a *tsunami* of anger. Modern marketing is all about *buzz*, about having your *finger on the pulse*, while in the political theater, a campaign and its leaders *act in concert* to produce a *movement* of followers

21. Schön, "Generative Metaphor."

22. To say that information is analogous to energy is perhaps underselling the connection between the two concepts, as physicists from James Clerk Maxwell and Ludwig Bolzmann to Albert Einstein and Stephen Hawking have shown that the relationship between energy and information is far reaching and subtle. So, e.g., Hawking's most famous result involved a relationship between energy and information that led him to predict on information-theoretic grounds that black holes must radiate energy. (For a readable summary, see Stuart Clark, "A Brief History of Stephen Hawking: A Legacy of Paradox," New Scientist, March 14, 2018, accessed March 1, 2023, https://www.newscientist.com/article /2053929-a-brief-history-of-stephen-hawking-a-legacy-of-paradox/.)

marching to the same beat. The political *piper plays a tune* and we *dance like puppets*; the *drummers* take us off to war, and in the *discordant cacophony* of contemporary culture, where it's hard to distinguish *signal* from *noise*, the propagandist can *drown out* voices of reason, and drive us into an *echo chamber* divorced of resonance with reality.

All of this is a long way from the tidy metaphor that popped meaning into a box. There is, to answer the question that heads this section, nothing *in* a word. Words are not like boxes, or pipes, or train carriages. Meanings are neither freight nor passenger. The resonance metaphor suggests that rather than being a "thing" inside or carried by another "thing," meaning is a process, a process that sustains an informational connection.[23] A word only *carries* meaning in something like the sense that Galileo's pendulums carried a beat.

On the conduit view, a semanticist's job would be no harder than delicately cutting off packaging to shine light on the content inside, but meanings, if we are right, are not the sorts of things that sit still while one tries to cast even metaphorical light on them. That is why the resonance metaphor is helpful to our project at this point. As we will discuss in subsequent chapters, idealizations that tend to come along with the metaphor that meanings are object-like are subtle and pervasive. It is far from clear what would constitute firm evidence for or against the content-delivery model of communication that accompanies the conduit metaphor, but it is problematically suggestive. We believe that the content-delivery aspect of the conduit metaphor sets traps.[24] It suggests, for example, that conventions relate terms only to contents that are in some sense neutrally shared. That conventions link words only to neutrally shared contents is not something to take for granted.

23. Here we use "information" in the very broad sense it has in Shannon Information Theory, and in discussions of information in physical systems. In this sense, a wave crashing on the shore carries information about the position of the moon and about far-off storms long since passed. The lay use of "information" is narrower, referring to what is newly and perhaps even explicitly conveyed about the world. When an utterance is described as "uninformative," what is usually meant is not that the utterance carried no physical information at all, but rather that it failed to describe anything unknown to the hearer.

24. Note that it is possible to use a conduit metaphor for information without assuming content delivery. Shannon Information Theory and the related development of Information Channel Theory illustrate exactly this. These models of information provide mathematical limits on the degree to which a stream of signals across a (possibly noisy) channel of limited bandwidth can result in information being shared between a source and a target, yet many of the results involve no assumptions at all about the particular process used to encode that information. Typically, no assumption is made that particular chunks of signal correspond directly to particular chunks of information. For a standard reference, see Cover and Thomas, *Elements of Information Theory*, and Hamming, *Coding and Information Theory*.

1.3. The Scholarship of Resonance

The idea of switching to a resonance metaphor is not new. For example, Keith Stenning, Alex Lascarides, and Jo Calder write that the "analogy of resonance is an important antidote to thinking that communication is merely about the transport of ideas."[25] We now discuss the work of some of the many prior scholars who advocate this antidote, inspiring our own use and development of the resonance metaphor. There is much we have learned from this prior work, but let us observe right away that our project is unlike any we know of in sociology, political science, linguistics, or philosophy (although we know of little philosophical work that uses a resonance metaphor at all). For in prior work, it is at least tacitly assumed that there is, in addition to resonance, some separate account of semantics or symbolic representation. By contrast, we seek to inject the "antidote" directly into the veins of the theory of linguistic meaning. Unlike any of the prior scholars whose work we will describe in this section, we propose analyzing all linguistic meaning as resonance, everything from the meaning of a morpheme to the meaning of a monograph, and we then use our account of meaning as resonance as the core element of our model of how language mediates the connections between people.

It is perhaps ironic that scholarship on resonance appears to have bloomed independently in a number of academic fields, with little apparent connection between these developments—a resonance zeitgeist spiriting itself into the fragmented landscape of contemporary humanities and social science. One large body of prior work is found in sociology, and in the borderlands between sociology and political science. This work is of direct relevance to the current project not merely because it uses the same physical metaphor, but because it concerns the same social and political issues. Prior authors in these areas have usually sought to account for what sorts of messaging resonates or creates resonance in social and political contexts. Resonance is explained at a pragmatic level, as perhaps involving holistic properties of a text. Sociological and political work on resonance barely touches on what linguistic meaning would have to be like to produce such effects. The same can be said of prior work on resonance in the field of linguistics: there is much discussion of how people use language to create emotional and social effects, and provide reinforcement or emphasis of the underlying linguistic meaning. The existence of an underlying linguistic meaning is simply assumed.

Let us turn first to work on the sociology of message framing, where resonance is a completely standard notion, especially in work on protest

---

25. Stenning et al., *Introduction to Cognition and Communication*, 8. Robert St. Clair ("Cultural Wisdom, Communication Theory, and the Metaphor of Resonance") is also explicit in contrasting resonance and transport metaphors for communication, and further contrasts the metaphor of resonance with a broader framing of social relationships and interactions in rhetorical terms.

movements. In the protest movement literature, springing from work of Robert Benford and David Snow, the question is, What makes a frame resonate?[26] For example, why would framing a message one way rather than another be more likely to induce someone to become active in a protest movement or attend a particular rally?

Although highly relevant to our project, the questions that Benford and Snow and followers ask is a slightly different one from the one we will ask in this chapter. For the moment, we will not ask why a communicative action resonates with someone, but rather what the resonances of that action are. Put differently, the framing literature tends to focus on why something is meaningful to someone, whereas we are considering the related question: what is the meaning? Here we must beg the indulgence of readers interested in questions raised by prior framing literature, for we will only return to the question of why a communicative action resonates with someone in chapter 3, after extensive further theoretical development.

Of particular importance to our project is Deva Woodly's analysis of the resonance of frames, which she applies to the messaging of political movements seeking to gain political acceptance.[27] Although it is set broadly in a tradition of political-frame analysis within which Benford and Snow's work is central, Woodly's focus is distinctive. Much work in that tradition of political-movement analysis centers on an empirical methodology that involves taxonomizing so-called collective action frames as regards what effects they seek to accomplish. Woodly's focus is more on the discursive features of arguments that make them resonate, which she achieves by leaning into a much older tradition, that of Aristotelian rhetoric, and by borrowing from twentieth-century scholarship in sociology and philosophy; in so doing, she argues for an analysis of what makes an argument resonate in terms of the way it is historically embedded in the culture of those it seeks to persuade.

26. The framing literature on resonance begins with Snow and Benford, "Clarifying the Relationship between Framing and Ideology." A central text of this work is now Benford and Snow, "Framing Processes and Social Movements," 611–39. Also highly relevant here is Gamson, *Talking Politics*, and Rodger Payne's "Persuasion, Frames and Norm Construction," which discusses coconstruction of resonant frames, paralleling moves we make when we introduce *accommodation* in chapter 6. Some recent work on resonance of frames (e.g., McDonnell, Bail, and Tavory, "A Theory of Resonance") takes a dynamic and interactional view on when resonance occurs that is very much in line with our own development. However, it remains the case that what is studied in this newer work is when resonance occurs and why, whereas we attempt to model *what* the resonances of an action are. Extending slightly from work on framing, Ottati, Rhoads, and Graesser ("The Effect of Metaphor on Processing Style in a Persuasion Task," 688) ask not when a frame resonates, but when a metaphor resonates, although there is a similar interest in the value of metaphor for persuasion.

27. Woodly, *The Politics of Common Sense*.

Woodly's arguments are grounded in extensive analysis of the trials and tribulations of two protest movements in the United States: the movements for equality of marriage rights and for minimum-wage laws. She demonstrates that the relative success of the marriage-rights movement in the United States correlates with the use of frames that in her sense are highly resonant. This means that arguments within these frames have just the right combination of new and old: new ways of looking at protest issues that work because they fit in well with preexisting ways of looking at core cultural concepts and practices. Woodly's work provides strong motivation for developing a better understanding of resonance, because she argues that proper deployment of resonant arguments can allow nonmainstream ("challenger") movements to create the conditions for political change. Woodly explains her project as follows: "I am not making the argument that successful movements are those that take advantage of serendipitous cultural resonances between their issue(s) and the prevailing ethos of a particular time. Instead, my claim is that movements can actually change the politics surrounding their issue through the disciplined use of resonant arguments over time."[28]

Let us give an example, adapting somewhat from her work: two highly resonant arguments used for same-sex marriage in the United States, a romantic argument and a stable monogamy argument. She has found that these arguments frequently co-occur in her sample of newspaper articles. The first uses the premise that the basis of marriage is love, and requires the additional, possibly unmentioned, premise that love is not specifically heterosexual. The second uses the premise that marriage promotes stability of relationships and monogamy, and requires the possibly unmentioned premise that stability of relationships and monogamy are desirable objectives independently of whether the relationship is heterosexual.

For each of the two arguments, the first premise is widely accepted within the background culture of US politics, and so doesn't need to be argued for. The second premises would seem to be more disagreeable to opponents of same-sex marriage. Yet it's also true that in both cases the second premise is a straightforward generalization from themes that are easily comprehensible even to opposing groups. It is in the nature of romantic love as it has been understood for millennia that it sometimes transgresses normative boundaries, and while opponents of gay marriage might choose to push the argument that homosexual love is itself in some sense unnatural, it is hard to even push the argument without at the same time recognizing and understanding the possibility of such love. For the stable-monogamy argument, again even opponents of same-sex marriage cannot help but understand the values of stability and monogamy, since those are two central values attached to their own conservative view of marriage. It would be rhetorically awkward for

28. Woodly, *The Politics of Common Sense*, 96.

conservative advocates of the restriction of marriage to heterosexual couples to offer an argument that stability and monogamy are inappropriate for same-sex relationships. More generally, what makes both arguments resonate is that they dig heavily into existing cultural schemas, giving them just enough twist to offer people a new way of looking at a problem, but not so much of a tug that they become unmoored.

Woodly's project, then, is to identify what it is about arguments that make them resonate and to show why this matters.[29] Our project overlaps with hers, but there are major methodological differences. The most glaring difference is that while we start from the way language functions and apply our model of language functioning to political examples, her work starts from deep analysis of political movements and tries to answer the question of how language functions in the cases she observes. Although coming from opposite directions, we see confluence in our projects.

Woodly talks about some arguments having resonances and others lacking them, but she doesn't extend this terminology to talk of argument X having resonances Y. For example, it's at least consistent with her account that the resonances of the romantic argument for marriage equality might be said to include nineteenth- and twentieth-century depictions in popular culture of romance culminating in marriage, as well as the strengthening practice through this period of people marrying for love. The framework we develop does allow us to talk of X having resonances Y, although we generalize such that X could be any communicative action and not just (the action of putting forward) an argument, and such that Y could be any feature of context,

29. In *The Politics of Common Sense*, Woodly gives two different analyses of resonance. The first, which we focus on in our discussion above, relates to the way that arguments use a shared cultural background for rhetorical advantage. She characterizes this background in terms of the Aristotelian notion of *endoxa*, i.e., understandings of how the world is shared by the majority, something close to what we term *collective attunements* in chapter 2. Woodly's second analysis of resonance is a more practical operationalization of the notion of resonance deployed in her quantitative empirical study of news stories. In this study, she creates a taxonomy of the main arguments appearing in the complete text of many hundreds of news stories on a topic (e.g., marriage equality), identifies each instance of each argument, and then uses statistical methods to make sense of the distribution of arguments. Departing from analyses of frames in the tradition that includes Benford and Snow's work, she defines a frame as a collection of commonly co-occurring arguments. She then characterizes a frame as resonant if it contains five or more commonly co-occurring arguments. Thus resonance on this second definition is a measure of the frame's ability to connect a significant number of distinct arguments. In our terms, we should say that the arguments that make up a Woodlyan frame resonate highly with each other, because each of them is found in the contexts in which the others are present, and we would further hypothesize that the reason for this is that the arguments cohere with each other to produce consonance of attunements when people accept the arguments together. While it is plausible that Woodly's quantitative measure relates to her discursive presentation of resonance in terms of shared cultural background, the nature of the connection is not obvious.

whether a style of depiction, a practice, a narrative, or a particular type of object (say gold rings, wedding dresses, and oversized cakes). When she talks of an argument being resonant, that translates for us, in the terms we define in the coming two chapters, as an argument harmonizing with the collective attunements of a certain community, or, more narrowly, as an argument harmonizing in a consonant way with that community.

Much work using resonance relates more closely to the development in the next chapter of the notion of *attunement*. In our terminology, an action has resonances, and people can be attuned to those resonances, as well as to all sorts of other things. Robert St. Clair's use of resonance perhaps falls into this category, as seen when he says, "Chants that accompany rituals . . . are sources of harmony . . . and are similar to vibrating tuning forks that beg others to join them in resonance."[30] As we understand his terminology, it is people who can be "in resonance."

In an influential sociological account of human relationships, what it is to lead a good life in the face of widespread alienation, and what this means for society, Hartmut Rosa also takes resonance as the central concept.[31] Here there is a significant difference in terms of goals, since in the current work we do not aim for a normative picture of how life should be lived, but for an account of how communication works. While there is much overlap, and while we draw from many of the same scholarly wellsprings as Rosa, the metaphor of resonance is also applied differently than in our work. For Rosa, resonant experiences connect different parts of a person's world, in a way that may be transformative. Rosa's (several) resonance relations are closely related to what we will term emotional attunements, involving affective relationships between people, and affective relationships between people and actions or things.

Given the difference in goals, we do not attempt here to do justice either to Rosa's work or to the growing literature it has seeded. That literature develops, critiques, and applies his account, especially in making sense of strongly resonant experiences that may center on a person's encounters with individuals who have had strikingly different life experiences that yet interlock with one's own lived history, or on encounters with a wide range of cultural artefacts whether movies, musical works, or museums. In a recent book-length treatment of Rosa's notion of resonance, Mathijs Peters and Bareez Majid observe that although resonance can be understood at large scales of time and culture, "it is not coincidence that . . . [they focus] on particular experiences that are vulnerable and brief."[32] They do not see Rosa's notion of resonance as being able in and of itself to sustain analysis of broad societal structures (or to provide a normative basis for such structures), but rather see larger-scale

30. St. Clair, "Cultural Wisdom," 80.

31. Rosa, *Resonance*.

32. Peters and Majid, *Exploring Hartmut Rosa's Concept of Resonance*, 150.

political and cultural currents as being reflected in the momentary experiences of resonance that are their central concern. Here there is a clear contrast with what we attempt in this volume. While we will, in section 3.9, consider what can make cultural objects resonate for a person, and while we will also, in section 6.4, proffer a related definition of what makes something meaningful to someone, our own focus is on developing a notion of resonance that can underpin communicative practice more generally, and at a societal level. For us, resonance is the basis of all communicative meaning, and does not come into play only during striking emotional or social experiences.

Within linguistics, John Du Bois has developed an important account of "dialogical resonance" centering on the way that speakers create connections within and across discourse, especially in spontaneous speech. The ensuing secondary literature builds not only on Du Bois's theoretical account, but also on the empirical methodology he developed for identifying resonance within spoken text, a methodology broadly set in the tradition of *conversation analysis*. Du Bois gives the following definition:

> Resonance is defined as the catalytic activation of affinities across utterances. Resonance is a property of relations between elements in discourse; as such it cannot be attributed to any element in isolation. It represents a developing process of activation and elaboration of certain aspects of the perceived relationship between comparable linguistic elements.[33]

Although Du Bois takes resonance to operate also at the level of systematic affinities people have for using the linguistic structures found in their social environment, his primary focus, and that of many following scholars, is on relatively short-term processes, whereby adjacent or nearby segments of text resonances depend on activation of working memory.[34] While Du Bois is careful to distinguish his notion of resonance from simple textual parallelism, he takes the notions to be intertwined, and paradigmatic examples of dialogical resonance involve clear repetition of discourse segments, often just a few seconds apart. While we will consider short-term attentional processes in this volume, there is a significant, and, we hope complementary, difference of focus in this regard. As we have

33. Du Bois, "Towards a Dialogic Syntax," 372.

34. An example of a well-developed project applying Du Bois's notion of resonance (although a wider range of relevant antecedent work is cited) is Mark Sicoli's analysis of Zapotec speech. He gives the following definition: "To resonate is to build signs that connect to and evoke the other through a parallelism of form that displays the common experience under development in the saying and doing of conversation as joint activity" (Sicoli, *Saying and Doing in Zapotec*, 17). As the definition suggests, Sicoli, in line with most literature adapting Du Bois's work, takes resonance to be a local property of discourse, albeit that he views the use of resonance as a somewhat conventionalized aspect of Zapotec speech practice.

emphasized repeatedly in this section, the ambit of our model is set at a broader level of communicative practice and long-term processes of ideological change.

A number of authors explicitly use the terminology of *attunement*, a philosophical example being the Wittgenstein scholar Stanley Cavell.[35] Cavell takes attunement to be a relationship only between people, whereas we will develop a broader notion that allows people to be jointly attuned to practices and all sorts of other things. Approaches to attunement like Cavell's, whereby attunement is a relationship between people, are found in a rich line of work developed especially by the sociologists Thomas Scheff and Randall Collins.[36] Again, we can think of the contrast between prior work and ours in terms of different questions we will seek to answer. The question posed in this line of sociological work is, simplifying massively, Who is someone attuned to (and why)? We, instead, will ask, What are people attuned to (and why)? And most importantly, our answer will be that one of the most important attunements people have is to the resonances of language.

To round out our discussion of the prior work on resonance on which we build, let us observe that one can think of what we are trying to achieve in this volume in terms of the program of the early behaviorist psychologist Ivan Pavlov. In his most famous experiments, he used a bell to activate his dog's appetite. As it happens, Pavlov experimented primarily not with a bell but with a metronome, which he found to be a more easily manipulable stimulus. Thus, the first behaviorist study of conditioning was a demonstration that autonomic salivary response can resonate with a pendulum, harkening back to Galileo's demonstration of how pendulums resonate with each other. More generally, the conditioning experiments of the behaviorist psychologists amount to a program of study of the development of what might be termed behavioral attunements animals have for the resonances of experimental and natural stimuli. We will not restrict ourselves, as the later behaviorists did, to the study of behavior independent of postulation of mental state, but we do take inspiration from the now highly unfashionable behaviorist paradigm. Like the behaviorists (and many others, especially in anthropology and sociology), we think that there is value in considering the actions of people independently of their conscious intentions.[37]

---

35. Cavell, *The Claim of Reason*. Although we find much to agree with in Cavell's Wittgensteinian, practice-based outlook, he differs sharply from us not only because he takes attunement to be only a relation between individuals (rather than between an individual and anything else), but also in that he seems to take the foundational nature of human attunement to suggest that much work on understanding language conventions is superfluous, whereas for us it is precisely human (collective) attunement that must be studied in order to understand what language conventions are and how they develop.

36. Scheff, *Microsociology*; Collins, *Interaction Ritual Chains*.

37. Let us give credit to two further prior (and well-developed) literatures that invoke concepts of resonance, both concerning psychology of language. Our model shares features with both of these antecedents, although our goals are somewhat different.

1.4. Associative Resonance

How could it be that something is meaningful but lacks content, or at least lacks anything for which the content metaphor is appropriate? Both as an intuition pump as a deeply problematic phenomenon in its own right, expressive language is a natural place to start investigating this question. It is somewhat obvious that ribald *fuck* and scatological *shit*, in their expletive uses, function partly by virtue of incongruous resonances, and it is hard to say what "ordinary content" could be attributed to either. If such epithets are content-laden boxes at all, then they are booby-trapped to explode on opening.

In the early and mid-twentieth century, philosophers studying expressives, indexicals, and performative utterances concluded that the study of natural language required different tools and resources than were available in "the formalist tradition," as David Kaplan calls it in his unpublished talk, "Ouch and Oops":

> Within philosophy and especially 20th-century philosophy, there are two great traditions of semantic theory, one a formalist tradition in which the great figures are all logicians: Frege, Russell, Tarski, Carnap, Church, and Kripke, and the other an anti-formalist tradition, in which the great figures are Wittgenstein, Strawson, Austin, and Grice. . . . The formalists for the most part study the idealized languages of science; the anti-formalists studied natural language, especially its context-sensitivity. It's from Wittgenstein that the slogan "Meaning is use" is derived.[38]

First, the term *resonance* is found in the *resonance model of reading comprehension*: see, e.g., O'Brien and Myers, "Text Comprehension: A View from the Bottom Up," and, for contextualization relative to other reading models, McNamara and Magliano, "Toward a Comprehensive Model of Comprehension." The resonance model of reading comprehension is a processing model concerned with the way earlier parts of a text affect the interpretation and integration of later parts of a text. The idea is that the effects are mediated by a passive process that does not require active inference, but is rather seen as a type of effortless psychological resonance, representation of the earlier text automatically affecting the building of new representations depending on degree of accessibility. Like our own model, resonance is seen as gradient, although the specific factors seen to affect the degree of resonance (e.g., textual similarity and textual distance) are specific to the domain being modeled.

Second is the notion of *motor resonance*: see Zwaan and Taylor, "Seeing, Acting, Understanding: Motor Resonance in Language Comprehension." Motor resonance concerns the activation of parts of the brain implicated in activation of motor signaling occurring as human movement-related tasks are perceived or comprehended, processes that have been argued to be mediated by "mirror neurons." The work relates to our discussion of mimicry, especially in section 6.4. The phenomena considered by Zwaan and Taylor are suggestive of the way in which language is "embodied," but we do not directly discuss embodied cognition or embodiment of language in this volume.

38. Kaplan, "The Meaning of Ouch and Oops," 2. Cf. fn. 40 in the Introduction.

The idealized artificial languages of science have limited indexicality, typically indexing the subject matter rather than the speaker; for example, they pertain to the structure of an argument, or the values of unknown objects through the use of explicit variables. They do not have slurs or expressives, albeit that one might detect a note of triumph in a logician's "QED." We do not find correlates of "I," "limey," or "wow" in, say, the language of calculus. Both formalists and informalists, historically, agreed that natural languages demanded a different approach to meaning than idealized languages of science. In his classic paper, "Demonstratives," Kaplan showed that one could add indexical and demonstrative expressions to a formal language (for example, to the predicate calculus) and provide a characterization of logical consequence for such languages. Thus, Kaplan showed that indexicals were not, after all, a barrier to the formalist tradition.

In "Ouch and Oops," Kaplan extends this project to expressives, including slurs. Kaplan suggests that expressive interjections like those of his talk's title do not have ordinary truth conditions, but rather *usage conditions*.[39] Thus, "damn" is a word a speaker uses as an adjectival modifier in a nominal when the following condition is met: the speaker is negatively disposed to the referent of the nominal. "Oops" is something you say when you've observed, in Kaplan's words, "a minor mishap." These usage conditions could be modeled as sets of contexts—the usage conditions for "ouch" are the set of contexts in which the speaker is in pain. Kaplan uses this to sketch a (nonstandard) account of logical consequence for expressives.

In his talk, Kaplan draws a distinction between descriptives and expressives—descriptives describe, whereas expressives express their contents. The content of an expressive is generally about the state of a speaker; for example, "ouch" expresses that the speaker is in pain. Kaplan relates his discussion of expressions of pain to Wittgenstein's, and this striking passage from the *Philosophical Investigations* makes clear the import of Wittgenstein's work both to Kaplan's project and to ours:

> Here is one possibility: words are connected with the primitive, the natural, expressions of the sensation and used in their place. A child has hurt himself and he cries; and then adults talk to him and teach him exclamations and, later, sentences. They teach the child new pain-behaviour.
>
> "So you are saying that the word 'pain' really means crying?"—On the contrary: the verbal expression of pain replaces crying and does not describe it.[40]

39. Kaplan, "The Meaning of Ouch and Oops."

40. Wittgenstein, *Philosophical Investigations*, 88, para. 241. Elsewhere, in material Wittgenstein was preparing for the *Investigations*, he makes a related statement, which is perhaps a passage Kaplan is referring to in his talk: "To say, 'I have pain' is no more a statement about a particular person than moaning is" (*The Blue and Brown Books*, 67). The logic of the tight connection that Kaplan draws between expressivity and indexicality

Wittgenstein's suggestion that an expression of pain replaces crying is consonant with our theme that whatever is needed to analyze such language, it is
not a standard notion of *content*, for it would seem at the very least somewhat
contrived to describe crying as having content.

Just as Kaplan's "Demonstratives" can be seen as an attempt to expand the
formalist tradition to indexicals, "Ouch and Oops" can be seen as an attempt
to expand the formalist tradition to account for expressives. Here is Kaplan's
analysis of "goodbye":

> I take it that the expressive (in this case, the word goodbye) has as its
> expressive content something like "You and I are now parting from one
> another for a significant period of time." Probably it doesn't any longer
> contain the elements of well-wishing, you know, the etymology of good-
> bye is from "God be with you," and probably well-wishing isn't any part of
> the expressive content any longer because I think nowadays if someone
> said goodbye and plainly did not wish the person well, you wouldn't think
> that that was an insincere use of goodbye, right? Goodbye seems perfectly
> acceptable to be used in that situation. So that's the expressive content.[41]

Kaplan says that the contemporary expressive content of "goodbye" corresponds to a proposition about the interlocutors' imminent separation.

In contrasting, as Kaplan does, the descriptive meaning of an expression
with its use, he says relatively little about what those uses might be. As against
a "normal declarative sentence," which "describes something," he says, "Let us
call an expression an expressive if it expresses or displays something which
either is or is not the case."[42] This suggests that an expressive may do one
of two things: expressing or displaying, although it's not clear whether he
intends any opposition between these two. However, any further hint as to
what expressives might do is lost in Kaplan's presentation, since he goes on to
analyze the semantic contribution of an expressive only in terms of the contexts in which it can be used, and not in terms of what its use is:

> Now I claim that "ouch" is an expressive that is used to express the con-
> tent that the agent is in pain, so what is the semantic information on
> this kind of model-theoretic analysis (if it is that)? The semantic infor-
> mation in the word "ouch" is represented by the set of those contexts at
> which the word "ouch" is expressively correct, namely, the set of those

---

mirrors the tight connection that Wittgenstein drew between the two, in remarks central to
what has become known in philosophy as "the private language argument." This is brought
out in the following characteristically aphoristic comment of Wittgenstein's, slightly later
in the same notes: "The man who cries out with pain, or says that he has pain, doesn't
choose the mouth which says it" (*The Blue and Brown Books*, 68).

41. Kaplan, "Ouch and Oops," 16.
42. Kaplan, "Ouch and Oops," 5.

contexts at which the agent is in pain. That set of contexts represents the semantic information contained in the word "ouch."[43]

So, the meaning of an expressive, according to Kaplan, is a set of contexts. Although Kaplan himself does not describe it in such terms, one might reasonably think that his usage conditions are analogous to Austin's *preconditions* on a speech act, the conditions that must prevail in order for someone to perform a licit act, such as sentencing someone in a court of law. So what Kaplan is discussing under the name of use conditions is what must prevail for someone to say "Ouch!," or at least what *does* prevail when people thus vocalize and they're doing so for appropriate reasons.

It is immediately clear that there is much more to say. Establishing that preconditions hold is not the most important part of what the various speech acts discussed by Austin do, and it doesn't seem to exhaust what some of the expressions Kaplan takes to be expressives do. Maybe saying "Ouch!" establishes that you're in pain, but analyzing greetings and farewells solely in terms of preconditions would leave too much unexplained. Why do we typically exchange greetings and farewells rather than simply having one person say "Hello!" or "Goodbye!" and why does a meeting bereft of these niceties seem so lacking, even when it is quite clear to everyone exactly when the meeting started and when it ended? Establishing the preconditions of individual actions of saying "Hello!" and "Goodbye!" might elucidate the social practices that these words play roles in, and elucidate the role that rituals of greeting and farewell play in establishing social connection, but it tells us very little about why those practices exist. It's as if we were to say that the significance of putting on your seat belt is that it is done after getting into a car, which would give it essentially the same significance as starting the engine. This would fail to clarify that belting up and starting the engine have totally different functions, and would fail to identify the significance of either within the broader practice of driving.

The view we develop in this book suggests that people taking part in a greeting ritual are not merely signaling the state they are in, but are cocreating a state, a state of affiliation as an interactional group, a state of joint attunement to common protocols, and a state of collective harmony. We can put it this way: greeting is not merely something an individual does when in a state of readiness to enter into an interactional relationship in order to signal that state. Rather, a relationship consists of connections between people, connections consist in joint behaviors and attunements, and greeting rituals are *joint behaviors that constitute part of such a relationship*. We should not look at the resonances of "hello" as merely reflections of a state that someone is in. Rather, we should look more holistically at the resonances of entire greeting rituals as part of an emergent cocreated state of interactional group membership.

43. Kaplan, "Ouch and Oops," 10.

Kaplan's theory of expressives does, however, give us a starting point. The starting point is the idea that expressive communicative actions reflect a pre-existing state, that reflection being a first example of what we will term the *resonances* of an action.

We will, for the purposes of this chapter, make a simplification and focus on what could be termed *correlational* or *associative* resonance, whereby things have resonance with each other if they tend to co-occur. Resonance can be dependent on considerably more complex relations of similarity or narrative fit, as we shall later see. But we will simplify and idealize dramatically here and define what it means for an action of a given type to have associative resonances with a feature of context in terms of the propensity of the feature to co-occur with a token of the action. The types of actions that are relevant are communicative practices, and what we are doing here can be seen as characterizing the abstract meaning of a communicative practice in terms of what the context tends to be like when the practice is performed.

We take the context to be the way things are, but relativized to parameters that are significant for a conversational interaction. Standard parameters include the time and location of the event, and/or the identity of an agent whose perspective is relevant, for example, the speaker or hearer. In the standard terminology of work on meaning in analytic philosophy, our contexts are *centered possible worlds*. Features of context include anything and everything. They include physical things like tables and physical events like rain, psychosocial features like someone's feeling of pain or of affiliation, and also cultural features, like the everyday practices that people tend to take part in, including communicative practices. However, our notion of context allows us to distinguish features around which the context is centered, like the current speech event (if any), the view to the left, what the individual around which the context is thinking at the time at which it is centered (if anything), and the weather in the same place but twelve hours earlier.

The following definition, which takes a practice to have an extension consisting of all the instances of the practice, provides the first step of the technical development of our model:

> **Associative resonances of an action:** A feature of context is a (positive) resonance of an action in the extension of a practice to the extent that an occurrence of the action changes the probability of that feature (positively).[44]

44. A related definition has been given as a general account of the meaning of animal alarm calls by Dezecache and Berthet, "Working Hypotheses on the Meaning of General Alarm Calls." They suggest the following definition of the meaning of an alarm call: "The particular set of circumstances in which calls occur more than expected by chance will be referred to as their 'semantics' or their 'semantic domain,'" (114). From a philosophical

So, if people are 90 percent more likely to have just experienced pain after saying "ouch" than if they hadn't said "ouch," then the strength of the resonance of the pain feature for this action is +90 percent.

Much of this book is concerned with societal practices, especially communicative practices, and the above definition of resonance provides a crucial component of our analysis of practice, and of the meaning of a practice. This is developed further in the next chapter. In talking of the meaning or resonances of a practice, one might be taken to refer only at a high level to the broad significance the practice has, whereas we are referring at a low level to the resonances associated with individual instantiations of the practice by virtue of instantiating it. For example, in talking of the meaning of the practice of exchanging rings in a wedding ceremony, one might refer to the cultural significance of the fact that a society has such a practice, a sort of sociological meta-analysis of the practice of exchanging rings. By the associative resonances of the action of exchanging rings, we refer to the significance that exchanging rings tends to have each time they are exchanged, not the significance for the culture of the fact that it has a practice of exchanging rings. However, and as will become important in part II of the book, it will turn out that resonances involve much high-level information, information about the ideology of the communities that perform them that goes well beyond the immediate significance that participants in a particular action, whether an action of ring exchange or an action of saying "ouch," are typically aware of.

In Bayesian terms, the strength of the resonance that an action has for a feature is the probability of the feature given the action minus the prior probability of the feature, what would be written in standard mathematical notation as p(feature| action) - p(feature).[45] When considering narrowly how

---

point of view, their definition is clearly Kaplanian, but with the extension that they consider probability boosts rather than uniform presence across uses of a call.

45. A number of standard Bayesian and information-theoretic notions could potentially be used in a definition of resonance. For example, we could have defined the strength of resonance between an action and a feature of context in terms of the *mutual information* between them. The definition we give is chosen both because it is the simplest that we could conceive of, and because it sets the stage for a strikingly straightforward definition of the presuppositions of an action, although we don't define this concept until chapter 5. Technically, associative resonances as we define them can be negative as well as positive. For example, a negative resonance of someone saying "ouch" would be the speaker feeling completely calm and relaxed, and a negative resonance of people greeting each other would be that they are in the process of parting. The existence of negative resonances plays no special role in this volume, and the reader can safely focus on positive resonance when we use the word *resonance*. However, we should note that when in chapter 6 we discuss the possibility of divergent accommodation, this could be thought of as accommodating (i.e., adapting) to selected negative resonances of the actions of out-group members.

utterances are interpreted by a particular hearer (or, more generally, a particular observer of a communicative act), it would suffice to consider the probabilities as subjective probabilities based on the hearer's prior information about actions of that type, and the probability boost as being a measure of the evidence that the action provided about the features of context. However, we understand resonances as being independent of particular observers, as inherent properties of actions qua instances of a given type of action, and we must be a little careful here.

There is a well-established (but controversial) tradition of analyzing probabilities as objective, so that, for example, the probability of decay of an atom of a particular isotope given the isotope's half-life might be regarded as independent of the observer, as an inherent propensity of the atom. However, we are concerned with intrinsically social actions, for which the word "objective" is not entirely apt. Although we can conceive of cases where this might be inadequate,[46] we will adopt a *frequentist* interpretation of probabilities. That is, it suffices for current purposes that the resonance of actions instantiating practices is in principle measurable in terms of frequency of co-occurrence, and frequency of occurrence of one without the other. What is crucial to such an interpretation is that it is clear what set of situations is to be considered in calculating frequencies, and hence probability boosts. We discuss this issue in section 1.8, below, and return to it in chapter 2, especially section 2.5.

Let us examine the resonances of an utterance of "ouch." To do this, we need to consider a set of contexts centered on someone saying "ouch" and compare it to a set of what we might call *index* situations. Resonances are probability boosts, and the probability boost is the difference between the probability of some feature given an utterance of "ouch" and the prior probability of that feature. The index situations are those that determine the prior probability. The choice of index situations is important, and we will have more to say about it, but for the moment let us consider a set of contexts centered on a randomly chosen living human. The features we will consider are (i) recent speaker pain, (ii) speaker being somewhat fluent in English, (iii) speaker being a living human, and (iv) the increasing cost of fish. Then:

   i. the probability of recent speaker pain given that the speaker said "ouch" is much higher than the prior probability of pain, so this is a strong resonance;

---

46. A case where the frequentist interpretation would not be easily applied would be a communicative practice that is rarely carried out but that is established by some sort of fiat, e.g., a religious ritual to be carried out in a certain rare circumstance, like the Second Coming of the Messiah. In principle, this ritual practice has a meaning, but it is not straightforward to express its resonances in terms of frequency-based probability, without considering frequency counterfactually, across alternative worlds in which the Second Coming occurred.

ii. the probability of English fluency given that the speaker said "ouch" is somewhat higher than the prior probability, so this is a medium- to high-strength resonance;

iii. the prior probability of the centered individual being human and alive is already high in the contexts being considered, so the utterance produces no probability boost, and this is not a resonance;

iv. there is presumably little correlation between people saying "ouch" and the increasing cost of fish, so there is only very low resonance, if any. To the extent that someone exposed to a sudden increase in fish prices might signal their feelings using such an exclamation, it is because that cost increase has caused them pain, or because they are jokingly exploiting the resonances of "ouch" to make an analogy with the feeling of pain salient.

Our analysis of resonances is intrinsically *scalar* rather than *categorical*. A scalar relation is one that, like the probability of A given B, admits of degrees. The standard entailment relationship of logic from Aristotle on is in this sense categorical. Kaplanian meaning is categorical insofar as it involves the set of contexts in which an expressive is used, and a given context either is or is not a member of that set. Resonance is thus obviously unlike Kaplanian meaning.

For purposes of comparison, a categorical notion of resonance can be derived by assuming some specific threshold degree of probability boost, so that we can talk of a feature of the context being a resonance of an action just in case the feature has that action as a resonance to that threshold degree. For example, that threshold could be the degree that could be a probability boost of .5, or a psychologically determined threshold, say the threshold that would tend to make a connection between the action and a feature noticeable to a random person chosen off the street who'd seen the action three or more times. Leaving aside the details of how the threshold should be set, we can easily define a Kaplanian meaning of an action as the set of contexts that have features that are resonances of the action. Extending our metaphorical terminology, we can also say that these contexts are resonances of the action.

Kaplanian meaning and resonance can both be related to what is referred to in biology, economics, and game theory as *costly signaling*. Costly signaling is the sending of a message in a way that requires significant effort, as opposed to cheap signaling, which is usually taken to include much vocal communication. Words are cheap. In many cases, what makes a costly signal effective is that it involves manifesting a property by putting effort into some action that could not have been performed were the property lacking. We could say, for example, that the Kaplanian meaning of driving to work is a complex proposition, something like the conjunction of the propositions that one has access to a vehicle in a drivable state, that one has the physical capacity and legal license to drive, that one has a workplace physically located at some drivable distance from one's current location, and so on. Therefore at least one way to signal this complex proposition or any of its entailments, a very straightforward and not easily refutable way, would be simply to drive to work. Putting in that effort obviously shows that you have the capacity to do so. In our terms, having access to a car is one of the resonances of the action of driving to work.

One can understand much real-world signaling in terms of resonance. Absent a medical condition, a resonance of burping after eating is that one has eaten a significant amount of food in a rapid or delightfully haphazard manner. This natural resonance then explains the fact that in some parts of the Middle East and Asia a mild burp after a meal has come to have a conventional nonnatural significance, a polite expression of the quality and quantity of the repast. It carries a convincing message to the extent that it is hard to fake. Thus does a burp become resonant.

Your capabilities are resonances of various actions you perform, specifically, and rather obviously, all the actions that evidence your capability. So, just as with the driving to work case, one can signal one's ability to invade a country by massing multiple divisions of heavily armed troops on the border, the resonance of this action providing compelling proof that one has the relevant military capacity. Other, more standard examples of costly signals are the provision of a lifetime warranty, indicating a seller's faith in the reliability of a product, and the ostentatious display of finery, whether a monarch's clothes and castles or a peacock's feathers. What such signals lack in subtlety and ease of performance, they make up for in clarity and probative value. Why? Because insofar as a particular costly signal depends on preconditions that are themselves incontrovertible, the signal is completely reliable. Costly signals have reliable resonances.

1.5. Revelations

What communicative act does someone perform when they utter an expressive? It is tempting to say that in uttering an expressive, speakers inform hearers of their state, so an expressive act would be an act of informing. This is unsatisfying, since it does not distinguish the act performed by saying "Ouch!" from the act performed by saying "I just felt a sudden sharp pain." Furthermore, if saying "Ouch!" is an act of informing, why is it that we would not normally describe an "Ouch!" that way? Suppose that Jason says "Ouch!" and David reports the vocalization by saying "Jason just informed me that he's in pain." The implication would be that David didn't think Jason had reflexively responded to pain, but rather had, perhaps humorously, exploited the convention that "Ouch!" expresses pain, and said "Ouch!" in order that David would recognize that Jason was sending a standard pain signal. Such labored ouches are not direct expressions of pain, in much the same way that saying "Ha, ha!" is not a direct way of expressing that you find something funny.

In fact, saying "Ha, Ha!"—like "Ha, bloody ha!"—commonly expresses not the amusement of true laughter, but, sarcastically, the opposite. Such cases of exploitation of a communicative convention are naturally analyzed as involving pragmatic reasoning to figure out the intention behind someone's communicative act, typically in the style developed by the philosopher Paul Grice.[47] More generally, Kaplan's account of expressive meaning is compatible with a Gricean explanation of how all uses of expressives convey information. The idea would be that when a speaker says "Ouch!" genuinely, a hearer who knows that "Ouch!" is something people say when they just experienced pain can reason that the speaker said "Ouch!" in order that the hearer would recognize their intention to convey that they just experienced pain. On this view, understanding someone who says "Ouch!" involves substantive theory of mind. We will not attempt to provide detailed arguments against such an account, but rather try to describe how a simpler, more direct account of expressive acts that doesn't revolve around communicative intentions could work. But what could it mean for something to be a direct expression of a feeling, and what would it mean for the effect on its hearer to be more direct than recognition of an intention to communicate that feeling?

The later Wittgenstein begins his quest for an account of meaning in the *Philosophical Investigations* with a nod sixteen centuries earlier, to St. Augustine. Here is a quote from the *Confessions*, going slightly beyond what Wittgenstein cited:

> My infancy did not go away (for where would it go?). It was simply no longer present; and I was no longer an infant who could not speak, but now a chattering boy. I remember this, and I have since observed how I learned to speak. My elders did not teach me words by rote, as they taught me my letters afterward. But I myself, when I was unable to communicate all I wished to say to whomever I wished by means of whimperings and grunts and various gestures of my limbs (which I used to reinforce my demands), I myself repeated the sounds already stored in my memory by the mind which thou, O my God, hadst given me. When they called some thing by name and pointed it out while they spoke, I saw it and realized that the thing they wished to indicate was called by the name they then uttered. And what they meant was made plain by the gestures of their bodies, by a kind of natural language, common to all nations, which expresses itself through changes of countenance, glances of the eye, gestures and intonations which indicate a disposition and attitude—either to seek or to possess, to reject or to avoid. So it was that by frequently hearing words, in different phrases, I gradually identified the objects which the words stood for and, having

47. Grice, *Studies in the Way of Words*.

formed my mouth to repeat these signs, I was thereby able to express my will.[48]

Perhaps the simplest communicative acts are the preverbal whimperings and grunts of which Augustine speaks, and this may be the earliest learned discussion of expressive meaning, notably presented with a Judeo-Christian revision of a Platonic nativist attitude toward the inbuilt nature of "sounds already stored in my memory" and toward "the gestures of their bodies . . . a kind of natural language, common to all nations." What caught Wittgenstein's attention, however, was Augustine's description of naming and pointing to objects, which Wittgenstein takes as inspiration for his celebrated *builders' game*:

> Let us imagine a language for which the description given by Augustine is right. The language is meant to serve for communication between a builder A and an assistant B. A is building with building-stones: there are blocks, pillars, slabs and beams. B has to pass the stones, and that in the order in which A needs them. For this purpose they use a language consisting of the words "block," "pillar," "slab," "beam." A calls them out;—B brings the stone which he has learnt to bring at such-and-such a call.—Conceive this as a complete primitive language.[49]

Wittgenstein's builders' game provides something like the level of simplicity and directness of communication that we are interested in here, a good starting point for the more complex cases we will turn to in later chapters. And "ouch" and "oops," like "block" and "pillar," are not costly signals. Yet even Wittgenstein's builders' game could be said to have an extra level of complexity to it beyond what we need for "ouch" and "oops," insofar as the builders are engaged in an interaction in which both players must act, whereas it is not obvious that "ouch" or "oops" require any action on the part of the hearer. Indeed, like many expressives, it is striking how natural it is to utter them when no one else is present. So let us first consider how these relatively noninteractional expressives function, and then turn to the interactional case.

For "ouch" and "oops," we agree with Kaplan that the primary function is to "display," that is, simply to manifest or reveal a state. We will term them *revelatory expressives*, as opposed to "hello," "goodbye," "please," and "thank you," which we will call *interactional expressives*. To utter a revelatory expressive is, as it were, to wear your heart on your sleeve. It makes sense that as social animals humans would tend to reveal various aspects of their states, including their feelings and their status, to those around them, because knowing something about each other enables us to coordinate more effectively. We find the metaphor of "wearing" apt because much of what people actually wear can also be seen as revelatory. The

48. Augustine of Hippo, *Confessions and Enchiridion*, ch. 8, para. 13.

49. Wittgenstein, *Philosophical Investigations*, 3.

crown, the bowler hat, and the peaked cap all reveal your place in society, and both the style of your jeans and the ring on your finger can reveal who you roll with. And although the use of "wear" involves a metaphorical extension, something else you can be said to wear is the expression on your face, which can be revelatory, expressing your feelings.[50] To say "Ouch!" is like briefly grimacing.

The idea we want to pursue, then, is that when someone wears an expression on their face, we can see what they are feeling, and that other revelatory acts function similarly. The standard Gricean view of the communicative function of declarative assertions[51] involves the following steps:

(i) the speaker has an intention to communicate (their belief that) the world is a certain way, and wishes for the hearer to recognize that intention;

(ii) the speaker produces an utterance that portrays the world as being that way;

(iii) the hearer grasps that portrayal;

(iv) the hearer recognizes the speaker's intention (or the speaker's underlying belief).

The Gricean view is idealized and covers only part of what is communicated, but it seems a reasonable description of the way in which much content is conveyed in a simple cooperative two-person act of assertion. Compare this to what happens in a simplified, passive model of perception:

(i) entities have externally detectable qualities that are correlated with their state;

(ii) an able observer perceiving those qualities recognizes that the entity has the corresponding underlying states.

When you perceive someone to be happy because they are smiling, the basic process, whether the smiler is a baby or an adult, is the second, perceptual

---

50. The presumed strong link between facial expressions and underlying emotions is such that many analyses of emotions take facial expression as the primary organizing principle behind taxonomies of emotional states, a classic example of such a facial-expression-based taxonomic organization being the Plutchik wheel (Plutchik, *The Emotions*). Further, even the adage "The face cannot lie," though clearly not literally true, has some psychological backing. Paul Ekman, famous for a theory of deception identification based on facial cues, comments (in a paper highly relevant to the current discussion), "When an emotion occurs, impulses are always sent to the facial muscles. There is no choice about that. We can choose to try to interfere with the appearance of that expression, we may be able to interrupt the action of the facial muscles, or dampen them so that nothing is visible, but we cannot choose to prevent the impulses from being sent to the facial nerve. We can also choose to make a set of facial movements which resemble a facial expression of emotion, but it will differ detectably from an emotional expression" ("Should We Call It Expression or Communication?," 336).

51. Grice, "Meaning," 383–85.

process. To put recognition of emotion in terms we will introduce in chapter 2 and discuss at greater length in chapter 3 (especially section 3.4), the observer becomes attuned to the smiler's emotional state because the observer is attuned to the practice of smiling. Attunement to the resonance of smiling enables a nonreflective and direct perception of that state, *direct* in the sense that the psychologist Gibson used that term in his development of a theory of visual perception.[52] There is no essential need for intention recognition.

Of course, an adult may feign a smile, and they may smile because they have the intention to convey happiness or some other message, and you may or may not perceive this intention, so the communicative process involved in understanding a smile may sometimes be more complicated. Crucially, it need not be. We may say in such a case that a communicative action drawn from the class of expressives is being used to perform a nonexpressive act, or at least is being use to perform something other than the expressive act with which it is most commonly associated.[53]

Likewise, when we recognize the pain of someone grimacing, or the pain of someone who utters "ouch," our recognition of the state of pain does not imply the recognition of an intention. That, we suggest, is the sense in which the communicative process associated with a revelatory act like saying "ouch" is simpler and more direct than that for an utterance of "I just felt a sudden, sharp pain." If anything, recognition of the significance of a revelatory act implies the absence of recognition of an intention, that is, the absence of recognition of an intention to act in a pained way in order to convey something that might or might not be reflective of the level of pain that the actor is feeling.

The directness of recognition of revelatory acts again suggests a respect in which the resonance metaphor is more appropriate for expressives than is the content-delivery metaphor. An expressive is an outer counterpart of what is always, at least in part, an inner state. Its presence in the air between speaker and hearer enables the hearer to become attuned to that inner state in much the same way as registering someone's red face allows you to become attuned to someone's state of excitement, and feeling their pulse allows you to become attuned more specifically to their heartbeat. A red face is not a box containing excitement; a pulse is not a box containing a heartbeat; and neither is "ouch" a container for painful content.

---

52. Gibson, "A Theory of Direct Visual Perception."

53. It might be said that all communicative acts are expressive, for even when one performs the act of asserting, one must express the thought that one then asserts. We suggest avoiding this terminology and talking of "depicting a thought" rather than "expressing a thought." A resonance of an utterance of a declarative sentence would then be the act of depicting a thought, and if this declarative is not part of a more complex sentence, then a further resonance would be the assertion of that thought. An utterance of a declarative can then be said to be primarily depictive rather than expressive (although it might additionally have some expressive resonances).

The idea we are proposing is that expressives should be thought of not as containing meanings, but as *sustaining social connections*. Use of revelatory expressives helps individuals become attuned to each other, in the sense that they allow the feelings of a person to become correlated with the model an observer has of those feelings. Our earlier technical definition of what it means for a feature of the context to be a resonance of an act is that the act is correlated with that feature. From a hearer's perspective, the act provides probabilistic evidence for the state, although the hearer need not be understood as reflectively weighing up this evidence. Such resonance is what allows a hearer to recognize a smile as the appearance of a happy person and to recognize an "ouch" as the sound of a person who experienced pain. Further, an observer perceiving the state of another may recognize what it would be like to be in that state themselves. So, resonance allows us to empathize with others whose states we can perceive. As discussed in section 3.9, if the connection between people is strong, one person may even feel another's pain, at least in attenuated form. Resonance can hurt. This is a theme that will become still clearer in section 10.2, where we apply our resonance-based approach to yet another type of expressive word, namely slurs. Slurs, we will argue, can not only reveal emotion, but also reveal ideology. Furthermore, slurs do not merely *reveal*, they also *inflict*, and sometimes they may inflict pain.

1.6. Interactional Expressives as Moves in a Game

Moving from the revelatory to the interactional case, we now discuss models of interactions as games, so that a standard game-theoretic approach can be used to model expressive acts, and we can make more concrete the technical underpinning for the resonance approach to interaction. Broadly, resonance between communicating agents is analogous to coordination in a game. However, the real world does not sharply delineate a definition of the game, the strategies adopted by players, and the individual token actions played. This takes us to a consideration of the difference between what is expressed and what the expression presupposes. This distinction, we argue, is crucial in the case of expressives, since the role they play in the social world hinges on presupposed resonances.

An example of a simple but devastatingly effective signaling system is given by insects in a colony under attack. They may release a specific pheromone that spreads appropriate defensive behavior, a concerted counterattack coordinated by a chemical cocktail. In game theory, a signaling system becomes part of a strategy, an idea famously developed in David Lewis's PhD thesis, which became his 1969 book *Convention*, where the concept of a *signaling game* is introduced.[54]

54. Lewis, *Convention*.

Let us say that in what we'll call *the coffee game*, there are a certain range of states {*hunger, thirst, sleepiness*} of a player named David (the sender), a certain range of actions {*moan, nod, blink*, . . .} that David can perform, and a further set of actions that consist of providing goods {*food, coffee, nothing*, . . .} that a second player, Jason (the receiver), can perform in response. Let us assume that Jason cannot directly detect David's state. We might suppose that there is a particular pattern of utilities associated with Jason's actions, so that there is, for example, higher utility to both players for *coffee* when David is in a state of sleepiness than for any other action, and suboptimal utility for *coffee* in any other state. Suppose that signaling is cheap, that is, that there is no significant inherent difference in utility between each of David's actions. In that case, it doesn't matter exactly what action David produces in any particular state. A communicative strategy for David would consist in a particular pattern of actions by David, for example, always nodding when sleepy. If Jason now has a strategy of performing action *coffee* when and only when David has performed action *nod*, the net result will obviously be that Jason provides the coffee exactly when it's needed, despite not being able to detect that state directly. If both players reliably stick to these strategies, then the combination of strategies will constitute a convention between them. The *sleepiness-nod-coffee* convention allows the two players to succeed in coordinating, and their joint work can proceed apace, with joint utility for both parties.

Given some facts about how often different combinations of states and actions happen, we can calculate the resonances of the action of nodding. Suppose further that David is sleepy 25 percent of the time, thirsty 25 percent of the time, and hungry 50 percent of the time. Suppose further that after some large number of iterations of the game, David nods 100 percent of the time when he is sleepy, 40 percent of the time when he is thirsty, and 0 percent of the time when he is hungry. The probability of David's states corresponds directly to their frequencies, so, for example, p(*sleepiness*) = 0.25. The boost that nodding gives to David having been sleepy is then p(*sleepiness*| *nod*) - p(*sleepiness*) = 1 - 0.25 = 0.75. As far as David's initial states are concerned, then, it can be seen that the resonances of nodding are *hunger*: -0.5, *thirst*: 0.15, and *sleepiness*: 0.75. It can be seen that once a convention like *sleepiness-nod-coffee* is somewhat in place, as in the above scenario, the strongest resonance of David's nodding, from among his prior states, is sleepiness. Likewise, if Jason always brings coffee when David nods, and rarely brings it otherwise, then both David's state of sleepiness and David's action of nodding will be resonances of *coffee*. An observation of the action *coffee* would provide evidence for both the prior state and the prior action.

Resonance in the coffee game is asymmetric in the sense that the actions of the sender and receiver are not similar. Symmetric resonance is exemplified by the spread of laughter or barking, whereas the resonances of David's nodding are asymmetric, more like the Pavlovian metronome than Galileo's pendulum.

The pattern *sleepiness-nod-coffee* is our first example of an interactional *practice*. It is much simpler than the more realistic practices we will be considering in future chapters. Crucially, it is the practice that gives actions their significance, or, as we will say, their resonances. That is, we will not be primarily concerned with what, if anything, David thinks he is communicating on any particular occasion when he nods, or with what Jason thinks David meant by nodding when Jason brings David coffee immediately afterward. Our focus will rather be on the significance of nodding within the context of a practice of doing so at certain times and with prototypical outcomes. This provides the blueprint for all the later analyses in the book: the resonances of a communicative action will be given by whatever practices the action can reasonably be taken to instantiate. Note that this does not mean that the intentions or other mental states of interlocutors are irrelevant to meaning as defined in terms of meaning, for it is quite possible for a practice to depend on any arbitrary aspect of an interlocutor's mental state, whether that be a state of surprise, a state of pain, or a state of intending to make a joke. But we are getting ahead of ourselves: the practice we're now considering doesn't involve mental states of surprise, pain, or intention, merely states of sleepiness, hunger, and thirst.

What does it mean to say that two people's actions are coordinated? It is easy to understand in symmetric cases where coordination simply means that all players do the same, but game theory is helpful in understanding what coordination means in asymmetric cases. The relevant technical notion is that of a *coordination game*. This is a game in which there are multiple solutions (technically, *equilibria*, e.g., *Nash equilibria*), and where players perform actions that accord with the same solution. In the above example, David and Jason coordinate on the strategy pair *sleepiness→nod* and *nod→coffee*, but an equally effective solution would have been the pair of strategies *sleepiness→blink* and *blink→coffee*. Thus, game theory provides one way of understanding what it means for people to be coordinated, or, as we will put it in the next chapter, to be *attuned* to each other dispositionally: they are attuned in the sense that they have matched strategies in a coordination game.[55] The sense of connection that people feel with each other might perhaps be related not only to their capacity to empathize, as discussed in the previous section, but also to how attuned they are in this technical sense. That is, the depth of connection we feel with someone might depend on how effortlessly we can coordinate shared dispositions that result in mutually advantageous outcomes to our interactions.

The fact that there is no a priori reason for players to prefer one solution to another in a signaling game is analogous to Ferdinand de Saussure's notion

---

55. We return to the nature of coordination in section 8.2, and provide a fuller definition.

of *arbitrariness of the sign* in natural languages.[56] That is, the coffee game illustrates not merely a convention, but an arbitrary convention, since other conventions would have done just as well. The development of the convention over multiple plays (it being an *iterated game*) illustrates a difference between costly signaling and cheap talk. Although conventional use of costly signals does emerge over time (the peacock's biologically costly feathers, for example, have a certain arbitrariness to them), costly signaling can operate without preexisting conventions: doing something that requires property X provides evidence that you have property X to a suitably perceptive observer. Thus, costly signaling builds on an existing resonance. On the other hand, cheap talk in the coffee game displays the emergence of an entirely new resonance. David and Jason initially dance to their own beats, but come to be attuned without negotiation or prior alignment of dispositions.

In the coffee game, nodding is an interactional signal: it functions as part of a strategic pairing of actions by distinct agents. But according to the definitions we've given, it is also revelatory: it is correlated with David's tiredness, and hence could potentially reveal that state to a suitably able observer. So what, then, is the meaning of a nod in the game?

On our proposal, the meaning of a nod is its resonances, a distribution of probability boosts of different features in the context. But in this section, we want both to contrast our proposal with a more Kaplanian approach, and to make a further argument that does not depend crucially on the fact that resonances are scalar. So let us also consider two variants of Kaplan's notion of meaning, just similar enough to resonance to make comparison easy, but categorical rather than gradient in the way that resonance is. Consideration of these variants will reveal stark differences between the Kaplanian approach and ours, while also highlighting a crucial issue that will be clarified in the coming chapters, the issue of which contexts are considered in defining resonance.

1.7. Differentiating Kaplanian Expressive Meaning from Resonance

Let us say that the *Kaplanian meaning of an action* is a function mapping features of context to 1 if the conditional probability of the feature given the action is 1, and to 0 otherwise. Before proceeding, let us touch on two somewhat obvious but inessential differences between how Kaplan actually defined expressive meaning and our definition of Kaplanian meaning. First, Kaplan talked about the meaning of an *expression*, whereas we talk of the Kaplanian meaning of an *action*, by which, properly speaking, we mean the Kaplanian meaning of a *type* of action or practice. At least when the actions in question are utterances, this difference is just terminological. Second, for

56. Saussure, *Course in General Linguistics*, 67–69.

uniformity with our notion of resonance, we have defined Kaplanian meanings as functions from features to probabilities, whereas Kaplan defined expressive meanings as sets of contexts. However, the Kaplanian meaning of an action corresponds to a set of contexts in an obvious way, that is, to the set of contexts that bear all and only the features the action maps to 1.

There is a third possible, or even probable difference with Kaplan insofar as it is not entirely clear what notion of context he was assuming in the "Ouch and Oops" talk, although one might potentially interpolate what he intended from his well-known writings on the topic elsewhere. A context, as we've introduced it, is just reality seen from a certain perspective, and we assume that this is a good enough match for what Kaplan had in mind for current purposes.

Above, we discussed contexts as relevant for an artificial game, the coffee game. We could stipulate that what we took to be reality was much reduced, and contained only the states and actions mentioned in the game, but this would to some extent belie the reason for using the artificial model in the first place. The intuition behind the game is that it is a simplified model of a real-world language community. So, again for the sake of argument, let us assume that in discussing the coffee game, reality has been fictitiously augmented with the two players performing their role in the coffee game, and centered on communicative episodes in the game.

As defined, the basic Kaplanian meaning of an action is a set that includes every feature that is found in all contexts of use. Since in all contexts the players are named David and Jason, part of the basic Kaplanian meaning of a nod is that the players are named David and Jason. Also, part of the basic Kaplanian meaning is that brown butterfly wings contain melanin, and that every mouse is self-identical. We will tackle these in reverse order, to bring out differences between Kaplanian meaning and the resonance model.

The last of these features of context, that every mouse is self-identical, is a tautology, as is every theorem of mathematics. In classical logics, tautologies have the very special property that they follow from every other proposition. As a result, in many standard approaches to meaning, tautologies are in some sense included in (or at least follow from) every declarative sentence. Relatedly, in many theories of belief based on classical logics, when one believes something, one also believes everything that follows from it, and hence all tautologies—what is known as the problem of *logical omniscience*. This is generally regarded by philosophers of language and linguistic semanticists as an acceptable price to pay given the benefits of the formal modeling systems they use, and many do not regard it as a negative at all. People do not exhibit logical omniscience, in the sense that they cannot recognize all the consequences of their beliefs, and would not recognize, say, Fermat's last theorem as following from, say, the statement "It's raining." Nonetheless, logical omniscience is commonly viewed as an acceptable idealization, justified by the clarity that logical models bring to models of both belief and meaning.

Given this background, it is not terribly surprising that the Kaplanian meaning of an action should fold in tautologies like the fact that every mouse is self-identical. Presumably, many theorists would not find it to be an objectionable property. However, let us point out that there is here a sharp difference between resonance and Kaplanian meaning. Whereas every tautology is part of the Kaplanian meaning of every expression, resonance has the reverse property: tautologies are never resonances of any expression. This can be seen by reasoning as follows: (i) the resonances of an action are features that are more likely in the presence of the action; (ii) tautologies are features of every context, which have a uniform probability of 1 in every context; and so (iii) tautologies never get a probability boost, and cannot be resonances.[57] Similar issues will arise in our discussion, in chapter 3, of how people harmonize their beliefs and other attunements. Quite generally, in this volume we try to avoid strong idealizations about people's reasoning capacities, including the idealization of logical omniscience. We leave a broader discussion of idealization until chapter 9.

We take it that the property that brown butterfly wings contain melanin is similar to a tautology insofar as it is a uniform physical feature of the real world, and thus a feature that holds in every context, independent of how that context is centered. Thus, by similar reasoning as for tautologies, this property is part of the Kaplanian meaning of every expression, but a resonance of no expression, at least if we anchor our contexts to the real world, which we do in this volume. Note here that this does not force resonances to always be veridical: even though situations in the real world in which real speakers have actual pain are resonances of "ouch," it does not follow that the speaker is in pain every time it is used. It merely follows that if people expressing themselves in this way were rarely in pain in the set of contexts used to define the resonance, it could not be a strong resonance.

To further elucidate the difference between resonance and Kaplan's conception of expressive meaning, let us move from one to the other via two intermediary steps. The first intermediary step is a version of Kaplanian meaning where probability plays a nontrivial role: what we can call for the purposes of this section the *probabilistic Kaplanian meaning* of an action is a function mapping features of context to 1 if the conditional probability of the feature given the action is above 0.5, and to 0 otherwise. The second intermediary step we can call the *categorical resonance* of an action: a function mapping features of context to 1 if the probability boost given by the action is above .5, and 0

---

57. Note that although tautologies cannot be resonances, both attitudes toward tautologies and actions of representing tautologies can be resonances. Thus, although it cannot be a resonance of the declarative "Mary is self-identical" that the context is one in which Mary is self-identical, it can be a resonance that the context is one in which this tautology is being depicted and that it is a focus of joint attention.

otherwise. By the probability boost we mean, as before, the difference between the conditionalized probability of the feature and the prior probability of the feature, and we call it categorical because it categorizes features as to whether they are resonances (value 1) or not (value 0). So, the categorical resonance of an action is a halfway house between the probabilistic Kaplanian meaning and regular resonance, like the former except based on the boosted probability of a feature of context, rather than absolute probability, and like the latter, except with all values above .5 pushed to 1, and all other values pushed to 0. In the regular resonance definition, the one we will be using in the rest of the book outside of the discussion in this section, features to be mapped into real values between -1 and +1, that is, the actual probability boost or drop of a feature given a certain action.

Let's consider the differences between Kaplanian meaning and probabilistic Kaplanian meaning. In the above coffee-game scenario where the *sleepiness-nod-coffee* conventions have emerged, both would assign values to David's states following his nodding of *hunger*: 0, *thirst*: 0, and *sleepiness*: 1. Similarly, the two notions agree as regards the players in the coffee game being named David and Jason, brown butterfly wings containing melanin, and mice being self-identical. Where the two notions come apart, obviously, is as regards features of context that are merely probable rather than certain; this has both positives and negatives.

Let's get what we take to be a negative for probabilistic Kaplanian meaning out of the way. The probabilistic Kaplanian meaning of David nodding includes the proposition that the next dice thrown anywhere in the world will not come up on six, and indeed that the last dice thrown did not come up on six. Indeed, this will be true of the probabilistic Kaplanian meaning of any type of communicative action that is not directly correlated with the value of the next dice thrown (and similarly, mutatis mutandis, for the last dice thrown). This is because if we consider a somewhat arbitrary non-dice-related set of the contexts centered on individuals at a certain time and location, say all those where David nods, then in a majority of them the next dice thrown will not land on six. This is obviously not a property of nonprobabilistic Kaplanian meaning. Neither does it hold for the resonance model: knowing that David had nodded would not boost your estimate of the next dice thrown coming up on six.

It might reasonably be argued that it is a mere artifact of our definition of probabilistic Kaplanian meanings that merely probable events are among the features connoted by all sorts of utterances. However, it does bring with it a striking advantage over the Kaplanian meaning. Suppose that just once somebody has said "ouch" without having first experienced pain, perhaps as a joke, perhaps to mislead, perhaps through misunderstanding of the convention, perhaps through some quirk of speaker performance, and so on. Whatever the reason, by the definition of Kaplanian meaning, speaker pain is then not a feature associated with, or expressed by, the utterance of "ouch." Indeed, nothing but tautologies and other eternal physical properties of the world are part of the Kaplanian meaning of anything. Absent some further work, Kaplanian meaning, and, by extension, Kaplan's own definition of the meaning of expressives, is so idealized as to be inapplicable to meaning in the real world, where no convention is followed 100 percent of the time.

Switching from Kaplanian meaning to probabilistic Kaplanian meaning provides at least one way of ameliorating the problem, although, as we've seen, that brings its own problems. One can also imagine variants of the latter with higher probability thresholds for associating features with actions, say 95 percent instead of 50 percent, but simply changing the threshold would not alter a fundamental weakness of the probabilistic Kaplanian meaning, namely, that highly probable features of context are signaled by every action, even if there is no correlation or causal connection at all between the action and the feature. Since, or so we imagine, conventions of language are broken more often than lightning strikes a speaker just after speaking, it follows that there is no way of setting the threshold such that (a) the probabilistic meaning will include what we would think of as conventionalized aspects of meaning, and (b) it is not the case that every action has as part of its probabilistic Kaplanian meaning that the speaker will not be struck by lightning just after speaking.

Here, categorical resonance helps. In the coffee-game scenario, categorial resonance gives the same pattern of values as for Kaplanian meaning and probabilistic Kaplanian meaning (again, *hunger*: 0, *thirst*: 0, and *sleepiness*: 1). Where categorial resonance differs is that it only associates features with an action if their presence in the context is correlated with that action. Therefore, the categorical resonance of an expression includes neither tautologies, nor laws of nature, nor uncorrelated high probability events like those involving dice throws and lightning strikes. And here we see a general advantage of resonance over Kaplanian meaning, since the regular resonance of an action is similar to categorical resonance in this respect: it does not assign any probability boost (or probability drop) to arbitrary features of context that are not correlated (or anticorrelated, respectively) with the action.

1.8. Which Contexts Count?

The question of what features of context are part of the Kaplanian meaning of an expression depends on the set of contexts that are considered. For example, if one were somehow able to restrict the set of contexts over which the Kaplanian meaning of "ouch" was calculated to just those in which people used it to express pain, then the Kaplanian meaning of "ouch" would express speaker pain, since the contexts where people were joking and so on would be excluded. It's doubtful that this would be a viable way of dealing with the failure of Kaplanian meaning to account for variability in language, such as uses of "ouch" in painless situations, because it is inherently circular, defining the meaning of expressions to be just what happens in the situations chosen because they have the features desired for the meaning. Nonetheless, the dependency of Kaplanian meaning on the particular set of contexts considered highlights an issue that for us is pivotal and affects all four models we considered in the last section, namely, Kaplanian meaning, probabilistic Kaplanian meaning, categorical resonance, and regular associative resonance. Indeed, the issue underlies the way that conventional meaning is transmitted and transformed over time, and also underlies the way that the same word can have different meanings to different groups. The issue is this: since we take the meaning (i.e., resonance) of an action to be a function of features of contexts in which people can make a choice as to whether to perform that action, meaning is not absolute, objective, and fixed, but rather is dependent on the choice of the set of contexts over which it is calculated. The question, then, is what set of contexts to use?

Even with respect to our simple coffee game, the answer to the question of which contexts to consider is not obvious, for it depends on what features we allow to vary in our contexts. If we restrict ourselves to contexts that are complete plays of the game and in which the *nod→coffee* convention has emerged and is followed all the time, such that nodding is performed always and only when David is sleepy, and coffee is delivered on exactly those occasions and on no others, then the expressive meaning of a nod might be described as a conjunctive proposition: David is tired and Jason is going to get coffee. But why take this notion of context? An alternative context for an action might be incipient, containing only information up to the time that the action took place. This seems like a good candidate for what Kaplan had in mind, but from a purely technical point of view we might equally well use posterior contexts, containing only information about what takes place after an action. We could say that the *incipient* expressive meaning of nodding in the coffee game is that David is tired, the *posterior* expressive meaning is that Jason will get coffee, and the *full* expressive meaning is the conjunction.

Yet why limit ourselves to contexts in which just one particular set of communicative conventions has emerged? In considering the expressive meaning of the move *nod*, we could also calculate the expressive meaning relative to much bigger sets of contexts, such as a set of all contexts including those in which David and Jason have started with no conventions and iterate the coffee game until one arises, whether that is the nodding convention or another, say that he blinks when tired. In that case, we would end up with disjunctive expressive meanings. For example, the disjunctive incipient meaning would be this: **either** there is a convention that David nods when tired and David is tired, **or** there is no convention that David nods when tired and David is not tired.

But why stop there? Why not consider the set of all contexts in which there is an act designated *nod*? These contexts would include games just like chess except that one nods when one resigns, and games that involve living an otherwise normal life, except that one nods when and only when one recognizes the emptiness of one's existence. Given a poor choice of a set of contexts, the current notion of expressive meaning of nodding would become distinctly unenlightening. For the notion of resonance to be at all helpful, we somehow need to find a set of contexts like Goldilocks's ideal chair: neither too big, nor too small.

Intuitively, the set of contexts that are "just right," in that they capture what resonance is supposed to capture, is what is likely to be informatively signaled by a given action. One thing we don't normally take an utterance of "oops" to signal is the fact that one tends to say "oops" after a minor mishap. That is, saying "oops" doesn't normally signal the presence of the very conventions that we follow when we use it. While we can, in providing language instruction, convey a convention by using it, signals are not typically used to communicate their own communicative conventions.[58] Conventions are features of context that are resonances of a signal, since every use of a signal provides evidence that the conventions surrounding that signal are in place. So, conventions provide an example of a feature of context that is a resonance of a signal, but which intuitively would not normally be considered part of the expressive meaning. There are many such features. When somebody says "oops," that provides evidence that they are not dead, and that they are neither a watermelon nor a prime number. And indeed, these features would be part of what Grice called the "natural meaning" of saying "oops." Crucially, however, while saying "oops" means that you are not a watermelon, "oops" is not generally used to communicate that the speaker is not a watermelon.

Our consideration of signals in the coffee game has brought forth a number of problems with Kaplanian expressive meanings. First, it's not clear what aspects of an interaction should be considered in a Kaplanian context, and second, it's not clear whether the conventions of communication can themselves be allowed to vary across Kaplanian contexts. However, we are not concerned with defending or extending Kaplan's notion of expressive meaning per se, since our notion of resonance is quite different. Even so, our discussion of a Kaplanian approach, and of how to deal with at least some of the problems in that approach, casts light on our proposal for analyzing meaning in terms of resonance.

---

58. Clearly most signals do not serve primarily to establish their own conventions. A large class of signals that challenge this generalization is found within handshaking protocols. These include saying "hello" to establish both English as lingua franca and availability for further communicative exchange, and computer-networking signals establishing data transmission rates or encryption standards. Yet even here, what is signaled is not the generalization that a given convention exists, but rather a more parochial fact, local to the communicative situation. Handshaking protocols usually establish which conventions are in use, not what the conventions are.

The resonances of an expressive include both incipient and posterior features, and among the incipient features are the prior conventions of meaning themselves, the very fact that the expressive has the resonances it does. In general, we do not regard the fact that resonances include both incipient and posterior features to be a shortcoming of our model. There is, on our view, no fact of the matter as to whether David's nod is more like an expression of tiredness or more like a request for future coffee, and no reason why resonances should be restricted to only one of these. However, we do think that it is intuitively clear that David's nod is not naturally thought of as signaling that there is a convention of nodding when tired. If the presence of this convention is a resonance of nodding, and if the meaning of nodding just is its resonances, then we are led inevitably to the following conclusion about our model:

> **Meaning/signal inequality:** What an action means is more than what is signaled.

This result will in fact be central to the account we develop in part II of the book. Much of meaning, we will argue, consists not in what is signaled, but in what is presupposed, and it is the presupposed part that is perhaps of greatest interest when considering the often-invisible transmission of ideology, for example, the very potent hustle of propaganda.

How, then, can we get the right set of features, a set that includes just what an expressive signals, and that leaves out all the features of context that are resonances that are not part of what is signaled? Over the coming chapters, we develop a two-pronged approach to this problem.

One prong of our approach to getting the right set of features involves using a standard method for restricting context: *presupposition*. Presupposition will be used to differentiate between what an action means and what it signals, or, more generally, between what an action means and what it does. We postpone discussion of presupposition until the second part of the book where, based on the notions of resonance developed in this chapter, we develop a radically different account of presupposition than is found in prior literature. However, the basic idea of how presupposition is relevant to the Goldilocks problem of finding a set of contexts that is neither too big nor too small, will already be clear to those readers familiar with prior presupposition theory. The presuppositions associated with an expression determine a broad set of contexts in which communicative interactions of a given type take place. For example, "oops," "ouch," and "pass the salt, would you darling" all share a common presupposition that some variety of English is being spoken. It is only relative to this subset of contexts that any one of the three is used, and none of them are standardly used to signal that we are in such contexts. Within that subset of contexts, each of them has its standard functions, for example, expressing that what the speaker takes to be a mishap has occurred. Presupposition will be used to distinguish between the complete set of resonances of an expression, which encode all the information that an observer could possibly derive from an utterance of the expression, and the smaller set of resonances that determine what an expression usually does, including what it is usually used to signal.

The question of which contexts should be considered in evaluating the resonances of an expression, and hence what can possibly be communicated by use of the expression, depends on psychological and social factors. The second prong of our approach involves extending our model in such a way that the resonances of communicative practices become reflections of the way these practices manifest in society. In the next chapter, we begin our exploration of how social and psychological factors constrain context choice, developing an account of what we term the *collective attunements* of groups of people. The set of contexts to be considered will be constrained by the existence of recognizable groupings of people, for which we adopt from sociological work the term *communities of practice*,[59] who are collectively attuned to a use of an expression, as well as to many other practices. The set of uses of an expression that are relevant to determining the resonances of that expression will be restricted to a set of interactions taking place within such a community of practice.

While there is clearly much work to do, we hope that in this chapter we have made the case that a theory of meaning centered on resonance rather than content holds promise. We are not claiming that theories of meaning that are framed in terms of "content" are inherently wrong just by virtue of using the term, or that they are wrong by virtue of implicitly invoking other aspects of the conduit metaphor or similar metaphors of transfer. Such metaphors are natural and easy given the culture in which both we authors and readers of this volume are steeped, and we accept that such metaphors often illustrate an idea helpfully. But we also think that framing the theory of meaning in terms of these metaphors presents dangers: the danger of structuring the theory around the metaphor without proper reflection, and the danger of focusing the theory only on phenomena for which the metaphor is apt, and to the exclusion of many communicative phenomena that are of societal and cultural significance. We are thus suggesting that it is a worthwhile intellectual

---

59. The notion of communities of practice was introduced in Lave and Wenger, *Situated Learning*. This notion was adapted and extended to the linguistic domain in Eckert and McConnell-Ginet, "Think Practically and Look Locally," 461–90. We talk of communities of practice in a way that significantly generalizes, and perhaps thereby distorts, the original use. The communities that Lave and Wenger discuss are primarily local, for example, comprised of those working together in a single building or company, and their interest was in the process of learning how people become enculturated to the norms and practices in such settings. We allow that communities of practice exist not only in this local sense, but also in arbitrarily larger groups across which cultural practices are shared, for example, all those affiliated with a particular political party.

exercise to attempt to approach the theory of meaning without reference to "content," and without some of the assumptions commonly associated with its use. We hope that the reader will indulge us in this, and will agree with us also that it is worthwhile to think through an alternative approach to communication that is as yet underexplored (although not unexplored), thence to see what fruit it brings.

It should be clear that resonance has some advantages over Kaplanian meaning. It might be argued that some of these advantages are not particularly surprising. After all, the relevant properties of resonance emerge directly from a straightforward use of Bayesian probability theory, itself a completely standard tool in many areas of research, in common use for analysis of communication and cognition, and the tool that provides the foundation of the bulk of contemporary work in computational linguistics. What is original in our project is not the use of probabilistic methods per se, but rather the way we leverage these methods to support the development of an account of meaning within society, an account in which meaning is essentially cultural and political.[60]

60. To be sure, our goal of developing a theory of meaning that is essentially cultural and political, a theory that centers social and emotional aspects of meaning rather than letting them play second string to an account of logical inference or truth conditions, is also not in itself original, as will be obvious to those readers familiar with the works of, say, Habermas or Foucault. Equally obvious to such readers will be that we take a quite different path than either of these figures, using quite different tools in quite different ways, and building on a range of prior scholarship that in large part was unavailable to them.

CHAPTER TWO

Attunement

Eye contact, although it occurs over a gap of yards, is not a metaphor. When we meet the gaze of another, two nervous systems achieve a palpable and intimate apposition.

So familiar and expected is the neural attunement of limbic resonance that people find its absence disturbing. Scrutinize the eyes of a shark or a sunbathing salamander and you get back no answering echo, no flicker of recognition, nothing. The vacuity behind those glances sends a chill down the mammalian spine. The prelimbic status of mythological creatures that kill with their gaze—the serpent-crowned Medusa, the lizardlike basilisk, hatched from a cock's egg by toads or snakes—is no accident. These stories create monsters from ordinary reptiles by crediting them with the power to project out of their eyes what any mammal can see already dwells within: cold, inert matter, immune to the stirrings of limbic life.

To the animals capable of bridging the gap between minds, limbic resonance is the door to communal connection. Limbic resonance supplies the wordless harmony we see everywhere but take for granted—between mother and infant, between a boy and his dog, between lovers holding hands across a restaurant table.

—THOMAS LEWIS, FARI AMINI, AND RICHARD LANNON[1]

2.1. You Must Remember This

Think of a favorite movie. Why does it resonate with you? Do you have a favorite line? Why does that line work? What ties it to its context? Conversely, what makes it . . . timeless?

If you're into old classics, you might think of the line "Play it, Sam!" from *Casablanca*, which was filmed eighty years ago, in the midst of the Second World War.[2] The movie is seen by some as the greatest of all time. A version of the line ("Play it once, Sam, for old time's sake") is uttered first by Ilsa (Ingrid Bergmann). It carries mystery. The audience has seen the conversation from its start, and no referent has been provided for the pronoun "it." Despite Sam's protestations ("don't know what you mean, Miss Ilsa"), it quickly becomes

---

1. Lewis, Amini, and Lannon, *A General Theory of Love*, 63–64.
2. Curtiz, *Casablanca*.

evident that Ilsa and Sam are very much on the same wavelength. To put this in the standard language of semantic theory, interpretation of the pronoun depends on common ground, and we infer that there is much common ground between Ilsa and Sam. The line is repeated by different characters, echoing in our minds, just as the referent of *it*, namely the song "As Time Goes By," provides a musical leitmotif. Together, they strengthen resonances across scenes, picking out dots between which we draw lines.

The second time we hear "Play it," the line is delivered by Ilsa's slick saloon-owning ex-lover, Rick (Humphrey Bogart). Rick's rendition is the best known, though typically misquoted as "Play it again, Sam." Although there is again no explicit antecedent for the pronoun, by this point we are well enough attuned to the characters that we know the referent immediately. But constant it is not: the referent changes: when Ilsa's husband, anti-Nazi resistance fighter Victor (Paul Henried) says, "Play it!" he is referring not to "As Time Goes By," but to "La Marseillaise," presented as a stirring symbol of free French resistance. Still, the resonances with the earlier occurrences of the line are strong. "As Time Goes By" has already been tied sentimentally to France with extensive flashback montages, and if Victor is not singing from quite the same score as Ilsa and Rick, he is nonetheless hitting shared themes. Despite their different nationalities (Norwegian, Czech, and "Drunkard," as Rick famously muses), we see the common ground of the movie's love triangle stars as much in their common use of language as in their common ideals, and in the united front they present against the evil of their day.

To watch the movie is, in part, to understand the attunements between the characters. But perhaps more important to our current project is the question of how viewers' attunements change as they watch the movie. How can we understand the way that the viewer is drawn in, and why?

Casablanca is not a pill that people swallow, or a box containing a set of propositions. That's not how it works. It works by engaging existing attunements and providing a path for people to focus their energies and emotions, through a process of what we will term *harmonization. Casablanca* has many resonances, and those resonances helped shape collective attunements both during the war and afterward, attunements to an ideology in which Americans are plucky yet indefatigable capitalists representing freedom in the face of authoritarianism, all in this together, everybody doing their bit, sometimes it's dirty work but the ends justify the means, and in which even one of the most intensely romantic loves must be sacrificed for the greater cause of country and freedom from oppression.

It is relevant here that the effects the movie has on the viewer are not mere random happenstance, for the movie was made with a quite explicit goal of drawing in a broad range of people and helping them see the world in a certain light. It is a movie that was made in the wake of the formation of the US Office of War Information under the directorship of Elmer Davis, which had issued a call for patriotic support of the war effort from the movie industry, and which was charged with overseeing a wide range of media production, including the output of Hollywood studios. Here's why Davis saw movies as an important part of the war effort: "The easiest way to inject a propaganda idea into most people's minds is to let it go in through the medium of an entertainment picture when they do not realize they are being propagandized."[3]

An overarching concept of interest throughout this book is attunement to ideology. We seek to describe a model of attunement that is relevant both for the strong resonances between the characters in a story, and for the ways in which something like a movie, which does not tell us what to believe or why, can be a powerful vehicle for ideological transmission. It is crucial here that attunements can change gradually. This may result from repeated exposure to propaganda or from exposure to a changed world; it is a well-worked theme in literature, history, and psychology that people may gradually become inured to events that were previously unimaginable but have become commonplace, and can adaptively develop ways of living in circumstances that they would have thought unsustainable. The gradualness of these processes implies, we think, that attunement is not an all-or-nothing thing, but that people can be attuned to something by degrees. We will be interested in this chapter and the next in the mechanisms by which degrees of attunement change. There are various sources of change in attunement, including reflective reasoning and random drift. Our interest is specifically in communication as a factor in creating, strengthening, maintaining, and destabilizing such attunements.

An ideology could creep upon an entire society gradually, without anyone in particular, even the elites, fully understanding the system they build and the ideology they propagate. At some point a country might find itself in peril, with no explicit theory of how it got there. In our view, what happens in such cases is this: the strong resonances of messaging it was exposed to (or exposed itself to) lead to it slowly becoming attuned to an ideology it cannot survive. But this is not to say that the effects of strongly resonant messaging are always so dire. *Casablanca*, in combination with a much larger collection of wartime messaging and educational policies, had positive effects for the war effort and for the country, effects of bringing people together, of developing common attunements.

Ideologies are cultural artifacts consisting of practices, attitudes, affect, and norms (we do not take a stand on the relative interdefinability of these notions). Assuming that ideologies are neither sourced from heaven nor innate, it must be the case that ideologies develop and are maintained through

---

3. Our discussion (and section heading) is informed by Stephen McVeigh, "You Must Remember This: Casablanca at 75—Still a Classic of WWII Propaganda," The Conversation, November 24, 2017, accessed March 1, 2023, https://theconversation.com/you-must-remember-this-casablanca-at-75-still-a-classic-of-wwii-propaganda-87113.

practices, including communicative practices.[4] People are attuned to ideologies, and they are attuned to the people who hold to those ideologies. An ideology, in the way we use it in this book, is at its most comprehensive comparable to what Rahel Jaeggi calls a *form of life*:

> What are we talking about when we speak of forms of life? In everyday usage, the notion of a form of life refers to a whole series of extremely diverse and more or less comprehensive phenomena. The nuclear family is a form of life from which one may try to escape with the help of alternative forms of life; the urban form of life is opposed to the provincial form of life; the forms of life in South Texas can be compared to those in Northern California. Studies are devoted to the fate of nomadic or the decline of bourgeois forms of life. Scholars analyze the forms of life of the Middle Ages, changes in forms of life in the modern era, but sometimes we speak in the singular of the modern or medieval form of life.[5]

Like Jaeggi's forms of life, ideologies, in the sense in which we employ it in this book, are *"ensembles of social practices,"* which are both "products and presuppositions" of our activities, both verbal and nonverbal.[6]

The remainder of this chapter introduces our model of attunement. Whereas resonance plays a similar role in our account to that which content plays in other theories of meaning, attunement plays the role that cognitive attitudes like belief play in other models of conversation and cultural transmission. What we will term *collective attunement* will then equate to what others have termed *common ground*, which is usually analyzed in terms of mutual belief or knowledge. Of particular interest will be collective attunement to practices, including speech practices. However, before we can analyze collective attunement, we need to introduce the concept of attunement as it relates to individuals, which is the function of the next section. In section 2.3, we discuss attunement to practice in the context of previous scholarship on practice, building especially on recent work of Rahel Jaeggi and Sally Haslanger. In section 2.4, we introduce the notion of collective attunement, contrasting it with standard models of common ground. With this notion of collective attunement in hand, we can then come full circle, in section 2.5, resolving a puzzle introduced in chapter 1. The puzzle centered on the fact that resonances depend on the set of contexts against which they are defined; absent a way of

---

4. There is a circularity here that we will brush up against again in this chapter, because the practices that help develop and maintain ideologies, and the norms of maintaining those practices, are themselves components of ideologies. But this circularity is, we take it, inherent to what we are trying to model, and is not in and of itself a shortcoming of the account.

5. Jaeggi, *Critique of Forms of Life*, 35.

6. Jaeggi, *Critique of Forms of Life*, 55.

regulating the set of contexts used, there is no fact of the matter as to whether a given feature of context is or is not a resonance. Our goal in section 2.5, then, will be to clarify the way that resonances can exist pseudo-objectively, as if floating free of any individual's associations or dispositions. Our solution depends on recognizing that the resonances of any particular communicative practice mirror the collective attunements that a certain group of individuals has to that practice, so that we must define resonances relative to interactive contexts that occur within a community of practice. We end the chapter, in section 2.6, by discussing some of the ways in which attunements change within a community, in the process relating attunement to a trio of central concepts in political theorizing: *ideology, persuasion,* and *power.* This sets the scene for the more detailed discussion of attunement change in chapter 3 and in the second part of the book.

2.2. Individual Attunement

Attunement has the following properties: (i) it is scalar; (ii) it is externalist, allowing high levels of attunement to something for which the agent has only the thinnest of mental representations; (iii) it does not require the agent's conscious awareness; (iv) it is not inherently propositional; and (v) it allows for groups to have attunements that individual members of the group lack. All of these properties will play a role in our account of the evolution and transmission of ideology.

In principle, a change in attunement may result from acceptance or rejection of an overt statement of some component of an ideology, but it is doubtful that exchange of explicitly stated ideological precepts is the primary communicative mechanism by which ideology is transmitted, transcended, or transmuted. Features of ideology can be communicated even when they are not what someone intends to communicate, and indeed they may be communicated by an act that was not intended to be communicative at all. More commonly, change results from observation of behavior that exemplifies or reveals practices or other aspects of an ideology; the behavior in question presupposes elements of the ideology. But this transmission process does not always increase attunement to existing ideologies.

The process we are describing does not simply reproduce ideology like a cultural Xerox machine. There are three reasons for this. First, the production of behaviors never perfectly exemplifies a broader practice, whether by intention or by accident. Second, a finite number of examples can never provide complete information as to the nature of the practice that they (imperfectly) exemplify. And third, when observing someone perform an action, the resulting change in an observer's dispositions never consists in suddenly gaining a tendency to behave exactly as the performer did, even if that should happen to be the observer's goal. In the case of ideological conflict, people may even seek to behave in a way that is as distinct as possible from the performance they observed, a process that, as we will see, has been much studied in communication studies and sociolinguistics.

People can be attuned to many different things, including power tools (if they know how to use them), the weather (e.g., by adjusting their wardrobe), and Catholicism (an ideology). Here's a working definition of attunement:

> **Attunement:** An agent is *attuned* to something to the extent that their state and behavior predictably evolve in accordance with its presence in the agent's context.

So, this notion of attunement is gradient, relating an agent to something else, which we may refer to as the object of attunement. Attunement is defined in terms of three further notions: *predictability, accordance of state and behavior,* and *presence in an agent's context.*

Predictability in the definition of dispositional attunement is inherently correlational, the degree of dispositional attunement being a measure of the degree to which the agent's behavior is correlated with the presence of something being in the context. However, the notion of predictability here is inherently more complex than that assumed in our definition of resonance in the last chapter, because we are now talking not simply about whether two things co-occur, but about whether a complex behavior is responsive to something's presence.[7]

We must also say more about the notions of *accordance of state behavior* and *presence in the context.* As regards presence in the context, let's consider the examples mentioned above. There is an obvious enough interpretation of *presence* for power tools: presence in a context could mean presence of an instantiation of the type in the physical environment of the individual on

---

7. A more general statement of predictability here would be as follows: given some class of models of an agent's behavior, predictability is a measure of the extent to which the best models that take into account the presence of a feature of context more tightly match the agent's behavior than the best models that do not take into account the presence of this feature.

We might alternatively use *explanation* rather than *predictability*, so that attunement would depend on whether a behavior was explained by the presence of the object of attunement. This brings in a rich but contentious literature on the nature of explanation. We note that, for better or worse, it is difficult to provide a measure of whether an agent is attuned to a tautology, or in cases of physical laws that hold universally or in all situations where an observation might easily be made. Thus, it would be difficult to say whether anyone was attuned to the proposition expressed by $1 + 1 = 2$, although it would be possible to evaluate attunement to the contingent and practice-dependent proposition that "$1 + 1 = 2$" is a tautology. Similarly, while finding out whether a creature was attuned to gravity would require observations of its behavior in zero-gravity contexts, it would be easier to figure out whether someone was attuned to a statement of a gravitational principle (say a statement of the inverse square law), e.g., by asking them.

whom the context is centered. But we might also interpret presence in the context to mean, less clearly, presence of the concept of power tools in the cultural context of the agent—that the agent's assumptions and practices contain or reflect that concept, for example. Both interpretations are relevant for us, and we will return to a similar ambiguity (regarding the question of when a practice is present in the context) in the next section. As regards dispositional attunement, it is not of import whether the concept of power tools is present in the cultural context; it will suffice to consider whether practices are present in an agent's context, practices that may involve particular physical artifacts.

For *weather*, we can take a similar tack as for the first interpretation of the presence of a power tool: weather is present in the context when an instance of it (say, light rain) is present in the immediate physical environment of the agent. If we want to speak instead of an ideology being present in a context, for example, *Catholicism*, we will need to think of contexts as cultural.[8] We have relatively commonsensical intuitions about when Catholicism is present in a context: it was not present in the contexts of agents in pre-Columbian South America, and some version of it is present in the context of many of the people of this area now. We will take presence of an ideology, such as Catholicism, to be best analyzed at the level of communities of practice, so the question of whether Catholicism is present in a context becomes a question of social affiliation: Catholicism is present for an agent if the agent is a member of a community of practice within which the specific practices of Catholicism are common (which does not necessarily mean that the agent themselves is a practitioner).

What is it for state and behavior to accord with the weather? Our characterization should be general enough to be neutral between different ways of attuning one's behavior to the weather. For example, someone might subscribe to a religion according to which one should expose oneself to the elements the worse it gets—in the cold, one should remove one's jacket, for example. This is a way of being attuned to the weather—as is the more standard way of adding clothing as the temperature plunges. Both of these are different ways of acting in reaction to changes in the weather.

How about power tools? Although someone who uses an electric sander to prop a door open acts in a way that is dependent on the object, the action of propping a door open is not one that is distinctively accomplished using an electric sander as opposed to some other similarly weighted object. A power

---

8. Complications arise when stating what it is for an ideology like Catholicism to be present in the context, because of the dangers of circularity: the presence of Catholicism might be taken to be evidenced only by the presence of adherents, i.e., people who are attuned to it. We are not sure there is a way around this circularity (which ultimately may apply also to the issue of the presence of the concept of power tools too).

tool has a range of potentialities, of which those lent by its weight alone are a small subset. Let us say that one behavior accords better with a power tool than another behavior does when the first depends more highly upon the potentialities of the object that distinguish it from other objects. However, since power tools are cultural artifacts, there is more to say.

Using an electric sander as a doorstop is acting in accord with (the presence of) the sander, but not to the same extent as using it to smooth wood, which relies on potentialities unique to sanding equipment, and, again, on standard practices.[9] The potentialities of such an artifact, and indeed the potentialities of any natural object that takes on an ideological role, depend upon the culture. Acting in accord with the potentialities of the object implies being disposed to utilize the object as an *affordance* in the sense of Gibson, meaning something that serves a function supporting an activity, so that a seat affords sitting and a pen affords writing.[10] Thus acting in accord with an object involves performing behaviors (the behaviors afforded by the object) that themselves may be culturally transmitted. So, attunement to the instrument will imply attunement to practices involving that instrument. Those practices may themselves have psychological and social dimensions that are connected to the physical practices. Power tools might have the potential to make some feel manly, and demonstrate to others that they are not confined to their office jobs. Yet the complications with power tools go deeper than the fact that the potentialities of a power tool are in part culturally defined.

The deep problem with talk of acting in accord with power tools is that absent culture, there is no such thing as a power tool. The very concept of a power tool is culturally bound, and the determination of whether something is or is not a power tool is not culturally neutral. So, it's not the case that we can talk of someone's attunement to power tools independently of their attunement to other aspects of culture. Attunements to a cultural artifact bleed into attunements to other aspects of the prevailing culture in which attunement to the artifact was attained. Learn to do something geeky, and you are likely to become better attuned to geek culture; learn to do something manly, and you are likely to become better attuned to male culture. As Jaeggi observes, "Practices are always 'practices in a nexus.'"[11] In our terms: it is both the case that practices are

9. Here we see why a notion such as mutual information might be helpful in modeling predictability. Using a notion like mutual information would establish both that the presence of a sander was correlated with an agent having a certain behavioral disposition, and that the presence of that behavioral disposition was correlated with the presence of a sander. This combination would constitute a reason to describe an agent as having a sanding disposition, and not, say, a door-stopping disposition that happened to involve an electric sander.

10. Gibson, "The Theory of Affordances."

11. Jaeggi, *Critique of Forms of Life*, 62.

resonances of other practices, and that they are objects of collective attunement in combination, so that attunement to one practice tends to imply attunement to many others. The resonances between various objects of attunement are central to an account of ideological maintenance and change.

Central to this chapter is the development of an account of dispositional attunement to practice. But as we've said (uncontroversially, we take it), there's more to an ideology than a set of practices. To understand attunement to ideology, we also need to understand affective attunement, cognitive (or attitudinal) attunement, and perceptual attunement. All are evident in the case of Catholicism.

Attunement to the ideology of Catholicism clearly involves affective attunement—feeling the same emotions as others in the community would in the relevant places and times. Without speculating on the nature of spiritual states, or their role in different varieties of Catholicism in particular, it is hard to imagine spiritual states not involving emotions of some sort, whether feelings of calm and well-being, or feelings of love or ecstasy. The central practice of prayer in Catholicism is associated with feelings such as adoration and humbleness, and affective attunement is also expected for the artifacts and other physical entities that support the practice and ideologies, for example, the Bible, the cross, and inspirational depictions. Affective attunement is, furthermore, central in the formation of in-group affinity within and across Catholic communities (i.e., positive feeling in the presence of in-group members, in-group practices, in-group ideology). What we are calling affective attunement, that is, certain patterns of emotional response, is not generally explicitly discussed in the theory of meaning—but it is starting more recently to emerge in theories of presupposition that seek to explain phenomena also of interest to us, such as slurs, as in the work of Teresa Marques and Manuel García-Carpintero.[12]

That Catholic ideology involves cognitive attunement, in particular the sharing of certain characteristic beliefs (the central case in the theory of meaning), is obvious. Catholicism is, after all, a faith. But the central tenets of the religion find their place in a broader web of attitudes, for example, beliefs about the way one should lead one's life, the respect different people in and out of the religious community are due, and beliefs that involve Catholic perspectives on everything from history and art to food and wine. It's not that there's one set of attitudes on these issues that all and only Catholics share, but rather that there are tendencies for Catholics to think in certain ways that are not so commonly shared among non-Catholics, and that are distinctive enough to

12. See Marques and García-Carpintero, "Really Expressive Presuppositions," in which they argue that "pejoratives in general and slurs in particular trigger normative, non-propositional presuppositions that require speakers and hearers to share some specific reactive attitude" (140).

be described as Catholic attitudes. Note here that the phrase "think in certain ways" bespeaks the fact that different types of attunements are not cleanly separable. We do not have one set of cognitive attunements and a separate, orthogonal set of dispositional attunements. The terms *cognitive* and *dispositional* characterize aspects of attunements, rather than strictly different types of attunement. Thus, to "think in certain way" reflects an attunement that is both dispositional and cognitive. Dispositions to reason and to judge necessarily have this character.

Last in our list of Catholic attunements, to be attuned to Catholicism is also to be perceptually attuned to it, to experience the world in a Catholic way. Catholics might perceive the world through different eyes than non-Catholics because they have different perceptual categories for events and objects they witness, and possibly also because at mass or elsewhere they might have (to borrow from William James) "varieties of religious experience" to which non-Catholics lack access.[13]

2.3. Attunement to Practice

The question of what *acting in accord* with a practice means varies enormously, from cases like driving where there are institutionalized methods for determining whether your behavior is legal, to cases like fashion where the fashion police aren't wearing badges, at least not this year.[14] What is relevant here is that Catholicism, driving, and fashion all involve, among other things, a host of practices. We must say more about attunement to practices, how that relates to a broader ideology, and about other types of attunement, going beyond attuned behavior. But before going on we must note that, like many before us, we were initially inspired by the work of Pierre Bourdieu.[15]

---

13. James, *The Varieties of Religious Experience.*

14. Jaeggi, *Critique of Forms of Life*, 67–73 (section 1.2), drawing on Georg Simmel, usefully distinguishes between fashions and forms of life, by appeal to such factors as the temporary nature of fashion, and the greater normative charge associated with forms of life. Our use of "ideology" encompasses both fashions and forms of life.

15. See Bourdieu, *Outline of a Theory of Practice; The Logic of Practice.* Two further authors who influenced us relatively early on in the development of our approach to practice are the anthropologist Alexander Duranti and the philosopher Olúfẹ́mi Táíwò. In *The Anthropology of Intentions*, Duranti provides a clear grounding of his position on intention against a background of work in philosophy of language (roughly what we term the *content-delivery model*), and provides arguments for the noncentrality of intention in his studies of speech practices in Samoa. Táíwò ("Beware of Schools Bearing Gifts: Miseducation and Trojan Horse Propaganda") argues that updating via privately held beliefs alone will not be a satisfactory account of the way propaganda works—one must be sensitive to "collective epistemic resources," as well as practices that people maintain independently of their beliefs. Our hope is that the framework we provide is adequate to this concern.

A theme of Bourdieu's anthropological and sociological work is that practices as cultural objects can be separated from the intentions of practitioners. This means that reproduction and innovation of practice do not need to be the result of conscious intention, and, from the perspective of an outside observer, that practices can be studied at least somewhat independently of what practitioners report as their intentions, if such reports are even available.

Bourdieu's development of a practice-based model that is not dependent on intention meshes naturally with the well-established idea that much of what is communicated is to a great extent left tacit or implicit, a web of presuppositions that are reflected in what is said, but is not completely explicit, and with the further idea that there is often no intention to communicate these presuppositions. As we will discuss in chapter 9, whether practices are taken to be performed intentionally or not, an approach that centers on intention and the recognition of intention is not likely to be well suited to the study of what we have called *hustle*, namely, that which is either communicated without intention, or is communicated without the recognition of communicative intention. Our model of resonance allows that the resonances of words exist at a community level, rather than at the level of individuals, and that these resonances can be significant in communicative interactions even when none of the conversational participants are aware that those resonances are in play. That is, the resonances of a communicative practice can affect change in attunement absent any intention for that to occur.

Comprehensive coverage of the voluminous literature on practice would be impossible here, even if we could claim to be fully versed in sociological and anthropological work on the topic, and we will not even attempt to connect to most of that literature.[16] We do not discuss the well-developed methodologies by which actual practices are studied. We will focus on Jaeggi's theoretical account, noting connections to parallel developments in the work of Sally Haslanger.[17]

Being attuned to a social practice means having dispositions that result in behaviors that match the practice. But what is a social practice? Jaeggi introduces her discussion of practices as follows:

> Practices in the most general sense are complex activities in which we engage alone or with others. Examples of practices are lining up at the checkout when shopping, making a bank transfer, inviting friends over for dinner, throwing a party, playing basketball, playing hide-and-seek with children, conducting a seminar, and taking an exam.[18]

16. An excellent and broad scholarly discussion of practice-based approaches is Rouse, "Practice Theory." For discussion more focused on methodologies for observing and describing practice, see Streeck and Mehus, "Microethnography: The Study of Practices."

17. Haslanger, "What Is a Social Practice?"

18. Jaeggi, *Critique of Forms of Life*, 56.

Jaeggi describes the essential features of her account of practice as follows: "Practices are habitual, rule-governed, socially significant complexes of inter-linked actions that have an enabling character and through which purposes are pursued."[19] We illustrate Jaeggi's multipart characterization with a particular kind of practice, in fact a particular *speech practice*, the practice of racist dog whistling, as developed through the Republican "Southern Strategy" discussed in the introduction. This is the practice of using terms like "welfare" or "inner city" for a political goal, say, to increase support for cutting taxes on the wealthy (say, by describing taxes as going to support "welfare programs").

> **Habituality:** The practice of racist dog whistling in this way had to be established, by repeated and *habitual* performance (think of Reagan's campaign against the "welfare queen").

> **Rule-governed:** To engage in the practice of dog whistling involves describing programs to be attacked using certain labels; the practice has *rules*, or at least has sufficient consistency in its form that observers can identify a categorical similarity across different instantiations of the practice. Philosophers and linguists tend to use the word "rule" in a nuanced way that does not necessarily require the presence of an explicit statement or requirement. This is certainly the case for Jaeggi, who indeed goes further, and allows that some rules governing a practice might not even permit of explicitation in principle.[20]

Sally Haslanger cautions against practices necessarily being frameable in terms of rules,[21] arguing rather that *descriptive normativity* is required for a regularity to be a social practice:

19. Jaeggi, *Critique of Forms of Life*, 61.

20. Jaeggi writes, "Just as some people apply grammatical rules correctly without being able to explain them, one can perform aspects of driving without having learned a corresponding rule—even though these rules can in principle be explicated. From these aspects of driving must be distinguished . . . those which are so closely bound up with experience that corresponding (formalized) rules cannot even be found or the rules would be far too complex to be illuminating or communicable at the practical level. Here it is not a matter of rule knowledge having become implicit or only existing implicitly; rather, these rules cannot even be formulated on account of the specific circumstances of implementation. Even the simple sequence 'carefully release the clutch until the gear engages and then depress the gas pedal' is a procedure that one can ultimately learn only by trial and error—hence only in practice—even if the sequence may be clear in principle in advance" (*Critique of Forms of Life*, 107).

21. Haslanger comments, "On one interpretation of practices, they are constituted by rules, and agents participate in the practices by intentionally following the rules, or at least (implicitly) taking the rules to provide reasons for their action. There are two standard concerns about this conception of practices. First, not all practices are constituted by rules (and, some would argue, we need a prior conception of practice to explain what it is to follow a rule)" ("What Is a Social Practice?," 234). Haslanger's second concern relates to the

Members of a group take the culture's concepts, scripts, and meanings to be normative for members of the group in the following sense: when encountering others who are similarly socialized, we implicitly begin with the assumption that they will do things in a particular way, taken to be the "right way." We may be surprised or feel entitled to criticize them if they don't.[22]

Despite this disagreement on whether rules are central to practices, we find that on this issue as on most we consider here, Jaeggi's analysis and Haslanger's are broadly consonant.[23] The disagreement seems to relate more to the nature of rules than to the nature of practice; given that Jaeggi suggests that rules can exist without practitioners being conscious of them, and in some cases without it even being possible in principle to make the rules explicit, it is not clear to us how much light could be shone in the gap between Jaeggi and Haslanger's accounts of practice on this issue. Jaeggi does not present an analysis of what rules are per se (beyond taxonomizing into different sorts and functions of rules), but what is clear from her discussion is that the crucial distinction between following a rule and performing a non-rule-based action is normative. Jaeggi explains that mere habits are not in this sense normative, because breaking a habit is not in and of itself something that opens one to criticism.

For example, if one is in the habit of putting pepper on one's food only after adding salt, then switching would be a change in habitual behavior, but not a normatively problematic change in dining behavior that would open one to criticism. On the other hand, dining practices are more broadly normatively constrained. There is extreme cultural variation as regards, for example, the appropriateness of belching at the table, or the constraints, if any, on what counts as a *finger* food, and dining behaviors are often actively regulated, with overt acculturation of children and foreigners who lack the local mores. Someone's dining habits may be in conflict with community norms, lacking

---

requirement of "intentionality" in the interpretation of practices she is considering, not the use of rules. Haslanger's discussion of intentionality jibes well with Jaeggi's, and it is in line with the view that we ourselves offer, i.e., the view that performing a practice does not depend on an intention to perform that practice. Later, she comments further on the variable significance of rules for practices: "Practices fall along a spectrum from explicitly coordinated behavior that is rule-governed, intentional, voluntary (e.g., games), to regularities in patterns in behavior that are the result of shared cultural schemas or social meanings that have been internalized through socialization and shape primitive psychological mechanisms governing cognition, affect, and experience (e.g., body comportment, verbal inflection)" (239).

22. Haslanger, "What Is a Social Practice?," 239–40.

23. The works of Jaeggi and Haslanger we focus on here share a similar vision and common intellectual roots, but appeared in the same year, presumably without either author having access to the other's work.

the proper etiquette, but any habits that are not perceived as themselves conforming to a societal regularity or maintained through societal regulation are not practices in the technical sense that we will assume.

As regards normativity, the practice of dog whistling is an interesting case, for it makes clear that there is a complex relationship between the norms governing practices and what is ethically desirable. There are communities on the political right wing that presumably think that acts that the current authors would describe as dog whistling are morally justified, whereas liberal academics, politicians, and journalists would not. The same communities who are among those most likely to label an act as dog whistling, and most likely to try to pinpoint the essential features of dog whistling justifying such a label, are those who take the activity to be problematic and who are also likely to try to restrict it. Similar considerations apply to all practices that we might term "hate speech" and to other communicative practices that simultaneously embody some community norms and controvert others. Sometimes controversial types of speech morph precisely because of these joint pressures, as when a slur or taboo word occurs in a slightly disguised form ("egad" and "zounds" being historical examples of the morphing of practices). Quite generally, norms that circumscribe the judgment of what counts as an instance of a practice are logically distinct from norms about whether performances of the practice are just or desirable, but not entirely separable.

As should be clear from the above discussion of rules, or maintenance of practice even if not explicitly regulated as such, the norms that constrain and define practices are taken by both Jaeggi and Haslanger to be understood at the level of communities, and not at the level of individuals. Haslanger's goal is explicitly to analyze "social practice," and it is a phrase that Jaeggi also uses on occasion. What Jaeggi describes as the "rule-governed" nature of practices is interwoven with what she describes as their social significance.

> **Social significance:** The norms that constrain and define practices are intrinsically social, regulated at the level of communities or societies, not by individuals.

Practices of dog whistling are socially significant both as regards the cultural background they rely on and as regards their function. Clearly, dog whistling can only be understood with the background of the social construct of race and its particularity in the American context. Within this practice, to describe programs (say) as "welfare" is to code them as strongly negative, associating them with increased laziness, for example, and drug use, all elements that tie in with a manifestly biased, socially constructed racial stereotype. The function of the practice is manifestly to drive political alignment on the basis of acceptance and use of such constructs.

Haslanger's and Jaeggi's characterizations link social practices together with group identity, in a way that our future discussion will exploit. To have a group identity is, minimally, to share in a set of social practices, and it may also require other elements, such as shared persona (in the sense of public manifestation, or comportment) and common ancestry or heritage. Our discussion of collective attunement in the next section, and the associated notion of a community of practice, both relate to group identity. We will briefly consider in chapter 3 the separate and in some ways stronger notion of *identity fusion*, which implies that people not only share various traits or practices, but see themselves as part of a common whole, to some extent merging personalities and developing a rich sense of collective agency.

We take it as definitional that the communicative practices we study in this volume are social practices, and that the politics of language is also definitionally social, but it should be noted that this is not quite the same as claiming that language is itself intrinsically social, a claim that some have denied.[24]

> **Enabling character:** The *enabling character* of practices refers both to the idea that practices often depend on other practices in order to even be possible (so, e.g., no amount of celebration would count as a wedding anniversary celebration absent the broader institutional practice of marriage), and to the idea that performing a practice causes changes that allow further practices to take place.

The practice of dog whistling has an enabling character in both senses. First, it is obviously enabled by a substantial linguistic background (as well as a social and political background), without which dog whistling would just be making sounds or squiggles on a page. Second, it reinforces unconscious racial bias, thereby enabling other practices of treating Black Americans as subordinate, for example, by discriminating in social activities such as job application or voter-rights support.

---

24. Much discussion of language centers around its function in cognition rather than communication. In some traditions, the goal of the study of language is taken to be primarily an investigation of a mental rather than social phenomenon. This is the case, for example, for the minimalist program in linguistics, which focuses on using language data to reveal a computational system common to humans (Chomsky, *The Minimalist Program*). For discussion of the related (but distinct) view that human language should be primarily considered as an internal mental system for the representation of thought, rather than a social system for communication, see Hinzen, "Narrow Syntax and the Language of Thought"; Reboul, "A Cognitive View of Language Evolution." The question of whether observable human language should be regarded as a mere surface manifestation of an underlying mental phenomenon is again related to (but distinct from) the idea that there is a language of thought, which may or may not mirror spoken language. Here Lev Vygotsky's suggestion that external language comes to dominate thought processes as a child develops (and which thus emphasizes the social as an influence on the mental), and Jerry Fodor's hypothesis of "mentalese," a form of mental representation that at least shares features with external language, are well known: Vygotsky, *Mind in Society*; Fodor, *The Language of Thought*.

Purposes: Practices serve a function which can be understood as the reason to perform them. The practice of dog whistling has clear *purposes*: to marshal unconscious racist bias toward political goals, such as cutting taxes for the wealthy, and destroying institutions or individuals to which one is opposed (e.g., opposition candidates or parties, the federal bureaucracy, the Walt Disney Company). Dog whistling has a purpose, in that it has predictable effects, would not exist if it did not have those effects, and certainly can be and often is carried out with the intention to produce those effects. However, Jaeggi is circumspect in her discussion of purposes, allowing that practitioners may not be aware of the purpose of a practice they engage in.[25] So, it is consistent with her view, and ours, that someone might dog whistle without intending to, and without intending to have the dog-whistle effects, such as reinforcing unconscious racial bias.

With these defining characteristics of (social) practices as background, we can now say more about what it means for some individual or group to be attuned to a practice. Simply plugging practice into our definition of dispositional attunement, we arrive at the following (which is simply a special case of the existing definition, not a new definition as such):

Attunement to practice: An agent is *attuned* to a practice to the extent that their state and behavior predictably evolve in accordance with its presence in the agent's context.

Instantiating the definition of attunement in this way leads to a type-token ambiguity briefly foreshadowed in our discussion of attunement to power tools above. At the type level, a practice can be present in a cultural context in which people tend to perform the practice, but at a token level, a practice can be present in a more temporally and physically localized part of the context in the sense that it is being actively instantiated, that is, performed, at a given time and place. That is, people can both be attuned to practices, and be attuned to particular instantiations of the practice. The latter notion, of being attuned to instantiations of a practice, will largely suffice for our purposes, but there is value to considering attunement at the type level too. Let us first

---

25. Jaeggi highlights the possibility of practices being performed without an intention to do so when she talks of the "active-passive" character of practice. She writes, "To assert that practices have purposes and that they are structured by those purposes is not to posit that they are based on intentions that are fully known," and later in the same passage, she continues, "Practices are to a certain extent subject-independent patterns of action that are still not entirely transsubjective; or, to put it in more concrete terms, they arise as it were through subjects and yet exist prior to them (and their intentions) and hence cannot be reduced to the intentions of the subjects concerned" (*Critique of Forms of Life*, 85).

consider an attunement to particular instantiations of a practice, and then return to consider the type level.

What are the tokens of a practice? This is a difficult question, relating closely to the subtle tension between the aforementioned views of Jaeggi and Haslanger regarding whether there are rules governing practices. Sidestepping the philosophically vexed question of what rules are, and hence whether practices can be defined by them, let us consider the tokens of a practice from a purely extensional point of view, as a certain type of regularity of behaviors. Rather than trying to specify in general terms when a regularity of behaviors constitutes a practice, let us simply assume that there are such regularities, and that the occurrences of individual tokens would be recognized by members of a community as belonging to the category. Note here that *recognizing* neither implies conscious recognition, nor does it imply a tendency to publicly label the actions as belonging to the practice (a metapractice), although it is common for practices both to be consciously recognized and publicly labeled or at least labelable. What we will call the *extension of a practice* is just such a set of recognizably like behaviors. Sometimes, but not always, these regularities are societally regulated, and occasionally they are even regulated through a separate formalized practice, perhaps bureaucratic or legal, but in focusing on the history of a practice, we generalize to a level that includes both regulated and unregulated practices.

The notion of an *extension of a practice* is metaphysically minimalistic relative to the denser and more theoretically substantive notions of practice itself offered by Jaeggi and Haslanger, and yet the extension of a practice is already a rich notion to work with. In recognizing a practice, community members must have access both to the context in which the behavior occurred, and to sufficient information regarding prior instantiations of the practice and the contexts in which they occur. Contexts are rich and include such features as the attunements of any participants in the practice. So, although the extension of a practice is minimalistic, it manages to be simultaneously just a form of behavior, and much more than that. For example, the extension of the British practice of drinking tea is simultaneously a bland pattern of physical actions involving a kettle, water, and other mundane trappings of British life, and also a set of rich contexts in which these actions take place, cold winter afternoons, moments after bad news, a favorite mug, the anticipation by the drinker of the first hot sip, a sense of well-being, and all the attitudes that make mundane trappings mundane to the participants in an event of drinking a simple cuppa, unremarkable to those whose lives they permeate, and yet paradigmatically defining of an entire society.

Drinking a cup of tea is a fleeting episode in a day, innocuous and commonplace. Yet it is woven into the fabric of society—into a nexus of other practices, as Jaeggi would have it—in such a way that it cannot be cleanly separated from other activities that co-occur, like the exchange of social niceties while enjoying the tea, or the practices that support tea drinking, such as dairy and tea production, water and power supply, and practices of mercantile exchange. Activities of all these sorts are present in the contexts of individual episodes of drinking tea. The extension of the practice of drinking tea is at once almost nothing and nearly everything.

For many practices, the extension is precisely what community members have access to as they acquire the practice, and indeed as they further shape the practice. Or rather, community members typically have access to a thin slice of the extension, a small subset of occurrences seen from a particular angle, with a patina of context. A toddler who witnesses adults drinking tea a few hundred times at a safe distance above where they play has access to almost nothing of the adults' experiences and attitudes as they sip and chatter. And yet almost nothing makes for a good start in life. A theme we shall return to is that people shape or extend practices over time by performing them idiosyncratically, and yet with sufficient similarity to prior occurrences that the new performance is seen as a novel instantiation of the same practice rather than as a completely separate practice. Whether a British three-year-old's imitation of tea drinking is actually an instantiation of the practice may be a little unclear to an observer, but soon enough most children will probably be so well attuned to tea drinking and its nuances that they perform the action without thinking twice, and with very similar attitudes and experiences to the adults who once surrounded them as they played. Yet other children will go on to drink tea in a slightly different way, with less sugar, say, or perhaps by staring at a screen instead of at another human while they drink. A practice steeps and develops new flavors.

Given that a practice has an extension that consists of individual instantiations of the practice, and given that a context is just reality centered on some individual at a particular time and location, we can easily state what it is for a token of the practice to be present in a context. It is simply for the relevant individual at a given time and location to experience the practice over an interval including that time and location, whether as an active participant or observer. The practice consists in a regular pattern of changes of contextual parameters over time, including parameters that concern the activity of participants and the attitudes of observers. To predictably act in accord with tokens of the practice is to be an individual whose behavior has a tendency to evolve in the way that is recognizable as a role of the practice, exemplifying the category given by the history of practice (and in contradistinction to categories of behavior identifiable as distinct and incompatible practices). It is, then, fairly obvious what it means for your behavior to predictably accord with the presence of the British tea-drinking practice in your context. Sipping a mug of hot tea made with a teabag of dusty Assam and Darjeeling varieties and with a spot of cow's milk is recognizably acting in accord with the standard British practice, but slurping sweet green watermelon-flavored tea with coconut milk and tapioca bubbles from a plastic cup through a giant straw is not. Dunking a biscuit (i.e., a cookie) into the tea fits with the practice, but dunking a croissant, celery, or your finger would not.

Put in terms of the last chapter, the resonances of the British practice of tea drinking include a positive probability boost for cow milk and for biscuit dunking, but not for tapioca bubbles, big fat straws, or the dunking of anything other than a biscuit. Acting in accord with the practice is having an increased tendency to do things for which the resonances provide a positive probability boost when participating in the practice. Not acting in accord with the practice, contrarily, would involve having an increased tendency to do things for which the resonances include a probability decrease.

Let us briefly return to the type-token ambiguity mentioned above. We have focused on attunement to a practice at the level of tokens in the extension of the practice. However, metapractices by which people regulate practices, communicate about the significance of practices, and sometimes consciously innovate practices, are set at the type level. Attunement to metapractices, say metapractices of maintaining the practice, can involve communicative actions about the practice being maintained at a type level. For example, a metapractice of maintaining tea-drinking practices, say by explaining that the milk should be put in the cup before the steeped tea is poured from the pot, involves communication about tea drinking at the type level. Metapractices may themselves occur in the immediate contexts of tokens of the practice, as when someone comments on proper tea-drinking practice during an episode of drinking tea, which means that the metapractices themselves can have a boosted probability in the resonances of the practice. Furthermore, since participants and observers of tokens of a practice will tend to be among those who engage in metapractices, even if they do not do so at a predictable time relative to their participation in or observation of the practice, attunements to metapractices will themselves tend to be resonances of a practice. Nonetheless, we suppose that many facets of practices discussed by Jaeggi and Haslanger are best understood at a type level, not only as regards regulation of a practice when rules and regulations are identifiable, but also as regards social significance and purposes, in Jaeggi's sense.

Attunement to a practice at a type level also buys us something that is not available at the token level in any obvious way. Attunement to a practice at a token level ensures that an agent will tend to act in accord with a practice when an instantiation of it is present in the context, but this does not in itself establish that an agent will initiate the practice when appropriate. To be dispositionally attuned to the practice of tea drinking is not merely to act appropriately when drinking tea, but also to have a tendency to drink tea when that would be appropriate, that is, to actively introduce tea drinking into the context on certain occasions, such as teatime.

At the type level, a practice is present for an individual when they are *in* a community among which participating in instantiations of the practice is common enough to be recognizable as a practice of that community, where by "in" we do not mean necessarily being a member of the community, but also include the broader sense of being among members of the community. This is roughly the sense of the proverb "When in Rome . . . ," which concerns the idea that when one is in a location one should perform local practices, even if one is not actually a member of the local community (i.e., one is in Rome, but not *romano/romana*, or, for that matter, Roman). Although we omit the math, it is a simple matter to use Bayes's Theorem and the resonances of a practice to calculate the set of occasions on which the practice itself has a boosted probability, and thus, when practitioners should be expected to initiate it. An agent who is attuned to the practice at the type level will be one who, when in a context for which the practice is present in the sense of being regularly practiced, not only has a tendency to act in accord with instantiations of the practice, but also has a tendency to initiate the practice in accord with its resonances.

Our focus on the extension of practices as histories of behaviors borrows from work in the psychology of categories and concepts over more than forty years, work heavily inspired by Wittgenstein's critique of rule-based categorization in his *Philosophical Investigations*. One prominent line of psychological work on categorization is exemplar theory, although, fittingly, it's perhaps more of a cluster of approaches than a line of work. Exemplar theory emphasizes the process of structuring data into groups, that is, exemplars, and views categorization as being heavily influenced by comparison with some or all members of those groups. So, these models can be seen as being relatively extensional models of conceptual categories, more focused on category building as structuring of data than as development of rules, or, for that matter, development of abstract prototypes against which new cases might be compared. While we take such work on categorization to be relevant to the categorization of practice, which is itself essential to our core notion of attunement to practice, we make no claims about psychological representation of practices, or of events more generally. Ours is not a model of categories as psychological exemplars, but as cultural exemplars. What we claim is that for the practices of most interest for the present volume, there need be no community-accessible representation of the practice that has priority over what people actually do, beyond collective memory of what has occurred (or, to put it more precisely in the terms of the next section, collective attunement to what has occurred).

While we make no commitments about psychological representations, we do take the nature of psychological representation to be important for the development of practice. For our immediate purposes, what is important is not exactly how the human mind works, but rather the fact, or so we assume, that there are strong commonalities in the way that human minds operate. It follows from this assumption that humans will share common ways of developing attunements in response to similar exposures to behavior, and this in turn must contribute to the development of stable practices in human communities.

For better or worse, modern "big data"-based natural-language processing is focused on models that start with an enormous repository of practices, and then try to reproduce those practices.[26] The field of machine learning is dominated by a highly empirical methodology in which systems are evaluated primarily on the basis of their ability to predict new instances of phenomena based on exposure to large numbers of prior instances. In this methodology, relatively little weight is given to whether the system's internal representation of a phenomenon is congruent with what we might think of as an intuitively or scientifically correct model, except insofar as our ability to understand those internal machine representations itself supports scientific and engineering progress in the development of systems that achieve even greater levels of empirical performance. That is, a majority of contemporary computer scientists, unlike more cognitively oriented AI specialists of bygone years, don't model the cognitive or affective state of humans performing a task; they just try to produce a system that has the right dispositions. In case they are trying to make a system appear human, they model human dispositions. When modern computer scientists build machines to perform the practice of answering questions, what they aim for is the system that most effectively replicates features of a data set of examples of humans answering questions, a data set that is taken to be a large enough sample of the practice that it can be assumed to be representative of it. A deep problem that we won't discuss in detail here is that the assumption of representativeness of a big data sample is often problematic, an unwarranted assumption leading to troublesome bias. Nonetheless, what we are saying can be put this way: maybe such a data set, if it really were representative, and if it really did encode context in a rich enough way, would be all that was needed to pin down what matters about the practice. That is, with a large enough set of exemplars of a practice, and enough context around them, one could, in principle, identify all the resonances of the practice, and hence all the information that would in principle be needed to model attunement to that practice.

The notion of attunement to a practice that we have so far described has involved only behavioral dispositions. If someone watches professional wrestling all day, it seems natural to say that they will become highly attuned to it, even if they do not thereby become disposed to body slam others over the ropes of a wrestling ring. They need not be *behaviorally attuned* to the practices performed by wrestlers. Someone could regularly fail to behave in accord with practice, even in the appropriate circumstances (dropped into a professional-wrestling ring, and still be hopeless at the practice), and yet be able to recognize the practice, understand it, and get excited by it. In such cases, there are *perceptual, cognitive,* and *emotional* attunements without behavioral attunement.

---

26. Here, let us also tangentially note that the communities of practice that must be modeled in the realm of political language are no longer solely human, but involve computational agents too. Computational propaganda is a fast-growing emerging field of study. See, e.g., the essays in Woolley and Howard, *Computational Propaganda.*

These are all valid notions of attunement, but they are not the notion of behavioral attunement that is a central focus of this chapter.

Dispositional attunement can also be more complex than in the cases we have considered. An agent's behavior may be adapted to the dispositions of others who follow a practice, even though the agent does not follow the practice. Examples would be somebody who avoids church on Sundays because it's too crowded, or a hunter who locates themselves (whether consciously or instinctively) within range of a watering hole at dusk, being thus adapted to the prey's practice of drinking then without necessarily following the practice themselves. We may speak in such cases of a *second-order* attunement to a practice, that is, an attunement to others' attunement to a practice. In that case, all the other cases of dispositional attunement to a practice we have considered, cases that involve a tendency to perform the actions that we might say constitute the practice, are *first-order* attunements. This distinction will be useful when we introduce the notion of collective attunement in the next section.

2.4. Collective Attunement and Common Ground

A standard story about communicative interactions, seen most obviously in David Lewis's and Robert Stalnaker's work,[27] focuses on the function of conversation to increase the store of shared information of the interlocutors. According to the story, information increase is a very public process. The shared information, what is known as the common ground, is by definition available to everyone involved. We are invited to think of the common ground in any conversation as like a big old scoreboard that hangs over the far end of a baseball field, except that instead of telling everyone the state of a baseball game, it tells us the score in a conversational game. The score determines what information is mutually believed about the world, as well as facts internal to the conversation, like whose turn is next.

There are some laudable aspects of this story, well known to philosophers, and some less laudable ones. The (Wittgensteinian) game metaphor is laudable. But the scoreboard metaphor is problematic. At the very least, communicative interactions that transmit ideology do not typically do so by displaying the ideology they transmit in ten-foot-high letters with 10,000-watt illumination on a stadium jumbotron. This aspect of the metaphor interests us mostly as a symbol of the way that the superficial topic of a conversation can distract from what is going on underneath.

We now develop a way of thinking about common ground in terms of attunement. This will provide an important building block for part II of the book, where we distinguish between the overt move made by a conversational

27. Lewis, "Scorekeeping in a Language Game"; Stalnaker, "Assertion."

act, and the *presuppositions* of the act. Presupposition will be central to our account of ideological transmission and conflict, as well as to analyses of linguistic phenomena involving social meaning and context dependence.

An attunement-based notion of common ground will have three properties that are either not available or not usually utilized in standard accounts of common ground. First, the standard notion of common ground is as something like a set of propositions, whereas, as discussed in the previous section, we allow attunement to various things that on most views are not propositions, for example, power tools, the weather, and Catholicism. Second, standardly the common ground, like the scoreboards of Lewis's youth, is black and white: a given proposition is either in the common ground or not; in contrast, attunement is a gradient notion, so that the degree of attunement can vary continuously. Third, whereas the common ground is usually conceived of as a complex attitude, we conceive of it in terms of the dispositions of agents, specifically, their dispositions to interact with each other.[28]

How can an account of individual attunement to context be extended to an account of how groups of individuals are attuned? Just treat groups as individuals! It turns out that this seemingly fatuous answer has significant benefits. Let us first state the definition and then explain how the approach differs from standard approaches and why that is a good thing.

> **Collective behavioral attunement:** A group of agents is behaviorally *attuned* to something to the extent that their collective behaviors predictably accord with its presence in the group's context.

Interest in the definition depends on there being nontrivial collective behavior, behavior that goes beyond the sum of individual behaviors. We take it that some inherently joint behaviors are not naturally analyzed at an individual level, for instance, having a conversation, moving a piano, playing a team sport, performing mass protest, and oppressing minorities. Given the existence of such collective behaviors, our definition simply mirrors the earlier definition of attunement for individuals, and directly leads to a notion of

---

28. We leave as an open question whether a more standard notion of common ground could be used in our account. Although it's not clear to us whether such a move would be enlightening, here are some reasons to think it is possible: (i) it is not inconceivable that relevant aspects of, e.g., the weather could be thought of as a special set of propositions; (ii) propositions could be probabilistic, and this might allow for the gradient effects we are interested in; and (iii) on some accounts, such as Stalnaker's, attitudes are themselves dispositional, so there is no sharp difference between a class of disposition-based theories of common ground and a class of attitude-based theories of common ground. However, it is relevant here that while common ground is standardly entirely symmetric, our notion of collective attunement is not: people can be collectively attuned to different aspects of the same practice. Collective attunement does not require that actors have the same dispositions, only that their collective behavior can be seen as a manifestation of dispositional attunements to the same features of context, for example, the same practices.

common ground. This notion will be useful in framing our account of how communicative actions undergird ideological change, but it will also help make sense of our account by allowing a straightforward juxtaposition to a more standard view.

> **Common ground:** The common ground of a group is the collective attunements of that group.

Each collective attunement has a certain strength, so that the common ground of the authors might involve a strong collective attunement to certain practices of arguing with each other, and a weak collective attunement to the price of fish. We do not here attempt to provide a quantitative measure of the different levels that collective attunement might have, but the fact that we assume that there is some measure guarantees various intuitive properties, like transitivity: if a group is attuned to X more than Y, and Y more than Z, then it will be attuned to X more than Z. For current purposes, it will suffice to know that we take collective attunement to be a partial order, whereby in some cases it is possible to say that a change resulted in an attunement becoming stronger or weaker than some other attunement, without specifying any quantitative level.

As will become clear, our use of a scalar notion of common ground is essential to our model, but to make it easier to think about the common ground, and to enable more direct comparison to standard approaches, we can approximate the common ground as a set:

> **Common ground (discrete approximation):** The collective common ground is (approximated by) the set of things to which the level of collective attunement of the group is high.

Here "high" might be defined, for example, as high enough that the attunement would be manifest to an observer, such as someone randomly plucked from the streets of New Haven who entered into a lengthy conversation with us.

Our view builds on the standard notion of common ground, and we now explain why the differences matter at an intuitive level. We will then outline reasons to think that our reconceptualization retains the efficacy of earlier accounts in dealing with a cluster of much-studied linguistic phenomena involving presupposition. This will set the stage for introducing our approach to social meaning and ideological change.

In a series of classic papers, Robert Stalnaker defined the common ground of a group to be equivalent to the set of propositions that members of the group mutually believe (or accept).[29] He models this set of propositions in terms of the set of possible worlds in which the propositions hold, although nothing in our discussion hinges on the use (or non-use) of possible worlds.

---

29. Stalnaker, "Pragmatic Presuppositions"; Stalnaker, "Assertion."

This notion of common ground was also assumed by David Lewis and has become the standard for subsequent scholars. Stalnaker used common ground as the basis for an analysis of presupposition and assertion. In Stalnaker's view, the (pragmatic) presuppositions of a speaker making an assertion are all the propositions in the common ground between speaker and hearer as the act commences. The effect of the assertion, once accepted, is then to change this set. In the cases that Stalnaker considered, the change consists of a strict increase of the common ground to include the proposition asserted by the speaker. Equivalently, an accepted assertion yields a strict decrease in the set of worlds in the common ground, by removing from the prior common ground any possible worlds incompatible with the proposition newly asserted.

On an idealized version of the standard Stalnaker-Lewis view, the common ground of a group has the following features:[30]

1. **Propositional:** the common ground can be thought of as a set of propositions;
2. **Discrete:** a proposition is either in the common ground or not;
3. **Highly accessible:** it is scoreboard-like, equally apparent to all members of the group;
4. **Intersective:** a strict subset of beliefs held by individuals;
5. **Incontrovertible:** the group cannot disagree about its own common ground.

We are confident that collective attunement can do everything that common ground does in standard semantic and pragmatic theory, in part because standard common ground is a special case of collective attunement. Yet collective attunement generalizes enormously. In a nutshell, the difference between the standard notion of common ground and the variant we are proposing is that our attunement-based notion has none of the above five properties.

First, a system of collective attunements is not propositional. It is not propositional because we can be attuned to things and people, as well as practices and power tools. We can be attuned to them dispositionally, perceptually, emotionally, and cognitively. For example, we can be disposed to perceive something in a certain way. Seeing a certain person as your partner rather than as a stranger, involves attunement to that person. That attunement is not naturally thought of as attunement to a proposition. Likewise, the emotional attunement of loving someone is not an attunement to a proposition, but to the person. A crowd's adoration of a preening demagogue involves a collective emotional attunement to that individual, but again what they are attuned to is not propositional. There may be reasons for their adoration, and it may be that the adoration can be explained by the fact that the demagogue is, or appears

---

30. "Idealized" because it's not clear to us the degree to which Stalnaker is committed to all of these claims about the common ground.

to be, in possession of various traits, but that does not make the fact of possession of those traits into what is adored. We can describe attunements and their objects using propositions, and then reason about them, but the fact that we can describe them using propositions no more makes the attunements propositional than saying "it was a hard edible fruit of the species *Malus domestica* that fell onto Newton's head" makes the apple into a proposition. Propositions can't fall onto people's heads.

Second on our list is the discreteness of the fact as to whether a particular proposition is in the common ground or not, as against the way that attunements can take values on a continuous scale of strength. An individual or group can be more or less attuned to a charismatic leader, to the fact that he is lying to them, to the thugs in the street, or to the practices of the leader's followers. The assumption that things are categorically either in or out of the common ground is an idealizing approximation. It is available to us, not a core part of the model (and neither do we take it to be desireable).[31]

As regards the high accessibility of common ground in the Lewis-Stalnaker model, it is unclear how seriously to take Lewis's scoreboard metaphor. Certainly, many philosophers, most obviously Stalnaker, would not assume that agents will always be able to make their beliefs explicit.[32] However, at the very least, there is a difference in emphasis between us and many of our predecessors working on common ground, since we are most interested in attunements that people are unaware of. Indeed, some of the most interesting collective attunements, for example, attunements to racist or sexist practices, are attunements of which many practitioners might sincerely deny awareness. By contrast, standard work does not distinguish between elements of the common ground that are manifest to all, and elements that are hidden.

The last two of the above five properties, intersectivity and incontrovertibility, also relate to hiddenness. As described above, on a standard view, the common ground of a group is a set of beliefs, a strict subset of the beliefs of the members of the group (that subset that they not only believe, but believe each other believe, and believe that each other believe they believe, and so on, recursively). However, our model has a weird property: something can be in the common ground of the authors of this book while neither Jason nor David is attuned to it.

---

31. One of Stalnaker's arguments that presupposition should be explained pragmatically rather than semantically is that "the constraints imposed by a statement on what is presupposed seem to be a matter of degree" ("Pragmatic Presuppositions," in *Context and Content*, 54). This does not, as far as we can tell, entail a thesis about the discreteness or not of the common ground, and the assumption that the common ground is discrete is typically made in presentations of the framework.

32. In "Intellectualism and the Objects of Knowledge," Stalnaker argues forcefully against the view that one can as a rule verbally articulate one's beliefs.

But are such failures of intersectivity really so odd? It is certainly not a novel thought that collectives of people have properties that members of the collective lack. Indeed, this can be said to be, from the point of view set out by Émile Durkheim, a fundamental and defining assumption of the field of sociology. Setting out what he takes to be a social fact, he states,

> There are ways of acting, thinking and feeling which possess the remarkable property of existing outside the consciousness of the individual.
>
> Not only are these types of behaviour and thinking external to the individual, but they are endued with a compelling and coercive power by virtue of which, whether he wishes it or not, they impose themselves upon him. Undoubtedly when I conform to them of my own free will, this coercion is not felt or felt hardly at all, since it is unnecessary.[33]

Although our primary motivation for avoiding intersectivity does not involve attunement to propositions, it may be instructive to consider the propositional case in order to facilitate comparison with the most standard view in analytic philosophy on its own terms, terms that mark it out as quite a different notion to that assumed by Durkheim. So let's briefly restrict attention to a narrow set of dispositions that concern propositions, namely the propensity to make assertions.

A group may jointly avow propositions, or an entire system of thought, that none of its members would individually defend, feeling collectively but not individually prepared to defend it. It should at least be clear that, whether this is normatively desirable or not, it is entirely possible for a group to jointly avow a proposition that some or even all members of the group would individually not avow. More generally, a group may have attunements that its members lack, so that an electorate may collectively support a candidate or proposition that many individuals object to, and a population may have collective dispositions to marginalize and oppress, when it would be a category error to even talk about the individuals having such dispositions. This shows a divergence from the standard notion of common ground, although perhaps not yet a difference to make the case that a switch from the more standard approach is merited. So what are the cases that we feel more clearly merit a departure from the standard approach?

The cases we find most interesting as a motivation for reconsidering the notion of common ground involve practices and ideologies. The thought that contexts, and perhaps common grounds, contain something *like* practices is familiar enough in semantics and formal pragmatics, in particular in semantic accounts of imperatives. In his analysis of different kinds of imperative-containing constructions, Paul Portner has added *to-do lists* to contexts, which

---

33. Durkheim, *Rules of Sociological Method*, 51.

formally represent plans, and some others have followed suit.[34] It's natural to think of an ideology as providing plans; certainly these notions are connected. Ideology, after all, is a source of descriptive normativity in Haslanger's sense—and so provides prescriptions for actions, often in the form of practices. Discussions in metaethics that treat prescriptions for actions as nonpropositional plans underlying normativity appeal to something like ideologies in our sense. Semantic discussions of expressivism that try to formalize these notions explore some of the same structural territory as us—adding something like normatively laden practices into the common ground. But less clear in such presentations is the way in which attunement to a single practice can yield radically different plans.

Our methodological outlook has been to look to social and political examples of speech to test the concepts and tools of standard approaches in the theory of meaning. Investigation of imperatives shows that consideration of ordinary speech acts even in nonpolitical usages reveals similar shortcomings—this is why semanticists who have been exploring semantic theories for imperative constructions have had to expand the toolbox, for example, by adding to-do lists or plans to contexts. Could one expand the toolbox enough without considering social and political examples? Our guess is one could not. Without considering social and political examples, certain essentially communicative phenomena will fall outside the purview of a theory meant to capture them. But whether we establish this in the current work is something only future research can decide.

Practices and ideologies operate not only at the level of the conversational interaction, the primary level at which the notion of common ground is usually applied in work on meaning, but also at a societal level. Consider any practice that involves specialization, such as American football, performing an orchestral symphony, or manufacturing various high-tech widgets. It could be the practice of forming a country's government. Or it could be a practice of overthrowing that government. In each of these cases, a collective is attuned to what we might call a *macro*practice (i.e., an essentially interactive, multiperson practice), and individuals, say individual musicians in the orchestra, are highly attuned to various *micro*practices (i.e., patterns of individual action), but it may sometimes be of little value to talk about their individual attunement to the larger macropractice to which they contribute their own specialized activity. In much the way that a dog may be better attuned to the practice of sniffing out prey than any human would be, so it is that collectives of individuals may be better attuned to some collective practices than any

---

34. Portner, "The Semantics of Imperatives," "Imperatives and Modals." See also Charlow, "Clause-Type, Force, and Normative Judgment," and Marques and García-Carpintero, "Really Expressive Presuppositions." This tradition is influenced by the pioneering work of Gibbard, *Wise Choices, Apt Feelings*.

individual could be. The practices of swarming, rioting, or oppressing minority groups are just not the sort of thing that an individual can become good at, and although sometimes there are individuals who are perceptually and cognitively attuned to the nuances of the collective process, or who intentionally instigate it, this is not necessary. Similarly, marriage is not the sort of thing that a single person could master, and it takes two to tango.

Attunement to a practice—the general case—is not sharing the same plan, in the sense of the same recipe for behavior. A quarterback in American football and their receiver are attuned to the same practice. Yet this joint attunement is poorly modeled by treating them as presupposing the same recipe of behavior. In virtue of being attuned to the same practice, the quarterback and their receiver enact very different plans of action. The quarterback and the receiver are enacting very different skills via attunement to the very same practice.

Attunement in this more general sense is essential to understanding oppressive or potentially oppressive relationships. When everyone has equal attunement to a joint practice, management of the process can itself be collective, but in a complex system with many specialized roles, it is often an emergent property that the management of the process be delegated to a minority. Thus, there is asymmetric control over resources and knowledge, which in turn presents those in a management role with the opportunity to maintain power over others.

For example, Russian landowners and serfs prior to nineteenth-century emancipation were collectively attuned to a style of agricultural production that no individual had complete competence in, but, equally, individuals were collectively attuned to a system of oppression. The system of oppression involved a range of behavioral dispositions (as well as attitudes) that could not be mastered by a single person, as they impose conflicting demands. The serfs, who were not allowed the luxury of education, usually learned little beyond the practices and culture of their forefathers, including not only practices essential to agricultural production but also practices of serving and showing deference to their masters.

Recall the above distinction between first-order and second-order-attunements. As regards first-order attunements, the serfs were no more attuned to the refined practices and etiquette of the nobility than were the nobility attuned to manual labor, and the serfs were no more attuned to practices of domination than were the nobility attuned to practices of deference. Nonetheless, they each had second-order attunements to the practices of others in society with whom they interacted, and were collectively attuned to the oppressive system within which they existed, including its attendant ideology, and to a vast set of subpractices that no individual could have been fully attuned to. And here it might be added that being emotionally attuned to a system does not mean liking it. Prisoners in a retribution-based penal system are supposed to suffer. If as a prisoner you enjoy the cut of the whip, you are not well-attuned to such a penal system. Lucky you.

Our model explains that even an oppressor may completely fail to understand the role they play. Just as someone may not appreciate that they are driving a getaway car from a bank heist, or that they inadvertently act as a drug courier every time they drive their truck across the border, likewise, people may not appreciate that they are contributing to a system of oppression. The way you carry yourself, the way you keep the floor in public conversation, the confidence you show at a job interview, which neighborhood you live in, and which schools your children attend, these are not faults per se, but they may reflect a system that fails many.

Relatedly, our view also explains what is sometimes called "racism without racists," the title of an influential book by Eduardo Bonilla-Silva.[35] It is clearly possible, on the model we have described, for a group to be collectively attuned to a racist practice, without any member having racist attitudes. We can explain how US policing could be a racist practice—one that continues the oppression of poor marginalized American communities, by appeal to racist attitudes in the past that led people to develop those practices, together with the furthering of practices devised by people with these attitudes, due to the continued attunement of groups to these practices. We might also speak of the dispositional attunement of *institutions* to practices, institutions like courts, police forces, companies, and political parties, to the extent that we can identify institutional behaviors, and say of these behaviors whether they are in accord with a given practice or ideology.

2.5. Attunement to Resonance

When one is "attuned to a practice," what one is attuned to is the pattern of activity circumscribed by the resonances of the practice. So, we can equally talk of being attuned to the resonances of the practice. We briefly touched on the relationship between resonance and attunement in our discussion of practice, in section 2.3, above, but other than that we introduced the two notions independently, as if they had no more in common than the metaphorical framing they share. As we will make clear in this section, the connection between them is much tighter than a mere framing. It is no exaggeration to say that as regards the role we give them in sustaining practice, the two concepts are mirror images of each other. This is what will enable us later in the book to move seamlessly between resonance and attunement, using whichever is most convenient. Specifically, when we want to talk of properties of a speech practice, we will focus on the resonances of that practice. In particular, our analysis of the *presuppositions* of communicative acts will be cast primarily in terms of

35. Bonilla-Silva, *Racism without Racists.*

resonance. When we want to talk about individual and collective psychological states, we will refer to attunement, or collective attunement (i.e., loosely,
common ground). This will be crucial for our discussion of *harmony*, and of
the related process of *accommodation*.[36]

In chapter 1, we introduced the idea of *resonance* as playing something like
the role that *content* often plays in accounts of meaning, although we intended
it to capture conventionalized communicative significance more broadly. We
emphasized that resonance operates at an interactional level, illustrated in
terms of a simple thought experiment, the *coffee game*. In the coffee game, a
practice emerges whereby when one person is sleepy, they nod, and when they
nod, the other brings them coffee. The game showed how conventional resonances can be an emergent property of iterated interactional situations. By
presenting our thought experiment in terms of a well-studied paradigm, the
two-player game, we adopted what we hope was a natural simplification. But
it was a simplification that obscured the way resonance functions within society. A book on political language necessarily concerns speech practices that
exist at the level of the polis, that is, a large speech community. We will now
consider how resonance functions within these larger groups, within what we
have been calling *communities of practice*. To do this, we must first say more
about what a practice is and what a community of practice is.

As discussed above, we avoid commitment as to how practices are represented psychologically, beyond assuming some sort of memory (which may
be "muscle memory" rather than explicit or clearly representational episodic
memory) of what has occurred. To achieve this, we need a general method
that, based on a history of actions, can compute for any two actions whether
they belong to the same practice. In this vein, we mentioned exemplar theory,
as developed in psychological work on concepts and categorization. But let us
here adopt a counterpart of exemplar theory found in exploratory data science
and machine learning, namely *clustering*. Clustering is an approach whereby
an algorithm automatically classifies data into groups of similar points. For
example, faced with data about the physical properties of animals, a clustering
algorithm might be used to guess how the animals are separated into different
species.

The practices within a community can be seen as a way of clustering
actions together, of viewing subsets of them as belonging to the same category.
Often, people introduce labels for practices, for example, labeling certain complex acts as acts of assertion, and certain other complex acts as acts of going
on a date. So, each practice is one cluster, a label on a subset of actions (or
complexes of actions). It is not, however, a simple clustering, in the way that
is standardly assumed in data analysis. Commonly, cluster labels are taken to

---

36. We analyze presupposition in chapters 4 and 5, harmony in chapter 3, and accommodation in chapters 6 and 7.

cleanly separate different groups of data points into non-overlapping sets. It may help to start by imagining a space of actions that is simple in this way, with like actions clustered together, and each action belonging to only one cluster, but it is as well to note right away that the real situation is more complex. Actions can belong to multiple practices, practices can be special cases of other practices, and patterns of actions can be broken down into smaller actions or patterns of actions that belong to further practices.

We are assuming, with Jaeggi, that practices are massively interconnected and interdependent, so the space of practices has a massively complex structure. Still, the basic idea of what a typical clustering algorithm in data science does is a good first approximation for what an individual must do when faced with the problem of making sense of the actions they experience. The individual assigns labels to actions (or at least groups them together, associating them with each other) with some level of confidence, collecting actions that are similar on dimensions that the individual determines to be useful for classification.

Let us move from an individual level to a group level. For a given community, let us define a set of recognizable practices as those clusterings of actions such that (i) there is a high tendency for individuals in the community to have similar clusterings, and also (ii) there is a high tendency for individuals in the community to perform the actions comprising the practices. These are the community practices.

To say that there is a high tendency for individuals in the community to have similar ways of clustering some set of practices, that is, that they classify actions similarly, is to say that they have strong collective cognitive (and perceptual) attunements to those practices. Similarly, to say that there is a high tendency for individuals in the community to perform the actions comprising the practices is to say that the community has strong collective dispositional attunements to the practices. So let us define a *community of practice* as follows:

> **Community of practice:** A community of practice is a set of individuals with strong collective attunements to a set of practices, such that no larger set of individuals has similarly strong or stronger collective attunements to that set of practices.[37]

---

37. Our use of "communities of practice" is set within a tradition whereby the term "speech community" refers to an arbitrarily large group who speaks something that can usefully be described as the "same" language. As previously noted in section 1.8, the way we use the term "community of practice" is more general than the use of the phrase in much work in sociolinguistics and theory of organizational learning. Whereas we allow groups of arbitrary size to be communities of practice, provided they distinctively share practices, there is a somewhat standardized use that is restricted to local settings. Eckert offers the following characterization of a community of practice: "A community of practice

Within such a community, there will obviously be a tight relationship between cognitive and dispositional attunements. We should expect that, ceteris paribus, the practice will be ongoing and that new performances of practices from that set will typically be taken to instantiate those same practices, and with a high level of agreement among community members.

We take the extension of a practice to be a strict subset of events that include members of a relevant community of practice as active participants. In section 1.4, we defined the *associative resonances of an action* in terms of a probability distribution over features of context, the idea being that some feature is a (positive) resonance of an action to the extent that the occurrence of the action implies a boosted probability for that feature. In principle, the probability boost for a feature can be calculated by taking the set of contexts in which the action has taken place, and comparing how much more often the feature is present in those contexts than it is in other contexts. What we are suggesting now is that the set of contexts relevant to such a calculation is determined by a community of practice. Communities of practice determine the extension of a practice, which in turn determines what contexts are relevant to calculating resonance, and the resonances of practices thus defined depend crucially on the identification of an appropriate community of practice, the community that contains the practitioners.

As Penny Eckert and Étienne Wenger explain,

---

is a collection of people who engage on an ongoing basis in some common endeavor: a bowling team, a book club, a friendship group, a crack house, a nuclear family, a church congregation." She goes on: "The value of the notion communities of practice to sociolinguistics and linguistic anthropology lies in the fact that it identifies a social grouping not in virtue of shared abstract characteristics (e.g. class, gender) or simple co-presence (e.g. neighborhood, workplace), but in virtue of shared practice. In the course of regular joint activity, a community of practice develops ways of doing things, views, values, power relations, ways of talking" (Eckert, "Communities of Practice," 683).

Etienne Wenger writes as follows:

> A community of practice defines itself along three dimensions:
> What it is about: its joint enterprise as understood and continually renegotiated by its members
> How it functions: the relationships of mutual engagement that bind members together into a social entity
> What capability it has produced: the shared repertoire of communal resources (routines, sensibilities, artifacts, vocabulary, styles, etc.) that members have developed over time.

Communities of practice also move through various stages of development characterized by different levels of interaction among the members and different kinds of activities. . . . Communities of practice develop around things that matter to people. As a result, their practices reflect the members' own understanding of what is important. Even when a community's actions conform to an external mandate, it is the community—not the mandate— that produces the practice. In this sense, communities of practice are self-organizing systems. (Wenger, "Communities of Practice: Learning as a Social System," 2)

One doesn't "do" a practice excised from the community. A practice is a way of doing things, *as grounded in and shared by a community*. The wearing of the right color of lipstick for the sake of being accepted is a practice by virtue of its role in getting accepted, not by virtue of its disembodied appropriateness. Practice always involves the maintenance of the community and therefore its power structure. Legitimacy in any community of practice involves not just having access to knowledge necessary for "getting it right," but being at the table at which "what is right" is continually negotiated.[38]

Exactly what counts as the relevant community for a particular practice is typically far from obvious. Thus it also follows that the extension of a practice is not fully determinate, and thence that the resonances are not fully determinate. We take this not as an inherent problem with the framework, but as reflective of real-world vagueness of social constructs, and of the fact that reasonable people may sometimes disagree about shades of meaning. For relatively stable practices, like the practice of saying "ouch," it will make little difference exactly what the community of practice is taken to be, within reasonable limits of space and time, but for other practices, like a relatively new meme generated on a particular message board, spread across social media, and just starting to lead to idiomatic usages in ordinary conversational interactions, it will matter greatly what is taken to be the relevant community of practice. Furthermore, this is not just an empirical matter, but may become normative.

People may actively police both the communities and the practices, attempting to constrain which actions count as exemplars of the practice. Many countries legislate the proper use of their national languages through special-purpose academies. An example of policing that gained national attention was the reactions of a broad slice of the US public to the "Ebonics" controversy in 1997, which occurred after the Oakland school board approved a policy allowing teaching of English to flexibly use the variety of English spoken by many of the students, that is, African American Vernacular English, a.k.a. Ebonics, a.k.a. Black English. A political and media firestorm followed, a firestorm in which the facts of what the Oakland school board was attempting to do were largely buried.[39]

---

38. Eckert and Wenger, "Communities of Practice in Sociolinguistics," 583.

39. We do not mean to imply that all who opposed the Oakland Schoolboard's policy were ignorant of the linguistic status of African American Vernacular English as a language variety in its own right, rather than being in some sense a degraded form of English, or what some might call "street slang." Some undoubtedly opposed the use of African American Vernacular English within the school district precisely because they recognized that it is a stigmatized language variety, and perhaps worried that so long as that variety was set

Although it provided a learning moment or two, the Ebonics firestorm was revealing of deep ignorance of the nature of language. Many believe that the language that much of the US population speaks is in some sense degraded both grammatically and morally, and there is deep collective angst at the possibility of what are regarded as standard varieties of US English being in some sense sullied by a vastly less prestigious variety playing any role in education. Implicitly, Black Americans were not being accepted as part of the community of practice for American English except when behaving in accord with the White majority. The urgent desire to push back against use of a particular language variety as a teaching tool is reflective not only of broader negative attitudes to the culture of an oppressed group, but also of a widespread perception that it is the proper role of educational establishments to defend the dominant culture. In other areas of education, say as regards religion, or as regards political attitudes in authoritarian states, common ways in which educational establishments standardize the language of students would be described by nonbelieving outsiders as a combination of policing and indoctrination—a point central to Althusser's discussion of schools as "ideological state apparatuses."[40]

Let us leave aside the admittedly important questions of language attitudes that come up at the level of language policy at a state level and within educational systems. We assume that identifying the community of practice relevant for a particular type of action must then involve a combination of facts about location, time, joint interests, and social identity. A community of practice may be as large as a nation, or even transnational, or as small as a family or work unit. Further, there may be no fact of the matter as to exactly who is in the community and who is not. One might consider a nation as a single community of practice relevant for various social customs, food preparation and consumption practices, child-rearing practices, and so on, but for any of these practices there will be smaller subcommunities for which the practices differ idiosyncratically but somewhat consistently, as well as larger or overlapping communities (say, English speakers around the world) among whom a subset of the practices is partially shared. Given these considerations, we cannot claim that relativizing practices to communities of practice immediately brings clarity to the definition of particular practices. Rather, we claim that the complexity of identifying the relevant community or communities is inherent to the process of identification and understanding of any social practice.

As discussed both in chapter 1 and in the current chapter, we do not understand resonances primarily in terms of the epistemic state of observers,

---

in a positive light in schools, students would continue to use it in contexts where they might draw that same stigma onto themselves.

40. Althusser, *On the Reproduction of Capitalism: Ideology and Ideological State Apparatuses.*

although we take the resonances of communicative actions to be precisely what allows communicative acts to provide information. Rather, we understand the probability changes that constitute resonance in terms of the collective behavior and states of all those involved in the practice, as well as in the state of the world more generally as it changes when the practice is performed. Let us return to the practice of saying "ouch" as an example. When a member of an English-speaking community of practice performs an act of expressing mild pain, one of the things briefly but dramatically boosted is the probability that they are engaged in making an "ow" sound, and that probability more or less quickly recedes, to be replaced by a high probability that they are making a "ch" sound. More generally, the resonances of a communicative action include boosts to all the typical features of situations in which that practice tends to occur, including features associated with the speaker (in this case, primarily emotional and behavioral) and features associated with the hearer (in this case, primarily cognitive and emotional, to the extent that a hearer might recognize pain and feel empathy).

Our relativization of resonance to community practices allows us to state two important postulates in cases involving the resonances of conventionalized, communicative actions, that is, communicative practices. We might term these postulates *non-idiosyncrasy* and *causal efficacy*. Both concern the standardization of language, the sorts of things that can become resonances.[41]

> **Non-idiosyncrasy postulate:** For a member of a speech community, the resonances of a speech act that follows the practices of that community are not dependent on idiosyncratic features of that individual, be they the speaker or audience member, but only on properties of the context in accord with which the practice is predictably used.

For example, the exclamation "ouch" is predictably used in situations when the speaker has experienced sudden pain, and its resonances include that property of the speaker, whether the speaker actually experienced such pain or not. Suppose that a particular speaker happens to idiosyncratically say "ouch" on a somewhat regular basis not when they are in pain, but rather when they are about to eat bacon for breakfast. If they are not part of a larger community of practice where their speech behavior is normal, then for any other English-speaking observer, the exclamation will be associated solely with resonances of prior pain, and not imminent bacon. Repeated actions that are recognized as the idiosyncratic behavior of only one individual and not the regular behavior of a meaningful class of individuals are not social practices, and for our purposes should be regarded as habits, not practices at all.

41. We are grateful to Justin Khoo and Timothy Williamson, discussions with whom helped us see the importance of these issues.

One of the most cited dialogues in philosophy of language, Lewis Carroll's Humpty Dumpty dialogue, famously touches on this point:

> "When *I* use a word," Humpty Dumpty said in rather a scornful tone, "it means just what I choose it to mean—neither more nor less."
>
> "The question is," said Alice, "whether you can make words mean different things—that's all."
>
> "The question is," said Humpty Dumpty, "which is to be master—that's all."[42]

In our terms, the master is not Humpty Dumpty, but the community of practice to which he belongs, for it is community practice that determines the meaning of a word, that is, its resonances. A community of one is no community at all.

> **Causal-efficacy postulate:** Within a speech community, speech practices will not emerge that have as resonances properties that can neither causally affect whether community members perform the practice, nor are causally related to effects of the practice that community members can recognize.

This second postulate also concerns the limits of conventionalization, but it concerns the types of features that can become conventionalized resonances for a community rather than the question of whether an individual can idiosyncratically determine the resonances for themselves. Imagine a situation in which "ouch" was used to express pain, but in which only a subset of people ever used the term, that subset being determined by an unobservable property. For example, it could be that the only people who ever said "ouch" were those whose maternal grandfather had once dropped a glass of milk. It would then follow in this hypothetical situation that the saying of "ouch" would boost the probability of someone having such a hapless maternal grandfather, at least for some suitably well-informed observer.

Care must be taken here as regards what we take community members to be able to recognize. When we experience pain, certain neurochemical pathways are active (or so we presume, though we lack relevant neuroscientific expertise). So, saying "ouch" boosts the probability that these pathways are active. Does it then follow that the resonances of "ouch" include certain facts about neurochemical pathways? We do not take it to be urgent for us to decide this matter here, but we are prepared to allow that the resonances might include properties of the context that, although not directly recognized by community members, happen to correlate with properties that can be recognized. In that case it might be that when ancient Greeks used the word ὕδωρ (*hudōr*, "water"), the presence of the chemical H_2O in a salient situation was a

---

42. Carroll, *Through the Looking-Glass*, 259.

resonance of the utterance, even though the ancient Greeks lacked knowledge of modern chemistry, a point familiar from the philosophical literature on *externalism*. One thing that would not follow from allowing for the existence of such resonances is that by virtue of Plato pointing at a glass and saying ὕδωρ, his student Aristotle could have become aware of the chemical structure of the liquid in the glass. More generally, the resonances of speech practices might include all sorts of things that neither the speaker nor the hearer is aware of, but which are nonetheless distinctive features of the contexts in which the practice is instantiated.

Let us now tie down a bit further the relationship between resonance and attunement. Earlier in the chapter, we defined attunement to practice as follows:

> **Attunement to practice:** An agent is *attuned* to a practice to the extent that their state and behavior predictably evolve in accordance with its presence in the agent's context.

The resonances consist in the set of features that are present in contexts of use, and as noted these include all the relevant facts about speakers, addressees, and other audience members or observers. So, for the state and behavior of agents to predictably evolve in a way that accords with a practice just means that the state and behavior evolve in line with the resonances of that practice. We arrive at the following, which describes the relationship between individual dispositional attunement and resonance, and which we take to have the status not of a new definition, but of something like a lemma, following from the definitions we have already given:

> **Attunement to practice (in terms of resonance):** An agent is *attuned* to a community practice to the extent that their state and behavior tend to evolve in accord with the *resonances* of actions belonging to the extension of that practice in the community.

So, slightly more narrowly, a dispositional attunement to a (part of a) practice is a tendency to perform the practice in contexts bearing features that are resonances of the practice. Further, membership of a community implies a tendency to be attuned to the resonances of practices that are prominent within that community. A member of a speech community will tend to have strong attunements to the resonances of the speech practices found in that community, and a member of a sports community will tend to have strong attunements to the resonances of whatever sports practices are found in that community. But since such communities often overlap, a member of a speech community will tend to have strong attunements to the resonances of the sports practices found in that community, and, vice versa, a member of a sports community will tend to have strong attunements to the resonances of the speech practices found in that community. The nexus of practices described by Jaeggi is mediated by overlapping communities.

Let's consider a simpler case, the coffee game. The community of practice consists only of the two players. The resonances of the only action that David performs include prior sleepiness, the physical act of nodding itself (the locutionary act), and Jason later bringing coffee. David has a dispositional attunement to behave in accord with these resonances, specifically by performing the action when he is sleepy, and also before Jason brings coffee, though of course he only has correlational evidence that Jason will react by bringing coffee. Similarly, Jason is dispositionally attuned to the practice. When he observes David nodding, he performs an action of bringing coffee. In this case, the two actions (David nodding and Jason bringing coffee), if they are perfectly correlated, completely share the resonances of a larger complex practice that involves both actions being instantiated.

The coffee game illustrates the sense in which resonance and attunement mirror each other. There is simply no difference between stating the resonances of the actions of nodding and bringing coffee, and stating David and Jason's individual dispositional attunements. To state the resonances is to state the dispositional attunements of the two members of this tiny community of practice, and vice versa. And this is entirely general. To state the resonances of a speech practice found in a speech community (or any practice in any community of practice) is just to state the attunements that members of the community tend to have to that practice, and vice versa.

2.6. Changing Ideology

No two instantiations of a practice are identical. Every time a practice is newly instantiated, differences between that instantiation and prior instantiations can have a small impact on what members of the community who were exposed to that instantiation judge to be correlated with instantiations of the practice, and this can then shift their attunements in a way that brings them either temporarily or permanently out of step with other community members. Practices change. They drift, may be affected by other cultural forces, and sometimes are shifted intentionally. A practice may vary considerably over time, or over space, as when there is a dialect continuum, such that small changes in a speech practice correlate with geographical location. A practice may vary relative to other variables, like social status, education, or genre. Consequently, it may sometimes be hard to identify a unique and stable community of practice within which there is a high level of collective attunement to the practice.

A stable practice is a fixed point of behaviors, emerging when there is a high degree of constancy of collective attunements to the practice over time and space. This will normally imply ongoing shared dispositional and cognitive attunement, that is, dispositions to produce new actions within the practice and high levels of agreement as to whether new events count as instances of the practice.

In case there is substantial stability of many practices, we can think of the community of practice in two ways. We can think of the community as its current set of members, or we can think of it as a collection of individuals over time, such that different individuals at different times would have similar attunements, and so, for example, would have a high degree of agreement as regards whether events instantiate the practice. Contrarily, sometimes a set of practices, or an entire community of practice, can be unstable and even die out. Since a community of practice can be understood as involving individuals spaced over time, it is possible to be the last speaker in a community of practice, albeit at this point the practice itself is inevitably highly attenuated. There may not be many speaking opportunities for that one speaker.

Here's a straw-man, assertion-based model of ideological transmission: people assert things, and other people accept them. Clearly transmission can take this form, but there are obvious reasons to doubt its generality. At the very least, there are other mechanisms of ideological transmission and information exchange. Actions can reveal a great deal to an observer, whether those actions are assertions or not, and even an assertion can reveal a great deal more than the proposition that is asserted. How so?

There is nothing mysterious about the mechanism we have in mind. Actions do not take place randomly, but rather are conditioned upon the state of the world. A daffodil blooms, and, unrelatedly, a coauthor sends a text. From the first, a honey bee, in natural harmony with the plant, might glean information to direct its nectar-foraging activities, and from the second, the recipient of the text, who enjoys a somewhat more complex harmony with the sender, might learn of some politician's latest outrage. The daffodil does not bloom in order to tell us that spring is in the air, and yet its blooming reflects that very fact. And a coauthor's text, whatever its content, may reveal that the recipient and their joint project with the sender haven't been forgotten. It may or may not have been intended to convey this. When we witness an event, we may infer that we are in the sort of situation in which such events occur. The more regularly an event takes place, the more clearly it might reflect its context. An event that involves humans interacting in such a systematic way that we can identify their interaction as an exemplar of a general practice can provide a great deal of information, if we know about the contexts in which such interactions tend to take place.

Every practice is potentially communicative, whether we would normally think of it as a communicative practice or not, because any instantiation of that practice reflects the fact that the context is one in which the practice tends to occur, and thus any instantiation of a practice provides an observer with information about that context. It follows that as regards specifically communicative practices, we get an informational double whammy: first, qua practices, they reflect context, and second, qua communicative practices, they have some functional signaling effect that both provides information about the context and changes it. The first, the way that a practice reflects its context, is what we will call, adapting standard terminology, *presupposition*. We reserve until part II of the book detailed discussion of presupposition, of the mechanism by which it supports the spread of attunement, and of its role in group identity and ideological conflict. For now, we merely seek to illustrate the way that ideology can be spread through changes in attunement that result from broad and perhaps repeated exposure to actions with strong ideological resonances, without the necessity of assertion. But first, let us state more explicitly what ideology amounts to within the resonance and attunement model.

So far, we said of ideologies (in section 2.1, above) that they are "cultural artifacts consisting of practices, attitudes, affect, and norms." On the view we have developed, cultural artifacts, as opposed to material artifacts, are no more and no less than collective attunements of groups of people. For an ideology, the relevant grouping is a community of practice, whether that community is a group of practicing Catholics, Democrats, or carpenters. Ideologies are then collective dispositional, cognitive, and emotional attunements among such groups, as well as attunements to metapractices that regulate practice. Ideology perhaps might be taken to include a separate dimension of moral attunement, but we will not discuss the question of whether moral attunement should or could be separated in any way from other attunements, or whether it would be useful to discuss ethical issues in terms of the attunement model. Leaving morality aside, we arrive at the following definition:

Ideology: An ideology is the system of collective attunements among members of a community of practice.[43]

The *ideological resonances of a practice* then consist in the increased tendency for practitioners to have attunements belonging to the broader ideology

---

43. Although we do not follow this line, we are sympathetic to Quill Kukla's suggestion that ideology is not merely a social construct, but also includes the spaces that society physically constructs. As Kukla says,

> Ideologies are built into practices and the material environment; they are not primarily or essentially "ideas in the head." Swanson says that an ideology "is a cluster of mutually supporting beliefs, interests, norms, values, practices, institutions, scripts, habits, affective dispositions, and ways of interpreting and interacting with the world" (forthcoming, 6). I like this list but would add even less idea-like phenomena such as buildings, aesthetic products, street signs, spatial divisions such as gates and hedges, and the like. ("Slurs, Interpellation, and Ideology," 9; see Swanson, "Slurs and Ideologies," for reference)

of the community, above and beyond attunement to the practice itself. The resonances can be innocent. An ideological resonance of the practice of saying "oy vey" is a tendency to eat bagels with a certain distinctive texture and density. The resonances can also be pernicious. The practice of labeling angry women as hysterical may have as a resonance an increased tendency to treat women as unworthy of hiring or promotion. Such practices take place within what we will call discriminatory ideologies:

> **Discriminatory ideology:** An ideology that includes attunements to in-group/out-group distinctions (a.k.a. us-them distinctions), and in which members of out-groups are valued less than members of in-groups, and hence as inherently deserving of less than equal treatment or resources.

To say that the ideological resonances of a practice are potent would then be to make the claim that instances of the practice have a powerful effect in shifting collective attunement within a community of practice, perhaps helping alter the makeup of subcommunities. We doubt the potency of the practice of saying "oy vey," but we suppose that various sexist speech practices, such as the labeling of women as hysterical, may be highly potent. Educational and religious practices often have potent ideological resonances, but so do practices of protest and practices of oppression.

Neither of the two definitions we have given, of ideology and discriminatory ideology, are inherently pejorative. According to the notion of ideology as we have characterized it, for example, everyone has an ideology. Even calling something a discriminatory ideology is not, in our sense, to evaluate the ideology negatively—for example, it may be acceptable to discriminate against Nazis as a group. In the literature on ideology, however, the dominant notion of ideology from Marx on has typically been pejorative in nature, the idea being that an ideology (such as the ideology of the ruling class that masks reality to subserve their interests) clouds people's perceptions and preferences.

We can distinguish two different senses in which the notion of ideology can be pejorative—a moral sense and an epistemic sense. A system of attunements is ideologically problematic in the moral sense if it contributes to the maintenance of unjust social hierarchies. A system of attunements is ideologically problematic in the epistemological sense if it masks socially important truths about the world. When scholars talk of ideologies pejoratively, they typically describe systems of attunement that are simultaneously epistemologically and morally problematic.

At least since the work of the sociologist Talcott Parsons, a nonpejorative view of ideology has also emerged. Parsons defines an ideology as "a system of beliefs, held in common by the members of a collectivity," adding also that the ideology should include some a norm of affinity to the collective and to shared goals of the collective used to guide action.[44] Our own nonpejorative notion of ideology is naturally seen as an extension of Parsons's notion, generalizing from beliefs to attunements, which then folds in the idea that the ideology should guide action since attunements can be dispositional.[45]

If the pejorative view prominent in Marxist thought and much critical theory is that ideology distorts reality, then a typical nonpejorative view, like that of Parsons, would be that ideology of one sort or another is both ubiquitous and necessary, that it is impossible to comprehend reality without the conceptual scaffolding of an ideology. We can then distinguish a third, radical view of ideology, turning the standard notion on its head. Quill Kukla expresses it as follows: "Ideologies need not be false; they are not sets of misrepresentations. While they in some sense represent social relations, these are not representations that cover over reality. Indeed, they play a role in constituting reality."[46] Taking this view to its extreme, ideology would neither be a mask that hides social reality, nor a tool for making sense of social reality, but rather ideology would be the primary construct from which social reality is derived. For our purposes, the weaker view expressed by Kukla suffices, that ideology is not merely some sort of observational or conceptual tool, but at least plays a role in constituting social reality.

We postpone to section 7.5 further consideration of the scholarly background against which this definition of ideology is given, although we must forewarn the reader that even there we make no attempt at a comprehensive discussion of prior literature on ideology, a topic that we could not hope to do justice to in this volume. We also do not attempt a detailed comparison with Jaeggi's notion of a "form of life," although that notion is closely related to our notion of ideology, especially in respect of being centered around practice. For the purpose of setting out our framework in these first two parts of the book, what we need of our notion of ideology is that (i) practices and not just propositions are central, (ii) both practices and propositional attitudes are tied to ideology via a notion of attunement shared across a community, and (iii) the community itself is bounded by the shared practices that define it. Thus our notion of ideology inherits the central role given to practice by Jaeggi, but also Haslanger, Kukla, and many others, notably Bourdieu.

In the light of our attunement-based approach to ideology, let us now briefly consider an oppressive practice, as an example application. Our interest here is in showing how the model we have developed can be used to explicate the efficacy of dehumanizing speech acts not merely as regards the immediate

44. Parsons, *The Social System*, 349. We are grateful for the extensive discussion of both pejorative and non-pejorative notions of ideology found in Eagleton, *Ideology: An Introduction*, 1–32; and Gerring, "Ideology: A definitional analysis."

45. For further discussion of the complex history of definitions of the term *ideology* see Gerring, "Ideology: A Definitional Analysis."

46. Kukla, "Slurs, Interpellation, and Ideology," 9.

effect of denigrating somebody, but as a way of driving ideological change. That efficacy consists in the ability of those acts to use an innocuous way of talking to smuggle across (if we may borrow from the conduit metaphor) a vast repertoire of attitudes and practices. Dehumanizing speech acts can achieve this by implicitly pivoting around a context that supports those attitudes and practices. As a hearer, you see the pivot and infer the context. That is the process we want to capture.

As the work of Lynne Tirrell has emphasized, when Rwandan Hutus repeatedly referred to Tutsis in the early 1990s as cockroaches and snakes, their actions presupposed, and brought together, many features of context.[47] Among those features are practices of treating Tutsis, and enemies more generally, in certain ways, practices of characterizing groups in terms of paradigmatic features, practices of using vivid analogies to achieve those characterizations, practices of speaking Kinyarwanda, and practices of talking specifically associated with cockroaches and snakes. This latter set of practices includes (i) bodily ways of manifesting fear and loathing, (ii) ways of speaking about them that characterize them as individually low and worthless and as collectively presenting a plague-like existential threat, and (iii) ways of eradicating them, violently and without remorse or mercy: one does not grant a cockroach a last-minute reprieve and offer it sustenance and a safe place to live with its growing family in exchange for a solemn promise to be just a little less roachy in the future. Without the existence of these three types of practice, reference to Tutsis as cockroaches and snakes would not be effective.[48]

But in what sense is reference to Tutsis as cockroaches and snakes appropriate? On the contrary, such talk is not appropriate. Rather, it is indefensibly immoral. We can say that it is inappropriate and immoral because we take as a fundamental precept that all human life has significant value. Yet to say this is beside the point, because the question we have posed is not quite the right one. The question we need to ask is not what makes reference to Tutsis as cockroaches and snakes appropriate, but what, counterfactually, would make it appropriate? To spell it out: what features would a context have to be like in order for it to be appropriate to refer to Tutsis as cockroaches and snakes? It would have to be a context in which Tutsis posed an existential threat, were of no human value, and where there would be no reason to show them mercy. If you were a Hutu who took yourself to be in such a context, you might be unable to empathize with Tutsis. A context in which one cannot empathize with other human actors is a fertile context for injustice or, in this case, genocide.

What the action of referring to Tutsis as vermin presupposed, then, was certain collective attunements, attunements relative to which the practice of genocide appeared justified, because it is only in a context involving such

47. Tirrell, "Genoçidal Language Games."
48. Tirell, "Genocidal Language Games."

collective attunements that talking that way would be appropriate. The Rwandan Hutu populace was repeatedly exposed to such presuppositions in many different forms, with broadcasts from the RTLM television station from mid-1993 onward being a primary mechanism for spreading such propaganda. The presuppositions were carried not only through analogy to vermin, but also through other speech acts that carried similar presuppositions, and through increasingly violent nonlinguistic acts.

A dramatic example of such a nonlinguistic act would be the killing of political opponents and ordinary Tutsis from the spring of 1994 on. All actions presuppose the appropriacy, or even reasonableness, of the practices they exemplify. So, a killing can presuppose the appropriacy of a practice of homicide by those who identify with the killers of those with whom the victim is identified. Assassinating a prominent political figure is ideal for such signaling, not only because the prominence guarantees publicity, but also because it is evident who the figure is identified with, it is evident who the enemies are, and it is evident that if the life of a high-status individual can be taken, then so can anyone else's. At the start of the Rwandan conflict, President Juvénal Habyarimana was shot out of the sky. Habyarimana was himself a Hutu, and the initial round of killings was presumably intended not merely to send signals, but also, and perhaps more importantly, to directly destabilize control structures; however, later mass killings focused on Tutsis.[49] This ethnically based targeting, combined with the increasing brutality of the killings, served to reinforce both the normalcy of a practice of killing Tutsis and the lack of mercy they were due. The machetes and clubs used in these killings mirror the methods used to kill snakes and cockroaches.

Suppose one were faced with repeated exposure to acts with extreme presuppositions. It's easy to suppose that one can simply ignore them. Suppose one regularly hears some group being talked of as vermin, and later learns that they are being exterminated in much the way that vermin are exterminated. It might be that with increasing exposure to such presuppositions, one comes to a slightly greater acceptance that the context is just as it has been presupposed to be. And so with each exposure, nonperpetrators become a little more like perpetrators, or at least share a way of talking about the actions that are perpetrated.

Similarly, a Nazi prison guard's action in referring to genocidal victims as if their bodies were no more than industrial materials presupposes a context that has features in which no respect is due to those victims and no remorse or guilt need be felt over their murder. In the context that the guard presumably both accepted and perhaps had helped promulgate, the victims lacked value as human beings by virtue of the groups they were identified with, whether

---

49. The fact that Habyarimana was a Hutu may have enhanced the strategic usefulness of his murder, since it made it easier for Hutu rebels to blame his death on Tutsis.

defined by religion, ethnicity, or sexual preference. It was a context that supported a range of individual and state-sanctioned practices that were not merely unfair, but inhumane. The prison guard's act of referring not only presupposed their own speech practice of describing the victims' corpses as they did, but presupposed a much broader range of practices in which, as a Nazi, and as a state worker, they were complicit. Likewise telling a sexist or racist joke presupposes a context in which certain negative stereotypes are valid, and in which social practices depending on the negative generalization are warranted.[50] In particular, the context will support practices that involve awarding differential reward, status, and opportunity to the "target"—or, perhaps better, the "victim"—of the joke, including the opportunity to have their voice heard. A laugh betrays consciousness of tension. But it also betrays a degree of acceptance of the perspective portrayed, and a degree of like-mindedness.

Presuppositions are commonly discussed at the level of individual sentences or utterances of those sentences. One respect in which we generalize the notion of presupposition is to move beyond the presuppositions associated with individual utterances, to consider instead the presuppositions associated with systematic patterns of language use. We have already seen that people can be attuned to practices, and, likewise, in the model we will develop, both the practices, and their attendant attunements, can be presupposed. So we may talk of utterances presupposing practices, or, indeed, of practices presupposing practices.

Let us turn to another example of a practice and its effect in changing collective attunement. The systematic exposure to sexist jokes may, over time, cause people to behave differently toward women, to engage in practices that not only denigrate women verbally, but cause them physical harm or curtail their freedom of action. When the authors were young, there was a ubiquitous and public practice of exchanging "my wife" jokes, often in the form "she's so fat/ugly/easy that . . ." or "I'm not saying she's fat/ugly/easy, but. . . ." This practice persists, although at least in public forums it's less prevalent. To be sure, there was always a certain uncomfortable edginess about such jokes, even though they were clichéd. The edginess was a necessary ingredient of the comic tension, but can also be seen in terms of Brown and Levinson's *positive politeness*. Positive politeness involves presenting goals as shared, and minimizing distance between the speaker and hearer. Positive politeness commonly involves evidencing common group identity and solidarity.[51] Both speaking of something

---

50. As discussed in section 10.2, some linguists and philosophers have argued that slurs' derogatory meaning or effects are best explained in terms of presuppositions. See, e.g., Cepollaro and Stojanovic, "Hybrid Evaluatives"; Marques and García-Carpintero, "Really Expressive Presuppositions"; Schlenker, "Expressive Presuppositions."

51. Brown and Levinson focus on politeness strategies as ways of managing speech that would otherwise threaten face. Positive politeness is opposed to negative politeness, which involves distancing: deferential, impersonal language and lack of imposition. We are using

that is mildly taboo and admitting problems with someone or something close to the speaker are ways of showing solidarity with the audience. You wouldn't say such a terrible thing about your spouse unless you trusted the person you were speaking to, would you?

In the United Kingdom, "my wife" jokes were a staple of public humor, and were common not only on the men's working clubs comedy circuit, but in variety shows both on stage and on television for mixed audiences of men, women, and children. They were in place at the workplace, and at home in the living room. There are many presuppositions associated with jokes of this kind. Most obviously, they reflect sexist values and their attendant dispositional attunements to focus on physical attributes of women and their sexuality, and to judge them harshly if they fail to adhere to the ideals of the attendant sexist ideology. Concomitantly, such humor reflects practices in which women's roles depend on their physical attributes and sexuality, rather than on their skills and intelligence. Comics reinforced these practices by telling the jokes, the media reinforced them by giving such comics a platform, and we all reinforced them whenever we joined the comic in laughing at women who fail to meet physical and sexual ideals. Suppose someone is regularly exposed to sexist jokes that either center on women's putative inability to comprehend technical matters, or implicitly suggest such inability by valuing other attributes. When such a person is confronted with a need to choose between asking a man or a woman for help with a technical issue, it would be surprising if that exposure had not contributed to a bias toward asking the man. Exposure to a practice of telling sexist jokes, a speech practice, leads to an increased dispositional attunement to other sexist practices, practices that are not limited to speech. In chapter 6, we will explicate such changes in attunement in terms of accommodation.

We reject any stark dichotomy between the speech practice of telling sexist jokes and attendant nonlinguistic sexist practices. Indeed, we regard the drawing of such dichotomies as insidious. There are two issues: first, speech bleeds into other types of action: if someone regularly describes another person as a pig, that person will probably come to think of them in a porcine light, and also naturally come to treat them with more disrespect.[52] One does not need to be a psychoanalyst to recognize that thinking of someone in a deeply

---

the term *positive politeness* in a slightly more general way than Brown and Levinson, since someone telling a joke is not lessening the effects of a specific face-threatening act. However, a joke, and unprompted politeness more generally, can be seen as mitigating potential future threats to face. Manifesting common group identity places the interlocutors in a position where they can potentially say things to each other that they could not otherwise, such as requesting help. See Brown and Levinson, *Politeness*, 101–29.

52. In Elisabeth Camp's work (e.g., "Imaginative Frames for Scientific Inquiry"), she argues that metaphors involve adopting a perspective—describing someone as a pig thus involves adopting a perspective that makes sense of this description.

disdainful way and treating them with disdain tend to go together, even if it would be theoretically possible for some superhuman to keep them apart. Second, even nonspeech practices are communicative: one portrays one's attitude toward other groups as much by the way one treats them as the way one talks about them. Both issues relate to discussion in the coming chapters. As regards the bleeding of speech into other behavioral dispositions, we suggest that we tend to harmonize across different attunements. As regards the communicative potential of nonspeech actions, the model we have introduced in the last chapter allows arbitrary actions to be associated with resonances, and one large class of those resonances, the presuppositional resonances, will be discussed in the chapters to follow. On the view we develop, all actions presuppose practices, and these are likely to be accommodated by others with whom we are socially affiliated. Both sexist jokes and acts of treating people of different genders differentially presuppose practices, and both seed future differential treatment. A further point is that dichotomies between disrespectful speech practices and other forms of harassment in any case tend to be drawn strategically, to defend disrespectful speech practices by artificially disassociating them from the nonspeech practices that are accommodated along with exposure to the speech practices.

But what is exposure to a practice? Exposure to a practice is not, or at least need not be, passive. By taking part in a practice, becoming a participant, we deepen its psychological hold on us. By telling sexist jokes, jokers thereby deepen their own attachment to the practice they are participating in. Jokers' actions have effects both on their audiences and on themselves. In this sense, sexist comics expose themselves. The social and psychological processes involved are not simple. For example, to the extent that some would view the act as shameful, performing the act may lead either to being shamed, or imagining that one is being shamed, and thence to defensiveness. Such defensiveness, and consequent discounting of alternate views, is one path that might, or might not, lead to an entrenchment of views and tendencies. Defending oneself against accusations of improper conduct may help inure the joker to the denigration of women. In this case, as for so many of the social phenomena that preoccupy us in this book, practice makes imperfect.

If participating in a practice is a form of exposure to that practice, the reverse is also true: exposure to a practice becomes a form of participation in the practice if one does not resist. And yet one often fails to resist. It is not obvious that merely hearing a sexist joke is always a form of participation in the speech practices surrounding sexist jokes. Yet, at least where some avenue for protest or rejection is available, it is hard to deny that exposure can be seen as tacit participation, whether one cringes "inside" or not.

One could say the same of viewers of pornography or portrayals of violence, of audience members in talks by extremist politicians and preachers, and of people whose idea of a nice afternoon is to watch circus animals jump through burning hoops or bulls being methodically tortured. It's the audience that has a choice of whether to participate, not the animal. If you have ever been a member of any such audience, it would seem pertinent to wonder how it has affected the way you are attuned to the social world, or how your reaction, or lack of reaction to the spectacle has changed the way others view you, or, more subtly the way you view yourself. Perhaps the true worry is this: how can we even know how the many sexist jokes we've heard have affected us?

Sexist jokes do not involve *assertion* of sexist stereotypes. They are a case of showing, not telling. The speaker shows us what the context they are attuned to is like, and what is normal in their society. The speaker shows us the stereotypical properties that women or classes of women are taken to have in this context, and shows us which ways of treating and talking about women are acceptable in it. But why should we accept what the speaker shows us, ways of thinking and being that draw lines that marginalize people, that denigrate ourselves if we are female, and that denigrate our own mothers and daughters whatever our gender? What pressure are we under? The answer is easy: it is social pressure. The positive politeness of a joke is an offering of the speaker's hand for a pact, an invitation to scrutinize the speaker's face up close, an implicit invitation to draw socially closer. Here is Sigmund Freud on the function of jokes:

> Since we have been obliged to renounce the expression of hostility by deeds . . . we have, just as in the case of sexual aggressiveness, developed a new technique of invective. . . . We are now prepared to realize the part played by jokes in hostile aggressiveness. A joke will allow us to exploit something ridiculous in our enemy which we could not . . . bring forward openly or consciously; . . . the joke will *evade restrictions and open sources of pleasure that have become inaccessible.* It will further bribe the hearer with its yield of pleasure into taking sides with us without any very close investigation, just as on other occasions we ourselves have often been bribed by an innocent joke into over estimating the substance of a statement expressed jokingly. This is brought out with perfect aptitude in the common phrase *die Lacher auf seine Seite ziehen* [to bring the laughers over to our side].[53]

At least in the moment of laughter or eye-rolling, you take on the perspective needed to understand a joke. You shift your perspective—that is, you *accommodate*, as we shall say in future chapters—at least for long enough to get the joke, but possibly for much longer, becoming more accepting of the perspective the joker has espoused, more likely to behave like the joke-teller does. By laughing when they laugh and thinking like they think, we become more like them. So there is a danger that when we understand a Hutu rebel,

53. Freud, *Jokes and Their Relation to the Unconscious*, 122–23.

or a Nazi prison guard, or a sexist comedian, we will empathize, understand where they are coming from, and take on board their way of thinking to some extent. Empathy itself has dangers. Might we even say that to accommodate the prejudices of malefactors is to become complicit in their crimes? If so, we pay a high price for laughter.

A central issue for a study of the politics of language is persuasion: how people persuade, what people find persuasive, and how people become persuaded. In our terms:

> **Persuasion:** What happens when communicative actions cause someone's attunements to shift to conform to some preexisting pattern with which their original attunements would have been in tension, typically through intent to produce that change.

As the earlier quote from Freud suggests, persuasion is often best achieved indirectly, for example, by humor rather than by explicit presentation of facts or opinions. Recent psychological literature on persuasion has generalized this idea, and typically adopts a two-process model separating the effects of explicit statements of reasons why someone should change their mind from other channels. The major lines of work descend either from Shelly Chaiken's opposition between *systematic* and *heuristic* persuasion, or from Richard Petty and John Cacioppo, who distinguish between *central* and *peripheral* routes that persuasion can follow.[54] Neither of these dichotomies match precisely onto distinctions between speech-act types, but, broadly, we can see both Chaiken's systematic persuasion and Petty/Cacioppo's central route as corresponding to the straw-man assertion model of communication from earlier in this section ("people assert things, and other people accept them").

The systematic and central approaches depend on the power of language to depict ideas that can be used as evidence in a deliberative process of drawing successive conclusions. By contrast, the heuristic and peripheral approaches to persuasion depend essentially on the power of resonance to drive re-attunement without evidentiary deliberation. This nondeliberative approach is well illustrated by the strategies of Hutu propagandists, discussed above. The propagandists persuaded people to develop dispositions to harm Tutsis, in part, by first encouraging a practice of labeling Tutsis as vermin, a process that involved exploitation of emotional and dispositional attunements toward vermin. Change in epistemic attunements was presumably a by-product of this process, but the new epistemic attunements of those influenced by the propaganda campaign were not formed primarily by presentation of propositional evidence that would justify the new beliefs that were formed.

---

54. Chaiken, "The Heuristic Model of Persuasion"; Petty and Cacioppo, "The Elaboration Likelihood Model of Persuasion."

The powers of speech are varied, although certainly, on our view, the power to drive attunement is foundational. Yet here it is unclear what it means to say of speech that it has power. According to Steven Lukes, "A exercises power over B when A affects B in a manner contrary to B's interests."[55] But as Lukes discusses at length, building on the typology of power introduced by Peter Bachrach and Morton Baratz, an interesting case occurs when someone changes another's understanding of their own interests, and hence perhaps changes their interests, by persuasion.[56] When persuasion takes place, someone may be induced to act without any demand being made explicit, and without the target of persuasion necessarily recognizing that any power has been wielded.

> **Power:** Let us say that an entity exerts power to the extent that the entity changes someone's state, shapes their interests, or causes them to act. An entity has power to the extent that it has the ability to exert power.

Note that this definition allows not only individuals to have power, but arbitrary groups or institutions too. Of relevance to our later discussion of oppressive language, in chapter 10, is that a community of practice can exert power.

We allow that some might wish to refine this definition in various ways, perhaps by insisting that power is only exercised when the effects are independent of or contrary to the affected person's prior interests. While this would be close to Lukes's specific analysis, several variants involving opposition to goals or preferences are found in the literature on power. As we read Lukes, part of the reason why political theorists have preferred to restrict the exercise of power to antagonistic cases that run against the interests of the affected party is that it is only in such cases that the presence of a power relationship might be empirically tested, by determining which party's interests were best served by an observable outcome. We are sympathetic to this desideratum, although it is not a driver in our work. From our point of view, the addition of a restriction to expressly antagonistic situations is problematic (and elsewhere, for quite different reasons, we oppose limitation of the field of study to expressly cooperative situations—see chapters 8 and 9).

We are interested in this volume in the power of words. We might define the *instrumental power* of words as the ability they give certain people to exercise power over others. But an interesting special case is the power that words give groups of people to coordinate and effect joint action. Whether in a protest movement or at a family dinner, the power of words to facilitate coordination shines as strongly as the power of words to foment conflict. We would not want to rule it out of court through definition. Restricting the notion of power

---

55. Lukes, *Power: A Radical View*, 42.
56. Bachrach and Baratz, *Power and Poverty*.

to adversarial cases would bring the danger of doing just that, making not only the notion of an individual having power over themselves, but also the more important notion of a group having power over itself, incoherent. Words can help grant a group such self-efficacy.[57]

Just as we have described the instrumental power of words, we could give a similar instrumental description of the power of a gun. We can also see the gun not merely as a device for wielding the power of an individual, but as having a certain power in and of itself, the power to cause pain or death. Similarly, we can see the power of words not as a power they give to speakers, but as an intrinsic power to effect change in others.

All words have intrinsic power in the sense that they can effect change in people, but the powers are idiosyncratic. Let us say that *exigence* is the intrinsic power of a communicative practice to affect participants that is hard to resist, independently of the intention of the speaker (or anyone else). The word "elephant" has the exigent power to make English speakers think of elephants. Jokes have the power to make us cringe or laugh. Slurs, as we will discuss in section 10.2, have many exigent powers. They have the power to draw attention to an ideology, they have the power to make a person's position within that ideology visible, and they have the power to affect people's feelings, and, in particular, to hurt people. All of these are hard to resist.

The power of words is not always the power of the speaker. For when words transmit ideology, the speaker may not understand what they are doing. That is certainly how Klemperer characterizes the insouciant uses by ordinary Germans, including Jews, of phrases that were part of the cocoon of Nazi ideology. We suppose the same was true of many Hutus repeating words seeded into the ground of their life by propagandists. But we suppose also that to the extent that any word is a container at all, it is like a piece of just-recovered driftwood, heavy with the ideology of the waters from which it has been dragged. A theme of this volume is that all our words are reflective of broader ideologies, and every speaker takes part in a social process of maintaining and transmitting ideology with every word they use. If so, then every one of us is engaged in part

---

57. Lukes contrasts his own conception of power with Hannah Arendt's. As he notes, Arendt's is set at a group level: "the human ability not just to act but to act in concert" (Arendt, *On Violence*, 44).

To analyze words as having the power to coordinate and effect joint action would be to take a leaf from Arendt's work. But note here that Lukes objects strongly to Arendt's approach and others of its ilk as "revisionary persuasive redefinitions of power which are out of line with the central meanings of 'power' as traditionally understood" (Lukes, *Power: A Radical View*, 34). Attractive as it might be, a revisionary persuasive redefinition of power does not appear to us to be essential to our project. It suffices for our purposes merely to note that quite varied conceptions of power are found in the literature, especially as regards whether it is defined at the level of a relation between individuals, or whether it is defined at the level of the group.

of a process of persuasion every time we open our mouth or text a friend, an act that plays a tiny role within the grand argument. This grand argument is no more visible to us than is the forest visible to an ant. A way of looking at this is that language is not just an instrument of power of an individual, wielded in order to achieve that individual's goals, but is also an instrument of power of a community of practice. The use of language by community members gives the community power over both its own members, and potentially, as we discuss in chapter 11, over those outside the community.

In the systematic or central approaches to persuasion, the persuader conveys the virtues of the position they wish to advocate explicitly and directly, without any attempt to hide what they are doing. These approaches exemplify what we call *straight talk*, and they are obviously the paradigmatic methods assumed in enlightenment-inspired approaches to deliberative democracy and free speech, as we will later discuss. (Straight talk, in which the intentions of speakers are transparent, is discussed more fully in chapter 8.) Heuristic persuasion, on the other hand, tries to persuade people without giving them the cognitively taxing task of evaluating complex information, instead offering them heuristic shortcuts. For example, Freud's nephew Edward Bernays famously helped persuade women to make a collective shift in their disposition to smoke and in their acceptance of other women's tobacco habits, by arranging for attractive, well-dressed society-type women to walk up and down Fifth Avenue puffing Lucky Strikes. Bernays helped Lucky Strike wield power surreptitiously. He offered a heuristic route, the same route later offered by thousands of smoking Hollywood film stars and by the iconic cigarette advertising icon, the Marlboro Man, caught by the camera lighting up on horseback, perhaps with lasso in hand, the epitome of rugged cool, and a resonant image. Instead of evaluating the pros and cons of smoking, you can just reflect on the behaviors of people you want to be like, people who resonate with you. Then use the following standard heuristic: *do what the cool kids do.*

Peripheral persuasion is, similarly, any approach to changing someone's mind, or their behavior, that doesn't appeal directly to rational deliberation, and instead uses emotional or indirect methods to sneakily effect a change. We can understand persuasion in the tobacco advertising cases as involving a peripheral route. The route is peripheral because it is not driven by epistemic attunement, but by emotional and social attunements, exploited in order to drive a dispositional attunement to smoke a particular brand of cigarettes. The visceral potency of dehumanizing language, the you-know-you-want-to-laugh-with-me tug of a sexist joke, and the subtle allure of an ideology portrayed indirectly through the actions of the sympathetic characters of *Casablanca*, all exemplify peripheral persuasion. The indirectness of these methods, designed to induce a passive change in attunement without need for conscious reflection, means that in none of these cases is there the transparency of communicative intention that is seen in what we term straight talk.

Peripheral persuasion, including any approach to persuasion that depends on tempting the audience to substitute heuristic shortcuts for rational deliberation, is then a special case of *hustle*. Hustle is an instrument of soft power.

The nondeliberative or semideliberative nature of attunement change is central to the development and transmission of ideology, and to the functioning of language that mediates these processes, that is, political language. In the next chapter, we consider these themes in both greater depth and greater breadth. We will discuss the significance of classic work in psychology and sociology for the model of resonance and attunement we have developed in order to bring out how change of attunement works, the process we term *harmonization*. An important theme of the developments there, in common with the literature on persuasion, is the nondeliberative nature of much attunement change at both individual and group levels.

CHAPTER THREE

Harmony

Conversing together is never comparable with the transfer of material.
In the understander, as in the speaker, the same thing must be developed
from the inner power of each; and what the former receives is merely the
harmoniously attuning stimulus. Hence it is also very natural for man to
re-utter at once what he has just understood.

—WILHELM VON HUMBOLDT[1]

WORDS HAVE POWER. They have power by virtue of their resonances. Resonance is key to a speaker's power over others. The resonant properties of words affect people emotionally and socially, and they shift their attunements. Here we get to the crux of what we seek to analyze in this chapter. We seek to analyze the effects that communicative acts have on people, the way this plays into group dynamics, and how this can have political implications.

Harmonization is our term for the process by which systems of attunement change. These changes can be at the level of systems of attunement of individual people, or at the level of collective attunements of a group or larger community. At both the individual level and the group level, a further distinction can be made, between (i) short-term changes in attunement activation, what might be called the immediate impression that a stimulus makes on someone, and (ii) more stable changes with predictable long-term effects. Examples of attunements becoming more or less activated in the moment include an attunement to the practice of using a certain word being activated by someone using that word, or an attunement to being shamed in some particular way being activated by something found to be shaming in just that way. Harmonization can also involve the wholesale creation of new attunements, or changes in the strength of existing attunements, as when a new word or a new concept is acquired, or when dispositions change such that the tendency to frame things in one way is partly replaced by a tendency to frame them in a new way.

Harmonization is an adaptive process. It is a matter of changing so as to accord with features of the environment. If that environment involves a certain action being performed, then we are in alignment with what is normal in the environment (and hence in alignment with the action) if our state develops in accord with the practice of which the action is an example. We are, in

1. Humboldt, *On Language*, 57.

this technical sense, in accord with an insult someone has hurled at us when we get riled up by it, since that is a normal part of societal practices of insulting people. But here it becomes clear that being in accord with the practice to which we are attuned does not imply being in individual harmony, or at least not positive harmony. When insulted, we are in internal discord. As the musical metaphor suggests, the dissonant harmony induced by the insult leaves a tension that must be resolved, seeking a new and more consonant harmony.

The most important drivers of harmonization in this book (especially chapter 6, where we connect harmonization to standard notions of *accommodation*) will be those related to identity and group cohesion. We feel consonance when we are in tune with those around us or those with whom we identify, and dissonance emerges when we are not in tune with them. It challenges our identity if we feel that we do not fit in with those with whom we identify. These issues, of identity and group cohesion, become particularly acute in the context of crowd behavior. The behavior of crowds calls for a theory of collective harmony, whereby the search for consonance and the avoidance of dissonance at a group level drives the behavior of groups.

So far, we have defined what the resonances of words are within a practice, and we have said what it is for someone to be attuned to something, but we have not explicitly put these together to talk about the different ways in which words can resonate with someone, and the power that words can thereby have over people. Relatedly, we have said little about the nature of the emotional and social power words have, or about how words come to have such powers. Further, we have focused on the resonances of individual things, and the attunements that people or collections of people have to individual things, including individual practices, but we have not talked about how the different attunements people have relate to each other. That is, we have not talked about the properties of systems of attunement. Ideologies are systems of attunements and their attendant practices. So, to talk about the transmission and development of ideology, which is the central goal of an account of the politics of language, we must in this chapter talk about how systems of attunements cohere and how they change in response to an external stimulus, whether that stimulus be the provocations of politicians, the banter of a plumber, or the chanting of a protest group.

We begin by discussing ways in which standard assumptions in what we have termed the *content-delivery model* of communication fall short. At this point we turn to prior literature, introducing prior work that will guide our own theoretical development. With this in hand, we describe some of the properties that a theory of harmonization of attunements must have so as to avoid the pitfalls faced by the content-delivery model. This is initially set at the level of individual agents, but in the last two sections of the chapter, we shift to the level of *collective harmonization*, that is, changes of attunement at the level of groups and communities.

3.1. Comprehension in the Content-Delivery Model

The traditional content-delivery model of communication, as we have characterized it, looks at language in terms of transport of neutral information that is packaged in a bundle of words. It is a straw man, insofar as many philosophers of language and linguists would certainly agree that aspects of it are at best idealizations. And yet it has been unclear what the alternatives to this way of looking at communication are. Also, and to us more worryingly, the model has tended to lead to a focus only on certain types of data for which it is a good first approximation. We have already suggested that the dichotomy of active speaker and passive listener is problematic, arguing that it is better to start with a model of communicative interaction in which one-way conversation is a special case. (Herb Clark and Deana Wilkes-Gibbs call this the "literary" model: "speakers refer as if they were writing to distant readers."[2])

We begin the analytic work of this chapter by considering what the content-delivery model, which tackles a single direction of information flow, suggests about the role of the hearer, and why that is problematic in its own right, especially in the context of political language and hate speech. This will lead us to a way of looking at the role of the hearer in terms of three processes that flow naturally from the attunement-to-resonance paradigm. The standard model allows for only one of the three, and even in that case prior scholars provide us with good reasons to doubt that the standard model gets it right.

As discussed in chapter 1, the content-delivery model can be seen as a special case of Michael Reddy's conduit metaphor, a special case in which the message has been packaged, as if words are little boxes for meanings. The hearer's role is to unwrap the packaging to find the content inside, and then, as if it were a surprise gift, make a judgment: can I accept this gift, and, if so, where can I put it? That is, if I accept what I have been given, how then should I integrate it into my system of beliefs?

Metaphorical it may be, but the metaphor is as ingrained in analytic philosophy as it is in broader contemporary culture. Because the metaphor is so ingrained, it is not seen as problematic that there are clear sociological divisions between subfields that focus on the *comprehension* problem, and those that focus on *integration* of the message, how a hearer accepts and internalizes what has been communicated. Within philosophy, the former issue, comprehension, is studied mostly in philosophy of language and the latter, integration, in epistemology. The problems resulting from this disciplinary division stem partly from the division itself and partly from standard assumptions in each of the subfields. Here are the problems:

---

2. Clark and Wilkes-Gibbs, "Referring as a Collaborative Process," 3.

1. *Neutrality of integration*: The cleavage implies that processes of comprehension and integration are independent. Formal work in epistemology commonly uses logics for representation of the message meaning. Integration is then analyzed in terms of a sterile artificial representation of the content of the message, abstracting away from the original form of the message. A consequence is that it is not the form of the message that affects its integration, but only the supposedly neutrally characterized information that is "contained" in the message.

2. *Short-termism*: The cleavage is allied with a focus on comprehension or integration of a single utterance, rather than on processes that involve long chains of interaction, perhaps spaced over multiple encounters between multiple people who might not themselves share common communicative goals.

3. *Passive transmission*: Comprehension is seen as a deliberative process of intention recognition. This biases study toward the analysis of how people use communication to progress toward goals. It is thus ill-suited to shed light on processes that occur reflexively (as is the case for much emotional and social resonance), and ill-suited to shed light on processes by which ideology is passively transmitted, let alone processes by which ideology evolves.

4. *Propositionality*: Within epistemology, the integration of communicative acts has primarily been studied in terms of how people change their degree of belief (their *credence*) in a proposition as they receive new information. So, the study of integration has almost exclusively concerned propositional knowledge. Models developed in this vein provide little insight into how language can produce emotional reactions or incite action.

5. *Deliberativity*: Although there has been a push in epistemology against idealized models, the field has been dominated by a picture of belief revision as deliberative reasoning, as if the hearer was a highly (perhaps even perfectly) rational detective or scientist carefully and unemotively sifting through evidence with no restriction on the complexity of reasoning employed. Real people have emotional, social, and cultural biases toward particular outcomes and have limited attention. There is typically no manifest chain of reasoning that can be reliably identified as explaining why someone has been affected by an utterance in a particular way.

6. *Noncompulsion*: The deliberative nature of the process assumed in the integration phase implies that hearers are free to make a rational decision about what to accept. On this view, we might think that a primary reason people would be hurt by an utterance (other than simply because they are upset that the speaker is behaving badly toward them) is that

they rationally accept that some proposition that has been asserted is true, and the truth of that proposition is itself hurtful. That is, one would be hurt when one learns bad news. Similarly, the only type of utterance that would make one feel good would be an utterance that conveyed good news that one decided to accept. No explanation is provided for language that directly triggers emotional reaction, in a way that circumvents processes of rational deliberation.

Let us use the term *deliberative uptake* to mean a multistage process like that assumed in the content-delivery model, consisting of comprehension, in which the meaning of an utterance is identified, followed by integration, in which a decision is reached deliberatively to accept the message and update one's mental state accordingly, or to reject it. The above set of six problems suggests that the way speech affects hearers is not well modeled as deliberative uptake.

Some of the ways in which deliberative uptake is inadequate are consonant with issues we have already raised in previous chapters. In particular, the process of uptake cannot be based on forming and then integrating a representation that is emotionally (or otherwise) neutral. But we also take the above six problems to show that even if the mental representations assumed were not neutral, deliberative uptake could still not be the sole process by which utterances affect hearers. Based on these shortcomings, we will describe an alternative model of how speech affects people in our resonance and attunement framework, a model in which a variant of deliberative uptake (minus the assumption of neutral representations) is supplemented with additional processes by which people change during and after conversational interactions.

Before proceeding, we should make clear that although the assumptions of the content-delivery model are, in varying degrees, common to much analytic philosophy, they are by no means standard assumptions in cognitive psychology. Much of our presentation in this chapter will be based on well-known psychological research. One important literature that we will not draw direct comparisons with is the psychological literature on reading comprehension.[3] Relative to the body of philosophical work we are critiquing, the intended domain of application of the psychological work is much more tightly circumscribed, its empirical base is much stronger, and its psychological foundations are far more nuanced. While we take inspiration from models of reading comprehension and will briefly allude to some further connections below, a crucial difference is that the reading-comprehension literature focuses only on factors affecting *individual* comprehension. We emphasize in this chapter the limits of approaches to meaning that assume something like a deliberative

3. See McNamara and Magliano, "Toward a Comprehensive Model of Comprehension," for an insightful and integrative discussion of the reading-comprehension literature. We thank Eyal Sagi for discussion on this topic.

uptake model in order to emphasize that such models cannot possibly capture interactive aspects of communication, and are not well-suited to capturing effects that occur at a group level. In this, the reading-comprehension literature in psychology is, by design, limited, albeit that, as a result, the reading-comprehension literature bears a limited resemblance to less psychologically sophisticated models of meaning in much of philosophy.

3.2. Cognitive Dissonance

When one is deciding between alternative courses of action, knowledge, it might be plausibly thought, is the only true coin of the realm.[4] If so, it makes sense to assume that when people are faced with clear disconfirmatory evidence, they simply drop false beliefs in order to better decide how to behave.

Now, imagine a human-like species for which the pipeline ran in reverse. These hypothetical animals would use their own behavior as a driver of what to believe, sticking with beliefs that conform to their behavioral tendencies, and refusing to accept evidence that ran counter to those tendencies. Surely a species displaying such irrational tendencies would quickly become extinct? Apparently not: the work of the psychologist Leon Festinger suggests that humans are in some circumstances just such unfortunate creatures. Or at the very least, we humans are very stubborn.

In contemporary epistemology, *fragmentation* is the splitting of representations of knowledge or belief into multiple self-contained segments. A primary motivation for the introduction of *fragmentation* into epistemic theorizing was the problem that contradictions raise for some formal frameworks in epistemology and the theory of meaning. At root, it is the idea that our minds are compartmentalized. Freudian psychology can be understood as resting on a particular version of this doctrine, and it's now a familiar part of everyday conceptions about how the mind works, how we deal with difficult life situations such as trauma. When we hear a story of a Nazi prison guard who in returning to his family transitions immediately from brutal abuser to gentle parent, it is nowadays natural to think of this in terms of compartmentalization, by which the guard maintains two personalities without experiencing tension between them. It is important here that, on the view we are describing, it is really personalities that are being maintained and not merely *personas*, public presentations of personality.[5]

---

4. See, e.g., Hawthorne and Stanley, "Knowledge and Action," for a development and defense of this view.

5. This is not to say that our account implies just this explanation of the hypothetical prison guard's psychology, which should be seen as an illustration of the power of the approach rather than as a diagnosis. The account allows other explanations. For example, if the prison guard is able to understand the prisoners as a threat to the motherland (and hence even to his own children's future), or, within his discriminatory ideology, as not

In mainstream epistemology, the equivalent of a system of attunements is systems of belief or knowledge. The technical usage of *fragmentation* within epistemology involves splitting the representation of knowledge (or belief) into multiple self-contained segments. It arises as a reaction to well-known problems with some of the most widely studied frameworks in epistemology, frameworks that take classical logic as their basis. Of these problems, the most relevant is that in classical logics anything can be derived from a contradiction. In classical logic, contradictions are like exploding mines: as soon as a contradiction exists within a system of propositions, classical logics allow all other propositions to be derived. It follows that as soon as someone believes things that contradict each other, they are also predicted to believe every proposition. The trouble is that it seems plausible that all of us at some time or other maintain beliefs that are inconsistent with each other, say thinking that you rushed out of the house late for work in the morning without having time to do anything else, and thinking that you let the cat out as you usually do after your morning coffee. Yet everybody can distinguish between things they believe and things they don't believe, even people that believe they let the cat out at 8 a.m. while also having a distinct memory of their morning actions that does not include anything to do with the cat. More generally, there is simply no evidence that having contradictory beliefs impairs our ability to reason and draw conclusions in the way that these classical models suggest would be the case.

Fragmentation has been suggested as a possible solution to this problem.[6] The idea is that in a situation where someone has inconsistent beliefs, their mental state should not be characterized as a single logically inconsistent representation of the world, but rather as two or more individually consistent representations, say one in which you let the cat out before going to work as usual, and another in which you didn't. This solves the problem, because now neither representation justifies fantastical inferences.[7]

---

worthy of decent treatment, then he may be able to reconcile his different dispositions at home and work. Note that the definition of a discriminatory ideology merely implies that outgroups are "inherently deserving of less than equal treatment or resources," but later in the volume, in section 10.3, we will introduce the notion of a *genocidally antagonistic social group*, a group whose ideology is such that the outgroup is viewed not merely as worthy of unequal treatment, but as deserving destruction.

6. See, for a first-rate recent discussion, Elga and Rayo, "Fragmentation and Logical Omniscience." Also recommended, with a wide range of perspectives and much new development, is the excellent collection of essays in Borgoni, Kindermann, and Onofri, *The Fragmented Mind*.

7. The use of fragmentation in classical approaches to belief offers a line of solution for the problem of contradiction and reopens problems for which standard models had solutions. That is, the solution creates a research program, that of determining how systems of propositions can be fragmented, how an agent with fragmented beliefs should modify their fragmented belief systems when faced with new information, and how agents with

In the late 1950s, Leon Festinger discussed situations in which people are faced with contrary *cognitions*, using the term "cognitions" with something like the breadth of our term "attunements," covering not only beliefs, but attitudes and behavioral inclinations more generally. For him, as for us, logical contradiction between beliefs is a special case of cognitions (or, as we would say, attunements) that are in tension. To describe this tension, he introduced a term that has entered everyday talk of human mental life: *cognitive dissonance*.[8] Its contrary, *cognitive consonance*, occurs when one cognition follows from another. The predictive value of the theory comes from the hypothesis that much human behavior is driven by the need to minimize dissonance. This minimization can result in stark departures from what we would normally describe as rational reactions to new evidence, especially when the level of dissonance created by that evidence is so high as to threaten one's psychological well-being.

We can put the issue Festinger tackled like this: when people experience high levels of dissonance, something has to give, and the question is, what? Festinger's answer, which is the lynchpin of a decades-long research program, allows that sometimes the dispositional and emotive tail will wag the epistemic dog:

> The maximum dissonance that can possibly exist between any two elements is equal to the total resistance to change of the less resistant element. The magnitude of dissonance cannot exceed this amount because, at this point of maximum possible dissonance, the less resistant element would change, thus eliminating the dissonance.[9]

Festinger can be seen as saying that as dissonance increases it will eventually result in change at the weakest link, the cognition (or, for us, the attunement, although not necessarily a cognitive attunement) that is held least dearly: let's call this the *weakest-link hypothesis*.

In some cases, we might reasonably interpret a failure to accept what should be compelling evidence as a sign of an underlying pathology. For

fragmented beliefs should reason. Our adaptation of fragmentation to systems of attunement can be seen as suggesting one direction that this research program might take.

8. The primary reference for the theory of cognitive dissonance remains Festinger, *A Theory of Cognitive Dissonance*. The other classic reference is the extended case study in Festinger, Riecken, and Schachter, *When Prophecy Fails*.

Although the heyday of cognitive dissonance theory within psychology has long since passed, it continues to be influential. Not only is the concept firmly entrenched in everyday folk psychology, but it continues to be used in scholarly work. For a recent overview, see Harmon-Jones, *Cognitive Dissonance*. A good starting point is the introductory chapter of the volume by Eddie Harmon-Jones and Judson Mills ("An Introduction to Cognitive Dissonance Theory and an Overview of Current Perspectives on the Theory").

9. Festinger, *A Theory of Cognitive Dissonance*, 28.

example, suppose an addict is faced with both expert warnings and direct experience of disastrous effects on others of the addiction. The addict might deny the evidence or minimize the extent or dangers of the addiction, and deny the seriousness of the behaviors they are engaged in so as to maintain their addiction, because facing those issues would introduce dissonance. In such a case it might be said that the addiction is, by its nature, more compelling than the compelling evidence. This is then a first example in which the contrariness of attunements extends across dimensions: the highly compulsive dispositional and emotional attunements of the addict are in conflict with evidence that might otherwise lead to cognitive attunements. These cognitive attunements would be *veridical* in the sense that if the addict had those attunements they would be better attuned to reality. Unfortunately, reality may be no match for the addiction.

The idea that beliefs can have a genealogy formed from our fears, confusions, and weaknesses, rather than reason, has, of course, a long philosophical pedigree. David Hume's work on religious belief is an obvious example.[10] Hume argues that humans have religious beliefs because they promise an easy resolution of frightening mysteries. On Hume's view, we have religious beliefs not because they are *rational*, but because they are *comforting*.

Festinger, like Hume, was also struck by the case of religious belief. This emerges in his extensive focus on cult members. Cult members are able to maintain systems of beliefs that appear patently absurd to outsiders, even in the face of what appears to be irrefutable disconfirmatory evidence. One might have thought that when a cult's raison d'être concerns a prophesy of a great event, and that event does not transpire, that would quickly lead to disenchantment among cult members. As Festinger discusses, on the basis of carefully researched historical and contemporary examples, religious and spiritual cults do not simply evaporate when the Second Coming, alien invasion, or end of the Earth fails to materialize on the appointed day. Rather, they often get stronger as a result.

A cult is not a set of propositions, but a set of people. A cult member is heavily invested in this community and in the way of life that binds them to that community—a community of practice and its attendant ideology. Within the cult, the members find like-minded people who are supportive of their lifestyle and actively reinforce their beliefs, but outside they face opprobrium. Thus, cult members are trapped in an epistemic dead end. Suppose the cult's central beliefs are critically challenged by events. The stronger the challenge, the more unbridgeable the gap between insider beliefs and outsider beliefs, the greater the likely opprobrium from outsiders, and the greater the probability that outsiders may not merely disdain but actively shame insiders. It is entirely in line with the weakest-link hypothesis that cult members should

10. Hume, *The Natural History of Religion*.

be unlikely to accept the disconfirmatory evidence at face value, for that would require a massive change in lifestyle and community, a change that has been made harder by the new evidence, not easier. Indeed, it may even be that the stronger the disconfirmatory evidence, the higher the cost of accepting it. If so, cult members are in a truly absurd position, since their social and emotional incentives run precisely opposite to what would seem to be an a priori epistemic principle, that a rational agent should be more likely to accept a proposition the stronger the evidence for it.

Festinger observed that facing damning counterevidence, cults often turn in on themselves, so that group members saturate themselves in a pool of like opinions, the cult members becoming ever more dependent on each other in the face of a hostile world. Sometimes this inward turn redoubles strength of conviction to such an extent that the group is able to follow it with an outward turn, attempts at proselytization becoming fervid. Festinger explains this latter effect in terms of the conversion of outsiders to the cause satisfying a need to reduce dissonance, by increasing the pool of those from whom cult members gain approbation.

The cases Festinger studied in most detail involve failures of cult prophecies. However, their morals apply more generally. The work suggests that members of a cult may be unable to recognize the failings of their leader, because recognition of such failings would create dissonance with a much larger set of practices and commitments. Again, it may even be that the more egregious the leader's behavior, the harder it will be for cult members to accept that behavior as a failing. If so, the oft publicized unusual behaviors of cult leaders (owning gold Bentleys, sexual antics, etc.) are not mere peccadilloes. Like external, real-world counterevidence, they may actually function indirectly to increase group cohesion. That is, the peculiarities of group leaders, a certain expectation-confounding other-worldliness, is a feature rather than a bug. Similar arguments apply to the fact that the cult way of life, in terms of daily practices, is often far from the mainstream. This is not an accident. The more unlike the mainstream, the greater the dissonance group members would feel in returning to that mainstream. The weakest-link hypothesis then suggests that the abnormality of everyday living practices within a cult is part of a psychologically sound strategy for maintaining cult integrity, since it leads to cult members having greater resistance to awkward facts than would be the case if their everyday life stayed close to outside norms.

Cognitive dissonance theory predicts that people should not be easily swayed by evidence that runs counter to practices that are central to their way of life, even very strong evidence. This implies that the epistemic state of a cult member can be quite strange. Here let us observe that fragmentation theory offers a path toward representing that epistemic state, since it allows people to simultaneously maintain contradictory beliefs. We note this not in order to propose a direct development of cognitive dissonance theory, or indeed of fragmentation theory, but simply as a way of underlining the fact that the two bodies of work are compatible. Later in the chapter, we will suggest a development of the resonance and attunement framework that combines ideas from both. But first, let us introduce one more big idea, an idea that in some ways is in tension with cognitive dissonance theory.

3.3. Nondeliberative Uptake

As described above, the content-delivery model suggests that when a hearer encounters a claim, they engage in a process of deliberative uptake: first the hearer must identify the proffered proposition without initially taking a stance on its verisimilitude; then, through a process of contemplation, the hearer must pass judgment on the truth of the proposition, either adding it to their stock of beliefs, or rejecting it. In a classic paper on how people process reportative evidence, the psychologist Dan Gilbert traces to Descartes the idea that comprehension is followed by a separate process of judgment as to the merit of the claim.[11] However, Gilbert sheds doubt on the idea that belief change is an inherently deliberative process in this way, and contrasts deliberative uptake with a view that he traces back to Spinoza.[12] On this second view, which we will term *nondeliberative uptake*, when an idea first enters our minds, it enters as a belief, and only later might we decide to reject it. Note here that though

11. Gilbert, "How Mental Systems Believe." Gilbert's paper has been influential in both psychology and philosophy. Our discussion draws on Gilbert and on work by philosophers Andy Egan ("Seeing and Believing") and Eric Mandelbaum, whose dissertation, "The Architecture of Belief," recapitulates and extends Gilbert's argument in crucial ways.

The Cartesian view appears centrally in Descartes's exposition of the method of doubt. The sixth of his "Principles of Human Knowledge" reads (in part), "We can refrain from admitting to a place in our belief aught that is not manifestly certain and undoubted, and thus guard against ever being deceived" (Descartes, *Selections from the Principles of Philosophy*, 36–37).

12. In the relevant passages of Spinoza's *Ethics*, he explicitly opposes Descartes's view, especially with regard to Descartes's explanation of why people sometimes perform errors in judgment. Spinoza's positive view is famously difficult to disentangle. However, we can see the inspiration for Gilbert's reading from the fact that Spinoza (i) says one way we form ideas is by comprehending utterances ("from the fact of having read or heard certain words we remember things and form certain ideas concerning them," notes to Proposition XL, Book II, *The Chief Works of Benedict de Spinoza*, 113), and (ii) says that someone who has an idea, or at least a true idea, can't help but believe it ("He, who has a true idea, simultaneously knows that he has a true idea, and cannot doubt of the truth of the thing perceived," Proposition XLIII, Book II, *The Chief Works of Benedict de Spinoza*, 114). Taken together, these imply that when you comprehend an utterance, you believe it—at least when the utterance is itself true. Jonathan Bennett, to whom Gilbert refers, provides a detailed and far more sophisticated argument for attributing something like Gilbert's view to Spinoza—see Bennett, *A Study of Spinoza's "Ethics,"* especially 159–62.

we use the term "nondeliberative uptake," Gilbert's model does not strictly concern whether uptake is deliberative, but the timing of any deliberation. His hypothesis is that people initially accept claims, and only later, as circumstances permit, consider more carefully whether they have, as it were, bitten off more than they can chew.

The idea of people too readily accepting what they hear, of being gullible, is an old one, familiar from antiquity. "This shows how little trouble most people take in their search for the truth—they happily resort to ready-made opinions," writes Thucydides after citing several common misconceptions.[13] Despite widespread recognition of the fact that all of us are to at least some extent gullible, the nondeliberative model of uptake remains challenging. It threatens what for many is presumably a deeply held conviction that we have free will in making up our minds, and do not simply accept the things people say to us automatically. However, in some cases, the nondeliberative view has immediate intuitive plausibility. Consider visual illusions. We observe something (say a straw apparently bent at an unexpected angle at the point it enters a glass of water) and only slowly recognize that the appearance is illusory (the straw is in fact straight). We will turn shortly to another class of cases, more central to our enterprise, where a process like the one Gilbert described is intuitive, or perhaps even rather obvious.

Whether Gilbert's model is intuitive or not, he offered a host of experimental evidence that human behavior is better modeled as nondeliberative rather than deliberative uptake. Much of the evidence in favor of the nondeliberative model depends on the ways that belief update changes when people are distracted or under pressure. The deliberative uptake model predicts that if the process of thinking about a proposition is interrupted or restricted by cognitive load, people should end up equivocal about the truth of the proposition, for they will not have had the opportunity to pass judgment affirming or denying it. On the other hand, the nondeliberative uptake model predicts that in the same circumstances, people should be likely to believe the proposition, even if it is inconsistent with other evidence they have previously been exposed to. To summarize a range of different experiments discussed by Gilbert: the nondeliberative uptake model seems to better fit the facts of how people under cognitive load change their minds in the face of new information. For example, people who are distracted in some way, and who are exposed to a proposition inconsistent with their prior beliefs, show a clearly increased tendency to manifest belief in that proposition afterward compared to exposure under lower cognitive load. This suggests, for example, that a great way to get people to believe peculiar things would be to broadcast on talk radio while they're driving.

13. Thucydides, *The Peloponnesian War*, book 1, 12.

Subsequent literature has made it clear that we should adopt a somewhat circumspect attitude toward the nondeliberative uptake model. Contra Gilbert's predictions, people sometimes shift to a deliberative stance, particularly when confronted with claims that challenge beliefs with obvious significance to them; that is, people can become epistemically vigilant.[14] The psychological literature here echoes a theme found in Stanley Cavell's interpretation of Wittgenstein on criteria of judgment. Using a notion of attunement related to our own, although it centers on attunement to others rather than to our more general notion of attunement to arbitrary features of context, Cavell writes,

> Appealing to criteria is not a way of explaining or proving the fact of our attunement in words (hence in forms of life). It is only another description of the same fact; or rather, it is an appeal we make when the attunement is threatened or lost. Official criteria are appealed to when judgments of assessment must be declared: Wittgensteinian criteria are appealed to when we "don't know our way about," when we are lost with respect to our words and the world they anticipate.[15]

On behalf of Wittgenstein, Cavell here suggests that when the attunements we have to the words of others are consonant with our forms of life, there is no need for deliberation in which reason ("criteria") is made explicit. In such cases, the understanding of others, our attunement to their words, amounts to what we have termed nondeliberative uptake. It is only when the speaker wishes to change our attunements in a way that clashes with our forms of life that we resort to the business of deliberation and challenge. We might say that ideological anomaly promotes vigilance, or, in our terms, that dissonance triggers deliberation.

Even if a strong claim that initial uptake with assertions is always nondeliberative is unwarranted, it's fair to say that a strong claim that initial uptake with assertions is always circumspect would be equally unwarranted. Based both on Cavell's Wittgensteinian considerations and the later psychological evidence, we have arrived at a tempered version of Gilbert's conclusions. As regards change of belief resulting from presentation of reportative evidence, uptake is sometimes relatively nonreflective, but can become circumspect when dissonance is experienced. We will talk more in this chapter about when dissonance is experienced, but to cut a long story short, that will typically be when attention is drawn to clashes between attunements, especially attunements that are strongly held, as will be the case for core ideological

14. See Hasson, Simmons, and Todorov, "On the Possibility of Suspending Belief." While Gilbert had shown that people under cognitive load have a tendency to process anything they comprehended as if it were true, Hasson and Todorov showed that the effect is only clear when the claim does not provide obviously usable information.

15. Cavell, *The Claim of Reason*, 34.

commitments. To get even further ahead of ourselves: to get someone to non-deliberatively accept propositions that clash to some extent with core ideology, it would be necessary to avoid drawing attention to the fact that you are doing so, to hustle, to sneak those ideas into the message rather than simply asserting them. We postpone discussion of a mechanism by which this is commonly achieved, presupposition, until the next chapter.

Our interest in this volume goes beyond changes in belief, belief being just one of many types of attunement. So let us now consider how change of other types of attunement works.

First, consider perceptual attunement, which we touched on implicitly in our earlier discussion of the bent appearance of a straight straw entering water. In paradigmatic cases of people sensing what is in their environment, no conscious deliberation is required to become aware of a stimulus and develop a percept. Indeed, the attunement model is an intellectual cousin of the so-called *direct perception* model introduced by the psychologist James Gibson,[16] whereby perception is understood not in terms of a process of forming percepts that must then be integrated into understanding, but in terms of an informational connection between what is happening in the world and the state and behavior of an agent. We have little to say about perceptual processes in general, but note that comprehension itself may be thought of as a perceptual process. On our somewhat Gibsonian view, the way people are affected by an utterance is not so much like the way Sherlock Holmes contemplatively follows a trail of clues, but the way an ant reflexively follows a trail of pheromones. The ant is in tune with its environment and incredibly sensitive to subtle differences about which it has no power to introspect.

Second, for dispositional attunement, while we may develop dispositions through conscious application of thought, this does not seem to characterize many examples of mimicry or learning how to perform a task like riding a bike. The immediate and noncontemplative nature of mimicry will be important in this volume, forming a central theme in our discussion of group behavior (in chapter 6).

Third, let us turn to emotional attunement, which we will consider at greater length. Emotions are often opposed to beliefs precisely because they are not thought to be deliberative, and feeling is not usually regarded as a species of "rational" thought. The question that Gilbert considered for belief was whether there is a reflective stage between comprehending a declarative sentence and coming to believe what it describes. For emotion, then, the question must be whether there is a reflective stage between comprehending an utterance and reacting to it emotionally. Although we must be careful not to make unwarranted empirical claims, it seems somewhat obvious that while emotional response can follow reflection, much emotional response is *more*

16. Gibson, "A Theory of Direct Visual Perception."

immediately reactive. Intuitively, once one understands that someone has said something complimentary (or insulting, or shocking, etc.), one can only dissociate from one's immediate emotional response slowly. That is, we tend to feel first and ask ourselves questions later.[17]

Words can therefore hurt us by a direct, causal process. Like sticks and stones, words have a power that can bypass the free will of the hearer to evade the harm, or at least make the harm difficult to avoid. In the context of the model that we have introduced in the last two chapters, this should come as no surprise. We have used a metaphor of resonance precisely because it analogizes communication to a physical process of energy transmission, such that a suitably "tuned" hearer will, by virtue of their attunement, be affected in accord with whatever is the conventionalized effect of the message.

We hypothesize that there are speech acts for which a primary function, and in some case the entire raison d'être, is that their conventional resonances include emotional effects on the hearer in particular contexts, whether positive emotional effects or negative emotional effects. For example, as regards the speech act of apologizing following a minor faux pas, one important function is the attendant effect of mollifying the addressee. Suppose that someone apologizes to another person who has just been mildly and not entirely intentionally discomfited by their actions. If the addressee is fully attuned to the practice of apologizing, and is also suitably attuned to the details of what happened, it would follow that they will be at least somewhat mollified, for that is part of what it means to be attuned to the practice.[18] The practice of complimenting is often instantiated through the performance of what appears to be an assertion. Yet its raison d'être is not providing information, but making someone feel good. Someone who has no tendency whatsoever to feel good

---

17. We don't wish to argue our case for what is fundamentally a question of empirical psychology on the basis of seventeenth-century philosophy, but we should be remiss not to note that it is hardly surprising that something like Gilbert's Spinoza-influenced model of nonreflective uptake should be plausible in the case of emotion. Emotion was central to Spinoza's project. His rejection of Cartesian dualism and his deterministic view of human nature implied that (bodily) emotional reactions and the functioning of reason should be of a piece. We should also note that as regards emotion, Descartes certainly did not argue for emotional reaction being essentially the result of reflection, so although there is a rift between the views of Spinoza and Descartes on emotion, it is not of relevance here.

18. Some might prefer to see the mollifying effect of an apology as a *perlocutionary effect*, in J. L. Austin's sense. We do not reject the concept of perlocutionary effects, but we do reject the possibility of drawing a line between illocutionary force and perlocutionary effects. In our view, the extent to which an effect is a conventional resonance of an action is linked to the regularity with which the effect is consistently associated with the action. That makes it an empirical question to what extent a mollifying effect is conventionally associated with apologizing. Mollifying is a resonance of apologizing just to the extent that apologizing tends to mollify. Likewise, making an interlocutor feel bad is a conventionalized resonance of the practice of insulting people to just the extent that insulted people feel bad.

when complimented, or, for that matter, to feel bad when insulted, is then not fully attuned to the practices. If nobody had such tendencies, the practices of complimenting and insulting would not even exist as such.

In the last chapter, we defined what it is for someone to be attuned to something. To repeat: an agent is attuned to something to the extent that their state and behavior predictably evolve in accordance with its presence in the agent's context. In the case of attunement to a practice, this means that the agent's behavior aligns with this practice. Thus, since it is normal after someone has just insulted you to feel bad, being attuned to the practice of insults thus implies that you are subject to this resonance, and, contrarily, if you completely lack any tendency to feel bad, then (lucky for you) you are not fully attuned to the practice of insults. (If you "get" the insult but do not feel hurt, then you have what we have termed a second-order attunement to that insult.) Similarly, but perhaps more tendentiously, since it is somewhat normal in the community for people to come to believe something that has just been asserted, someone attuned to the practice of assertion should then have a predilection to come to believe assertions.

To say that people have such tendencies or predilections does not imply that they have no choice but to feel bad when insulted, or to believe what is asserted. It also doesn't imply that uptake is nondeliberative, for the fact that someone's state has a tendency to evolve in this way does not in and of itself determine whether their state tends to evolve this way through conscious reflection, or through some other mental process. Furthermore, the difficulty of learning how other people's mental states are evolving while they are engaged in a practice presumably makes it difficult for temporally fine-grained requirements on the evolution of mental states to become conventionalized as parts of the resonances of communicative practices. However, if the development of a certain mental state is a resonance of a practice in certain types of context, then we should expect the mental states of community members engaged in the practice to evolve accordingly by default in contexts of those sorts.

In contexts where the opinion of the insulter matters, then, an insult should hurt by default, and in contexts where the opinion of an asserter is trusted, an assertion should be accepted by default. It would at least be unsurprising if such default behavior were implemented through something like the nondeliberative uptake process that Gilbert describes. This means that, at least in certain contexts, people's states evolve semiautomatically in line with whatever is normal for the practice. In such contexts, it would be mentally effortful to fail to withhold belief in an asserted claim, and mentally effortful to avoid feeling bad when insulted. A deliberative uptake model, by contrast, is suggestive of similar mental effort for acceptance of a claim as for rejection of a claim, and were the deliberative uptake model extended to emotional impact, it would imply equal mental effort to feel bad when insulted as to maintain one's composure. The idea that an utterance can affect people's emotional state immediately, as they comprehend it, and without reflective deliberation, will be important as we consider in this chapter and later in the volume the functioning of hate speech, and of slurs in particular.

The takeaway from our consideration of nondeliberative uptake is simple: while some of the effects of communication on hearers are doubtless mediated by reflective deliberation, others are clearly not. The question, then, is which effects are more deliberative, and which are more, to use Gibson's term, direct. Put in terms of modern psychology, the hybrid position we advocate resembles what are known as dual-process models, in which some processes are automatic and easy, and others are reflective and effortful, as in our brief discussion of models of persuasion in chapter 2.[19] But here we make no commitment to such processes being psychologically distinct or independent, and we merely take it that there is abundant psychological evidence that some processes tend to be more reflective and effortful, and others less so. From this point of view, we should not be asking whether it is Gilbert's Spinozan- or Cartesian-influenced model that best describes how communicative acts affect people, but rather which uptake processes are more deliberative, and which are more automatic. We will be returning to this question in the next chapter, where we study a large class of communicative effects not explicitly considered

19. While the various dual-process models that have been proposed are not without their detractors, it would be difficult to overstate the ubiquity of such models in modern psychology, especially cognitive and social psychology. A commitment we are carefully avoiding is to what is sometimes known as a *strong* dual-process model, which would imply a clear distinction of fast and automatic processes from slow and deliberative processes, perhaps even a neurophysiological modularization. We take the issues of how distinct the processes are, and how they are implemented in the brain, to be empirical, and clearly beyond the scope of this book. The narrower idea we are suggesting—that Gilbert's model be seen in terms of dual-process theory—is not original, but it is found in a classic analysis of people's tendency toward acquiescence, i.e., people's bias to respond to information questions affirmatively: see Knowles and Condon, "Why People Say 'Yes.'" For an overview of dual-process theory in cognitive psychology, see, e.g., Evans, "In Two Minds: Dual-Process Accounts of Reasoning." For social psychology, see Gawronski and Creighton, *Dual Process Theories*. The clearest nontechnical introduction to dual-process theory is Kahneman, *Thinking, Fast and Slow*. A defense of some controversies surrounding dual-process models is Evans and Stanovich, "Dual-Process Theories of Higher Cognition." For a philosophical introduction to and analysis of dual-process theory, see Samuels, "Dual-Process Theory as a Theory of Cognitive Kinds." Further extended discussion of dual-process theories in a philosophical context is found in literature on implicit bias. Since implicit bias is by definition not easily accessible to processes of rational deliberation, the very idea of implicit bias is suggestive of a dual-process view. For extensive discussion of the dual-process view and alternatives to such a view, in the context of implicit bias, see the introduction and many excellent chapters in the first volume of a collection edited by Michael Brownstein and Jennifer Saul that kick-started interest in implicit bias in philosophy: Brownstein and Saul, *Metaphysics and Epistemology*.

by Gilbert (or, for that matter, Spinoza and Descartes), namely, the effects of *presupposition*, roughly the collectively assumed background behind an utterance. As will be seen, a wide range of evidence suggests that much presupposition processing, especially the processing of presupposed framings, is highly automatic. While Gilbert may have been only half right as regards uptake with assertions, the evidence suggests he might have hit the mark regarding uptake with presuppositions.

3.4. Individual Harmony

Our discussion in the last two sections concerned what prior literature tells us about how people adapt to new information, how people re-attune. We drew the following conclusions:

(i) Communicative effects are not, or at least not always, a matter of deliberatively weighing evidence, and at least some uptake may occur semiautomatically.

(ii) The processes that determine how our cognitive attunements change inherently involve noncognitive attunements, such that logical consistency cannot be the prime factor. Attunement change is based on a more holistic property of systems of attunements, so that, as we put it above, the emotive and dispositional tail has the potential to wag the epistemic dog.

(iii) If we sometimes accept information without fully considering its implications, then we must sometimes end up with contradictory beliefs, which implies that our beliefs must in some way be fragmented. Generalizing, there at least are several ways we can deal with the problem that would occur when attunements are at odds with each other: we can drop or fail to develop some of the attunements, or we can compartmentalize, avoiding dissonance by fragmenting the space of attunements into subspaces in which there is less conflict.

We now discuss one way these insights might be brought together into an account of harmonization, the special way that groups of attunements evolve. Our starting place is the goal of harmonization: harmony. We will consider two subtypes of harmony: individual harmony and collective harmony. The first is discussed in this and the following sections, and collective harmony is introduced in sections 3.7 and 3.8.

We begin with individual harmony, defined as follows:

Individual harmony: What is experienced emotionally when one is aware of how one's attunements relate to one another, a sense of consonance (positive harmony, or just harmony when this will not cause confusion) or dissonance (negative harmony).

Consonance: The experience of manifest coherence of systems of attunements.

Dissonance: The experience of manifest incoherence of systems of attunements.

This then leads to a derivative definition of harmonization:

Harmonization: The process by which groups of attunements evolve in order to bring about positive harmony.

One way in which the musical metaphor seems to us apt is that it suggests that people may at times find a limited degree of dissonance acceptable, and even in a certain way a positive, provided it is followed by a suitable resolution. This comports with our intuitions about human behavior. For example, people may actively seek the discomfort of learning so new that it does not fit with their preconception, which may involve experiencing a lack of coherence for a while, with the hope that this will eventually bring them to a new stage of harmony in which there is greater consonance.[20]

Our definitions of consonance and dissonance involve several further notions, referring to (i) coherence and incoherence, (ii) the idea of a *system* of attunements, and (iii) the idea that coherence or incoherence can become *manifest*.

Although we further discuss coherence in the context of narrative, in section 3.5, for the most part we leave it unanalyzed. What we do want to stress is that coherence is not just logical consistency of sets of propositions, and indeed it cannot be, because we do not take attunements to be purely propositional. For example, a dispositional attunement to play a competitive sport may cohere with a cognitive attunement to the effect that playing this sport is healthy, as well as cohering with emotional attunements whereby sporting performance brings pleasure, but conflict with a cognitive attunement such as a belief that playing this sport is not a wise use of limited time, a dispositional attunement to sit at home and watch this sport on TV, and an emotional attunement involving a fear of losing.[21]

---

20. Although Festinger does not talk of harmonization in this way, he does allow that people can sustain a degree of cognitive dissonance. Indeed, it is an important theme of his work that only massive dissonance can drive a radical change in beliefs or behaviors.

21. To be clear, it's not that we are claiming the relevant attunements could not possibly be rendered in propositional form, and logical methods used to analyze coherence. Standard logical methods are just not a great fit to the problem of analyzing coherence, e.g., because we take it to be a scalar notion.

The bulk of this section is taken up with exploring the broad idea that fragmentation creates subsystems of attunements that have a tendency to be activated together, and across which coherence or incoherence might be sensed.
For current purposes, it suffices that coherence and incoherence among
attunements will normally only become manifest when those attunements are
simultaneously activated. Conscious higher-order reflection on one's attunements could also lead to evaluation of attunements being coherent or incoherent, but as we understand the psychological literature, such conscious processing is usually not taken to be the source of felt consonance or dissonance.

The resonance-based framework revolves around association, and the
approach we now take to developing an account of systems of attunement, and
thence harmonization, centers around a consideration of what it is for one
attunement to be associated with another.

The prestige of association as an explanatory tool in psychological work
has swung backward and forward for centuries. The proposal developed in
this volume is not strictly associationist, insofar as we don't make any assumption at all that attunements themselves are just a matter of association: in
principle, an attunement could involve arbitrary algorithmic processing. We
certainly make no claim that association is the be all and end all of mental processing. Rather, we think, as so many have found before us, that for a relatively
simple idea, the mechanism of association has remarkable power. This power
explains why association remains an important theme in modern psychology,
albeit tempered with many other mechanisms.

We think that the power of association is underutilized in most contemporary theories of the semantic and pragmatic function of language. Our
theory of how words carry meaning is somewhat associationist, with the crucial distinction that the associations we are interested in are regularities shared
by members of communities of practice and would not exist if they were not
sustained by feedback loops within such communities. What we assume about
human psychology is, in line with our account of word meaning, about to get a
little more associationist. Just as Hume considered that thoughts can become
associated with each other when the sense stimuli that trigger the thoughts
regularly co-occur, so we will consider under what conditions attunements can
become associated with, or dissociated from, each other.

On the view we have developed, people associate a word with its resonances.
That is, the resonances of communicative actions just *are* associations, albeit
associations created and perceived collectively by the members of a community of practice. To be attuned to something is to associate different things
with each other as a group, for example, to associate the different behaviors
and effects that constitute a practice with each other, and to conceive of that
grouping as a single practice. Some of these associations are of the body as
much as they are of the mind. We might say that a word is, in part, a certain
type of association between the physical behaviors that produce it, the prior

contexts it is used in, and the functions it has, as well as with other behaviors that, taking a more interactive stance, tend to be performed by interlocutors when the word is used.

In terms of how they relate to systems of attunements, we suggest that fragmentation and association can profitably be seen as two sides of the same coin, a single property: we propose that fragmentation is no more and no less than dissociation. To see what this means, start with the idea that attunements can be active or inactive, depending on whether we are performing an activity that depends on those attunements. When someone is playing chess, their attunements to chess will be active, and when they are not thinking about chess at all, those attunements will be inactive. For two attunements to be associated is for there to be a pattern of coactivation. However, conversely, there are patterns of deactivation, by analogy (and perhaps it is something more than mere analogy) to neural connections, which can be excitatory or inhibitory. We suggest that fragmentation derives from the fact that attunements do not each exist in a vacuum, but rather are associated or dissociated with each other in the sense that activation of one attunement tends to lead to activation or deactivation of others to varying degrees. Pedaling a bike is tightly associated with steering the bike and maintaining balance, but less associated with facts about how bike riding works in terms of the physics of balance and the mechanics of the bike and the body, and still less associated with the practices of playing chess, frying fish, or voting. This is just to say that biking dispositions are somewhat compartmentalized relative to other attunements. More generally, if there is any systematicity at all to the associations between attunements, that is, if there is any systematicity to the patterning of which attunements are commonly active together and which are rarely active together, then fragmentation is inevitable within our model of attunement.

To switch to a more holistic level, consider again the Nazi prison guard who goes home to their family and is a loving, tender parent. How does compartmentalizing work so effectively, so that their brutality in one context does not bleed into the other? From the point of view of an associationist model like ours, it would be more surprising if such a person *failed* to compartmentalize. The guard is engaged in different practices at different times, and our model offers no intrinsic reason for there to be a strong connection between the two. Of course, as onlookers, we see both patterns of behavior simultaneously, and the contradiction between brutality and tenderness is manifest to us. But to think this way is to fail to see through the prison guard's eyes. In one context, they focus hawklike on untrustworthy objects of disdain and hatred who must be subjugated, and in another they proudly gaze upon beloved and delicate children to be nurtured.

Our model of fragmentation depends on different attunements being differentially active. When we talk about levels of mental activity for different attunements, we are implicitly talking about attention and how it changes. Leaving aside for simplicity the difference between conscious and unconscious mental activity, the attunements that are active help define our attention. The spotlight of attention consists in active attunements and all the things that play a role in the particular application of those attunements, for example, the combination of bike-riding attunements and the bike and the road and the feelings in our body as we ride. Attention is in and of itself an important topic. It doesn't take a political savant to recognize that attention is exploited by manipulative political messaging, and is relevant to the evolution of public concern even when not directly exploited. Earthquakes lead only to a temporary increase in attention to earthquake safety, and although we are unaware of any direct empirical comparison, we suspect that collective attention to the misdemeanors of politicians has an even shorter half-life. One reason for this is that politicians and their media representatives actively distract us, bringing new things to our attention, so that we no longer attend to what they wish to distract us from.

To model attention, whether on a more classical view or in the attunement framework, some machinery must be added. We simplify by amalgamating the notions of attention and mental activation, which in psychology are distinct notions. This simplification is not intended to represent a theoretical stance, but rather a placeholder for future work. Let's adopt the following recipe: whatever your favorite model of a mental state (say, a set of propositions, or a set of attunements), add to it an *activation function*. The activation function maps each of the constituents of the mental state to a number, a level of activation. If your favorite model of a mental state was pairs of propositions and their credences, then the new model would consist of a function from pairs of propositions and credences to activations. Our favorite model of a mental state is a system of attunements, so we now have a function from attunements to a pair consisting of (a) a level of attunement and (b) a level of activation. An oversimplistic illustrative implementation of attention, for any of the above variant models of a mental state, would simply map unattended objects to 0, and objects in the *spotlight* of mental attention to 1.

Before going on, let us point out here that the moves we have made so far are not at all radical. Within philosophy, at least philosophy of mind, discussion of attentional processes has been on the rise in recent years,[22] and in work on attitude shift and framing in political science, one of the dominant formal models for the last four decades uses attention in a way quite similar to our own. We are thinking here of the expectancy value theory of attitude developed by Martin Fishbein, partly in collaboration with Icek Ajzen.[23] In that model, an individual's attitude toward an issue is a weighted sum of

22. See, e.g., Seemann, *Joint Attention*; Watzl, "The Philosophical Significance of Attention"; and Eilan et al., *Joint Attention*.

23. Ajzen and Fishbein, *Understanding Attitudes and Predicting Social Behavior*. A

evaluations of particular attributes and the salience of those attributes. On this view, persuasion operates not necessarily by presentation of new facts, but by use of framings that shift attention, directing salience toward the attributes for which evaluations are in line with the framer's goals.

The moves we will now make, and indeed predecessors of our terminology, are also found in the reading-comprehension literature. In the *landscape model* of reading comprehension, developed by Paul van den Broeck and colleagues, conceptual representations are activated at different levels determined by what was previously read and integrated and background knowledge; the mental state of the reader is seen as a vector mapping concepts to levels of activation, a vector that changes dynamically as text comprehension proceeds.[24] In this and other reading-comprehension models, the representation of the text that is formed is affected by the requirement that a particular reader has for textual coherence, and the effort the reader puts into the search for a representation that is globally coherent. In our terms, readers seek a harmonious understanding of the text, and they search through a space of possible representations when faced with dissonance. But note here that while some models of reading comprehension focus on active and strategic integration of material into their mental representations of the text, others focus more on passive, automatic processes. In one branch of the literature, these automatic processes are described using a resonance metaphor: new representations are formed partly as a result of resonances with previously activated conceptual representations.[25]

Let us now add a little geography to the mental landscape of our harmony model, by assuming the existence of an *inter-attunement distance* that associates any two attunements with a positive value, the distance between them.[26] The *inter-attunement distance* represents the level of association between the attunements, that is, the degree to which activation of one attunement is likely to lead to activation of the other. This creates something like *neighborhoods of thought*, that is, sets of attunements that tend to be simultaneously activated

---

helpful overview of framing theory that discusses the expectancy value theory model is Chong and Druckman, "Framing Theory."

24. Linderholm et al., "Fluctuations in the Availability of Information during Reading." We thank Eyal Sagi for discussion of the reading-comprehension literature. Models in this literature and associated literature on discourse analysis are more thoroughly and computationally articulated than is our own proposal, and a natural line of development of the harmony model would use this prior work as a starting point.

25. O'Brien and Myers, "Text Comprehension," as discussed also in section 1.3, fn. 34.

26. Our talk of a mental landscape rather obviously recalls the notion of "mental space" developed by Giles Fauconnier. There are strong similarities between the two. In particular, he targets types of reasoning, for example, reasoning involving analogical mappings, that are not well accounted for in standard logics. The classic reference is Fauconnier, *Mental Spaces*. Another body of work that puts a spatial metaphor to work in analyzing conceptual structure is due to Peter Gärdenfors, e.g., *The Geometry of Meaning*.

to some degree because the *inter-attunement distances* are low. The landscape of attunement for a person is the sum of their neighborhoods of thought. Our model now consists of two functions: a function from attunements to a pair of a level of attunement and a level of activation, and a function from pairs of attunements to distances.[27] This immediately creates the possibility of attunements that are in some sense inaccessible, an intuition that is basic to Freud's tripartite model of the mind, and that Freud explained with a suggestively spatial metaphor in a 1933 lecture:

> Symptoms are derived from the repressed, they are, as it were, its representatives before the ego; but the repressed is foreign territory to the ego—internal foreign territory—just as reality (if you will forgive the unusual expression) is external foreign territory.[28]

As already stated, we are not attempting to theorize the difference between conscious and unconscious processing, and we will not invest our model with foreign territories as such. We merely take the proximity between two attunements to be a measure of the probability that activation of one attunement will lead to activation of the other.[29] Given that this chapter builds on an associative theory of resonance and attunement, it is natural that the inter-attunement distance be given a Humean interpretation: proximity between attunements corresponds to strength of association,

---

27. Alternatively, we could use a function from attunements to a triple of a level, an activation, and a location in an abstract mental space, from which distance could be calculated. This would then bring up a question of what the geometry of mental space is like, how many dimensions it needs, and what axioms it follows. There is no special reason to assume a Euclidean two- or three-dimensional space, except that it is so conceptually familiar as to be the obvious starting point for work on this sort of model.

28. Freud, "The Dissection of the Psychical Personality," 57.

29. Using a standard technical approach, one might take the distance between two attunements to be the negative log of the probability that one will activate the other, so that a distance of zero implies that when one is activated, the other is always activated, and that as the distance tends to infinity, the probability of simultaneous activation tends to zero. However, using formal definitions of this sort would be overstating the power of the landscape model, which must remain metaphorical, at best a useful source of intuitions. For it is far from clear that activation tendencies of attunements can in fact be modeled using a Euclidean space. To see why, suppose that attunement A has a high probability of being activated when exactly one of attunement B and attunement C are active, but that attunements B and C have a significant probability of coactivation. There is no way of representing these dependencies by placing A, B, and C in a spatial arrangement, and predicting coactivation solely on the basis of probabilities defined as described. Thus it might be better to think of the landscape metaphor not as directly representing the probability of coactivation between attunements, but rather as representing one source of constraints on coactivation, and allowing that there might be additional factors determining how attunements interact.

or, in contemporary psychological terminology, the degree to which attunements prime each other.

A simple implementation of the inter-attunement distance might map the distance between any two concepts concerning, for example, family to zero, any two sports-related concepts to zero, and any pair of a family thought and a sports-related thought to one. This would mean that familial thoughts were all interrelated, sporting interests were all interrelated, but family thoughts were unrelated to sporting interests. That would yield exactly two neighborhoods of thought. A minimalist model of attention could then consist in a stipulation that if some attunement is activated at level 1, then all attunements at distance 0 from it are activated at level 1, and all attunements at distance 1 are activated at level 0, that is, that only one of those neighborhoods could be activated at a time, like street lights in a county experiencing power shortages. Hey presto! We have created a model of an agent with a two-track mind. The agent has three cognitive states: total inattention (emptiness of mind), thinking about sports, and thinking about family.

A more sophisticated model might not only have gradient distances and activations, but also allow flexibility in whether attention was focused on a narrow region of mental space, or was somewhat diffuse and dispersed over a larger region. In such a model, the landscape of attunement would not absolutely determine where an agent's attention was directed, but would rather provide defaults for how attention would evolve absent mindful control. It would then require effort to focus on only one of two attunements with a strong association, or to simultaneously activate two attunements that were not tightly associated. That is, we might relate patterns of attention to processing cost. A high cost would be incurred by focusing attention simultaneously on highly disconnected regions or on only a small part of a highly connected region, and a low cost to a pattern of activation in which only a cluster of highly connected attunements were activated, and no other highly connected attunements were activated.

Let us apply some of these ideas in terms of the examples we have introduced in the chapter, starting with the prison guard who lives a double life. For the prison guard to see what we see would require an act of reflection as regards the relationship between different practices they engage in, and such reflection would inevitably be painful. That is, it would create dissonance. Nazi prison guards who managed to maintain double lives with equanimity were, we speculate, precisely those who avoided performing such inconvenient acts of reflection, and thus were easily able to maintain the boundaries between mental compartments. The boundaries arose naturally as a reflection of the intrinsic compartmentalization of the guards' different roles in life, and reflection is precisely what their discipline mitigated against, discipline instilled in them through propaganda, training, and workplace and family practices. We are obviously not experts on prison-guard psychology. We intend this example of the sort of account of a real-world behavior that might be given in the framework we have developed only as an illustration and an intuition pump. What it illustrates is that fragmentation is hardly a surprising addition to our fundamentally associationist model. It is rather a natural consequence. And there are two related intuitions that we hope the example pumps, one concerning dissociation of practices, and the other concerning avoidance of dissonance.

Earlier, we noted a problem that a model of fragmentation imposed on top of a classical logical representation faces, namely the problem that there is no clear basis on how sets of propositions might be fragmented. In our terms, the prison-guard example suggests that at least one (on reflection, unsurprising) source of separation between groups of attunements is the separation of practices in someone's life. On the view we have developed, it would be unsurprising if a professional logician were far from logical when cooking or arguing with their spouse, because there is a real-world separation between the practice of being a logician and the practices of being a cook or a spouse. Although a logician might well reflect on the relationship between the two, there is nothing forcing them to do so. At this abstract level, which leaves aside the important moral differences between the two cases, the difference between the philosopher and the prison guard is simply the degree of dissonance that simultaneously embracing the different facets of their life might bring.

This takes us to the second intuition suggested by the prison-guard example. Our discussion of the separation of practices might be thought to make an implausible assumption about the prison guard. A skeptic might ask how someone who spends so much of their lives behaving in such dramatically opposed ways could possibly be so unreflective that they do not become aware of, and perhaps then obsessed by, the (to outsiders) obvious tension between their different "forms of life." This is where the concept of cognitive dissonance comes to the fore, although our framework introduces a possibility that was not present, or at the very least not explicit, in Festinger's work. Put in everyday terms, our hopefully somewhat commonsensical suggestion is that a prison guard might fail to reflect expansively on the tension between their different forms of life precisely because to do so would be painful. In terms of our framework: preferring consonance, the guard avoids a mental activity that would bring dissonance, and so conveniently allows the two practically separated parts of their life to also remain mentally fragmented.

Before considering the ramifications of this reasoning for our framework, let us note that we have brushed upon a question that has filled volumes. Are the perpetrators of great evils, and in particular heinous war crimes, in some sense deeply bad people before they commit crimes against humanity, or are they merely "ordinary men" who become twisted by propaganda and the extraordinarily violent and perverse situations in which they find themselves?[30] We do not take a position on this issue here, beyond noting that converging lines of historical and psychological research suggest that it is common for people to have the potential to adopt inhumane practices in situations where they have extreme power over others.[31] What we do want to note is that the type of compartmentalization that emerges in our framework mirrors a twist on this question, a Freudian twist now so familiar in psychoanalytic work as to perhaps seem unremarkable. For we might also ask whether the perpetrators of great evils are sometimes *still* ordinary people in other walks of life. The geography of attunements at least allows the possibility that the same person be depraved in one form of life, and saintly in another.

Returning to the role of cognitive dissonance in our framework, recall that Festinger argued for a position whereby people's epistemic attitudes can be swayed by avoidance of dissonance, as when someone fails to accept evidence that would challenge their dispositions and desires. But in the cases Festinger discussed, the issue was discussed on the assumption that acceptance of evidence is a binary: one accepts the evidence or fails to accept it, and, more generally, one either does or does not believe things. In terms of attunements, this would amount to either having an attunement or not having it. Our attentional account of systems of attunement brings a further possibility.

Since harmony is an experience of the relationship between attunements, one can avoid felt dissonance by suppressing some subset of the attunements that would otherwise be in tension, and not only by eliminating or avoiding attunements. If suppression meant permanent suppression, such that suppressed attunements were never activated, there would be no practical difference from Festinger's model. But suppression need not be permanent or total. Leaving aside Freud's well-known claim, cited above, that repressed ideas or tendencies can still be psychologically active, suppression in our model can be temporary. Fragmentation allows that two sets of attunements can be in complementary distribution: one set is active only at times when the other set is suppressed, and vice versa. Thus, there are at least two ways of avoiding

---

30. See Browning, *Ordinary Men*.

31. We are thinking of two controversial lines of work. The first is one of the most influential, and highly criticized psychological studies ever run, the Stanford Prison Experiment: Haney, Banks, and Zimbardo, "Interpersonal Dynamics in a Simulated Prison." Leaving aside the deep issues of scientific ethics that the experiment immediately raised, we should note that the specific conclusions usually drawn, to do with conformation to social roles, have been questioned—see, e.g., Le Texier, "Debunking the Stanford Prison Experiment." Further, the study did not have a large sample size, and it is unclear to what extent the behavior of the participants reflected only their own understandings of the social roles that they were given (prisoner or guard), rather than the expectations of the experimenters. The second line of work involves Stanley Milgram's equally terrifying and famous experiments showing that people will obey authority figures who ask them to perform acts that harm others. The general conclusion that somewhat randomly chosen people can easily be manipulated into acting oppressively is by now well demonstrated.

dissonance: first, there is the Festinger approach, of abandoning the weakest attunements that are causing felt dissonance, and of refusing to take on new attunements that would cause such dissonance, and second, there is the option of pushing attunements that would combine problematically into separate domains of the attunement landscape, such that they are rarely or never coactivated, with the consequence that it is easy to ignore the fact that they are in tension.

Politics is rife with contradiction and hypocrisy. A politician might fight for freedom of speech and simultaneously propose legislation that curtails it, for example, by banning books or legislating against issues being discussed in the classroom. The question is one of why supporting a strategy that simultaneously suggests support for antagonistic goals, undermining the ideals it advocates, does not lead to cognitive dissonance. Part of the answer is that neither fighting for freedom of speech nor legislating what educators can say is propositional. They are behaviors. There is little tension between the behaviors for one who does not wish to reflect on the relationship between the ideals behind them.

3.5. Narrative Harmonization

Attunements can be structured in complex ways, ways that are not completely captured simply in terms of coactivation or inter-attunement distance. Most obviously, attunements to simple practices can jointly constitute attunement to a complex practice. Attunement to the practice of speaking a language is like this, consisting of attunement to many simpler subpractices. A related type of structure is that imposed by a narrative or plan. A plan relates attunements to each other by enabling goals to be met by organized performance of separate actions, so that the plan calls for joint or sequential activation of attunements. Narratives can provide much richer structure than this, determining not only courses of action, but also ways of understanding the world and our place in it. Our goal in this section is to show in outline how narrative structure may be a source of coherence for attunements, and hence a driver of harmonization.

Jack Balkin lists some of the things "we use narratives for," clearly for him a partial list:

1. Remembering events in temporal sequences.
2. Ordering and organizing the past.
3. Explaining human action in terms of plans, goals, and intentions.
4. Understanding our own selves and motivations through autobiography.
5. Giving causal explanations of events.
6. Creating expectations about the future.

7. Internalizing expectations about how to behave in social situations and interact with others.

8. Providing scripts that tell us how to understand social situations, engage in social conventions, and assume social roles.

9. Creating notions of what is ordinary and extraordinary, expected and unexpected, canonical and deviant in social life.

10. Accounting for deviations from what is ordinary, expected, or canonical.

11. Creating social myths and shared memories that unite groups we are part of, frame their experience of contemporary events, and produce shared expectations about how the group is supposed to behave.[32]

Hearing a commotion in a restaurant and looking over to see one patron with wine on their clothes and another in the act of leaving the restaurant, we rapidly construct a narrative as to what occurred. We may be right and we may be wrong, but we certainly use our ability to access a store of narratives to rapidly interpret a small amount of evidence in a rich way. This is not always a good thing. At time of writing, there is a US national news item of a familiar type: a Black pastor, the Reverend Michael Jennings, was watering a vacationing neighbor's petunias and hydrangeas while they were on vacation, and another neighbor called the police on him because they took him to be engaging in suspicious activity. Police approached him, and, even though he had a watering hose in his hand and identified himself as a pastor watering his neighbor's plants, they arrested him. For both the person who found the pastor's actions suspicious and the police, the narrative that came most readily to mind in seeing a Black man in the yard of a nice house involved criminality.[33]

We often relate narratives by uttering a series of sentences.[34] But, following Rachel Fraser, we reject thinking of narratives as characterizable in terms of a list of sentences.[35] Fraser rejects the set-of-sentences model, essentially

---

32. Balkin, *Cultural Software*, 189.

33. See Eduardo Medina, "Alabama Pastor Is Arrested while Watering Neighbor's Flowers, Video Shows," *New York Times*, August 31, 2022, https://www.nytimes.com/2022/08/31/us/black-alabama-pastor-arrested-flowers.html.

34. Arthur C. Danto argues that histories must incorporate what he calls "narrative sentences," ones that encode, informationally, a future perspective on past events (*Narration and Knowledge*, chapter 8, 143–81). We suggest a stronger thesis, that narratives cannot be reduced to narrative sentences.

35. Fraser, "Narrative Testimony." She summarizes her approach as follows: "Just as the Stalnakerian model of conversation takes simple testimony to be a conversational technology aimed at opinional co-ordination, I take narrative testimony to be a conversational technology which aims at perspectival co-ordination" (4028). There is much overlap between our approach and hers. If it is allowed that perspective can be cashed out in terms

because narratives have to be holistically coherent, in a way that cannot always be captured by a string of sentences. It is because we approach interpretation with narratives that we can make coherent sense of a string of sentences—not the other way around.

The coherence brought by a narrative, then, is not simply logical consistency.[36] When attunements are structured according to a narrative, the coherence of those attunements will depend on how well they match the narrative, and how coherent the narrative is. Narratives involve events and actors. The events are often sequenced, or at least are usually connected in some way, and the actors have characteristics of importance to the story that may include, for example, taxonomic kind, personality, personal circumstances, societal functions, or identity. Both events and actors may be given valuations, as when an event is calamitous, or an actor is a hero or villain. Let us say that a *narrative frame* is an abstract template that consists of (i) a set of principal actors that have particular characteristics and relationships with each other, (ii) a set of connected events that involve those actors and locations and lead to particular changes affecting the actors, and (iii) optionally, valuations of some of the actors, behaviors, or events. An *instantiation of a narrative frame* is then a narrative in which the abstract events, actors, and locations of the narrative frame are identified with particular events, actors, and locations. To be *cognitively attuned to a narrative frame* is to have a disposition to see groups of events, actors, and locations as instantiations of that frame. Importantly, such a disposition can bring with it a tendency to reason and act based on the narrative frame.

Suppose someone experiences dissonance among attunements because a disposition to act in a certain way is not justified by what they know about the world. Then narrative instantiation can potentially enable harmonization via a backfilling process (the narrative equivalent of abductive reasoning in

---

of attunements, as we do in section 6.4, then narrative harmonization is akin to her notion of perspectival coordination via narrative testimony.

36. To say that we are not the first to emphasize differences between narrative coherence and logical consistency would be to make a massive understatement. Plato made the contrast between rhetoric and rational argumentation in a passage of the *Gorgias* that is famously dismissive of both sophists and rhetors: "as cosmetics is to gymnastics, so is sophistry to legislation, and as cookery is to medicine, so is rhetoric to justice," a passage that culminates in the aphorism that "[rhetoric does] in the soul what cookery does in the body" (Plato, *Gorgias*, 33–34). From Aristotle on, logic and rhetoric have been seen as complementary, and the contrast between them has arguably been a pillar of Western thought. A more recent line of work begins with Walter Fisher's *Human Communication as Narration*, where he develops a model of "Narrative Rationality" in which narrative forms are seen as a source of "good reasons" in and of themselves, and not merely as aesthetically pleasing or emotionally laden persuasive techniques that must play intellectual second fiddle to logical argumentation. For critical and scholarly discussion, see Stroud "Narrative Rationality."

logic). That is, the person experiencing dissonance fills in their understanding of the world on the assumption that the world conforms to the narrative. Just as when someone observes smoke and then infers abductively the presence of fire, one may find oneself alone and then draw solace from the idea that one is on a hero's quest. What we will term *narrative harmonization* is a change in a system of attunements based on the supposition that real-world characteristics of individuals, relationships, and events match the characteristics found in a narrative, and that behaviors portrayed positively in the narrative are normatively desirable.

To take a simple example, consider the narrative frame of the saying "The early bird gets the worm." Suppose that someone desirous of some prized object acts too hastily to obtain it, and fails, thus producing dissonance. They may bring coherence to their action by mapping themselves onto the early bird actor in the narrative frame, the prized object onto the worm, and their disposition to act quickly onto that of the early bird. Within this framing, their attunements are seen as coherent at a high level, even though in this particular case the prize was not obtained.

Since narrative harmonization can involve treating a narrative frame as normative, it can be used to justify behavior using the narrative. But it is possible that someone's attunements to a narrative go further than justification of behavior using the narrative, and that they actually behave according to what the narrative suggests is desirable. If someone has a tendency to behave by analogy with characters drawn from a narrative frame, we can say that the individual is *dispositionally attuned to that narrative frame*. Much education and indoctrination are based on the idea that stories serve as models for behavior and misbehavior. The idea is presumably that attuning people dispositionally to the narrative frame of a holy book, or for that matter a book of folk tales, is a more effective way to inculcate in them a set of ideological practices than simply telling them what to do.

Let us note here that in invoking narrative frames, we do not claim to have provided a theory of when attunements are coherent, but rather to have related the question of when attunements are coherent to the question of when narratives are coherent. Although we will not attempt to provide a general account of narrative coherence, it is broadly clear what the components of such an account might include. Narrative coherence presumably depends in part on the ease of identifying causal connections between the events in the narrative, and the degree to which the interplay of actors within the events is explained by their characteristics and relationships. However, we suppose that a theory of narrative coherence would be a psychological theory, and so might also invoke gestalt principles involving the organization of the narrative. For example, a theory of narrative coherence might involve the presence of clear parallelisms or contrasts, such as the implied parallelism between the early bird and other birds implicit in the proverb, the clear contrast in how early the different birds were, and the clear contrast as regards who got the worm.

A narrative may suggest a plan of action, but it may also serve to help us understand what is happening without suggesting a future course of action. It is important to realize that the story does not need to be made explicit, because our culture comes replete with a stock of narrative frames, and a single word may have sufficient resonance to invoke one. For example, on February 15, 2022, the lieutenant governor of Texas, Dan Patrick, sent out the following tweet, which, since it refers in an ugly way to faculty at the University of Texas at Austin, and since it was followed up at a press conference with a threat to dismantle the University of Texas tenure system, happens to hit close to home for us:

> I will not stand by and let looney Marxist UT professors poison the minds of young students with Critical Race Theory. We banned it in publicly funded K-12 and we will ban it in publicly funded higher ed. That's why we created the Liberty Institute at UT.[37]

Dan Patrick's use of a poisoning metaphor immediately conjures a narrative frame in which anybody can identify the main roles: academics = villains, students = victims, Patrick = savior. In the framing of this tweet, critical race theory obviously has a role familiar from history, mythology, and fairy tales: poison. The use of narrative frames allows persuasive rhetoric to be effective without defining its terms. In the example, the term "critical race theory" has no clear definition, and it has never received a clear definition from those on the right attacking it, though it is clear that their use presupposes a far broader notion than is employed in literature on critical race theory in legal scholarship. In the mouths and tweets of right-wing politicians and journalists, it is not a term that refers to a series of concepts with which a reasonable person might agree or disagree; it is a role in a narrative. We discuss the demonization of critical race theory, and its relationship to racist politics, in chapter 11.

Plans and narratives provide alternative ways in which attunements are structured, but they also provide alternative ways in which tension between attunements can be introduced or dispelled. For example, someone may feel tension when faced with a need to perform an action that takes them further from their desired goal, but that tension could be somewhat resolved when the action is seen as part of a larger plan that will eventually take them to that very goal. That is, a plan can explain why one is doing something undesirable, by justifying it as a necessary subgoal of the original goal.

Narratives are more general than plans, since they intertwine combinations of actions more deeply with ideology, and with issues of identity,

---

37. Dan Patrick, @DanPatrick, Twitter, February 15, 2022, accessed March 1, 2023, https://twitter.com/DanPatrick/status/1493694009600053250?ref_src=twsrc%5Etfw.

character, and society. Narratives can be aspirational, helping to set goals for an individual by offering models for behavior. A narrative can create tension by suggesting that an individual is diverging from standard behavior, or, contrarily, dispel tension by explaining behavior as conforming to a standard template. People can be led to perform extreme acts that would otherwise create unsustainable personal tension, such as acts of war, if they see these acts as part of a heroic story in which their actions play a positive role in establishing a greater good.

Narratives and plans provide organizational frameworks that group attunements together. Relatedly, narratives and plans affect attention. They direct attention by providing default expectations of sequencing and colocation of events. They thus drive processes of fragmentation, or potentially defragmentation, as when we start to see something in one part of our lives as a metaphor for something in another, and thus as exemplifying a common narrative frame. Narratives can also influence attention by enhancing vividness of particular situations or events. Like stereotypes, and often in tandem with stereotyping, narratives provide schemas that enable people to better focus on and remember certain things, or at least to focus on how the narrative depicts those things. The narrative can tell us which tensions to focus on, for example, the tension created by a perception of threat or loss. Likewise, the narrative can also bring about harmony, by drawing our attention away from dangers or inconsistencies, and toward things that are consonant with our self-image and well-being.

Harmony, then, need not require our beliefs to be explained scientifically or logically, but rather to be integrated, to be given a meaning in the context of some general structure. If so, then harmony can be achieved not only by drawing valid inferences, the method usually associated with logic and science, but also by assimilation to patterns and schemas. To recognize something as fitting into a pattern is not to deduce anything, but merely to categorize it. Narrative harmonization is sufficiently powerful that it might allow an entire *form of life* to be categorized, to fit comfortably into the interwoven patterns of a complex tapestry of stories.

3.6. Priming Hate

The associationist model we have sketched provides a way of thinking about an important process for the politics of language, namely priming. By exposing people to words that are associated with practices, and perhaps inciting them to repeat or chant those words, attunements to the associated practices may themselves become activated. Mere exposure to the right words may help get an audience into the right frame of mind, a frame in which they are attuned to a demagogue's speech or a crowd's behavior, and perhaps are even somewhat pliant. This is not to say that such processes are always problematic. Practices of ritual chanting of scriptural verses and mantras, whether individually or en masse, are widely felt to be beneficial, simultaneously combining the apparent opposites of being a grounding discipline and spiritually uplifting.

As we have noted, Lieutenant Governor Dan Patrick's invocation of *critical race theory* is rhetorically functional even though in its right-wing usage the term lacks clear definition. The phrase does not function primarily to help the speaker convey a precise proposition, but to raise to prominence a web of associations. This web of associations helps form a tightly connected region of attunements, a segment of an ideology. In a similar vein, but with less ideological density, consider the function of Donald Trump's repeated use of epithets, such as "Crooked Hillary," to label his political opponent Hillary Clinton. The obviousness and superficiality of his strategy in no way blunted the power of the relentless jab to prime an association between Clinton and crookedness. It is hard to believe that anyone who experienced the 2016 US election campaign would not, as a result of both this phrase and the constant chanting of "Lock her up!" exhibit at least some priming effect whereby after hearing the word "crooked," the word "Hillary" was primed, and vice versa.

To take another much-discussed example, consider the significance of priming for group stereotypes. Such stereotypes are involved in a wide range of race and gender vocabulary, including racial and gender epithets. The model of attention we have outlined suggests that once language has activated an attunement to a certain categorization, perhaps using a racial or gender stereotype, further attunements might then become activated. A hearer who is exposed to a labeling of someone using a term for which there is a strong stereotype would activate inferential attunements that involve tendencies to draw further conclusions about the individual who has been so categorized, as well as further dispositional and emotional attunements. These in turn might lead to ways of treating that individual and ways of feeling about that individual that fit within the ideology of the hearer. Thus, we might say that a stereotype is not merely a set of default properties; it is a doorway into an ideology and to all the emotions and practices that belong within it.

In all these cases of priming, our claim is not that a hearer is necessarily powerless to resist associations that have been seeded by a history of occurrence of words in certain contexts, but that it will cost a hearer effort to keep a clear head. For example, it does not follow from our account that those who experienced the 2016 election had no choice but to develop a dispositional attunement to treat Hillary Clinton as the less ethical of the two candidates, but it came to require at least some effort to keep a clear head and to recognize that the association between her name and criminality was planted in our heads independently of any clear evidence about her behavior.

Priming is reflexive activation of one attunement by another, an association between attunements. Political persuasion is partly a matter of strengthening the associations between some things, so that associations with other things will be weakened. For example, in the aftermath of mass-shooting tragedies in the United States, right-wing politicians reliably mention mental-health problems, as well as "good guy with a gun" rhetoric, distracting from one of the primary causes of the tragedies, namely, the ease with which bad guys, mentally ill or not, can get guns. Similarly, if voters are able to rapidly recall a narrative regarding some politician's stance on crime, that could reduce their tendency to think about economic or welfare stances when voting.

The obverse of priming, where activation of one attunement suppresses activation of others, is a natural consequence of our basic assumptions. This is what creates the possibility of what might be termed *distractive priming*, whereby the fact that processing of one thing has been facilitated may mean that processing of something else is attenuated. The psychological connection between priming, on the one hand, and attention and distraction, on the other, is a complex one. Attention and distraction are inherently short-term processes, while priming effects can be long lasting, and can affect processing without having a direct effect on attention. Indeed, the fact that someone is primed to process something in a particular way can potentially reduce the amount of attention that the processing requires. We thus resist making strong claims about exactly how priming relates to attentional effects. What we can say is that politicians both distract people in the short term, moving the conversation away from topics that they would rather people not think about, and also use distractive priming as part of longer-term strategies.

Here, let us draw a connection with nondeliberative uptake, which we use not to refer to Gilbert's theory of hearer belief revision per se, but to the idea that some effects of communication are effortless and semiautomatic. One effect of communication is the impact on attention, and this impact is for the most part beyond deliberative control, as illustrated by the well-worn "Don't think of an elephant!" conundrum (to which we previously alluded in our discussion of the exigent power of words, in section 2.6). Politicians seek not only to drive attunement in a desired direction, but to control attention and prime certain ways of reacting to what people attend to. Thus, a theory of political language is also a theory of political psychology, and must analyze attentional and associative processes at both short and long timescales.[38]

3.7. Mass Coordination

For some purposes, it's better to characterize a gas thermodynamically than in terms of its component molecules. More generally, sometimes the best way to look at a complex system is holistically, at the level of the system rather than at the level of its constituent parts. In work on communication, Chomskyan linguistics has focused exclusively on language as a function of individual human

38. We thank Eyal Sagi for discussion.

psychology, while, in contrast, much work in sociolinguistics and communication studies is set at the group level. As will hopefully have been clear from the earlier chapters of this volume, we see value in both levels of description. While we defined what it is for an individual to be attuned to (the practice of using) a word, we also distinguished individual attunement from collective attunement, and we analyzed the conventional resonances of words as collective attunements across a community of practice. But so far in this chapter we have only described harmonization as an individual-level process.

In this section, we motivate the idea of considering harmonization at a group level, by considering cases in which the behavior of groups seems special, a thing in its own right that is perhaps most naturally analyzed, at least in part, at the level of the group rather than at the level of the individual. We begin with a simple biological example to pump intuitions, and then move to considering two more "big" ideas from prior literature, in fact from over a century ago: *contagion* and *collective effervescence*. These ideas illustrate the interest in group-level description, and also provide inspiration for development of our notion of collective harmony.

To prime the intuition as to how a theory of collective harmony might deliver value that a theory of individual harmony cannot, let us consider a relatively extreme case: the behavior of a colony of ants engaged in foraging activities in your kitchen. The ants have recently discovered a way of getting from their nest, accessed via a crack in the wall behind the sink, to your well-stocked larder. Without even realizing that a bidirectional highway of ants stretches across your kitchen, you wander bleary-eyed into the room, slide a chair out from under the table and slump into it. In the process you squash some ants and block the foraging line. Although it might be possible to argue that at the level of the individual ants there is a sort of dissonance, because they don't have a clear pheromone-laden path to follow, this level of analysis is neither clearly motivated nor clearly revealing of what then happens: individual ants have little clue what is going on at a global level. Yet, in the course of just a few minutes, a new foraging line develops, circumnavigating the chair you pulled out, and reconnecting your larder to the place the ants call home. It is relative to the level of the ant colony that we can give a functional explanation: (i) the ants were collectively engaged in an evolutionarily optimized foraging activity; (ii) the changes you unconsciously imposed on their environment disrupted this activity; (iii) collective behavior was then suboptimal insofar as the nest was not being actively stocked; (iv) they collectively reoptimized until they determined a new locally minimal path between nest and larder, thus returning to optimized foraging activity as before.

The collective change of behavior of the ants in your kitchen is extraordinary. It is remarkable that they can coordinatively solve a logistically complex problem using only very simple chemical markers to communicate. The communication processes of ants are powerful, but rely on simple heuristics: innate and attunements, if you will. It is by now somewhat well understood scientifically how some species of ants optimize for their environments, even though the detailed functioning of the individual ant as a computational system remains a hard scientific problem. Collective change can be explained without reference to individual ants having a detailed representation of the organization of the space they were negotiating, or dispositions that would allow them to precisely navigate that space in the absence of other ants. While we could talk of individual ants reharmonizing their dispositional attunements in reaction to dissonance created by lack of clear pheromonal signposting, what we want to suggest is that the standard explanation (in terms of processes of pheromone trail reinforcement combined with semistochastic variation in individual ant behavior) is really a story at the level of collective harmony. It is the ant collective that deals with the dissonance introduced by your sleepy entrance into the kitchen, and it does so by reharmonizing its collective behavior so that the ants are collectively attuned to their changed environment.

CONTAGION

Gustave Le Bon's 1895 *Psychologie des foules*[39] introduces the idea of contagion as a process within crowds, using it to compare the effects of the crowd to those of hypnotic suggestibility:

> Contagion is a phenomenon of which it is easy to establish the presence, but that it is not easy to explain. It must be classed among those phenomena of a hypnotic order. . . . In a crowd every sentiment and act is contagious, and contagious to such a degree that an individual readily sacrifices his personal interest to the collective interest.

Though Le Bon does see crowds as bringing forth a positive and altruistic side of human nature, he harps on the idea that masses of people are driven by emotion rather than pure reason, stating that the crowd's "collective observations are as erroneous as possible, and that most often they merely represent the illusion of an individual who, by a process of contagion, has suggestioned his fellows."[40]

Le Bon's work was, for a while, influential. Its political significance is seen in the mutual admiration between Le Bon and Mussolini, who in one interview is reported to have said of Le Bon, "I don't know how many times I have re-read his *Psychologie des foules*. It is an excellent work to which I frequently refer," and in a later meeting, made extensive reference to Le Bon both for

39. Le Bon, *The Crowd*, 10.
40. Le Bon, *The Crowd*, 31.

political justification and for his explanation of political method, specifically the idea that the crowd is irrational and driven by emotion.[41]

Le Bon's contemporary Gabriel Tarde also spoke of contagion, in his 1890 *Les lois de l'imitation* (*The Laws of Imitation*). Tarde used the term in a much broader sense than Le Bon, to refer not merely to the spread of emotion and behavior in a crowd, but to the spread of arbitrary elements of culture within and between societies. He thus essentially invented what Richard Dawkins later termed cultural *memes*, although Tarde's phrase *chose sociale* (social thing) was clearly not as contagious as Dawkins's *meme*.[42] Tarde saw the contagion of culture (he also talks of diffusion) as being explained in terms of a fundamental drive toward imitation, which in turn he saw as an automatic, unconscious, nondeliberative process. As he writes, memorably, "Society is imitation and imitation is a kind of somnambulism."[43] We do not think that society is just imitation, or that all imitation is unconscious in the way that Tarde is suggesting, but we do think both that imitation is central to ideological transmission, and that the process is often somewhat nondeliberative—more Spinozan than Cartesian, if you accept Dan Gilbert's historical framing. Here let us note that in an important series of articles, Lynne Tirrell, taking a cue from Victor Klemperer, exploits the metaphor of disease contagion in her

---

41. Nye, *The Origins of Crowd Psychology*, 178.

42. Dawkins introduces the term *meme* in *The Selfish Gene*, describing it as "a unit of cultural transmission or a unit of *imitation*" (192, emphasis in original), and as a shortened form of "mimeme," making the connection with imitation, and hence the similarity with Tarde's work, particularly striking. However, Dawkins appears to have been unaware of his predecessor, whose work has enjoyed a renaissance only more recently. Tarde's conception of cultural evolution is seen clearly in passages like this one: "In the beginning of societies, the art of chipping flint, of domesticating dogs, of making bows, and, later, of leavening bread, of working bronze, of extracting iron, etc., must have spread like a contagion; since every arrow, every flake, every morsel of bread, every thread of bronze, served both as model and copy. Nowadays the diffusion of all kinds of useful processes is brought about in the same way, except that our increasing density of population and our advance in civilisation prodigiously accelerate their diffusion, just as velocity of sound is proportionate to density of medium. Every social thing, that is to say, every invention or discovery, tends to expand in its social environment, an environment which itself, I might add, tends to self-expansion, since it is essentially composed of like things, all of which have infinite ambitions" (Tarde, *Laws of Imitation*, 17).

To dig somewhat further back historically, Tarde observes that Pliny the Younger had used of contagion in this way, talking of the contagion of religious belief. The context is a letter to Emperor Trajan regarding the dangers posed by the spread of Christianity (as opposed to worshiping Trajan himself and the Roman pantheon). Pliny explains that "the contagion of this superstition has spread not merely through the free towns, but into the villages and farms." He continues, on an optimistic note, "Still I think it can be halted and things set right" ("Letter to Trajan").

43. Tarde, *Laws of Imitation*, 87. Tarde himself takes inspiration from Adam Smith in recognizing the importance of imitation.

analysis of toxic language.[44] The point here is that ideologically problematic speech practices not only spread like diseases, but they harm like diseases too, even though the harmful effects on different groups are quite distinct. Sometimes toxic speech is debilitating due to the pain it causes, and sometimes toxic speech causes harm to those who encounter it only insofar as the attunements to the discriminatory ideology it induces are themselves intrinsically problematic.

COLLECTIVE EFFERVESCENCE

In his 1912 *The Elementary Forms of the Religious Life*, Émile Durkheim gave a theoretical interpretation of religious life in an aboriginal Australian society that was based on the ethnographic work of other scholars. The groups Durkheim discussed were totemists, investing objects with mystical power, and each of the groups he studied in central and northern Australia regarded things that named or characterized their group as having particularly strong magical powers. If you can imagine a nation that worshiped its own flag, or a gun or a cross, or in which, to take an example from earlier in this chapter, the incantation of words like *freedom* and *equality* could leave people spellbound, then you perhaps get the basic idea of totemism, albeit totemic objects may be particulars rather than abstract types, and can be more directly causally efficacious in the totemists' lives.

Durkheim's work is an important antecedent for our account of harmony, and at a general level, Durkheim's account fits naturally with our own. First, as has become common in anthropological and sociological work, practice occupies center stage: there is discussion both of prohibition of practices as undesirable or taboo, and of positively approved or required ritual. Second, he emphasizes (and here he is reacting to an individualism that already pervaded much intellectual thought at the time) that the right level of analysis for religion is not the individual but the collective, in line with his general views about the subject matter of sociology. As he states in his introduction,

> Religious representations are collective representations that express collective realities; rites are ways of acting that are born only in the midst of assembled groups and whose purpose is to evoke, maintain, or recreate certain mental states of those groups. But if categories are of religious origin, then they must participate in what is common to all religion: They, too, must be social things, products of collective thought.[45]

---

44. Tirrell, "Toxic Speech: Toward an Epidemiology of Discursive Harm"; "Toxic Speech: Inoculations and Antidotes"; "Discursive Epidemiology."
45. Durkheim, *The Elementary Forms of Religious Life*, 9.

The aspect of Durkheim's account that most obviously inspires our own is his introduction of the notion of *collective effervescence*. One understands the term in Durkheim's work primarily by example, but we would define it based on his work as a charged emotional state of activity that reigns when the individual wills of a group of people is collectively engaged in an activity that captures their entire attention and channels it into the cocreation of a single joint event. Alternatively, this definition can be rendered in terms of the account developed in this chapter.

> **Collective effervescence:** A state in which behavioral and emotional harmony within a close-knit group dominates the collective attention of that group to the exclusion of anything else.

Given that collective effervescence involves a peculiarly narrow focus of joint attention over a sustained period, it might be said that it is analogous to a flow state in the sense of the psychologist Mihaly Csikszentmihalyi.[46]

Note that we have taken the liberty of not including the presence of religious ritual into the definition of collective effervescence, although all of Durkheim's examples are of religious ritual. Thus, our definition allows that collective effervescence might spring up among sports fans, ravers, and political protesters: it needs only that there are simultaneously activated collective behavioral and emotional attunement, serving to galvanize joint activity. So, on this broad interpretation, there is collective effervescence during Orwell's Two Minutes Hate, a daily ritual in the novel *Nineteen Eighty-Four* in which the masses scream with rage at the principal enemy of the state:

> In a lucid moment Winston found that he was shouting with the others and kicking his heel violently against the rung of his chair. The horrible thing about the Two Minutes Hate was not that one was obliged to act a part, but, on the contrary, that it was impossible to avoid joining in. Within thirty seconds any pretence was always unnecessary. A hideous ecstasy of fear and vindictiveness, a desire to kill, to torture, to smash faces in with a sledge-hammer, seemed to flow through the whole group of people like an electric current, turning one even against one's will into a grimacing, screaming lunatic.[47]

If there is collective effervescence in the distinctly dissonant harmony of the hate-filled space of Orwell's fiction, there is equally collective effervescence

---

46. Csikszentmihalyi, *Flow*. Csikszentmihalyi characterizes flow as an "optimal experience" in which an individual is willingly absorbed by whatever they are doing, i.e., their attention is undividedly focused on one activity. He also talks of flow, not just coincidentally, in terms of "inner harmony" (217, and elsewhere). So collective flow would involve an outer or collective harmony and the joint attention of a group, freely given and focused on a single group activity.

47. Orwell, *Nineteen Eighty-Four*, 133.

during the singing of "Happy Birthday" at a children's party, young eyes glowing, the sound of smiles in voices more enthusiastic than tuneful, candles on the cake flickering. What all these occasions have in common is that a group of people brought together develops self-reinforcing, short-term collective dispositions that dominate their attention. In both cases, it is hard to resist being drawn into the group activity, and individual will is submerged.

While Durkheim's work still seems fresh and relevant to us, let us also point to a new series of studies that explicitly targeted collective effervescence across a range of multiday secular mass gatherings (e.g., festivals like Burning Man, where there is an ethos of self-growth and community engagement). The studies can be seen as offering support to Durkheim's ideas, but perhaps the greater importance of the work might rest in the transformative power that the participants reported, with positive prosocial effects such as increased generosity. While the net positives and negatives of the gatherings are difficult to evaluate, the work at least suggests a positive path in a society where alienation is rife. We might say that whereas Orwell's vision, very much in line with Carl Schmitt's fascist philosophy, was of feelings of alienation channeled into hatred for a common enemy, the more hopeful path offered by these studies involves methods to overcome personal alienation by channeling attention toward common humanity.[48]

3.8. Collective Harmony

We now define harmony at the group level by close analogy with individual harmony at the level of individuals.

> **Collective harmony:** The emotions jointly experienced by members of a group due to the way different group members' attunements relate to each other. This may be an experience of collective consonance, when there is manifest coherence of attunements, which implies a high degree of collective attunement, or collective dissonance, when there is manifest incoherence of attunements.

The special properties of collective harmony, and, we hope, its distinctive explanatory value, derive from the fact that a central term in the definition, *manifest coherence* (or *incoherence*), comes to have a special significance in the group setting. We will consider what it is for attunements to be coherent, and what it is for that coherence to be manifest, in turn, and sketch how the definition can be applied to group behavior and attitudes.

48. See Yudkin et al., "Prosocial Correlates of Transformative Experiences." Note that the presence of hallucinogenic drugs at festivals was a predictive factor in the studies, but far from being the sole explanation of the effects observed. Schmitt's more troublesome vision is expounded, for example, in *The Concept of the Political.*

Coherence is a matter of whether different attunements are mutually supporting. For individual harmony, we focused on support relations that might be across highly dissimilar attunements, for example, cognitive attunements like a belief in the value of riding a bike and dispositional attunements like the ability to ride one. At the group level, one person's attunements can be supported by the presence of others with the same or similar attunements. So, coherence of attunements across a group is partly a matter of the extent to which attunements are shared, a notion that doesn't make immediate sense at the level of the individual.[49]

Likewise, what it is for coherence to become manifest is quite different at an individual and group level. At the individual level, it is to be understood as involving an introspective psychological process that can involve attunements of any type. At the group level, evaluation of coherence is mediated. Attunements become manifest through behavior. We cannot directly evaluate coherence of attunements, but only evaluate the coherence of what we see, hear, taste, smell, and feel, attunements projected onto the big screen of embodied action and sensation. Nonetheless, the impression made by the behavior of others is not only one of intellectual comprehension, but of empathic identification. The expression "mind-reading" is suggestive, but it does not adequately capture this. It is not emotion reading but emotion mirroring that is at stake.[50] At least for some emotions, it is experience of what

49. We have been assuming that there is no sense in which an individual can have the same attunement twice, but for completeness let us note that it is logically possible to make sense of the idea of a single person having shared attunements, provided they are shared across distinct aspects of the individual's life. A version of the landscape model described above might allow that different clusters of attunements both include some particular attunement, without mutual activation across the systems. Thus, the prison guard might have an attunement to vigilance when with their children, and an attunement to vigilance when with prisoners, and yet without vigilance in the first role activating other attunements associated with the second role. More generally, the sharedness of attunements across aspects of a person's life would be a matter of the extent to which they have the same personality when playing different roles. This consideration then naturally suggests an analogy whereby we consider the question of the extent to which different individuals sharing attunements might come to have not merely a shared "identity" but also a shared personality, but we refrain from speculating further as to the analogies to be found between individual psychology and group psychology.

50. In *The Theory of Moral Sentiments*, 4–5, Adam Smith discusses empathic emotional response in the context of seeing someone on the rack: "By the imagination we place ourselves in his situation, we conceive ourselves enduring all the same torments, we enter as it were into his body, and become in some measure the same person with him, and thence form some idea of his sensations, and even feel something which, though weaker in degree, is not altogether unlike them. His agonies, when they are thus brought home to ourselves, when we have thus adopted and made them our own, begin at last to affect us, and we then tremble and shudder at the thought of what he feels. For as to be in pain or distress of any kind excites the most excessive sorrow, so to conceive or to imagine that we

others are experiencing, and thence also motivation, a drive to do what others are doing. And this we take to be uncontroversial. There is a large literature on the topic of emotional contagion and its physical basis and motivational consequences, much of this literature taking emotional contagion to be a secondary effect of physical mimicry of emotional presentations.[51] It is apparently not just laughter that can be infectious.

We can pick out a further property of the manifestation of coherence of attunements that is distinctive at the group level: simultaneity, or, at larger time scales, the property of being contemporaneous. People demonstrate the similarity of their attunements by activating them in similar contexts, and people cannot be in a more similar context than when they are present at the same place and time. Density and size of a crowd are factors here: it is obvious that a behavior will become highly manifest when displayed in unison by a huge number of copresent people, or by a large number who are very close to the observer.

So, immediacy is crucial to collective harmony. At scales of days and above, and at the physical scale of villages and above, this presence of attunements changing in synchrony with each other underlies fashion, the fact that a mode of dress, thought, and expression must be à la mode in order to fit. Gabriel Tarde's discussion of contagion as a slow process of cultural diffusion was largely set at these time scales.[52] On the other hand, Le Bon's crowd contagion and Durkheim's collective effervescence both involve the rapid activation of attunements, and sometimes rapid development of new attunements seen in new behaviors, simultaneously deployed through conspicuous behavior. The behavior is often conspicuous not only because it may be raucous and

---

are in it, excites some degree of the same emotion, in proportion to the vivacity or dullness of the conception."

51. Much of the large and diverse literature on emotional contagion focuses on the process by which one person is, as the disease metaphor would have it, infected by another. A somewhat standard definition of *primitive emotional contagion* is "the tendency to automatically mimic and synchronize facial expressions, vocalizations, postures, and movements with those of another person and, consequently, to converge emotionally" (Hatfield and Rapson, "Emotional Contagion," 153–54). Some more recent literature identifies relatively small but statistically significant effects in big data studies of emotional contagion in social media. A by now somewhat infamous study shows the effects in a study of Facebook users (problematic because the feeds of these users were manipulated without their consent): Kramer, Guillory, and Hancock, "Experimental Evidence of Massive-Scale Emotional Contagion." Emotional contagion effects on the Twitter platform are discussed in Ferrara and Yang, "Measuring Emotional Contagion in Social Media."

52. This is not to say that Tarde did not consider contagion at fine time scales. His discussion of the development of a "group mind" in a crowd hinged on the possibility of rapid imitation and repetition, and foreshadowed recent work in social psychology on identity fusion, briefly discussed below.

exaggerated, but because it is highly distinctive, in that it is a type of behavior that would not be seen on other occasions.[53]

In our terms, Durkheim's collective effervescence consists in highly cohering and distinctive attunements being activated synchronously within a group that shares a strong bond of common identity. The effervescence serves to reaffirm that identity and provide a potentially transformative experience by providing participants with a situation in which they can develop and experience attunements that they otherwise would not.

Synchrony of action is central to our understanding of Durkheim's collective effervescence. In the case of chanting the same chant, clapping and marching to the same beat, synchrony involves a pattern of repeated simultaneity. But we should note that synchrony does not simply mean simultaneity, and in other cases it is more complex. Call and response patterns involve careful timing, as do crowd reactions to a central performer. In sports, synchrony is seen in everything from the careful timing of a single throw and catch combination to the extraordinary synchronization of a larger play in a team sport. We might say that in all these cases, a combination of strong joint identity, high synchronization, and great distinctiveness of behavior leads to something akin to the collective effervescence that Durkheim described.

Crowd contagion is naturally understood in these terms. A situation in which attunements of the group are immediately manifest is one in which those attunements can spread rapidly. If the group shares a relevant identity, sharing attunements will produce consonance, leading to powerful feedback loops in which any attunement that is shared by a portion of the group can become rapidly shared by larger portions to whom the attunement is manifest. For some attunements, like basic emotions of panic and excitement, the

---

53. Both the distinctiveness and the synchrony of actions during episodes of collective effervescence is memorably described by Durkheim:

> On every side one sees nothing but violent gestures, cries, veritable howls, and deafening noises of every sort, which aid in intensifying still more the state of mind which they manifest. And since a collective sentiment cannot express itself collectively except on the condition of observing a certain order permitting co-operation and movements in unison, these gestures and cries naturally tend to become rhythmic and regular; hence come songs and dances. But in taking a more regular form, they lose nothing of their natural violence; a regulated tumult remains tumult. The human voice is not sufficient for the task; it is reinforced by means of artificial processes: boomerangs are beaten against each other; bull-roarers are whirled. It is probable that these instruments, the use of which is so general in the Australian religious ceremonies, are used primarily to express in a more adequate fashion the agitation felt. But while they express it, they also strengthen it. This effervescence often reaches such a point that it causes unheard-of actions. The passions released are of such an impetuosity that they can be restrained by nothing. (*The Elementary Forms of Religious Life*, 217–18)

shared identity of cohumanity may suffice to support rapid spread and mutual reinforcement.

Although for some purposes merely having the common identity of being human, or perhaps "being there," can trigger contagion effects, as when an arbitrary crowd gathers around a spectacle, for some collective attunements, narrower identities are relevant. These might include collective attunements that are peculiar to the specific environment, such as attunements to playing sport for a sports team, or attunements to familial habits of eating and arguing and celebrating in family settings, or attunements to a specific vocabulary of protest peculiar to a rally of a particular political stripe. A crowd will have a stronger tendency to contagion when they share identity. But here the feedback loops become more complex. In the case of a rally or protest, part of the logic of the event is that development of the identity goes hand in hand with synchronous display of attunement. The more people jump up and down or shout the same slogans or songs in time with each other, the stronger the common bond of joint identity becomes, and the stronger the consonance created by further synchronous action.

In a crowd, and especially in ritual settings, feedback loops encourage the formation of collective emotions and behaviors that would not result from individual attunements of group members in other circumstances. In other words, in these settings, some aspects of individual agency are lost or transformed. This is an idea that is quite clear in the work of Tarde, Le Bon, and Durkheim. The idea has resurfaced in various overlapping strands of contemporary psychological work, notably in the concept of *diffusion of responsibility*, seen in John Darley and Bibb Latané's explanations of the *bystander effect* (whereby people are less likely to take responsibility to act in an emergency situation the more other people are present), and in the concept of *identity fusion* introduced by William Swann and Michael Buhrmester.[54]

As Herbert Kelman and Lee Hamilton argue, diffusion of responsibility played a central role in the perpetration of Nazi war crimes:

> The Nazi extermination program was carried out by a vast bureaucracy in which many functionaries—from Adolf Eichmann down to junior clerks—sat at desks, shuffled papers, arranged train schedules, and carried out a variety of other tasks without having to consider the final product of their efforts. The perception of personal causation was reduced not only by the dissociation of each functionary's contributory acts from the human consequences of those acts but also by the

54. Darley and Latané, "Bystander Intervention in Emergencies"; Swann et al., "Identity Fusion." The theory of identity fusion is further developed in Swann et al., "When Group Membership Gets Personal." See also Whitehouse and Lanman, "Ritual, Fusion, and Identification"; Swann and Buhrmester, "Identity Fusion." For discussion of diffusion of responsibility in the bystander effect, we thank Eyal Sagi.

diffusion of responsibility within the bureaucracy. The more people are involved in an action, the less likelihood that any one of them will see herself or himself as a causal agent with moral responsibility.[55]

The bystander effect does not depend on people having a common social identity; the original work by Darley and Latané in fact suggested that people's tendency to dissociate themselves from moral responsibility to act when others are present was not highly correlated with at least one type of identity, namely gender identity. Rather, the bystander effect can be seen as a passive failure to take significant individual action when in any group situation. It is not so much groupthink as group avoidance of potentially dissonance-yielding action.

If *diffusion of responsibility* depends little on social identity, *identity fusion* goes in the other direction: it can be thought of as particularly strong type of identity-based psychological bond between people in a group, although in some ways identity fusion is also somewhat independent of what are often thought of as social identities, for example, those based on gender, age, occupation, or sexual orientation. Central to social identity are aspects of self-image and self-presentation that serve as exemplars of some group. For example, someone for whom being American is an important social identity might see their predilection for burgers as natural. However, that same person might also see their enjoyment of French New Wave cinema as idiosyncratic. Or if one has a Catholic social identity, one might find oneself to be in some ways a bad Catholic, without thinking there is anything bad about Catholicism.

So, one's personal identity is distinct from one's social identities: the social identities inform the personal identity, but are not confused with it. Identity fusion, on the other hand, involves seeing oneself and a group as not entirely separate. Someone whose identity is strongly fused with the United States would see a harm done to them as a harm done to the United States (i.e., as anti-American), and, vice versa, would take a harm to the United States as being very much like a personal insult. Further, it is quite possible for identity fusion to take place with a group with whom one feels no strong social identification, as when a group coalesces for some arbitrary reason not connected with social identity, and the primary thing shared is the experience itself. Based on extensive studies of people's behavioral predilections and how those predilections relate to their degree of identity fusion, it has been suggested by Bill Swann, Michael Buhrmester, and other researchers that identity fusion is a far more powerful motivator for actions on behalf of a group than is social identity (see fn. 54 on p. 163 in this section for references). Someone who merely feels that they fit in well with a national ethos is less likely to shoot or take a bullet for their nation than is someone who doesn't clearly distinguish themselves and their country.

---

55. Kelman and Hamilton, *Crimes of Obedience*, 165.

The potential of the concept of identity fusion to explain examples of apparently "selfless" action makes the concept important for our project, and for any work on political persuasion. We do not claim to offer a new analysis of identity fusion, but we do see such processes of submergence of the self as being naturally described within the framework of collective harmony that we have laid out in this section. If identity fusion is a possible end point of harmonization with a group, then at least part of what must have happened when such a point is reached is that one's idiosyncratic individual attunements become deactivated, relative to strongly activated collective attunements of the group. As we have seen, at least in some settings, like those at large political rallies, the consonance gained by people jointly activating attunements can lead to strong positive feedback loops.

Under these conditions, if attunements and attention are pushed in a certain direction, collective harmonization may overwhelm individual preferences. And the thing about large political rallies is that they are carefully oriented to give just such a push. Attendees are offered hats to wear and signs to wave, insurgents are planted in the crowd to act enthusiastically in line with the behavior that is desired, the stage is set up as a focus of attention, perhaps with huge Big Brother screens to bolster the effect of amplification and spotlights. And most of all, after a string of somewhat mediocre henchmen speak, the great leader emerges. The leader is a peculiar and extreme person, at once dominant and full of machismo, and at the same time almost a caricature of himself, so odd that one cannot take one's eyes off him. It is no accident that the great charismatic leaders are often such strange people. As we commented in our brief discussion of spiritual cult leaders, above, this strangeness is a feature, not a bug. For it is one way of being sure that they will be magnets for attention. And attention, when it is joint among thousands of people, becomes a driver of collective harmonization, leading to a condition of collective effervescence in which the active attunements of any individual are the active attunements of the group. It is a scary situation to behold as an outsider. For what one sees if one is sufficiently far removed, perhaps watching a decades-old newsreel, is thousands of spellbound people chanting and moving together like puppets, as if the demagogue has somehow stripped them of their free will.

Let us consider here the role of the ideas we introduced in sections 3.2 and 3.3, fragmentation, cognitive dissonance, and nondeliberative uptake. That the processes we have described in this section are largely nondeliberative is fairly clear from the literature on the topic: it is generally agreed that emotional contagion is nondeliberative, and there is a similar case to be made for many of the other processes underlying collective harmonization within a crowd environment.

As regards cognitive dissonance theory, recall Festinger's weakest-link hypothesis, which suggested an explanation of cases where people's emotional and dispositional attunements appear to drive their epistemic attunements. According to this principle, people have a tendency to do whatever is easiest to avoid dissonance. Thus, people will tend to suppress whichever attunement is most conveniently suppressed in order that they do not feel conflicted. Suppose that a participant at a political rally has a cognitive attunement that runs counter to the sentiment expressed on the stage before them, say a belief in the equality and goodness of all set against the speaker's blatantly racist rhetoric. Someone who focuses on such a righteous belief will face extreme dissonance.

Which will be easier: ceasing to applaud and scream with everyone else, or ceasing to focus on the belief? By the simple expedient of attending to the rally and not attending to the belief, the immediate feeling of cognitive dissonance is avoided. The attendee has not necessarily ceased to hold the righteous beliefs, but they have compartmentalized them; that is, they have fragmented their mental state in such a way that the conflicting attunements are not simultaneously activated. This allows their attention to stray away from what, from our external moral perch, they ought to have focused on, a belief in what is good, and hence a conclusion that the activities around them are not. Fragmentation is what makes this move possible, for absent the possibility of fragmentation, which consists only in dissociating the belief from actions that conflict with it, the attendee would have faced a more blatant choice with a high personal cost: stop participating in the rally, or stop believing in equality and goodness of all.

This defensive strategy of compartmentalizing is complementary to a separate effect of propaganda that we have discussed, for example, in the context of the state declarations prior to the US Civil War (outset of chapter 1). Propaganda may lead to a reframing of what equality consists in, so that cognitive attunements are adjusted; such basic notions as equality and freedom can be subverted so as not to be discordant with the racist overtones, or overt racism, of right-wing rhetoric and action. We suppose that whereas changes of attention that suppress a strongly held cognitive attunement so that its relevance is not apparent may happen in the blink of an eye, transformations of such attunements are commonly slower. This is surely a process that happens more at the time scale of the cultural diffusion processes discussed by Tarde, not in the context of crowd dynamics discussed by Le Bon.

3.9. What Resonates and Why

In chapter 1, we argued for the development of a theory of meaning based on resonance rather than content. After summarizing prior literature on resonance in communication, we started to develop our own account. That account went in a different direction from most prior literature in the following way. Prior scholars have typically been interested in what makes something resonant, or when something resonates with an audience, for example, what makes a framing of a political goal resonant for a target audience within a movement or for potential recruits. We have not defined what makes an action resonant. Rather, we defined what the resonances of an action are, using that as the basis of a theory of meaning intended to be rich enough to model broadly political and sociolinguistic phenomena. In following this path, we left aside the question of what makes something resonate with someone. We have outlined a theory of meaning but said nothing about what makes meanings special. If you like, our theory of meaning says nothing about what makes something feel deeply meaningful. Although not normally put in such vaguely spiritual terms, that is an issue of central import in analysis of political messaging. The framing of a political debate is not arbitrary, but shaped by the question of what makes meanings special to people, that is, the question of which frames resonate with which audiences in which contexts.

There is a reason why we could not state back in chapter 1 what makes something resonant, what makes its meaning special. There we presented a highly idealized model of the resonances of individual signals within an interaction that made no reference at all to the broader culture of the agents involved in the interaction. However, prior literature makes it clear that the question of what makes something resonant is deeply entwined with the cultural context of those involved. For example, Deva Woodly argues for a theory of resonance that depends crucially on "common sense" cultural background. As she puts it,

> Resonant arguments, and the frames that they combine into, are able to influence people's political understandings and social imaginations more forcefully than other kinds of information and evidence because they inhabit a special discursive space in which background notions, common logics, and new ideas are aligned in a harmonious way.[56]

We agree. In our terms, the notion of what it is for something to resonate with an audience cannot be analyzed at the level of the associations of the individual signal, and not even at the level of what it is for an individual to be attuned to that signal, but rather must be analyzed in terms of how the associations of the signal relate to broader systems of attunement of that audience, for it is only at that level that the question of whether attunements are "aligned in a harmonious way" arises. Adapting the intuition in the quote from Woodly to our own framework, we arrive at the following definition of the extent to which something is resonant, or equivalently, how much it resonates:

Degree to which something resonates: Something resonates (positively) for a group or individual to the extent that it induces increased (positive) harmony for them.

56. Woodly, *The Politics of Common Sense*, 97.

The above definition of the extent to which something is resonant is not limited to the question of when frames resonate, but applies to arbitrary events or objects. Seeing someone give away their last gummy bear might resonate, as a type of narrative resonance, if you will. A picture of a rainbow might resonate. And so might a peculiar man with a small mustache. Nonetheless, we will focus in this section on the question of when frames resonate.

To take a standard example from the framing literature, much political discourse seeks to explicate issues in terms of civil rights. Indeed, in political science literature, "civil rights" is often used as a label for what Benford and Snow term a "master frame," because it is not issue specific, but rather is generalizable to multiple areas.[57] As Benford explains,

> Typically, once a social movement fashions and espouses a highly resonant frame that is broad in interpretive scope, other social movements within a cycle of protest will modify that frame and apply it to their own cause. For example, once the US civil rights movement of the 1950s and 1960s experienced a number of successes based on an equal rights and opportunities frame, several other movements, including the American Indian, women's, gay and lesbian, Chicano/a, and Gray Panthers, adopted and proffered a similar frame to their specific movement campaigns.[58]

Civil rights framings are resonant for those people for whom those rights form central organizing principles in their ideology. For these people, a framing that casts an issue in terms of civil rights might produce a sense of individual harmony if it connects together disparate attunements into a way that makes their system of attunements more coherent. To take the example of same-sex marriage in the United States, someone who feels dissonance at the idea of an institutional change, and thus specifically dissonance at the idea of legal and civil change to recognition of same-sex marriages, may be able to overcome that dissonance if they can come to see same-sex marriage not as a divergence from historical precedent and prevailing ideology, but rather as an expression of the central features of the ideology that shaped their modern nation. Looked at this way, it is the past in which rights were distributed unevenly that is anomalous, and a future in which a wider range of people have access to those rights is consonant.

What makes a framing resonant is often not just its ability to tap into a wealth of prior attunements, but to do so effortlessly, so that it is processed with little conscious deliberation. Sticking with same-sex marriage and related LGBTQ+ issues, a good example is the use of the phrase "Love is love," which at the time of writing has been spread widely around the United States on

57. Benford and Snow, "Framing Processes and Social Movements," 618–19.
58. Benford, "Master Frame," 366.

"We believe . . ." yard signs proclaiming a range of values perceived to be under threat following the election of Donald Trump in 2016. The tautology "Love is love" might seem provocatively asinine, but that is part of the point. Who could disagree? Or, to tie into our discussion of deliberativity in this chapter, how much does one really need to think before agreeing?

The resonance and hence power of the adage "Love is love" derives from the fact that it allows LGBTQ+ issues, and same-sex marriage in particular, to be understood in terms of collective attunements that have become central to contemporary US ideology. The first collective attunement, discussed at length in Woodly's analysis of the same-sex marriage movement, is the idea of romantic love as the central component of a good marriage, an idea that is not globally recognized at present, and was not dominant in the United States until relatively recently (within the last century). Part of the power of the adage is that some of those who are opposed to same-sex marriage are among those most likely to subscribe not merely to the view that love is central to marriage, but that romantic love has no place outside of marriage, or at least of courting with marriage as a goal. The second collective attunement is the idea that romantic love does not answer to any higher principle, but is entirely and inherently a matter of personal choice. It is relevant here that romantic love has since ancient times been seen as inherently transgressive. In literature and mythology around the world, romantic love is often in tension with other prerogatives. For this reason, the mere fact that someone might find same-sex union to be in tension with their ideology does not necessarily mean that they cannot recognize same-sex love as being an expression of "true" love. These two collective attunements then tap into the civil-rights frame. If marriage is the idealized state for those in a state of love, and love is entirely a matter of personal choice, it follows from attunements to personal freedom that marriage among those of an age to make such choices should be unfettered by further institutional restrictions. The simple slogan "Love is love" is resonant in large part because it connects unobjectionably to collective attunements that are core parts of the ideology of a wide range of people at whom the message is targeted.

We have defined what it is for something to resonate positively in terms of harmony and its attendant feeling. However, the point of a framing in politics, say a civil-rights framing of same-sex marriage issues, is not just to make individual people feel good, if it even achieves that. The point is to persuade people, to cause them to change attitudes and behaviors to which they were resistant. It is central to the mechanism of persuasion that by tying an issue, say same-sex marriage, to broader ideology, to what Woodly refers to as "common sense" and Jaeggi refers to as "forms of life," the crafters of political messages create the potential for dissonance. The process is not complex, but let us spell it out.

Suppose there is some goal idea (or behavior, or emotional attitude) to which a person targeted by a messaging campaign is not attuned. Now suppose that this targeted individual shares other collective attunements, for example, accepting principles that they and most people around them see as common sense or obvious, and that the message crafter finds a framing that establishes a way to link the goal idea to those collective attunements. If the target recognizes that the goal idea is natural in the light of the connection to those collective attunements, for example, because the goal idea can be seen as an expression of shared principles, then they will feel a tension. Harmonizing by accepting the goal idea can then resolve this tension. That process is straightforward enough, basically similar in structure to the way any argument works to convince someone of something that they have not previously embraced, except that it applies to arbitrary attunements and not merely to belief in propositions. But we can now go further, to the group level.

By adopting the goal idea, or other intended attunement, a targeted individual will have attunements that are in alignment with members of the political movement for which the message crafter is advocating. They can thus derive harmony not only through consonance of attunement of the goal idea with their broader ideology, but also through consonance of their attunement with attunements of others. At the same time, they may feel dissonance with others who do not share attunement to the goal idea. Shifting someone's mind on an issue may therefore be part of a process of peeling them off from one group and aligning them with another. This has strategic implications. It might be that the best political strategy is not always to hit an issue head on, where it will create immediate dissonance if recognizably associated with a group with which the targeted individual does not feel social alignment, perhaps to the extent of preventing effective communication. It might be better to start with less obvious behaviors and issues that can indirectly incentivize. For example, start by getting them into church, and only then work on aligning their faith with the rest of the congregation. Or bus them to the rally, and then get them shouting and jumping and wearing the same hats and T-shirts. Or, if you want people to align with attitudes or behaviors of a group that stereotypically drinks a lot of lattes, you might find it easiest to start by giving away some free latte vouchers, and only move onto civil rights and "Love is love" framings later.

Here it is significant that something can be resonant for a group first, and for individuals only secondarily. A chant, a slogan on a hat, or a march along a certain route might resonate with a group in part because the group finds it easy to become behaviorally aligned while chanting, while wearing the hat, or while marching. That might lead secondarily to resonance for the individuals, and to identification with the crowd. At least sometimes, it is only thereafter, in a very indirect process, that the meaning of the chant or slogan, or the significance of the route of the march, or what was witnessed along the route, itself take on special significance for the participants. It is not just that the behavioral tail can wag the cognitive dog, but that what resonates with a pack of dogs can drive the individual dogs secondarily, through processes of collective effervescence that we have described.

To our knowledge, the most theoretically sophisticated extant analysis of frame resonance other than Woodly's is that of Terence E. McDonnell, Christopher A. Bail, and Iddo Tavory, who take their philosophical inspiration less from Aristotelian rhetoric, as she does, and more from the pragmatist tradition of Dewey, James, and Peirce.[59] McDonnell et al. agree with the bulk of prior work that embedding a frame in the cultural milieu is crucial for frame resonance; they take this factor to have been overemphasized and to have encouraged a view of resonance as a fixed property of a framing or other cultural object, independent of who is using the frame or being exposed to it, and independent of the particular context in which the frame is used. What they take to have been underemphasized, drawing on the pragmatist tradition, is what the frame does for people in particular contexts, the functional load it bears in helping people work through problems experienced in particular ways at particular times, and in helping motivate action appropriate to those contexts. As they say, "Cultural objects are not relevant unless employed to solve a problem," so we should see "resonance as an experience emerging when affective and cognitive work provides actors with novel ways to puzzle out, or 'solve,' practical situations." They go on (making explicit their debt to Peirce),

> Resonance is a specific kind of experiential effect (or interpretant), emerging at the same time that actors come to see the world in a new light. . . . It is thus only through the effect of signs that meaning-making is completed, and such effect cannot be encapsulated by an analysis of cultural objects but must also take into account the habits of thought and action through which an interpreter experiences such an object.[60]

Resonance, on this view, is not a fixed property, but something that occurs as people "puzzle out" (a phrase they draw from Peirce) a problem, come to see aspects of the problem in a new light, and imbue aspects of the problem situation with new meaning. Furthermore, this does not happen only at an individual level:

> Instead of focusing on patterns of interaction among individuals, resonance can also be studied via analysis of interaction among groups, organizations, or other collective actors within broader social arenas such as the public sphere. . . .
>
> We can see resonance occur on a macro level as different organizational actors come together and converge on a cultural object—as

59. McDonnell, Bail, and Tavory, "A Theory of Resonance."
60. McDonnell, Bail, and Tavory, "A Theory of Resonance," 3.

in the unification of Gay and Lesbian social movement organizations around "queer" identities.[61]

As we have made clear, we view resonance as being usefully analyzed at a collective rather than individual level. We also agree with McDonnell et al. as regards resonance being more than just cultural embedding, and having a problem-solving character. This is reflected in our definition. Our definition does not refer to a fixed state of a frame or other cultural object, but rather to its ability to induce harmonization.

Let us make the relationship to problem-solving explicit. A problem is something that causes dissonance, a clash between a desire to change or understand things, and other attunements that mitigate against such change or sense-making. On our definition, a framing will be resonant for an individual or group facing such a problem precisely when it provides a way to overcome such dissonance, for example, by reinterpreting the situation in such a way as to produce consonance between attunements.

We have not discussed what psychological processes determine the intensity of feelings of dissonance or consonance, and we do not claim to have the relevant psychological expertise, but it is consistent with the account we have proposed (i) that harmonization, especially at the group level, need not be an instantaneous process, but can occur gradually and as the result of a string of interactions, and (ii) that the fact of there being an extended process that people engage in is a contributor to the strength of consonance experienced (or indeed to the build-up of dissonance in case no resolution to the problem is found). This latter point, as regards the importance of process, relates to the broader intuition that we gain more satisfaction from solving problems that we have attended to for a while than from those that we solved more or less instantaneously, since in the latter case we perhaps didn't see them as "real" problems at all. This idea fits in naturally with the musical metaphor: sophisticated composers do not simply provide consonance at all times, but rather exploit discord, resolving tension only once the dissonance has become manifest and perhaps even unnerving. A feeling of harmony is not a long-term state, but a reaction to change.[62]

61. McDonnell, Bail, and Tavory, "A Theory of Resonance," 8.
62. Let us note a desideratum of a theory of resonance, as seen in McDonnell, Bail, and Tavory's discussion:

> A pragmatist approach enabled us to distinguish between resonance and Durkheimian moments of "collective effervescence" [Durkheim, *The Elementary Forms of Religious Life*] or Collins's [*Interaction Ritual Chains*]. Rather than the heightened emotions one feels when engaging in ritualized interactions with objects, an experience that draws attention to and reinforces group beliefs and commitments, resonance produces heightened emotions as people come to novel solutions. Resonance, then, is closer to Dewey's (1934) notion of "having an experience" [Dewey, *Art as Experience*]—resulting from a process of

The examples we have given above are largely concerned with political framings and with what is commonly called the cultural resonance of those frames. Even though they take embedding in preexisting culture to have been overemphasized, McDonnell et al. see themselves as contributing to the development of a theory of cultural resonance. Yet in all the cases we have discussed, and in accord with McDonnell et al.'s account, resonance might result not only because of broad properties of a culture, but from individual peculiarities of an experiencer. Something is personally resonant with someone when it induces harmony by manifesting consonance of attunements that are distinctive to that individual. By contrast, cultural resonance, the greater concern of this book, and of the prior literature on political framing, is harmony resulting from consonance with the distinctive attunements of an ideology, the distinctive collective attunements of a community of practice.

3.10. Conclusion

In this chapter, we have developed an account of harmonization at both the individual and group levels. It is designed to help describe both political processes at different scales, a range that includes personal interactions, social media, and mass rallies. The resulting framework has properties that are quite unlike those found in more standard content-delivery models of communication. To end, let us consider one by one what we presented as the central relevant features of the content-delivery model, and the ways in which our analysis of harmonization changes the picture.

1. *Neutrality of integration*: In the content-delivery model, the form of the message is just packaging. But harmonization is strongly affected by form: people may become attuned to forms of collective activity before they fully develop matching cognitive attunements. A political rally, to state the obvious, is more about form than content.

2. *Short-termism*: The content-delivery model has led to a focus on comprehension and integration of a single utterance. Harmonization can be both faster and slower. There are important communicative effects

---

"undergoing" that leads to consummation when an unexpected solution is found. ("A Theory of Resonance," 9)

The desideratum, then, is that a feeling of resonance be separated both from feelings of collective excitement, and from the sense of consonance with a community of practice experienced by those performing established behaviors ritualistically, i.e., in a highly standardized way. It should be noted here that our definitions of collective effervescence and resonance are related but distinct, since we define collective effervescence in part in terms of maintenance of joint attention, which does not play a direct role in our definition of degree of resonance. Although we do not analyze Collins's model in the same depth, we discuss it further in chapter 6, where we consider the process of ideological transmission in terms of accommodation, in particular accommodation of practices.

that are faster than deliberative integration (or non-integration) of a message, but there are also much longer-term processes, whereby consonance or dissonance may develop slowly, and whereby the effects of multiple concordant communicative interactions can slowly drive re-attunement and fragmentation across large subsystems of attunements.

3. *Passive transmission*: Whereas the content-delivery model centers on a deliberative process of intention recognition, we have emphasized the nondeliberative character of many communicative processes. In particular, people do not have full control over how they will react to hateful speech, to the excitement of a group, or over what political messages will resonate with them.

4. *Propositionality*: We have emphasized the central role that change in dispositional and emotional attunements plays in communication. The power of words rests in large part on their ability to drive emotion and action. As we have seen, the power to shape beliefs may follow from that power, because harmonization does not give priority to cognitive attunements. Our Festinger-influenced model allows that rational deliberation over propositionally represented evidence may sometimes play second fiddle.

5. *Deliberativity*: We do not deny the existence of processes of belief revision as deliberative reasoning, but inspired by Gilbert's research, as well as by classic work on collective effervescence and group contagion, we have emphasized that both many short-term effects of communication, and many longer-term effects of harmonization, are largely nondeliberative.

6. *Noncompulsion*: The nondeliberativity of many aspects of harmonization implies that people can be affected by communication in ways they would not wish. The immediate resonances of hateful speech may include the driving of attention and felt pain. A mass rally may semi-automatically arouse duplication of activation patterns within attendees, and a compulsion to harmonize with the group.

To close this chapter, let us briefly consider an important example in which the concepts we have discussed are important, in particular the notion of dissonance. Festinger's best-known work on dissonance concerned cults, but the term "cult" is negatively charged. Those inside a cult would not describe it as such. Applying the term "cult" to a group also suggests that a group is small enough that its ideology can clearly be distinguished from that of the mainstream. Nonetheless, there are times when a broad majority of people collectively exhibit behavior that fits well with the cults that Festinger described.

Let us briefly consider the way people think and behave with respect to the environment in a time of dramatic climate change. It turns out that being told regularly, in the language of science, that the climate is in a death spiral that will kill and displace millions or billions of people, has remarkably little effect. People of all stripes continue to vote, consume, exploit, and argue in much the same way as before. To many people, it is those worrying about climate change who appear to be in a cult-like group, the climate-change alarmists. After all, what is science if not a sort of cult?

It is more convenient to believe that these alarmists have a secret agenda, say destroying our way of life, or drawing attention to themselves, and thus cannot be trusted, than it is to believe that they are right. It is more convenient because accepting that the scientists are right would imply change in behavior on a massive scale, a radical reorganization of economic priorities at a global scale that would challenge core assumptions of the dominant consumption and growth-based ideology. What humans are now doing in continuing to act as before while the planet burns around us is structurally highly similar to the way cult members successfully bury their collective heads in the sand and refuse to accept what should be powerful evidence. The big difference, of course, is that a small cult behaves the way it does in part because of how it is seen by outsiders, and this factor cannot play the same role when the group being considered is not small, but makes up a sizeable portion of humanity. Yet the dynamics are the same. Change of behavior creates more short-term dissonance than would acceptance of fact, and so behavioral inertia wins out, and humanity plunges ever onward in the direction of catastrophe.

Does Festinger's theory, or the account of harmony and resonance we have developed, teach us anything about how climate-change messaging should operate? There is no low-hanging fruit here, no easy one-step solution that we can offer, but we can make some observations.

First, if it is true that part of the problem of convincing people of the significance of climate change is that the need for them to change their own way of life produces dissonance, then it follows that messaging should not necessarily emphasize personal sacrifice except possibly when part of a heroic narrative. The message may often be that action on climate change is what is needed in order for people to maintain their lives, rather than that dealing with climate change begins with people disrupting the patterns they are used to. Considerations of dissonance suggest that calls to change individual patterns of consumption may therefore be counterproductive.

Second, work on framing in protest movements suggests that there often are resonant frames to be found even in the face of stubborn long-term problems, frames that can allow people to understand those problems in a new light. These frames do not come out of nowhere. A movement that remains stuck with a limited selection of frames that resonate with only a subset of people is unlikely to be successful in growing and winning over converts, as seen, for example, in Deva Woodly's extensive discussion of US fair-wage movements, whose extensive local successes have not been duplicated at a national level.[63] When people actively explore different framings, they sometimes discover new framings that work. It is not for us to say whether it would be more effective to use a social-justice framing, for example, a framing in terms of the rights of unborn children to life on a clean planet, or a framing in terms of the rights of the planet itself as an actor rather than as a physical system, or any other framing. It is a creative exercise to explore and develop new framings and narratives, and an empirical question what frames will work with what groups and when they should be deployed. What we take from the traditions this chapter builds on is that the development of ways of thinking and talking about climate change is of comparable import to the development of scientific understanding of the problem. For without a way to bring collective harmony on the issue to a large enough global community, the political will for change will remain lacking.

63. Woodly, *The Politics of Common Sense*.

PART II

Presupposition
and Ideology

CHAPTER FOUR

The Psychology of Presupposition

In this world, while "race talk" is by no means unknown . . . racism is located as well, and very importantly, in an undercurrent of presuppositions that provide no moments of awkwardness or embarrassment for participants, and that permit White privilege to be taken for granted.

—JANE HILL[1]

4.1. Common Ground and Common Enemies

It is intuitively obvious that when people communicate, they take a lot for granted, that they assume, that is, they *presuppose*, many things that their interlocutor is probably already familiar with. These presuppositions form the very fabric into which our communicative acts are woven, without which communicative connection would be difficult to sustain. To switch metaphors, the most basic role of presuppositions in our resonance-based theory of communication is analogous to the role played by a carrier signal, the frequency you turn the dial to if you have an old-fashioned radio. On this analogy, the physiological and neurological makeup of humans is like a tunable radio or walkie talkie, and the conventions of a particular language are like a setting on the dial, which determines the frequency of the carrier signal. When we talk, we presuppose a common setting. Presuppositions fix the basic conventions of communication, sufficiently to provide a stable background relative to which the modulations of the primary intended message can be recognized.

The carrier-signal analogy is hopefully illuminating, and yet it might suggest too limited a role for presuppositions. Presuppositions don't stop at the level of shared community practices, but go arbitrarily deep, including shared values when talking to someone who shares a taste in music or game shows, shared humanity when conversing with another human, and even some level of shared dispositions and attunement to reality when we talk to a pet or the latest gizmo on our smartphones. Unless we are poets or academics studying communication, we typically become conscious of these carrier signal-like

1. Hill, *The Everyday Language of White Racism*, 47.

presuppositions only when they fail, as when an accent or an unexpected locution suggests: you're not from around here, are you?

Beginning with the work of Gottlob Frege and Peter Strawson, the literature on presupposition made a significant break from the intuitive idea that
people presuppose things (a break that Robert Stalnaker later suggested had
been a mistake). Instead of talking about people presupposing things, much
of the linguistic and philosophical work on presupposition suggests that it is
people's words or utterances that do the presupposing. Thus, for example, the
act of saying "Sarah is at home" presupposes the identifiability of Sarah from
use of the word "Sarah." This move ushered in a rich line of work on how
presuppositions are encoded in language, driven by the discovery of a set of
phenomena that could not easily be explained in models of language that did
not distinguish between presupposition and other types of meaning.

Of particular relevance for the current project is the phenomenon of *presupposition projection*, which will play a major role in this chapter. Presupposition projection is the remarkable ability of presuppositions that are *triggered*
deep within a complex utterance to pop out, the presupposition behaving
much as if it occurred without the complex material around it. For example,
suppose someone says, "Most of us doubt that Sarah is at home." The speaker
is clearly not committed to the claim "Sarah is at home," and yet does appear
committed to the identifiability of Sarah, which occurs inside this embedded
clause. Here is a similar naturally occurring example. When the journalist and
broadcaster Walter Cronkite said, "It is doubtful that the awesome image of
this bomb will ever—or should ever—be erased," he was denying something,
and yet the presupposition that a particular mutually identifiable image of a
bomb was awesome is clearly something that he was committed to, and took
to be uncontroversial.[2] Such examples illustrate the way that presuppositions
allow people to reveal and share their commitments without making an overt
claim that they hold those commitments. This ability to say things without
being obvious means that presuppositions have a special role in persuasion,
and more generally, in ideological transmission, and that is why we are devot-
ing part II of the book to them.

Because presuppositions tend not to be the focus of attention in a communicative interaction, they can fly beneath the radar. For that reason, presupposition is often exploited in communication, as a way to manipulate someone
by using the presuppositional resonances of an action to shift someone's attunements without them realizing it. As Edward Herman and Noam Chomsky
commented in an interview: "There is a firm elite consensus on the legitimacy
of state violence—in fact, it is a simple presupposition, which is much more

2. Walter Cronkite is quoted in Senate Resolution 68, "To Establish a Select Senate
Committee on Technology and the Human Environment," 404.

insidious than assertion."[3] Scholars such as Marina Sbisà, Rae Langton, Caroline West, and Mary Kate McGowan have focused on presupposition as a central mechanism by which speech enables ideological transfer.[4] In this chapter, we use examples from experimental psychology and literature to illustrate these effects, and thus justify these authors' choice, and our own, of focusing on presupposition as a central mechanism of hidden ideological transfer. We will also demonstrate the importance of a related process, *accommodation*, which is the standard term for the way people adapt to presuppositions. Accommodation is typically a subconscious process that, as we will later argue, is heavily influenced by social, emotional, and dispositional attunements that are difficult to account for in standard models. We will suggest that accommodation is simply harmonization driven by social cues in the speech context. In cases of

3. Mullen, "The Propaganda Model after 20 Years: Interview with Edward S. Herman and Noam Chomsky," 12. As the interview makes clear, this is in line with what Herman and Chomsky had said in their milestone work on propaganda, *Manufacturing Consent*. However, in *Manufacturing Consent*, Herman and Chomsky do not use the terminology of presupposition theory, but rather talk of "assumptions." For example, in discussing the framing of the Vietnam war in terms of US victimhood justifying military action as retribution rather than as being inherently aggressive (in the introduction to the 2011 edition of the book), Chomsky and Herman state, "It is compelling evidence of the propaganda service of the mainstream media that throughout the war they accepted this basic propaganda assumption of the war managers, and from that era up to today, we have never found a mainstream editorial or news report that characterized the U.S. war against Vietnam, and then all of Indochina, as a case of aggression" (*Manufacturing Consent*, xxx). At a more general level, the developments in the current volume are compatible with the themes explored in *Manufacturing Consent*, which excels in providing historical evidence for the systematicity of processes that have yielded a relatively high degree of political conformity in the United States, conformity as regards central tenets of foreign policy, largescale military actions, and fundamental organization of the economy.

Although we do not pursue this agenda here, it would be natural to study in our own model Herman and Chomsky's seminal analyses of the framings used by politicians and mainstream media, the way in which much mainstream media tends to fall into line with regard to certain types of government policy, and, resulting from these, the ways in which public attention is effectively controlled, or at least limited. Framing, already discussed in chapter 2, will again be discussed in section 4 of the current chapter. The broader processes of alignment they consider would, in our terms, be mechanisms by which collective harmony is reached, with journalists and editors both individually and collectively dispositionally attuned to accept the easy story that governmental organizations, advertisers, and the businesses that own the presses provide, and to avoid the dissonance of reporting on stories or angles that would run counter to their own interests. Attention is an important part of our account of harmony, but we stop far short of attempting to describe in detail complex collective attentional processes at a national level as Herman and Chomsky do.

4. Presupposition and accommodation play a central role in, e.g., Sbisà, "Ideology and the Persuasive Use of Presupposition"; Langton and West, "Scorekeeping in a Pornographic Language Game"; Langton, "Blocking as Counter-Speech"; McGowan, *Just Words*.

both presupposition and accommodation, we rework these notions here and in subsequent chapters to fit into a model that centers their role in ideological transfer.

This part of the book, then, develops an account of presupposition, and the related process of accommodation, in terms of the notions of resonance, attunement, and harmony presented in part I. The literature on presupposition is large. An academic career could be founded merely on writing handbook articles about it. The purpose of this chapter is to introduce presupposition and show its significance for our project, setting the stage for the coming theoretical development.

Let us make a distinction among types of resonance that will help make sense of the division of labor between this chapter and the next, with the caveat that it is not, for us, an important theoretical distinction, but rather one that is practically useful in introducing presupposition to the reader. The distinction, which is gradient, is one of transparency, and thus relates to the notion of hustle. The division of labor simply involves beginning with relatively more obvious cases where a resonance is transparent, and then turning to the more subtle presuppositions that we take to be central to ideological transmission and change.

Any resonance that is highly salient for a practice is, in the sense intended, transparent, in that it is clear that it is associated with the practice. For example, saying "What she ate was a sandwich" makes the sandwich salient, and does not draw attention to the female who did the eating, which is backgrounded, but the existence of a female whose eating is under discussion would presumably seem obvious to the participants. So, some resonances are not merely transparent but highly salient, some are not salient but are transparent, being readily discernible given the grammatical form of a construction, commonsense knowledge about meaning and use, or dictionary definitions, or other factors that make the resonances culturally salient.

There are also resonances that are less readily discernible, neither salient nor transparent. For example, "The cat is on the sofa" has a readily apparent resonance that its use co-occurs with situations in which a cat is salient. This salience arises by virtue of practices involving the sentence's constituent words and practices of combining them. But the sentence also has as a resonance that the speaker is within a certain community of practice, namely English speakers, and that in this community there are certain practices of using the word "cat." This resonance is not one that would normally be salient among conversational participants when the sentence is produced. On the view we will develop, both the somewhat salient resonance that there is a cat, and the (typically) less salient resonances concerning the practices involved in producing it, are presuppositions. In neither case would it presumably be obvious to most English speakers that they are specifically presuppositional resonances, and indeed this classification is not one that we necessarily expect other academics who study linguistic meaning to agree on.

In this chapter, we will be concerned primarily with presuppositional resonances for which it is somewhat evident that they are resonances, although, crucially to many of the cases we will discuss, it is not so evident that they are presuppositional. These are the examples that are clearest for introducing and motivating the concept of presupposition. In the next chapter, we will turn to presuppositional resonances that are significantly less obvious, cases where the resonance itself is not necessarily evident, and the question of whether it is presupposed or not is not something normally considered.

Presupposition theory revolves around the explanation of distinctive patterns of inference and around the technical machinery needed to model such inference patterns. Our presentation does not focus quite so directly on inference but on influence: we focus on the use of presupposition to persuade. In the next two sections, we consider classic work in psychology through the lens of presupposition theory. We discuss two lines of experimental work: Elizabeth Loftus's work on leading questions in eyewitness testimony and their effects on long-term episodic memory (section 4.2); and equally famous work by Amos Tversky and Daniel Kahneman on prospect theory, which relies on differential effects on people's choices resulting from linguistic framing in terms of gains or losses (section 4.3). In both lines of work, presuppositions are crucial to the way that experimental subjects are manipulated. In the Loftus experiments, presuppositions guide subjects into a certain understanding of how to interpret what they have seen, and in the Tversky and Kahneman experiments, presuppositions guide subjects into seeing the choice before them in a certain light.

The presuppositional constrictions considered in sections 4.2 and 4.3 include many grammatical devices: definite descriptions, questions, temporal subordinate clauses, and verbs expressing change. In section 4.4, we consider what might at first appear to be an innocuous part of the grammatical machinery of language: pronouns. We start by considering literary cases in which authors use pronouns to establish common ground. In these cases, the author places strong presuppositional demands on the reader, effectively jumping into the middle of a story as if the reader already knew who and what it was about. We then give examples of a similar, widely discussed trick in political persuasion, using an *us* versus *them* pronominal distinction to present as if already established a common ground of who is a friend, and who is an enemy.

All of the many presuppositional constructions we will consider demand collective attunement. When that attunement is not present, people usually harmonize with their interlocutors without even realizing it, sliding effort-lessly right onto their wavelength. Hearers don't so much read the speakers' minds as meld with them. A mind meld might seem magical, but what we are describing requires no special powers. People's ability to establish con-nection, what we have termed *harmonization*, is no more fantastical than is the ability of musicians to play in tune with each other. We pay attention to what a group around us is doing and do something that matches what they do. Perhaps an even stronger statement can be made: as we pay attention to those around us, and unless we actively resist it, we become who they are, or who they seem to be. That is a strong claim, and yet such realignment of identity is precisely what the propagandist seeks.

Collective attunement extends what is seen in most work on common ground in philosophy of language and linguistics. One way it extends the standard notion is by incorporating social perspective and emotion, rather than being limited to factual information. Here an unexpected vista comes into view, a surprising connection between the dry mental accountancy seen in standard theories of how we calculate the reference of pronouns and the stirring of passions of hate speech. Both are used strategically to establish common ground. Yet no common ground is stronger, or more motivating, than hatred of a common enemy. This chapter takes us on a journey from presuppositions that draw people into particular beliefs, to presuppositions that draw people into groups that are cleaved along antagonistic societal borders.

4.2. A Collision of Language and Psychology

You witness a multiple automobile accident and are soon being interviewed by a police officer on the scene. You're asked,

How fast were the cars travelling when they smashed into each other?

"35 miles per hour," you respond. Your friend, who also witnessed the collision, is being separately interviewed. Your friend is asked,

How fast were the cars travelling when they hit each other?

Your friend says, "25 miles per hour." The higher answer you gave could have as much to do with bias in the question as with the actual speed of the vehicles. Specifically, the word "smash" in the question you were asked prob-ably had a different effect than the word "hit" in the question your friend was asked. Yet you would deny that there was any such effect: as far as you are concerned, seeing is believing, and you are just reporting what you saw. A week later, you and your friend are each contacted by an insurance claims adjuster, who asks, among other things, "Did you see any broken glass?" You think you might well have seen some, but your friend is confident there wasn't any shattered glass. You should reflect on the fact that despite what you remember seeing, your friend may well be right. You may remember glass although there was no glass. A biased question like the one you were asked a week ago may have had a greater impact on your long-term episodic memory than did the colliding cars.

Such effects were first reported by psychologists Elizabeth Loftus and John Palmer,[5] and they have been reproduced robustly in many further experiments. The demonstration of the effect of wording on judgments of speed and on long-term memory of the event is part of a seminal group of studies by Loftus, studies in which she showed that eyewitness testimony is unreliable and highly susceptible to the methods used to obtain that testimony. This work led to substantive changes in the US criminal-justice system. The wording of the questions above is verbatim from their experiments, in which subjects saw a video of a car crash. The difference of 10 m.p.h. is roughly the average difference found in those experiments for the different wordings of the question, and people who are asked the "smashed" question are about twice as likely to later report having seen glass than those who are asked the "hit" question.

What is the nature of the bias in the automobile collision questions? In the original paper, Loftus and Palmer didn't discuss this, beyond saying that the verb *smash* "biases [the] response," that the interviewer "supplies a piece of external information, namely, that the cars did indeed smash into each other," and that the questioner "is effectively labeling the accident a smash," and hence having an effect on memory representation. However, in a paper the following year in which she considered a wider range of data, Loftus identified the relevant linguistic mechanism: *presupposition*.

Although Loftus says little about the nature of presuppositions, we understand her idea as follows: the presuppositions of utterances are aspects of the wording that reflect assumptions of the speaker. The apparent assumptions of a questioner as reflected in the presuppositions of the question can change the hearer's representation of an event under discussion without the hearer realizing that this is happening. The standard view in linguistic theory at the time that Loftus was writing (although it was also challenged at around the same time) is that presuppositions can be conventionalized: when a linguistic expression is conventionally associated with presuppositions, the expression is called a *presupposition trigger*.

The most widely discussed example of a presupposition trigger is the definite article "the," a definite description being said to presuppose existence of the entity described. The opposition between "the" and "a," which lacks this existential presupposition, is the basis of some of the experimental designs Loftus used to show that presupposition was crucial in biasing recall of observed events. Subjects were shown videos and then asked questions of the form "Did you see X?" where X contained either a definite description

---

5. Loftus and Palmer, "Reconstruction of Automobile Destruction."

or an indefinite description. So, for example, some subjects were asked "Did you see the broken headlight?" which presupposes the existence of a broken headlight, while others were asked "Did you see a broken headlight?" which does not carry this presupposition. In numerous variants of this setup, it was found both that the presence of a presupposition trigger led to greater initial false responses, and that the presupposition trigger led to greater rates of false memory a week later.[6]

Returning to the original example in this section, how is presupposition at play in the *smash/hit* case? Although we will expand upon the explanation in terms of resonance, the basic analysis is easily stated in terms of standard presupposition theory and two well-studied classes of presupposition trigger: wh-questions and temporal subordinate clauses. All wh-questions ("how" being considered a wh-question despite its spelling) are standardly analyzed as carrying presuppositions. Asking the question "Why did you pay?" uncontroversially presupposes that you paid, as do "When did you pay?" and "How did you pay?"[7] Likewise, temporal subordinate clauses, which can be headed not only by "when" but also by "before," "after," "until," and "while," are all standardly analyzed as carrying presuppositions. Thus, the sentences "The shopkeeper smiled before / after / when / until / while you paid" all uncontroversially carry the presupposition that you paid.[8] Thus even if the

---

6. The headlight example is from Loftus and Zanni, "Eyewitness Testimony." There have been studies showing that the issues are complex. Zanni and Offermann, "Eyewitness Testimony," showed that the definite article did not lead to higher false memories for subjects high on a neuroticism scale, while Singer and Spear, "Cleft Constructions," show that at least in cases involving recent textual antecedents, subjects are as sensitive to erroneous information presented through some types of presupposition trigger as they are to information presented more directly.

7. While one can respond "I didn't" to any of these three questions, this is usually taken by presupposition theorists to be a denial of a presupposition rather than an answer to what has been asked. Note here that all of the following are at least mildly infelicitous: "#I don't know whether you paid, but why/when/how did you pay?" (The fact that "If you paid, why/when/how did you pay?" sounds better is exactly what is predicted on standard analyses of presupposition, since this is understood as asking a question that only needs to be answered if the assumptions in the antecedent of the conditional are true.) Note that although questions are, as stated, standardly analyzed as carrying presuppositions, the evidence is indirect, since standard tests for presupposition rely on projection tests, which cannot easily be applied to questions. However, if indirect questions like the *why*-question in "Mary wondered why you paid" are used, projection tests (discussed below in the main text) become easier. An argument based on this methodology would run as follows: (i) consider the pair "Mary wondered why you paid" and "Mary didn't wonder why you paid"; (ii) observe that both carry an implication that the addressee paid (and similarly for *when* and *how*); so (iii) this behavior under negation is strong evidence for the presence of a presupposition carried by the question.

8. The standard argument that temporal subordinate clauses carry presuppositions depends again (for this is standard in presupposition theory) on projection tests. In the

experimental stimuli had not been in the form of a question, there would have been a presupposition.

Given the presence of constructions standardly analyzed as presupposition triggers, it is clear that any question of the form "How fast were the cars traveling when they X-ed?" will be associated with a presupposition that the cars X-ed. For one group of subjects X is "smashed into each other," and for the other it is "hit each other." So, whatever the meaning differences between "smash" and "hit," those differences are transformed into presuppositions in the experimental stimuli at hand. Consequently, if we can figure out what those lexical meaning differences are, we will then know what the differences are in the overall presuppositions of the questions.

The basic difference in lexical meaning is clear. Although "smashed" and "hit" can describe an overlapping set of circumstances, "smash" is used only to describe high-energy collisions, whereas "hit" is used to describe collisions independently of the energy of the collision. You can *hit* the ground running, but if you *smash* into the ground, you're likely to stay there; "violently smashed into" is common, as we found in simple textual searches on the large corpus of books made available by Google Ngram, whereas "softly smashed into" appears not to have occurred in any published book prior to this one. Likewise, neither "slowly smashed into" nor "delicately smashed into" occur even once in a truly gigantic text collection. By contrast, it's easy to find cases of "delicately hit" and "slowly hit."[9] Similarly "the feather/pillow smashed into" don't occur, but "the plane/bullet smashed into" are (unfortunately) not uncommon. The fact that feathers, pillows, planes, and bullets all *hit* things provides clear evidence that "hit" is not restricted to either low-energy or high-energy collisions, while the fact that "smash" combines with

---

case of "The shopkeeper smiled before / after / when / until / while you paid," the standard approach is to consider embedding the entire sentence in an environment like that provided by a possibility modal. We then construct "Perhaps the shopkeeper smiled before / after / when / until / while you paid," and note that while it does not entail that the shopkeeper smiled, it still carries the implication that the addressee paid. This is evidence that while it is not presupposed that the shopkeeper smiled, it is presupposed that the addressee paid. Similarly, we can embed in the antecedent of a conditional: "If the shopkeeper smiled before / after / when / until / while you paid, that makes me suspicious." Again, the implication that the addressee paid survives, evidencing the presupposition. The presuppositions of temporal clauses have been recognized for a half-century, a thorough early discussion being found in the dissertation of Heinemaki, "Semantics of English Temporal Connectives." For a somewhat more recent discussion of presuppositions of a subset of temporal clauses, see, e.g., Beaver and Condoravdi, "A Uniform Analysis of 'Before' and 'After.'"

9. Our evidence for differences in frequency of such constructions comes from Google Ngram searches. These were performed at https://books.google.com/ngrams. A sample search is generated by the following query: https://tinyurl.com/mr37m78c. The corpus used for these searches is so large that the number of words in it is the same order of magnitude as a person might be exposed to in an entire lifetime, hundreds of millions, we estimate.

planes and bullets but not with feathers and pillows demonstrates again that "smash" is exclusively used for high-energy collisions.

Let us note in passing another difference between "smash" and "hit" that is of interest for the current project, although our suspicion that it is relevant to the original Loftus and Palmer results must be seen as purely speculative. This concerns what we have called *resonance*. While neither "hitting" nor "smashing into" an object implies a change in the object, smashing prototypically has a significant effect. Imagine that you're strapped for cash and buying a car, and you learn of two that are for sale, one that another car smashed into, and one that another car hit: which do you think will have the lower price? Furthermore, a direct object of "smash" (i.e., X in "smash X" rather than "smash into X") is substantially changed as a result: it is, in fact, smashed. We can hit something over and over precisely because hitting it may have little effect. But how many times can you smash something without putting it back together in the middle? Even though "smash into" lacks the entailment of partial destruction that "smash" combined with a direct object has, the resonances of the latter form might get activated even by the former, so that having conceptualized an event as involving something smashing into something else, we also come to represent it, associatively, in terms of things getting smashed. More generally, both communicative actions like uttering "smashed into" and noncommunicative actions like smashing into something have resonances, and those resonances may depend on arbitrary contingencies concerning the practices they instantiate, or similarities between these practices and others as perceived by an observer.

It is clear that there are significant differences in the implications and resonances between "smash" and "hit." Furthermore, as argued above, their positioning in the experimental stimuli (within a temporal subordinate clause that is itself embedded in a wh-question) implies that all these differences become differences in presuppositions in the case at hand. Whereas in the *hit* case what is presupposed is a collision between cars, in the *smash* case what is presupposed is a collision that is associated with high-energy and substantial structural changes in those vehicles.

Biased question experiments like those run by Loftus and colleagues demonstrate that presuppositions are particularly effective at influencing people's memory of an event, even overriding what they have directly perceived. Why is this? Three relevant factors are widely discussed in the literature on presupposition: first, presuppositions are normally taken to be uncontroversial; second (and now we must introduce some standard terminology), presuppositions *project*; and third, presuppositions are *accommodated*. Of these, the apparent uncontroversiality of presuppositions, discussed at least since Stalnaker's classic work on presupposition,[10] is self-explanatory. If Jason says,

---

10. The idea that presuppositions are taken for granted and uncontroversial is discussed in Stalnaker, "Pragmatic Presuppositions," in Stalnaker, *Context and Content*, 135–48. Taking

"The rain is getting heavier," his use of the definite article *presupposes* the existence of rain, and he seems to take this proposition to be less controversial than the *new* information he's presenting, namely that it's getting heavier. It's clear why uncontroversiality might be relevant for the effects Loftus observed: one would expect experimental subjects to be less circumspect and less careful when they integrate information that is linguistically marked as uncontroversial, than they would be in integrating other information, and thus the subjects might not take as much care to check presupposed information against their prior memory representations as they would with other information. In terms of our discussion in chapter 3, it is plausible that presuppositions are commonly subject to nondeliberative uptake.

In the classical examples of presupposition, interpreters regularly see them as commitments of the speaker, even when they are embedded in a larger construction that would otherwise prevent inferences about the speaker's commitments. This phenomenon is called *projection*. Questions are an example of an embedding construction that blocks the speaker's commitments. For example, when you ask, "Did Jason come to the party?" you're clearly not committed to Jason having come to the party. Two other construction types that also typically block speaker commitments are negation and possibility modals, words like "maybe" and "could." Normally these block commitments. If you say, "Maybe Sam likes tennis" or "Sam doesn't like tennis," or, for that matter, "Maybe Sam doesn't like tennis," you're not committed to Sam liking tennis.

Now, consider this example from an MSNBC article: "Maybe Trump doesn't realize that his Opportunity Zones policy has been exposed as a sham."[11] The writer appears *committed* to the proposition that Donald Trump's policy has been exposed as a sham. The commitment of this proposition remains even under the words, "maybe" and "doesn't," which, as we have seen, typically block commitment. Why? Because *realize* is a *presupposition trigger*, and the propositional complement of *realize* ("his Opportunity Zones . . . sham") is presupposed, and thus somewhat immune to the commitment-blocking effect of the modal and the negation.

Presuppositions can also project from questions, despite the fact that the primary function of questions is to find out about commitments, not to make them. For example, consider the following question from Trump:

Was Andy McCabe ever forced to pay back the $700,000 illegally given to him and his wife, for his wife's political campaign, by Crooked

Stalnaker's work as a starting point, Scott Soames built uncontroversiality into his definition of "utterance presupposition"; see his "How Presuppositions Are Inherited."

11. Steve Benen, "The Problem with Trump's Proof That He's Helped the Black Community," Maddowblog, MSNBC, June 3, 2020, accessed March 1, 2023, https://www.msnbc.com/rachel-maddow-show/problem-trump-s-proof-he-s-helped-black-community-n1223426.

Hillary Clinton while Hillary was under FBI investigation, and McCabe was the head of the FBI??? Just askin'?[12]

The question is whether Andy McCabe was forced to pay some money, so clearly Trump is not committed to him having paid this money. Indeed, it presumably being a rhetorical question, Trump in fact seems committed to the opposite. However, there are a number of presuppositions in the question. You can only *pay* something *back* if you had it in the first place, and the question presupposes that McCabe received this money. There are a number of other presuppositions, including the propositions that there was $700,000 illegally given to McCabe, that McCabe has a wife who had a political campaign, that Hillary Clinton is appropriately referred to as *Crooked Hillary Clinton*, that Clinton was under FBI investigation, and that McCabe was the head of the FBI. The question form appears to introduce a reasonable issue for discussion (perhaps suggesting that after answering it negatively, we might ask ourselves *Why not?*), but Trump uses the question to present all this presupposed information, which projects from the question, as if it were uncontroversial.

The paradigm Loftus introduced employs a sneakiness similar to Trump's question: presuppositions embedded in questions project, and are accepted as reasonable by a significant percentage of subjects, who are perhaps distractedly making a good-faith effort to answer the question that has been asked. They wouldn't even be able to answer the question directly if they didn't treat the presuppositions as true. Hearers do what's needed in order to coordinate with the speaker, for example, by answering their questions if they possibly can. This coordinative adjustment is a part of the process of collective harmonization discussed in chapter 3. We can also understand it in terms of what the philosopher Donald Davidson terms *principles of charity*, although Davidson himself does not distinguish clearly between presupposed and nonpresupposed information.[13] Davidson suggests that in order to understand an interlocutor, we use a *principle of coherence*, whereby we understand them as having an internally consistent worldview, and a *principle of correspondence*, whereby we do our best to take what they are talking about to correspond to aspects of the world that we ourselves are sensitive to, or at least would be sensitive to if in the speaker's position. Thus, if someone alludes to *the rain*, to a time when cars *smashed into* each other, or to *the $700,000 illegally given* to someone, we will assume that these descriptions are part of a rationally coherent way of looking at the world, and that they are parts of the world that we ourselves could detect if we have not already done so. When someone asks

12. Trump's tweet of September 12, 2020, is cited by Michael S. Schmidt, "Comey and McCabe, Who Infuriated Trump, Both Faced Intensive I.R.S. Audits," *New York Times*, July 6, 2022, accessed March 1, 2023, https://www.nytimes.com/2022/07/06/us/politics/comey-mccabe-irs-audits.html.

13. Davidson, "Three Varieties of Knowledge," 158.

a question, we instinctively interpret the question charitably, accepting that the things apparently referred to in the question really exist, and using these charitable assumptions as the basis for proceeding with the conversation in accord with the speaker's designs.

In later work, Davidson describes the charitable impulse of speakers in terms of "a policy of rational accommodation," that is, a policy of adapting to interlocutors so as to understand them.[14] This terminological shift is apt. Accommodation, which has been a central notion in presupposition theory since David Lewis introduced the terminology forty years ago,[15] is the process that yields the most significant difference between presupposed and nonpresupposed information. Lewis and others working on semantics and pragmatics have since understood accommodation in a broadly similar way to Davidson, as a process by which hearers adapt to the demands of the speaker. In our terms, hearers adjust some of their attunements to match those of the speaker in a process of harmonization. Although Lewis sees accommodation at play in a number of processes, the example that he discusses at greatest length and that has taken a firm hold in subsequent literature involves accommodation of presuppositions. The idea is straightforward: when someone says something that presupposes something to be true that the hearer did not previously believe, the hearer can accommodate by adjusting their beliefs in line with the presupposition. So, for example, Trump's eighty-five million Twitter followers could (before he was banned from that social-media platform) accommodate to him by accepting, erroneously, the existence of a massive illegal payment to McCabe.

Although our own analysis of accommodation as a special case of harmonization differs somewhat from those in most Lewisian literature, we are in agreement with prior scholars as regards a simple point that is crucial to the current discussion: accommodation of presuppositions is a different process than regular uptake of the primary speech act a speaker has made.

In particular, standard analyses suggest that, when a speaker makes an assertion, this is seen as a negotiable proposal for addition to the common ground. However, the standard view is that presuppositions are presented as nonnegotiable. If presuppositions must be accommodated, this tends to occur in a relatively automatic way that is not subject to extensive deliberation.[16] If presupposition accommodation typically happens in an automatic way when it happens, then it is not subject to deliberation.

14. Davidson's shift of terminology is explicit in his 1984 Lindley lecture, appearing in Davidson, "Expressing Evaluations."

15. Lewis, "Scorekeeping in a Language Game."

16. The description of presuppositions as nonnegotiable is found, for example, in AnderBois, Brasoveanu, and Henderson, "Crossing the Appositive/At-Issue Meaning Boundary," and in two works by Sarah Murray: "Evidentiality and the Structure of Speech Acts," and "Varieties of Update."

Let us however distinguish the *automaticity* of accommodation from its *rapidity*. The gradual acquisition and improvement of skills has a large nondeliberative element. When someone learns to hit a jump shot in basketball, they train and improve gradually though nondeliberately and automatically via practice. Accommodation can also work this way, particularly in the accommodation of practices (e.g., speech practices). The claim that accommodation is automatic and nondeliberative does not entail anything about its rapidity.

The term *accommodation* was not used in this way when Loftus and colleagues published the original studies discussed above, but the paradigms they created depend on experimental subjects' accommodating unsatisfied presuppositions. These and further studies have demonstrated that accommodation of presuppositions can lead to people developing false memories, with no awareness that those false memories arose through the use of language that leads them to accommodate false information.

Describing the series of experimental paradigms she created, Loftus explains that "information was introduced via presuppositions in questions, a technique which is effective in introducing information without calling attention to it."[17] That is, presupposition is a mechanism that can allow information to be smuggled into a person's mind, as it were, below the radar, nondeliberatively. In short, it is no surprise that foundational theorists such as Langton have centered this notion. It is one ideal communicative mechanism for ideological transfer.

4.3. Valence Framing

It is apt, writing in the midst of the Covid-19 pandemic, that we next turn to an only mildly adapted version of the famous "Asian Disease" problem developed by psychologists Daniel Kahneman and Amos Tversky,[18] which involves an experiment designed to probe the effects of *framing*. The very framing of a disease as "Asian" has become an intensely political matter during the pandemic, what would be described as a question of *issue framing* or *attribute framing* in the political-science literature on framing that we have commented on at various points in part 1 of the book (sections 1.3, 3.4, and, especially, 3.9). The experiments we now turn to were among a group of studies playing a pivotal role in developing the overlapping fields of experimental and behavioral economics, and that are now standard fodder for introductory psychology courses. The research emerged in a separate tradition from other work on framing we have discussed, in psychology rather than political science. What is at stake in the experiments is not some particular attribute of a problem, like the country of origin of a disease, but rather the question of whether something is set in a positive light, in terms of potential gains, or in a

17. Loftus, "Leading Questions and the Eyewitness Report," 571–72.
18. Tversky and Kahneman, "The Framing of Decisions," 453.

negative light, as a loss. This glass half-full versus glass half-empty difference is sometimes termed *valence framing*.[19]

We now present the experiments and the standard analysis, briefly set that analysis in the context of the resonance framework introduced in part I of the book, and then turn to the question of how presupposition can help make sense of some aspects of Kahneman and Tversky's reasoning about the "framing effect" (as they termed it) that they observed. We begin with the experimental stimuli, reproduced from the original study.[20]

Context:

Imagine that the United States is preparing for the outbreak of an unusual Asian disease, which is expected to kill 600 people. Two alternative programs to combat the disease have been proposed. Assume that the exact scientific estimates of the consequences of the programs are as follows:

Loss-framing decision problem:

i. If program A′ is adopted, 400 people will die.
ii. If program B′ is adopted, there is a one-third probability that nobody will die and a two-thirds probability that 600 people will die.

In the original study, 78 percent of subjects chose the option that preserved a one-third probability of nobody dying. However, it will come as no surprise that the wording of the choices is crucial. In a second condition, subjects saw the same initial context, but wording in terms of lives saved rather than lost.

Gain-framing decision problem:

i. If program A is adopted, 200 people will be saved.
ii. If program B is adopted, there is a one-third probability that 600 people will be saved and a two-thirds probability that no people will be saved.

This reversed typical preferences, as a clear majority (72 percent) in this condition preferred the safe option, a guarantee of lives being saved. These experiments, and the attendant effects, are among the most reproduced in

---

19. Chong and Druckman, "Framing Theory." For an application of valence framing to electoral issues in political psychology, see, e.g., Bizer and Petty, "How We Conceptualize Our Attitudes Matters."

20. Kahneman and Tversky, "Choices, Values and Frames." The context and framing conditions are presented using the text from the original study, but with our headings and numbering. The design is between-subjects, so subjects had only seen one of the two framings when making their choice.

psychology, although many studies have differed in important respects from the original.[21]

The stimuli are designed in order to reveal departures from the predictions of classical decision theory, based on the assumption that people maximize expected utility. The experiment is designed so that all four options have the same expected utility, since in each option there is an overall expectation that 200 people will live and 400 will die.[22] Thus, expected-utility theory suggests that in both conditions, subjects will be indifferent to the options, predicting a roughly 50/50 split in both conditions, and certainly no reversal of preferences from one condition to the other.

Kahneman and Tversky explain the data using one part of what they term *prospect* theory, a theory in tune with our project insofar as it focuses on the context-sensitive nature of human decision-making. Options looked at from one angle can seem very different than from another; they present quite different prospects ("prospect" coming from the Latin *prospectus*, "view"). The central idea relevant to the preference reversal in the Asian Disease problem is that people have diminishing sensitivity to increasingly large gains or losses. This idea is essentially as old as the above method for calculating expected utility, both being products of the Swiss polymath Daniel Bernoulli, over three centuries ago.[23]

In standard decision theory, it shouldn't matter to your choices on simple decision problems whether you're a billionaire or a pauper. But think about the difference between how happy you'd feel if someone gave you a free ticket in a lottery and you won nothing, versus how you'd feel if you won a hundred dollars. A pretty big difference, right? Now think about the difference between how happy you'd feel if you won a million and how you'd feel if you

21. Of particular note are the reproductions in the Many Labs Replication Project, which used materials very close to the originals, and the 1998 meta-analysis of Kühberger, recently updated and extended by Steiger and Kühberger. Overall, these studies have shown that the effects are robust in close replications of the original, although the effect size is smaller than found in the original study, and somewhat robust in studies that vary significantly from the original. See Klein et al., "Investigating Variation in Replicability"; Kühberger, "The Influence of Framing on Risky Decisions"; Steiger and Kühberger, "A Meta-analytic Re-appraisal of the Framing Effect."

22. Assuming that (negative) utility is proportional to the number of deaths, the expected utility of option (i), a one-third probability of 0 dying (i.e., 600 saved), and a two-thirds probability of 600 dying (0 saved) gives $\frac{1}{3} * 0 + \frac{2}{3} * 600 = 400$ deaths expected (200 expected to be saved). This obviously gives the same as the expected utility of option (ii), which is presented as a guaranteed 400 deaths (again, 200 saved).

23. The ideas emerged in Bernoulli's solution to the St. Petersburg lottery problem: Bernoulli, "Exposition of a New Theory on the Measurement of Risk." Technically, the property of classical decision theory that Kahneman and Tversky are arguing against is the property of decision problems being invariant under addition and subtraction of a fixed sum to all options, a property that is already lacking under Bernoulli's analysis.

won $1,000,100. Not so much difference! That is, as the gains grow big, we become increasingly indifferent to small further gains. Contrarily, whereas a loss of $1K would count for most of us as a pretty bad day at the races, few of us would say there's a great deal of difference between a day when we lost $50K and a day when we lost $51K. Of course, in each case the difference, $1K, is the same. We might say that the prospect of that $1K is very different at a distance of $50K than it is right up close.

The effects follow immediately. Each time a big number is presented (600 saved or 600 dying), that number is effectively discounted slightly more than the smaller numbers (400, 200, or 0). To see the effects of discounting in an oversimplified way, try replacing every occurrence of 600 by 500 in the problems, but leave everything else the same. It is immediately clear that in the loss framing, option ii, the risky option, has higher expected utility, because what was 600 deaths risked has become 100 deaths less awful. Similarly, in the gain framing, the risky option suddenly has lower utility than it had before, because the 600 saved has been replaced with 500 people saved. Hence in this case we get a preference reversal: as Kahneman and Tversky put it, people are risk averse for gains.[24]

We can see Kahneman and Tversky as having revealed a problematic idealization in classical economic theory. The traditional, idealized model takes any object of desire, whether it is people being alive rather than dead, or a sum of money, to be equally desirable whatever the situation. But as we have seen, this idealization does not match intuition. A hundred dollars is a nice little gain, but has less value to you when judged as part of a gain of a million: on top of a million it seems remote and unimportant. What Kahneman and Tversky tell us is that value is not absolute, but is relative to some reference point. And moving that reference point may even turn a perceived gain into a perceived loss or vice versa. This, they claim, is what happens in the Asian

24. We note that our characterization of the problem suggests a hypothesis that, to our knowledge, has not yet been directly tested in the large literature on this problem: perhaps what is discounted is the numeric values themselves, not the utilities of the different options. That is, perhaps people don't merely have skewed perceptions of the value of 600 deaths (or lives) relative to 400 deaths (or lives), but rather have skewed perceptions of the quantity 600 relative to the quantity 400. This together with a standardly observed additional effect of negativity dominance, that whatever people feel bad about has heightened salience or significance relative to what they feel good about, would yield the standardly observed S-curve of value, steeper for negatives than positives, at the heart of Kahneman and Tversky's model. If this were true, then in an affectively fairly neutral issue like how far away an unnamed object is, we should still see similar effects. Thus it would be predicted that option (i) will be preferred in the following judgment: "Which is further away: (i) something definitely 400 miles away, or (ii) something with a ⅓ chance of being 0 miles away, and a ⅔ chance of being 600 miles away?" We speculate that if there is any such effect, it is smaller than the effects Kahneman and Tversky hypothesize.

Disease problem. They say that *framing* the decision problem using the word "save" sets up a reference point in which the default state is people dying, so that people tend to view the problem in terms of possible gains, whereas framing the problem using the word "die" sets up a reference point in which the default state is people being alive, so that people tend to view the problem in terms of possible losses.

Kahneman and Tversky's modeling is convincing. However, their use of the term "framing" labels a phenomenon without providing any insight into how it relates to the lexical semantics of the expressions as conceived of in linguistics, philosophy of language, or lexicography. Neither does their notion of framing relate in any way that's been made explicit to standard notions in the theory of how language is used, pragmatics. It is not at all obvious where in the theory of meaning Kahneman and Tversky's notion of framing resides. Let us now consider in general terms how their notion of framing might relate to resonance, attunement, and the standard concept of attention, which played a big role in our discussion of harmonization, and then turn to the issue of more immediate import to the current chapter, the relevance of presupposition.

There is a lot going on in the frames used in the Asian Disease problem, and even more going on in the many other variants in the literature that we are not considering here. At the very least, we can reframe the framing discussion in our own terms, by saying that the difference between the conditions is one of resonance: the *saving lives* wording has different resonances than the *people dying* wording. In these terms, probably the most important difference between the wordings concerns the fact that people have different emotional attunements to uses of "saving lives" than to uses of "people dying"; that is, the first has an emotionally positive resonance, and the second has an emotionally negative resonance. We can also say, relatedly, that the two wordings have different attentional effects. Whereas "saving lives" draws attention to a positive aspect of the outcome, "people dying" draws attention to a negative aspect of the outcome.

Neither of these differences in resonance have to do with reference point setting per se. They have rather to do with how people feel about the outcomes, and what people focus on. Let us now consider what Kahneman and Tversky's analysis that the two framings induce different reference points amounts to. The mechanism by which "save" sets up a reference point in which the default state is people dying is not mysterious. It's presupposition. You can only save money that you would otherwise have had to spend, you can only save time if you expected a task to require it, and you can only save people's lives if they were otherwise going to die. Describing an action as "saving" presupposes an expected loss, although certainly the presupposition is not as transparently worn on the sleeve of the word "save," the presupposition trigger, as with many other cases discussed in this chapter. It's a testament to the siloed nature of academia that the framings in the Asian

Disease problem stimuli have not, to our knowledge, been analyzed explicitly in terms of presupposition before.[25]

We know this is a case of presupposition rather than some other aspect of the meaning, because the standard diagnostic for presupposition, the property of *projectivity*, tells us. To use this test to figure out whether an expression presupposes some feature of context, we check whether we would normally expect that feature to be present in both simple positive uses of the expression, and in uses where the expression is embedded in a way that would tend to suppress a speaker's commitments, say because the utterance expresses a denial, a question, or a hypothetical, and the ordinary meaning is thus not asserted but questioned, denied, or merely hypothesized. (For detailed discussion of projectivity, see section 5.4.) So let's test the claim that uttering "save X" presupposes the expectation of loss of X (or at least damage). First, it's clear that this holds for a simple positive use of "save X." We see this in the names of thousands of organizations using a "Save the X" template, everything from "Save the Amazon" to "Save the Zambizi," names that only make sense under the assumption of a clear and present danger to X. Now we can look at embeddings. Here are three headlines using the verb "save," with embeddings involving negation, a question, and an expression of possibility:

The Pandemic Won't Save the Climate.[26]

GM/UAW Strike: Will the Strike Save the Cadillac CT6?[27]

Pilsen Residents Say Landmark Designation Might Save Buildings, But It Won't Stop Gentrification.[28]

---

25. One of the most influential discussions of the crucial features of the Kahneman and Tversky framing effect, Levin, Schneider, and Gaeth, "All Frames Are Not Created Equal," does not mention presupposition as a possibly relevant factor, and neither do the metastudies cited earlier (see fn. 21 on p. 194). Moxey and Keren ("Mechanisms Underlying Linguistic Framing Effects") discuss the Asian Disease problem in the context of an account of presupposition denial, but do not explicitly discuss the role of presupposition in the Asian Disease problem. Note that we must emphasize that we are not claiming that presuppositional setting of the reference point is the only factor creating what Kahneman and Tversky term the "framing effect." This hypothesis would be difficult to maintain given that some close variants of the experiments, including some used in Kahneman and Tversky's classic studies, use wordings that do not have such strong reference setting presuppositions, e.g., wordings that talk about the number of people who are alive rather than the number of people saved.

26. Headline, *Foreign Affairs*, May 7, 2020, accessed March 1, 2023, https://www.foreignaffairs.com/articles/2020-05-07/pandemic-wont-save-climate. The subhead, tellingly, is "Don't Expect the Clear Skies to Last."

27. Headline, *Automobile*, September 17, 2019, accessed March 1, 2023, https://www.automobilemag.com/news/general-motors-gm-uaw-strike-plants-cadillac/.

28. Headline, WBEZ Chicago, October 29, 2020, accessed February 23, 2023, https://www.wbez.org/stories/pilsen-residents-say-landmark-designation-might-save-buildings-but-it-wont-stop-gentrification/31fd3199-a5ca-4c72-9c45-e2b54a64feb1.

It is clear that in the context assumed by the writers and editors, there is severe danger of damage or loss to the climate, the Cadillac CT6, and buildings in Pilsen, respectively. This illustrates the projective behavior we hypothesized, and so, based on its projective behavior, "save" is a presupposition trigger, triggering a presupposition of expected loss. Hence, the two options in the gain-framing condition for the Asian Disease problem presuppose that the context is one in which mass death is anticipated.

All lexical predicates that denote a change of state or the lack of it presuppose some initial state, so that, for example, "stop smoking" and "keep smoking" both presuppose prior smoking. So, no diagnostic testing is required to demonstrate that the two constructions involved in the framing of the Asian Disease problem, "X's life will be saved" and "X will die," clearly have a further common initial state presupposition, namely that X is alive. But unlike in the "save" case, the verb "die" is not associated with a lexical presupposition that someone was expected to live or expected to die. There is only a normal default assumption of continuity, which implies that living things are expected to continue to live unless there are reasons to expect otherwise. However, this isn't part of the meaning of "die." The contrast between "save" and "die" in this respect is illustrated by fact that the first version of the following constructed example is odd (as indicated by the hash), while the second version is fine:

There had been nothing threatening the patient's life, and . . .

a. # fortunately, the doctors saved him.
b. unfortunately, he died.

One further nuance is that even leaving life-and-death decisions aside, *saving* something is stereotypically good, while the expected state that saving prevents is bad. We can add to this obvious fact that the inherent goodness of *saving*, an aspect of its positive affective resonance, is presupposed. We can see this by comparison with the verb "prevent." That the two verbs are different is clear: if someone is sick, you can *prevent* them from getting better, but you cannot *save* them from getting better. That this difference stems from the verbs' presuppositions is evidenced by how the presuppositions of "save" project, for example, in questions. The nonsense question "Did David *prevent* Jason from being splogged?" tells us little about whether being splogged would have been a good thing, whereas the question "Did David *save* Jason from being splogged?" clearly implies that sploggings are best avoided. Thus, *to save* is inherently good in just the sense that it involves prevention of an expected outcome that is presupposed to be bad.

Recall that we said that the Kahneman and Tversky account was incomplete. The problem is that their account includes only a partial explanation of what linguistic properties of the experimental stimuli cause subjects to set the reference points they use in making their decision. What Kahneman and

Tversky say is that one stimulus pair involves a framing in terms of gains, and the other involves a framing in terms of losses. This is fine as far as it goes. But we can now say more.

As a preliminary, note that if we are right, then there's a sense in which the two experimental conditions are not symmetrical, because one framing carries more relevant presuppositions than the other. Specifically, the *save* condition is the more semantically interesting case, in that it has the rather special presuppositions just discussed, whereas *die* just carries the normal presupposition of any change of state verb (that the entity in question is in a state such that the transition is possible, i.e., in this case that the subject is alive). Further, although your own moral stance may suggest otherwise, as regards lexical meaning the badness of *death* is at most a presupposed affective resonance, and not a presupposition that something *dying* is inherently bad. If you're a vermin exterminator, the more cockroaches die, the better. So, let's begin with the assumption that it's the special context in which you're trying to save human lives in a pandemic that makes mass death a bad thing.

The story goes like this, then. First, since people dying presupposes that they are alive, in the same way that any transition presupposes its start state, the loss framing tends to push the reference point as one where people are alive. Since human deaths are bad, the stimuli in the loss framing do indeed express losses relative to that reference point. Let us note in passing that this setting of the reference point is somewhat in tension with the description given to all subjects in both conditions, which in our slight variant is "a disease that is expected to kill three million people worldwide."

Second, since "save lives" presupposes a strong expectation of death, and describes actions that will potentially lead to outcomes other than what is expected, the gain framing sets up a reference point in which people are expected to die, and in which the outcomes are reversals of this expectation. Since death is both bad in this context and presupposed to be bad by "save lives," that reference point is seen as having lower expected utility than what is achieved by taking either of the *life-saving* options. Thus, the second formulation of the disease problem is a framing in terms of gains.

In both cases, the framing effects are produced by presuppositions embedded in the experimenter's language. We can then understand uptake by experimental subjects as presupposition accommodation. Experimental subjects harmonize so as to have a short-term collective attunement with their interlocutor, implying a disposition to reason about the problem in a similar way. In one experimental condition, collective attunement implies a disposition to reason about the problem as if it involves potential gains, and in the other condition it implies a disposition to reason about the problem as if it involves potential losses. If we take someone's *perspective* in this experiment to mean the reference point used for conceptualizing the problem, then what the results of the experiments suggest is that there is a fairly high level of attunement to the experimenter's proffered perspective. This is not to say, by the way, that we are claiming that subjects require a complex theory of mind to perform this experimental task. People simply have tendencies to harmonize, tendencies that need not be the results of deliberation. But here let us note that we are not alone in claiming that deliberation is not essential to the process of developing common ground. For example, Elisabeth Camp takes a similar line in discussing quite different phenomena: she has argued in her explanations of both metaphors and slurs that subjects simply have a tendency to accept the perspective that's offered to them.[29]

Analyzing the Asian Disease problem in full would require further discussion of exactly how the above presuppositions interact with the numeric quantifiers in the examples (a type of interaction that one of us has studied[30]), as well as a more thorough discussion of the specific properties of the context set up for both the *save* stimuli and the *die* stimuli. There is, furthermore, a much broader experimental paradigm involving reference point setting through framings, and that is itself part of an even broader set of paradigms involving interactions between attention and decision-making. What you pay attention to affects how you weigh different things in your judgments and decision-making. As discussed in the last chapter, attention is shifted by communication when we harmonize with our interlocutors and develop shared attention with them. We described these attentional effects of communication in terms of collective harmonization, suggesting that processes of collective harmonization can be studied at radically different time scales, anything from the instantaneous mimicry and mind reading of conversational interlocutors to the larger time scales of cultural diffusion. Joint attention of the sort relevant to the current discussion drives short-term collective attunement, the shared attunements we have at the level of fractions of a second or minutes. These shifts in attention are an important vehicle for propaganda, precisely because the cause of the shift is often not apparent to us. That the shift occurs at all, and especially that it's typically beyond our conscious control, demonstrates how subtle a power others can have over us, which is why manipulation of attention is widely used in persuasion.

Even a moderately comprehensive discussion of how existing psychological results of reference-setting paradigms, what is usually called *grounding*,

29. For example, Camp explains, "An author or narrator also presents the facts of the fictional world from a certain perspective, *which she expects us to share*" ("Two Varieties of Literary Imagination," 117, emphasis added). On the subject of slurs, Camp writes, "The automatic nature of semantic understanding in general, along with the fact that perspectives are intuitive cognitive structures only partially under conscious control, means that simply hearing a slur activates an associated perspective in the mind of a linguistically and culturally competent hearer" ("Slurring Perspectives," 343).

30. Beaver, "When Variables Don't Vary Enough."

relate to our project would require a book in itself. The larger literatures on attention and joint attention would require much more. So, we desist from further such discussion here. It suffices for our immediate enterprise that we have shown how the *framing* terminology used by Kahneman and Tversky and in much following literature in cognitive psychology and behavioral economics can be related to the presupposition terminology more standard in linguistic semantics and pragmatics. As we saw, this terminology is not unknown in cognitive psychology, since it was already employed by Loftus and followers. The *smash/hit* and *save/die* paradigms reveal that a single linguistic mechanism underlies two quite distinct cases by which bias is transmitted to a hearer without their becoming aware of it. That mechanism is presupposition accommodation.

4.4. Marking Our Common Ground

"It was now lunch time and they were all sitting under the double green fly of the dining tent pretending that nothing had happened."

That is an odd way to start a section. What makes it even odder than typical sentences in this book is obvious: you can't tell to whom "they" refers, or, for that matter, when "now" is, or recover anything more about the identity of the dining tent. Words are triggering presuppositions of a rich common ground in which various entities are joint objects of attention, and the presuppositions are unsatisfied.

The pronoun and definite description presuppose entities jointly available for reference, and the use of past tense and the unresolved temporal marker "now" presuppose a commonly identifiable time interval. These constructions presuppose objects of such high salience that the speaker's strategy assumes a full description is not necessary for coordination. And yet, the quote is the beginning not only of this section, but also a short story, by Ernest Hemingway.[31]

Presuppositional attunement is a central mechanism behind the formation and maintenance of us-them distinctions. We will concentrate in this section on the presuppositions of pronouns. By focusing on the presuppositions of pronouns, the way their use calls for *joint attention to a shared referent*, we can shed light upon how linguistic mechanisms can be used to bond and to divide.

To utter a pronoun in a sentence is to signal that a presupposed object of joint attention plays a certain role in the proposition the sentence expresses. The sentence "She disagrees, doesn't she?" would be odd out of the blue, because it is neither clear who "she" is, nor what claim she disagrees with. Presupposing joint attention to a female individual and a claim would be fine

---

31. Hemingway, "The Short Happy Life of Francis Macomber," 263.

in a context where you had just asserted, "Everyone says the queen should abdicate in favor of her son." In that case, to say "She disagrees, doesn't she?" would be to suggest that the queen disagrees with the claim that she should abdicate. Insufficient context is available when the sentence is used out of the blue for much sense to be made of it.

Absent an appropriate context, you could imagine simply accommodating the existence of a female and a claim so that the sentence conveyed merely that some girl/woman disagreed with something. Similarly, you can accommodate referents that you conceptualize merely as *whoever the hell the speaker is thinking of.* These strategies provide you with a way of interpreting the sentence, but they miss the point: you still don't know which things the speaker was presupposing to be centers of joint attention. In addition, you haven't managed to discover the proposition that the speaker expressed, merely a proposition that approximates what the speaker expressed and yet isn't *about* the same objects.[32]

The presuppositions of pronouns are a little different than those of other constructions we've discussed in this chapter. As should be clear, they're much harder to accommodate, a fact discussed in earlier literature and confirmed in empirical work.[33] If the speaker presupposes that two cars smashed into each other, it's obvious what to accommodate: that the cars smashed into each other. Similarly, if the speaker presupposes a way of thinking about a decision problem in terms of a reference point where some number of people are expected to die: just accommodate that reference point. But if the speaker presupposes joint attention on something and you've no clue what it is, you can't accommodate by attending to that thing. Here are your options: either give up, as the reader may have done with "She disagrees . . . ," or else take a leap of faith. The leap of faith amounts to accommodation by guesswork, filling in the referent as best you can, perhaps hoping that its identity will become clearer as discourse proceeds. But the speaker is asking a lot of you.

Sometimes, the speaker, or writer, does ask a lot of you. Here's a tweet that's circulated as we've been writing this book, a quote from F. Scott Fitzgerald:

32. In a situation where someone eavesdrops on a conversation that they are not intended to be a full party to, the hearer has no choice but to accommodate anything and everything presupposed by the speakers, or at least accommodate that the speakers take the context to satisfy the presuppositions. An everyday situation where this would occur would be overhearing a conversation in an elevator, and hence David Beaver and Henk Zeevat refer to the process the hearer must go through as "elevator accommodation" (Beaver and Zeevat, "Presupposition and Accommodation," 12–13). One can accommodate unresolved presuppositions in an elevator that one could not stomach in a normal conversation.

33. Tonhauser et al., "Toward a Taxonomy of Projective Content."

They were careless people. . . . They smashed up things and creatures
and then retreated back into their money or their vast carelessness, or
whatever it was that kept them together, and let other people clean up
the mess they had made.[34]

It was cited in the *New York Times* as having taken on a "new resonance."[35] The
general nature of that resonance is of interest for us, but we want to focus on
just one question: who does "they" refer to in the tweet? It is notable that what
has been elided from the original Fitzgerald quote actually provided referents:
the original began "They were careless people, Tom and Daisy—they smashed
up things." It certainly might be argued that the fictional Tom and Daisy are
still the referents of the tweet, and doubtless some of those reading the tweet
remembered the book, which they might well have read in high school. But what
gives the tweet a new resonance is presumably the fact that the quote can be
seen not as about the fictional Tom, Daisy, and their ilk in the 1920s, but about
their counterparts in today's world. But who, exactly, is being talked about? It's
presumably not the group referred to by "they" in the idiomatic template "**They**
don't call me X for nothing," if indeed that "they" can be said to refer to a group
at all, rather than being a sort of expletive place-holder. Neither is it the same
group referred to by "they" in the slightly less idiomatic but not uncommon
"They finally caught [description or name of criminal]," where the reference of
"they" is vague. Given this vagueness, it is not obvious that it makes sense to ask
what the pronoun refers to. It might be better to say that the pronoun marks a
role, a role that is presumably occupied by a societally relevant group like the
local or national police. The sentence does not clearly mean anything more than
the passive "[description or name of criminal] was finally caught."

The "they" of the tweeted quote does not include among its referents the
thousands of people who retweeted it. Neither is it the same "they" as in the
following National Rifle Association ad from 2017. Here we've highlighted relevant occurrences of "they" and "their," as well as "we" and "our":

They use **their** media to assassinate real news. **They** use **their** schools
to teach children that **their** president is another Hitler. **They** use **their**
movie stars and singers and comedy shows and award shows to repeat
their narrative over and over again. And then **they** use **their** ex-president
to endorse the resistance.

All to make **them** march, make **them** protest, make **them** scream
racism and sexism and xenophobia and homophobia. To smash

34. Natalie J. Ring, @HistoryCounts, Twitter, October 2, 2020, accessed February 19,
2023, https://twitter.com/historycounts/status/1312092169612726273?lang=eu.

35. Ian Prasad Philbrick, "A 'Great Gatsby' Quote Takes on New Resonance," *New York
Times*, October 7, 2020, accessed March 1, 2023, https://www.nytimes.com/2020/10/07
/books/great-gatsby-quote-trump.html.

windows, burn cars, shut down interstates and airports, bully and ter-
rorize the law-abiding—until the only option left is for the police to do
their jobs and stop the madness.

And when that happens, **they'll** use it as an excuse for **their** outrage. The
only way **we** stop this, the only way **we** save **our** country and **our** freedom, is
to fight this violence of lies with the clenched fist of truth. I'm the National
Rifle Association of America, and I'm freedom's safest place.[36]

Just as we noted in chapter 2 that when the line "Play it, Sam" is uttered in
Casablanca, the referent of the pronoun "it" is not explicit, so it is that in this
advertisement the referent for "they"/"their" is not explicit. We do learn that
"they" have a rightful president, obviously Donald Trump. We are to infer that
Trump is not another Hitler. "They" also have an ex-president, Barack Obama.
We are told that "they" use Obama for the nefarious purpose of endorsing the
resistance. And why do "they" use stars, shows, and an ex-president? Answer:
"to make them march," etcetera. For the intended audience of the ad, only one
thing matters about the referent of any of the third-person pronouns: it's not
"us." The "we" of the final paragraph are the right-minded Americans who recognize the danger "they" pose. These people's country and freedom are apparently
in danger, for the NRA is offering to "save" them. As an aside, although "save" is
not the object of discussion in the current section, it is no coincidence that the
same word is being used in an NRA ad as in an experimental stimulus designed
to introduce bias, a word with a clear presupposition of incipient danger.

The NRA ad above is not unusual as regards its use of an antecedentless
they to prime common attunement to an unidentified evil group. We have not
made a quantitative estimate, but, impressionistically, the device is common
in propagandistic discourse we have studied. Here are two "Qdrops," that is,
messages posted by Q, creator of the QAnon movement, a personage who, fittingly for the world's number-one conspiracy theorist, may not exist:

Their need for symbolism will be their downfall.
Follow the Owl & Y head around the world.
Identify and list.
They don't hide it.
They don't fear you.
You are sheep to them.
You are feeders.
Godfather III.
Q[37]

36. Dana Loesch, "The Violence of Lies," National Rifle Association ad, December 12,
2018, accessed October 12, 2020, https://www.youtube.com/watch?v=169zQ1g-*Ulo*.

37. QAnon post is numbered 184 and dated November 21, 2017, https://qanon
.news/Q#.

Why are we here?
Why are we providing crumbs?
Think MEMO.
BUILDING THE ARMY.
Not convinced by this spreading?
You, the PEOPLE, have THE POWER.
TOGETHER you are STRONG.
APART you are weak.
THEY WANT YOU DIVIDED.
THEY WANT RACE WARS.
THEY WANT CLASS WARS.
THEY WANT RELIGIOUS WARS.
THEY WANT POLITICAL WARS.
THEY WANT YOU DIVIDED!
LEARN!
FOR GOD & COUNTRY—LEARN!
STAY STRONG.
STAY TOGETHER.
FIGHT, FIGHT, FIGHT.
This is more important than you can imagine.
Q[38]

For an uninitiated reader of Q's many musings, the lack of explicit antecedents for the pronouns would seem to be the least of your interpretative problems. But this is to miss the point of these QAnon posts, which are supposedly revelatory leaks of classified information from a well-placed governmental source. With their crazy swerves between Koanic profundity, telegraphic urgency, and surrealist absurdity, Qdrops are to leaked government secrets what the sound of one hand clapping is to music. To borrow an expression from Gertrude Stein, *there's no there there*: it's all resonance and no facts. Indeed, to say there are no facts is an overstatement: it is hard even to find clearly stated propositions. Lack of explicitness, juxtaposition of suggestive, emotive imagery, epigrammatic imperatives, and puzzling allusions are all central to the QAnon practice. What is demanded of the reader is not uptake of information, but the embrace of contradiction and omission, and preparedness to see whatever is unexplained as something that has been intentionally hidden. What is presupposed is not just a particular collection of facts or referents for pronouns and other gnomic nominals ("the owl & Y head," "crumbs," "MEMO") but collective attunement to a deeply paranoid way of thinking and talking. And once you've accepted this presupposed common ground, once you've been, as QAnon adherents put it, "red pilled," your world will never be the same again.

---

38. QAnon post is numbered 563 and dated January 19, 2018, https://qanon.news/Q#.

Let us note in passing an interesting complication that we will not discuss in detail here. As the reader may have observed, the Qdrop involves a sophisticated three-way distinction not covered by the standard *us-them* dichotomy, a distinction between *us, you,* and *them.* Q seems sometimes to appeal directly to the reader, and sometimes to appeal to the reader indirectly, as part of the (presumably inclusive) second-person pronoun plural collective *we/us.* It is perhaps of relevance here that the identity of the anonymous Q is of an insider-outsider, hiding within the body of federal government, distinguished from other government officials by their revelatory understanding, but also distinguished from their legion supporters, who are taken to be outside the government machine, and not privy to the special access that Q has to what is really happening in the circles of power. The combined use of *you* and *we/us* is resonant with Q's nuanced position, at once one with their audience, and simultaneously a person apart, able to address them from a distant perch.

Returning to a very different but equally subtle use of an unresolved pronoun in an alternate world, why was the "it" in the *Casablanca* line "Play it, Sam!" not given an explicit referent? As we discussed in chapter 2, this device manifested common ground between the characters of the movie. But unresolved pronouns also serve to pull an audience into a narrative. Adding to the Hemingway quote with which we started this section, here are some more literary first lines that use this device (with emphasis added to the unresolved pronouns):[39]

> "**He** was born with a gift of laughter and a sense that the world was mad." (Raphael Sabatini[40])
>
> "**He**—for there could be no doubt of **his** sex, though the fashion of the time did something to disguise it—was in the act of slicing at the head of a Moor which swung from the rafters." (Virginia Woolf[41])
>
> "**He** was an old man who fished alone in a skiff in the Gulf Stream and **he** had gone eighty-four days now without taking a fish." (Ernest Hemingway[42])
>
> "Deep one night **he** was trimming **his** nose that would never walk again into sunlight atop living legs, busily feeling every hair with a Rotex rotary nostril clipper as if to make **his** nostrils as bare as a monkey's, when suddenly a man, perhaps escaped from the mental ward in the same hospital or perhaps a lunatic who happened to be passing, with

---

39. In briefly surveying the first lines of several hundred novels in English, mostly from well-known authors, we found no prominent examples with completely antecedentless female pronouns. We can only speculate as to why antecedentless male pronouns are apparently much more common, but will resist the temptation to do so.

40. Sabatini, *Scaramouche,* 3.

41. Woolf, *Orlando,* 13.

42. Hemingway, *The Old Man and the Sea,* 5.

a body abnormally small and meagre for a man save only for a face
as round as a Dharma's and covered in hair, sat down on the edge
of **his** bed and shouted, foaming,—What in God's name are you?"
(Kenzaburō Ōe[43])

"Thanks to **his** rare talent for keeping a diary over an extended period
of time without missing a single day, **he** was able to cite the exact
date **his** vomiting started and the exact date it stopped." (Haruki
Murakami[44])

"It was a wrong number that started **it**, the telephone ringing three times
in the dead of night, and the voice on the other end asking for someone **he** was not."[45] (Paul Auster[46])

"It was like **so**, but wasn't." (Richard Powers[47])

"**They** shoot the white girl first. With the rest **they** can take **their** time."
(Toni Morrison[48])

As a literary device, the unresolved pronoun presents the reader with a conundrum. On the one hand, someone is speaking to you as if there were already
sufficient common ground for you to resolve a pronoun, but on the other hand,
there is no such common ground. The device biases you, as it were, to read
on, for there is no other way to resolve the pronoun and the tension it has
created.[49] So in part the unresolved opening-line genre is parallel to what we
see in some online clickbait: "Use this one simple trick to . . . ," but the literary device, unlike this type of clickbait, offers at least a hint of a conversation

43. Ōe, "The Day He Himself Shall Wipe My Tears Away," 1.

44. Murakami, "Nausea 1979," 151.

45. We take it that the opening "It" is an expletive pronoun in a cleft structure of the
form "it was X that Y" rather than an unresolved pronoun, though it's not clear that there's
any fact of the matter. Similar comments apply to Richard Powers's opening line.

46. Auster, *City of Glass*, 7.

47. Powers, *Galatea 2.2*, 3.

48. Morrison, *Paradise*, 3.

49. The device of opening a novel so as to present the impression of common ground
when in fact it is lacking can also be achieved using expressions other than unresolved
pronouns. In each of the following cases, we can think of the missing information in terms
of an implicit question:

"You better not never tell nobody but God" (Alice Walker, *The Color Purple*, 1).
Question: Tell what?

"In the late summer of that year we lived in a house in a village that looked
across the river and the plain to the mountains" (Ernest Hemingway, *A Farewell to Arms*, 3). Question: Which year is "that year"?

"Many years later, as he faced the firing squad, Colonel Aureliano Buendía was
to remember that distant afternoon when his father took him to discover ice"
(Gabriel García Márquez, *One Hundred Years of Solitude*, 1). Question: Later
than what?

joined midway, as if the reader had just asked the author to tell them more about somebody's life.

Authors of fiction are connoisseurs and controllers of context. To stretch the terminology of *low* and *high* context slightly from its standard anthropological use (where it is used to talk about differences in culture), a literary author can present a low-context situation, in which there is little assumed common ground, as if it were a high-context situation, in which there is a great deal of common ground. Authors manipulate context not only to seduce readers into the web of their stories, but also to portray everyday situations in which there are clashes of assumed context. A beautiful and very relevant example is found in Flannery O'Connor's short story "Everything That Rises Must Converge." The young central protagonist, Julian, and his mother, both White, have just stepped onto a bus in the US South shortly after racial integration, and we focus on Julian's mother (already salient):

> She sat forward and looked up and down the bus. It was half filled. Everybody was white. "I see we have the bus to ourselves," she said. Julian cringed.
>
> "For a change," said the woman across the aisle, the owner of the red and white canvas sandals. "I come on one the other day and they were thick as fleas—up front and all through."
>
> "The world is in a mess everywhere," his mother said. "I don't know how we've let it get in this fix."[50]

Flannery represents a high-context Southern White culture, deeply infused with racism, in which everyone present understands tacitly what everyone else is saying. The use of pronouns, which is just one way Flannery constructs that high context, is striking. When Julian's mother says "we have the bus to ourselves," the reader immediately realizes that she can't mean that the two of them have the bus to themselves, for the bus is half-filled. She means there are only White people on the bus. Thus, that single, simple utterance, apparently not directed at Julian but thrown out into the air of the bus, presupposes an *us-them* distinction in which Blacks are the other, not named, but referred to in a way that is at once implicit and shockingly blunt. The second woman's rejoinder refers to the unintroduced other, Black people, with a third-person pronoun, and, in case there was any doubt at all about the deeply racist attitudes being portrayed, uses the standard dehumanizing trope of comparing out-group members to a parasitic infestation—the truly awful "they were thick

50. O'Connor, "Everything That Rises Must Converge," 10. Fittingly, the first word of the story is a pronoun. Although the referent is revealed later in the same sentence, it's only by linkage to Julian, who himself has not been previously introduced: "Her doctor had told Julian's mother that she must lose twenty pounds on account of her blood pressure, so on Wednesday nights Julian had to take her downtown on the bus for a reducing class at the Y."

as fleas." Julian's mother is clearly in agreement with the sentiment. Her repetition of "we" in the final utterance offers solidarity, albeit while sharing discomfort and accepting collective blame.

The antecedentless pronouns in the NRA ad (and likewise in the Qdrops) are functionally similar to the literary cases. The use of pronoun in the ad for which no referent has been made explicit has a strong presupposition, the presupposition that in comprehending the ad you have as objects of attention the same sets of individuals as Dana Loesch, the narrator. In every one of the above literary cases, the author soon makes entirely clear who is being referred to, but in the NRA ad, there's simply no clear reference, as in most propagandistic cases with which we are familiar. We are never granted the resolution of a full noun phrase describing the group in question, just the hammering repetition of awful properties the group has. You hear the hammer strike but have to imagine the wall it is demolishing. That is rhetorically powerful.

In work that was influential as Nazi ideology took hold in prewar Germany, Carl Schmitt argued that the distinction between *friend* and *enemy* is central to politics. In creating a political formation, entity, or group, one must appeal to a "they" against which "we" are to be compared. Schmitt writes,

> The enemy is not merely any competitor or just any partner of a conflict in general. He is also not the private adversary whom one hates. An enemy exists only when, at least potentially, one fighting collectivity of people confronts a similar collectivity.[51]

The NRA ad is a political ad, and the Qdrops are seeding alienation from the existing body politic—they call for the formation of a political alliance, by opposing it to another political group, a "they" against which "we" are to be compared. Such propaganda calls on the friend-enemy distinction to simultaneously resolve the "us" and "them" pronouns. But resolution does not feel effortful. We don't need the referents for the NRA's antecedentless "they" to be named because, to the extent that there is any definite reference, we can effortlessly figure out who "they" is supposed to refer to: it is, like "He Who Shall Not Be Named,"[52] the common enemy.

Recall here the discussion of the term "critical race theory" in chapter 3. We suggested there that this term, in its right-wing usage, lacks clear reference to particular concepts or practices, but is rather a role in a narrative, like the flag of the enemy. It is meant to evoke a narrative of existential threat. The fact that the term "critical race theory" works so well to evoke existential

51. Schmitt, *The Concept of the Political*, 28.

52. The phrase "He Who Shall Not Be Named" entered popular culture from J. K. Rowling's *Harry Potter* novels, where it is used to refer to the archenemy, Voldemort. In the magical world of the novels, words have the power to invoke more than shared reference, so the reader is being asked to imagine that there might be very special reasons for using a pronoun rather than a name.

threat evidences the fact that it is not causing the intended audience to worry excessively about the exact definition of the term, even though there are, as yet, no psycholinguistic studies of whether use of the term causes processing difficulty.

The "they" of the NRA ad, or of the Qdrop examples, has a similar function to "critical race theory." Again, despite its unclear reference, it does not appear to be hard to swallow. The pronoun marks only otherness, identifying a role in an easily recognizable narrative frame as being filled by an indistinct horde of out-group foes. In this narrative frame, what is under attack is a form of life that is presumed to be shared by a collective that includes the speaker or writer and other right-minded people who wish to protect American values and practices from liberal extremists. This collective is the "we" of the third paragraph of the NRA ad. To the extent that "we" has any clear reference, it is partly defined by opposition to "they." By positing a "they," "we" are united. But just like "they," it is perhaps better to think of "we" not as a specific grouping but as a role in a story: the good guys. The audience is presupposed to consist of good guys.

The use of such *us-them* labels helps build group cohesion in two ways. First, the mere use of a pronoun with no explicit referent presupposes collective attunement. Secondly, the vile properties ascribed to the out-group and the positive motives or beliefs ascribed to the in-group reaffirm the intended audience's feeling that the group they are part of is the right one.

For you to have the same sets of individuals in mind as Loesch does, it must be exceedingly obvious what those sets are. If you're hooked by the NRA strategy, attuned to the right things, then you'll feel like your attention is on the same things as Loesch, and you won't worry too much about the details, for instance about exactly which people are in the extension of *they* and which aren't. The NRA *they* is a maximal group of bad actors, the *other*, if you will, and whatever groups you hate must be subsumed within that maximal group. The group is understood as homogeneous, as acting in concert to tear down everything you love, with differences within that group of others minimized or seen as irrelevant. Likewise, the in-group is homogeneous: if you're one of *us*, that's all we need to know.

If you don't or won't share Loesch's values, the ad will probably make you bristle. Assuming common ground is a way of welcoming those who can accommodate into the in-group, but it can be just as powerful in alienating outsiders. In this, Loesch's style of speech is welcoming for its target market, but it is also divisive, separating those with her from those against her. It is a paradigm case of making friends by identifying common enemies. And the presence of common enemies, we speculate, is such a strongly motivating type of common ground that it is ideal for directing attention. A focus on a common enemy can distract from inconvenient details, like the fact that Q never evidences any coherent political philosophy, or the fact that the NRA represents large corporations that have a vested interest in particular political policies, and can drive attention to a commonality between in-group members that can help forge a political movement, or a social identity. In this, there is a surprising confluence between the bonding effects of in-group uses of slurs to label a common enemy (though not *reclaimed* uses of slurs—see chapter 11), and the use of *us-them* pronominal distinctions. This is a surprising fact about language, for at first blush it would be difficult to identify linguistic categories that have more obviously different functions than pronouns and slurs. Politics, as they say, makes strange bedfellows.

CHAPTER FIVE

Presupposing Practice

If the practices of the members of the same group or class are more and better harmonized than the agents know or wish, it is because, as Leibniz puts it, "following only [his] own laws," each "nonetheless agrees with the other." The habitus is precisely this immanent law . . . laid down in each agent by his earliest upbringing, which is the precondition not only for the co-ordination of practices but also for practices of co-ordination, since the corrections and adjustments the agents themselves consciously carry out presuppose their mastery of a common code.

—PIERRE BOURDIEU[1]

OUR JOB IN THIS CHAPTER is to provide a theoretical description of presupposition in terms of resonance that can illuminate its role in persuasion specifically and in the maintenance and transmission of ideology more generally. That burden of explanation will not be carried by presupposition alone, but through a combination of presupposition and accommodation. An action carries presuppositions, and it is the accommodation of these presuppositions that results in many cases of unobvious transmission, maintenance, and even creation of ideology. However, we defer detailed discussion of accommodation to chapter 6, where accommodation is tied to the broad processes of psychological and social alignment introduced in chapter 3, harmonization.

The work of this chapter is at once conservative and technically radical. We analyze a standard concept, namely presupposition, in a novel way, developing an approach that differs from others in the huge prior literature on the topic in at least two respects. First, whereas presupposition is standardly categorical, so that something either is or is not presupposed, for us presupposition is a matter of degree, as is the case for all resonances. Second, whereas presuppositions are standardly taken to be propositions, for us presuppositions are resonances, which may or may not be propositional.

It is true that various prior theories extend presupposition to other potential objects beyond propositions, such as questions under discussion. But these are treated as extensions of a basic notion of propositional presupposition. On our model, by contrast, presupposition is not, in the first instance, a relation to propositions at all. Each word belongs to a speech practice (usually more than one). Using a word is a manifestation of a speech practice. Manifesting

1. Bourdieu, *Outline of a Theory of Practice*, 80–81.

a speech practice by using a word simultaneously presupposes, among other things, that very practice. On our account, then, it might be said that the most basic thing presupposed is a practice. Presupposing practices, including speech practices, is a core example of presupposition, and not an afterthought.

Both the gradience and the nonpropositionality of presuppositions have immediate consequences. In models where presupposition is categorical, there is little room for nuance, and it is hard to make sense of the observation that some presuppositions project more vigorously than others.[2] This emerges naturally in a gradient theory of presupposition. In models where presuppositions are propositional, accommodation involves change in beliefs. But if what is presupposed is a practice or an emotion, then accommodation can become a change in behavior or emotion.

We begin this chapter by rehearsing some of the properties of the model introduced in part I and by showing what is missing. Then, in section 5.2, we plug the gap with a probabilistic account of presupposition that straightforwardly extends our probabilistic theory of resonance, setting that probabilistic proposal against a background of existing accounts of presupposition. In the remaining sections of the chapter, we first discuss various consequences of adopting the new model of presupposition (sections 5.3–5.5), and then, in section 5.6, segue into the discussion of accommodation that follows in chapter 6.

5.1. What More Do We Need from a Theory of Resonance?

Instead of thinking of meaning in terms of *content*, as if words were little packages with the meaning wrapped up tightly inside, we have suggested using a metaphor of *resonance*, a metaphor already employed in fields such as social-movement theory and advertising. On this view, the communicative function of language is not to transfer packets of information, but to establish connection. We went on to make a terminological distinction between attunement and resonance. Whereas things resonate, only animate beings can have attunements, which involve their dispositions, attitudes, or emotions. Things resonate by virtue of people being attuned to them. That is, something carries resonance by virtue of people recognizing or creating patterns of connection between that thing and anything else, including their own behavior or emotions. For example, a favorite cup may carry a cocoa resonance and various associated feelings because that's what you like drinking from it: you are attuned to a relationship (which you created) between the cup and cocoa, and similar cups may not resonate with you as strongly. However, the most important resonances for us are those attached not to individual habits, but to community practices. Practices of drinking cocoa may carry resonances of

---

2. Tonhauser, Beaver, and Degen, "Gradience in Projectivity and At-Issueness."

cold winter nights or of spiritual connection to ancestors, depending on the community that practices them.

A falling apple recalls Newton, where a bite of the apple evokes Eve, Snow White, or Steve Jobs. But what of specifically communicative actions or, more generally, interactions? They are special because resonance, on our view, is not merely incidental for a communicative interaction: it's the whole point. To see a practice as communicative is to understand it as having a function of creating a dependency between the attunements of individuals, to produce *connection*.

Approaching communication in terms of the connection created by collective attunement provides a setting in which to study nonideal communicative practices, for example, lying and insulting. Both lying and insulting yield a mixture of what we might term positive and negative connection, positive because they create common attunement as to what the speaker is publicly committed to, and negative because both tend to produce misalignments of attitudinal, emotional, and dispositional attunement. Indeed, they not only tend to produce such a mix of alignment and misalignment, but they are also intended to produce them.

In developing the resonance-based framework, we simplified in many ways. For example, we set aside the details of how, for example, emotional and similarity-based resonances of actions might be studied, and we focused on what we termed *associative resonance*, which measures the extent to which some feature of context co-occurs with an action, that is, the extent to which that feature tends to be present in the contexts in which the action takes place. We showed how this idea is related to a prominent approach in the literature, from the philosopher David Kaplan, who identifies the meaning of an expressive action like saying "ouch" with whatever is common to its contexts of use.

The notion of context we need is inherently "shifty," in that small changes of contextual anchoring can dramatically change what it is appropriate to say. It does not suffice for a felicitous use of "ouch" that there is, as Dickens's Mrs. Gradgrind put it, "a pain somewhere in the room"[3]; the pain must be the speaker's. That is, we need a notion of the context of an action such that we can differentiate between the *local* situation of that action and other *nonlocal* situations. Such a notion of context would enable us to say, for example, what the (local) state and (nonlocal) history of the speaker is like for any particular instance of the practice of saying "ouch." To take another example, consider the telling of a well-known, off-color joke. The local situation includes immediate properties of the particular joke-teller and audience, while the nonlocal situation includes not only more distant histories of those individuals, but also more general properties, like any tendency for tellers of this joke and their audiences to be prejudiced. In looking at the general properties of a practice, we should expect features of interest to be such things as the time in which it is

3. Dickens, *Hard Times*, 234.

being instantiated, and the attunements, group identities, and social relationships of the interactants. Thus, features of the context of an action must be
indexed to the action they are being related to as regards time, place, and the
identities of actors involved in various roles.

While the need for indexicality is a common feature of our proposal and
Kaplan's, a big difference, following a pattern that will now have become
familiar to our readers, is that we suggested that the relationship between
actions and features should not be black and white. That is, instead of thinking of a dichotomous notion of meaning whereby a feature of context either
is or is not part of the Kaplanian meaning of an action, we suggested a scalar
notion of resonance. On the model we proposed, something is an associative
resonance of an action to the extent that it is more likely given that the action
occurred than if it had not occurred.

In chapter 2, we introduced collective attunement as a variant of the standard notion of common ground, and in chapters 2 and 3, we showed how
many social and political phenomena might be modeled in terms of mechanisms that produce a shift of individual or collective attunement. So, political
persuasion consists, in part, in the use of resonant messages that lead people
to harmonize around attunements activated by the politician. In introducing
presupposition in chapter 4, we presented a number of cases suggesting its
centrality for shifting attitudes. So political persuasion must consist, in part, in
the use of messages that presuppose the ideas and perspectives that the politician favors. It would appear, then, that we are faced with an embarrassment of
riches, two distinct approaches to modeling political persuasion and ideological shift more generally. The goal of the current chapter is to show that these
two approaches are not merely complementary, but describe different aspects
of the same broader process of cultural transmission.

Here, let us return to a big theme of this book, *hustle*, which in turn
can be related to the well-established psychological literature on persuasion
(see section 2.6). As we defined it in chapter 2, persuasion consists in shifting someone's attunements in a way that would have been in tension with
their prior attunements. One strategy for persuading is to use a straight-talk
strategy, overtly suggesting reasons for adopting a new attunement. However,
doing so is difficult, because persuasion is needed precisely when the new
attunement is in tension with prior attunements, producing recalcitrance.
Literature in psychology and communication studies suggests that, instead,
persuasion often works through indirect routes that induce change of attitude through methods other than directly explicating reasons for the change.
Whereas in deliberative presentation of reasons the intentions behind the
argument are explicit at every step of the way, this is not the case for these
alternative, indirect forms of persuasion.

To take a famous example, an ad campaign that seeks to convince people
to buy a certain brand of cigarettes through presentation of a rugged cowboy

smoking does not make manifest the intention to convince in this way; it does not make manifest that you should smoke that brand because that will imbue you with characteristics of the cowboy. Quite generally, indirect routes to persuasion are not based only on straight talk, but involve hustle. That is, indirect persuasion involves at least some communicative actions in which the persuader is not overtly manifesting their intention to change someone's mind, even if it is clear that the persuader is more broadly engaged in such an act. It is obvious that a politician holding a baby in the crowd is hoping to attract more votes, but as soon as one cynically recognizes the act of holding the baby as motivated by electoral considerations rather than prosocial loving tenderness, the persuasive value of the act is diminished.

When we see a cowboy smoking or a politician holding a baby, we are not seeing assertions; we are just seeing people performing practices. The performance is crafted so as to appear incidental, as if we just happen to have caught the individual in the act of smoking or cradling, an act that is not portrayed as exceptional for the individual as normal. In a sense that we will attempt to make clearer in this chapter, the very act of smoking or cradling presupposes the appropriacy and structure of those practices, as well as the normalcy of the cowboy or politician performing them. We are not asked to see the acts as normal; we are simply presented with the acts, and their normalcy is presupposed. Thus, nobody tells us to take on board the gentle resonances of the scenes we observe; we simply do so as part of our regular perceptual function of becoming better attuned to the world around us.

We will not make too much of the role of presupposition in cases like the smoking cowboy or the cradling politician. Invoking presupposition here perhaps adds little analytic understanding to these particular cases beyond what the resonance framework might already offer. But the examples serve to focus attention once again on a repeated theme of this volume, the wide range of ways that persuasion operates without assertion. Nonassertive persuasion is central to propaganda and to political hustle more generally, and presupposition is one of the most well-studied mechanisms by which people change their attitudes independently of assertion. The examples we presented in chapter 4 were chosen to illustrate the function of presupposition in indirect persuasion, often in the context of speech acts such as questions in which no information is asserted at all.

To see why the model we introduced in part I of the book does not suffice to do the theoretical work we need, note two interrelated properties of associative resonance. First, it is *timeless*. The associative resonances of the practice of ordering an espresso at a cafe include the speaker needing a boost, the addressee being a barista, the speaker being perhaps a little sleepy before the act, the speaker receiving a small cup of concentrated liquid caffeine, and, hopefully, the speaker being somewhat livelier afterward. Some of these are states prior to the act, some after, and some overlap. The notion of associative resonance does not distinguish. The second property is closely related: our correlational notion of associative resonance is *noncausal*, so the mere fact that a practice has a certain resonance does not tell you whether that resonance should be thought of as a cause of the action, an effect of the action, or merely something that happens to co-occur with the action for independent reasons.

The work that is needed in this chapter, what is missing so far from our account of associative resonance, hinges on the oft-repeated fact that correlation is not causation. What we need to do is to distinguish the things that a communicative action is correlated with from those it causes. The features of context with which a communicative act is merely correlated will be what we identify as the presuppositions (or, more fully, the *presuppositional resonances* of the act). Correspondingly, the things that a type of act tends to reliably cause are the equivalent of what in speech act theory is termed the *illocutionary* and *perlocutionary effects* of the act, although these will not be a focus of the chapter. It is the presuppositions of the act that drive the process of *accommodation*, while the standardly recognized effects of the act are manifested through a separate process, roughly what is standardly termed *uptake*.

Having located presupposition within the resonance framework, we will spend the remainder of this chapter tying the resonances of interactions more tightly to the attunements of the interactants and studying the properties of the model of presupposition that results. Specifically, we argue that the model better accounts for the complex inferential behavior that prior empirical work on presupposition has revealed than do existing models of presupposition, and furthermore that the scalar nature of the resonance framework provides a novel perspective on a question that has played an important role in prior literature on presupposition, the question of whether presuppositions are conventionalized.

5.2. Presuppositional Resonance

We now build both on standard notions of *presupposition* and on the cluster of concepts that J. L. Austin referred to as conditions on the felicity of speech acts, sometimes called *preconditions* in later literature, although for him preparatory conditions were a subset of a larger set that might be generically referred to as *felicity conditions*.[4] Before proceeding, a short recap of relevant parts of the long history of work on presupposition is in order.

In the modern era, work on presupposition dates back to Gottlob Frege and Peter Strawson. They suggested the idea of presuppositions as necessary conditions for a sentence to be meaningful. According to this view, "I have to

---

4. Austin, *How to Do Things with Words*.

get my sister from the airport" would be meaningless absent the existence of a sister. Of the many later evolutions of the idea, two, both originating in the early 1970s, are especially relevant here. Robert Stalnaker's pragmatic presupposition centers on the notion of common ground that we have already discussed, and we will return to it shortly. The other is the notion of presupposition in dynamic semantic models, first suggested by Lauri Karttunen. Karttunen suggested that we think of sentential clauses as updating a context, with contexts being sets of propositions. A presupposition is then a proposition that must be in the prior context in order for a sentence to be used to perform an update. For example, only contexts containing the proposition that the speaker has a sister could be updated with "I have to get my sister from the airport." So, whereas in the Frege/Strawson model there is no temporal priority between what is presupposed and the content expressed, the dynamic model has an explicit procedural interpretation; presuppositions, as might be anticipated on etymological grounds, are *prior* conditions.

The bulk of formal work on presupposition focuses on the presuppositions of sentences or utterances of sentences, rather than on presuppositions associated with arbitrary speech acts. The model we will propose can be seen as a development of this line of work, but it also shares much in common with Austin's notion of the *preconditions* of a speech act. The preconditions of a speech act include both propositions that a speaker and hearers must believe in order for a speech act to be appropriate, and also social requirements, for example, the condition that the speaker is legally or otherwise empowered to perform the act in question. As Austin writes, making the connection to presupposition explicit:

> We might say that the formula "I do" presupposes lots of things: if these are not satisfied the formula is unhappy, void: it does not succeed in being a contract when the reference fails . . . any more than [the statement that "John's children are all bald" made when John has no children] succeeds in being a statement.[5]

Putting Austin's observation into our terms, the act of marrying two people by declaration, and the act of referring using a possessive description ("John's children") are alike: they are both communicative practices. Each practice is shaped by a history of use—the extension of the practice, as we termed it in chapter 2, that has yielded conventional patterns of interactive behavior. The pattern involves certain properties that contexts have when the practice is used, and certain ways that performance of the practice changes the context. In one case, when the context involves a person playing a certain role within the larger practice of a marriage ceremony, the effect of performing the subpractice of saying "I do" is to advance the ceremony in such a way as to enable

5. Austin, *How to Do Things with Words*, 51.

the enactment of the marriage itself shortly thereafter. In the other case, when the context makes some guy called "John" identifiable as such, and if this guy has children in the (possibly separate) context under discussion, the effect of the act is to make those children a topic of conversation. Further things can then be said of them, for example, that they are bald, or that they need to be picked up from the airport. What is needed is an account of the presuppositions of communicative practices that is general enough to be usefully applied in both cases.

Stepping away from the historical backdrop, our immediate goal is to give a theory of the presuppositions of communicative practices that accounts for a range of properties of presuppositions, including (i) their ability to leak out of embedded contexts, that is, their *projectivity*; (ii) the fact that they seem to circumvent the ordinary process of information update, often being *accommodated* without attracting the degree of reflection, awareness, or public deniability that we might expect for standard uptake of a speech act; and (iii) their iceberg-like combination of vastness and near invisibility. This last property of presuppositions derives both from the fact that presuppositions help determine our way of seeing the world (and it's hard to see a telescope while looking through it), and from the fact that they are not usually a focus of attention in a communicative interaction.[6] We seek to explain these properties.

The approach we now develop hinges on the solution to a conceptual problem alluded to in the first section of this chapter, closely related to issues raised in the final section of chapter 1. Put bluntly, we must deal with the fact that the notion of resonance does not distinguish between the background of an action and its effects. What we must now pinpoint, then, is the background of a practice, the things that typically populate the context of the actions comprising an instantiation of that practice before they take place, and without which the actions would not even function as an exemplar of the practice to which it belongs.

Our recipe for extracting the background is roughly this: start with all the correlational resonances of the practice and remove any resonances that are effects of the actions. At least, that would be the recipe if the resonances were simply a set of features. However, there is no set of features that are the resonances of an action. Resonance is a matter of degree. So, what we will do is subtract the degree to which some feature is an effect of an action from the

6. What we refer to here as "presupposition" is related to other standard concepts like "tacit knowledge" and "implicit assumptions" or to Camp's "perspective" (e.g., in "Two Varieties of Literary Imagination"). Against this background, the idea that complex systems of presuppositions can be virtually invisible should not be contentious, since the idea that complex assumptions provide a lens through which one sees the world and yet are themselves invisible until revealed by careful investigation has long been central to the entire enterprise of philosophy.

degree to which something is a resonance. It follows that what we need is a measure of the degree to which something is an effect of an action.

Let us simplify drastically by leaving unanalyzed the nature of causality. Having made this enormous shortcut, the problem turns out to be easy: the degree to which something is an effect can just be identified with the probability that a feature is caused by the action. We'll call this the *effect probability*. We can now define a dynamic notion of the presuppositions of practices, which we will term the *presuppositional resonance* of a practice for a feature, as the difference between the associative resonance and the effect probability. Our theory of presupposition in terms of associative resonance, itself defined in chapter 1, is then given by these three equations relating a practice to a feature:

1. Associative resonance = p(feature| instantiation of practice) – p(feature)

2. Effect probability = p(instantiation of practice-caused feature)

3. Presuppositional resonance = Associative resonance – Effect probability

These simple equations give us a numeric measure of the extent to which a feature is a presuppositional resonance of a practice, that is:

Presuppositional resonance = p(feature| instantiation of practice) – p(feature) – p(instantiation of practice-caused feature)

We have defined the presuppositions of a practice, but not the presuppositions of an action, that is, a token or instantiation of a practice. This is complicated by the fact that an action can simultaneously instantiate multiple practices, as when uttering "I would like some more cake" simultaneously instantiates the practice of speaking English, the practice of combining a subject and a verb to make a sentence, the practice of asserting, and the practice of requesting. For the moment, let us characterize the presuppositions of actions that instantiate multiple practices in this way as being exactly the presuppositions of the practices that are instantiated (combined using standard probability theory).

In thus characterizing the presuppositions of individual actions, we are temporarily sidestepping two difficult and important issues that have already come up in our discussion of the resonances of an action in a community of practice (section 2.5). First, the question of whether an action instantiates a practice is itself a biased question, assuming a dichotomy. Actually, it's a matter of degree: an action may be taken to instantiate a practice even if it differs substantially from prior examples of a practice, or it may be taken to partially instantiate a practice, and in either case it is far from clear what the presuppositions should be. Second, the question of whether an action instantiates a practice is one that reasonable people may disagree on. Who decides? Is it a matter of the speaker's intentions? Do other interlocutors or an audience get a say in the matter? An observing linguist or anthropologist? We will not address this issue in this chapter, save to note that it gets to the heart of why many theorists have adopted practice-based accounts in the first place, namely to produce a theory of action that is not centered on the intentions of actors.

Our account of presupposition is inspired by the dynamic accounts of presupposition and speech act models we've discussed. Despite this inspiration, our definition of the numeric measure of presuppositional resonance will perhaps be seen by practitioners in that domain as a radical departure (perhaps even an overly radical departure), since it doesn't closely resemble any of the standard definitions of presupposition in the literature. Most obviously, in *being scalar*, it departs both from both standard dynamic notions of presupposition and the standard notion of a precondition of a speech act. By contrast, the standard notions are *categorical*: it's taken to be a yes/no question whether a given utterance has a certain presupposition, and similarly for the notion of the precondition of a speech act. As in our discussion of collective attunement in chapter 2, a comparison with the more standard approach might be made by introducing an approximation to our scalar notion. Thus if we set a threshold probability, we could say that a feature of context is categorically presupposed by a practice if its presuppositional resonance reaches the threshold.

There's another somewhat related way that our account differs from many prior accounts: on the view we have proposed, presuppositions are not necessary conditions for an act, but *tendencies*. It may be of solace to any conservatively minded readers that necessary conditions for an action to take place will always have positive presuppositional resonance. Well, almost always! In fact, there's an interesting type of case where something that on traditional accounts would come out as a necessary condition, and hence as a presupposition, has zero presuppositional resonance. That is the case of tautologies. On standard accounts, an utterance of "The cheese factory is smelly" would presuppose that seventeen is a positive number, simply because the latter is a tautology, and hence "necessary" in classical logics. Our model does not have this property. The fact that seventeen is a positive number, although it may be true in every context, is not a presuppositional resonance of any practice. This follows directly from the fact that it is not a resonance at all: its probability does not get boosted by any action, because its probability is always 1.

In chapter 2, we took the reader through an account of common ground as collective attunement, and common ground is the central concept in Stalnaker's theory of pragmatic presupposition. Readers might then reasonably have expected our account of presupposition, like Stalnaker's, to take our adapted version of common ground to be the main ingredient in our definition of presupposition. Instead, we adopted a definition of the presuppositions of a practice that doesn't mention common ground (even indirectly, as collective attunement). This might seem a significant departure from a large subset of existing accounts, but it is not quite as significant as it might appear to be, because our definition sneaks collective attunement in through the back door. The back door in question is the fact that resonance is a very rich notion.

Let's go back to the presupposition literature. We can think of presuppositions in some accounts as providing a relation between sentences, so the sentence "The king of France is bald" presupposes the sentence "There is a French king." In other accounts, presupposition can be thought of as a relation between utterances and propositions, where an utterance is a production of a sentence by a particular speaker in a particular context. The importance of using a notion of utterance presupposition rather than sentence presupposition is manifest in the case of a sentence involving a first-person pronoun, like "my" in "my husband." An utterance of "My husband is late again!" would presuppose the proposition that the speaker of that utterance has a husband, and it would be hard to express this presupposition cleanly in terms of the presuppositions of the decontextualized sentence alone, since the sentence is, as it were, separated from the speaker's husband, if not completely divorced.

Having observed the importance of an utterance-based notion of presupposition in cases where a sentence is indexical, that is, indexes the utterance situation, it then becomes apparent that the issue was present with the classic "The king of France is bald." On a natural reading, that sentence implicitly indexes a time at which it is uttered (although there may be another, less obvious reading where the sentence spells out a generic claim about French kings, rather than referring to someone reigning at time of utterance). In "Pragmatic Presuppositions," Stalnaker goes in a different direction. For him, presuppositions aren't used to describe properties of sentences or utterances: pragmatic presuppositions are attitudes of people, a relation between a person and a proposition that holds when the proposition is in the common ground of the speaker and whoever the speaker is talking to. So according to Stalnaker, it is at best unhelpful to talk of an utterance of "My husband is late!" presupposing that the speaker has a husband, and we should instead say that the speaker has, when making the statement, presupposed that they are married.

We agree with Stalnaker that a notion of common ground is central to understanding presuppositional phenomena. Where we disagree is that, unlike Stalnaker, we see considerable utility in considering the presuppositions of utterances, or more generally, of behaviors, or, more generally still, of certain classes of behaviors, that is, practices. Although we will give a more detailed argument when we discuss the nature of *accommodation* below, the intuitive reason why we hold this view can be summed up as follows: there exist properties of language that are clearly conventionalized, since they identifiably recur with different occurrences of the same communicative practice (e.g.,

utterances of certain words), and which are needed to explain the communicative effects of those practices, and yet which have these effects somewhat
independently of the psychology, attitudes, and expertise of the person saying
them. A clear example is racial slurs: like grenades, they are still dangerous
when thrown by a child who doesn't understand what they are doing. When a
child uses a slur, a lot is presupposed, including the structure of the practice
itself. More generally, the resonances of actions are only partially determined
by the people performing them, and the conventions responsible for such
effects of words and other communicative actions are presupposed not by the
users, but by the uses.

How then, does common ground, which we have generalized to collective
attunement, bear on presupposition? Presuppositional resonance encodes all
the prior resonances of a practice. Given that interactants are involved in every
instantiation of the practice, and that each set of interactants has collective
attunements, it follows that the distinctive regularities in those attunements
will be part of the presuppositional profile. For example, the presuppositional
profile for a telic verb like "stop" might register a tendency for interactants
to be collectively attuned to a preexisting process, so that when someone
says, "Mary stopped smoking," there might be not only a presupposition that
Mary smoked previously, but also a presupposition that this is in the common ground. Similarly, if there is a distinctive tendency for people who use
the expression "caffè mocha" to have an above-average collective attunement
to the location of the nearest Starbucks coffee house, then that will be represented in the measure that the presuppositional profile derived from performances of the "caffè mocha" act attributes to the collective attunement of interactants to that location. To take a more politically relevant case, given that
there is a distinctive tendency for people who use the word "inner city" in certain contexts to be collectively attuned to anti-Black racist ideology, then that
will be in a presuppositional resonance of the practice of saying "inner city" in
those contexts. Therefore, certain uses of the word "inner city" will constitute
evidence of the political leanings of the interlocutors.

Although the presuppositional profile is not defined in terms of common ground, it nonetheless yields a sort of normalized common ground, a
pattern of distinctive collective attunements prior to an interaction. Let's call
the *attunement profile of a practice* the subpart of the presuppositional resonances that involves collective attunements of interactants.

As previously, we can give a discrete approximation of the typical common ground of a practice as the set of features of context that are above some
threshold (e.g., 50 percent) in the attunement profile. Thus, we arrive at a
variant of Stalnaker's pragmatic presupposition. It's like his notion insofar as
it involves the common ground of the interactants, but it is unlike his notion
because it is not the actual common ground of those involved in any particular
interaction, but is rather related to what an observer might discern about the

common ground (qua collective attunement) on the basis of knowledge of the extension of the practice. The extension of the practice includes all sorts of things that somewhat consistently hold in the contexts in which the practice is performed. These include the collective attunements of interactants.

Echoing classic work on externalism in philosophy of language from Hilary Putnam, one consequence of attaching presuppositions to actions and practices rather than to people is that interactions involving novices can carry similar ideological presuppositions to interactions involving experienced practitioners.[7] Consider kindergarten name-calling, say one kid trying to get a rise out of another using a homophobic slur. It might be that neither kid has a clear sense of the sociological background of the slur (a situation that one of the authors experienced in the schoolyard). Despite lacking understanding, the name-caller is somewhat attuned to a practice of homophobic slurring, and the name-caller's action has unfortunate, or even painful resonances. Without knowing exactly what they are doing, the kid invokes a homophobic ideology, a resonance presupposed by the practice of using that term. Clearly, if the slur were only used by kids who knew nothing of the history of the practice, the practice would over time transmogrify. We would no longer be able to say that collective attunement to a homophobic ideology distinctively attached to the practice. But if kids use the practice as part of a broader community of practitioners attuned to the practice, then the presupposition will be maintained. Furthermore, the name-calling little kid has just taken a step toward mature attunement to the ideology, albeit that full attunement is going to require both practice and observation of the community of practitioners, plus, as we will discuss in the next chapter, some affinity to that community.

We've seen that practices carry presuppositions. But the reverse is also true: practices can be presupposed. Similarly, the ideologies in which those practices are collective attunements can be presupposed. How can a practice be presupposed? Recall that the extension of a practice is just a history of interactions understood as belonging to the same category. They are understood as belonging to the same category because they bear similarity to each other, because certain features tend to recur among these interactions, and collectively these features are distinctive. Features can recur in at least the following ways, all of which may overlap: (i) there can be a tendency for the practice to take place in environments bearing that feature or in which that feature is found at a distinctively high rate; (ii) there can be a tendency for interactants to themselves bear that feature; or (iii) there can be a tendency for the feature to be a collective attunement of the interactants. Let's first consider a simple case of geographical restriction of a tendency, and then consider how one practice may be presupposed by another practice.

---

7. Putnam, "Meaning and Reference."

Suppose that there is a distinctive tendency for people speaking with a certain accent to be in Rome. Speaking with this accent then has a high presuppositional resonance with the location Rome, which is presumably why we would label it a Roman accent. There are also tendencies for the interactants performing the practice of speaking with that accent both to be located in Rome at the time of the act, and to have a history of location in Rome, especially while young. Finally, there is a tendency for those speaking with the accent to be attuned to Rome, dispositionally, emotionally, and attitudinally. Thus, speaking in the accent is correlated with behaving in a way that is sensitive to the geographical organization of Rome, having strong emotions with regard to Rome and all things Roman, and having a set of distinctive attitudes about Rome, for example, beliefs, hopes, and regrets, including metalinguistic knowledge of the Roman accent itself. Furthermore, one would expect these to be collective attunements of Romans.

What practices do practices presuppose? They have presuppositional resonances both with practices that occur at similar locations and times, and with practices with a heavily overlapping set of practitioners. Thus, practices of male friends drinking beer at a pub might have had, or still have, presuppositional resonances for practices of telling sexist jokes, and vice versa. But equally, the practice of telling sexist jokes might have resonances with male practices of behaving toward women in ways that make them feel uncomfortable, for example, the practice wolf-whistling, the practice of ogling, or practices of commenting on women in a way that reflects sexist stereotypes about their appearance and demeanor, prioritizing sexual attractiveness and quiet submissiveness over intelligence, independence, and forcefulness. Similarly, the practice of telling sexist jokes may resonate with discriminatory hiring and professional advancement practices if, as we suppose is the case, those who tell such jokes tend to belong to subcommunities in which the rate of these further sexist practices is elevated.

Practices carry presuppositions of collective attunement at very different levels of temporal granularity. At one end of the spectrum are patterns of short-term dispositions and mental states. The various practices involved in playing a complex board game (e.g., moving a piece in chess) commonly presuppose short-term collective attunement of the players to the state of play. Similarly, the subpractices of driving, for example, taking a left turn, presuppose collective attunement of drivers in the immediate vicinity both to the local road layout and to each other's planned trajectories and vehicular maneuver capacities. Likewise, linguistic practices presuppose short-term collective attunement. At a level that for most people is consciously inaccessible, the practice of uttering a phoneme presupposes collective attunement to the prior phoneme, since that affects its production. The practice of making a contribution in a conversation presupposes collective attunement to whose turn it is. Even those who interrupt will normally be so attuned, for people do not interrupt in the same way as they hold the floor.

Let us return to an example that we discussed in the last chapter (section 4.4), the practices of using pronouns. Pronoun use presupposes the ability to rapidly develop joint attention on an entity with suitable number and gender characteristics. This presupposition often holds in the context in which a pronoun is used precisely because prior speech acts have introduced a suitable entity into discourse, making it jointly salient. But as we have also seen, pronouns are often used in cases where the presupposition of collective attunement to the referent of a pronoun is not met by virtue of mention in the immediate discourse context. In such a case, the speaker may be exploiting the standard conditions under which a pronoun is used to give the impression of collective attunement, the impression that the hearer is being treated as a confidante, while simultaneously engaging the audience by forcing them to do some thinking. Who is this "he" or (apparently less commonly) "she" the author is talking about? Or, in more political speech, who are "they"? More critically, are you one of "us"?

The spectrum of collective attunement presuppositions runs from short time scale attunements that must be analyzed in terms of attention and other real-time mental processes to long-term attunements that concern ideological convictions and identity. The presuppositions of pronouns run the gamut, with the innocuously hidden and yet painfully sharp presuppositional resonances of us-them distinctions unwinding a strand of barbed wire through humanity, and forcing the hearer to choose an ideological side. More generally, even an utterance of a short word or phrase can be rich in presupposed ideological resonances. An "Oy vey!" resonates with very different ideological overtones than a "Mamma mia!" Neither of them have the vile ideological resonances of a "Heil Hitler!" or, to take an example from Lynne Tirrell's work, of the Kinyarwandan "Inzoka!" ("snake!") used as a specifically racial taunt amid the crumbling social strife that presaged the Rwandan genocide.[8] Our account of slurs, to be presented in chapter 10, will not be a purely presuppositional account, because understanding the practice of slurring must involve what slurs do as well as what they presuppose. Nonetheless, presupposed resonance plays a central role in that account, and slurs provide clear cases of presupposed and frequently dehumanizing ideology, whether that ideology is racist, sexist, homophobic, or, for that matter, liberal-phobic. Standard accounts of presupposition, for example, as necessary conditions for interpretation, have limited value in explaining such effects.

5.3. Conventional Meaning

As we discussed back in chapter 1, David Kaplan identified the meaning of an expressive term (a class that includes racist and sexist slurs, as well as his favorite examples, "ouch" and "oops") with the set of contexts in which the

8. Tirrell, "Genocidal Language Games."

term is used. Kaplan was using a standard approach to meaning whereby a set of contexts is equivalent to a proposition that might be spelled out as a big conjunction, each conjunct representing something that holds in every single one of those contexts, and such that the conjunction together entails anything that's true in every single one of them. We noted that using this idea brings with it a problem: since the contexts of use of the term all have the property that they include the convention by which the term expresses what it does, it follows that the Kaplanian meaning includes the convention itself. Yet surely, when you utter "ouch," you are not expressing the fact that there is a convention that one says "ouch" when in pain, albeit your utterance might convey evidence to this effect to someone unfamiliar with the convention. The problem is easily resolved in terms of presupposition.[9] In this section, we'll make the solution explicit by exposing more clearly the difference between what is presupposed and what is expressed, briefly discuss how expressive meaning relates to compositional meaning, and show how in both cases the model we have proposed leads to an account of conventionality that is somewhat different from those in the literature.

"Ouch!" If the message just expressed is not the conjunction "speaker pain is expressed by 'ouch,' and I'm in pain," then what is it? An utterance of "ouch" presupposes the convention and expresses the pain. But how do we know that? Apart from being obviously silly, why is it wrong to say the reverse, that is, that "ouch" presupposes pain and expresses a convention? This question is answered straightforwardly by the account of presupposition above. There is a high tendency for interlocutors to be collectively attuned to the convention prior to use of "ouch," but there is not such a high tendency for interlocutors to be collectively attuned to the pain prior to utterance. Thus, the first attunement but not the second is presupposed. As for what is communicated by the expressive, it is natural to extend our account in terms of the change in collective attunements. So, we might say that the message communicated by a signal is what interactants tend to become more collectively attuned to by virtue of the signal being used. (Those familiar with dynamic semantics

9. It will have occurred to some readers that perhaps the problem we identify with Kaplan's proposal could be solved in terms of his distinction, in separate work, between character and content. The idea would be that the character of an expressive is a function from contexts to a Kaplanian meaning. So, in contexts in which there is a convention that "ouch" expresses pain, the Kaplanian meaning of "ouch" is then the set of all contexts in which "ouch" would appropriately express pain. Perhaps this could be made to work, but it would certainly require a careful slicing and dicing of contexts. At any rate, our point here is not to "fix" Kaplan's proposal, but rather to use the problem to illustrate how we differentiate what is at issue from what is presupposed. Our approach could even be seen as building on Kaplan's account of indexicals, as it has a similar two-dimensionality. On our view, it is only relative to a context that a given behavior can be seen as instantiating a practice, and only relative to a context that practice can then have whatever effects it does (say, expressing a proposition, promising something, or slurring).

will immediately see that this is just a variant of a fairly standard dynamic account of meaning and presupposition, with roots in the work of Irene Heim and Lauri Karttunen, although it also has much in common with Robert Stalnaker's pragmatic model of assertion.[10])

Let us shift from expressives like "ouch" to larger, compositional sentences. Consider an utterance of "Either it's raining or it's snowing." What is expressed by the word "raining," what is expressed by the first disjunct, and what is expressed by the entire utterance? We will say that in all three cases ideas are expressed. "Raining" expresses an idea corresponding to an abstract property that a situation might have; "it's raining" expresses an idea corresponding to a proposition about a particular situation at the time of utterance; and the entire disjunction expresses an idea corresponding to yet another proposition, a slightly weaker one. Of course, such an utterance would normally be used not merely to express an idea but also to perform an assertion. Whenever you assert something, you simultaneously instantiate the practice of expressing an idea and the practice of asserting it. On this view, whereas the first disjunct involves only an expression (or description, or presentation) of a way that things can be, the full utterance is involved in two distinct acts that involve its meaning, the expression of a certain idea, and the assertion that the idea corresponds to reality.

Uttering "it's raining" is very different from uttering "ouch." The first expresses an idea, and can be used to assert it, while the second expresses pain, which is not the right category of thing to be asserted. Nonetheless, they come with overlapping presuppositions, both presupposing not merely the specific practices needed to use them, but the much larger family of practices involved in speaking English. And to the extent that people who say "it's raining" or "ouch" tend to share cultural tendencies different from people who say "il pleut" or "aïe," those cultural tendencies, everything distinctively involved in anglophone ideology, will also be presupposed to at least a mild extent. When we observe people saying "il pleut" or "aïe," we obtain a lot of evidence about them and their circumstances. Unlike someone who says "it's raining" with a British accent, they are vanishingly unlikely to have eaten baked beans on toast for dinner last night. Yet someone who says "il pleut" does not thereby signal what they did or didn't eat for dinner last night; that is not part of the message standardly encoded by this signal. Such information is a presuppositional resonance of the signal.

This takes us to a tricky issue: to what extent are presuppositions part of the conventional meaning of an expression? Some might take the fact that the presuppositional resonances for "ouch" and "aïe" encode information not only about the practices of expressing pain but also about what you ate for dinner

---

10. Heim, "On the Projection Problem for Presuppositions"; Karttunen, "Presuppositions and Linguistic Context"; Stalnaker, "Assertion," "Pragmatic Presuppositions."

as being a reductio ad absurdum of the claim that these resonances have any intrinsic connection to conventions of language. And indeed, perhaps it is. However, we should like to suggest that the absurdity rests not in the concept of presuppositional resonance, but in the idealization that there is a small, finite set of things that are part of the conventional meaning of an utterance of a word.

We don't think that conventionality of the bulk of speech practices is black and white, but rather take it to vary continuously, so that some aspects of a practice, including a speech practice, may be more conventionalized than others. Note that although we have exemplified the noncategoricity of conventions in terms of differing degrees of presupposition (an issue that will become important in the next section), we believe it applies equally to the principal message communicated by a signal. In the domain of meaning, this vagueness is a natural concomitant of our assumptions about practice, for if the extension of a predicate is determined by its history of practice, then there should be borderline cases for which conventions less clearly determine its correct application than for central examples. To take classic cases from Eubulides and Wittgenstein, respectively, it is not clear exactly what counts as a *heap*, nor what counts as a *game*.[11]

This is not to say that categoricity is not an essential part of grammar and communication, a point to which we shall return. The meanings of "heap" and "game" certainly exhibit the hallmarks of categoricity, as do judgments of grammaticality in many cases. Our point here is not to claim that there are no categories, or that there is no categoricity, but rather to point out that in our descriptions of linguistic conventions we often make simplifying assumptions. The idea that there is a binary fact of the matter as to whether a particular action instantiates standard speech practice, that is, that grammatical conventions define completely strict categories for which one can state sufficient and necessary membership conditions, is an *idealization*. It is a useful idealization. It underpins generative linguistics, allowing syntacticians to equate grammars with sets of strings. But it is not an idealization that has clear empirical backing, and it is not an idealization that holds sway throughout linguistics. In studies of language change, as in the subfields of historical linguistics and sociolinguistic variation, it is standard to look at changes in progress as involving tendencies that are in the process of *freezing* into standard practice, or that continue to shift without fully stabilizing, or that are in competition with other practices without there being a uniformly preferred choice. Certainly there are ways of modeling such processes in terms of standard methods with categorical generalizations, for example, by considering people's knowledge of language to consist in mixtures of generative grammars (e.g., by assigning

---

11. Wittgenstein, *Philosophical Investigations*, 3. It remains contested whether Eubulides is the originator of the paradox of the heap, and no text of his survives.

a probability to each grammar).[12] However, to model people's knowledge of language this way and allow every speaker in a community to have different mixtures is really to accept that the idealization of categorical grammatical conventions fails, and to offer a model that makes sensible conservative use of existing methods. If knowledge of language is knowledge of grammar mixtures, then that is as much an argument against exclusively categorical conventions as a spectrum of increasingly fishy merpeople would be an argument against exclusively categorical speciation.

5.4. Projection

Having discussed the relationship between the message communicated by a signal and its presuppositional resonance, we now pivot to an account of presupposition projection. That is, in this section we will discuss the distinctive behavior of presuppositions in utterances that involve embedding one construction inside another. The nondiscrete model of presupposition (and collective attunement more generally) that we have adopted has more flexibility than standard approaches. We will argue that this gives it a significant advantage in accounting for the complex properties of projection that have emerged in recent linguistic work.

As we have noted, projectivity is of interest not only as a curious linguistic phenomenon, but also for its particular significance in an account of the politics of language, since it helps explain why presuppositions are important vehicles for hustle.[13] Presuppositions allow manipulative people to subtly bias questions, and, more generally, to affect hearers' attitudes and dispositions without performing the type of assertive act that would make the intention to effect such change explicit. But for the moment we will focus on the abstract patterns of presupposition projection in their own right, and on how those patterns may be explained.

In section 4.2, we considered the presuppositions of the following Trump tweet, which among other things carries the presupposition that $700,000 was illegally given to Andy McCabe:

> Was Andy McCabe ever forced to pay back the $700,000 illegally given to him and his wife, for his wife's political campaign, by Crooked

---

12. The mixtures of grammars approach can be found, for example, in the work of historical linguist Tony Kroch (e.g., "Reflexes of Grammar in Patterns of Language Change"). Such methods are also common in computational models of language acquisition, with much work using probabilistic context-free grammars (which allow each grammar rule to be associated with a probability).

13. We are far from being the first to see presupposition as playing a central role in manipulative language. For example, in *Sold on Language*, Julie Sedivy and Greg Carlson argue that presupposition is an important device in advertising.

Hillary Clinton while Hillary was under FBI investigation, and McCabe was the head of the FBI??? Just askin'?

What makes this an instance of *presupposition projection* is that a presupposition seems to jump out of a complex construction rather than being affected by that construction in the way that ordinary nonpresupposed meaning would be. Let's start with where the presupposition comes from, the *presupposition trigger*. Triggers are normally thought of as grammatical constructions, for example, a nominal phrase headed by the word "the." We see the grammar of a language as a practice, a collection of communicative actions seen as exemplifying a whole. Words have many facets. You may look at printed words and see something physical, as physical as the book or screen you're reading from. But those word tokens embody a part of the broader grammatical practice. It is at this level, as embodying grammatical subpractices, that we can talk of a word or construction being a presupposition trigger.

The presuppositional resonances of a practice can be thought of as measuring how presupposed a particular feature of context is: the more strongly a feature is distinctively present in the contexts where the word occurs, the greater the degree to which it is presupposed. How does this explain projection? Rather than immediately attempting to resolve the general issue, let us first get our terminology straight and consider a narrower framing of the question. In the previous chapter, we said that certain constructions, like negation and questions, block commitments, so that, for example, whereas someone who uttered "It was raining" would be committed to a certain fact about previous weather, someone who uttered the question "Was it raining?" obviously would not be. Another term used in the literature is *nonveridical*. A linguistic construction that embeds or modifies others is *nonveridical* if the truth of sentences involving that construction does not depend on any proposition expressing material they embed or modify being true. Questions and negations are said to be nonveridical because they can be felicitously used independently of whether any sentence they modify expresses something true, or something the speaker takes to be true. The notion of nonveridicality allows us to give a narrow definition of projection in line with most prior work on the topic:

> **Propositional projection:** A construction is a trigger for a projective proposition if both unembedded uses of the construction and uses of the construction in nonveridical environments provide evidence of speaker commitment to the truth of that proposition.

For example, an unembedded use of "It was raining" commits the speaker to (i) grammatical and lexical practices such as those involving use of the word "rain" and its gerundive form "raining," (ii) there being a mutually identifiable past interval and location under discussion, and (iii) there having been rain then and there. Which of these commitments survives embedding in the more complex construction "Perhaps it was raining"? Clearly, the first and second commitments survive, and not the third. Why? Why does the act of asserting the basic sentence carry many of the same presuppositions as asserting the modal variant?

In a celebrated 1974 paper, the linguist Lauri Karttunen inverted the concept of presupposition projection.[14] The term "projection" suggests that presuppositions jump somewhat explosively out of constructions; we might think of Karttunen's proposal as the idea that patterns of presupposition related inference result not from how presuppositions *project out* of constructions, but rather from how features of context *tunnel in*. To say that a presupposition of a construction A projects when embedded in a larger construction B is then to say that both A and B are normal utterances in contexts where the presupposition holds, as if features of the outer context in which B is uttered have tunneled in to become part of the context in which A occurs. As regards the clause "it was raining," the argument would go as follows:[15]

(i) expressing a thought using that clause is appropriate in contexts in which interlocutors speak English and in which a past interval of time is salient;

(ii) this is true also of the local context in which the clause occurs when embedded under a modal;

---

14. Karttunen, "Presuppositions and Linguistic Context." Karttunen's model of presupposition is closely related to Stalnaker's. Both propose to explain presuppositional data in terms of the contexts in which utterances occur, and both allow that these contexts will be updated dynamically as conversation proceeds. However, Stalnaker's model cannot properly be described as an account of presupposition projection, because the pragmatic model of presupposition he develops does not assume that presuppositions are conventionally associated with particular constructions, i.e., presupposition triggers. If there are no presupposition triggers, it doesn't make much sense to ask what happens when presupposition triggers are embedded. A further difference between Karttunen's work and Stalnaker's is that while Karttunen details exactly how local contexts in which presupposition triggers occur may be different from the broader, global context in which a complete utterance occurs, Stalnaker does not attempt any such detailed description, and indeed in much of his work he seems committed to there not being a useful notion of local context that differs from the global context of utterance.

15. The Karttunen-derived explanation of projection suffices for our purposes here, but we note that alternative explanations might be compatible with our general approach. In particular, we are thinking of an explanation in terms of *at-issueness* as proposed by a group including one of the current authors (see Simons et al., "What Projects and Why"). The idea would be that the history of practice is used not merely to determine what features of the context are normally present when a given construction is used, but also what issues are under discussion. Projection would then tend to occur when a construction is used that indicates that some feature holds in the context, but when the question of whether that feature holds in the context is not itself under discussion.

(iii) by default, we should expect the local context created by the modal to be the same as the global context of utterance as regards these features;

(iv) therefore, the contexts in which the modalized variant can be appropriately used should be the same in relevant respects as contexts in which the nonmodalized version can appropriately be used; and thus

(v) projection is observed: presuppositional properties associated with the unembedded clause are also associated with the embedded clause.

The Trump tweet above involves embedding in a question construction rather than under a modal. Let's just go through why this is a case of presupposition projection, simplifying the tweet slightly for the sake of clarity. Consider the unembedded clause in (1). If (1) was uttered, the speaker would be committed to $700,000 having been illegally given to Andy McCabe. But this would equally be the case if (1) was negated, modalized, or turned into a question, as in (2), (3), and (4), respectively. Thus this speaker commitment has the hallmark of presupposition: it projects.

1. Andy McCabe was forced to pay back the $700,000 illegally given to him.
2. Andy McCabe was not forced to pay back the $700,000 illegally given to him.
3. Perhaps Andy McCabe was forced to pay back the $700,000 illegally given to him.
4. Was Andy McCabe forced to pay back the $700,000 illegally given to him?

So, given that the commitment that $700,000 was illegally given to Andy McCabe is a presupposition, we can now say why it projects. First, definite descriptions are commonly used in the practice of referring. Successful use of a description results in a context in which there is joint attention on an object, and this joint attention then allows further practices to take place that depend on such attention, for example, acts of predication.[16] Contexts in which acts of referring occur involve the distinctive presence of something matching the description well enough to be identified, so the presence of such an object is a presupposition. The context created by embedding the clause containing the description in a question, as in the original tweet, does not differ from the

---

16. Definite descriptions have various uses other than referring, e.g., in "Jason is not the only author of this book," where the description "the only author of this book" is non-referential. Such examples are used by Coppock and Beaver in "Definiteness and Determinacy" to motivate associating definite descriptions with a presupposition weaker than is normal in other approaches, a presupposition that there is at most one object satisfying the description.

global context of tweeting in any relevant way. Therefore, the speaker's commitment must hold in the global context of the act of tweeting. Trump has thus succeeded in conveying his commitment to McCabe's shadiness inside a question, as if McCabe having received such money were a widely accepted and unremarkable feature of context, and not something new or controversial, something one might expect to be asserted rather than presupposed. As it happens, Trump has a penchant for presupposing bad things about Andrew McCabe. We leave it to the reader to unpack the presuppositions of the tweet that follows. (Rubric: one point each for explaining the role of the telic verb "continue," which presupposes that the pre-state holds, and the role of embeddings involving the modal verb ["let"], negation, and imperative mood.)

> Republicans, don't let Andrew McCabe continue to get away with totally criminal activity. What he did should never be allowed to happen to our Country again. FIGHT FOR JUSTICE![17]

Neither is Trump the only one in his orbit using embedded presupposition triggers to communicate untruths. In case you need yet another exercise in unpacking presuppositions, here is former New York City mayor Rudy Giuliani embedding the presupposition trigger "find out" under the negative adverb "never" and a presumably rhetorical question at a press conference on November 19, 2020, dedicated to undermining confidence in the results of the national election that had just taken place: "Are you seriously going to want me to take seriously the secretary of state of Michigan when the secretary of state of Michigan never bothered to find out that the votes in her state were being counted in Germany by a Venezuelan company?"

Presupposition projection turns out to be a messy business. Presuppositions are normally differentiated from ordinary meaning (what is sometimes termed *at-issue* meaning) using evidence from projection, but there is now a long literature presenting examples in which projection does not occur. For example, the factive verb "realize" is normally taken to be a presupposition trigger, because it is associated with projective inferences. The basic inference is seen in the fact that (1) implies the truth of the factive complement, the inference to the truth of (4). What makes this inference projective is that it is also seen in examples (2) and (3), in which "realize" is embedded under negation and in the antecedent of a conditional, respectively.

> (1) Jason realizes that I'm in a bar right now.
> (2) Jason doesn't realize that I'm in a bar right now.
> (3) If Jason realizes that I'm in a bar right now, he'll text me to get back to work.

17. Donald J. Trump, @realDonaldTrump, Twitter, November 10, 2020, accessed February 20, 2023, https://twitter.com/realDonaldTrump/status/1326194143132082178?ref _src=twsrc%5Etfw.

(4) The speaker is in a bar at the time of utterance.

In general, factive verbs (thus, not only "realize," but also, e.g., "know," "regret," and "discover") are usually analyzed as presupposition triggers. But now consider this example, introduced by Lauri Karttunen a half-century ago:[18]

(5) If I realize later that I have not told the truth, I will confess it to everyone.

Example (5) does not imply that the speaker has not told the truth, but only that the speaker leaves open that possibility, so in this case the factive complement of "realize" does not project.

It was the variability of projection data, as seen in examples like (5), that led Stalnaker to propose his pragmatic account of presupposition. In advancing a pragmatic approach that he argued was more appropriate to such inconstant inferences, he avoided talk of presupposition triggering. He suggested that presuppositional inferences should be derived not by considering the conventional meaning of expressions to determine what is presupposed and what is not, but rather by considering the facts pertaining to a particular utterance and the conversational situation in which it takes place, and in particular what our knowledge of the conversational situation would lead us to take to be in the common ground of interlocutors.

On our reading of his early papers on presupposition, Stalnaker offers there a strong methodological hypothesis: although it is possible for meanings of expressions to have conventionalized presuppositional requirements, there is in fact no need to postulate such requirements, since presuppositional phenomena can be explained entirely in terms of speaker presuppositions. On this view, there is simply a tendency for people to use factive verbs when the factive complement is in the common ground of the interlocutors, and this is not a fact about the meaning of factive verbs per se. It's only a tendency, so there are counterexamples, as in Karttunen's example (5).

We certainly agree with Stalnaker that there is such a tendency. Indeed, the notion of presupposition we have developed is like Stalnaker's insofar as it allows such tendencies, rather than depending on necessary conditions for interpretation, as would be the case in some semantic theories of presupposition. Where we *disagree* with Stalnaker is as regards the significance of this fact. Stalnaker assumes that conventional meaning is categorical—there is a conventionalized connection between a term and something else; it must manifest in every context. We reject this as an idealization about conventional meaning, one that we do not think should be built into our models.

18. Karttunen, "Some Observations on Factivity," 64. The example is his (25b). For naturally occurring data involving nonprojection of factive presuppositions, see Beaver, "Belly Button Lint Colour."

On our view, tendencies to draw inferences are part and parcel of the history of the practice of using words, and the conventional meaning of those words is given by nothing besides history. In general, our attunement-based model allows for part-time presuppositions, in which weak conventions might in some cases lead to only weak evidence that a presupposition holds in the context of utterance, while allowing that sometimes it doesn't.[19] This much is in the spirit of the clarifications Stalnaker has offered regarding his account in more recent work:

> Claims about what sentences presuppose should be understood as claims about what cooperative speakers can normally be expected to be presupposing when they use those sentences. A presupposition "trigger," on this way of thinking about the phenomena, is an expression or construction that signals, for one reason or another, that a certain presupposition is being made.[20]

Our agreement with Stalnaker here is partial. What we agree with is his suggestion that presuppositional effects reflect tendencies among speakers. We do not, however, think that "claims about what sentences presuppose should be understood as claims about what cooperative speakers can normally be

19. Note that the possibility of part-time presuppositions in our model makes the account in some respects like that of Gerald Gazdar's *Pragmatics, Implicature, Presupposition, and Logical Form*. This is hardly surprising, since we and Gazdar owe a common debt to Stalnaker's pragmatic model of presupposition. However, our model differs from Gazdar's in that we allow some constructions to trigger presuppositions more strongly than others. In contrast, for Gazdar every use of a trigger introduces a defeasible preference for the presupposition to be accepted, and there is no difference in the strength of this preference from one trigger to the next.

20. Stalnaker, *Context and Content*, 94. We note in passing that a much stronger view than that expressed in this passage, namely the view that presupposition theory could get by only with mention of speaker attitude and without mention of conventionalized properties of linguistic expressions, would lead to a contradiction in Stalnaker's account. The problem concerns cases of informative (what he later terms *anticipatory*) presupposition. Let us make the strong assumption that knowledge of language does not involve knowledge distinguishing presuppositions associated with particular constructions from other types of content. Now suppose that a speaker utters a sentence like "I don't have time to feed the cat" to someone who they realize doesn't know they have a cat. On the strong view suggested by Stalnaker's early work, these cases involve a pretense by the speaker that the presupposition is in the common ground, when in fact it is clear that this is not so. The question then would be, How is the speaker manifesting the pretense? Since the only relevant behavior being performed by the speaker is uttering a certain expression ("the cat"), the pretense must consist in uttering that expression. But in that case, uttering the expression constitutes acting as if the presupposition in question is in the common ground. The use of the expression, in other words, must signal that the speaker has a certain presupposition, and a speaker's knowledge of the expression must include the knowledge that the expression provides such a signal. But this is inconsistent with our initial assumption. Therefore, knowledge of language must involve knowledge distinguishing presuppositions associated with particular constructions from other types of content.

expected to be presupposing." We think that claims about what sentences of a given type presuppose are claims about the typical contexts in which those sentences arise, or, more generally, that claims about what communicative actions drawn from a given practice presuppose are claims about the typical contexts in which those practices are performed. One type of property found in contexts in which practices are performed is the presence of collective attunements of various sorts among the interlocutors. As we suggested in section 2.4, collective attunement plays much the same role in our framework as common ground plays for Stalnaker, and common ground is precisely what Stalnaker takes speakers to presuppose. But we have emphasized that the collective attunements we are interested in are neither limited to being beliefs, nor limited to the speakers involved in the interaction, and indeed may not specifically be attunements of any of the individuals directly involved.

The presuppositions of an action provide evidence as to the collective attunements of the community of practice that gives the action its communicative significance. These presuppositions include arbitrary attunements, and not merely beliefs: the bundle of attentional tendencies, dispositional attunements, emotional attunements, and cognitive attunements that make up an ideology. Claims about what sentences presuppose should be understood in part as claims about the ideology of the relevant community of practice within which the sentence has meaning.

Given that we are not only interested in propositional commitments of the speaker, but interested in arbitrary features found in the context of communicative acts, let us propose a generalization of the notion of propositional projection defined earlier in this section:

> **Projection of resonance:** A construction is a trigger for a projective resonance if both unembedded uses of the construction and uses of the construction in nonveridical environments tend to carry that resonance to a significant extent.

Note that we do not limit this to presuppositional resonances. In this part of the book, we are focused on presuppositional resonances, because we believe they are central to the transmission of ideology and to ideological evolution and conflict. But it is not only presuppositional resonances that project. Of particular importance when we come to discuss hate speech in detail in chapter 10 will be the projection of attentional and emotional resonances, and these resonances can be effects of communicative actions rather than presuppositions. Consideration of hate speech has proven problematic for standard theories of presupposition projection in part because certain features associated with hate speech, slurs in particular, are what has been termed "hyper-projective."[21]

---

21. Camp, "A Dual Act Analysis of Slurs," 39.

When a presupposition is said to be projective, the nonveridical embedding environments that are considered include, inter alia, negation, conditionals, questions, and imperatives. One type of environment that is usually not used as a diagnostic for presupposition is what we might call metalinguistic environments, such as indirect speech reports, quotative environments, and abstract discussions in which aspects of linguistic constructions are discussed in the abstract. Metalinguistic environments generally have been assumed to be what Lauri Karttunen termed "plugs" to presupposition projection.[22] So, for example, suppose David says the following:

> Jason said, "My sister is late!"

It has generally been held that David would be not committed to Jason having a sister, despite this being a presupposition associated with what Jason purportedly said. Likewise, theorists working on presupposition would typically assume that in giving an example sentence, like that above, the authors of a book do not thereby become committed to the presuppositions triggered within the example sentence. In fact, Jason does not have a sister, although the fact that we feel a need to clarify this might give pause for thought.

The details of how presuppositions project in metalinguistic environments remain underexplored, perhaps because projection in such environments has been assumed to be so limited that they could not usefully be used as diagnostics for presupposition. Absent much data on projection of presupposition from metalinguistic environments, we will only note that our framework allows that there could be partial projection, in which a presuppositional resonance is weakened by embedding in a metalinguistic environment, but not eliminated. What is empirically clear is that some resonances of slurs project quite strongly from metalinguistic environments. This is in fact the reason that we, like many authors, avoid even mentioning the N-word (as opposed to referring to it indirectly with the awkward locution "the N-word"). Hyperprojective resonances are those that are clearly not plugged, but project from metalinguistic environments.

> **Hyperprojectivity:** A construction is a trigger for a hyperprojective resonance if both unembedded uses of the construction and uses of the construction in metalinguistic environments (including indirect speech reports and quotation) tend to carry that resonance to a significant extent.

The contemporary scholarly discussion of presupposition projection kicked into high gear after Terence Langendoen and Harris Savin introduced what they termed "the projection problem for presuppositions" a half century ago. They defined this as the problem of relating "the presuppositions and

22. Karttunen, "Presuppositions of Compound Sentences," 174.

assertions of a complex sentence . . . to the presuppositions and assertions of the clauses it contains."[23] Let us generalize. The projection problem for resonance is the problem of relating the resonances of a complex communicative event to the resonances of its parts. Of particular interest to us later in the book will be the resonances of complex communicative events involving embedded hate speech.

5.5. Categoricity

The resonance-based model of presupposition does not make a clean distinction between what is categorically presupposed and what is not categorically presupposed. We can imagine that some might view this as a shortcoming. The flexibility of the model would, at the very least, be unnecessary if there were clear evidence that in fact there are clear categorical differences, that is, evidence that the grammar makes a sharp distinction between presupposition triggers and nonpresupposition triggers. In that case Occam's razor might suggest a simpler account would be a better account. Continuous models are often hard to work with analytically, so why bother? But maybe there is a bigger problem. Could it be that the type of continuous model we are proposing is not merely methodologically awkward, but is in a deeper sense a poor fit for human speech practices, because those speech practices involve categorical distinctions where our model doesn't?

We will now consider the question of whether grammars have clear categories of presupposing and nonpresupposing constructions, what we will term the question of *presuppositional categoricity*. But first it is helpful to think about what categorical differences in grammars look like more generally, itself a specific instance of the age-old question of what conceptual categories of any kind are like.

Categoricity has been much studied not only in abstract philosophical and mathematical terms, but also experimentally in cognitive psychology, especially in the area of categorical perception. Categorical perception is often studied in terms of the emergence of perceptual boundaries between categories, this emergence leading to two properties that we may think of as the hallmarks of categorical perception. First, people make sharp judgment

---

23. Langendoen and Savin, "The Projection Problem for Presuppositions," 55. Note that their statement of the problem uses the term "assertions" to mean something like entailments, since they do not appear to be taking sentences or clauses to be performances of assertive speech acts. Their statement of the problem can be related naturally to Frege's principle of compositionality, that the meaning of a larger unit must be a function of the meaning of the parts and their mode of composition. Langendoen and Savin can be seen as saying that if Fregean compositionality is right, then it must apply to presuppositions too, and the projection problem is the problem of determining how composition affects presuppositions.

changes at transition points between categories. So, if someone is exposed to a sequence of stimuli that gradually change (say a sequence of computationally morphed cartoons starting with dog-like images, but becoming increasingly cat-like), we tend to see a sudden transition in which images people will confidently describe as cats, rather than a gradual decrease in confidence of the images' dogginess and increase in confidence of the images' cattiness. Second, people show much greater ease distinguishing two stimuli that fall on either side of a category boundary than they do distinguishing two stimuli in the same category. Thus, if shown two doggy pictures a few minutes apart, people may not be confident in saying whether it was the same picture, whereas if people are shown a dog picture and then a cat picture a few minutes apart, they are much more likely to decisively and confidently identify them as being different, and that may be so even if the first two images were more physically distinct than the second two.

The effect that it can be hard to tell the difference between two things in the same category if you haven't explicitly learned to make such distinctions is known as *within-category compression*. It's responsible for the fact that if you led a sheltered childhood and then met people of an ethnicity you were not exposed to, you might at first have found yourself embarrassingly unable to distinguish them from one another.

As it happens, one of the classic studies in categorical perception was a study of perception of language; we are thinking here of the highly influential work of Alvin Liberman and colleagues[24] on the perception of consonants, work that created a standard paradigm in acoustic phonetics. As background, consonants (and speech sounds more generally) can be thought of as existing in an acoustic space involving combinations of frequencies distributed over time. For example, both "ba" and "da" correspond to an initial sudden burst of sound energy across the spectrum, followed by a disappearance of much of the high-end energy and a rapid transition into the base frequency and formants characteristic of the production of an "ah" sound. The sounds "ba" and "da" are very obviously distinct as regards the mechanics of production (the first involving lip closure, and the second a closure of the tongue against palate), and, introspectively, we feel that the two sound very different. However, from a physical point of view, the acoustic differences are subtle enough that it needs a little practice to tell the difference just by looking at spectrograms. Furthermore, the question of how to specify the difference at a technical level is a difficult one, because people produce slightly different sounds from each other when saying what we might think of as the same thing, and, indeed, vary from one production to the next, and also because hearers will identify a range of sounds as being "ba" or "da." That is, if we think of the acoustics of "ba" and "da" in terms of acoustic space, they are not points but zones in that

---

24. Liberman et al., "The Discrimination of Speech Sounds."

space, with a range of physical event types that are heard as "ba," and a range that are heard as "da." What does it mean, then, to say that these sounds are categorical in nature?

The experiments run by Liberman's team involve hearers identifying sounds produced by a speech synthesizer, with examples of sounds drawn from an area of acoustic space that includes canonical "ba," "ga," and "da" sounds, but which also includes examples of sounds that are intermediary between these. The experiments, which involved both making judgments on individual sounds and making decisions as to whether two sounds were distinct, demonstrated both the above hallmarks of categoricity: sharp boundaries emerge with rapid changes in category identification across those boundaries, and high within-category compression, it being much more difficult to tell the difference between two "ba" sounds than between a "ba" and a "da," even if the former pair of sounds were somewhat more physically distinct than the latter.

Let us return now to presupposition: is there reason to think that there is a categorical difference between constructions that bear a presupposition and those that don't? There are certainly clear cases of both, but there is no evidence of presuppositional categoricity analogous to that found in work on categorical perception. In fact, on the contrary, recent work on presupposition projection is highly suggestive of there being degrees of presuppositionality, and perhaps even a continuous space. This work, in part joint with one of the current authors, involves people's judgments as to what follows from an utterance or text, in particular judgments regarding inferences that involve projection, cases involving embedding in a nonveridical environment of a construction thought to be associated with a particular feature of context.

The studies involve either constructed experimental stimuli or texts extracted from a corpus, and in either case subjects perform judgments as to whether projection occurred. What has emerged in this work is, first, that there is great variance in constructions standardly identified as presupposition triggers as regards the strength of projection effects, and furthermore that this variation is observed somewhat independently of the embedding environment. The literature on presupposition might be taken to suggest that in the relatively simple cases studied in the experimental work, people should have sharp judgments on whether a presupposition projects or not, but that is not the case: confidence in a projective inference doesn't appear bimodal at the individual or group level. Neither do we observe a bimodal split between presupposed and nonpresupposed inferences when looking across different constructions.

For example, if we consider the presuppositions standardly associated with the factives "know" and "discover" (i.e., the presupposition that the complement is true), we find that projection is significantly stronger for "know" than for "discover." If we then compare both of these with the presupposition standardly associated with the construction "stupid to" (as in "Jason was stupid to coauthor with David," presupposing that Jason did coauthor with David), we find significantly stronger projection for "know" and "discover" than for "stupid." And if we compare these with a standardly analyzed presupposition of "only" ("Only Jason cried," presupposing that Jason cried), we find that projection in this case, while still clearly present, is weaker than for any of the other three.[25] Furthermore, it turns out that typically projective inferences are found even in cases that are not standardly taken to be presuppositional, for example, for the complements of the verbs "believe" and "say." Consider the sentences "He doesn't believe that he lost the election," and "He won't say that he lost the election," both which involve embedding a nonfactive verb under negation. When someone hears such sentences, there is a significant chance they will conclude that the speaker is in fact committed to it being the case that whoever is under discussion lost the election. Summarizing: constructions standardly analyzed as presuppositional seem to have varying presuppositional strengths (as measured by projective inferences), and even constructions standardly analyzed as nonpresuppositional have properties that could be described as weak presuppositions insofar as they sometimes lead to typically presuppositional inferences.

We do not wish to argue that a clear case has been made that presupposition is an inherently noncategorical phenomenon. Rather, we would seek to put the shoe on the other foot: categoricity of presupposition is an idealization that may be helpful for formalization, but is not yet rooted in empirical research, there being no analogue in this area of the work in categorical perception discussed above. There is, at present, no clear evidence that it is a categorical matter whether a construction carries a presupposition or not. Until such evidence is found, we would suggest that a sound research strategy is to be open to noncategorical models and to recognize that in assuming categoricity one is making a convenient idealization that so far lacks direct support.

Whether a theoretician chooses to make an assumption of categoricity will presumably depend on their immediate goals, for example, the particular slice of data they are looking at, but one thing should be clear from the discussion in this section: assuming categoricity will not always make the linguist's life easier. If your goal is to analyze the sort of projectivity data discussed in this section, you would be hamstrung attempting to produce variable projectivity results in a categorical model. On the other hand, a resonance-based account along the lines we have sketched could readily be applied to such data. Indeed, the results on projectivity just discussed suggest a potential methodology for quantifying the presuppositional resonances of different constructions,

25. The cited results are found in Tonhauser, Beaver, and Degen, "Gradience in Projectivity and At-Issueness." For a corpus study of projection involving a wider range of constructions and embedding environments, see de Marneffe, Simons, and Tonhauser, "The CommitmentBank."

whereby a feature of context would have a presuppositional resonance strength for some construction that is proportional to the degree of projectivity found empirically, once other factors have been controlled for. We will not pursue such an approach here. Our goal in this section has been more modest: to clarify what categoricity of an account of presupposition would mean, and establish the plausibility of a noncategorical model of presupposition along the lines we have proposed.

5.6. What Else Is Missing?

We have now set forth the main elements of our view on how meaning relates to context, a view that we hope might support analysis of aspects of social and political discourse that are not well described under standard idealizations in the theory of meaning. We started the chapter with a missing piece. We had suggested that many of the effects that concern us in this volume depend on presupposition, but we had not said what the presuppositions of an action are like. This lacuna was particularly pressing, given that in the first part of this volume we developed a theory of meaning in terms of resonance and attunement, notions that are not discussed in any prior model of presupposition.

Our treatment of presupposition generalizes standard approaches in two ways. First, we treat context dependence as intrinsically scalar, allowing different degrees to which an act is revealing of (or dependent on) aspects of its context. Second, the types of presupposition we consider are not typically discussed. In particular, an act may presuppose social practices, including the communicative conventions of the act itself.

Let us return to the explanations of the effects of biased questions in two lines of experimental work in cognitive psychology, Elizabeth Loftus's studies of recall and memory, and the empirical studies on which Daniel Kahneman and Amos Tversky founded prospect theory. In both cases, the experimental effects hinge on the framing of the question. In Loftus's work, framing a question in ways that evoke properties or constituents of scenes that were not present causes people to "remember" the scene differently. In Kahneman and Tversky's work, framing a decision problem in terms of gains causes people to make different choices than if the problem were framed in terms of losses, an effect that would not be predicted in a simplistic application of classical utility theory to human decision-making. Loftus herself has advocated for the role of presupposition in the memory paradigm we discussed, and we argued that presuppositional analyses are appropriate for both the memory and prospect theory paradigms.

Quite generally, while it is possible to offer a framing explicitly, for example, in negotiation ("Do you think we might put it this way . . . ?"), it is far more common for a framing to be presupposed. What does it mean for a framing to be presupposed? A framing is a communicative practice, a practice of using certain expressions for some purpose. In the cognitive-psychology examples, the framing expressions are taken to provide a particular conceptualization of an issue or an event, for example, a conceptualization of a vehicle collision as involving high energy if the verb "smash" is used, or a conceptualization of the effects of a health program as offering a positive gain if it is described in terms of lives "saved." The well-worn example of pro-choice versus pro-life framings for abortion can be seen as providing a conceptualization in this way, but it also suggests that frames are something more. Each of these abortion framings is a broad rhetorical practice that doesn't merely describe a state of the world in a particular way, but offers a key dichotomy around which abortion debates can be structured. Much of the literature on framing concerns complex rhetorical practices used to do things other than describe situations or outcomes; for instance, a frame may serve to motivate protest, unify a group, or deride opponents.

Having recognized that frames do not merely describe, but have other functional effects too, we can see that the description of frames in the cognitive-psychology cases as merely offering ways of conceptualizing an issue is unnecessarily limiting. It might be that a relevant effect of using the word "smash" is to engender excitement, and it might be that there is a dramatic difference between the emotional resonances conjured by talk of "lives saved" as against "lives lost." Further, it might be that there are dispositions associated with thoughts of gain that are quite different than dispositions associated with thoughts of loss, for example, a disposition to play it safe in the first case, and a disposition to gamble to avert disaster in the second. On the model we have described, frames can not only presuppose particular conceptualizations, but can also carry emotional and dispositional resonances as part of their presuppositional profile.

Given these considerations, we feel that our account of presupposition not only explains core aspects of examples we have discussed, like the ability of the framing presuppositions to project from within questions, but also offers some novel directions for further study. And yet the story so far is incomplete, for there is one central component of the explanation of the effects of frames in the previous chapter about which we have said very little: accommodation. That is, we have provided an account in which the presuppositions of the experimental stimuli in the experiments we discussed there can be modeled, but we have left completely open the question of how hearers adapt to those presuppositions.

In standard models of communication as information exchange, accommodation is what allows presuppositions to be informative. In the next chapter, we will suggest that a generalized notion of accommodation can not only account for standard cases of informative presupposition, including the adaptation subjects apparently perform in response to deviously framed experimental stimuli, but can also play a central role in describing the transmission of ideology, ideological conflict, and the crystallization of separate groups. These are big claims, and they may seem fanciful to those who are familiar with the literature on presupposition in philosophy of language and formal semantics/ pragmatics. Here a crucial difference between prior work on presupposition and our own becomes significant. Prior work focuses on presuppositions about the world or about what has been said earlier in a discourse, and in these models, accommodation, as noted, explains how these presuppositions can be informative, effectively allowing repair of faulty contexts in which there is a mismatch between interlocutors' beliefs. Once we move to considering presupposed norms and practices, and once we allow that accommodation involves not only modification of beliefs, but also modification of behaviors and dispositions, and once we also consider the motivations for accommodation in terms of joint behavior at the level of groups of arbitrary size, accommodation becomes something far more remarkable. It becomes an engine of societal change.

To get a sense of what we take to be the importance and breadth of application of accommodation, note that we will suggest that it can provide a way of understanding aspects of what Judith Butler termed *performativity*, which she develops as part of an anti-essentialist model of categories such as gender.[26] Butler's notion of performativity has had an impact on many literatures and is a central notion in current *third-wave* sociolinguistics, building on a long line of work in sociology that begins with Erving Goffman's use of the term *performance*. (Butler's use of performativity is presumably influenced by both J. L. Austin and Goffman, but it is clearly unlike Austin's in that it is not restricted to a narrow set of sentence types. Goffman's theatrically inspired notion of performance[27] is broad, encompassing all aspects of the way someone acts during an extended encounter.) Folk models of social identity, often used at least tacitly in scientific and humanistic scholarship, are essentialist in the sense that they treat categories such as gender and ethnicity as fixed, and regard people's behaviors as allowing them to mark their identity relative to these fixed categories. Butler's seminal work swept the rug from under this view, explaining how people's behaviors can dynamically redefine or create the very social categories they differentiate. Our view borrows heavily from this perspective. As we will develop the account, accommodation might be said to be not only *informative* but also *formative*, contributing to the cascading development of new social categories, behaviors, and groupings in overlapping chains of successive social interactions.

26. Butler, *Gender Trouble*.
27. Goffman, "Presentation of Self in Everyday Life."

CHAPTER SIX

On Parole

All the world's a stage,
And all the men and women merely players:
They have their exits and their entrances;
And one man in his time plays many parts.

—WILLIAM SHAKESPEARE, *AS YOU LIKE IT*, ACT 2, SCENE 7

Each society demands of its members a certain amount of acting, the
ability to present, represent, and act what one actually is. When society
disintegrates into cliques such demands are no longer made of the
individual but of members of cliques. Behavior then is controlled by silent
demands and not by individual capacities, exactly as an actor's perfor-
mance must fit into the ensemble of all other roles in the play. The salons of
the Faubourg Saint-Germain consisted of such an ensemble of cliques, each
of which presented an extreme behavior pattern. The role of the inverts
was to show their abnormality, of the Jews to represent black magic
("necromancy"), of the artists to manifest another form of supranatural
and superhuman contact, of the aristocrats to show that they were not like
ordinary ("bourgeois") people.

—HANNAH ARENDT[1]

6.1. Vox Populi

A dictionary clings to language by the tail. Communicative practice rushes forth, caring not for ideals of stability of form or determinacy of meaning. There is no fact of the matter as to where a communicative practice is going. There is no fact of the matter as to where it's been; there is just a history of instantiation of which no individual has ever experienced more than a tiny slice. If ideologues seem to succeed in tying a practice down for a generation or two, what is left in the hands of their heirs is hollow ritual. Practice must live free to remain vital. The power of political communication rests on its ability to draw attention, drive attunement, and differentiate adversaries. This is achieved through an ever-evolving mixture of repurposed *spandrels* (to hijack

---

1. Arendt, *The Origins of Totalitarianism*, 84–85.

a term from evolutionary biology[2]), new enough to catch the eye and ear, and old enough to be recognized. To understand the politics of language is not merely to understand the catchphrase du jour, but to understand the processes that make such phrases effective, and the processes that make them rot.

Although this volume is entitled *The Politics of Language*, our goal is not to detail the role of some particular set of linguistic constructions found in political rhetoric. The words and phrases of any particular political moment are in constant turmoil. Even when some phrases, like "law and order" or "states' rights" recur, they recur with new resonances. Though in no way improved, neither a Confederate flag nor a noose hanging from a tree mean quite the same as they once did. The already borrowed "Make America Great Again" of the Trump presidency will never be the same "Make America Great Again" again. A word repeated is not the same word but an echo of the original, with all the resonances it has acquired along the way: *plus c'est la même chose, plus ça change*. Jorge Luis Borges takes this idea as far as it can go in his story *Pierre Menard*, in which Menard is imagined not to copy Cervantes's *Don Quixote*, but to reauthor fragments of it from scratch centuries after Cervantes. The new version is word for word identical with the original despite being written independently, centuries later. As Borges tells us, "The Cervantes text and the Menard text are verbally identical, but the second is almost infinitely richer."[3]

Sometimes there are functional motivations for performing a communicative action in something other than a way that prototypically exemplifies prior practice. Such a motivation arises whenever there is a need to distinguish between one signal and another. A peacock's best bet for impressing the peahens is not to have tail feathers indistinguishable from those of his fellow peacocks, but to have bigger and brighter tail feathers than any of the others. The extra tail-feather production can only be achieved if the peacock is in excellent condition, and even then it will be a drain on resources. But if there wasn't a price, it wouldn't be costly signaling. Thus the practice of tail-feather signaling, once started, does not remain fixed, and neither does the cost: an evolutionary tail-feather fashion race ensues.

Or suppose, to use an example from sociolinguist Penny Eckert's seminal Detroit high-school study, consider a teenage girl who has a need to mark her membership in an anti-establishment grouping, the Burnouts.[4] The Burnout

---

2. Gould and Lewontin, *A Critique of the Adaptationist Programme*. They observe that certain architectural structures (such as the semitriangular spandrels found at the intersections between domes and supporting columns) emerge out of engineering need, but then become architectural motifs in their own right, even though the original need has vanished. They use this as a metaphor for biological traits that have functions quite unlike those that originally led them to evolve.

3. Borges, *Labyrinths*, 42.

4. Eckert, *Jocks and Burnouts*.

pronunciation of "fight" sounds a bit like "foyt," and black makeup is in. Should she pronounce "fight" just like the average Burnout, or might she have reason to push it to more of an extreme? Would she aim to look like an average member of the group, or would she be tempted to dab just a bit more makeup on, you know, so everybody really knows who she is? The distinctive accent and dark makeup may not win favors with the teachers, or elite jobs down the road, but if there wasn't a price, it wouldn't be costly signaling. Thus do vowels and cosmetics evolve.

Or consider a political candidate trying to stand out from all the politicians that have gone before, much despised for having looked after their own and not the bulk of people in the country. One way of differentiating oneself would be to break norms and push boundaries of what is acceptable. Such a strategy will garner enemies. But here, again, the price is the point.

Clearly, there are sometimes reasons to perform a practice not as it has been typically performed before, but in such a way as to clearly distinguish performance of the practice from performances of variant practices. This is closely related to the point Ferdinand de Saussure was making when he remarked that "in language there are only differences," a central theme of his work.[5] The practice of producing the vowel in "fight" needs to be distinguished from the practice of producing the vowel in "feet," just as Burnouts need to distinguish their practice of producing the vowel in "fight" from the practices others use when pronouncing "fight." Each individual performance must strike a fine balance. It must be sufficiently like other performances of the practice to be seen as an instance of the class, and yet sufficiently different from performances of other practices so as to minimize the possibility of confusion.

The need to differentiate one practice from another places limits on a norm-based account of practice, for in a norm-based account an optimal action would be one that epitomizes the practice it instantiates. Our point here is that a communicatively optimal action is often not one that epitomizes a communicative practice, but rather one that most *clearly* instantiates the practice. Clarity of performance demands not merely faithfulness to a prior practice, but distinction from others.

Saussure's dictum applies at the level of differences in speech practices marking differences in social identity. The consequences of the social need for distinctiveness for speech practices can be divided in two.

First, there is selective pressure to perform in a key that is incompatible with the keys of groups from which one's own group is distinguishing itself. Recognition will be easy if members of one group dress or wear their hair or speak in ways that out-group members wouldn't, or if they all manifest beliefs that are antithetical to the out-group creeds. Further, faking group

5. Saussure, *Course in General Linguistics*, 120.

membership will be harder under the same conditions, when playing in the key of the group risks censure by the rest of society. For some, to wear extravagant makeup might or might not be as hard it would be for an Ephraimite to pronounce the "sh" of "shibboleth," but to wear such makeup would be to take a public risk, albeit one that many others have chosen to take. The example suggests that the same features that play into the key of a social group, and thus support collective harmony within that group, may also in some circumstances be sources of dissonance. There may be dissonance for individual group members, who could belong to multiple overlapping groups, each tuned to distinct keys, and there may be dissonance caused in society more broadly.

Second, there is pressure for the key of a social group to evolve. This is true partly for reasons given above: drift is inevitable unless explicit work is done to maintain conventions, and regular change in practices makes them harder to imitate. But there is a further reason: however distinctive a behavior is, it can always be made more distinctive by performing it in a way that is less like the behaviors of those in other groups. It is furthermore quite possible that after regular exposure to an attunement, or because of change in other attunements, out-group members will cease to be surprised by it, and cease to attend to it, thus bleaching its value as a marker.

Here let us make a brief excursus to examine another important scholarly connection and its significance for political propaganda. Saussure's focus on differentiation in language is mirrored by the more general analysis of individual and cultural differentiation developed a couple of decades later by the anthropologist Gregory Bateson on the basis of his studies of the Iatmul people of Papua New Guinea. Bateson defines what he terms *schismogenesis* as "a process of differentiation in the norms of individual behaviour resulting from cumulative interaction between individuals."[6] The processes we exemplified above are what he terms *complementary schismogenesis*, when behaviors of individuals or groups coevolve to become increasingly differentiated. He opposes this to *symmetrical schismogenesis*, in which accentuation of the same pattern of behavior occurs simultaneously in opposed individuals or groups as a result of pressure to outdo competition. A classic example he gives is of ever more extreme boasting behavior among males in a group he worked with, but examples of similarly unstable evolution of progressively more extreme behavior are found in many arms races, both metaphorical and, unfortunately, literal.

Bateson's concept of schismogenesis is not merely analytic, but has seen strategic use in the political sphere. During World War II, Bateson's roles included application of schismogenesis to sow discord in Japan through the use of "black propaganda."[7] This involved Bateson operating a fake Japanese radio station from Burma and Thailand, for example, transmitting

---

6. Bateson, *Naven*, 175.
7. Becker, "The Nature and Consequences of Black Propaganda."

variants of Japan's own wartime messaging that were sufficiently exaggerated to undermine confidence in the veracity of the original. One of us has defined *undermining propaganda* as a "contribution to public discourse that is presented as an embodiment of certain ideals yet is of a kind that tends to erode those very ideals."[8] *Black propaganda* goes further. It is a contribution to public discourse that is misrepresented as from a committed group member yet is of a kind that tends to erode that very group. The insight that Bateson and other subversive political propagandists have used is that societies are systems that are at best only in an unstable equilibrium. In terms of the resonance metaphor, this system is prone to fracture when energetically stimulated.

The engineering iconoclast Nikola Tesla famously claimed to have shaken buildings almost to the point of collapse with a carefully tuned pocket-size oscillator, and he is variously reported to have boasted that he could have toppled the Brooklyn Bridge or the Empire State Building, and that he did cause an earthquake.[9] The application of schismogenesis to black propaganda can then be understood by physical analogy with the type of machine Tesla claimed to have produced, or the smaller-scale phenomenon of wine glasses shattering when exposed to a carefully pitched voice. Black propaganda is an attempt to induce catastrophically disruptive tumult within a group using apparently innocuous messaging that resonates with members of the group. Despite its apparent mildness, the messaging progressively shakes the group from the inside, driving it away from equilibrium and making it ungovernable.

Similarly divisive messaging strategies appear to be a mainstay of contemporary social media disinformation campaigns.[10] It is perhaps helpful to understand the mechanisms of such campaigns, as Bateson did, as simply leveraging existing social processes to sow division in a target group. It immediately becomes clear that while in certain types of propaganda campaign the goal is to always stay on message, we should not be surprised to see that in others neither truth nor consistency is central. This latter characteristic is most obvious in the so-called *firehose of falsehood* approach to propaganda exemplified in the disinformation campaigns of Putin's Russia.[11] We return

8. Stanley, *How Propaganda Works*, 69.

9. Biographer James O'Neil writes as follows:

> "So powerful are the effects of the telegeodynamic oscillator," said Tesla in reviewing the subject in the thirties, "that I could now go over to the Empire State Building and reduce it to a tangled mass of wreckage in a very short time. I could accomplish this result with utmost certainty and without any difficulty whatever. I would use a small mechanical vibrating device, an engine so small you could slip it in your pocket." (*The Life of Nikola Tesla*, 144)

10. Guess and Lyons, "Misinformation, Disinformation, and Online Propaganda"; Jayamaha and Matisek, "Social Media Warriors."

11. Paul and Matthews, "The Russian 'Firehose of Falsehood' Propaganda Model." The firehose of falsehood differs in many ways from the black propaganda of earlier years, for example, because it does not uniformly target an enemy but rather targets Russians and

to these broad issues of political group dynamics in the next section, but for now we will focus on consideration of the processes of individual and group adaptation. These processes support the communicative fabric of communities of practice, but provide the substrate for disruptive propaganda as well as for constructive government and social development.

In this volume, we do not focus on truth, but on resonance, and we do not study language as a fixed construct, but as a collection of societal practices in constant tension and development. The model we have been building up provides a way of looking at evolution of meaning that is rather different from that found in more standard models of meaning, whether that of Richard Montague or J. L. Austin. These models analyze meaning in terms of a single, determinate set of rules. It's not that Montague and Austin did not recognize the possibility of change or its societal importance, but that they abstracted away from change in order to lay bare the structure of the beast on their dissection table, frozen, as it were, in time. In studying the social and political workings of language, we think it important to start with the idea that the functions of expressions of ordinary language do not hew to fixed rules, but are determined by the living conventions of practice. The extensions of practices change with each instantiation, and what counts as a distinct practice can change as rapidly as our recognition of what counts as a distinct community of practice. The fission of a practice into distinct subpractices (say, a "fight" subpractice and a "foyt" subpractice) is a natural concomitant and indeed integral part of the fission of communities into distinct subcommunities in which processes of schismogenesis are inevitable, and can sometimes be accelerated by active social engineering.

In our version of a Wittgensteinian practice-based account of conventional communicative function, the meaning of an expression is not given by a lemma in a dictionary, or even by a short list of lemmas. Rather, there is a history of usage, what we have termed the *extension* of a communicative practice, and the functions the expression has had on different occasions of use form a cloud of resonances. Interlocutors can coordinate on a function on a particular occasion of use to the extent that the functions the expression seems to have had when used in comparable contexts are sufficiently narrowly circumscribed for the purposes at hand. To adapt an example from a well-known discussion of naming, from psychologist Roger Brown, if an adult uses "dog" in talking to a child, they might successfully coordinate on reference to the animal before

---

foreigners alike, and because at least part of its function seems to be to create a situation in which it is hard to know what information can be trusted or which sources are credible, thus effectively blanketing populations in such a layer of disinformation that democratic decision-making is infeasible. However, there are strong similarities with black propaganda, e.g., in the use of professional Internet trolls and bots that infiltrate online discussion groups and social media, presenting themselves as in-group members while deploying subversive messages.

them, and not its collar or the chew toy in its mouth, even if the child also uses "dog" to refer to arbitrary large quadrupeds including cows and horses.[12] Similarly, to use Quine's famous skeptical argument for the impossibility of reliable translation, one can imagine successful coordination on the reference of a use of "gavagai" (by a speaker of an unknown language when in the presence of a rabbit) being at least equally robust.[13] Such coordination does not depend on the presence of identical conceptual representations among interlocutors. It merely depends on there being sufficient similarity in cognitive and other attunements to serve the immediate purpose, whether that commonality arises as a matter of genetic predisposition, similarity of experience, or congruent acculturation.[14]

Communicative practices at once serve as pivots enabling coordination, and yet shape-shift. In the remainder of this chapter, we will study how communicative practice evolves in terms of the resonance model of practice and presupposition laid out in the last five chapters, focusing on how the process of accommodation used in the account of presupposition can be generalized and explained.

Our discussion of accommodation addresses a gap in our account of resonance. The work of Rae Langton, Caroline West, and Marina Sbisà, and much other work besides, has suggested that accommodation is the mechanism by which the presuppositions of communicative actions wield their power, as well as being the process underlying the effectiveness of much manipulative language in politics, advertising, and everyday life.[15] We agree, and will go somewhat further, suggesting that accommodation is a central mechanism by which multiple linguistic interactions over time lead to ideological change. It is the place in the theory of meaning where slow processes of adaptation are accounted for.

Standard accounts model accommodation as a process in which a sharp single change takes place to fit the perceived needs of an interaction. On this view, accommodation is not a good candidate to explain long-term effects of the ideological resonances of language. We aim to improve on this situation,

---

12. Brown, "How Shall a Thing Be Called?," 14–15 and 18–19.

13. Quine, "Translation and Meaning," 28–33.

14. The question of the extent to which linguistic practices build on a common genetically inherited substrate is a matter of extreme controversy. We do not take a stand here. Nothing we say about the development of attunement toward practices depends on a particular level of innate shared disposition, or indeed on any significant level of predisposition toward specifically linguistic practices. An example of evidence of linguistic sensitivity in young infants, suggestive of the interpretation that significant aspects of human linguistic competence is in some way already built in at time of birth, is found in Waxman and Markow, "Words as Invitations to Form Categories."

15. Langton and West, "Scorekeeping in a Pornographic Language Game"; Sbisà, "Ideology and the Persuasive Use of Presupposition."

by providing a way of thinking about accommodation whereby it becomes clearer how small changes within individual interactions can lead to long-term ideological change, whether that change is for better or for worse.[16]

Accommodation does more than plug a gap in our resonance-based model. The term "accommodation" is used in two highly divergent bodies of work. One is in analytic philosophy of language and formal pragmatics, and the other is in sociolinguistics, social psychology, and communication studies. The two bodies of work do not involve any visible signs of significant scholarly cross-fertilization, such as cross-citation. Indeed, at first glance, these lines of scholarship appear to have little more in common than a coincidence of nomenclature, although it is at least the case that both approaches take accommodation to be an interactional, adaptive process. In this chapter and the next, we will suggest that there is value in viewing these two bodies of work on accommodation as part of a single generalized picture of adaptation in interactional situations. Just as we can speak of behavioral attunement and cognitive attunement, so we can speak of behavioral accommodation and cognitive accommodation, and these two types of accommodation, roughly speaking, correspond to the types of accommodation found in the two literatures.

6.2. Accommodation as Harmonization

The view that we develop in this chapter is that in considering the evolution of practice, accommodation is the engine of change. It is not merely a special type of comprehension. Accommodation is a force shaping both our individual performances and the practices and ideologies that come to define the groups we are aligned with. So how will we analyze it? Here's the soundbite:

Accommodation is harmonization to context.

Large societal and cultural structures must be understood in terms of individual human interactions. The large structures are not only reflected by those local interactions, but indeed can be said to consist in local interactions and to be transformed by them. This idea is at the heart of the adaptation of Durkheim's work to the study of conversational interaction by Erving Goffman, a shift in focus made completely explicit in Thomas Scheff's conception of *microsociology*,[17] and developed further in Randall Collins's *interaction ritual theory*.[18] Collins summarizes (in the abstract of a central paper) his

16. Michael Barnes also rightly argues that accommodation must be gradual in order to account for the phenomena it is being used by Langton, Sbisà, and others to explain. However, Barnes does not supply a model of accommodation that is gradual; see his "Presupposition and Propaganda."

17. Scheff, *Microsociology*.

18. Randall Collins, *Interaction Ritual Chains*.

view in a way that recalls both Durkheim's account of rituals and Festinger's account of dissonance:

> Individuals continuously negotiate [social] coalitions in chains of interaction rituals in which conversations create symbols of group membership. Every encounter is a marketplace in which individuals tacitly match conversational and emotional resources acquired from previous encounters. Individuals are motivated to move toward those ritual encounters in which their microresources pay the greatest emotional returns until they reach personal equilibrium points at which their emotional returns stabilize or decline.[19]

How do individuals "tacitly match conversational and emotional resources acquired from previous encounters"? How can a negotiation take place implicitly? Our answer is that a history of practice is encoded in the presuppositional resonances of conversational actions, and that the implicit parts of the negotiation involve adaptive moves of accommodation, driven by preferences for individual and collective harmony. We will not engage closely with Collins's proposal in this volume, but if our interpretation of his model is on the right track, then what his account demands is a theory of interactional accommodation. In the rest of this chapter, we will explain what we think such a theory must involve and then apply it to one of the hallmarks of the contemporary political scene: polarization and the formation of echo chambers.

A slur, a sexist joke, or a casual dismissive gesture can change future attitudes and behaviors. We have suggested that the presuppositional profiles of denigrating acts like these include discriminatory and oppressive ideologies. Spread and acceptance of these ideologies takes place when exposure to the acts leads observers to internalize the behavior of typical interactants, deepening their attunement to the ideologies that are prominent in the presuppositional profiles of the act. Each interaction might have only a small effect on an audience member, whose grasp of the act will be incomplete. On a first exposure to a slur, a watching kid may grasp no more than that they've observed a practice of someone expressing heightened negative emotion toward members of a group, perhaps with the group itself not being clearly delineated as far as the kid is concerned. Nonetheless, over the course of subsequent exposures to this and related behaviors, and with the help of bootstrapping achieved through mimicry, and thus learning by doing, the kid can develop the discriminatory dispositions they have observed. The mechanism whereby attunement to presuppositions is deepened is *accommodation*. Extending slightly the soundbite at the start of this section, here's a definition:

---

19. Randall Collins, "On the Microfoundations of Macrosociology," 984.

Accommodation: Accommodation is harmonization triggered by the perceived context of communicative interactions.

According to this definition, accommodation is a process of adaptive change in a conversational setting. But not just any change. First, it is specifically *harmonization*. Second, it is harmonization to the perceived *context* of interactions.

If accommodation is harmonization, then accommodation is a psychosocial process whereby a system of attunements changes so as to yield increased consonance for an individual or group. Our use of "harmonization" implies that people can accommodate to different degrees. This is in line with our model of presupposition, which is also scalar, but contrasts with the all-or-nothing models of accommodation that are standard in analytic philosophy and theoretical semantics/pragmatics. As we shall see later in the chapter, the process of finding consonance can also yield a certain type of dissonance, so the claim that accommodation yields consonance is nontrivial. Note also that the definition of accommodation does not limit it to being a psychological process of just one agent, and does not limit it to being a process in the head of a hearer, both of which are common assumptions in prior work. On our view, accommodation can be an adaptation of any participant in an interaction, or an observer of the interaction. In particular, speakers may accommodate as they speak. Indeed, accommodation is not limited to individuals, but can be analyzed at a group level, whereby what is harmonized is not an individual's attunements, but a group's collective attunements. Accommodation at the group level might involve the people of an entire nation harmonizing in a way that is triggered by the contexts they observe in TV sitcoms or election campaigns. A pliant population accommodates by coming to speak and act in ways that are partly determined by the models set in front of them, using the mannerisms of sitcom stars and smoking with the calm style of a Marlboro cowboy.

We say in the above definition that accommodation is triggered by the *context* of an interaction. Why do we emphasize context? Because this is what distinguishes accommodation from *uptake*. By *context*, we are referring to the situation in which an interaction takes place, and not to the new situation created by the predictable effects of conversational moves within the interaction. Consider an instance of the command "Hand over the money!" uttered in a bank. The context includes physical features, such as the location and the visible appearance of the interlocutors, and various sociocultural features, like the cultural significance of the bank, the roles of those who work in it and visit it, and a mass of social practices that are taken by default to be shared among those in this space, including speech practices. According to the model of presupposition developed in the last two chapters, the complex communicative action of issuing the command can supplement this context. But how does this supplementation work? That is precisely where accommodation comes in to provide the missing link in the story so far.

Recall that a feature of context is a resonance of a communicative practice to the extent that an occurrence of the action changes the probability of that feature (section 2.5). A bank robber demanding "Gimme the money!" instantiates many different practices, including the practice of speaking English, the practice of definite reference, the practice of using an imperative to command, and the practice of robbing a bank. All of these have resonances. Some of these resonances are features of the context that results from the communicative action, features that are sufficiently associated with instantiations of the practices in question that they can be seen as somewhat predictable effects. Examples are the hearer recognizing what the speaker is asking for, the hearer becoming publicly committed to giving the speaker what they have demanded, the hearer actually giving the speaker what they have demanded, and the hearer getting scared.

The presupposed resonances of a practice are features of typical contexts in which the actions take place. Here, presuppositional resonances include the presence of money to be handed over, the ability of the hearer to provide cash without the normal paperwork, and a power relationship sufficient to coerce the addressee into performing this distinctive financial transaction. The fact that someone has performed practices with certain presupposed resonances provides a clue as to what the context is like, or at least what the speaker takes the context to be like. A hearer, if they are attuned to these same practices, can then leverage the presupposed resonances of a communicative action to adapt to the situation. The hearer changes the way they are attuned to aspects of the context reflected in the communicative action directed at them. This adaptation is accommodation.

In the simplest cases that we consider first in this chapter, the adaptation monotonically increases collective attunement between interactional participants. Their individual harmonization, as each interactant adapts to the presuppositions of the other's actions, is part of a broader process of collective harmonization taking place as a conversational interaction or relationship unfolds. A well-studied special case of such collective harmonization is the process known as *grounding*, whereby interactants develop shared understanding of their environment and shared ways of talking about issues of interest to them within that environment. Grounding is then a process involving layered accommodation of presuppositions, although it might also involve metadiscourse, explicit negotiation about the assumptions to be made and the speech practices to be adopted.

It is important to realize that while accommodation, on our view, always involves harmonization, harmonization is more general: it can include explicit negotiation, and it can also involve reactions to features of the environment that are neither communicative nor social. Suppose you are attuned to swans being white and observe something that appears to be a black swan, and that you then gradually adapt, modifying in some way your beliefs or your understanding of your perceptions. This is harmonization, but it is not accommodation, since it was not triggered by the perceived context of a social interaction.

6.3. Beyond Scorekeeping

In the midst of our discussion of presupposition in the last two chapters, we also introduced the logico-linguistic tradition of work on accommodation, which, at least as regards use of the term "accommodation," dates to David Lewis's foundational 1979 paper "Scorekeeping in a Language Game."[20] This tradition takes accommodation to be a repair strategy, whereby a hearer's beliefs change in order to enable comprehension of what a speaker has said, or in order to reflect what a speaker appears to have assumed is common ground. Accommodation played a central part in our explanation of various phenomena. Although in some cases we invoked accommodation to clarify phenomena that are not normally explained in terms of accommodation, even there our use was quite standard from the point of view of work on presupposition. For example, our explanations in chapter 4 of framing effects both in Kahneman and Tversky's work on prospect theory, and in Elizabeth Loftus's work on memory, depended on experimental subjects accommodating framing presuppositions.

Our account of accommodation is, we freely admit, more powerful than is needed to account for the bulk of data on presupposition accommodation in linguistic theory. Harmonization is a leviathan, and the standard well-worn examples, as they are normally described, are small fry in the sense that they require neither attention to social and emotional factors, nor a general theory of dissonance and mental landscapes in which compartmentalization and self-deception are possible. In essence, most of the work for these cases is done by the way people recognize context, and very little work is done by harmonization.

Let us recap the explanations of classic psychological experiments we presented in chapter 4. Suppose that an utterance, involving a strategically deployed how-much question and when-clause, presupposes that two cars "smashed" into each other. The hearer knows that "smash" is an expression standardly used in a context of a high-energy collision, and simply has to take the same perspective as the speaker appears to have, recognizing that the current context is the normal type of context in which the expression is used. Harmonization here consists in nothing more than blithely adopting the perspective of those with whom you are engaging.

The explanation is similar for many standard cases in the logico-linguistic tradition. When a speaker uses the description "my sister," a hearer can then

20. Lewis, "Scorekeeping in a Language Game."

recognize, simply adopting the same perspective as the speaker, that they are in the sort of context in which such a description would be apt, that is, one in which the speaker has a sister. Unless the hearer previously had reason to doubt the existence of said sister, there need be no complex chain of reasoning of the form "Wow, that's weird. The speaker is acting as if they believe that they have a sister. I wonder why they have this belief? That my interlocutor would not only have this belief but also seem to take it for granted that I have this belief is creating dissonance for me, for it reflects a difference between our beliefs. How can I resolve it? I know, I'll adapt my beliefs, and henceforth will believe that the speaker has a sister." No, what normally happens is that by virtue of their competence in the same speech practices, which includes an implicit understanding of the presuppositional resonances of the utterance, the hearer somewhat automatically develops exactly the attunements that the speaker's act presupposed. That is, and though we don't think it controversial, we are hypothesizing that most accommodation of this sort is nondeliberative.

Similarly, the speaker may not have reasoned in a terribly complex way when using the phrase "my sister," and may not have considered the probability that the hearer would be familiar with the sister's existence. The fact that a speaker would assume things with which the hearer is not familiar indicates not that they probably did some complex reasoning about what pretenses they could get away with, or what would be the optimal way to convey the desired information to the hearer, but rather exactly the opposite. The speaker may have done no careful *audience design*, and may not have deliberated at all about how to describe their sister in the way that, say, the joint authors of an academic monograph might deliberate about what the audience could be expected to know. The upshot of these considerations is that the type of harmonization needed to account for the effects of presupposition in these cases is very restricted: it is merely collective harmonization of interactants. This collective harmonization centers on a preference for the consonance produced by speaking and thinking like others in the group you are in. We do not need a very complex model of attention, or a complex model of reaction to psychological dissonance, in order to account for such cases.

Most speakers do not function like the writers discussed previously, in the final section of chapter 4, who strategically began novels with unsatisfied presuppositions as to the referents of pronouns. When a speaker says something with presuppositions unknown to their interlocutors, we should not by default conclude that they are masters of sophisticated audience design, but rather that they have probably engaged in no conscious audience design at all. It is not a trivial fact that both speakers and hearers tend to adopt fairly lazy communicative processing strategies. Interlocutors assume that their communicative practices are sufficiently robust that they will manage to jointly coordinate on many of the same features of context, even without explicitly discussing or reasoning about those features. This fact is closely related to the more general phenomena of mimicry to be discussed in the next section, a good default approach to developing coordination, and it is not particularly controversial. However, unlike most speakers, both experimental psychologists designing stimuli and novelists composing the first line of a novel are skilled manipulators. Thus, they don't merely act in accordance with a context, but can design a context that has no prior existence. It's because of experimental psychologists and novelists, as well as propagandists, that we have been careful to include in our definition of accommodation the word "perceived." In accommodating, people don't necessarily harmonize to the real-world context in which we are situated, but can harmonize to a perceived context, whether recognizing that they are doing so (as perhaps may be true in the case of a mysterious pronoun opening a novel), or not (when successfully duped by psychologists and propagandists).

Unconscious adoption of the perspective of an interlocutor might be said to be on the ground floor of a theory of harmonization, and does not in and of itself demand the towering edifice above it. Indeed, many of the more interesting cases, the cases for which upper stories of the building are needed, are those in which accommodation does not take place, in which an audience questions a presupposition or refuses to accept it, even in the face of the dissonance this creates in the conversational situation. Although it is far from being a default, such accommodation failures are not uncommon in political discussion, or, more generally, in conversations between people with strong affinities to groups that are in conflict. In such cases, the refusal to accept framings or go along with tacit assumptions might potentially be the basis of fruitful negotiation, but refusal can easily lead to communicative breakdown. This is a topic we will be returning to throughout the chapter, and especially in section 6.6, where we consider the role of systematic conversational breakdown in cases of extreme political polarization.

As should be clear, accommodation is typically subconscious. Or, at least, most accommodation is not sufficiently attended to that the subject in a psychological experiment would later report that their judgments depended on accepting assumptions implicit in the experimental stimuli. Most subjects in experiments we have discussed presumably neither attend to bias in the framing of the stimulus questions, nor consider alternative framings. As we have noted, for Lewis, accommodation occurs in the blink of an eye. There is something right about this, and something wrong. What's right about it is that since accommodation typically occurs as an autonomic and relatively non-deliberative process, the actual time spent adapting to a particular speaker may be short, and the amount of time we are aware of adapting to the speaker may be negligible or zero. This lack of attention to accommodation is precisely the reason presuppositions make such excellent vehicles for hustle, and thus explains why the manipulative use of presupposition is a key strategy for politicians and advertisers alike. What's wrong with Lewis's blink-of-an-eye claim is that it assumes accommodation to be an all-or-nothing thing: some feature either is or is not in the conversational score. Accommodation may happen rapidly, but it may also be the case that what happens rapidly is a small change, and that the net effect of a lot of small changes is in effect a gradual process, a process that appears more like slow adaptation to prevailing attunements of a community of practice, acclimatization to its ethos and mores, than like a sudden volte-face.

To repeat part of the passage from Lewis we have cited earlier: "If at time t something is said that requires presupposition P to be acceptable, and if P is not presupposed just before t, then—ceteris paribus and within certain limits—presupposition P comes into existence at t." This is clearly an unhelpful way to think about the process of accommodating practices. If we have practices as core examples, central cases of accommodation must be regarded as taking much longer, say the length of a childhood, or of an extended propaganda campaign. In the examples that motivate the standard theory, accommodation of a proposition can reasonably take place in real time as we process an individual utterance.

Suppose Elly says, "I am picking my sister up from the airport," and Allie accommodates the proposition that Elly has a sister. This sort of process is so rapid that it is hard to find evidence of extra time being taken to accommodate presupposed material above and beyond the time taken to process similar expressions when the presupposition is already known to the hearer. Contrast this with the types of cases that are central for us, for example, when executives describe people solely in terms of their work efficiency and their interlocutors increasingly treat those too old or infirm to work with ever more disdain. The time course of this process might be measured not in dozens of milliseconds but in dozens of PowerPoint presentations. To be sure, there might be rapid and unconscious periods of adaptation during each Power-Point presentation, but each of these episodes feeds into a much longer-term process of harmonization that might lead the hearer to become gradually inculcated in a particular technocratic way of thinking, or might eventually lead to such dissonance that they eventually cut themselves off from their in-group, and leave for greener pastures.

Here we hope the reader is beginning to see how viewing accommodation as harmonization might constitute a major shift in presupposition theory. Whereas previously accommodation of presuppositions was understood as a sort of short-term online belief revision process, we are suggesting that it involves not only belief revision, but also behavioral and emotional adaptation, and that these processes of adaptation might take place across a wide range of time scales. Furthermore, a process of adaptation that takes place across multiple sales meetings and business lunches is not simply a process in which one person produces an utterance with a presupposition, and another reacts to it. Accommodation is a social process, and groups can accommodate, collectively harmonizing to the jointly perceived contexts of multiple conversational interactions. It is a process in which multiple hearers are affected by multiple presuppositions in multiple utterances by multiple speakers, and in which many of the hearers will themselves also play the role of speaker. That is, accommodation becomes an interactive process involving feedback loops. Thus accommodation need not simply be a reshaping of attunements to better fit a context, but can become an evolving process of group change that, while triggered by a particular misalignment with context, ends up yielding a succession of collective re-attunements that have no simple relationship with the original misalignment. We should expect this process to be deeply affected by the social organization of the group within which accommodation is occurring, because, for example, power relationships and factors such as identity and role will affect who pays attention to whom, and thus the dynamics of who adapts to whom and in what way.

Consider the rippling effects of accommodation to the presuppositions of a new meme and its associated metadiscourse, say the #metoo movement that began in 2017. Following a spate of reporting on victims of sexual misconduct, and in many cases criminal sexual assault, a single Twitter posting encouraging people to post their own victimhood stories under the #metoo hashtag inspired an explosive cascade of responses. The phenomenon included tens of millions of #metoo social-media posts within days. Such effects need to be seen holistically, at the level of a large community, not at the level of individual interactions. There is thus a parallel to individual accommodation at the level of groups. Since such processes lead to change in collective attunements, we could naturally call what is occurring *collective accommodation*. It is collective accommodation not merely to a new speech act, but a new speech practice. That practice evolved, and continues to evolve, as does the community of practice within which the practice exists, each use of the hashtag adding to the extension of the practice, and members of the ever-changing and increasingly global community accommodating as they perceive differences between their attunement to the practice and what they perceive to be the broader collective attunement. What is collectively accommodated may be collective attunements that are not even analyzable at the individual level. For example, one might optimistically hope that #metoo led to a reduction in the level of certain types of oppression, but the disposition to oppress is itself not a disposition at an individual level. Virality of a meme and oppression are like war, famine, and mass extinction. They can only be understood at a systemic level.

In the rest of this chapter, we discuss the process of accommodation at a group level. We argue that harmonization helps us understand the accommodation of types of attunement not considered in the standard Lewis-Stalnaker type models we have discussed so far, and we further describe how accommodation might be usefully seen as central to group-level processes of ideological transmission and change.

6.4. Tuning In to Others

We have at various times in this volume talked of *perspectives*, and of how people shift perspectives, or take the perspective of another. These notions will be of particular import in chapter 7, where we discuss the concept of neutrality. But what is a perspective? In terms of our model, a perspective on a set of features of context is a distinctive system of attunements to those features. Similarity of perspectives on a set of features for a group of people then equates to the group having what we have termed *collective* attunement to those features.

Given this way of explicating *perspective*, we can then say what adopting someone's perspective consists in. To adopt some individual or group's perspective on a set of features of context is to accommodate toward them as regards attunements to those features, harmonizing sufficiently that one's attunements to the features are similar to theirs. Extending this definition of perspective shift, we might say that to *empathize* is to temporarily adopt someone's perspective, especially by harmonizing with and attending to emotional attunements and behaving in accord with them. The fragmented nature of the landscape of attunements allows such temporary perspective-taking to occur without greatly impacting an agent's other attunements. We can, in the moment, take on aspects of someone's thoughts and feelings, even their personality, but compartmentalize, much as does a method actor. The method actor inhabits their role not only mentally, but physically, and yet in an instant can return to their more familiar persona, like Sherlock Holmes miraculously whipping off his disguise before a befuddled Watson.

We will now argue that our definition of accommodation as harmonization to context implies that it can be manifested not merely passively and epistemically, as a Lewisian change in cognitive attunements, but performatively, as short-term change in behavior within an interaction. How so? Well, if accommodation is harmonization to the context of communicative interaction, then it follows that it can involve reactions to arbitrary features of that context. What are the relevant features of context? They are features of context presupposed by the utterance, and features that are salient to the interaction. This could potentially include the physical space within which the interaction is held, or the medium of communication, but the most important features are features of the interactants themselves. Accommodation might be a response to any feature of an interactant, including the identities they are seen as representing, the way they are sitting, and the way they are talking. But what response? Since harmonization is a process of finding consonance across a system of attunements that is not restricted to cognitive attitudes, accommodation could include an emotional response or a dispositional response.

Furthermore, a dispositional response might be long-term or short-term, and a short-term dispositional change might be registered by a perceptible alteration in behavior. Thus, accommodation could produce an emotional-behavioral response to someone, say, smiling, relaxing, or lighting up a cigarette, or becoming visibly or audibly angry, tense, or threatening.

Let us term behavioral adaptations to conversational context *behavioral accommodation*. Behavioral accommodation is not studied in the logico-linguistic tradition but in a separate psychosocial tradition of work that was initiated in the early 1970s by Howard Giles, a tradition now called Communication Accommodation Theory.[21] The primary area of theorizing in Communication Accommodation Theory is the effect of the social relationship between interlocutors on their interactional behavior, considering factors such as status and ethnic or gender identity. For the most part, the focus is on the degree to which behaviors converge or diverge, although some work considers more complex social behaviors, like the telling of jokes. Seen at a high level, both the logico-linguistic and social traditions treat the default and most common types of accommodation as coordinative, whereby interactants come to think alike, act alike, and see themselves as alike. Thinking alike, in the sense of having common beliefs, is the notion of accommodation prominent in the logico-linguistic tradition; acting alike, and seeing ourselves as alike, are central to the psychosocial tradition. The psychosocial tradition also considers the case of interactants who behaviorally manifest their differences. We will suggest that such cases are in fact not exceptions to the generalization that accommodation is coordinative, but we postpone that discussion to the next section. Our goal in the remainder of this section is to describe the social basis of coordinative accommodation.

It seems reasonable to postulate that the reason we accommodate to others is that we care what they think about us. William James's description of our sensitivity to the views of others, and the sense in which that feedback shapes how we see ourselves, remains apt:

> A man's Social Self is the recognition which he gets from his mates. We are not only gregarious animals, liking to be in sight of our fellows,

---

21. Giles's introduction of what is now known as Communication Accommodation Theory began with his thesis, "A Study of Speech Patterns in Social Interaction." A standard overview is Giles, Coupland, and Coupland, "Accommodation Theory." Note that both Giles's work and the recent discussion of accommodation in psychological and computational analysis of dialogue (e.g., Doyle and Frank, "Investigating the Sources of Linguistic Alignment in Conversation") is substantially predated by the use of the term "accommodation" popularized by Jean Piaget in his developmental work in the 1950s. For Piaget, accommodation concerns children's adaption of their mental schemas to fit features of the environment. Piaget is perhaps a direct antecedent of both Giles's and Lewis's usage of accommodation, since Piaget explicitly mentions accommodation in social interaction, commenting, e.g., "accommodation to the point of view of others enables individual thought to be located in a totality of perspectives that insures its objectivity and reduces its egocentrism" (*The Construction of Reality in the Child*, 356–57).

but we have an innate propensity to get ourselves noticed, and noticed favorably, by our kind. No more fiendish punishment could be devised, were such a thing physically possible, than that one should be turned loose in society and remain absolutely unnoticed by all the members thereof. . . .

Properly speaking, a man has as many social selves as there are individuals who recognize him and carry an image of him in their mind. To wound any one of these images is to wound him. But as the individuals who carry the images fall naturally into classes, we may practically say that he has as many different social selves as there are distinct groups of persons about whose opinion he cares. He generally shows a different side of himself to each of these different groups. Many a youth who is demure enough before his parents and teachers, swears and swaggers like a pirate among his "tough" young friends.[22]

It seems safe to say that our feelings of consonance, or dissonance, are hugely dependent on our perceptions of the behaviors of others. Which others? In the above quote, James simply says that it is others "about whose opinion [one] cares." But whose opinions do we care about?

Psychological work on personal and social-identity theory[23] suggests that people's social behavior can be thought of in terms of a balance between (i) conformity to groups to which one feels affiliation, (ii) the constraints of social roles which one plays, and (iii), as emphasized in Social Distinctiveness Theory,[24] competing needs for individual self-determination and distinctiveness within one's in-groups. This idea of optimal social distinctiveness is central to Thomas Scheff's *Microsociology*. The close relationship between Scheff's model and our own is apparent in the following passage, in which he relates his model to Émile Durkheim's notions of *mechanical solidarity* (similarities of experience and practice, enhanced by joint ritual, and weakening in modern society) and *organic similarity* (social and work-functional

---

22. James, *The Principles of Psychology*, 294. James goes on to distinguish one particular social self: "The most peculiar social self which one is apt to have is in the mind of the person one is in love with. The good or bad fortunes of this self cause the most intense elation and dejection—unreasonable enough as measured by every other standard than that of the organic feeling of the individual. To his own consciousness he *is* not, so long as this particular social self fails to get recognition, and when it is recognized his contentment passes all bounds" (294). That is, inner harmony and relationship harmony can sometimes be hard to distinguish.

23. Good introductions to Social Identity Theory and Identity Theory are, respectively, Tajfel et al., "An Integrative Theory of Intergroup Conflict"; Burke, "Identity Control Theory." We strongly recommend the overview of both in Hogg, Terry, and White, "A Tale of Two Theories."

24. Brewer, "The Social Self"; Hornsey and Jetten, "The Individual within the Group"; Leonardelli, Pickett, and Brewer, "Optimal Distinctiveness Theory."

complementarity and interdependence, increasingly dominant for large, modern, urbanized populations):[25]

> Too little distance produces overconformity, just as too much produces underconformity. Some balance seems to be necessary to allow for the system to maintain coherence, a mixture of tradition and change.
>
> Although at first sight the level of differentiation seems similar to the distinction Durkheim made between mechanical and organic solidarity, the overlap is slight. Durkheim's distinction is strictly behavioral; it does not encompass the main elements in [psychiatrist Murray Bowen]'s idea [of social bonds within families], which concern internal as well as external states. Organic solidarity concerns cooperative behavior. Optimal differentiation in Bowen's sense concerns intellectual and emotional attunement, mutual understanding as well as behavioral interdependence.[26]

As the earlier passage from James suggests, pressures for similarity and differentiation may be felt through observation of the behavior of others with whom we interact. Such feedback might be in the form of explicit praise or criticism. But it might also take the form of nonverbal behavioral accommodation such as semitransparent feedback given by bodily orientation, gesture, and facial expression, or still more subtle feedback based on the level of attention we receive.

One way in which someone's behavior manifests their attention to us is via its responsiveness to our own behavior, even if that response has no inherent emotional valence. If someone catches a ball you have thrown across a crowded football field, or catches a glance that you have shot across a crowded room, then they are paying attention to you. They care about you in at least a very limited sense. Note here that if you are static, then you do not provide a clear opportunity for your interlocutor to accommodate to you, since absence of major movement is a default. If it is important, whether for coordinative or emotional reasons, to know that people are paying attention, and

---

25. Durkheim, *The Division of Labor in Society*.

26. Scheff, *Microsociology*, 5. Note that although the notion of *attunement* mentioned in this quote plays a similar functional role in Scheff's theory as it does in ours, the two notions are defined quite differently. Scheff's attunement is a relation between people who may be attuned to each other to a greater or lesser degree if they are jointly paying attention to the same things and have shared understanding. On our view, attunement is a relation between an individual (or group) and anything else, with attunement to another individual (or group) being a special case. Thus for us, people being attuned to each other implies that they have common attunements to other things, which is not how Scheff uses the term. He does however talk of "attunement of thought and feeling" (*Microsociology*, 106), so our talk of cognitive and emotional attunements can be seen as an extension and to some extent precisification of Scheff's terminology.

if responsiveness provides a way of gauging attentiveness, then it would be adaptively beneficial to keep shifting, so that each shift offers an opportunity for response. If every time one person smiles the other smiles, and when one crosses their arms the other crosses their arms, and when one tells a joke the other laughs, then they know they have each other's attention.

From a young age, people take cues about how to behave from those that represent the groups with which they are affiliated. Among the earliest studies demonstrating this effect systematically were the "Bobo doll" experiments conducted sixty years ago by the psychologist Albert Bandura and collaborators, building on a preexisting line of experimental research in imitative learning.[27] Kids aged three to five got to watch how adults interacted with large wobbly dolls: some adults were violent toward the dolls, while others were gentler. When the kids were later left alone with the dolls, their play tended to mimic the actions they had witnessed, acting aggressively toward the dolls if that's what they'd seen, and more gently if they'd witnessed adults doing so. Crucially, the extent to which they mimicked certain behaviors depended on what can be interpreted as an in-group/out-group variable: kids were more likely to reproduce verbally aggressive behavior by an adult of like gender.[28]

Leaving aside the extent to which we can draw strong conclusions directly from these old experiments, what is clear is that Bandura's study has been hugely influential in work on how aggression spreads, and on mimicry in the absence of reward. As regards effects of in-group status, there have now been many studies showing differential preferences for imitation of behavior by in-group members.[29] To put these results in our terms, without making any strong claim that we are doing more than redescribing them: (i) people (and especially children) have a tendency to accommodate to interactional behaviors they have witnessed by harmonizing with those behaviors, by developing dispositions to behave in the same way; and (ii) people are more likely to accommodate to in-group members than out-group members because the need to harmonize with a group is dependent on the affinity felt toward that group.

27. Bandura, Ross, and Ross, "Transmission of Aggression."

28. For levels of physical aggression, kids in general took their cues more from male investigators than female investigators. Whether this is because aggressive females were seen as acting against stereotype, or because female investigators are generally mimicked less in such experiments, or whether it is just statistical happenstance, we leave open.

29. For adults, see, e.g., Yabar et al., "Implicit Behavioral Mimicry." Imitation effects are strong among those facing ostracism from in-group members: Lakin, Chartrand, and Arkin, "I Am Too Just Like You." For infants and children, studies showing effects of group membership on mimicry include Watson-Jones, Whitehouse, and Legare, "In-Group Ostracism"; Buttelmann et al., "Selective Imitation"; Howard et al., "Infants' and Young Children's Imitation of Linguistic In-Group and Out-Group Informants"; Genschow and Schindler, "The Influence of Group Membership on Cross-Contextual Imitation."

It is far from surprising that people are disposed to act like those they perceive to be of their kind; birds of a feather, after all, have been known to flock together. What makes humans special in this regard is that both the feather and the flocking are cultural artifacts, and that a single individual can wear many feathers, each of which marks membership of groups that themselves each flock in many ways. For humans to be birds of a feather is for them to jointly accept membership and trappings of a category that humans themselves have constructed. These constructed categories may be loosely based on naturalistic concepts, like race and gender, or not, as in ideological groupings or football team allegiances. For humans to flock, in the broad metaphorical sense we intend, is not merely for them to gather together physically, but to exhibit arbitrary common behaviors. To flock is to form a community of practice.

Cultural flocking produces feedback loops: our behaviors come to define our categories, the wearing of the feathers that mark out the community itself being a community behavior. To take an example that has been a focus of feminist academic study for many years, gendered behaviors help define what it is to have a certain gender.[30] Similarly, to be a redneck is no longer to be a fair-skinned person who labors under a Southern sun, but to exhibit whatever dispositions and attitudes have come to loosely define a clustering of people who are unlikely to self-identify as rednecks at all. Even without self-identifying as rednecks, the clustering of behaviors and attitudes that out-groups dismissively refer to as stereotypical of rednecks may be strong enough that it brings people together at the church, the concert, the racing circuit, and the polling booth.

Category-defining behaviors, and hence the categories themselves, are dynamic. If highly visible people in a group develop a tendency to use social media in a new way, or party, parade, or pray in a new way, others in the group will have a tendency to accommodate those new practices, that is, fashions. And once the practices become identified with the group, part of the group's standard social scripts, the group's identity will in turn become identified with the practices, producing a cycle of renewal. We see in this dynamicity an abstract similarity with the suggestion above that dynamically shifting behavior can be adaptively advantageous in verifying attentiveness and thereby underpinning coordination. At the group level, too, change itself can be a positive adaptive trait, and not merely an inevitable effect of drift. If social-identity markers are static, then they might be easily appropriated by other groups or mimicked by outsiders wishing to join a club that the members might rather keep exclusive. If social-identity markers evolve dynamically, like a changing password at the door, then the club will be harder to get into. Stay trendy.

---

30. The classic work taking this anti-essentialist approach to gender is that of Judith Butler, in particular her book *Gender Trouble*.

While natural properties such as age and skin tone clearly play a role in providing perceptually accessible markers for many groupings, what we're talking about here is the question of what cultural devices serve to identify the members of social groups. That is, we are interested in what attunements people in groups need to have in order to be recognized by each other. Although arbitrarily complex protocols are possible, a simple principle is obvious: the more distinctive attunements members of a group share, the easier it will be for them to recognize each other. To return to an earlier metaphor, the distinctiveness of these attunements is analogous to a musical key: you recognize others in your groups when they play in keys that you like to play in, that is, when they behave in a way that manifests dispositions consonant with yours.

The term "key signature" is apt, but a key is more than a distinctive squiggle: it both identifies and defines a group, helping to make membership of the group and the individual attunements that form the key *meaningful*. There is, then, a collective harmony in a social group when there is a clearly defined and recognized key collectively accommodated by the group that conveys meaning to the group members. The key is a pattern of group-appropriate attunements, such that individual group members can manifest their membership by displaying attunements in that key, such that other group members are perceptually attuned to the meaning of the key, and such that when group members perceive someone playing in that key, what they perceive is a fellow group member. A given performance in this key may or may not make group identity apparent or salient for out-group members.

A key may be difficult to reproduce because it is a form of costly signaling and the cost is too high for many; it may be difficult to reproduce because it keeps changing, as we just suggested; or it may be difficult to reproduce because it has the quality of a shibboleth—virtually imperceptible or practically irreproducible for those not in the know. Parts of the key may be invisible to those not paying attention, as with a key ring or carabiner hanging in a particular way to signify gender identity. The choice of hanging keys for this function itself carries suggestive resonances that go beyond a mere lexical coincidence with our use of the term "key." And parts of the key may be literally invisible: you see (say) a local shop-keeper cordially greeting a police officer, but as the two shake hands, each of them sees a fellow mason.

What is important here is that accommodation is a process that can cause things to become both inwardly and outwardly meaningful. Accommodation supports feedback loops of group adoption of some styles, and group avoidance of others. But meaningfulness as we are using it here is a slippery concept, and so let us say a little more about how we are using it.

In talking of meaningfulness, we are not talking about the meanings of formal semantics as developed in the Western analytic tradition from Frege on, or at least not *just* about these post-Fregean formal semantic meanings. It is clear that in ordinary talk the word "meaningful" is ambiguous: it certainly implies symbolism, significance, or richness of resonance, but can also be used in a valuative sense. For something to be meaningful in this sense is akin to it being resonant as we defined it in section 3.9. There we said that something resonates (positively) for a group or individual to the extent that it induces increased (positive) harmony for them. But we want to suggest that this only partially captures what we are trying to get at by *meaningfulness* in this section, which has to do with identity.

> **Meaningfulness:** Something is inwardly (/outwardly) meaningful for some individual or group to the extent that it resonates for them (/for others) in a way that activates attunements that are distinctive of their identity.

The definition is intended to allow for people have complex or perhaps even multiple identities. Crucifixes might be inwardly meaningful to someone qua their Catholicism, but a particular crucifix might be especially meaningful to them because they have worn that particular object for many years, or because it has other important personal associations connected with its history. To see what we mean by outward meaningfulness, consider the ambiguity of the old proverb "the clothes make the man." It can be understood both to mean that your clothes signify your character to others, and that your clothes are part of who you are (cf. the similarly ambiguous "you are what you eat").[31] The first is outward meaningfulness, and the second inward meaningfulness.

The definition of meaningfulness also allows that it is not merely objects that are meaningful. Practices, too, can be meaningful. In the case of clothes, it might be that the wearing of certain types of clothes is more meaningful than the clothes themselves. More generally, any behavior can become meaningful. An example of central relevance for us is that talking in a certain way can be meaningful, whether talking in a way that is a hallmark of origin, gender orientation, class, or education.

Note also that although we have talked in this section about what is meaningful in a positive way, our definition of what it is for something to resonate (in section 3.9) allows something to resonate negatively when it leads to dissonance for a group. Hence, inward and outward meaningfulness can also be negative, as when something makes negative stereotypes associated

---

31. The most natural interpretation for "the apparel oft proclaims the man," Pollonius's advice to his departing son, in Shakespeare's *Hamlet*, is that the clothes signify the nature or status of the wearer, but the sophisticated use of clothing to represent character in *Hamlet* is open to deeper analysis. Brillat-Savarin's eighteenth-century "Dis-moi ce que tu manges, je te dirai ce que tu es" (Tell me what you eat, and I'll tell you who you are), although ambiguous, suggests that your eating habits are diagnostic of, and perhaps central to your identity, while Feuerbach brought out a distinctly metaphysical interpretation in his later punning variant "Der Mensch ist, was er isst" (A person is what they eat). (Our thanks to Hank Southgate for discussion.)

with the group salient. Racist imagery and paraphernalia involved in racist practices can be meaningful in this negative way. Perhaps the most shocking examples are duplications of paraphernalia that has been involved in violence against members of the group, such as nooses, torches, and clothing typical of lynchings in the United States. A racist might tell a gas-chamber joke knowing exactly how it might be meaningful to any Jews who hear it, the way in which it will resonate negatively, the dissonance it will cause.

Let us return to the idea suggested by William James that we depend for our own sense of harmony on the attention and responsiveness of others with whom we are affiliated. Other than by performing explicit acts of reassurance, how can you provide evidence to someone that you are paying attention? And what is the simplest way of being responsive to them? Here's a general way of achieving both, already hinted at by examples we have considered: do whatever they do, mimicking any aspect of their behavior that isn't independently governed by the needs of your role in the interaction. If they cross their legs, you cross your legs; if they talk fast, you speed up; if they smile, you smile; if they say it was "absolutely awful," then as you nod and make a pained expression, say "absolutely awful!"

The *chameleon effect*, that is, short-term behavioral mimicry extending to arbitrary behaviors such as foot shaking that have no conventionalized communicative significance, is known to be largely automatic and unconscious.[32] Nonetheless, such mimicry logically requires a basic level of attention to your interlocutor's behavior and constitutes the simplest and most flexible response strategy that establishes such attention: any time you either don't have a conventional response to your interlocutor's behavior and don't have the time to compute a new response, repeating what they did will not only show that you were attending at some level, but will also show by direct demonstration that you are attuned to their behaviors. This type of mirroring also serves to make interlocutors feel good, a case of what is described in the pragmatics literature as *positive politeness*. By acting the same way that someone else acts, you show implicit approval of that way of acting, and register your similarity and hence closeness to them, mitigating the negative effects of any demands you may place on them.

As regards coordination, mimicry of speech practices amounts to adopting common communication protocols, and a background of bodily norms against which to evaluate gestures. The robustness of communication depends upon people not simply using a one-size-fits-all set of conventions for every aspect of communication, but rather adapting as needed. In an environment where someone is not able to hear you clearly, it may be important to speak slowly and loudly, and when speaking to a child, it may be important to use basic vocabulary. A good general way of adapting to the needs of your interlocutor is

32. Chartrand and Bargh, "The Chameleon Effect."

to adapt your speech to be more like theirs. There's no better way of being sure they will be familiar with the words you use than by choosing words that you have heard them say, and a decent way of choosing topics they will be interested in hearing about is choosing topics you've heard them discuss. Indeed, the associative workings of the mind mean that often both you and your interlocutors will be primed by the words and topics already mentioned, as well as by other aspects of the commonly accessible speech situation, meaning that there will be a happy coincidence between what one of you finds easy to produce and the other finds easy to comprehend. Furthermore, since speakers of the same language in the same speech situation will tend to exhibit similar priming effects, they will have a natural tendency to use similar words. Thus priming supports convergence of speech behavior, while simultaneously supporting success in coordination.

The upshot of all these considerations is that there are functional pressures for behavioral convergence of group members not only at the level of identity marking, but also at the level of individual conversational exchanges. This is a central plank of Communication Accommodation Theory, initially focusing on accent patterns in speech.

In some of his earliest work on the topic, Giles recognized the complementary possibility of divergent behavioral accommodation (to be discussed in the next section), and he explained convergent behavioral accommodation in terms of the need for social approval:

> If the sender in a dyadic situation wishes to gain the receiver's social approval then he may adapt his accent patterns towards that of this person, i.e. reduce pronunciation dissimilarities—*accent convergence*. On the other hand, if the sender wishes to dissociate himself from the receiver (maybe because of unfavourable characteristics, attitudes, or beliefs), then there may exist tendencies opposed to the receiver, i.e. emphasize pronunciation dissimilarities—*accent divergence*.[33]

Giles's earliest studies showed convergent behavioral accommodation among Welsh speakers of English, who, when positively disposed toward their interlocutor, used speech features that were more typical of the English of Wales when talking to other Welsh people, and speech features that were more typical of the English of England when talking to English people. That is, various speech features converged with those of the interlocutor, whether Welsh or English.[34] Similar results were found in an experimental study of Canadian

---

33. Giles, "Accent Mobility," 90, emphasis in original.

34. It is tempting to describe this situation, somewhat colloquially, as Welsh speakers speaking with less of a Welsh accent when speaking to English people than when speaking to Welsh people. This description, however, builds in a presupposition that the dialect spoken in Wales involves an "accent" relative to so-called "Received Pronunciation" paradigmatically spoken in England, which is then presupposed to be neutral. To talk of one

French-English bilinguals, in which experimental subjects were presented with recordings by a nonpresent speaker and then asked to record a description for the same speaker. The more the recording involved perceived adaptation to the style of the subject, the more the subject expressed approval of the speaker, and the more the subject adapted their own speech to the perceived style of the recording they'd heard.[35]

Let us define convergence and divergence in a way that encompasses accommodation across logico-linguistic and social traditions:

> **Convergence/divergence:** Accommodation is *convergent* toward a second party (an individual or group) when it results in a monotonic increase of the level of collective attunement with that party, *divergent* when it results in a monotonic decrease of the level of attunement with that party among some system of attunements, and *mixed* when there is a combination of convergence and divergence to the same party.

On this definition, accent convergence or divergence would involve changes in a system of short-term dispositional attunements governing active speech production, changes that result in a net increase or decrease in the similarity of relevant phonetic features (say, features of a vowel affected by placement of the tongue during production).

In the decades following Giles's introduction of accommodation as a socially motivated behavior among interactants in a speech situation, Communication Accommodation Theory has been vastly extended. It now includes matching of arbitrary aspects of communicative style and posture, for example, gesture, gaze, bodily position, code-switching, word-choice, syntactic construction, and speech rate, and even performance of complex acts such as telling jokes or making personal disclosures, and other behaviors that can be understood in terms of positive politeness. Many instances of behavioral accommodation have been documented in political contexts, for example, when politicians speak with a more Southern accent to sound like children of the South, when they drop the "g" in "-ing" to sound folksy,[36] or when they dress down and roll up their sleeves to look more like the people they're speaking to.

Studies of word use show that across a very wide range of conditions, people "style match" lexically, meaning that as an interaction proceeds they increasingly use a common vocabulary.[37] Since this vocabulary includes functional words

---

dialect being more neutral than another, is, however, to make a political statement, and to presuppose such neutrality is to leave the same politics perniciously implicit.

35. Giles, Taylor, and Bourhis, "Towards a Theory of Interpersonal Accommodation."

36. Purnell, Raimy, and Salmons, "Defining Dialect, Perceiving Dialect, and New Dialect Formation."

37. A good starting point to what is termed Language Style Matching (LSM) in the literature, but which focuses on lexical similarity, is Niederhoffer and Pennebaker, "Linguistic Style Matching in Social Interaction."

that correlate with the syntactic constructions being employed, this same data is also indicative of matching at the level of syntactic complexity and construction choice. Notably, lexical style-matching effects are found even in somewhat adversarial situations, such as business negotiations, hostage negotiations, and police interviews.[38] Of course, the fact that a situation is adversarial does not imply that there is no desire at all for mutual social approval, and certainly doesn't imply that there aren't other social benefits to be gained from coordination, which is essential to successful negotiation. In non-adversarial situations, there is evidence (though we must be careful in moving from correlation to causation) that lexical style matching is functionally expedient: groups engaged in problem-solving tasks in which style matching occurs tend to be more productive.[39] Style matching is positively correlated with whether people who have just met will go on to form a romantic relationship, and is correlated with measures of how well a relationship is going.[40]

The literature on mirroring and mimicry includes study of the underlying neurological processes involved. It is not our goal here to study the neurological underpinnings of mirroring behaviors, but we think it's worth considering whether there might be general principles underlying those behaviors, a reason why mirroring makes sense as a part of normal communication. Let us suggest briefly a line of explanation that is complementary to explanations in terms of marking of politeness or group identity, although it rests on principles that are used in Peter Burke's development of Identity Theory.[41]

Burke adapted an approach from Perceptual Control Theory[42] in which perception is modeled in terms of a feedback loop. Rather than just passively

38. For a study of negotiation in an experimental setting, see Ireland and Henderson, "Language Style Matching, Engagement, and Impasse in Negotiations." For an analysis of police-negotiation transcripts, see Taylor and Thomas, "Linguistic Style Matching and Negotiation Outcome." Police interview data is reported in Richardson et al., "Language Style Matching and Police Interrogation Outcomes." For a final case of adversarial lexical style matching, consider the fact that participants in a presidential debate style match, and that the degree of style matching is predictive of audience approval: Romero et al., "Linguistic Style Matching in Presidential Debates." See also Carrera-Fernández, Guàrdia-Olmos, and Peró-Cebollero, "Linguistic Style in the Mexican Electoral Process."

39. Gonzales, Hancock, and Pennebaker, "Language Style Matching."

40. For the importance of lexical style matching in speed-dating interactions, see Ireland et al., "Language Style Matching Predicts Relationship Initiation and Stability." A later speed-dating study, by McFarland, Jurafsky, and Rawling ("Making the Connection"), revealed the significance of three types of mimicry (laughter, function word use, and speech rate), but the picture is complicated both because the men and women do not value mimicry in the same way, and because the models include many other factors. Correlative evidence of a relationship between lexical style matching and relationship health is found in three archival studies in Ireland and Pennebaker, "Language Style Matching in Writing."

41. Burke, "Identity Processes and Social Stress."

42. For Perceptual Control Theory in the words of its somewhat iconoclastic primary developer, see Powers, *Behavior: The Control of Perception*.

waiting to receive signals, the perceiving animal actively adjusts its physical state and perceptual processing so as to maintain constancy of the stimulus, so that at least some aspects of perceptual processing become a special case of the broader biological process of homeostasis. Simple examples of perceptual feedback are the dilation of the pupil in response to reduced light or the tracking with eyes or head of a moving object so as to maintain a constant position in the (highest acuity part of the) visual field. For identity, Burke cites an example that had previously been studied experimentally, the example of people who perceive themselves as dominant engaging in more dominant behaviors when feedback suggests they are perceived as submissive.

Burke's model can be seen as cashing out the idea we began this section with, from William James, that our social selves are reflections of the views of others on which our positive self-esteem depends, so that failure to reflect what we aspire to causes dissonance. This is made explicit in the following passage from Michael Hogg, Deborah Terry, and Katherine White:

> The perception that one is enacting a role satisfactorily should enhance feelings of self-esteem, whereas perceptions of poor role performance may engender doubts about one's self-worth, and may even produce symptoms of psychological distress. . . . Distress may arise if feedback from others—in the form of reflected appraisals or perceptions of the self suggested by others' behavior—is perceived to be incongruent with one's identity. According to Burke . . . , identities act as cybernetic control systems: they bring into play a dissonance-reduction mechanism whereby people modify their behavior to achieve a match with their internalized identity standards.[43]

Let us speculatively suggest how a feedback model like Burke's, and like that found in a host of technologies since the invention of negative feedback control almost a century ago, might apply to mirroring within an interaction. As well as observing others, people self-monitor. Suppose then that, following general principles of biological systems, people wish to maintain a relatively constant perceptual environment, due to the higher processing load brought about by perceptual variation, and the greater difficulty of identifying meaningful signals when set against a variable background. In that case, they will make whatever behavioral changes they can to control and reduce such variation. It immediately follows that whenever there is a discrepancy between the signal they obtain by self-monitoring and the signal they maintain by monitoring another, they will feel a pressure to reduce that discrepancy, and will adjust their behavior until the perceptual difference vanishes. So if you hear yourself talking faster than your interlocutor, you will feel a pressure to slow down, and if you perceive a difference between the sound or effect

---

43. Hogg, Terry, and White, "A Tale of Two Theories," 257.

of the words you are using and the sound or effect of the words someone else is using, you will feel a pressure to make your words more like theirs. If someone raises their voice, you talk louder, and vice versa . . . "Why are we whispering?"[44]

Independently of whether anything like the feedback mechanism we have described is a useful way of thinking about the types of mirroring behaviors that form the simplest cases of behavioral accommodation, it gets at an important general point. Convergent behavioral accommodation, which is a process of harmonization within a group of conversational interactants, might not merely be polite in-group marking, but is also functionally advantageous. So far we've suggested some low-level reasons why it might be functionally advantageous, related to the ability to recognize signals: behavioral convergence reduces distracting variation, makes the communicative situation more predictable, and provides a baseline from which potentially communicative discrepancies in behavior can be judged. But there is also a higher-level functional reason for behavioral convergence that is higher-level insofar as it concerns complex interactional practices that are used to perform arbitrarily complex communicative actions, and not merely duplicated individual behavior indicative of identity and rapport. The higher-level function is the coordinative development of the communicative practices themselves.

Theoretical linguists and analytic philosophers have long been enamored by generative models of language, models that allow a finite formal system to produce an infinite number of forms, and express an infinite number of meanings. As if the infinities in such models were such a big deal! The problem is that the infinities in question are not nearly big enough. Consider the fact that no two adult speakers have the same lexicon. If Jason uses a word in a way that is unfamiliar to David, David's supposed ability to give meaning to an infinite number of forms will not be of direct use, since he won't be able to give meaning to the form in question. Looked at this way, infinite generativity could be as much a handicap as a benefit, for it is a corollary of infinite generativity, and one that on the basis of personal experience seems entirely plausible, that there are an infinite number of sentences in Jason's grammar that David cannot completely understand.

---

44. The process of harmonization, and hence accommodation as we use that term, is akin to what Jean Piaget termed *equilibration* (Piaget, *The Development of Thought*). Piaget's discussion of this process reveals that he sees it as a high-level extension of regulatory processes that operate in perception-behavior feedback loops that are biologically fundamental: "Self-regulations are the very nature of equilibration. These self-regulations come into play at all levels of cognition, including the very lowest level of perception" (Piaget, "Problems of Equilibration," 10). We will not attempt a detailed mapping of Piaget's triad of *assimilation, accommodation,* and *equilibration* into our own use of the terms *harmonization* and *accommodation,* and also leave it open how our discussion of imitation might be related to Piaget's extensive work on imitation in infants.

Generalizing, not only does every speaker's system of grammatical attunements differ slightly from that of every other speaker, but every interaction places novel demands on the interactants. These demands cannot be met by deployment of a fixed tool-for-every-occasion Swiss Army knife bequeathed to us by our forebears, however ingenious, but rather require processes of dynamic optimization of communicative practices. These processes have been studied extensively in work of psychologists of language and sociologists and sociolinguists in the Conversation Analysis tradition, work that focuses not on the infinity of forms and meanings that an individual speaker can produce or comprehend, but on the patterns of interaction seen in individual conversations. An important result from that work (although it seems obvious after the fact) is that rather than simply using a common stock of conventions, people innovate new conventions during their conversations. For example, when faced with a novel task that involves selecting shapes, people collaboratively develop efficient descriptive language, starting off with longer descriptions, and honing in on shorter, name-like descriptions.[45]

Both explicit and implicit negotiation of meaning are seen in studies of dialogue.[46] Explicit negotiation might involve people proposing a practice, perhaps saying what they mean or what they are going to mean by an expression, but explicit negotiation may also be part of a repair sequence. After someone has signaled failure to understand, there might be a corrective move with clarification or substitution of an alternative expression, and sometimes metadiscussion of how expressions will be used. Negotiation of meaning is implicit when a use of an expression that is novel to some audience member is unannounced, and the novelty is not explicitly acknowledged. In such cases, what *grounds*[47] the conversational move—that is, establishes that there is joint understanding of what move has been performed—is at most a general acknowledgment of understanding, perhaps a back-channeling nod or confirmatory vocalization, and perhaps merely the absence of a furrowed brow or other manifest signs of confusion.

---

45. Wilkes-Gibbs and Clark, "Coordinating Beliefs in Conversation." They give the example of a subject in an experiment involving the description of shaped objects who initially identified a shape by saying "All right, the next one looks like a person who's ice skating, except they're sticking two arms out in front," and later refined the description to "the ice skater" ("Coordinating Beliefs in Conversation," 28).

46. A good general discussion of the processes involved in multiple types of communicative coordination is Pickering and Garrod, "Toward a Mechanistic Psychology of Dialogue." See also Clark and Wilkes-Gibbes, "Referring as a Collaborative Process"; Clark and Gerrig, "Understanding Old Words with New Meanings"; Larsson, "Ad-hoc Semantic Systems," "Grounding"; Healey, "Expertise or Expertese?"; Hawkins, "Coordinating on Meaning in Communication."

47. Clark and Brennan, "Grounding in Communication."

Accommodation is harmonization to context. When the context is a task you are trying to complete, dissonance would be created if your language did not allow you to perform that task efficiently. The dissonance is avoided by dynamically altering dispositional attunements to match the needs of the context, for example, by developing a disposition to refer to a salient object using a name or short description. Since the bespoke language behaviors people use in response to short-term conversational needs are adaptations that are not entirely predictable on the basis of broader community practice, they involve behavioral accommodation.

Any novel communicative behavior extends the prior history of language practice with an instance that diverges from what the hearer has previously observed. The hearer must then find a consonant way of adapting to the novel behavior in the conversational context, and this adaptation is accommodatory. The hearer both accommodates to the particular instance of a novel behavior by finding a consonant understanding of the behavior, and changes their dispositions to understand and possibly also produce the behavior they have observed. The hearer presumably also accommodates cognitively, recognizing how the new practice functions, and adapting to any further presuppositional resonances of the new behavior. The bottom line is that the process of implicit negotiation of meaning, and more broadly implicit negotiation of novel language practices, is one of accommodation by interlocutors. We use the term *collaborative language accommodation* to refer to collective harmonization around novel language practices, whether primarily implicit or involving overt metalinguistic moves of negotiation. The takeaway from this discussion is that the robustness and flexibility of human language rest not on the infinite generativity of fixed individual grammars, but on a social trait of humans: accommodational adaptability. In what follows, we will suggest how the alliances and group rivalries of the social and political world depend in large part on people's choice or ability to engage jointly in collaborative language accommodation.

6.5. Marching to Your Own Drum

The Communication Accommodation Theory literature is replete with examples of people not accommodating to their interlocutors, or accommodating in a way that is somehow suboptimal. While all such behaviors have sometimes been labeled *nonaccommodation*, most writers currently speak even of people whose communicative adaptations result in increased behavioral distinctiveness from their interlocutors as accommodating, hence our talk of *divergent accommodation*. The literature also includes many examples of people *underaccommodating*, so that adaptations to the interlocutor can seem perfunctory, or *overaccommodating*, as when a caregiver adopts a style that reflects in amplified form the slowness or limited active vocabulary of an elderly person, or *misaccommodating*, which can happen when someone adapts to their stereotypical preconception of how their interlocutor speaks rather than adapting to actual speech behavior.[48]

Our definition of accommodation does not require that interactants converge as regards thought or behavior. However, we suggest that accommodation always involves convergence, even if it produces divergence among interlocutors in a particular speech situation. In terms of our above definition of convergent, divergent, and mixed accommodation, divergent accommodation with one party should then involve convergent accommodation to another. So our claim that accommodation always involves convergence does not entail that all divergent accommodation is in fact mixed accommodation (although this is also an interesting hypothesis), because mixed accommodation, as defined, involves simultaneous convergent and divergent accommodation to the same party.

Consider again the paradigmatic example from Communication Accommodation Theory: a Welsh person is in conversation with an English person, finding the latter (or what they represent) to be irksome. In such cases, Welsh people sometimes speak with more distinctively Welsh English speech than they would otherwise, thus diverging from their interlocutors. Similarly, people often adopt a speech style that emphasizes the characteristics of their own gender identity when speaking to someone presenting as having a distinct gender identity. While it is logically possible for someone to diverge from their interlocutors without doing so in a way that conforms to any existing pattern, recent work in Communication Accommodation Theory suggests that divergent accommodation from an interlocutor is best seen as involving convergence to some other attractor. This attractor would be a group toward which accommodators (in the above example, the speakers) have greater affinity than they do to those they diverge from, and with whom they wish to mark their common identity. One of many overviews of Communication Accommodation Theory puts the idea as follows:

> Convergence is defined as a strategy through which individuals adapt their communicative behavior in such a way as to become more similar to their interlocutor's behavior. Conversely, the strategy of divergence leads to an accentuation of differences between self and other. A strategy similar to divergence is maintenance, in which a person persists in his or her original style, regardless of the communication behavior of the interlocutor. Central to the theory is the idea that speakers adjust

48. One of several good overviews of the relevant literature is Gallois, Ogay, and Giles, "Communication Accommodation Theory." For extensive annotated references to both the Communication Accommodation Literature and to semantic literature in the Lewisian tradition, see Beaver and Denlinger, "Linguistic Accommodation."

(or accommodate) their speech styles in order to create and maintain positive personal and social identities.

Giles (1978) also invoked Tajfel and Turner's (1979) social identity theory of intergroup relations (SIT), and [Speech Accommodation Theory] thereafter has largely (but not solely) relied on the framework of SIT to explain the motives behind the strategies of divergence and maintenance. Why should one choose to appear dissimilar to another? Referring to similarity-attraction theory alone would mean that the motive driving divergence or maintenance behaviors would be to appear dislikable, or at least that the speaker's need for social approval is low. Invoking the intergroup context, SIT explains the adoption of these strategies through the desire to signal a salient group distinctiveness so as to reinforce a social identity.[49]

Although at least some aspects of accommodation may be based in perceptual and behavioral mechanisms that require no attention to or awareness of social function, the idea that divergence is a performance of social identity rather than an arbitrary marking of distinctness suggests to us a generalization:

Social Alignment Hypothesis: Accommodation by an interactional participant promotes confidence in the nature of their attunements to identities or to groupings with which coordination is valued.

Convergence is the base case in which only the interactional group and its subparts need to be considered. In this case, accommodation by an interactant increases their attunement (or perception of attunement) to the group of other interactants. Thus the collective attunement of the interactional group is increased. According to the hypothesis, when an agent marks their distinctness from an interlocutor by diverging from them, we need to consider at least two groups. The agent reinforces their identity as a member of another group by convergence to that group, that is, by adopting dispositions, emotions, or attitudes that are distinctively associated with the second group.

Corollary of Social Alignment Hypothesis: Divergent accommodation from some individual recognized as belonging to a group occurs to promote confidence in membership of an alternative group or commitment to a contrasting identity. Nonaccommodation (maintenance), seen as stubborn refusal to adapt, similarly promotes confidence in

49. Gallois, Ogay, and Giles, "Communication Accommodation Theory," 123. The term *Communication Accommodation Theory* (CAT) has become standardized in place of *Speech Accommodation Theory* (SAT), as the purview of the work has extended from early work centering on speech styles to a broader consideration of communicative style and performance. The references in the quotation are to Giles, "Linguistic Differentiation between Ethnic Groups"; and Tajfel and Turner, "An Integrative Theory of Intergroup Conflict."

affiliation to an alternative group or commitment to an contrasting identity.

Note that divergence of behavior from another interactant need not connote nonmembership in their group(s), but could equally indicate difference of positioning within the same group, for example, within the same family. This is why we say that accommodation provides confidence in *the nature of* attunement to identities or to groupings, rather than simply indicating the fact of attunement. The fact that someone behaves so as to mark distinctive identity within a group, or to mark membership of a subgroup, need not indicate any lack of affiliation to the larger group, and need not indicate a lack of cooperativeness. A theory of accommodation must allow for the fact that groups have structure and that individuals have positions within that structure, positions that can be demarcated by distinctive behaviors. A theory of accommodation that uniformly predicted ever more blurring of distinctions of behavior within groups would not be a very good theory.

The social alignment hypothesis leaves open the possibility of mixed accommodation, whereby someone accommodates convergently and divergently with respect to the same person or group. Consider two people with different gender identities in conversation. They may simultaneously exaggerate style features associated with their own gender identities, for example, the pitch of their voice and their body posture, and yet style match on other features, such as speech rate or word choice, to the extent that such matching is perceived as gender neutral. So their pitch and body-posture accommodation is divergent (though converging to their own gender grouping), and their speech rate and word-choice accommodation is convergent.

Such simultaneous convergence and divergence might equally take place with respect to accommodation of attitudes. For example, suppose two mildly antagonistic interlocutors from different social groupings are discussing who they do and don't hang out with, and one of them says, "I would never be seen hanging out with my loser goody-two-shoes brother!" The addressee might convergently accommodate the belief that the speaker has a brother, and that the brother is somewhat inclined to doing what society, school, or parents expect of him, and yet draw further conclusions at odds with the speaker's beliefs, for example, that the brother is probably a decent guy and not a loser at all, and perhaps that, contra what the speaker seems to assume, the fact that someone is a goody-two-shoes is no reason not to hang out with them.

We speak of an increase of *confidence* in attunement, rather than of an increase in attunement simpliciter. This allows for two twists. First, there is the idea considered earlier in the chapter (section 6.1) that by performing an exaggerated form of a practice, by being, as it were, more Catholic than the pope, an actor might better manifest their affinity to a group than by performing a more standardized version of the practice. By performing in a way that overshoots the standard practice of what we can call the *target group*, that is, the group they are manifesting alignment with, the actor increases the confidence of any spectator in judging that they belong, or wish to be seen to belong, to the target group as opposed to any other salient group, for example, the group to which an interlocutor they are diverging from belongs. Second, and more generally, our reference to confidence allows that people might converge with what they perceive to be the behavior of another interactant or group rather than with the actual behavior. So, some cases in which accommodation is not fully convergent, for example, cases of underaccommodation and overaccommodation, can then be understood not as someone behaving in a way that connotes difference, but rather as someone behaving in a way that connotes similarity. The behavior represents the actor's best attempt to behave as they think the individual or group they are mimicking behaves.

A different way of putting both twists is that accommodation need not produce convergence to the attunements of a group, but to the attunements of a stereotype of a group. To return to a Wittgensteinian point, a social practice does not have a single standardized form, but rather consists in a history with much variation, and, furthermore, any one individual has only a small window on the history of a practice they are attempting to produce. So the best anyone can possibly do in producing that practice is perform it in a way that is recognizably like the way they take it to be currently appropriate to perform that practice, and it is inevitable that what they will converge to is not any particular way of performing the practice (for no one way of performing is privileged above others), and is not an ideal version of the practice (there being no ideal), but rather is something like a stereotyped version of the practice that the actor has interpellated.

One phenomenon discussed in Communication Accommodation Theory that the social alignment hypothesis seems at first to say nothing about is true nonaccommodation, or maintenance, in which an actor does not adapt their social behavior or speech style in any way in reaction to the particular circumstances of an interaction. Such failures could result from a lack of adaptability, including simple insensitivity (as when someone fails to perceive an acoustic feature that has significance for their interlocutor but not for them), but could also, on occasion, be better seen as performative stubbornness. But what does it mean to say that an actor does not adapt in any way? To say this is to suppose that there is a fact of the matter as to how the actor would have behaved had the situation been in some way normal, and to claim that the actor has not adapted to the difference from normality. But there is no normal. There is just a sequence of interactions that someone experiences in the course of their life, and behaviors that they exhibit in these situations.

Only someone suffering from an extreme clinical condition, such as death, can truly be said not to have adapted to the social situation in which they are located, and we might question to what extent in such extreme cases a person is a full participant in a social interaction. Everyone else adapts, if only to a small degree, to every new situation. To the extent that the adaptation is small on some measure, that is because only a small adaptation is needed for the actor to maintain harmony. Such cases show not that someone is failing to behave in a way that increases confidence in their identity, but rather that someone is adapting to their interactional situation precisely in the way that maximizes confidence in their identity. When there is social pressure to adapt, and when an actor is taken to have the power to adapt, that actor's resoluteness and consistency of self-presentation become a strong indicator of their confidence and investment in their distinctive presentational style. So, when in this book we talk of *nonaccommodation*, what we mean is not failure to accommodate simpliciter, but failure to accommodate to some significant subset of the attunements of some particular interactant.

On this view, the very act of maintaining a speech style is a form of accommodation to a group, manifesting our alignment with and positioning within that group, that is, our social identity. Indeed, far from expecting people to mimic their interlocutors faithfully, we expect people to actively maintain their own speech styles, physical deportment, and even attitudes. People who mimic too much are often seen as ridiculing those they imitate, or else as being Janus-faced, shiftily vacillating, capricious and shapeless, lacking spine.

Contemporary individualist Western mores demand of people that they "be themselves." But to be yourself, socially at least, is to manifest that you are being yourself, and to manifest a way of being is to use a style that is recognized as a style. But that suggests that even something as supposedly individualistic as being yourself might involve accommodation to some combination of social groupings; it is in the context of other social groupings that ways of being carry any public meaning. We might then say that your accommodation to a social situation is the way in which you adapt to that situation, and if someone appears inflexible or somewhat constant across a wide range of social situations, then we might say that they perform with a relatively narrow band of accommodation to their interlocutors, and are constantly adapting their performance in such a way as to maintain high confidence in their affiliation to a fixed complex of identities.

The suggestion, then, is that we are always accommodating, always performing our social identity with greater or lesser adaptation to the key of those around us. This is not a new thought—to return to Shakespeare, "All the world's a stage." Yet Shakespeare's metaphor might be taken to imply that people have preassigned roles, and that in performing these roles, we follow preexisting scripts determined by the role. Judith Butler famously suggested a far more radical view of performance in developing her strongly anti-essentialist view of gender and other identities as socially constructed. For Butler, not only does the performance of gender establish one's gender identity, but, furthermore, it is the history of performance of gender identity, and the associated practices that assimilate these performances into a wider web of meaning, that are constitutive of the gender identity itself.[50] These ideas, worked out in detail and applied in her epochal *Gender Trouble*[51] and other works, are already clear in a classic 1988 essay, "Performative Acts and Gender Constitution: An Essay in Phenomenology and Feminist Theory," and indeed are completely explicit in the stunning introduction to that work:

> Gender is in no way a stable identity or locus of agency from which various acts proceed; rather, it is an identity tenuously constituted in time—an identity instituted through a stylized repetition of acts. Further, gender is instituted through the stylization of the body and, hence, must be understood as the mundane way in which bodily gestures, movements, and enactments of various kinds constitute the illusion of an abiding gendered self.
>
> . . .
>
> If gender is instituted through acts which are internally discontinuous, then the appearance of substance is precisely that, a constructed identity, a performative accomplishment which the mundane social audience, including the actors themselves, come to believe and to perform in the mode of belief.
>
> . . .
>
> In opposition to theatrical or phenomenological models which take the gendered self to be prior to its acts, I will understand constituting acts not only as constituting the identity of the actor, but as constituting that identity as a compelling illusion.[52]

As should be clear, our understanding of identity performance, and of practice more generally, is strongly influenced by Butler, although we make no attempt here at a detailed discussion of her program, or a detailed reckoning of what we owe. We will also not explore Butler's powerful idea that recognition of the performative aspect of gender norms provides a way of undercutting and contesting gender norms, a call to action that she frames at the end of her essay as a warning. She cautions that if the performative nature of gender "is mistaken for a natural or linguistic given, power is relinquished to expand the cultural field bodily through subversive performances of various kinds."[53]

---

50. The thought that communities of practice ground social kinds, which are every bit as part of the natural world as other kinds, is explored and defended in detail in the analytic tradition by Sally Haslanger, in *Resisting Reality: Social Construction and Social Critique.*

51. Butler, *Gender Trouble.*

52. Butler, "Performative Acts and Gender Constitution," 519–20.

53. Butler, "Performative Acts and Gender Constitution," 531.

6.6. Echo Chambers

As we have defined it, a community of practice is an ideologically bound social group. It shares a distinctive set of collective attunements that harmonizes across dimensions, the ideology being precisely these collective attunements. To be a social group, its members must feel identified with the group and the ideology. To be ideologically rich, the group's collective attunements must include a wide range of attitudes and practices that determine many aspects of how individuals should live their lives and how they should behave socially and politically. Ping-pong players do not form an ideologically rich group. Catholics do.

All ideological groups are *harmonic attractors*. By this we mean that entering the group resolves some dissonance, and leaving the group produces dissonance. Note that this allows the ideology to be far from any ideal of harmony: it may be that members feel dissonance because of the behaviors of other members of the group, behaviors that may or may not be consonant with the ideology, and it may be that there are contradictions within the collective cognitive attunements (i.e., the belief system) of the ideology, or misalignments of cognitive attunements and emotional or dispositional attunements. What makes the group a harmonic attractor is not that the collective attunements of the group are perfectly consonant, but that leaving the group would produce more dissonance than staying in it.

There is nothing inherently bad about richly ideological communities of practice. They can give life meaning, at least in the restricted sense of meaningfulness that we offered in the last section. Richly ideological communities of practice range from villagers tied together by common heritage and, perhaps, occasionally, willful ignorance of other ways of life, to protest groups tied together by common cause against injustice. They also include cults of many different flavors and degrees of connectedness. To use the term "cult" is, of course, to make a strongly negative normative valuation. To call a group a cult is to say that it is an ideologically rich grouping for which the collective attunements are reprehensible, or even abhorrent. For example, it may be manifest to an outsider that the cult's belief system is manifestly inconsistent, that the group is poorly attuned to reality, that the emotional attunements of members are so strong as to prevent normatively desirable deliberation, or that practices of the group are unhealthy or immoral.

Some cults, like the contemporary QAnon movement, are labeled with the term "conspiracy theory." While there is some merit to the term, to which we'll return, it is misleading. Calling it a "theory" suggests that what is central to the ideology is a certain set of propositions believed by adherents. If anything, QAnon is not a conspiracy theory but a *conspiracy practice*, a practice that includes not only various discursive practices but also pseudo-investigative processes for revealing any crumb of evidence, all of which will increase consonance of group members. Some of those discursive practices are for belittling or bamboozling opposition and interpreting counterclaims or negative evaluations directed at the group as evidence of the desperation of outsiders. One prominent set of discursive practices involves the Qdrop, whereby an enigmatic message apparently from the leader Q is released, the message following a template of Delphic inscrutability and pseudoprofundity that is in equal parts guru and Goebbels, an impenetrable call to action to protect *us* from *them*, abounding in juxtaposition of highly resonant terms that have no clear extension or connection. The extent to which the discursive practices of Q diverge from mainstream society speech practices is best seen in examples of Qdrops, like this one that we discussed earlier:

Symbolism Will Be Their Downfall

Their need for symbolism will be their downfall.
Follow the Owl & Y head around the world.
Identify and list.
They don't hide it.
They don't fear you.
You are sheep to them.
You are feeders.
Godfather III.[54]

Given the centrality of distinctive practices in any cult, we make a mistake when we focus on untenable beliefs that cult members apparently hold. It matters not that neither Scientology nor QAnon forms what regular enlightenment-style thinkers would consider a logically consistent set of ideas, for an ideology need not comprise a set of logically consistent ideas. It needs to be a strong harmonic attractor. Manifestly, both QAnon and Scientology are exactly that. Whatever incongruities we see within the group, their practices mean that members are able to live with any dissonance they feel, and they would experience greater dissonance in transitioning out of the group, into a world that is manifestly hostile to them, than they would by remaining within the fold. They can, furthermore, avoid strong feelings of dissonance if they are able to maintain a landscape of attunements, in the sense of section 3.4, in which inconsistent attunements are separated into separate neighborhoods of thought, and this separation, or *fragmentation*, can be supported by narratives that explain the appearance of inconsistency. For example, the narrative that the enemy intentionally sows confusion can suggest that it is not worth paying attention to otherwise irremediable inconsistency. Thus the inconsistency may be, to use a standard spatial metaphor for the organization of thought, pushed to the back of one's mind.

The further point we wish to make about the term "conspiracy theory" relates to the fact that it reflects two-way disdain. When we label someone a "conspiracy theorist," we are negatively evaluating that person's own negative evaluation of the actions of some other societally important group. The term "conspiracy theory" correctly captures both the mistrust felt for some other group and the validation of that mistrust in terms of an analysis of that group's actions as self-serving. Conspiracy theories are a paradigmatic example of *us-them* politics. They often go hand-in-hand with hatred: when people hate a group, they interpret the group's actions as self-serving, and such interpretations justify or amplify the hatred.

It is important to realize that it is social and emotional attunements, especially attunements that might eventually motivate actions in support of a cause, that are of greatest fundamental import politically, not the strange and often inconsistent description of the world that provided the ostensible import of the conspiratorial rhetoric. In this regard, conspiracy theorizing is just one of many associated discursive practices that are politically significant because they engender strongly pro-in-group and strongly anti-out-group sentiment and drive attunement toward behaviors that go beyond the bounds of accepted democratic practice.[55] But it is also important to realize that when we bandy around the label "conspiracy theory," we may ourselves be playing a role in us-them politics, accepting that there is an unbridgeable epistemic gulf between us (the clear thinkers) and them (the confused). "Conspiracy theorist" is a slur. That is not to say that the terms "conspiracy theory" or "conspiracy theorist" should not be used, but that we should recognize that to use them is not merely to label, but also to take both epistemic and moral high ground.

Let us say that an *antagonistic ideological social group* (or, equivalently, an *antagonistic community of practice*) is a community of practice for which a central feature of the ideology is a strongly negative collective emotional attunement to some other social group. While there have always been such ideologies, Carl Schmitt made explicit the idea that a negative view of others is a distinctively positive or even necessary element of effective government.[56] What he characterized as a friend-enemy distinction was obviously a fundamental plank of Nazism, the Nazis being a paradigm case of a strongly antagonistic, richly ideological social group.

---

55. In focusing on the social role of political messaging rather than on belief formation, we follow a line that is clear in Hannah Arendt's *The Origins of Totalitarianism*, and which has recently been developed by Megan Hyska ("Propaganda, Irrationality, and Group Agency," "Against Irrationalism in the Theory of Propaganda"). Drawing on an Arendtian analysis of propaganda as primarily functioning to create or destroy social groups, she makes a distinction between *propaganda* as "group-forming speech" and *indoctrination* as "group-addressing speech" ("Propaganda, Irrationality, and Group Agency," 231). We take it that this is a distinction of function rather than a clear separation of practices, since it is not evident to us why a particular message or systematic messaging strategy could not serve both roles. We would hesitate to classify Qdrops as being exclusively group-forming or group-addressing.

56. Schmitt, *The Concept of the Political*.

In a polarized political environment, the dominant ideological groupings differ on the most salient social and political issues and practices, and those ideologies are central to identity. It follows that most people will either be well aligned or sharply misaligned on the most salient social and political issues and practices. The resulting social effervescence, in which those with whom one is aligned express aligned views, leads in turn to increasing crystallization of attitudes, by which we mean in-group similarity of attitudes across multiple issues, in-group similarity of discursive and other practices, and widespread inflexibility of both attitudes and practices. We see examples of such crystallization now, for example, in studies showing correlations between attitudes toward race and immigration and attitudes toward climate change, issues that are, on their face, somewhat orthogonal.[57]

When does a society become politically polarized? The mere presence of antagonistic ideologies is not sufficient. On the contrary, a nation can become largely united in its antagonism toward an outside group or power or toward an internal group that constitutes only a small minority. This was Schmitt's point. Polarization involves the growth of an ideologically rich grouping that is collectively strongly antagonistic toward a significant group of others in the same society. Political polarization occurs when the targets of antagonism themselves represent or are allied to a politically powerful group. In an extremely polarized situation, for some large ideological grouping, the target of antagonism is everyone who is not part of the grouping. As such a situation is approached, a high level of mutual antagonism between groupings, always present to some extent in a two-party democratic system, is inevitable, a nadir of us-them politics.

The philosopher C. Thi Nguyen distinguishes between *epistemic bubbles* and *echo chambers*.[58] An epistemic bubble forms when the voices of certain groups or institutions are excluded by omission—there is just no access to them. Echo chambers arise when "other relevant voices have been actively discredited."[59] In an echo chamber, you may hear other voices, but you will not give them any credence, as they have been discredited as sources of information. Conspiracy theories are characteristic mechanisms by which to discredit sources of information, and so are central to the formation of echo chambers. Echo chambers, as Nguyen describes them, pose a more serious

57. Cf. Dan Kahan ("Ideology, Motivated Reasoning, and Cognitive Reflection") on polarization. The empirical studies he reports on suggest that alignment of attitudes within groups is largely driven by preferences for commitment to ideas that signal membership of and loyalty toward those very groups. As he writes, "As a form of 'identity self-defense,' individuals are unconsciously motivated to resist empirical assertions . . . if those assertions run contrary to the dominant belief within their groups" (408).

58. Nguyen, "Echo Chambers and Epistemic Bubbles." We do not adopt Nguyen's terminology here, so for us an echo chamber need not involve active policing of outside views.

59. Nguyen, "Echo Chambers and Epistemic Bubbles," 141.

social epistemic problem than epistemic bubbles. As Nguyen points out, an epistemic bubble can be "burst" by simply introducing omitted information. To dismantle an echo chamber, you have to unravel or bypass the system by which legitimate sources of information are discredited.

How might such a chamber develop? An echo chamber forms when only the practices of insiders resonate strongly inside a group. The problem of echo chambers (as opposed to mere epistemic bubbles) is not merely that other voices cannot be heard or accepted, but that they do not resonate at the right frequency. Yet it is not just voices that are drowned out. In the echo chambers of extreme ideological groupings, many *practices* may cease to resonate, including characteristically democratic ones—practices of treating people equitably, or practices of respecting scientific or other kinds of institutionally expert advice.

Looking at echo chambers this way suggests the sense in which impermeability to outside views is not merely failure of uptake. Our model suggests that the following is a fairly clear route to the development of echo chambers:

Antagonistic Echo Amplification

1. Ideologically distant groups have incommensurable practices, values, and emotions.
2. In a dialogically healthy environment, such gulfs can be at least partially overcome by joint negotiation of meaning (whether implicit or explicit).
3. But such negotiation of meaning depends on collaborative language accommodation.
4. Behavioral accommodation to the practices of others, a crucial step in collaborative language accommodation, is known to be limited by antagonism between groups.
5. So, in the presence of at least one ideological grouping displaying somewhat generalized out-group antagonism, communicative coordination between members of that group and others will be rare.
6. The social alignment hypothesis predicts that an emotionally polarized environment will become an epistemically and dispositionally polarized environment.[60]

60. That is, when in-group members converse primarily among themselves, there is a well-documented tendency for their attitudes to become more extreme by accommodating only to each other, and if anything divergently accommodating on those occasions when they are in contact with others. This tendency is seen in Festinger's work, discussed in section 3.2. More recent studies are summarized by Cass Sunstein as follows:

> We can sharpen our understanding of this problem if we attend to the phenomenon of group polarization. Found in many settings, it involves likeminded people going to extremes. More precisely, group polarization means that after deliberating with one another, people are likely to move toward a more extreme point of view in the direction to which they were already

7. It follows that once a significant ideological grouping displays generalized out-group antagonism, a negative feedback loop will set in, amplifying the echo of collective attunements within the in-group, and causing ever-increasing divergence from other societal groupings.

Note here that while a tendency for divergent accommodation away from out-group interlocutors would exaggerate the speed of the breakdown of deliberative democratic processes, the high probability of nonaccommodation in the face of a disdained out-group member suffices for our argument.

Consider the implications of this argument for the literature on framing. Absent accommodation, frames and modes of reasoning used by other parties will not be adopted, because they will not resonate (in the sense defined in section 3.9). There will thus be no uptake for ideas couched in those frames or justified by such reasoning. Divergent accommodation of language practices may exaggerate this process further, say, for example, if one party offers pro-choice argumentation, and the other uses pro-life frames, with no possibility for compromise. The problem then is that even when voices that use other frames are heard, as is indeed common in public debate, an ideologically polarized audience will be unable to fully grasp the message of their out-group, and a fortiori that message cannot be taken up.

Consider arguments made by George Lakoff to the effect that if Democrats wanted to persuade people, they should push back on Republican framing with their own frames.[61] We find much to like in Lakoff's discussion, and certainly agree that framing practices are strategically central in politics, as discussed in sections 3.5 and 3.9. However, if we are right about the role of

---

inclined. With respect to the Internet, the implication is that groups of people, especially if they are like-minded, will end up thinking the same thing they thought before—but in more extreme form, and sometimes in a much more extreme form.

Consider some examples of the basic phenomenon, as studied in more than a dozen nations. (a) After discussion, the citizens of France become more critical of the U.S. and its intentions with respect to economic aid. (b) After discussion, whites predisposed to show racial prejudice offer more negative responses to the question of whether white racism is responsible for certain conditions faced by African-Americans. (c) After discussion, whites predisposed not to show racial prejudice offer more positive responses to the same question. (d) After discussion, a group of moderately pro-feminist women become more strongly pro-feminist. (e) Republican appointees to the federal judiciary show far more conservative voting patterns when they are sitting on a panel consisting solely of Republican appointees; and Democratic appointees show far more liberal voting patterns when they are sitting on a panel consisting solely of Democratic appointees. (Sunstein, "Democracy and Filtering," 59)

We are assuming that the tendencies Sunstein discusses extend to dispositional and emotional attunements, and not merely cognitive attunements.

61. Lakoff, *Know Your Values and Frame the Debate.*

nonaccommodation in polarization, then Lakoff's policy conclusions were at a minimum perilous, and possibly even counterproductive. We agree with Lakoff that some sort of pushback on frames is needed. The problem is that if this were implemented simply by having Democratic politicians insist on using preferred Democratic framings, then they would fail to get their message across at all in a polarized environment. If you use your own frames, and those frames do not resonate for the other side, then the other side is unlikely to accommodate. You may as well not have spoken. Indeed, you may have unwittingly encouraged divergent accommodation, in which case you have only promoted the very polarization you sought to overcome.

One way to be heard by someone who is deeply opposed to you is to find a messenger with whom they empathize, a medium that they'll tune into, and talk to them in their own language. Yet talking to someone in their own language is not so easy. A further conclusion suggested by our argument, though again we might be seen to be stating the obvious, and not offering a concrete way to put it into effect, is that a root cause of runaway echo chamber formation is generalized antagonism, for it is intergroup rivalry that makes incommensurable positions unbridgeable. There is, then, little prospect for voices to be not just heard, but also understood, so long as enmity reigns. If there is to be reconciliation of attitudes, it must go hand in hand with a restoration of empathy for those with different identities.

Restoring empathy and trust, especially when confronted with mechanisms such as conspiracy theories that would need to be unraveled in order to do so, is complex and difficult. Fortunately, such a personal approach is not the only way to address the problem of echo chambers. A *social identity* is a pattern of attunements, attunements to particular communities of practice, and attunements shared with others in that community. Each of us has several, indeed many, social identities. Each one of us is a member of multiple organizations—a citizen of a country, a member of a synagogue or mosque, a player on a softball team. Instead of going to war with frames, or one by one trying to unravel personal mistrust between individuals, one could try appealing to another social identity, one that is not defined by the problematic echo chamber. Somebody who may be opposed to one politically may share a social identity as a fellow vegetarian, or a fellow athlete, or even a fellow citizen, and can be appealed to by messages that activate shared social identities rather than opposed ones.

Ideally, in times of emergency, a healthy democratic country is one whose citizens come together across these different social identities, their identity as fellow citizens being paramount. Good leadership in a democratic country activates shared identity, so that what people have in common becomes more meaningful than what sets them apart. This is a prerequisite if every voice is to be heard, the fundamental principle of democracy itself.

PART III

Idealization

CHAPTER SEVEN

Neutrality

We must take sides. Neutrality helps the oppressor, never the victim.

—ELIE WIESEL, NOBEL PRIZE ACCEPTANCE SPEECH[1]

TIME AND AGAIN, in this book, we have argued that central concepts in the theory of meaning, for example presupposition, are characterized in a way that is not adequate to the generality of the phenomena they were introduced to explain. And a theme running through these pages has been that this characteristic failure of generality is a consequence of problematic idealizations in the study of speech. In this part of our book, we raise this underlying theoretical vein of our book to the surface.

In this chapter, and the next, we single out two idealizations for extended critique. These are the idealizations of *neutrality* and *straight-talk*. We have chosen these two idealizations for several reasons. First, because the objections to them are different in character, developing both gives us a broader sense of the ways in which idealizations can distort. Secondly, we have chosen these concepts for their broader importance to democratic political philosophy. The problems we raise for them arise from the study of speech. However, the problems these idealizations contribute to range considerably wider. Finally, in chapter 9, the last chapter in this methodological section of the book, we place critiques of idealizations in the theory of meaning into the larger context of debates about "ideal theory" in other areas of philosophy.

This chapter concerns the ideal of neutrality. Our conclusion is a kind of deliberate misreading of the quote from Elie Wiesel at the start of this chapter. The quote suggests and justifies a *moral* imperative, echoing in stark terms a long history of warnings of the dangers of neutrality. We instead interpret "We must take sides" metaphysically: it is impossible to be neutral. More narrowly, the main thesis we defend is that words can never be neutral.

We began this book with the concepts of resonance, attunement, and harmony. These three concepts can be seen, respectively, as generalizations of meaning, belief, and logical consistency. Words have various resonances. The resonances allow communication of attunements, and harmonization settles the attunements of individuals and groups into coherent wholes. The resonances may be rich, including all the elements of ideologies. A language is a web of resonances that gives flesh to its speakers' social identities. We will

1. Reproduced in Wiesel, *Night*, 88.

argue that the model of speech we have built upon these conceptual general-izations is in tension with natural language ever being neutral. Among other things, we deny that speech can ever lack all but denotational resonances. If you idealize away from resonances that are nonneutral (in the sense we discuss), you idealize away from important linguistic reality. In the case of neutrality, we argue that the idealizations are especially distorting, misrepresenting under-lying metaphysics.[2]

7.1. A Neutral Space for Reasons?

Let us say, provisionally, that discussion is *neutral* if perspective and attun-ement to social location are irrelevant to the understanding and evaluation of each move in the discussion.

Here is a natural way of thinking of how propaganda impairs democracy. Democracy is conceived as a space of neutral deliberative reason. In such a space, participants in a discussion solely focus on exchanging reasons. Since the space of deliberation is neutral, it is devoid of biased perspectives. Since it is devoid of biased perspectives, the best argument wins. Why, according to this picture, do we not live in a democracy? Because propaganda prevents the neutral exchange of reasons. Propaganda wields perspective as a weapon, sometimes explicitly, other times covertly, masking perspective behind a facade of apparent neutrality. Propaganda excites emotion and fosters in-group bonding, impeding rationality. Propaganda is thus a threat to the realization of the democratic ideal. Propaganda and ideological discourse are barriers to the neutral space of reasons that is the liberal ideal.[3]

2. Material from this chapter first appeared in Beaver and Stanley, "Neutrality," and we gratefully acknowledge Matthew Congdon for very useful editorial comments as we prepared the journal version. Alice Crary provided a powerful response in her "Neutrality, Critique, and Social Visibility." Although this chapter has been revised and expanded with material that connects it to the rest of the book, the central lines of argumentation are as in the original journal article, and we do not directly respond to her comments and criti-cisms in this revised version. Nonetheless, her response and conversations with her over the years have changed our thinking, and this has affected the final form of the chapter and the book as a whole. In particular, her comments regarding the importance of ideas in the post-Wittgensteinian ordinary-language tradition, and on certain strands of work within feminist philosophy, have led to us more clearly reflecting, at various points in the book, connections to work of Wittgenstein and Cavell, on the one hand, and work on standpoint epistemology, on the other.

3. Note that one might consider a weaker understanding of a "neutral space," whereby while the space is neutral, the reasons expressed within it are not. Some might imagine a physical space such as a Roman forum as having this quality. We will not discuss this approach, save to note that we do not see that the mere fact of a forum being a physical space rather than an animate agent or a speech act makes it intrinsically neutral. A physical space embodies practices and comes to have resonances intrinsically tied to those practices. There was nothing neutral about a Roman forum, since only certain types of individuals

Such a position is naive, because of course even the most committed public-reason liberal can grant that there are important appeals to emotion, for example, to address gaps in democratic culture. In a more sophisticated vein, one could allow that some propaganda—some appeals to emotion, to a persuasive force not backed by reasons—could be necessary to achieve democratic ends.[4] When some of the population is in the grips of ideology, reasons will not work to free them. Ideology can block considerations of reason.

On this picture, even for democratic ends, propaganda is sometimes necessary to shock people out of ideological barriers. But it is *only* as a way station to the democratic ideal of neutral deliberative reason. Speech that resonates emotionally with people, bonding them via emotions such as empathy, can perhaps play a role as a means to realizing democratic ideals. But ultimately, the idea goes, a true democratic space of reasons does not involve speech whose function is to resonate with an audience via means other than the provision of reasons. Public reason is, on this picture, incompatible with perspectival content.

Such a neutral conception of public reason is not required even for high-church epistemic democracy. W. E. B. Du Bois's essay "Of the Ruling of Men" is an epistemic argument for democracy. Du Bois argues that only by including everyone's voice will one devise good policy:

> Continually, some classes are tacitly or expressly excluded [from democratic participation]. Thus women have been excluded from modern democracy because of the persistent theory of female subjection and because it was argued that their husbands or other male folks would look to their interests. Now, manifestly, most husbands, fathers, and brothers will, so far as they know how or as they realize women's needs, look after them. But remember the foundations of the argument—that in the last analysis only the sufferer knows his sufferings and that no state can be strong which excludes from its expressed wisdom the knowledge of its mothers, wives, and daughters. We have but to view the unsatisfactory relations of the sexes the world over and the problem of children to realize how desperately we need this excluded wisdom.[5]

would ever be heard there, and debate within the forum was firmly couched in terms of the pervading ethos. Physical spaces, like online spaces for debate, are not inherently any more neutral than a so-called neutral arbiter can be, for brief discussion of which, see below. We thank Leah Ransom for discussion of this issue.

4. Examples may be controversial, because part of the point of an emotional appeal is to supplant complacency and stir controversy, whether the goals are otherwise reasonable or not, and sometimes we may consider the emotional reactions to such appeals themselves to be in some sense reasonable, or at least appropriate. Consider the case of "abolitionist propaganda" discussed in Brooks, *Bodies in Dissent*. Henry "Box" Brown's panoramas exhibiting the brutality of American slavery were meant to appeal directly to emotions, but the strong emotions they evoked were appropriate to the inhumanity of slavery.

5. Du Bois, "Of the Ruling of Men," 83.

Du Bois's argument is explicitly epistemic, but it concerns highly subjective perspectives. Du Bois's argument is that we need the insight from highly subjective perspectives for good policy, and no amount of learning or good intentions will suffice to make policy without them.

Though the idea of a space of neutral "unsullied" public reason is not necessary to defend some kind of version of deliberative democracy, it nevertheless proves tempting as a model. In commenting on the arguments of Catharine MacKinnon and Rae Langton to regulate pornography, Judith Butler asks, "If pornography performs a deformation of speech, what is presumed to be the proper form of speech? What is the notion of nonpornographic speech which conditions this critique of pornography?"[6] Butler adds dryly, "Though neither Langton nor MacKinnon consults Habermas, their projects seem to be structured by similar cultural desires"; Butler is suggesting that their projects require an idealized speech community in which the only consideration is (to use Habermas's phrase) "the force of the better argument."[7] The temptation to appeal to an ideal of neutral public reason is easy to slip into, even when one does so unawares.

In Alice Crary's 2018 paper, "The Methodological Is Political: What's the Matter with 'Analytic Feminism'?" Crary critiques this picture of the antidemocratic nature of emotional or antirational appeals in public discourse. In particular, she criticizes it for presupposing a picture of idealized public discourse as a neutral space of reasons. Using as an example the account of propaganda in Stanley's *How Propaganda Works*, since it is for her a paradigm case of how not to proceed, Crary questions whether it is reasonable for feminists to view radically antiestablishment methods that undercut enlightenment-style

---

6. Butler, *Excitable Speech*, 86. Butler is commenting on MacKinnon, *Only Words*, and Langton, "Speech Acts and Unspeakable Acts."

7. Here Butler is referring to a thread that runs through much of Habermas's work, the idea that in rational communication, argumentation can play a role in the search for truth that transcends the particular perspectives and goals of interlocutors, and the interlocutors can be convinced not by each other, but by the force of the arguments themselves: "Argumentation can exploit the conflict between success-oriented competitors for the purpose of achieving consensus so long as the arguments are not reduced to mere means of influencing one another. In discourse what is called the *force* of the better argument is wholly unforced. Here convictions change internally via a process of rationally motivated attitude change" (Habermas, *Moral Consciousness and Communicative Action*, 160). Elsewhere, Habermas comments that interlocutors "are bound by presuppositions of communication and rules of argumentation that define 'the space of reason.' In this 'space' reasons can float freely and unfold their rationally motivating power unimpeded so as to affect the mind . . . in the right way" (Habermas, *Truth and Justification*, 140). The above quote from Butler makes the point that the concept of a deformation of speech presupposes that there is some sort of pure, undeformed speech, unsullied by ideology. Butler can be seen as standing in a philosophical tradition that critiques the possibility of reasons that transcend the socially embedded perspectives of reasoners. We also stand in this tradition. Reasons cannot float freely.

rationalism as a short-term tactic en route to a new and better "neutral conception of reason." She views such an approach as deeply flawed, and says of
its advocates:

> They recognise the practical need for ethically non-neutral methods. At
> the same time, they claim that these methods are as such non-rational
> and should therefore only be used—as crucial but also intrinsically
> problematic and therefore merely temporary instruments—for clearing
> away obstacles to the creation of a space for debate that is maximally
> neutral and, as the thinkers in question see it, hence rationally and
> politically sound. This is the stance that Jason Stanley, for instance,
> defends in his recent, widely discussed book on propaganda. Despite
> regarding all propaganda as non-neutral and hence as non-rational
> and politically problematic, Stanley allows for indispensable or, in his
> terms, "non-demagogic" types of propaganda that are at times "neces-
> sary" for dismantling ideological formations that distort what he sees
> as the neutral space for democratic discourse.[8]

In the framework developed in this volume, the notion of "a neutral space
of reasons" for discourse is incoherent and epistemologically problematic.
It is incoherent, because utterances of words unavoidably are tied to speech
practices that locate speakers in histories and social roles. Perspective is
inherent to communication.

If our model of speech is correct, the ideal of a neutral space of reasons is also
epistemologically problematic. It is epistemologically problematic because,
given that *ought* implies *can*, taking it as an ideal suggests it is possible to
avoid thoroughly unavoidable communicative effects of speech practices. It is,
therefore, an ideal that occludes reality. It is a dangerous ideal.

Our model undermines the ideal of neutral reasoning. But perhaps this
just shows that our model of speech is problematic, insofar as it cannot make
sense of the notion of a neutral space of reasons. In what follows, we will critique the motivations and indeed the very coherence of this ideal. In the end,
it emerges as a virtue of our model that it cannot make sense out of it, rather
than a problem.

What would ground the ideal of a "neutral space for democratic discourse"?
One would need to think of linguistic meaning as having a certain kind of neutrality, that language has a nonideological core that is the subject of semantic
and pragmatic theory. According to this containment-metaphor-based model,
the "core" of meaning is some sort of neutral, objective information, with a
denotation independent of the speaker.

But first—what is "neutral, objective information"? Our discussion here
is necessarily speculative, as we are not committed to the coherence of the

---

8. Crary, "The Methodological Is Political," 48.

notion. We begin with its source in the analytic tradition—the work of Gottlob Frege. Frege's preferred notion of meaning, which he called sense, was a kind of neutral informational content. Frege recognized that there were aspects of meaning that were not neutral in his preferred sense. But he rejected these as irrelevant to his "official" notion of meaning. We will argue that these aspects are conventional, and we can understand them as such.

7.2. *Frege on Sense versus Tone*

In Frege's mature philosophy of language, from 1892 on, there are two levels of meaning: sense and reference. The reference of a proper name is an object, so "Mark Twain" and "Samuel Clemens" have the same reference. But, famously, Frege argues that in such cases the two names may have different meanings, as it is possible to believe that Mark Twain is not Samuel Clemens, without irrationality (or, to return to the classic example that Frege used, that Hesperus is not Phosphorous). These different meanings, the different meanings associated with "Mark Twain" and "Samuel Clemens," Frege calls *senses*. Here are five doctrines Frege holds about senses:

1. The sense of an expression is the way the expression presents its referent.[9] "The Evening star" and "The Morning star" present the same referent, Venus, in different ways.
2. The sense of an expression is what one must grasp in order to understand the expression.[10]
3. The sense of an expression is its reference in opaque, or indirect, contexts, such as in the '...' of "John believes..."
4. Sense *determines* reference, at least in the *minimal* sense that a difference in reference entails a difference in sense.
5. Some senses, the *thoughts*, are the ultimate objects of truth and falsity.

On this picture of meaning, each word has a meaning, the way it presents its referent, and the thought expressed by the sentence is composed of the meanings (senses) of the words the sentence contains. The thought is what is believed, and it is what is judged true or false.

In "Logic" and elsewhere, Frege draws a distinction between sense and what he calls *tone*. From the distinctions he draws between sense and tone, we can draw a conclusion about Frege's views of senses. It is that senses are neutral and aperspectival:

9. "It is natural ... to think of there being connected with a sign ... besides that to which the sign refers ... also what I should like to call the sense of the sign, wherein the mode of presentation is contained" (Frege, "On Sense and Reference," 57).

10. "The sense of a proper name is grasped by everyone who is sufficiently familiar with the language" (Frege, "On Sense and Reference," 57–58).

If we compare the sentences "This dog howled the whole night" and "This cur howled the whole night," we find that the thought is the same. The first sentence tells us neither more nor less than does the second. But whilst the word "dog" is neutral as between having pleasant or unpleasant associations, the word "cur" certainly has unpleasant rather than pleasant associations and puts us rather in mind of a dog with a somewhat unkempt appearance.[11]

Frege's argument that the two sentences tell us the same thing is that they have the same truth conditions, namely, they contain the same information about the world. Consider someone who objects to the view that the two sentences "This dog howled the whole night" and "This cur howled the whole night" give us the same information, holding that the second sentence also expresses the information that the speaker holds a negative view toward the dog. Frege writes,

> We assume that the first sentence is true and the second sentence is spoken by someone who does not actually feel the contempt which the word "cur" seems to imply. If the objection were correct, the second sentence would now contain two thoughts, one of which was false; so it would assert something false as a whole, whilst the first sentence would be true. We shall hardly go along with this; rather the use of the word "cur" does not prevent us from holding that the second sentence is true.[12]

Frege holds that senses of words are the elements relevant to the truth or falsity of what is said by sentences containing them. Since tone is not relevant to truth or falsity, it is not part of sense. This Fregean picture has developed into the view that the core of the theory of meaning is the study of meaning properties relevant to truth or falsity of the assertion. Since the differences between "cur" and "dog" are not relevant to truth and falsity of assertions, they are not relevant to the theory of meaning.

From our perspective, Frege's argument is problematic because it privileges the semantic predicates "true" and "false" over other predicates of communicative acts, and by focusing on these predicates, it also implicitly restricts the purview of the theory of meaning to acts of assertion and the truth conditions of sentences that are asserted. Speech does not merely attune people cognitively, to properties of the external world, but also attunes them emotionally, socially, and dispositionally. Speech that attunes people to emotions can be wounding or inspiring. When it also attunes people to the world, it can simultaneously be true or false. Given that speech can attune us to emotions and practices, we should not from the outset privilege the metasemantic predicates "true" and "false."

11. Frege, "Logic," 140.
12. Frege, "Logic," 140.

There is another thought articulated here by Frege that is natural and widespread. It is that the "normal" words, like "dog," are "neutral as between having pleasant or unpleasant associations." The idea that a theory of meaning can ignore tone receives a kind of illicit support from the fiction that nonneutral words have neutral counterparts. Do they?

7.3. Evaluative Predicates and Value-Laden Concepts

Many *concepts* are inherently evaluative. Consider concepts from virtue ethics, like the concepts of generosity or cruelty. These "thick" moral concepts mix descriptive and evaluative elements, and even perhaps affective ones. The practice of calling an action "generous" is a practice of praising that action. The practice of calling an action "cruel" is a practice of condemning it. The reason there is no neutral counterpart of "generous" is not merely that the term involves perspective, but that it involves positive valuation. It is not clear how any development of Frege's notion of tone could be of much use here. It seems to us at the very least unhelpful to say that the sense of "generosity" is neutral, but that it has a negative tone.

Few would want to suggest that words like "cruel," "vindictive," "selfish," and even words for "thin" moral concepts like "right" and "wrong," have neutral counterparts. But this is surely not just a matter of language, not just a question of there happening to be certain words that are used evaluatively. Surely, if people can be said to have concepts corresponding to words like "cruel" and "generous," then they have concepts that are intrinsically evaluative. It's not merely that our words are neither neutral nor built on a neutral core, but that our ways of categorizing the world are neither neutral nor built on a neutral core.

We do not attempt to give in this volume a theory of concepts or categories. But we will say this. We can see no reason to assume that the way people categorize is in any sense neutral, and there also is no reason to assume that categorization is in some sense restricted to purely epistemic attunements. Whether the notion of a purely epistemic attunement is coherent is not obvious to us, but we would certainly want to allow that a person's categories might involve perceptual, emotional, and dispositional attunements. People's concepts of everything from cotton wool and knives to Bach fugues and jokes may be inseparable from how they perceive them, how they feel about them, and how they use them. But if at least some concepts that words pick out are not in any interesting sense neutral concepts, but are rather intrinsically laden with value, then it is not clear what it would mean for a word that has such a concept as its meaning to have a neutral counterpart. The neutral counterpart would have to be a concept that is not value-laden. But then what would make that concept the neutral counterpart of the original?

We have no idea what you get if you neutralize the concept of being selfish, but we think it would of necessity lack the things that make the concept of being selfish what it is; it would not be a neutral version of the original concept, but rather a different concept altogether. This suggests to us that for at least some words, not only do they lack neutral counterparts, but they could not possibly have neutral counterparts. In such cases, to restrict attention to a neutral core would be to lose almost all of the fruit.

There is, then, good reason to say that some words lack neutral counterparts. Whatever the relationship between "mom" and "mother," it is not that the latter corresponds to the neutral core of the former. Neither the word "mother" nor the concept of motherhood is neutral, either ideologically or emotionally. But let us go further and consider a case in which the existence of a neutral counterpart has been taken as obvious. If the neutral counterpart hypothesis can be argued to fail even here, then the case for neutral counterparts as a useful component of semantic theorizing is on rocky ground indeed.

7.4. "Dog" versus "Cur"

The Fregean example of cur is suggestive, but misleadingly so. "Cur" is not merely rare, but essentially never used in contemporary English with the sense of dog + <negative affect>, except by philosophers of language. If it is so hard to come up with an example of a word conveying tone that the standard examples are themselves vanishingly rare, then how important can tone be? Contrary to the impression that the example "cur" gives, we suggest that tone is ubiquitous.

Let us start with the supposedly neutral counterpart "dog," which we choose precisely because of its apparent innocuousness. An unpretentious word, certainly. Old English. And clearly the least marked noun to describe a dog, or at least the most obvious word to use. But neutral? What would it even mean for it to be "neutral"?[13]

Consider first the fact that the etymological history of English words correlates to the register in which they are used. Thus, those Old English words, like "child" and "chip" and "chin," which are still in common use, tend to be understood as ordinary colloquial, plain English words. Anglo-Norman vocabulary is more varied in its register, with "beef," and "blue," and (in the United Kingdom) "bucket" being broadly distributed across registers, but "citizen," "commodity," and "conspiracy" carrying a decided edge of specialization, education, and privilege. And more obviously Latinate or Greek vocabulary presumably provides many of the five-dollar words in Mark Twain's aphorism "Don't use a five-dollar word when a fifty-cent word will do." Such language tends to sound cultured or learned—from "amorousness" and "abdominal" to "phobias" and "philosophy." The point here is not that these etymologies provide any hard and

---

13. We are inspired here by Jennifer Foster's discussion in "Busting the Ghost of Neutral Counterparts."

fast rules as to the extrasemantic significance of words. Rather, etymology provides a way of sorting words into heaps, and once the words are in those heaps, broad differences in usage and connotation become obvious. Simply categorizing words by length, or by frequency, would achieve almost the same as sorting by etymology.

Let us now propose that "dog" is inherently tonal, introduce natural objections, and then at least partially rebut them. It is obvious first that "dog" is often used in phrases that have negative connotations. Although there are certainly expressions in which "dog" is used positively, the negative resonances in English are mirrored by the fact that the "recurring themes in common idioms in languages such as French, German, Italian, and Spanish, are those of: low status/worthlessness, futility, unhappiness, competition/aggression."[14] Such associations surely creep into many uses of "dog." And "dog" being, as noted, an unpretentious Old English word, will also carry its unpretentiousness with it wherever it goes. One might, of course, use or mention the word "dog" in a pretentious utterance, but that is true of even the most mundane function words like "in" and "a": one should not expect an unpretentious word to significantly reduce the pretention of a pretentious sentence any more than one should expect lightweight clothing to lower the weight of an overweight wearer.

A number of objections surface at this point. One might accept that when one uses the word "dog," various connotations connected with the attitudes and social positioning of the speaker are available, but deny that those have to do with the meaning of the word. One might, perhaps, say that some of the connotations reflect nothing about the meaning of "dog" but rather its usage. And one might say that yet other connotations have nothing to do with the word "dog," but rather are associations we have with the concept represented by "dog," associations we could in principle have even if we didn't know the word "dog." And one might note that "dog" is often used without any conscious intention to display unpretentiousness, or, for that matter, a negative attitude toward "dog." Doesn't this suggest that if there is any such coloration, it is not part of the conventional meaning of the word?

Let us tackle the last of these first. Does the potential lack of conscious intention imply a lack of convention? Although, as we will see, the possibility of unconscious invocation of tonal meaning is significant, we do not take that possibility to directly bear on the issue of whether or not a given tonal coloring is a conventional aspect of a word's meaning. At risk of an argument from authority, let us borrow a line of thought with such philosophical pedigree

---

14. The quote is from a posting by Livia Miller, "Writing Doggedly: Dog Idioms from around Europe," on the Oxford Dictionaries OxfordWords Blog on July 11, 2013. At time of writing, this post is no longer available on the OxfordWords website, but is accessible at https://web.archive.org/web/20130718093339/http://blog.oxforddictionaries.com/2013/07/dog-idioms-europe/.

that it is part of the canon of undergraduate philosophy of language: Putnam's externalism, as previously invoked in section 5.2.[15] A use of "beech" conveys the meaning of "beech" rather than "elm" even if the speaker does not have a sufficiently advanced conceptualization of either beeches or elms to distinguish between the two, for example, being unaware of the fact that the base of beech leaves is more symmetric than that of elm leaves. If the speaker lacks conceptual distinctions, then clearly the communicative intention cannot involve conscious access to those distinctions. Therefore, the argument would go, one can utter something with a certain meaning without necessarily having conscious access to all aspects of that meaning. And a fortiori, one can utter something that conventionally carries a certain tonality without conscious awareness of that tonality. Just as one can, as the schoolyard rhyme suggests, be a poet and not know it, so can the tone of one's words reveal piety or pride, and cause offense or delight, all despite any lack of conscious intention. Even the words of a tone-deaf speaker may carry tone.

The framework we developed in parts I and II is, among other things, one way of developing Putnam's approach to externalism. Where he justified an externalist account of meaning in part on the basis of the existence of experts who could in principle pass judgment on the proper application of botanical terms like "beech" and "elm," we instead depend on collective attunement in a community of practice. We suggested, in chapter 2, that collective attunement of a group to a practice does not imply full individual attunement by the members of the group. So, for us, what differentiates the resonances of "beech" from the resonances of "elm" is the differences in the way they are both used within a community of practice, that community being, roughly, the English-speaking world, or any large and highly connected subpart of it.

Furthermore, we defined the resonances of an action in such a way that they do not essentially depend on the intentions of a particular actor, but on the extension of the practice that the action instantiates, an extension that is defined relative to a community of practice. On our approach, it would be possible for some practice to develop that crucially depended on intention, and indeed there can be practices for which the primary communicative function is to indicate one's purpose, but, equally, a practice can become conventionalized in such a way that intentions are not central or strong resonances. To clarify: what we mean by saying that a resonance is not central is that there are other stronger resonances, and what we mean by saying that a feature of context is not a strong resonance of a practice is that an action instantiating that practice is only associated with a low probability boost for that feature. Given our probabilistic approach, even when a certain type of intention is associated with a practice, it will not follow that the intention is present at every or even most performances of the practice. To return to an example that has been an

15. Putnam, "Meaning and Reference."

intuition pump throughout this book, one can analyze the functioning of the practice of saying "ouch" without supposing that an intention to express pain is a strong resonance, although such an intention may be analyzed as a weak resonance, present on some occasions of use but not others.

What of the idea that what we have identified as the potential tonal components of "dog," the unpretentiousness and a somewhat demeaning attitude toward dog-like things, are not part of the meaning of "dog"? It is intuitive to analyze the claimed negativity as being an attitude toward dog-like things, rather than part of the meaning of the word. And it seems plausible to say that the unpretentiousness of "dog" is no more and no less than a fact about usage, associated with our knowledge of register rather than with our knowledge of the meaning of the word. We have two replies, one somewhat defensive, and the other accepting.

Our more defensive reply is that we cannot see a clear empirical basis for discriminating tone as part of expression meaning from tone as either associated with an underlying nonlinguistic conceptual category, or from tone as a matter of usage. We can, on the contrary, see at least one argument for considering at least some of the tonality of "dog" a part of its meaning. We can think of this using Grice's notion of *detachability*. Detachability is a diagnostic criterion for whether an aspect of meaning is conventional or conversational, although, as we will discuss later, it is by no means clear that the criterion is a coherent one. Grice describes an inference associated with an expression as "nondetachable insofar as it is not possible to find another way of saying the same thing (or approximately the same thing) which simply lacks the [inference]."[16] So let us ask: is the unpretentiousness of "dog" detachable?

The word "canine" used as a noun (or indeed the Latin *Canis familiaris*) would presumably be taken by Grice as having the same extension as "dog," but contrast strongly in pretentiousness. So it is possible to find another way of saying "the same thing (or approximately the same thing)" that lacks the inference in question, namely the inference that the speaker is acting in an ordinary, humble, or unpretentious way. It is less clear whether the words "canine" or "hound" carry similar negative connotations as "dog," though certainly they are not found in the same negative idioms. We do not live in a hound eat hound world. It anyway seems that, by Grice's criterion, at least the inference of unpretentiousness is detachable from the concept represented by "dog," and therefore this inference should be considered to be conventionally associated with the word "dog."

Here is a fact: use of one and the same word on different occasions can exemplify different speech practices. This simple fact has ramifications for a test like detachability. There are regular speech practices, involving use of

---

16. Grice, "Further Notes on Logic and Conversation," 43. Grice is here discussing the difference between entailments and what he terms "conversational implicatures."

"dog," that have negative connotations. Use of the phrase "dog eat dog world" is a clear case. There are other speech practices, which uses of "dog" also can exemplify, that lack any obvious negative connotations, and that may indeed have positive connotations. The occurrence of the word in the phrase "dog show" is a clear case. The word "dog" is associated with all of these speech practices. Which speech practice a particular use of "dog" exemplifies is communicatively relevant. We have here many conventional associations, rather than none.

Communicative actions are relevant for coordination in a particular context. The word "dog" is typically used as part of a practice of unpretentious speech; it fits into a way of speaking that is appropriate in particular contexts. Whether a particular use of "dog" exemplifies a practice of this kind is a context-dependent matter. The context-dependence of practices is built into our model, much like the context dependence of indexicals. We have not exploited much of the power of probability theory in our account so far, restricting ourselves to the correlative connection between an action and a feature. But the same mathematical framework allows arbitrarily more complex dependencies. In principle, the resonances of a single practice could involve a high probability of feature A whenever feature B is present in the context, and a low probability of feature A whenever feature B is absent. The question for us would not be whether a meaning can in principle be like that, but whether such a meaning is likely to become conventionalized and remain somewhat stable in a community of practice. That is, there is an empirical question of the extent to which members of a speech community categorize a range of actions involving a complex dependency of this sort as belonging to a single practice, and the extent to which, contrarily, the speech community will categorize the range of actions as belonging to two distinct practices, one used in contexts where B is present, and one where B is absent.

A word exemplifies a speech practice or practices, the practices that are salient in the context in the sense that the presupposed resonances of the practice are a good match for that context. Being a good match implies both that in such contexts there would be a significant probability of the practice being performed, and that the practice does not have strong positive resonances with features absent from the context, or strong negative resonances with features that are present. And it is the practices that are salient in the context, those it is recognizable as exemplifying, that determine the communicative effect of uttering it (including its referential content, which, as Kripke emphasized, is determined by speech practice).

The examples we have discussed lead us away from a model of communication that privileges a notion of neutrally descriptive denotation as central to meaning. If the speaker and hearer both know that Mary has exactly one pet and that it's a Labrador, then in saying "Mary's X is missing her," many values of X would lead the speaker and hearer to become jointly attuned to the same property of the world, for example, X = "dog," "doggy-woggy," "puppy-wuppy," "damned dog," "hound," "pet," "Labrador," or "lab." That two expressions attune conversational participants to the same properties of the world is consistent with these expressions having all sorts of other communicative effects. What other sorts of linguistic phenomena suggest a similar moral?

7.5. Speech Practices

In *The Language of the Third Reich*, Klemperer describes the propaganda of the Third Reich under which he lived. The speech practices that were pervasive under National Socialism, the subject matter of the book, were sufficiently distinctive as to give them a name, *Lingua Tertii Imperii*, or LTI:

> The LTI only serves the cause of invocation. . . . The sole purpose of the LTI is to strip everyone of their individuality, to paralyze them as personalities, to make them into unthinking and docile cattle in a herd driven and hounded in a particular direction, to turn them into atoms in a huge rolling block of stone.[17]

Klemperer's book is a focused description of LTI, of characteristic Nazi speech practices.

The first chapter of Klemperer's book, "Heroism: Instead of an Introduction," is devoted to describing the symbols associated with German cognates of the term "heroism," what he describes as the "uniform," in fact the "three different uniforms," of the word. The first uniform was that of the "blood-soaked conquerors of a mighty enemy," the image of the original stormtroopers of the 1920s. The second uniform was that of "the masked figure of the racing driver," representing German success at the beloved sport of auto racing. The third uniform was that of the wartime tank driver. These are the symbols that the term "heroism" evoked. In all three cases, the symbols were "closely tied up with the exaltation of the Teutons as a chosen race: all heroism was the sole prerogative of the Teutonic race."[18]

Klemperer writes,

> What a huge number of concepts and feelings [the Nazi cast of mind, the typical Nazi way of thinking] has corrupted and poisoned! . . . I have observed again and again how the young people in all innocence, and despite a sincere effort to fill the gaps and eliminate the errors in their neglected education, cling to the Nazi thought processes. They don't realize they are doing it; the remnants of linguistic usage from the preceding epoch confuse and seduce them. We spoke about the

---

17. Klemperer, *The Language of the Third Reich*, 20–21.
18. Klemperer, *The Language of the Third Reich*, 2–7.

meaning of culture, or humanitarianism, of democracy and I had the impression that they were beginning to see the light, and that certain things were being straightened out in their willing minds—and then, it was always just round the corner, someone spoke of some heroic behavior or other, or of some heroic resistance or simply of heroism per se. As soon as this concept was even touched upon, everything became blurred, and we were adrift once again in the fog of Nazism . . . it was impossible to have a proper grasp of the true nature of humanitarianism, culture, and democracy if one endorses this kind of conception, or to be more precise misconception, of heroism.[19]

Klemperer is here saying that there is a distinctive National Socialist speech practice. In this speech practice, only Aryans are described as "heroic." Use of the word "heroic" attunes an audience raised under National Socialism to a practice of treating Aryans as better than non-Aryans. Indeed, the function of the speech practice of heroism myths in Nazi ideology is to attune audiences to such a practice. Use of the term "heroic" also attunes the audience to emotions, resonating positively with images of Storm Troopers and race-car drivers, and (presumably) negatively to images of cosmopolitan decadence, to homosexuality, and to swarthy Slavic or Semitic faces. Klemperer claims that those raised under National Socialism react to the use of the term "heroic," and similar vocabulary, inadvertently—the use of the term leads the audience to have positive emotional attunements to certain images and negative emotional attunements to others. A Nazi propaganda poster from 1940, set in a characteristic gothic font and with emphatic capitalization, attributed the following quote to Hitler: "HEROISMUS ist nicht nur auf dem Schlachtfelde notwendig, sondern auch auf dem Boden der Heimat" (Heroism isn't only needed on the battlefield, but also on the soil of the homeland). In Nazi ideology, "heroism" was part of an Aryan supremacist speech practice. It became a conventionalized property of "heroism," or at least of the German "Heroismus," to be a constituent of such a speech practice.

If we think of using words as exemplifying speech practices, we can understand how they can have conventional significance over and above the contents they are used to present. A use of the word "heroism" in Germany in the early 1940s conveyed a wealth of associations, in virtue of the Nazi speech practices that such a use exemplified. A noun like "stormtrooper" was used to predicate a property of some individual. A certain set of individuals were in the extension of the predicate, namely the stormtroopers. One of the things the term "stormtrooper" could be used to do was predicate membership of this set.

Philosophers sometimes talk of the "ordinary denotation" of an expression, although this is not part of our own technical development. For such

19. Klemperer, *The Language of the Third Reich*, 2.

philosophers, the ordinary denotation of "stormtrooper" would be the property of being a stormtrooper, which they may or may not have distinguished from the property of being in the extension of the term "stormtrooper." For some, following the line most clearly developed by Rudolf Carnap and Richard Montague, one aspect of the denotation, its *intension*, would be a somewhat more sophisticated variant of this property. The notion of intension plays a similar role in contemporary theory of meaning as Frege's notion of *sense* played in his account, although Frege himself didn't provide any very clear analysis of what senses are, beyond that they are modes of presentation. On the Carnap/Montague view, the intension would not just be a set of individuals, but a property that varies depending on how the world is, essentially a function from the way the world is to the set of individuals that would be in the extension of "stormtrooper" if the world was that way. No such notion of denotation can adequately capture what is expressed by "stormtrooper." What "stormtrooper" expresses is not just membership of a set, but placement within a complex social world seen from a certain perspective. And use of "stormtrooper" was not just expressive. The use of "stormtrooper" in Nazi Germany helped make the Nazi world what it was, in virtue of the practices its use exemplified.

There are many mechanisms that play a role in forming an ideology. With Jack Balkin in his theory of "cultural software," we focus on *symbolic forms*, which, in his words, "carry units of cultural transmission."[20] Nazi ideology embodies a way of thinking of Aryans and a way of thinking about Jews, and these ways are carried in the speech practices that constitute it.

Nazi ideology is an extreme example of an oppressive ideology. It brings out in vivid ways how ideologies can unjustly create hierarchies of worth. But any way of talking about other beings brings with it attunement to emotions, images, and suggested practices. If one is asked to "go out with the guys," one can make a free choice about one's decision—but the language in which the invitation is offered will elicit emotions that will influence one's choice. The emotions will be different if one asked to "meet with mutual acquaintances," even if the shared references are the same. Ignoring the force of such emotions, the result of the framing of an invitation, is missing a vital function of language. It is a function of language that is missed if one only focuses on neutral shared references of words.

Let us pause to recall (from section 2.6) that in our descriptive sense of "ideology," not all ideologies are oppressive. An ideology helps to guide us through a complex world by giving us shortcuts and strategies in the face of an overwhelming mass of information. An oppressive ideology involves shortcuts that impose or reinforce hierarchies of ethnicity, gender, or other dimensions that should not be set into hierarchies of value. A liberatory ideology involves

20. Balkin, *Cultural Software*, 102.

practices that undercut or disrupt such hierarchies. And some ideologies are just habits, practices, and concepts that help an agent maneuver the world in mundane, practical ways—to find food, for example.

As we have seen in the previous section, we do not need to move to extreme cases, such as National Socialist speech practices, to see that words can conventionally signify much more than the extensional properties of the world they are used to present. This is a fact about conventional significance that is far more general. When speakers use words like "dog," they also exemplify speech practices that are located within ideologies and manifest a particular perspective. The words "stormtrooper" and "dog," although nouns of very different stripes, are alike in respect of both having the trivial property that their resonances are not neutral. We can call the property trivial for a simple reason: not only are resonances never neutral, but it is entirely unclear how it could possibly be the case that a practice could arise that had neutral resonances. Practices arise within communities of practice. At a minimum, a practice carries as a resonance the ideological perspective and social location of the practitioners. There is no such thing as a neutral practice. The idea of a neutral practice makes no more sense than the idea of a neutral ideology.

The function of an ideology is to create a set of presupposed shared meanings—not just common beliefs, but attunements to more than just the beliefs that we associate with the entities, events, actions, and properties under discussion. A full theory of language should allow us to model these presuppositions. That is, a theory of language should allow us to model not just the commonly shared beliefs that our words presuppose, but commonly shared attunement to emotions and practices associated with ways of referring to objects, actions, and events. It should allow us to model the degree of attunement that reflects differential attachments to these ideologies. Oppressive ideologies clearly frame the social world with charged emotions—but even casual conversation persuades along dimensions that cannot simply be captured by considering "neutral" shared references.

7.6. Perspective

In sketching the neutral picture of content within standard theory, we began with the work of Gottlob Frege and his distinction between sense (neutral content) and tone. The picture Frege sketches in 1897 neglects indexicality, words like "I," "here," "now," "this," and "that," whose reference shifts with context. A central moral of the last half century of discussion of indexicality is that it seriously compromises any putative commitment to neutrality of meaning. Any defense of neutral meaning against our skepticism must reckon with this moral, which is, as it were, internal to the ideology of analytic philosophy of language and mind.

John Perry famously argued in "Frege on Demonstratives" that the moral of indexicality is that nothing could play all of Frege's five roles of senses.[21] Frege seems committed to the hypothesis that the linguistic meaning of the first-person pronoun "I" is always the same. Given that sense is supposed to be linguistic meaning, this means that "I" has the same sense in every context. For Frege, a sentence expresses a thought by virtue of how the senses of the words in the sentence combine. So, under the hypothesis that the sense of "I" is constant, if President Obama were to utter in 2015 "I am the President of the United States," he would express the same thought as the one David Beaver would express by using that sentence at the same time. But then the thoughts would have the same truth value. However, the thought President Obama would have expressed would be true, and the thought David Beaver would have expressed would be false. Therefore, the thoughts are different after all. Frege must abandon one or more of the roles of sense.

In the end, Frege comes around to recognizing the failure of the picture of sense he had earlier addressed. When he addresses the topic of indexicals in his paper "The Thought," he decides that the word "I" has different senses in different contexts (his discussion shows clear commitment to role 4, that a difference in reference entails a difference in sense).[22] He abandons the *publicity* of sense, on the grounds that each person's first-personal way of thinking of themselves is accessible only from that person's perspective. The sense of an occurrence of "I" is only accessible from one perspective. It is not a sense that is aperspectival, and so, as John Perry and others have long pointed out, Frege's own discussion violates the thesis of the neutrality of meaning. On Frege's preferred view, our first-person thoughts cannot be grasped by others.

Frege's initial discussion of first-person thought, the *de se*, has had a tremendous impact on the theory of meaning. It could rightly be said that the problem of perspective is one of the perennial issues of the last century in the theory of meaning in the analytic tradition. There is a lengthy tradition of defending Frege's view that first-personal thoughts are not shareable. As Gareth Evans argued, Frege's view that first-person perspective is not sharable is consistent with Frege's commitment to the objectivity of thoughts—in the sense that a first-person perspective is an objectively existing perspective, albeit only capable of being grasped by one person.[23] Evans embeds his defense of Frege's position in Frege's theory of meaning, employing senses rather than modal semantics. But Frege's view of irreducibly unshareable first-person thoughts is not bound to this theory of meaning. David Lewis took the notion of an irreducibly first-person perspective so seriously that he altered his basic conception of content, moving from propositions as sets of

21. Perry, "Frege on Demonstratives."
22. Frege, "The Thought: A Logical Inquiry."
23. Evans, "Understanding Demonstratives."

possible worlds to propositions as sets of centered worlds, worlds centered upon a first-person perspective.[24] Lewis's technology is baked into the notion of resonance we have developed, since resonances involve probabilities of features occurring in a certain type of centered context. Building on Lewis's work, Robert Stalnaker has argued for the coherence and importance of "a notion of informational content that is not detachable from the situation of a subject, or from a context in which the content is ascribed."[25] In short, the thought that informational content is irreducibly perspectival is deeply embedded inside the analytic tradition in the theory of meaning.

Suppose that what is meant by perspective is not a generalized notion like that introduced in the last chapter (the attunements to a set of features of context that some individual or group has), but is rather something like Lewisian content. Let us term such a notion "indexical perspective." Then one may, in an effort to achieve something like neutrality, attempt to detach perspective from discourse by appeal to a language stripped of indexicality, say for the purposes of science. Addressing the historian's attempt to conceal perspective from their language, Roland Barthes writes,

> As a matter of fact, in this case, the speaker annuls his emotive person, but substitutes it for the "objective" person: the subject subsists in its plenitude, but as an objective subject; this is what Fustel de Coulanges called, significantly (and rather naively), "the chastity of history." On the level of discourse objectivity—or lack of signs of "the speaker"—thus appears as a special form of image repertoire, the product of what we might call the referential illusion, since here the historian claims to let the referent speak for itself. This illusion is not proper to historical discourse—how many novelists—in the realistic period—imagine they are "objective" because they suppress signs of "I" in the discourse! . . . We know the absence of signs has a meaning too.[26]

Discourse that appears to lack perspective is often a way of masking a perspective.[27] Even if one doubts that indexical perspective is ubiquitous in empirical discourse, it is nevertheless very often present when it appears not to be.

It has been widely recognized that irreducibly perspectival content poses challenges to idealizations about rationality and communication, how to retain and build on a core of information over time, and how to share that information with others. In short, the modifications in the theory of meaning required to incorporate the ubiquity of irreducible and shareable perspectives pose

24. Lewis, "Attitudes *De Dicto* and *De Se*."

25. Stalnaker, *Our Knowledge of the Internal World*, chapter 3.

26. Barthes, "The Discourse of History," 132.

27. Statistics may be biased, but this is not in any straightforward way a case of hidden indexical perspective.

challenges to the notion of a neutral deliberative space of reasons for shared rational inquiry. There are many creative solutions—for example, Sarah Moss has argued that to each perspectival proposition (*de se* proposition), there corresponds a nonperspectival (*de dicto*) proposition that can "rationally stand in" for that perspectival content in communication and learning.[28] Moss's solution of finding a *de dicto* "stand in" for each *de se* proposition (like the approach of Stalnaker[29]) relies on denying a core motivation intuition of the *de se* literature—that two people (Lewis's "two Gods") can share all their *de dicto* beliefs, while differing on their *de se* attitudes. It seems to be generally conceded, by such solutions, that differences in individual perspectival contents must supervene on differences in ordinary (*de dicto*) contents. If individual perspectival content runs as deep as Lewis and Evans hold, then it does raise significant problems for how to make sense of neutral debate.

Andy Egan's work on the problem of the *de se* is an attempt to alter the framework of the theory of meaning in more substantial ways than Moss, not by finding a *de dicto* ("neutral") counterpart of *de se* belief, but by relativizing the fundamental notions of the theory of meaning, such as the common ground of a conversation and (accordingly) presuppositions, both of which can have *de se* content. Different roles involving the same *de se* common ground (speaker, or hearer) result in grasping different propositions (the speaker grasps a proposition about themselves when uttering, "I am tired"; the addressee grasps a proposition about the speaker, while both speaker and hearer have *de se* attitudes toward their joint common ground, relativized to themselves).[30] This is a distinct way to alter the theory of meaning to account for something like shared discourse information—but the *information* that is shared, on this account, is not the same. Only components of that information are shared, as when you and we are thinking of different scenes involving the same number of daffodils.

The moral of the extensive literature on individual perspective over the past two decades is that we are already stuck with a difficult problem of

28. Moss summarizes this aspect of her account as follows: "Each de se proposition you believe is equivalent with some de dicto proposition, given what you believe with certainty. This sort of de dicto proposition is something you convey to your audience, and something they come to believe. Furthermore, your audience already has some de se beliefs about their relation to you. So they also come to believe some de se propositions: the consequences of their standing de se beliefs and their acquired de dicto information" ("Updating as Communication," 235).

29. Stalnaker, *Our Knowledge of the Internal World.*

30. Egan expresses his conclusions about the inherently perspectival nature of meaning as follows: "attempts to quarantine *de se* content in the philosophy of mind, and maintain a pristine philosophy of language dealing only in *de dicto* contents, are doomed to fail. Once we let *de se* content into our philosophy of mind, there's no viable way to keep it out of our philosophy of language altogether. It at least gets in to the pragmatics" ("*De se* Pragmatics," 159).

objectivity at the very heart of orthodoxy in the theory of meaning. Just the problem of the *de se* alone raises significant conceptual difficulties for the concept of a neutral space of reasons for deliberation.

Andy Egan's theoretical interest in the *de se* was a small part of his contribution to the large literature on relativism, a major topic of research in philosophy of language in the last two decades. Perhaps the signal work of this era is John MacFarlane's *Assessment Sensitivity*.[31] An assessment-relative theory of meaning is one that takes norms governing notions like agreement or disagreement to be relative to a context (or standard) of assessment. If there is such a thing as a neutral debate, it would presumably have to involve agreement or disagreement about the same propositions. The central theoretical task facing any assessment-relative account is to make sense out of such agreement and disagreement, in other words, to make sense out of the fundamental concepts of rational debate.

Most work on assessment sensitivity is driven by examples in which a robust sense of objectivity is in any case misplaced. For example, one of the central motivating examples for this revision to the theory of meaning is predicates of personal taste, as in "is tasty."[32] These are domains in which it is easier to see how one might abandon commitment to a genuine neutral space of reasoned debate. However, we might imagine, as in the case of the *de se*, that the problem of social perspective is more general, and indeed ubiquitous.

Oddly, given the centrality of the problem of the *de se*, and the recent exploration of the conceptual foundations of assessment sensitivity, analytic philosophers working in the theory of meaning have been more reluctant to explore the consequences of theorizing about *social* perspective as a node or element in the theory of meaning. The goal of revising the theory of meaning to accommodate an irreducibly first-person perspective has been central to almost every tradition in the analytic theory of meaning. But there is considerably less discussion of how to alter the theory of meaning to account for social perspective, and less discussion of the sorts of linguistic phenomena that would raise the issue in the first place. As we have seen, there does not seem to be a legitimate objection in principle to such a program, as subsequent work on assessment-relativism has shown.

The literature on assessment sensitivity concerns how truth is evaluated. But the notion of a social perspective need not be theorized as a parameter of *truth* assessment. Elisabeth Camp has shown that perspective does not need to be theorized simultaneously with the evaluation of truth, or as a question of how a predicate "is true" is applied to sentences or propositions. In a pioneering set of papers, she has argued that perspectives are implicated in

---

31. MacFarlane, *Assessment Sensitivity*.

32. Classic papers include Lasersohn, "Context-Dependence"; Egan, "Disputing about Taste."

"political discourse, intimate interpersonal arguments, informal commentaries on movies—anywhere that intuitive interpretation is at stake."[33] Camp's perspectives are comparable to the landscapes of attunement introduced in the analysis of harmonization in section 3.4, determining what concepts and dispositions tend to be activated together in a person's thought, and they can be seen as a direct antecedent of our proposal.

Camp has applied her account to a range of issues. She suggests that perspectives are central to understanding essential features of metaphors, in particular their lack of paraphrasability.[34] She has also argued that perspectives are necessary to understanding how slurs derogate—by introducing derogating perspectives.[35] (We will return to the treatment of slurs in chapter 10.) In short, over the years, Camp has given a systemic case, considering a variety of different linguistic constructions and phenomena, for the importance of perspective as an essential tool in the theory of meaning.[36] Suppose someone wished to maintain the possibility of democratic debate as involving a neutral space of reasons. They would not only need to counter worries arising from arguments that point of view is inherent in the very notion of a propositional claim, but they would also need to sidestep the worry that every claim is associated with some perspective, some way of thinking about the claim involving implicit priorities about what to think about. It is entirely unclear what it would even mean for a perspective, in Camp's sense, to be neutral. But let us not here make the contentious claim that every utterance involves a perspective in Camp's sense, or a social perspective of any sort. For the purposes of this section, what we take from Camp's work is the more minimal claim that she provides a tangible demonstration that it is coherent to develop a theory of meaning within which social perspectives might play a central role.

Social perspective is often conveyed in narrative form, or with respect to background narrative frames, as discussed in section 3.5.[37] Full interpretation of

---

33. Camp, "Imaginative Frames for Scientific Inquiry," 308.

34. Camp, "Metaphor and That Certain 'Je Ne Sais Quoi.'"

35. Camp, "Slurring Perspectives."

36. Samia Hesni has made related arguments that intuitions about linguistic felicity are responsive to social location. She observes that contrasting intuitions as regards the felicity of sentences like "Muslims are terrorists" and "White men are terrorists" have as much do with the identity of the interlocutors as to do with facts in the world ("Normative Discourse and Social Negotiation," 87–88). Hesni's argument is that if we wish to capture the evidential basis of the theory of meaning—speaker intuitions—we must theorize about social situatedness.

37. We recommend Rachel Fraser's "Narrative Testimony" for explicit discussion of the relationship between narrativity and perspective, which she summarizes as follows: "In successful narrative testimonial exchange . . . speaker and hearer become co-ordinated not only with respect to the informational content of the speaker's testimony, but also with respect to the content's representational format. Such co-ordination gives rise to perspectival dependence" (4032).

speech requires a background of narratives, which must augment the "simple picture" that assigns objects, properties, and relations to expressions. It is against a background of narrative that we interpret speech, not vice versa. But if this is so, then what would neutral speech be? Could it be speech in which the underlying narratives were neutral? If the concept of a neutral story makes any sense at all, we doubt that a neutral story would be any good. But independently of this value judgment, neutral narrative does not seem to us a fruitful direction on which to ground a more general notion of neutral speech, for the concept of a neutral narrative is at best ill-defined, and at worst incoherent. It is unclear what it would mean for a story to be neutral, to be a way to frame patterns of events that is free of ideology.

Could neutral speech could be speech that is entirely bereft of narratives? Let us suppose for a moment that speech bereft of narrative is a coherent concept. Let us also leave aside what seems to us a natural view, that speech bereft of narratives would be far from ideal, and would in fact be tragically impoverished. The sense in which speech bereft of narratives would not be neutral is simple. Far from being neutral, narrativeless speech would be a particular and rather narrow subspecies of discourse. It would be exceptional and extraordinary. It would be speech that did not support narrative modes of thought like those we discussed in chapter 3, modes of thought that many have taken to be central to human culture (cf. our discussion in section 3.5 of narrative harmonization).[38] Preferring narrativeless speech to more common modes of human discourse would require a particular ideological position. We should call it an extreme position. Whether extreme or not, it would not in any sense be a neutral position. Hence the hypothesized narrativeless speech would also

---

38. It might be suggested that narrativeless discourse would be scientific. We will not contest whether there could be such a thing as narrativeless scientific discourse, but it is doubtful that actual scientific discourse is narrativeless. Here is Walter Fisher on the issue: "There is no question . . . that scientific discursive practices are rhetorical, whether involving the specialized audience of scientists or the generalized audience of the public. In both instances, rhetorical motives and rhetorical means are at work—the desire to gain adherence, adaptation to audience constraints, and the use of strategic, persuasive symbols, including charts, graphs, pictures, metaphors as well as empirical data and well-formed arguments. Justification to convince a specialized audience and translation for a generalized audience are both rhetorical 'doings,' practices" ("Narrative Rationality and the Logic of Scientific Discourse," 22). In his earlier, and seminal, *Human Communication as Narration*, Fisher makes a related statement that bears on the supposed neutrality of argumentation in scientific discourse: "The most fundamental difference between narrative rationality and other rhetorical logics is the presumption that no form of discourse is privileged over others because its form is predominantly argumentative. No matter how strictly a case is argued—scientifically, philosophically, or legally—it will always be a story, an interpretation of some aspect of the world that is historically and culturally grounded and shaped by human personality. Even the most well-argued case will be informed by other individuated forms besides argument, especially by metaphor" (49).

not be neutral. It would be the speech of ideologues who fancied their speech better than that of the bulk of humankind.

Narratives are not the only structures against which we interpret strings of sentences; we can add to this list stereotypes, value systems, perspectives, prejudice, framings, practices, identity, and affect. Each of these notions is unlikely to be straightforwardly reducible to another. Jessie Munton has recently argued that prejudice is not adequately captured by false beliefs about a group, negative affect, or prejudicial behavior.[39] According to Munton, prejudice toward a group is rather a problematic way of organizing information about that group—one that gives certain features more weight than they should receive. Prejudice, on Munton's view, is a problematic *salience structure*, one that makes certain features of group members more salient than they ought to be. If what I say can presuppose prejudice, and prejudice is a salience structure, then perhaps, to model speech, we need to think of presupposition as a relation, not just to information, but to something psychologically richer.

We have presented an account of presupposition that makes this concrete. In the model of presupposition developed in chapter 5, a practice can presuppose any system of attunements that is commonly present among the participants in the practice. Further, as we argued in section 3.4, attunements are organized into landscapes that encode activational relationships. Thus one attunement may selectively activate others, and hence determine a default flow of attention, as when, absent external stimuli to redirect attention, one follows through steps of an argument, a story, or a plan. Our model allows such structures to be presupposed by a practice, provided that the presence of the structure is in a position to affect whether the practice is performed (the *causal efficacy postulate* of section 2.5). We believe the model thus allows us to capture the idea present in prior work (in particular, in the work of Camp and Munton) that in presupposing a stereotype, we do not merely presuppose a set of facts, but also presuppose tendencies to focus on some characteristics rather than others.

We could, perhaps, attempt to individually add each of the major notions we have mentioned in this section—narratives, framings, prejudice, identity, etc.—to an ultimate theory of communication, characterizing each as we go. However, our hope is that by this point in the book the charitable reader is starting to get a feel for how such developments might be advanced. Perhaps the reader is even sympathetic to the possibility that the model we have proposed already does some of the work that might be demanded of these notions. Rather than picking through each of the many further notions that we have discussed, let us try to consider a broader context in which they can be seen as playing their own roles. The broader context is that of *ideology*, which we defined in chapter 2 as follows:

39. Munton, "Prejudice as the Misattribution of Salience."

Ideology: An ideology is the system of collective attunements among members of a community of practice.

The term "ideology" is used in a bewildering variety of senses, as befitting the fact that the study of ideology has been central to philosophical theorizing dating back at least to Plato. Raymond Geuss defines the broadest sense of ideology, "ideology in the descriptive sense," as including "the beliefs the members of a group hold, the concepts they use, the attitudes and psychological dispositions they exhibit, their motives, values, predilections, works of art, religious rituals, gestures, etc."[40] In this sense, ideology is not pejorative—every group has an ideology—but rather is something like a worldview, understood broadly enough to include practices. As emphasized already in this chapter, our definition of ideology is ideology in such a descriptive sense.

Pierre Bourdieu writes, "Every established order tends to produce (to very different degrees and with very different means) the naturalness of its own arbitrariness."[41] This is a central function of an ideology. An ideology creates a set of presuppositions—what Bourdieu calls "doxa," "the class of what is taken for granted . . . the sum total of the theses tacitly posited on the hither side of all inquiry."[42] Among the doxa in Bourdieu's sense—the presuppositions imposed by ideology—we include more specific notions, such as narratives, stereotypes, practices, and so forth. This too is how Bourdieu thought about these notions—as Judith Butler writes, emphasizing the materiality of doxa, realized as practices and habits, "'Rules of the game' are, quite literally, incorporated, made into a second nature, constituted as a prevailing doxa."[43]

Across very different paradigms in the theory of meaning, philosophers have held that first-person perspective is something that must be modeled, to account for an essentially dominant view that first-person perspective is ubiquitous and theoretically central.[44] We have seen a two-decade attempt to make sense more generally of disagreement about less than factual seeming domains. There is thus no obstacle in principle that theorists of meaning in the analytic tradition have had to the centrality and importance of perspective—indeed, they have been theorizing it as a parameter of truth. We have argued in this section that once it is already granted that the theory of meaning must be adjusted to account for first-person perspectives, there is no obstacle to

40. Geuss, *The Idea of a Critical Theory*, 5.

41. Bourdieu, *Outline of a Theory of Practice*, 164.

42. Bourdieu, *Outline of a Theory of Practice*, 178.

43. Butler, *Excitable Speech*, 154.

44. In chapter 3 of *Know How*, Jason Stanley argues that first-person perspective does not pose distinctive issues for a broadly Fregean theory of content—it is just one kind of mode of presentation. Using similar considerations, Herman Cappelen and Joshua Dever argue in *The Inessential Indexical* that the focus on the specialness of *de se* thought to the theory of meaning has been misplaced.

exploring the ways in which perspectives, narratives, and, overall, ideologies, structure communication.

7.7. Against Neutrality as an Ideal

The thought behind neutrality is that the core of communicated denotation is nonideological. On this way of understanding neutrality, the core information conveyed in a communicative action is neutral because it does not in any way convey something about social perspective.

But, as we have argued, ideologies are constituted in part by social practices. And speech practices are paradigmatic examples of social practices. In *The Language of the Third Reich*, Klemperer writes,

> Nazism permeated the flesh and blood of the people through single words, idioms and sentence structures which were imposed on them in a million repetitions and taken on board mechanically and unconsciously. . . . Language does not simply write and think for me, it also increasingly dictates my feelings and governs my entire spiritual being the more unquestioningly and unconsciously I abandon myself to it.[45]

Klemperer here forces us to take seriously the thought that National Socialist ideology consists in large part of certain speech practices. It is for this reason that denazification took the form of constraining and minimizing those speech practices.[46] The result of denazification was a more open, inclusive, and democratic German society. Denazification is an example of restrictions on speech practices leading to a strengthening of democratic norms.

Social practices include "cultural schemas," such as "rules of etiquette, or aesthetic norms, or such recipes for group action as the royal progress, grain riot, or democratic vote, or a set of equivalences between wet and dry, female and male, nature and culture, private and public."[47] A speech practice embodies a schema in this sense, a way of speaking of the world, characteristically the social world, in a way that assigns different groups social roles and positions. In so doing, a speech practice reflects a perspective on the world. These speech practices thus help constitute ideologies—social perspectives on the world (according to one reading of Elisabeth Camp's work, speech practices are the result of such perspectives, which give rise to them).

If we think of a use of a word as occurring within a speech practice, then we can see that there will standardly be communicative effects of using that word

45. Klemperer, *The Language of the Third Reich*, 14.
46. In the work of Elisabeth Camp, perspectives *give rise* to speech practices. One might disagree with the priority claim inherent in Camp's work, though. Perhaps perspectives are also in part constituted by habits of behavior, including speech behavior. This, we take it, is what Klemperer is urging.
47. Sewell, "A Theory of Structure," 8.

over and above attuning an audience to a common object, property, or relation. By using one word rather than another for the same thing, "dog" versus
"canine," for example, we locate ourselves within one speech practice rather
than another. The speech practices our words exemplify locate us socially, and
often politically. Different speech practices can use some of the same tools—
that is, can employ some of the same words. One and the same word can
exemplify, in one context one speech practice, and in another context, quite
a distinct one. So, different uses of one and the same word can communicate
quite different things, depending on the speech practice they exemplify. But
this is not the *lack of linguistic convention*—it is *participation in multiple
linguistic conventions*.

The connection between presupposition and practice makes particularly
vivid the problems with a model of speech that focuses on neutral debate as
an ideal. Words are always embedded in speech practices, which are elements
of ideologies. All speech will locate its users in this way. If we ignore this fact,
or pretend it is something we can idealize away from, we are liable to overlook
the effects of the speech practices that words exemplify. The use of a word can
cue us to the social location of a speaker, to their identity, their socioeconomic
class, gender, or race. We might say that the ideal of neutrality is problematic
insofar as it masks the way that speech essentially presents the world within a situated perspective. Though we take this to be true, it does not quite go far enough,
for it focuses on the limiting nature of the ideal of neutrality for assertions,
that is, communicative acts whose primary purpose is to present the way the
world is. Before considering other communicative acts, let us turn briefly to
one of the most important lines of epistemological work in recent years.

As we have noted, not all ideologies are oppressive. Some standpoints
bring with them epistemological advantages, which is the central thesis of
standpoint epistemology. There are various versions of standpoint epistemology.
There are some according to which the thesis is a truism—being in a certain social
situation leads you to have more fine-grained knowledge about it, for example. There are some according to which it is a weighty metaphysical claim.
For example, if certain social situations can be *transformative*, in the sense
of Laurie Paul, they can give you access to information that you cannot have
without that experience.[48] This is a *weighty* standpoint epistemological claim.
If standpoint epistemology is true, then certain social perspectives can aid
you evidentially. Since speech practices are parts of social perspectives, ways
of talking can presuppose ways of thinking about the world that are more
epistemologically advantageous.

All communication takes place with respect to a context of practices, which
licenses the communicative acts constitutive of the communicative exchange.
Understanding the interplay between utterances and different background

48. Paul, *Transformative Experience*.

ideologies is essential to understanding what is communicated and to which audience. On our model, there is no sense to be made, as long as one is using words in a living language, of the possibility of reasoning free of a set of background practices. And such situated background practices affect the rhetorical force of one's chain of reasoning. If standpoint epistemology is correct, knowing that someone is speaking from a privileged epistemic perspective can even be relevant to deciding whose views carry the most weight. From this more realistic perspective, the very *coherence* of an ideal of neutrality is questionable.

Let us strengthen that. Considerations from standpoint epistemology suggest that the coherence of an ideal of neutrality is questionable as applied to knowledge, and equally to the act of assertion. What of other communicative acts? As we have discussed in this volume, borrowing heavily from the tradition of work that runs through Wittgenstein and Austin, people do much in communication besides asserting things about the world. People greet each other, express feelings of pain, happiness, or love, sentence others to jail, joke, threaten, promise, pray, offend, and thank. When at a Black Lives Matter march people in unison repeat "Sandra Bland! Say her name!" they are not asserting anything, and neither is anything being asserted when at a Donald Trump rally people repeat "Lock her up!" The ubiquity of nonassertive speech acts in ordinary discourse, as well as explicitly political discourse, leads to a significant problem for the ideal of neutrality. And here it does not even matter whether we talk of "ideal" in the sense of idealization, that is, theoretical abstraction or simplification, or "ideal" in the sense of preferred way of doing things. The problem is not with the word "ideal," but with the word "neutral."

The problem is that communication consists of actions drawn from practices. Just as it is unclear what a neutral perspective would be, it is also entirely unclear whether there is any coherent notion of a neutral action or of a neutral practice. Take the mundane practice of greeting. What one might be tempted to describe as a neutral greeting would, in many contexts, appear standoffish for its lack of effusiveness. No greeting is neutral. One cannot joke neutrally, pray neutrally, or sentence someone to death neutrally any more than one can cross a road or kill a fish neutrally. It is simply a category error to apply the term "neutral" to the act of crossing the road or killing a fish. One can at best cross the road or kill a fish without manifesting one's feelings, but that is not to act neutrally in any interesting sense, and it is not a sense of neutrality that would seem to be of great interest either to philosophers of language or political theorists.

There is another sense in which an action can be neutral, as when someone acts as a "neutral arbiter." In this sense, to call the action "neutral" is to say that the actor gave no net benefit to any of the parties in the affair being arbitrated. This concept of neutrality is prominent in political debate. It is related to what is meant by talk of a country's neutrality in a war, although in this case something weaker might be meant: that a government's public actions do not so decisively favor the victory of one side that these actions should themselves be considered acts of war. It is the also sense most relevant to the Wiesel quote that "Neutrality helps the oppressor" with which we headed this chapter, which concerns people's moral obligation to speak up when systematic oppression is growing around them. Silence may be golden, but it is the oppressor who has a need to trade in its currency, for an absence of speech is an absence of dissent.

We see then that just as speech is never neutral, so it is with silence. Silence registers tacit acceptance of the staus quo. But here let us note that in *The Origins of Totalitarianism*, while Hannah Arendt does see silence as an important aspect of the onset of totalitarianism, she develops a more nuanced view than Wiesel, grounded in a broader historical study of totalitarian movements in the twentieth century. The problem is not only silence in the face of overt acts of oppression such as beatings on the street and firing of Jewish workers in 1930s Germany, but the more general failure of people to speak up when national government systematically overlooks, or even supports, gross inequality. In describing the circumstances within which totalitarian regimes grow, she observes that "democratic government had rested as much on the silent approbation and tolerance of the indifferent and inarticulate sections of the people as on the articulate and visible institutions and organizations of the country."[49] That is, the silent acceptance of oppressive systems and the forced silence of the oppressed are, for Arendt, properties of an unjust society, whether superficially democratic or not. Such a society is ripe for totalitarian takeover. Under the guise of giving the oppressed and powerless a voice, totalitarians create a chaos of noisy and violent dissent in democracy in order to displace democracy in favor of an oppressive system that better suits them.

To describe a speech act as neutral in the sense of not benefiting specific sides in an adversarial situation is to presuppose some very specific distinctions, such as who the relevant parties are, and what constitutes harm or benefit. That is, to arbitrate neutrally in this sense is to act in a way that a particular ideology determines is neutral. But if neutrality of a speech act is to be relativized to an ideology, then it is of limited practical or theoretical interest. Practically, an ideology-dependent measure of neutrality cannot serve as a very general tool for arbitration between ideologies. Theoretically, to accept neutrality as a relative notion is to accept the impossibility of the project of defining a coherent notion of neutrality with the qualities that it was purported to possess, allowing words in some sense to stand above the fray, elevated from the whims of mortals, impartial as the stars above. In some religions, the word of sacred texts is understood to have such qualities, but for anyone standing in

---

49. Arendt, *The Origins of Totalitarianism*, 312.

a tradition of post-enlightenment rationalism, the ideal of neutrality cannot possibly be so lofty.

There is, as we have seen, a substantial literature on the topic of rescuing agreement and disagreement in the presence of various kinds of perspectival relativity. One solution, taken in the assessment-relativity literature, is to limit the scope of claims of perspectival relativity to cases in which there isn't a sense of shared objective reality—a paradigm example being judgments of taste.[50] The terrain looks different in the case of social perspective—one cannot focus on a limited set of contexts in which social perspective is irrelevant (as we have urged). One might think this raises a profound problem for this investigation. One might, that is, think that the ubiquity of social perspective means that we must compromise on the existence of robust truth claims.[51] Fortunately, this is not so. Though social perspective is ubiquitous, it need not be a *parameter of truth assessment*, as seen in Camp and Munton's work.

In our account, the possibility of a robust theory of truth rests on the fact that attunement is not limited to social categories and practices: there is also attunement to physical properties of the world. Within the community of practice that makes the exchange meaningful in the first place, uptake of a true claim about the world will result in attunement to the world as it actually is, and not merely as it happens to be understood.

There is an analogy to be drawn here with perception, and with Gibsonian direct theories of perception in particular.[52] Modes of perception differ dramatically, with sight, touch, and hearing revealing different qualities of the world in different ways. Furthermore, one individual's hearing and neurological processing may differ arbitrarily from another's. Perception is not neutral, whether one is wearing rose-tinted spectacles or not. Yet different individuals with their different perceptual apparatuses may become attuned to the same physical facts in the world, say the proximal onset of a storm. Similarly, and although communicative practices vary arbitrarily, the statement "It's going to rain" can be true when uttered in a particular context by virtue of the fact that uptake of the claim by a member of the English-speaking community

50. See Lasersohn, *Subjectivity and Perspective*. The major work on Assessment Sensitivity is MacFarlane, *Assessment Sensitivity*. MacFarlane considers five applications, to taste, knowledge, statements about the future, and epistemic and deontic modals.

51. That is, the ubiquity of social perspective does not mean that social perspective must then play an analogous role in truth evaluation to the role played by parameters in MacFarlane's account of predicates of personal taste (MacFarlane, *Assessment Sensitivity*). For MacFarlane, this would undermine the defense he gives of a type of limited relativism, avoiding the pitfalls of taking all truth claims to be inherently unstable. He achieves this defense by separating those claims that depend upon parameters of evaluation from those that do not, an approach that would become untenable in the form he gives it were all truth claims relative to a parameter of social perspective.

52. We touched on Gibson's work in section 1.5 and elsewhere in part I. The relevant reference is Gibson, "A Theory of Direct Visual Perception."

following the practices of that community would attune that person to a property of the world. Every claim is ideologically relative, and claims about the weather are no exception, but that does not preclude there being a fact of the matter as to whether a claim made by a member of a specific community of practice on a particular occasion is true or not.

To be clear about our position, we are not claiming that for any particular class of statements it is practical, or even possible, to robustly assess the truth value. The existence of statements for which it is possible to robustly assess truth clearly does not imply that the truth of any significant class of statements can be robustly assessed in this way. What we have in mind here are not just issues of vagueness and paradox that have dogged philosophy for millennia, as might be seen in the question of whether it is raining when a single drop falls. We are thinking also of cases in which aspects of ideology, and their constituent practices, are contested. For example, any claim involving a gendered term, including commonplace terms like "man" and "woman," enters upon ideologically contested territory.

There are then at least three problems to overcome in assessing the truth of a claim involving contested terms. First, there is the ancient problem of vagueness. In our terms, this means that for some claims it may be impossible to determine sufficient history of practice for all the constructions used in the claim such that it is clear whether the physical nature of the world and the conventions of the community of practice determine the claim to be true, or determine it to be false. Second, there is the problem of contestation, which implies that different people may see the same claim through different ideological lenses, with the implication that even though there may be a fact of the matter as to whether a particular statement is true within a particular community of practice, people may contest the truth of a sentence because they do not share collective attunement to the same ideology, and may even sometimes intentionally contest the truth of a sentence as a proxy for contesting ideology. Third, there is a problem of irreducibility of perspective. By this we mean that even if there are particular properties of the world that would determine whether a certain statement within a particular community of practice were true, there could not possibly be a neutral way of paraphrasing the truth conditions of the statement.

Regarding the third issue, the point is that paraphrasing involves reframing, but not *deframing*. Paraphrasing produces a new symbolic object that one must interpret with a specific ideology. One may well have clarified in the process, perhaps shifting a complex issue into more easily understandable sub-issues, but in doing so one has not removed perspective. In fact, one has potentially muddied the waters, since the process of paraphrasing introduces ideology in two ways, first thorough the intrinsically ideological practice of paraphrasing itself, and second through the ideological practices that make the constructions in the paraphrase meaningful. This is so whether the paraphrasing is into natural language (the paradigmatic case being the famous instance of Tarski's truth schema "'Snow is white' is true iff snow is white"[53]), or into the mathematical terms of contemporary formal semantic theory.

The practice of labeling certain claims as true, we submit, is connected to the propensity of those claims to attune people to properties of their environment, both properties of the world and properties of their speech community. At the same time, the practice of labeling things as true may also (much like the practice of labeling things as neutral or objective) play other roles, like the role of pushing or enforcing the priority of an epistemic standpoint. Developing a resonance-based theory of the practice of labeling things as true is not a project we take on in this volume. Quite generally, we think that while plenty of attention has been paid to the nature of truth, insufficient attention has been paid to the role of nonpropositional aspects of language.

While we have emphasized that there is much at stake in communication beyond truth, our proposal is not at all to do away with the notion of truth in favor of, say, a radically relativistic view on which the truth of claims is just a personal or even community preference. The relativization we are urging is not a relativization of the sort discussed in the assessment-sensitivity literature, where truth can be taken relative to a parameter of taste or a potential future history. We hope to help explain attributions of predicates like "arrogant," or "sad," to an assertion, attributions that reflect socio-emotional attunements people may have to the assertion—not to explain how attributions of truth are more complex than they appear to be.

We have argued that speech attunes us to ideologies, which harmonize narratives, practices, affect, values, principles, goals, and expectations, so that there is no "simple" attunement to things. Further, we have de-emphasized the role of truth in the theory of meaning: nowhere in this book do we offer a definition of a truth predicate in terms of our model of meaning. The fact that we do not focus on the nature of truth only reflects our opinion that it has been overemphasized in much prior work; it does not reflect any conviction that defining truth would be a mistake. However, both our denial of simple attunement to things and our de-emphasis of truth may lead some to a legitimate worry. The worry would be that the path taken in this book, and in this chapter in particular, is toward a relativist abyss in which all communicative acts are epistemologically equal, none cleaving more tightly to reality than any other.

We do not believe that our commitment to speech as pervasively ideological forces us to sacrifice a kind of robust realism. Attunement to ideology does not preclude attunement to reality. On the contrary, attunement to sophisticated ideology, for example scientific theory, can support far more nuanced attunement to reality than would otherwise be possible. While the question of

53. Tarski, "The Semantic Conception of Truth and the Foundations of Semantics."

what reality consists in is complex, since culture and cultural objects are part of it, we hold that it is always a legitimate question whether a particular communicative act better attunes people to reality or not. Furthermore, we doubt that as complex a communicative system as a human language could possibly have evolved if it did not have at least a strong tendency to help attune interlocutors to reality. It is not the case that realism is in tension with the ubiquity of social perspective, and realism about communication does not depend on there being such a thing as neutral speech.

To make this discussion more concrete, consider an example. Suppose that just as you are starting to cross the street, an onlooker who has observed an oncoming truck shouts, "Watch out!" and you leap back to the safety of the sidewalk. There is no interesting sense in which the onlooker's panicked exhortation was neutral, and we would not normally describe such a speech act as true or false. Fortunately, it did better attune you to reality. So it is with all communication: whatever social, emotional, and dispositional attunements a particular communicative act brings, the question of whether the act is suited to the context in which it is used is a practical one. Among the ways in which an act can be suited to its context is the way it attunes interlocutors to physical aspects of that context. We submit that it is quite possible for a theory of communication that eschews neutrality to nonetheless support a robust realism, because the theory will distinguish the contexts in which acts attune people to reality from those in which they do not.

The considerations in this chapter suggest that there are significant problems with the concept of neutrality. Let us consider what follows from that. First, are particular claims about specific stretches of discourse being neutral coherent, or are they false? Second, to the extent that the notion of neutrality is coherent enough for such claims of neutrality to be false, could it nonetheless be the case that the ideal of neutrality is one worth aiming for, even if it is never actually attained? The answer to both of these questions depends on what notion of neutrality is being assumed. If what is meant is discourse that lacks any ideological perspective—what might be termed "ideological neutrality"—then any claim of neutrality would be incoherent, and indeed the ideal of neutrality would be incoherent too. Discourse occurs in a language, and a language is embedded in an ideology, so discourse cannot be free of ideology. Furthermore, a claim of ideological neutrality consists only in a failure to recognize that alternative perspectives could add anything to the discussion. So such a claim is not only incoherent, but itself cannot possibly be part of a neutral discussion. To claim ideological neutrality is to claim epistemic and communicative supremacy over groups that do not adhere to the speaker's ideology. Such claims are thus examples of what are often termed "power moves," paradigmatic examples of a communicative action for which social location is relevant.

Let us return to the provisional definition of neutrality of a discussion from section 7.1, whereby neutrality demands that "perspective and attunement to social location are irrelevant to the understanding and evaluation of each move in the discussion." Let us allow that perspective need not be completely irrelevant, because we might reasonably say that a primary goal of discussion is to change someone's perspective. That is, according to the definition of perspective given in section 6.4, the goal of discussion might be to change someone's attunements to a set of features of the context.

Let us instead limit what must be irrelevant to presupposed perspective: while an effect of a neutral discussion might be to change perspective, perspectival presuppositions and social location should be irrelevant. But even with this limitation of perspective to what is presupposed, perspective will always be relevant to understanding the moves in a discussion, for the simple reason that there can be no understanding of discussion about features of context without prior perspective on at least some of those features. Furthermore, as we have argued, all language has presupposed resonances of social location, starting with membership of the interlocutors in common communities of practice, without which there could not be mutual understanding of what is said.

We can go further along this line: if we are going to idealize about discussion, then, to put it in our own terms, we might say that if an ideal discussion were going to achieve anything, it would be collective harmonization. Harmonization is an increase of collective attunement, such as collective attunement to the world (or "common knowledge," to use the standard term), and this brings with it the possibility of enhanced future coordination. If one of the functions of an ideal discussion is to create collective attunement, and thence enhanced coordination, then it is hard to understand how social location could ever be irrelevant.

While we have not considered every possible definition of neutrality, we have considered a range of issues related to the concept of neutrality in this chapter, and they draw us to the following conclusions. First, if neutrality is to be coherent at all, it must be a limited notion. Ideological neutrality is incoherent, and neutrality might at most be applied to a subset of moves in discussions, those that describe the world, and not to speech acts in general. Second, when claims of neutrality of human language are made, they are false: as we have argued, even the most mundane language is socially located and has a host of resonances. Third, we doubt that neutrality is coherent as a speech ideal. Not only do we see no good reason why emotional appeals to, say, inequity in social location could not be components of healthy discussion, but we also see the purpose of discussion as intrinsically social. A theory of human discourse predicated on an ideal of neutrality, whether descriptive or prescriptive, would necessarily be incomplete, for it would omit the purpose of human discourse.

CHAPTER EIGHT

Straight Talk

Confronted with an analysis . . . the code traffickers quickly turn into hard-core literalists who say things like "How can it be racist to be for equality?" or "My objection is simply to preferential treatment for anyone," or "I just want decisions to be made on a basis that is fair." Such demurrers invoke a plain meaning philosophy of language and also claim a transparency of intention: "I just mean what I say, and what I say is both innocent and upright." The question is one of motives.

—STANLEY FISH[1]

One man's transparency is another's humiliation.

—GERRY ADAMS[2]

IN THE PRECEDING CHAPTER, we discussed and critiqued the ideal of neutrality of discourse. Since discourse is invariably shaped by social practices it presupposes and exemplifies, discourse is never neutral with regard to perspectival features such as (for example) social position. In this chapter, we discuss the limitations of another somewhat idealized conception of discourse—*straight talk*. *Talking straight* is about being *transparent*, keeping your communicative intentions up-front and obvious.

Neutral discourse has some intuitive and pretheoretic commonalities with straight talk. We can easily imagine the liberal ideal of discourse democracy to be a kind of *neutral straight talk*—discourse that lacks a perspective and is fully transparent. We saw in the last chapter that neutrality of discourse is incoherent, as perspective is essential to human discourse. An ideal that fundamentally misrepresents the nature of its domain is epistemologically problematic.

The ideal of neutral discourse represents discourse as ideally free of perspectives. Neutrality as an ideal would lead one to think that transforming nonideal discourse into ideal discourse involves removing perspectives one by one until the ideal of neutrality is achieved. But discourse, as we have argued,

---

1. Fish, *There's No Such Thing as Free Speech*, 90.

2. Adams is cited in "N.Ireland Process: Where Did It Go Wrong?," CNN, October 22, 2003, http://www.cnn.com/2003/WORLD/europe/10/22/n.ireland.hold/. The context was negotiations over the IRA's decommissioning of arms. In the above quote, Adams, the leader of the political party associated with the IRA, Sinn Fein, was indicating that full disclosure of exactly what arms the IRA had in its possession and was decommissioning would be humiliating to the movement.

is essentially perspectival. Utterances of words characteristically exemplify speech practices, which locate their users socially. You cannot remove a perspective from a speech practice, except insofar as what you then have is a distinct speech practice, with its own perspective. Most ideals mask reality by making it seem that reality is closer to the ideal than it actually is. The ideal of neutral discourse masks the gap between it and reality in a more problematic way. Speech is fundamentally perspectival. If you remove speech practices, you lose speech, and speech practices are perspectival. The ideal of neutral discourse masks reality by completely misrepresenting the *nature* of the gap between it and reality,

What about the ideal of straight talk? Here, we do not deny the bare coherence of straight talk. And perhaps it is logically possible to communicate fully transparently, though the ubiquity of speech practices makes that unlikely (as we shall see). Nevertheless, the ideal of straight talk is problematic in the theory of meaning, as it masks so much of what such a theory is responsible for explaining. To understand how much of what this ideal masks, we turn to what we call *hustle*—the large body of talk exchanges that are not transparent, which constitute most or perhaps all of linguistic reality.

8.1. Defining Hustle via Straight Talk

A communicative action is transparent, if the speaker thinks that the hearer will consciously recognize the communicative action as the action it is. The *straight talk* in an utterance consists in those communicative acts the speaker performs transparently. Discourse is straight talk if it is composed solely of straight talk. The *hustle* in an utterance is all the communicative actions performed through that utterance that are not straight talk. In a nutshell, and to allow the use of *hustle* as a verb:

Hustle is what people do with words nontransparently. They hustle.

To see where this is going, let us note that hustle, thus defined, covers two major classes: (i) manipulative acts and (ii) communicative actions we perform but are not conscious of performing. First, suppose a speaker is manipulative. For example, imagine us intentionally rushing you into signing a document without a careful reading of the fine print by suggesting that we have to leave in a few minutes. ("Busy, busy, busy!" one of us smiles, and looks down at an ostentatious watch.) We intend that you do not recognize the subterfuge; the speaker's real goal in rushing you is to get you to overlook the fine print. Since we *intend* that you do not recognize it, and we also *believe* that you will not recognize it, the action of suggesting that we have to leave in a few minutes involved hustle (even if it happened to be true), namely convincing you to sign without reading the fine print. Secondly, hustle includes *unconsciously performed* communicative acts. Since we authors don't know what actions we're performing unconsciously, we'll pick on a fictional, but plausible, third party as speaker.

Deep in the bowels of a British city, a female executive is carrying a stack of legal documents, and a male denizen of the office says, "Need some help with that, love?" The executive finds the offer, and the manner of asking, condescending, and replies as she strides past, "How about you go fetch me a coffee . . . black, no sugar. Thanks, LOVE!" The male worker knows he has been put in his place, but does not have a deep understanding of why or how. As he heads to the break room to get the coffee, he mumbles, shrugging, "I was only trying to help" to the small audience that witnessed the event. By offering help, the male worker suggested his addressee's inadequacy for the task she was undertaking, and by referring to her as "love," his utterance suggested, as far as she was concerned, a socially inappropriate level of familiarity between them, implying that she had equal or lower status. At the time of utterance, the male worker did not think he was implying inadequacy or familiarity, and certainly wasn't attempting to get his addressee to believe something that he himself did not. Indeed, it is plausible to us that in such a case the male worker might not even consider the possibility that his words could be taken in such a negative light. If so, then it is clear that at the time of utterance he did not believe that his addressee would believe that he was performing the actions of suggesting inadequacy or familiarity. Therefore, these suggestions were hustle.

Although there are practices that intrinsically involve hustle, such as lying and dog whistling, we have suggested ways in which hustle might accompany a much wider range of communicative actions, perhaps even all communicative actions. We have emphasized that hustle is central to the transmission of ideology and explicated mechanisms. Hustle has thus been central in this volume. Yet it is not one of the building blocks of our resonance-based framework: none of our core definitions of resonance, attunement, harmony, presupposition, and accommodation mention hustle. The reverse is also true: hustle is not itself a resonance-theoretic notion. It is a general communication-theoretic notion that could be applied independently of the specific theoretical framework.

We can put it this way: *hustle is about the failure of an idealization, the idealization of straight talk.* The idealization is at the heart of models of meaning in a tradition of work developed by Paul Grice, which centers on the idea that for the speaker to mean something always involves a recognizable communicative intention. This is not to say that hustle cannot be modeled in frameworks based on recognition of communicative intention, but it would need to be modeled as an explicit divergence from what is taken to be ordinary communication. By contrast, the resonance framework was created to avoid strong commitments regarding the role of intention in communication, and without an idealization of straight talk. We no more control the resonances of the words we use than we control a mischievous genie, perhaps prepared to do our bidding after we release it from a bottle, but only in its own impish way.

The resonances of particular communicative actions derive from complex systems of practices, including practices of making sounds, practices of using words, practices of arranging the words, and rhetorical, interactional, and pragmatic practices. Although, as noted, certain practices that are of interest in theorizing the politics of language exist specifically because they can consistently be used to hustle, hustle applies at the level of the action, not at the level of the practice.[3] Thus we can speak of the resonances of actions drawn from a practice being hustle on one occasion, and not hustle on another. Take pronouns, for example. The resonances of a pronoun such as "them" include joint salience of some group. That is: the use of the pronoun gives a probability boost to a certain feature of context, and that feature is the joint salience of some group. The relevant group will normally be manifest to interlocutors, and the intention to refer to it will commonly be obvious. But in section 4.4, we discussed cases in which the identity of the referent is not shared at all, and in which a pronoun is deployed strategically to give the illusion of such common ground. In such cases, the pronoun is not merely being used in a way that capitalizes on the presence of common ground. Rather, the use of the pronoun has disguised a function of creating or reinforcing common ground. The presence of such a strategic intention is not necessarily manifest to the hearer, and so the resonance of joint salience in such cases involves hustle.

Hustle in many of the cases discussed in chapter 4 was presumably intentional, but it need not be. Furthermore, hustle need not be a bad thing. Creating common ground, for example, is usually seen as a good thing, and the fact that the mechanism behind the creation of common ground is not always overt does not thereby make it inherently problematic. Let us make some distinctions we can use in the remainder of the chapter. Hustle could be:

1. *intended* if the sender intends it not to be transparent;
2. *incidental* if not intended;
3. *unconscious* if the speaker is not aware of performing the action;
4. *detrimental* if it is against the interests of the hearer;
5. *malign* if it is intended and detrimental, and *malicious* if the sender recognizes that malignance; and
6. *congenial* if at the time of the communicative act, the sender does not consider it to be detrimental hustle associated with that act.

3. This is not to say that the term "hustle" could not be defined at the level of practice. There are communicative practices for which a primary function is to hustle, for example boasting, lying, or dog whistling, and so one might reasonably talk of these as "hustling practices," or some such.

Hustle is a broad and heterogenous class. It should be clear from this list that what is left out by the idealization of straight talk is a great deal of speech.

Let's consider the Gricean approach mentioned above, where what something means hinges on what communicative intentions can be recognized. The assumption of recognizable intentions is even more central to Grice's enterprise than the assumption of cooperativity (which we will discuss below). Without the assumption of cooperativity, Gricean reasoning doesn't warrant pragmatic inferences, and pragmatic inferences are its trademark success. But without the assumption of joint recognition of intentions, not even literal content is conveyed. Loosely, according to Grice, an indicative utterance carries as part of its meaning a certain proposition if (a) the speaker intends that the audience will think that the speaker believes that proposition, and (b) the speaker intends that the speaker and hearer jointly recognize that the utterance is intended to yield that effect.[4] This is what he calls *nonnatural* meaning, that is, the type of meaning achieved via communicative intention (as opposed to the smoke-means-fire type of *natural* meaning). One of the great virtues of Grice's model of meaning is that it covers both literal meanings and the pragmatic implications that Grice termed *implicatures*. Let us illustrate the centrality of intention recognition to Grice's model with a simple case of implicature.

Suppose that at some point Jason did not wish to go jogging with David. He therefore developed an intention that David came to believe that it was a bad time for them to go out jogging. Jason said to David, "It's raining." David and Jason jointly recognized that Jason intended to achieve several effects by saying that. One was that David came to believe that Jason thought it was raining, that is, David came to believe that Jason believed the literal content of the sentence he had uttered. Another was that David came to believe that Jason believed that it was a bad time for them to go jogging, that is, David identified and accepted an implicature of Jason's utterance. As a result, David actually did come to believe that Jason believed it was a bad time for them to go jogging, and indeed that it was a bad time for them to go jogging, thereby fulfilling Jason's wishes.

When Jason told David, "It's raining," was that straight talk? To a first approximation, where we only consider the communicated propositions that it was raining and that it was a bad idea to go jogging, yes. The action of communicating these propositions was certainly straight talk, since Jason believed David would recognize that he was communicating them, and we have considered no other effects. But when someone says something, there's no end to the inferences that a hearer might draw. It just so happens that as a result of Jason's utterance, and the sound of Jason's voice as he produced it, David came to believe, among other things, that Jason had not fully recovered from

4. Grice, "Meaning," 383–84.

his previous night's revelry, and yet that Jason had not entirely lost the ability to communicate in English. Jason intended neither effect, and, in his somewhat diminished mental state, did not even have a belief that he would cause David to draw these inferences. So if we're going to be strict about it, even Jason's benign comment on the weather was not straight talk, although the additional hustle was both congenial and incidental. But note here that our definition of hustle is only as tight as its component terms, so that a generous conception of what Jason *believed* will lead to a correspondingly more restricted conception of which of the acts he performed were *hustle*.

While incidental hustle is, by definition, congenial, it may or may not be malign. It cannot be malicious. Intended hustle, on the other hand, could be congenial, malign, both congenial and malign, or not only malign but malicious. Suppose that on the morning before Sofia gives a big presentation, her boss says to her, "Don't worry. Perhaps these guys aren't as tough as everybody says!" Sofia didn't have any prior indication that she'd be presenting to (what everybody says is) a tough crowd. The information was offered in the form of a presupposition, as if completely uncontroversial, and Sofia accommodates it readily. This causes Sofia to ramp up her presentation and give a really aggressive pitch. As it happens, the group she is presenting to does not like aggressive pitches, so that they sit stone silent after her presentation, causing Sophia great embarrassment. It is immediately clear that she has lost the deal.

If Sophia's boss did not intend for Sophia to decide to change her presentation, then causing that effect was incidental, but detrimental. If, on the other hand, her boss did intend that she would react to his comment by giving a particularly aggressive pitch, but thought that this would be beneficial, then her boss's comment, qua action of realigning Sophia's presentation style, was congenial but malign. If her boss not only intended to cause Sophia to make her pitch more aggressive, but also knew that this was not what was needed, then her boss was being actively malicious.

8.2. Coordination and Cooperation

The notions of cooperativity and coordination will be important for us, so let us now consider how they relate to each other. First, as the terms are ordinarily used, coordination, unlike cooperation, does not imply benefit or intended benefit to others. Secondly, coordination does not require as high a degree of agency as does cooperation.

Coordination of activity between entities occurs when their behaviors are correlated in such a way as to make the behavior of one predictable given knowledge of the behavior of the others. Since coordination does not imply mutual benefit, one can coordinate with another's actions in a purely self-serving manner. David might coordinate his trips to bars with trips of Jason's, knowing that Jason will pay for expensive cocktails and without any desire to help Jason to reach personal objectives. We should not describe David's actions as cooperative in this case, unless we take Jason as having a mutually recognized goal that is more easily reached as a result of this generosity.

Coordination does not require a high degree, or indeed, at the limit, any degree, of agency. That is, coordination can occur without any intention to coordinate. Note first that we can coordinate our actions with the activity of inanimate entities. We can even coordinate our actions with nature itself. For example, we might coordinate our gardening activities with the vicissitudes of the weather or coordinate our religious activities with the phases of the moon. Unless nature is itself agentive and benefits from our actions, these are not examples of cooperation.

Note further that our actions may be coordinated with those of others even if there was never an intention to so coordinate. For example, in his little-known work as an undercover FBI agent, Jason was once forced to hide in the trunk of a mafia boss's Lincoln Continental, a spot that a somnolent, or possibly recently deceased rival gang member by the name of Joey "Fangs" Napoli was already partially occupying, along with a set of slightly bloody golf clubs. Fortunately, the Continental has a large trunk. For several hours, Jason's movements were coordinated with those of the mafia boss. Fangs's movements too were coordinated with that of the mafia boss, as were the golf clubs', although the latter two facts were true by design. Neither Jason nor Fangs was cooperating with the boss any more than the golf clubs were, and neither the boss nor the driver of the Continental had any desire to bring Jason along for the ride.

To *cooperate*, agents must choose to perform actions that enhance the probability that both they and others will reach their goals. To say that the activity of one entity is coordinated with that of another is to make a much weaker claim: it is to say that the activity of the first is dependent on that of the second. This dependency implies that knowing how the second acted would alter our best estimate of the probability of the first entity's having acted as it did. To say that agents coordinate their actions (and not merely to describe their activity as coordinated) is to make a subtly stronger claim: it is to suggest that they *choose* actions in an interdependent way. On the strong idealizing assumption that agents are performing their actions as the result of rational choices, coordination implies that it is in their mutual interests to act in a coordinated fashion.

Since we will be using game-theoretic concepts below, it is helpful to relate our descriptions of cooperation and coordination to those standard concepts. Cooperative game theory concerns strategic problems in which it would be of interest for agents to use conventions to govern their activity, and even to subjugate their actions to an enforcing agency that verifies compliance with the conventions, thereby providing a guarantee of mutually beneficial coordination. Thus, cooperation involves coordination for mutual benefit, and conventions should be expected to emerge precisely when there is repeated occurrence of situations in which coordinated behavior for multiple parties is favored.

The point of current relevance is that what is understood as cooperative behavior, and thus the sort of behavior that cooperative game theory seeks to help us understand and regulate, is the sort of behavior a group might jointly opt to have externally enforced, because guaranteeing such action is maximally mutually beneficial. Take, for example, the most famous game-theoretic example of all, the *Prisoner's Dilemma*. If two criminal accomplices recognize that in the future they might be in jail, and each is offered the chance to defect against the other, then it would be advantageous for them to set up a way to enforce nondefection. Mutually assured destruction, as we all know, can be a great motivator, even if it does little to help us sleep at night. Thus, the accomplices might agree that a third party is to observe their behavior, and if one of the two accomplices defects (by confessing to the police), then the defector is to be punished in some heinous way, for example, involving harm to their family. Having mutually agreed upon a mechanism guaranteeing such painful retribution, both parties will be confident of their cooperation with each other and not with the police, should they ever be apprehended. Thus, agreeing to possible retribution actually enhances their expected future payoff.

Now consider a communicative action that involves intended hustle. In order for there to be intended hustle, there must, by definition, be something believed not to be transparent to some second player, to whom the action must appear identical to another action that lacks any hustle. It follows, trivially, that there is such an alternative action: one just like the first, except lacking the hustle. This alternative action is the move that the second player takes the first to have made. It also follows that it would be problematic to assign payoffs such that the full set of players (a so-called *grand coalition* in game theory) would jointly agree to a regulation enforcing the first action rather than the second, for the simple reason that at least some players could not even distinguish the two actions. Therefore, communicative actions that involve intended hustle are not fully cooperative in the technical sense that they would not be accepted by a grand coalition in cooperative game theory.

This establishes that hustle is not fully cooperative in a technical sense, but we can go further: it is also the case that selfishness in action engenders hustle. If an action (or, more generally, a strategy, or, more generally still, a strategy profile for a subcoalition of agents) is selfishly motivated and is potentially suboptimal for other players, then that action has the following two properties. First, the type of action is not one that a coalition would choose as a norm in those circumstances, that is, the action is not suitable for conventionalization in the narrow sense of cooperative game theory. Second, players taking such actions have a motive for hiding exactly what they did, keeping some of the desired effects of their actions secret. For it is only if their actions are disguised in this way that their defection can be expected to be unilateral, so that they make just the gains they anticipate, and the audience does not have the opportunity to reorient and redress some of those gains. This motive for secrecy becomes stronger when the reputation of senders with the audience is itself of value to the sender. It becomes stronger still when there is a societal norm governing the type of action performed and there is the possibility of onlookers observing or learning of the defection, thus damaging the sender's reputation in society at large.

Summing up these considerations, we see both that lack of cooperativity in communicative behavior has a natural tendency to align with the use of intended hustle, and (our earlier conclusion) that communicative actions involving intended hustle are not fully cooperative. Admittedly, the argument was formulated using a very particular and technical sense of what cooperation is, but the broad outlines of the argument are, we think, quite intuitive. It is even somewhat obvious, once one reflects on it, that people who are communicating in a noncooperative fashion might do well to hide their noncooperativity. Perhaps the claim itself is less remarkable than the fact that philosophers of language and linguists (including ourselves) have seldom reflected on the fairly intuitive relationship between nontransparency and noncooperativity, at least not in their lives as scholars.

Let us say that communication is *coordinative* to the extent that its effects enhance coordination, where we include here coordination of attitudes, emotions, and behaviors. For example, once upon a time, Jason screamed in terror, thus representing, although somewhat overeffusively, his emotional attitude toward a scary scene in a political documentary. As a result, David shared his terror. In this situation, coordination of emotional attitudes occurred, so in our terms there was, at the very least, a coordinative element to the screaming act.

The above arguments from cooperative game theory suggest that it may sometimes be useful to draw lines differently than our hustle terminology at first suggests, since talk involving hustle can be fully cooperative, provided it is unintended hustle. If we lump together straight talk and unintended hustle, we get what we will call *prosocial communication*, communication that lacks intended hustle. For example, since Jason did not have a hidden agenda, his screaming act was prosocial.

A bee doing a dance is performing a communicative act, but is not being communicatively transparent, because bees, so far as we know, lack beliefs that their communicative actions will have effects. The communicative actions are all hustle. But it is presumably all incidental hustle. Now, a bee's dance surely enhances coordination, which is a necessary condition for saying that the communicative act of dancing is cooperative. And since the bee also has no intention to be nontransparent, that is, all bee hustle is incidental, we can in fact say that in dancing the bee is prosocial, and in this respect is just like Jason screaming. Our readers may even feel it is apt to describe the bees themselves as cooperating. To describe them as such is to frame them as self-actuating intentional agents, whether that is intended literally or metaphorically.

As with bees, to describe a person as cooperative when they perform a socially significant act reflexively is to use an intentional framing, or to take an *intentional stance*, as Daniel Dennett would have it.[5] Generally, we will find it easier to describe the person as cooperative the more deliberate and the less reflexive the action. Thus, a parent giving a distressed child a hug is cooperative, but someone screaming or sharply intaking breath is usually not aptly described as cooperating, even though their act may be prosocial in our technical sense, and fully cooperative in the sense that it enhances coordination and involves no intentionally hidden meaning. When Jason told David it was raining, which he did sincerely, he was certainly coordinative, since he (intentionally) enabled us to coordinate a complete absence of physical exercise for an entire day, and it was prosocial because there was no intended hustle. On the other hand, if Jason had told David the same thing in order to spare David the embarrassment of being outrun, that would have been coordinative but not completely prosocial. In such a situation, there is intended hustle in Jason's persuasive actions, even though that hustle is congenial.

Our definitions lead to some subtle distinctions. Consider: David has bees, knows where a new source of pollen is, knows about bee communication, and has built a robotic bee. He remotely controls his robot bee to perform a dance for the colony, just as a regular bee would, indicating where the pollen is. As a result, the bees' psychological states change, leading them to fly to the new source of pollen. Now, if a bee performed the same dance as David's robot bee, that act would have been prosocial, and fully cooperative. But David, communicating via robot bee, had a communicative intention that he did not intend the recipients to recognize. Indeed, he knew that the recipients were unable to recognize communicative intentions. Like bee hustle, David's hustle was congenial, but unlike bee hustle it was intended. Therefore, although the communicative act was in all relevant behavioral respects identical to the one that a bee would have performed, and although the bee's actions would have been prosocial, David was not being fully prosocial. On the contrary, he was being manipulative. On this terminology, you are not being fully prosocial if, for example, you covertly manipulate your child.

8.3. Leading Questions

Rhetoric, whether in the service of power or money, is clearly very successful in manipulating people. But how successful? Here is one result: asking people even *purely hypothetical questions* unconsciously shifts their subsequent preferences and behavior in often dramatic ways. In a study coming

---

5. Dennett, *The Intentional Stance.* For evidence that treating an entity in a joint task involves a substantively different mental representation of that entity, see Gallagher et al., "Imaging the Intentional Stance."

from a marketing perspective, by Gavan Fitzsimons and Baba Shiv, subjects were told in advance that they would be asked purely hypothetical questions.[6] One group was asked,

> If strong evidence emerges from scientific studies suggesting that cakes, pastries, etc. are not nearly as bad for your health as they have often been portrayed to be, and may have some major health benefits, what would happen to your consumption of these items?

Subjects were told that the study "was about the effects of a change in environment on how consumers express opinions about products," and so were directed into another room and offered a choice between snacks on a display cart placed between the rooms: chocolate cake or fruit salad. Another group, the control group, was not asked any hypothetical questions.

In the control group, 25.7 percent chose cake. In stark contrast, subjects who were merely presented with the hypothetical question, and no further elaboration, selected the cake 48 percent of the time. Merely telling subjects to "please think carefully before you respond to the question" to prepare to justify their answer later increased cake selection from 48 percent to 66 percent. And subjects were clearly unaware of having been manipulated by the hypothetical question. Without exception, they denied that their preferences or their behavior were influenced by the hypothetical question in subsequent in-depth interviews. When asked whether they accepted that cake had major health benefits, every subject reported that they did not accept this and recognized that the question was hypothetical. And *every single subject* maintained that their choice was unaffected by being asked the hypothetical question.[7]

We already gave many examples, in chapter 4, of leading questions, although they were not hypotheticals, that is, not presented in the counterfactual mood. Let us consider a political example that is similar to the cases studied there, in that it contains a presupposition trigger of a type that has been widely discussed in the relevant semantic literature (the verb "know"), but is also similar to the unhealthy pastry case, in that it involves a hypothetical being used to shape preferences. Karl Rove was George W. Bush Jr.'s campaign manager in the 2000 Republican primary that pitted Bush against John McCain. Before the South Carolina primary, Bush's campaign polled prospective Republican primary voters with the following hypothetical question: "Would you be more likely or less likely to vote for John McCain if you knew he had fathered an illegitimate black child?" McCain had an adopted daughter

6. Fitzsimons and Shiv, "Nonconscious and Contaminative Effects of Hypothetical Questions."

7. Fitzsimons and Shiv, "Nonconscious and Contaminative Effects of Hypothetical Questions," 234.

from Bangladesh, and her skin tone is much darker than that of McCain or his wife. Presumably the question resonated strongly with certain voters. Bush subsequently won South Carolina.

Clearly, hypothetical questions can be and are used as vehicles for intended hustle. Hearing hypothetical questions can change the way people think about an issue, priming an association so that when thinking about one thing, something else becomes salient. That is, the hustle can be thought of in terms of the power of the hypothetical question to coerce a change in the landscape of attunement, without conveying explicitly that certain propositions are true or false. This effect is not transparent to the hearer: that much is evidenced by the fact that hearers in the Fitzsimons and Shiv study denied any effect of the question.

A question can hustle whether the speaker intends such effects or not. Suppose that a professor asks a student, "Have you read Adorno on this topic?" The professor might honestly intend this as a question of information, and yet the student might as a result (i) develop an intention to read Adorno, (ii) feel they should previously have read Adorno, and (iii) feel put down. If the professor does not intend these relatively predictable effects, then causing them is unintended hustle, whether or not the hearer actually recognizes them as effects of the utterance. In that case, the professor is prosocial but somewhat incompetent. Conversely, if the speaker does intend the effect, but does not intend that the hearer will recognize this intention, then that is also hustle, that is, intended hustle. One can imagine, if the professor's communicative goal is satisfied, the student walking away from the conversation feeling somewhat down, without being able to identify exactly why. In that case, the problem with the professor is clearly not one of incompetence but temperament. Only if speaker and hearer mutually recognize that both the effects and the recognition of those effects were intended would causing the effects not be hustle. In that case they could be analyzed as (particularized) Gricean implicatures.

The act of pragmatically implicating, at least in the sense originally introduced by Grice, is inherently prosocial, because it depends on transparency of intentions and a hearer's ability to recognize those intentions. As Grice says, implicatures are *calculable*, meaning that a hearer can recover the reasoning that leads to the pragmatic inference. However, this prosociality seems to disappear if the use of implicature is motivated by a desire for plausible deniability that would have been unavailable had the relevant inference been stated explicitly. The professor saying "Have you read Adorno on this topic?" and intending for the hearer to recognize their inadequacy, can insouciantly deny that any such insult was intended. Similarly, the professor could indirectly deny that any such insult could possibly have been intended by self-deprecatingly saying, for example, "I haven't read him myself, but was just wondering." On the other hand, the professor who goes on to say, "You haven't read Adorno? You should be ashamed of yourself!" has made the insult explicit, and closed down any easy avenue for denying it.

If one effect of asking the question about familiarity with Adorno is that the student feels bad, then there is an element of malign hustle, and possibly malignant hustle if the professor intended the student to feel bad. Of course, it is impossible to say on the basis of a canned one-sentence example that the net effects would not be positive for the hypothetical student in the long term, but if the professor actually intended to cause the student to feel, for instance, marginalized and ignorant, even if only in the short-term, then we can say that there is a component of malignant hustle in the communicative act. Furthermore, even if the professor intended overall to benefit the student, the indirect approach of shaming them in order to spur them to greater future scholarship, if not a transparently stated strategy, would not be prosocial.

Rove's push-polling question quite clearly involved malignant hustle. Rove's intention may have been that those taking the poll, as well as others deceived by the ensuing whispering campaign, would come to have false beliefs. Or maybe his intention was not to instill false beliefs, but rather to produce an emotional effect, to instill suspicion or concern. The development of a concomitant whispering campaign (of which this is a textbook case) would itself be intended hustle. Even if we generously ascribe to Rove the belief that a vote for Bush would be in the voters' long-term interest, we take it that causing people to wrongfully suspect falsehoods to be true is inherently problematic. Perhaps this may be pardoned in some circumstances, perhaps in a scientific study such as the psychological experiments in which subjects were hustled by questions in chapter 4, or in the Fitzsimons and Shiv study. However, misleading people in a way that is designed to sway their voting behavior in a democratic election of national import is not excusable in the same way. We feel no need to varnish the claim that Rove and his team acted maliciously toward the voters. It seems reasonable to extend our terminology and say that when hustle is malign, it is not merely not prosocial, but simply *antisocial*. Karl Rove's election tactics constitute a paradigm case.

8.4. Plausible Deniability

The Gricean ideal of speaker meaning involves a communicative intention that the intention itself becomes mutual knowledge. This strong requirement of mutual knowledge is how the notion of overtness must be cashed out: an intention is fully overt if the speaker and hearer have mutual knowledge of that intention. When the speaker and hearer are regarded as having such a strong mutual epistemic commitment, denial is contradictory. As Richmond Thomason writes,

> Most conversational implicatures, I think, are meant; and in fact the response "I didn't mean that" can always be used to renounce an implicature.[8]

8. Thomason, "Accommodation, Meaning, and Implicature," 345.

Thus, if it is on the conversational record that a speaker has asked, "Are you busy tonight?" the speaker cannot deny having asked whether the hearer is busy without denying the conversational record itself. There is no room here for plausible denial.

Elisabeth Camp writes about the speech act of insinuation that "what is distinctive about insinuation" is that a speaker who insinuates is "prepared and able to coherently deny" the insinuated content.[9] For example, if someone, after being stopped for speeding, utters "can we take care of this quickly?" they can deny offering a bribe when they are accused of so doing. Camp labels this "implicature with deniability," though we regard this as understating the degree to which the Gricean framework is challenged by this sort of phenomenon.[10] The Gricean framework cannot make sense of the range of linguistic phenomena that allow for plausible deniability.

When there is an intention of plausible deniability, there is an absence of complete transparency about whether an inference was intended, and so, by our definitions, there is hustle: the talk is not entirely straight.

When Hans Gruber in the movie *Die Hard* says, "It's a very nice suit, Mr. Takagi. It would be a shame to ruin it," there is a clear suggestion that if Mr. Takagi does not cooperate, then the speaker will inflict serious bodily harm upon him, with collateral damage to the suit.[11] In this case, where Gruber has previously asked for a code, and is holding a gun, we might naturally say that the implicated proposition is that if Takagi doesn't give Gruber the code, Gruber will shoot. But the degree to which the suggested proposition can be fully specified is variable in such cases.

In a scene in the movie *The Lincoln Lawyer*, an ethically challenged client, Louis Roulet, who has broken into lawyer Mickey Haller's home, says to him, "That's a cute picture of your daughter, Hayley. She's very pretty. She's got soccer practice tomorrow, right?"[12] There is a clear implication that if the Haller does not do Roulet's bidding, his daughter will suffer.[13] In cases like this, the lack of mutual knowledge of what is implicated is evident: it's in the nature of insinuation that it is unclear exactly what proposition is insinuated.[14] Roulet's

---

9. Camp, "Insinuation, Common Ground, and the Conversational Record," 45.
10. Camp, "Insinuation, Common Ground, and the Conversational Record," 46.
11. McTiernan, *Die Hard*.
12. Furman, *The Lincoln Lawyer*.
13. In the conversation in *The Lincoln Lawyer*, the tables are soon turned:
   Haller: Don't.
   Roulet: Don't what?
   Haller: You think you're the first client to ever threaten me with my family?
   Roulet: Huh? All I said was she's pretty.
   Haller: Are you scared, Louis? Because where you are, right now . . . you're in a very dangerous place.
14. See Fricker, "Stating and Insinuating," who makes this central to her account.

is not merely a veiled threat, but a vague threat. It is difficult to identify with confidence a single, well-defined proposition that the speaker intends to convey. In this case, the criterion of mutual knowledge for an overt communicative intention is certainly not met.

Given the presence of a range of ill-defined propositions that are somewhat plausibly but not necessarily intended as implicatures, we are clearly dealing with intended hustle, although what we have is not complete opacity for the hearer, but rather semitransparency. Indeed, the hustle in these cases goes further than nontransparency as regards what propositions are intended. One wants to say that it is clear that he is not primarily complimenting Haller's daughter and not primarily requesting information when he, superficially, asks about her soccer practice, but rather that the main action he is performing in uttering the entire three-sentence sequence is one of making a threat. But what threat is he making? If we cannot determine this, then we are not merely in a position of being unable to say what propositions Roulet is insinuating; we are also in a position of being unable to say, or even to know, in detail, exactly what Roulet is doing. Insinuation is a weapon of power, and the power is amplified by the ability to mask the details of the action, creating uncertainty and demonstrating that the insinuator holds all the cards.

The power relationship inherent to threatening insinuation is what is at play when it is subverted in Monty Python's "Army Protection Racket" sketch, in which two wannabe mafiosi attempt to place untoward pressure on an army officer:

DINO: How many tanks you got, Colonel?

COLONEL: About five hundred altogether.

LUIGI: Five hundred, eh?

DINO: You ought to be careful, Colonel.

COLONEL: We are careful, extremely careful.

DINO: 'Cos things break, don't they?

COLONEL: Break?

LUIGI: Well everything breaks, don't it Colonel. [*He breaks something on the desk.*] Oh dear. . . .

LUIGI: How many men you got here, Colonel?

COLONEL: Oh, er . . . seven thousand infantry, six hundred artillery, and er, two divisions of paratroops.

LUIGI: Paratroops, Dino.

DINO: Be a shame if someone was to set fire to them.

COLONEL: Set fire to them?

LUIGI: Fires happen, Colonel.

DINO: Things burn.[15]

---

15. Chapman et al., *Monty Python's Flying Circus*, 97–98.

Things do indeed burn. We leave readers to draw their own conclusions about the nature of brothers Luigi and Dino Vercotti's hustle, and, for that matter, about the role of hustle in subversive humor.

To pick one more classic cinematic scene, consider the lengthy discussion between hitman Jules Winnfield and small-time student drug-dealer Brett in the movie *Pulp Fiction*.[16] Jules's palpable menace early in the scene (i.e., before it gets bloody) seems to stem not from any particular threatening speech act, but from his insouciance as he discusses breakfast and helps himself, with manifestly unnecessary urbanity, to Brett's Big Kahuna burger. Jules's casual demeanor shows that he will have no compunction in performing acts that transgress the bounds of normal society. It quickly becomes obvious that Jules can act as he wishes, and that Brett is totally in his power. But as the scene unfolds, neither Brett nor the audience can be quite sure what Jules is doing. Menacing insinuation is part of Jules's modus operandi, a fact he makes explicit later in the movie, when he famously explains why he likes to dramatically recite a (partly fake) Bible quotation to his victims: "Now . . . I been sayin' that shit for years. And if you ever heard it, that meant your ass. You'd be dead right now. I never gave much thought to what it meant. I just thought it was a cold-blooded thing to say to a motherfucker before I popped a cap in his ass." If Jules just thought it was a cold-blooded thing to say to a motherfucker, and never gave much thought to what it meant, then it was a paradigmatic case of hustle. It was paradigmatic because there was no straight talk at all, and the function of Jules's performance would presumably have been somewhat opaque to his victims, who, unfortunately for them, did not have a lot of time to think about it.

We would offer that perhaps the violence-prone among us are in the habit of making indirect threats and vaguely menacing insinuations for three distinct although related reasons. First, obviously, there is plausible deniability itself: it is hard to prosecute the Grubers, Roulets, Winnfields, or Vercottis of this world if they make their threats indirectly and with the possibility of denial. The second involves exploitation of the status of the proposition as plausibly deniable. While the mere fact of forcing the hearer to use their imagination to identify what actions the speaker has planned might add to the vividness of the threat, the suggestion that whatever is planned is so heinous that it cannot be talked about publicly amplifies the menace to a new level. The third is that the uncertainty raised by the lack of clarity of the intended message can itself be a source of distress either for a single addressee like the unfortunate Mr. Takagi, or for a larger audience among whom the uncertainty sows discord, both because they disagree about what was meant and how clear it was, and because they find it hard to know how to react to an individual who blatantly violates both norms of assertion, as well as norms of ethical behavior.

16. Tarantino, *Pulp Fiction*.

This latter property of insinuation is crucial to Jules's menacing behavior in *Pulp Fiction*. His control of the situation depends in part on his ability to appear to know exactly what he is doing, while nobody else does, and to be able to confirm or deny whatever he likes, while nobody else can.

We doubt that any of this reasoning was explicit for President Trump when, during the 2016 US election campaign, he famously commented of his opponent, "If she gets to pick her judges, nothing you can do, folks. Although the Second Amendment people—maybe there is. I don't know."[17] But it is clear that the speaker in this case understands very well that vagueness of a threat, and its deniability, can add to the menace. Indeed, the casual looseness with which an insinuation is dropped adds considerably to the effect, in part because it suggests that the speaker is not someone who can be reasoned with or trusted to stick within the narrow confines of traditional mores. The impossibility of reasoning is central to the so-called *madman* approach to diplomacy, a tactic that, within the United States at least, appeared until recently to have been left in the dust of Nixon's fall from grace. It is also one aspect of the firehose of falsehood style of propaganda used in more recent times by Vladimir Putin's regime (as discussed briefly in section 6.1).

By its nature, intended hustle requires cognitive sophistication: to hide something effectively, one must have a good understanding of the person one is hiding it from. Thus, if your best strategy involves lying or misleading, guaranteeing deniability, dog whistling so that different groups get different messages, or seeding the ground for a whispering campaign, you will be best off if you are working with a team of lawyers and PR specialists who either help you plan your move or clean up the mess afterward. The availability of such infrastructural support is one reason why politicians find it relatively easy to utilize intended hustle in their campaigns. Craven media is another.

To close this section, let us note a critical and perhaps underappreciated fact: there is a strong political asymmetry in the availability of hustle as a public rhetorical strategy. Veiled threats, insinuations, and simulated madness are all more easily and readily wielded by an authoritarian than by a democratic idealist, and all these devices quite obviously function rhetorically by way of intended hustle.

Here is a somewhat obvious premise: politicians advocating democratic ideals are thereby committed to a high degree of transparency. It follows not only that intended hustle should be inimical to them, but also that the costs of mounting a campaign involving intended hustle are potentially high. For if it is revealed that the democratic idealists are acting in a covert way, then they will immediately be revealed as hypocrites of the highest order. In contrast, a politician supporting authoritarian ideals has not thereby made any strong

17. Trump is quoted in Corasaniti and Haberman, "Donald Trump Suggests 'Second Amendment People' Could Act against Hillary Clinton."

commitment to transparency. Therefore, the reputation of authoritarian politicians is not greatly endangered by the revelation that they have acted in a covert way. Indeed, it may even be a badge of pride. The values of authoritarianism are centrally dominance and power; the goal is to win. Being ineffective will lose an authoritarian status; being opaque will not. The supporters of liberal ideals must be prosocial in order to live what they speak, or else expect to suffer electoral consequence. On the other hand, an authoritarian can not only survive the revelation that they are antisocial, but use this as positive evidence of their stop-at-nothing tactics. The calculus is then that voters desperate for large-scale change will readily choose to have a stop-at-nothing strong man on their team, not merely *in spite* of antisocial infractions against democratic norms, but because of them.

8.5. Hustle and the Development of Speech Practice

Whereas for intended hustle there is transparency for the speaker and opacity for the hearer, speech practices can lead to opacity for either speaker or hearer. In the former case, we have what we termed above *unconscious hustle*, a special case of *incidental hustle*. When you identify what seems to you to be, say, sexist language, but the speaker appears to be naively unaware of the overtones that so disturb you, that is incidental hustle.

Since mortal agents are incapable of having full access to the context and assumptions against which what they say or hear has meaning, everything that has been said or will be said by human beings will involve some degree of opacity for both speaker and audience. The inevitability of incidental hustle means that we literally cannot have a full appreciation of what any sentence means. We cannot know all the resonances, any more than we can know the full history of the air we breathe. Furthermore, miscommunication, by its nature, involves incidental hustle. For, any case of miscommunication is a case where the requirement of straight talk is not met: if miscommunication has occurred, then there cannot possibly be mutual knowledge of the communicative intention to express whatever it is that was misunderstood.

Whether the inevitable opacity of meaning is a problem depends in part upon your goals. If your goal was to communicate just exactly one thing and nothing else, you would have a problem. But if your goal is, say, to increase coordination, then the fact that your utterances can have more meaning than you put into them is certainly not a problem per se. It may indeed be a benefit, the sort of thing a poet might strive for on occasion. That is, it is at least possible to intend to achieve a certain effect on an audience, and to succeed in having that effect, and yet not to understand at all the mechanism by which your words produced that effect.

We submit that it is not only poets who might benefit from incidental hustle, but societies. We want to suggest, on the basis of mechanisms considered in the first two parts of the book, that incidental hustle can play an important role in the formation of group bonds and identities.

By engaging in a certain speech practice, one associated with a group to which the speaker or hearer both belong, say a common ethnic identity, interlocutors may increase coordination and collective attunement. As the community of practice develops, certain practices may become inwardly and outwardly meaningful to the practitioners (in the sense of section 6.4), without most of the practitioners recognizing that this process is occurring, and perhaps without anyone intending for it to occur.

Consider Canadian raising. This is a property of Canadian (and upper Midwest US) English affecting the sound of many words, so that, for example, "flout" sounds like "float" would in other varieties of English. It seems likely that the vast majority of productions contributing to the development of Canadian raising involved no conscious awareness of the ongoing sound change or what its exact rules were. People just did what their parents and acquaintances did, and for various reasons (like limited contact) felt no pressure to do what people across the border were doing. That is, accommodation to the in-group by huge numbers of people, adapting their vowels to those of the people around them, led to collective harmonization around a shared practice. Later, the distinctive practice may have become meaningful in and of itself, as a marker of identity, but it need not have developed as a conscious reaction to anyone else's speech style, and indeed need not have developed with any strategic intent.

Though the example involves sound change, it should be clear that similar considerations might apply in cases of so-called semantic drift, whereby words change their meaning over time. This may happen in a community of practice of any size, whether a nation, a political movement, a cult, or a chatty pair of friends. Neither speaker nor hearer needs take stock consciously of the resonances their language has gained by being used previously within the group to which they belong. And yet, even without such awareness, the use of in-group language may improve communicative coordination among the interlocutors and contribute to cooperative success within the group more broadly.

8.6. Is Straight Talk Central?

By enumerating a range of applications, we hope we have set out a case that hustle is a worthy area of study in communication, and thereby that an idealization of straight talk is unreasonably limiting. One might protest that there are special foundational roles that are played by speech that fits into the straight-talk model. Is there, in the philosophy of language, a case for the "foundational nature" of straight talk? We discuss two arguments within philosophy of language for the view that speech that fits the idealizations of the standard model has a distinguished role. The first is David Lewis's theory of metasemantics in his paper "Languages and Language." The second is Paul Grice's theory of implicature.

The project of semantic theory involves taking an assignment of semantic values to words in context and explaining how they combine to form the compositional semantic interpretation of the whole sentence, or perhaps the discourse. Semantics links a sentence like "dogs bark" to its literal interpretation, a tendency dogs have to make a certain noise. And the study of semantics does include difficult theorizing about the nature of the meanings, the semantic values, or words. For example, does "dogs" in "dogs bark" refer to a kind? Or is it rather a predicate of dogs, in which case perhaps the sentence "dogs bark" has an unpronounced generic quantifier that binds the subject of that predicate, as in "generically for x such that x is a dog, x barks"? Pragmatics is the study of aspects of the message conveyed by a linguistic act that are not part of the semantics. Metasemantics is a distinct project entirely from either semantics or pragmatics. Metasemantics is the project of explaining (roughly, because the word "meaning" is here used pretheoretically) why linguistic expressions have the meanings they do. Lewis's "Languages and Language" is a contribution to the project of metasemantics.

Lewis's distinctive take on how to proceed in metasemantics requires preliminary explanation. Lewis takes languages to be mathematically defined abstract entities, functions from words (and larger expressions, such as sentences) to meanings (or "semantic values"). Languages are defined by recursive definitions of truth, as in the classical Tarskian definition of truth in terms of satisfaction. This sets up the problem of Lewis's paper, which is to describe the relation between groups of people, or populations, and these abstract languages. The relation Lewis describes in "Languages and Language" is what yields his answer to the question "Why does this population speak this language?" and hence derivatively, the answer to the metasemantic question of why expressions have the semantic values they do.

So the goal of David Lewis's "Languages and Language" is to describe what makes it the case that a given population P speaks a given language L, where languages are here conceived as functions from syntactic strings to semantic values, "semantic systems discussed in complete abstraction from human affairs."[18] Lewis's answer is that the population P uses the language L if and only if "there is a convention of truth and trust in L. To be truthful in L is to act in a certain way: to try never to utter sentences of L unless one believes it true in L. To be trusting in L is to form beliefs in a certain way: to impute truthfulness in L to others, and thus tend to respond to another's utterance of any sentence of L by coming to believe that the uttered sentence is true in L."[19]

18. Lewis, "Languages and Language," 166.
19. Lewis, "Languages and Language," 167.

If Lewis's analysis of what it is for a population P to use a language L is correct, then "straight talk" has a foundational metasemantic role. It is when we engage in straight talk, using language to say what we mean and mean what we say, that we engage in the kind of use that underlies the truism "meaning is determined by use." On this account, straight talk, where we are speaking truthfully and seriously, determines what language we are using. Since the language we are using is a function from symbols to meanings, on Lewis's picture, straight talk is a central element in the metasemantic story explaining why we mean what we do by our words. Hustle is not.

In "Coordinating with Language," Jessica Keiser convincingly responds to Lewis.[20] Here is an objection Lewis considers toward the end of "Languages and Language."[21] There could be some people, let's call them "New Yorkers," who use a language, but whose typical use of that language involves sarcasm, innuendo, and other forms of speech that is not what one might think of as straight talk. Based on consideration of these hypothetically hustling New Yorkers, Lewis argues that we need to characterize a notion of *serious communicative speech situation*, and he claims that it is uses of language in serious communicative speech situations that determine whether or not that population uses a particular language, abstractly conceived. There is much work to be done to justify Lewis's claim here.[22]

A serious communicative situation, for Lewis, is a situation that "exists with respect to a sentence S of L whenever it is true, and common knowledge between a speaker and a hearer, that (a) the speaker does, and the hearer does not, know whether S is true in L; (b) the hearer wants to know; (c) the speaker wants the hearer to know; and (d) neither the speaker nor the hearer has other (comparably strong) desires as to whether or not the speaker utters S."[23] Lewis's

20. Keiser, "Coordinating with Language." One objection we can sketch but do not defend is related to "Foster's Problem" for truth-conditional semantics. The theory of meaning Lewis employs, possible-worlds semantics, tends to underdetermine meaning. "Hesperus is a planet" and "Phosphorus is a planet" have the same truth conditions but different meanings. Even more problematically, the predicates "is red" and "is red and Peano Arithmetic is incomplete" have the same possible worlds truth conditions, but clearly have different meanings. A convention of truth will help link populations to languages in Lewis's sense, with possible-worlds semantics values, but is less obviously helpful with more realistic theories of meaning that individuate content more narrowly than truth conditions.

21. "Suppose they are often untruthful in L because they are not communicating at all. They are joking, telling tall tales, or telling white lies as a matter of social ritual. In these situations, there is neither truthfulness nor trust in L. Indeed, it is common knowledge that there is not" (Lewis, *Languages and Language*, 183).

22. Jessica Keiser (*Non-Ideal Foundations of Language*, chapter 2, 17–41) persuasively advances these and other theoretical objections to Lewis's metasemantic picture. She goes on to provide a detailed alternative version that does not accord straight talk a foundational metasemantic role.

23. Lewis, "Languages and Language," 183.

proposal is that a population P uses a language L if and only if there is a convention of truthfulness and trust in L in serious communication situations. But why think that the only uses of language that are meaning-determining are ones that occur in serious communicative situations?

Using the sentence "Hannah is in New York" in lying to someone is not a serious communicative situation. Nevertheless, someone using "Hannah is in New York" to lie is still using the words with their meanings in L. Why think that these uses are not meaning determinative? If I sarcastically say, "Trump will be a great president," my use of the name "Trump" still denotes Trump. Political discourse is not generally made up of serious speech situations. But words are nevertheless used with the meanings they have in the language. Mutatis mutandis for sentences uttered in other nonserious speech situations. All that use somehow fixes the fact that population P uses language L.[24] Why think that there is any story about the connection between use and meaning simpler than this?

Keiser recommends that we think of it another way. Perhaps our New Yorkers are *always* sarcastic, *always* joking, *always* intending to amuse at the same time as inform. Lewis's view entails that they do not then speak a language. That consequence is just false. We can imagine New Yorkers as described, and they would speak a language.

Perhaps the claim is conditional; it's enough to establish a convention if members of a population were to be in serious communicative situations with respect to sentences of L, they would have a convention of truth and trustfulness in L in those situations. But why privilege serious communicative situations? Couldn't there be semantic properties of language that only are brought out by uses of sentences to do more than convey information in a jointly cooperative project? Would an analogous claim about phonological and grammatical properties, that they are all revealed in serious communicative situations, be at all plausible?

There is no independent reason to think that all the semantic properties of a language are brought out by straightforward information exchanges. Many people do not find straightforward information exchanges particularly natural means of communication, and it's just not at all clear why we should think such environments are special in that the kind of use in these situations completely determines the language a population is using (or, in perhaps more natural terms, completely determines all the semantic properties of words).

Meaning is determined by use, to be sure. But there is no reason at all to think there is any kind of magical formula for determining which uses are meaning determining, no reason to think that we can characterize in advance

24. Or speaking in a framework we find more natural than Lewis's, these facts fix the meaning conventions for the words of the language, now considered as a symbol system independently of an interpretation.

a class of uses that has a special, exhaustive role in the determination of meaning. And so there is no reason to accept Lewis's characterization of the central class of cases that do all the work of metasemantics, and hence no case for privileging speech that fits the standard model.

That said, even if Lewis's metasemantic theory were correct for some portion of language, what might be called descriptive language if it were cleanly separable from the rest of language, it is irrelevant to our project in this book. That fact would not justify the use of the standard model as a guide to what is of overall importance in the theory of meaning. If we seek an explanation of how linguistic communication functions, we must have a model that treats hustle and straight talk on a par. This is consistent with an account that assigns a special metasemantic role to straight talk for just some aspects of language. The goal of metasemantics on the Lewisian picture is to state what makes it the case that a population uses its words to mean what they do, that is, speaks the language that they do. Speech that fits the standard model may have a special metasemantic interest for some, say those studying the theory of reference. However, that should not lead us to privilege the model in a different task, giving a theory of linguistic action. A theory of linguistic action must extend beyond actions of description.

Are there other reasons to give a special role to transparent communication? In Grice's classic work on implicature, he analyzes implicatures, a class of messages delivered by utterances that are typically not semantically encoded by their words and modes of combination. He relies upon one of the idealizations we criticize: that, in general, speech is a cooperative enterprise. One might take this as evidence that cooperation is the right model to assume, as it explains even a good deal of apparently noncooperative speech.

Here are two related rebuttals of the claim that Grice's analysis of implicature essentially relies on constraining attention to cooperative contexts. The first is from Jennifer Saul.[25] If you tell someone who's expecting you to do some errands "I'm on my way!" while in fact you're at home, you could reasonably be said to have lied. It matters not that you (claim to) intend to mean that you're "on your way" to fame and fortune, since that's not a contextually appropriate completion. Saul suggests you have lied if you (correctly) believe all contextually appropriate completions to be false. She is arguing that a central notion of Grice's account, namely what is said, must be analyzed in a quite specific way to account for the difference between lying and misleading. This implies that considering noncooperative contexts can shed light on notions fundamental to Grice's account, and that ignoring them may lead to incompleteness. Underscoring this point, "Conversational implicatures are often exploited as a way to mislead without lying."[26]

25. Saul, *Lying.*
26. Saul, *Lying,* 76.

Here is a second and somewhat more direct reason to think that an account of implicature cannot rely on an assumption of cooperation, although it is closely related to the version of Saul's argument above. Whereas the first argument shows that in cases where interlocutors might incorrectly assume full cooperation, implicatures are still generated, we now turn to adversarial cases. Here it is manifest that interlocutors cannot make any strong assumptions about cooperativity. In Nicholas Asher and Alex Lascarides's 2013 paper "Strategic Conversation," they point out that implicatures are generated even in clearly noncooperative speech situations, such as clearly antagonistic courtroom cross-examinations.[27] Some of Saul's key examples of misleading speech are courtroom cases as well. By focusing on cases where there is no basis for strong assumptions of cooperativity, Asher and Lascarides conclude that we need a more general theory to explain implicatures, one that does not accord Gricean cooperativity any special status. One might also grant that strong cooperative principles like Grice's principle of cooperation explain some features of speech, including many classic cases of implicature. But that is far from admitting that cooperative speech situations have a foundational role. Hustle is vastly more varied than the study of implicature.

To generalize from these two arguments using the terms we introduced in section 8.2, we must still be able to identify what is said in the case of utterances that are not *prosocial*.[28] We sketched there a general argument for the view that non-prosocial actions, that is, communicative actions involving intended hustle, are not fully cooperative. We do not wish to claim that it is an easy project to identify what is said when people hustle, merely that a theory that ruled out the possibility of identifying what is said in such cases would be of extremely limited interest in a theory of communication. Indeed, we should prefer a theory of meaning that accounts for what is said in overtly antagonistic situations that might arise in a courtroom or in an election campaign, and even for the antisocial utterances deployed by political manipulators like Karl Rove in his push polling operations.

It should be clear that hustle is a category considerably more expansive than just lying. This should be obvious, because unintended hustle is not lying. But is intended hustle simply lying? Lying involves an (intended) mismatch of belief between speaker and hearer as regards the proposition the speaker intends to communicate. It's useful to show in detail that such a mismatch is neither a necessary nor a sufficient condition even for intended hustle.

Consider the example of Linda and Sofia, who will celebrate their anniversary on Friday, that being, coincidentally, their regular weekly date night. Linda wants to go to a certain restaurant to celebrate, L'Auberge du Philosophe, and

---

27. Asher and Lascarides, "Strategic Conversation," 15–16.
28. We thank Jennifer Saul for discussion of ways in which hustle might be a considerably broader category than what she calls "misleading" in *Lying*.

wants Sofia to believe that she would really enjoy eating there on their anniversary. They have not discussed their anniversary, and Sofia has in fact forgotten about it. On Tuesday Linda mentions that a colleague of hers clearly earns too much, as he goes to L'Auberge du Philosophe twice a week, and insists on regaling her with mouth-watering tales of their most special concoctions. Apparently, the menu du jour is always fantastic. Linda appears blissfully transported to another place as she reports on these tales. On Wednesday, Linda is reading, and looks up and smiles at Sofia. Sofia asks Linda what she is reading, and she replies, truthfully, "It's a review of L'Auberge. Five stars!" Later that day, Sofia impulsively calls L'Auberge, thinking it's been awhile since they treated themselves to a really special meal. She is fortunate enough to find that there's a free table that very Friday. Suddenly, she has a further thought . . . August 12, what is special about that day? "It's our anniversary!" she blurts out to the receptionist. This leads to a somewhat more personal conversation than she had intended, but the receptionist is demure throughout. Blushing a little as she puts down the phone, she thinks, *Good catch, Linda will really enjoy eating at L'Auberge on our anniversary! I'm so glad I thought of taking her there!*

In the story of Linda and Sofia's anniversary meal, Linda succeeds in causing Sofia to believe a certain proposition, namely that Linda would enjoy eating at L'Auberge on their anniversary. Because of Sofia's apparent cluelessness, with which the authors cannot help but identify, Linda's plan could easily have failed. It is nonetheless the case that Linda intentionally caused Sofia to believe the proposition in question by virtue of producing two utterances. That proposition, furthermore, is one that Linda herself believed. It is also the case that what Linda said was literally true. Yet we would describe this as congenial hustle on Linda's part. It is congenial because the speaker intends that the hearer comes to believe something that the speaker thinks is true, and the speaker thinks that it is in the hearer's interest to believe it. Yet it is hustle because the speaker did not think that the hearer recognizes the speaker's true communicative action. Thus Linda's actions are not fully prosocial, but to the extent that the mistaken beliefs Sofia formed are not harmful, Linda is not being actively antisocial.

Congenial hustle is common in conversations with children. If we tell a child that going on a hike in the park would be fun, we might receive in return a contradictory response, followed rapidly by a hardening of the child's attitude. For this reason, a caregiver might avoid what psychologists would term the *central* route to persuasion, which operates by presenting the target with facts and arguments (as introduced in section 2.6). Instead, we might mention either to the child, or to another addressee within earshot of the child, how good the ice cream is at that little place just down the road from the park entrance. Psychologists of persuasion call this a *peripheral* route.[29] In follow-

---

29. Petty, Goldman, and Cacioppo, "Personal Involvement as a Determinant of Argument-Based Persuasion."

ing this route, we do not intend that the child recognizes our communicative intention. Of course, we have only the child's best interests at heart, and mean no harm by our communicative sleights of hand (which is not to say that they will not come back to haunt us as the child gets wiser, and we do not).

The anniversary and ice cream examples illustrate the possibility of hustle without dishonesty on the part of the speaker as regards the literal content of the utterance. The speaker is not trying to get the child to believe something false; what we have here is hustle, but it is not lying. There is no intended mismatch here between speaker and hearer on whether the literal meaning is true. There is a mismatch as regards the speaker's underlying intention, but for child-directed speech it is far from clear how seriously we could take the view that understanding usually involves intention recognition in the first place. The prevailing view is that theory of mind (which is understood in psychology as a capacity, rather than as a scientific theory) is a developing trait in young children. This implies that intention recognition emerges gradually rather than being central to all child communication.

Next, we illustrate the possibility that speakers might intend that a proposition they do not themselves believe will come to be a belief of the hearer by virtue of a communicative act. Suppose Sofia thinks it will rain, but Linda doesn't. They discuss this and agree to disagree. Linda knows the umbrella is in the closet, but Sofia doesn't know where it is. Linda says, "The umbrella is in the closet." Sofia comes to believe that if she goes to the closet and fetches the umbrella, it will lower the chances of getting wet. Linda intends Sofia to believe that, and Sofia knows that she does. However, Linda does not believe it herself, since she believes that the probability of rain is zero. She has been cooperative. (One might even say Linda is displaying supererogatory communicative behavior. She is not merely cooperating, but playing along with what she sees as a misguided worldview to keep Sofia happy.) Question: is Linda hustling? Intuitively, no, because she is being, at least as regards the issues of immediate relevance, completely transparent. This exemplifies the nonsufficiency of the mismatch condition. Hustle is not about mismatch per se, although of course mismatch of belief is a necessary precursor not only to hustle but to communication itself; individuals with identical beliefs have limited need to exchange information about the world. No, hustle is not about mismatch. It's about transparency.

In considering the ice cream case, the umbrella case, or, for that matter, Saul's *Lying, Misleading, and What Is Said* (which has extensive moral dimensions beyond what we have discussed), we of course are aware that lying and misleading are topics of perennial philosophical and political concern. So far as we can see, the developments in this volume do not bear on Kant's famous arguments that lying is morally indefensible. But what of the even stronger claim one might make that hustle is morally indefensible, and thus that all talk should be straight talk? We must certainly deny any such claim, but not on moral grounds. We must deny it because it ignores the inevitability of hustle in human communicative practice.

What, then, of the ideal of straight talk? Most speech hustles. Adopting the idealization of straight talk would make hustle fall outside the ambit of the theory of meaning. We rejected the idealization of neutrality because it is incoherent. Straight talk is not entirely incoherent. Straight talk might be a useful political concept, or a guiding ideal for discourse in an ideal language, say for mathematical or logical inquiry. The straighter your mathematics, the better, it might be claimed. But as an ideal guiding model building for a theory of meaning for natural language, it should be rejected. Building concepts and tools drawn only from consideration of data that is straight talk will result in a partial theory at best. In parts I and II of this book, we developed concepts and tools for a novel theory of meaning. These concepts and tools—and the theory—were straightforwardly based on speech that was hustle, which compromised the core of our data throughout. Even the "oops," "ouch," and nodding behaviors of chapter 1 were analyzed in practice-theoretic terms that, despite being inherently interactional, involve no reference to communicative intention.

If one centers hustle, one is immediately led to recognize the centrality of speech practice to a theory of meaning. The ideal of straight talk masks the importance of speech practice. We have no proof that some of the tools and concepts of our theory of meaning, like the concepts of resonance and attunement, could not be derived from consideration of straight talk alone. But this is not how we derived them and assigned importance to them. We have no a priori argument against straight talk as an idealization, but in developing our theory, we have totally ignored it.

CHAPTER NINE

Philosophy and Ideal Theory

In philosophy we often compare the use of words with games and calculi which have fixed rules, but cannot say that someone who is using language must be playing such a game. But if you say that our languages only approximate to such calculi you are standing on the very brink of a misunderstanding. For then it may look as if what we were talking about were an ideal language. As if our logic were, so to speak, a logic for a vacuum. Whereas logic does not treat of language—or of thought—in the sense in which a natural science treats of a natural phenomenon, and the most that can be said is that we construct ideal languages. But here the word "ideal" is liable to mislead, for it sounds as if these languages were better, more perfect, than our everyday language; and as if it took the logician to shew people at last what a proper sentence looked like.

—LUDWIG WITTGENSTEIN[1]

WE HAVE THUS FAR EXPLORED two idealizations at length: neutrality and straight talk. We argued at length against both. We begin this chapter by situating our project first within the broader ambit of traditions across philosophy that critique idealizations. We precisify the target of ordinary-language philosophy—the idealizations of "ideal-language theory." We conclude by showing that the theory we have developed in part I of this book, centering on resonance and attunement, demonstrates that ordinary-language objections to these idealizations about language cannot be rescued by standard defenses of ideals in epistemology.[2]

9.1. Nonideal Epistemology and Beyond

When economists, philosophers, and political scientists study *rationality*, they commonly take as a model an agent with an infinite amount of time to reason and perfect logicality. This perfectly rational agent has utilities ordered linearly, to allow their preferences to be thought of as a utility function that orders choices along a dimension that can easily be ranked, for example, as an amount of money as measured in dollars. They use their knowledge to

---

1. Wittgenstein, *Tractatus Logico-Philosophicus*, par. 81.
2. Material from this chapter first appeared in 2018, as Beaver and Stanley, "Toward a Non-Ideal Philosophy of Language."

flawlessly perform judgments, and combine that with their preferences to make irrefutably optimal decisions. Their actions conform perfectly to the results of these decisions. The attitudes and dispositions of the rational agent are in perfect harmony.

It is quite clear that individual persons are not the perfect rational agents of the study of rationality. We do not have an infinite amount of time to make decisions. As a consequence, we simply cannot consider every possibility, as this would take infinite time. It is even clearer that we lack perfect logicality; we are prone to errors in reasoning and not just when we are tired. How relevant to understanding humans are the properties of perfectly rational agents with no memory limitations? How relevant are the properties of such models to the study of anything of genuine scientific concern?

There have been a number of challenges over the past fifty years to standard models of rationality.[3] The standard model of rationality emerges from the study of the mathematical properties of idealized agents. But one might reasonably adopt another approach, one that begins with actual agents and the limitations they face. In philosophy, this is the *naturalist* project in epistemology. Naturalizing epistemology requires us to think of the agent that we study as located in space and time and limited accordingly.

Naturalism leads philosophers to consider the constraints due to the physical location of the knower. But the physical location of the knower is also a *social* location. The social location of a speaker is what is relevant to understanding whether they have a standpoint of special authority over their subject matter. To take an obvious example: if someone has a disability, they have a social location with special authority over the obstacles facing someone with that disability. Someone who is hearing impaired generally knows what it is to be hearing impaired better than someone who is not hearing impaired, as both authors of this volume can attest, having each experienced both functional and impaired hearing.

Naturalism in epistemology and philosophy of science made it difficult if not impossible to ignore the "situated knower" of feminist epistemology, critical race theory, and Marxism. Charles Mills writes,

> Though mainstream philosophy and analytic epistemology continued to develop in splendid isolation for many decades, W. V. Quine's naturalizing of epistemology would initiate a sequence of events with unsuspectedly subversive long-term theoretical repercussions for the

3. For critiques of neoclassical economics' assumption of rationality, see, e.g., Herbert Simon's argument for a notion of "bounded rationality" in "A Behavioral Model of Rational Choice"; Hollis and Nell, *Rational Economic Man*; Tversky and Kahneman, "The Framing of Decisions." For but a few critiques of rationality assumptions in philosophy, psychology, law, and other social theory, see Cherniak, *Minimal Rationality*; Elster, "When Rationality Fails"; Thaler and Sunstein, *Nudge*.

field. . . . If articulating the norms for ideal cognition required taking into account (in some way) the practices of actual cognition, if the prescriptive needed to pay attention (in some way) to the descriptive, then on what principled basis could cognitive realities of a supra-individual kind continue to be excluded from the ambit of epistemology? For it then meant that the cognitive agent needed to be located in her specificity—as a member of certain social groups, within a given social milieu, in a society at a particular time period.[4]

In her *Stanford Encyclopedia of Philosophy* article "Feminist Epistemology and Philosophy of Science," Elizabeth Anderson raises a concern about idealizations in much of epistemology. Anderson is concerned about the narrowness of scope of the evidence that analytic epistemologists have used as the basis of their theorizing. She argues that this artificially makes certain knowledge claims paradigmatic, and others unusual, difficult cases to explain. But this is due merely to the narrowness of the idealizations, not epistemic reality:

> Mainstream epistemology takes as paradigms of knowledge simple propositional knowledge about matters in principle equally accessible to anyone with basic cognitive and sensory apparatus: "$2 + 2 = 4$"; "grass is green"; "water quenches thirst." Feminist epistemology does not claim that such knowledge is gendered. Examination of such examples is not particularly helpful for answering the epistemological problems that arise specifically in feminist theory and practice. What is it to know that I am a woman? What is it like to be sexually objectified? Why is it that men and women so often have dramatically divergent understandings of what happened in their sexual encounters? How can we arrange scientific practices so that science and technology serve women's interests? These kinds of questions make other kinds of knowledge salient for feminist epistemology: phenomenological knowledge, de se knowledge, knowledge of persons, know-how, moral knowledge, knowledge informed by emotions, attitudes, and interests. These kinds of knowledge are often gendered, and they can influence the propositional claims people are disposed to form and accept. This has critical implications for mainstream epistemological conceptions of knowledge, insofar as the latter are based on false generalizations drawing only from examples of ungendered knowledge.[5]

Feminist epistemology has been widely taken to be successful in vindicating Anderson's concern about the traditional examples of analytic epistemology. When one looks more broadly at epistemology, including political

4. Mills, "White Ignorance," 14.
5. Anderson, "Feminist Epistemology and Philosophy of Science," section 1.

examples, previously mysterious cases—such as the *de se*, or knowing how—become less so. It may have appeared that the content of basic knowledge claims was timeless, aperspectival, and value-neutral. But if so, that only shows that the notion of a "basic knowledge claim" was playing problematic ideological work in restricting examples. We have precisely similar concerns to the ones Anderson here gives voice about the theory of meaning.

Our specific understanding of the issues has been shaped by Charles Mills's 2005 paper, "'Ideal Theory' as Ideology," in which Mills calls attention to the dangers of an analogous situation in political philosophy, the privileging of a methodology of studying cases under certain liberal idealizations.[6] One example is Rawls's restriction to "well-ordered societies," which in *A Theory of Justice* he sees as "cooperative venture[s] for mutual advantage."[7] Mills calls this methodology "ideal theory." Despite the label, Mills's concern with ideal theory is not that it employs ideals. Mills is clear that any normative theory employs ideals. His critique is rather of the view that the primary, or the "foundational," project of political philosophy is to construct a theory of justice for institutions and states under certain particular idealizations, idealizations that mask or marginalize many of its central topics.

Consider the concept of *social change*. To study social change, one needs to theorize from a broader class, one that includes both societies that are not "well-ordered" in Rawls's sense and ones that are. To consider as "foundational" only the questions that can be posed by restricting one's attention to societies and institutions that fit the ideal model suggests that the question of social change is not as fundamental of a problem.

Perhaps Mills's greatest concern is that the methodology of ideal theory will lead to "silence on oppression":

> Almost by definition, it follows from the focus of ideal theory that little or nothing will be said on actual historic oppression and its legacy in the present, or current ongoing oppression, though these may be gestured at in a vague or promissory way (as something to be dealt with later). Correspondingly, the ways in which systematic oppression is likely to shape the basic social institutions (as well as the humans in those institutions) will not be part of the theory's concern, and this will manifest itself in the absence of ideal-as-descriptive-model concepts that would provide the necessary macro and micro-mapping of that oppression, and that are requisite for understanding its reproductive dynamic.[8]

In political philosophy, defenders of "ideal theory" in Mills's sense can maintain that by "fundamental" they mean something other than "important."

6. Mills, "'Ideal Theory' as Ideology."
7. Rawls, *A Theory of Justice*, 4.
8. Mills, "'Ideal Theory' as Ideology," 168–69.

Explaining oppression and social change is important, maybe (ideal theorists could grant) equally important to questions that are "fundamental." But by "fundamental," the ideal-theoretic political philosopher means something else, perhaps "prior." A case can be made that the questions of ideal theory are prior, because we need to know the principles of justice before we can even state the goal of social change. But to address the question of what the principles of justice are, one does not need to first address the question of social change. This, to the ideal theorist in political philosophy, grants priority to their inquiry.

Similar questions arise in the theory of meaning. Presumably we can envisage a world that is purely prosocial, in which there is only straight talk and incidental hustle, but no intentional hustle (a world lamentably bereft of stand-up comedy). But can one be intentionally hustled if there is no straight talk? Suppose that intentional hustle modally depends on the existence of straight talk, but not vice versa. Is that a basis of a case for restricting our theorizing in one mode to straight talk? Such priority need not exclude an investigation into the question of why we so often get hustled.

There are differences in the initial plausibility of objections and responses to idealizations in political philosophy and the philosophy of language. One (at least apparent) disanalogy is that there has never in human history been a well-ordered society. In other words, there has never in human history been a society that fits the ideal model in Rawlsian political philosophy. This is a broad problem for ideal models in political philosophy. But at least superficially, this is not as widespread a problem for idealizations about speech (though it is in the case of *some* of these idealizations, such as that of neutrality, which we argued was not so much impossible to achieve as it is incoherent). If so, it suggests that Mills's concerns are more pressing in political philosophy than in the theory of meaning, as the idealizations are more extreme.[9]

But another disanalogy between the political philosophy case of ideal theory and the theory of meaning case suggests the opposing moral, that the methodological problem posed by the idealizations in the theory of meaning is *worse*. If we grant that even theorizing about social change presupposes a conception of justice, but not vice versa, then there is at least some understanding of priority that attaches to ideal theory. In contrast, it is no part of, for example, Grice's project to provide an account of cooperative communication that then yields the concepts most central to the study of noncooperative communication. From this perspective, the methodological problem in the theory of meaning is worse.

In both the case of political philosophy and the theory of meaning, there are legitimate concerns about the ideological function of ideal theory. Mills's

---

9. The concession that there are many actual talk exchanges that meet the standard model is just for the sake of argument. As will emerge below, we are not ourselves convinced of this.

contention in "'Ideal Theory' as Ideology" is that the ideal-theory approach to political philosophy has an ideological function, to conceal the importance of notions such as ideology, social change, and oppression. If ideal theory is "prior," then these other notions are "secondary." A similar concern arises in the theory of meaning. If what is "important," "central," and "prior" are the prosocial aspects of language pertaining to the conveying of information, then other effects of speech are "secondary." This can obscure the ways in which aspects related to "tone," expressive meaning, and connection to ideology are central to understanding the ways in which speech functions. If we only concentrate on the information conveyed by someone's speech, we ignore the myriad other effects, both intentional and unintentional, in which speech impacts audiences. These concerns about the ideological effects of ideal-theory approaches are analogous.

Yet the disciplinary sociology of political philosophy and philosophy of language differ significantly.[10] Though to some extent the topic of oppressive or subordinating speech has not been accorded the same level of theoretical centrality as other work, it is hard to attribute the difference between the large amount of work on apolitical examples in the theory of meaning and the lesser amount of work on political examples to a problematic hegemonic ideological formation in the theory of meaning. There is simply no dominant philosophy of language tradition akin to John Rawls's program in political philosophy, or Jürgen Habermas's, both of which share analogous ideal-theory assumptions. Contemporary theorists of meaning in philosophy and linguistics belong to many different traditions.

Our background for the most part is in the logic and semantics tradition. In this tradition, natural languages are treated with the tools developed for the interpretation of the formal languages of logic and mathematics, which lack many of the properties of natural languages. Arguably, such formal languages lack what Frege termed "tone," at least in the sense that they are not intended to model anything beyond truth and logical consequence. Insofar as terms in these formal languages belong to speech practices, they are such marginal speech practices as to cast little general light on the study of human communication more broadly. It is the tradition of "ideal-language philosophy." By design, and despite important methodological changes in philosophy associated with the development of "ordinary language" philosophy in the mid-twentieth century, this tradition seeks to hide much of what happens when ordinary people talk.

Challenging the methodology of ideal political philosophy became central in political theory and political philosophy as academic disciplines in the 1990s and thereafter. But challenging ideal-language philosophy has a much

---

10. Historians of philosophy have argued that similar ideological exclusions caused by disciplinary formations functioned to exclude work in modern philosophy by women, e.g., O'Neill, "Disappearing Ink."

older tradition. J. L. Austin's 1962 *How to Do Things with Words* specifically targets idealizations about language. The central target of the book is "the descriptive fallacy," that "the business of a statement can only be to describe some fact."[11] Austin argues ultimately that there is not even a distinguishable species of speech that is pure description, a claim that our model bears out. Ordinary-language philosophy is defined against "ideal-language philosophy," precisely in that the idealizations of the latter, the ideal properties of formal languages, were argued to misrepresent linguistic reality.

The affinities between Austin's project and ours run deep. Our focus on practice rather than proposition is an extrapolation of his program in which conventions of language concern not merely representational techniques, but ways of doing things. Further, the concept of presupposition, the focus of part II of this book, is utterly central to Austin's critique. Austin initially attempts to draw a distinction between performatives and constatives, where performatives have preconditions, and constatives just state something to be true or false. But, as Austin eventually concludes, we can think of preconditions for performatives as their presuppositions, which constatives have as well.[12] A practice has preconditions, and a description of the world presupposes practices that give that description its stability and meaning. We have argued, following Austin, that the same concept of presupposition is at issue in both cases. With Austin, we suspect that there are problems with the very division of speech into doing and describing, and our model bears this suspicion out. Like Austin, we recognize the need to operate with a concept of presupposition that does not depend on such a division.

9.2. The Content-Delivery Model

In this section, we precisify the idealizations of "ideal-language philosophy" by focusing on something like Austin's descriptive fallacy. In this book, we have caricatured the ideal-language philosophy approach as assuming models of communication involving a particular variant of Reddy's conduit metaphor. Communication is seen as a cooperative enterprise of exchanging contents to interlocutors in the purpose of a common goal, and delivering them to each other in some sense *inside* little packets of words. Speech, according to the conduit model, is a *content-delivery system*.

---

11. Austin, *How to Do Things with Words*, 1.

12. Austin's brief discussion of the relationship between preconditions and presuppositions culminates as follows: "Here we might have used the 'presuppose' formula: we might say that the formula 'I do' presupposes lots of things: if these are not satisfied the formula is unhappy, void: it does not succeed in being a contract when the reference fails (or even when it is ambiguous) any more than the other succeeds in being a statement. Similarly the question of goodness or badness of advice does not arise if you are not in a position to advise me about that matter" (*How to Do Things with Words*, 51).

If we think of speech as a content-delivery system, it is natural to develop tools, concepts, and resources that isolate the content-delivery aspect of language as precisely as possible. Aspects irrelevant to the content-delivery model can be filtered by idealizations. The use of language to evoke emotion or social bonding, or to negotiate social station and rank, distracts from the function of language to deliver information, and hence are aspects that should be filtered out of the core evidence for building a model of speech as a content-delivery system. Concepts, tools, and resources that are abstracted from speech as a content-delivery system can perhaps later be applied to these other functions of language, or they can be studied as peripheral uses of language.

How might one form idealizations that isolate speech as a content-delivery system? It's natural to focus on one speaker and one hearer—the person who delivers the content and the recipient of that content, and to think of them as engaged in a cooperative rational enterprise. It's natural to abstract away from obstacles to smooth content delivery by speech—to think of the agents in our model as maximally open to the reception of content, with their intentions fully transparent, and to think of the various determinants of content as maximally mutually accessible. If the function of speech is to deliver information about a shared objective reality, it's natural to think of conventions of language connecting words to neutral bits of information. If speech is content delivery, we can and perhaps should abstract from social roles and power relations. The conception of speech as centrally and most basically a conduit of information leads to what we can think of as *the standard model*, determined roughly by the following idealizations:

DIALOGUE: A talk exchange is between one speaker and one hearer.

COOPERATIVITY: Speaker and hearer are cooperating in the service of a set of common interests.

RATIONALITY: Interlocutors are perfectly rational: they are computationally unlimited, reason scientifically and logically rather than emotionally, and have consistent preferences.

TRANSPARENCY: Utterance meaning, including presupposition and implicature, is characterized by a unique set of communicative intentions that are mutually and readily consciously recognizable.

SHARED CONTEXT: Features of context relevant to interpretation must be mutually known in order that a unique content can be identified.

NEUTRALITY: (i) Conventions associated with words assign them a core of neutral and aperspectival meaning; (ii) at least some expressions are completely neutral, in the sense that perspective and attunement to social location are irrelevant to their meaning; and (iii) the neutral core of the meaning of a nonneutral expression is paraphrasable in neutral terms.

SOCIAL HOMOGENEITY: The linguistic community is socially homogeneous, and utterance meaning is computed without reference to social roles, affiliations, power relations, or personalities.

LANGUAGE HOMOGENEITY: Conventional meanings are determined primarily at a level of recognized languages, which may have millions of speakers. Speech practices of individuals or subgroups, registers, styles, differences from one communicative medium to another, and rhetorical frames of particular conversations, are not central.

PROPOSITIONALITY: Content is packaged into neat units, one proposition per utterance, and the primary point of communication is to convey these propositions with assertive speech acts.

FORCE: The primary level for studying communication is the illocutionary force of the utterance, which is a function of the underlying content.

EXTENT: The individual utterance is the bearer of significant semantic properties. Properties of larger discourses, or temporally discontinuous exchanges, need to be considered only by extrapolation from the single utterance case.

These ideal-language idealizations result in a picture of speech designed to explain how it can be true or false. But we began this book by promising to explain how speech could also be harmful, violent, or dangerous. In crafting our theory, we considered as evidence a wide range of speech that is clearly nonideal according to this model. As we will try to show in chapter 10, although perhaps this is not in itself surprising, applying the tools and resources we derived from study of speech that is nonideal makes it much easier to explain what it is about speech that makes it harmful, violent, or dangerous. We contend that it is the ideal-language model itself that makes it mysterious how speech can have these properties, as well as many more positive properties, like being friendly, soothing, or clear. One might have thought that the last of these, the property of clarity, would be exactly what ideal-language models would be good for. Yet even here they fail, for as any educator knows, what is clear to one person is not clear to another, and this can only be understood once one drops idealizations like *rationality*, *shared context*, and *social* and *language homogeneity*.

While we have documented many cases in this volume of prior scholars who have denied particular idealizations, from Wittgenstein and Austin on, we have certainly gone further than others who, like us, work broadly in a tradition of analytic philosophers like Frege, Austin, Grice, and Montague. Though there are surely ways in which we ourselves have simplified and abstracted from the complexities of real-world speech, we have nonetheless proposed a framework that eschews all eleven of the above idealizations. Recapping material from the last eight chapters, let us rehearse some of the principal points that separate our proposals from much prior work.

DIALOGUE: Neither a crowd chanting in unison nor a dog-whistling politician intending to have different effects on different audiences fits the standard model. We have taken such data as central and discussed mechanisms for modeling communication at the level of groups. We make no assumptions about the assemblage involved in interactional events, or about the audience.

COOPERATIVITY: Our model assumes communication to be coordinative, but not inherently cooperative. Our practice-based model supports analysis of intended hustle, which we have argued to be a common feature of noncooperative communication.

RATIONALITY: We have argued that nondeliberative processes are central to communication, and we have suggested that the descriptive resonances of words (the way in which occurrences of words relate to features of the world) should not be privileged over emotional resonances.

TRANSPARENCY: We have argued against an idealization of straight talk, and we have suggested that hustle is central to communication. The practice-based model of communication does not make strong assumptions as regards intention recognition. Recognition of intentions is an important aspect of communication, but it should not be assumed in the modeling of such central communicative processes as mimicry and emotional response.

SHARED CONTEXT: Our model applies in cases such as dog whistling where context crucially differs between audiences. We have also emphasized that much accommodation is gradual, and that accommodation can be divergent, with the net effect that mismatches between contextual assumptions are an intrinsic part of communication.

NEUTRALITY: We have argued that the concept of a neutral core is incoherent. All words come with perspective, and there is no such thing as an inherently neutral act.

SOCIAL HOMOGENEITY: Social resonances are as important in our model as descriptive resonances, and heterogeneity of groups and practices is at the core of our analysis of intergroup interaction, for example, processes of othering and the formation of echo chambers.

LANGUAGE HOMOGENEITY: We take as central situations of discursive conflict in which speech practices themselves are at stake, and in which groups compete for dominance of their preferred rhetorical frames. The language practices themselves are subject to both convergent and divergent accommodation, rather than being assumed constant across the community.

PROPOSITIONALITY: The haze of resonance associated with words is neither restricted to a single proposition, nor restricted to being propositional at all. Neither emotional resonances nor behavioral resonances nor resonances involving shift in attention are naturally thought of as propositions being exchanged between interlocutors.

FORCE: We have emphasized effects of utterances that go beyond the illocutionary force of the utterance, and indeed go beyond what is sometimes described as *perlocutionary* force (intended side-effects of an utterance). Every word in an utterance carries its own resonances, and the most important effects may be connected with accommodation of background rather than uptake of illocutionary force.

EXTENT: Resonances of a practice are defined in terms of its extension, a history that dynamically changes with each utterance. Each utterance helps shape the resonances of future utterances whether temporally close or distant. Oppressive speech consists of oppressive practices that cannot be fully understood by consideration of the effects of isolated oppressive speech acts alone. Many processes of accommodation and ideological change are gradual.

We hope it is clear that the framework we have set out does not rest on these particular idealizations. We accept that the exact idealizations of particular proposals in the literature vary widely. We also accept that the exact status of the idealizations also varies. Sometimes they are implicit in the choice of data, but never made explicit; sometimes, as with rationality, they are explicit simplifications but are not taken to be realistic commitments; sometimes, as with cooperativity in Grice's work, they are regarded as communicative assumptions that structure reasoning whether they hold or not; and sometimes, as with neutrality in much post-Fregean work, they are strong theoretical commitments. At the very least, we take any of the idealizations we have listed to potentially restrict the empirical domain of inquiry in developing a theory of meaning in communication. Thus, they are no innocent assumptions.

One way to object to a putative ideal model, determined by a set of idealizations, is by rejecting one or more of the ideals. But this does not mean that an ideal-theoretic methodology is inescapable. After all, it may be that each and every idealization, each way of limiting the data set for the study of speech, results in some unacceptable exclusions, ones that distort the theoretical concepts in a field built on speech situations that abstract from them. This is a possibility in the theory of meaning.

9.3. The Ideal/Nonideal Debate in the Theory of Meaning

The validity of ideal theory as a method in philosophy is an issue that is essentially as old as the discipline of philosophy itself. In *The Republic*, Plato develops his theory of justice by describing what he regards as an ideal city-state, which, on his view, perfectly embodies justice. And toward the end of Book V, Socrates is asked to address how the ideal model he sketched could even be possible:

"But, Socrates, if we allow you to go on like this, I fear you will never come to the point of discussing the matters you put aside in order to say all that you have just said. Those matters, you recall, raised the question whether a city such as you have described could ever be a real possibility and how that possibility might be realized. Were your city to be duly constituted, I am among those ready to admit that it would be a boon to its citizens. . . . Let us take it for granted that these and countless other advantages will accrue to the city so constituted. But let us leave off belaboring these points. Excluding all other considerations, what should be done? The reverse."[13]

The impossibility of realizing ideals is, we can say with some justification, the original nonideal concern for ideal theory. It is originally raised in the domain of political philosophy. And though Socrates takes this concern seriously, he has an answer that plausibly undermines it. Socrates argues that the concern can be dismissed, because it misconstrues the methodology of ideal theory in political philosophy, at least as he employs it. His goal in describing an ideal city is to allow a measure of how close we are to that (perhaps impossible) ideal of a just city. According to this defense of the ideal-theoretic method in political philosophy, providing an ideal allows one to have a measure to use to assess how close a given actual state is to that ideal. And that goal doesn't require that the model determined as fully ideal has to be possible to realize at all.

The debate between ideal and nonideal methodologies has roiled political philosophy in recent years. But ideal-theoretic methodologies are employed in a variety of disciplines in philosophy, and debates and concerns about them are broader than just political philosophy. And as we have already discussed several times, and as one would expect, the debate is different across areas of philosophy with different domains. Socrates's position that the goal of political philosophy is to provide a measure of closeness to his ideal city is a claim about what should guide practice in political philosophy. But a similar view about what should guide practice in the philosophy of language would be manifestly absurd. The goal of philosophy of language does not even tangentially include helping to measure how close actual given discussions in language are to speech in an ideal model, whether it is an ideal model structured by the idealizations we discussed in the previous section, or one that is more general. Maybe this is what we are doing in political philosophy. But this just isn't what we are or should be doing in philosophy of language.

For the sake of expediency, in the discussion to follow, which compares debates about ideal theory between disciplines, we will consider the idealizations that structure the content-delivery model as our example of an ideal model in the theory of meaning. However, our discussion is of broader

13. Plato, *The Republic* 188–89 (471c–e).

significance, its conclusions relevant for ideal models that employ much less demanding idealizations.

On the ideal-theoretic approach underlying the content-delivery model, speech is, most centrally, a content-delivery system. If so, the thinking goes, it makes sense to form idealizations that allow us to focus on this function, abstracting from other functions. One kind of defense of ideal models is to argue that the idealizations are chosen carefully to limit attention to speech that is theoretically particularly generative. Because of the supposedly special nature of this subtype of speech, research just on it yields concepts and tools that are in fact applicable to functions of speech that are not obviously means of content delivery. For example, one function of speech is to bond speaker and audience into a common social identity, which does not on the surface appear to be a function of speech that is explicable on the content-delivery model. But the advocate of the content-delivery model could defend its idealizations by maintaining that when speech functions to bond speaker and audience into a common social identity, it does so by means of sharing content—content about a common enemy, for example. Bad speech, on this model, is a kind of *misinformation*.

Arguing that the idealized model provides surprising resources to account for speech that apparently falls out of its purview is not the only way to defend ideal models in philosophy of language, though it is perhaps the most difficult. Another kind of defense of ideal models can also be applied here, familiar even in the hard sciences. One could argue that the kind of speech that falls outside the ideal model is in some sense peripheral to theory, a kind of mere noise in its status as evidence for forming concepts. Yet a third defense of ideal models appeals to a distinction between the "pure" version of the inquiry, and an "applied" version. For example, one could argue that the study of functions of speech outside content delivery is an *applied* study, to be contrasted with the pure study of the content-delivery function of speech, and as such may not be equally worthy of studying.

Some defenses of ideal-theoretic methodologies transfer to debates in other disciplines, or at least make some kind of minimal sense. Also, some concerns about ideal-theoretic methodologies transfer between disciplines. Consider Charles Mills's objections to two idealizations of Bayesian epistemology, which fall under Mills's lens in "'Ideal Theory' as Ideology." A first idealization critiqued by Mills is that of "idealized cognitive capacities":

> The human agents as visualized in the theory will also often have completely unrealistic capacities attributed to them—unrealistic even for the privileged minority, let alone those subordinated in different ways, who would not have had an equal opportunity for their natural capacities to develop, and who would in fact typically be disabled in crucial respects.[14]

14. Mills, "'Ideal Theory' as Ideology," 168.

Second, Mills decries the assumption of "an idealized cognitive sphere":

> Separate from, and in addition to, the idealization of human capacities, what could be termed an idealized cognitive sphere will also be presupposed. In other words, as a corollary of the general ignoring of oppression, the consequences of oppression for the social cognition of these agents, both the advantaged and the disadvantaged, will typically not be recognized, let alone theorized. A general social transparency will be presumed, with cognitive obstacles minimized as limited to biases of self-interest or the intrinsic difficulties of understanding the world, and little or no attention paid to the distinctive role of hegemonic ideologies and group-specific experience in distorting our perceptions and conceptions of the social order.[15]

Mills's concerns about idealizations in epistemology carry over to the case of the idealizations of the standard model of communication. Speech can be oppressive via its content—if you claim that a group is essentially criminal, the oppressive effects can (largely? entirely?) be captured by the content of your claim. But insofar as there are oppressive properties of speech that are not reducible to content, the idealizations function to mask them. If, for example, a *practice* of speaking is oppressive, that fact will be filtered out by the idealizations; a way of mocking the LGBT community by speaking in a certain pitch is oppressive, but not via its content. Manipulative speech can reinforce hierarchies, operating via nontransparent intentions that allow for plausible deniability (think of the use of dog whistles in political speech). And occluding manipulative speech by theoretical idealizations may be regarded as itself a kind of manipulation.[16] Occluding manipulative speech is politically problematic, reinforcing existing social hierarchies by masking the existence of practices that support and maintain them. Mills's concerns about two central highly idealized concepts in epistemology generalize to related concerns about some widely (though not universally) assumed idealizations in philosophy of language.

We have seen that versions of the impossibility argument against idealizations exist across various philosophical disciplines. But even when the same basic objection to idealizations does transfer across disciplines, targeting other idealizations with the same problem, the *replies* may not. As we have seen in Socrates's defense of the "impossibility worry" for ideal models in political

---

15. Mills, "'Ideal Theory' as Ideology," 169.

16. It is not just manipulative speech that these idealizations occlude—social bonding and the creation of in-groups and out-groups are processes that do not simply work by the delivery of content. And on the model we provided in parts I and II of this book, these functions of speech are not derivative from content delivery, or at least they are not derivative from a process that operates anything like that in the paradigmatic models of content delivery described by the idealizations we considered in the last section.

philosophy, it is possible to respond to this objection by appealing to the aim of political philosophy. However, nothing like his response has any plausibility in the philosophy of language.

The "impossibility objection" arises in epistemology as well, and here too the most plausible replies are nonstarters in the theory of meaning. Here is a difficult version of the impossibility objection, arising against idealizations in Bayesian epistemology, as stated by David Christensen:

> As many people have pointed out, attaining probabilistic coherence is far beyond the capacity of any real human being. Probabilistic coherence, after all, requires having full credence in all logical truths— including complicated theorems that no human has been able to prove. It also places constraints on beliefs about logically contingent matters—constraints that go beyond human capacities to obey. . . . The fact that this sort of "logical omniscience" is built into probabilistic coherence has led many to doubt that coherence can provide any sort of interesting normative constraint on rationality.[17]

There are of course also, as Christensen proceeds to point out, similar idealizations with deductive rationality; for the same reasons, we do not know all the deductive consequences of our beliefs.[18]

In the final paragraph of *Putting Logic in Its Place*, Christiansen replies to the version of the impossibility objection as it arises against idealizations in Bayesian epistemology:

> Furthermore, philosophy in general, and epistemology in particular, need not be directed toward external practical ends. We surely may philosophize because we hope (perhaps optimistically) to help people improve themselves cognitively. But just as surely, epistemologists need not restrict their efforts to improving our educational system, or to producing popular manuals for cognitive self-help. We may philosophize because we want a better understanding of ourselves—of our cognitive natures and our situation in the world. We may philosophize because we want a better understanding of rationality itself.[19]

We find it problematic to pose the options as being between an epistemologist who restricts their efforts to improving our educational system, an epistemologist who produces popular manuals for cognitive self-help, and an epistemologist who wants a better understanding of rationality itself. Christensen's way of

---

17. Christensen, *Putting Logic in Its Place*, 150–51.

18. This is a problem with the idealized model of Bayesian epistemology that (nonaccidentally) has a direct correlate in the case of the possible-worlds theory of meaning, as discussed in the context of *fragmentation* in section 3.2.

19. Christensen, *Putting Logic in Its Place*, 178.

setting up the options imposes immediately a distinction between the applied study of a subject matter, and the pure study of that subject matter; only the third kind of epistemologist would count as a pure epistemologist. This distinction has proven to be politically problematic. In the case of all such disciplinary distinctions, the study considered to be pure is associated with more prestige.

Christensen's defense of the unattainable ideals of Bayesian rationality is that it is an exercise in a kind of idealized Platonic inquiry, an attempt to grasp the form of rationality. This project, he argues, requires abstracting from the limitations of reality that are obstacles to the manifestation of ideal rationality. However, as in the case of Socrates's reply to the impossibility objection to his ideal model of a city in *The Republic*, the defense that Christensen envisages for ideal-theoretic epistemology just doesn't get to the starting line in philosophy of language. The expressive functions of speech, the functions of language to bond and share identity, are *genuine functions of speech*—they are not in any sense "practical applications" of a pure theory of speech, for example as content delivery. Moreover, the theory we have developed makes this vivid. In that theory, cognitive attunement is at the same level as affective attunement, or attunement to identity. If the model of meaning we have developed is on the right track, then standard defenses of ideal theory in epistemology cannot possibly be replicated here. It's hard to think of idealizations in the theorization of communication that could be defended on the grounds that they lay language bare by focusing on its true function. Rather, too many of the idealizations in the theory of meaning function to cover up important roles that language plays in society, leaving an impoverished and artificial theory of communication incapable of being extended beyond toy examples.

In recent work, Herman Cappelen and Josh Dever end up at a position that is in some ways similar to our own, and in some ways distinct:

> Our job for this volume was to clarify the distinction between Ideal and Non-Ideal Philosophy of Language. We've ended up rejecting the distinction. However, maybe there's another, closely related distinction that is useful. This volume has in its title the phrase "social and political philosophy of language." What does that category pick out and what is it contrasted with? At the risk of appearing to be incurable curmudgeons, we are going to also reject that category as fairly useless. What could it possibly pick out? Maybe it's an attempt to pick out speech by people who are politicians or people who talk about political/social topics. If that's the remit of social-political philosophy of language, then it should be concerned with sentences like:
>
> > "We should increase the sale tax on cigarettes because that would give the city more money for schools and it could reduce cancer rates."

> "The price of parking on city streets should be increased because it is not fair that public property should be rented to car owners for very little money."

That's what the vast majority of "political speech" is like. It's just "ordinary speech." It's not special in any way. It doesn't constitute a distinct subset of speech.[20]

Though our arguments differ, we agree with Cappelen and Dever that there is no sharp distinction between ideal and nonideal philosophy of language, and we have shown in detail that it cannot possibly be an entirely parallel debate to the ones in epistemology or political philosophy. We have argued that idealized philosophy of language cannot be argued to be prior to nonidealized philosophy of language, and indeed this is in line with the fact that work in the ordinary-language tradition has always actively questioned simplifying idealizations that see language as a purely representational system. But it is an idealization to assume that categories must be sharp in order to be useful, and the question of whether nonideal philosophy of language is sharply delineated from ideal philosophy of language is distinct from the question of whether the category "nonideal philosophy of language" is a useful one. We do not take a stand on this latter question here, but note that the editors of the handbook in which Cappelen and Dever's argument appears, the *Routledge Handbook of Social and Political Philosophy of Language*, apparently found the distinction to be useful, at least as an organizational device.

In the opening of the *Routledge Handbook*, the editors, Rachel Sterken and Justin Khoo, define the remit of the volume as bringing together "work on how language shapes and is shaped by social and political factors."[21] We agree with Cappelen and Dever that social and political language is not a separate category of language. It is a central tenet of this volume that all language is social and political. But we disagree entirely with their conclusion that "social and political philosophy of language" is "fairly useless." Rather, we presume we are in agreement with Khoo and Sterken. "Work on how language shapes and is shaped by social and political factors," which constitutes social and political philosophy of language, has become a lively subarea of academic research, building especially on the work of feminist and race scholars; we take it that progress in this subarea is essential to progress in philosophy of language.

We have argued that some of the most well-known defenses of ideal models in political philosophy and epistemology are simply absent in the case of

20. Cappelen and Dever, "On the Uselessness of the Distinction between Ideal and Non-Ideal Theory," 101. Their view, which perhaps is in part a riposte to an early presentation of our work on idealization at the 2017 conference on Philosophical Linguistics and Linguistical Philosophy (PhLiP), is echoed in the first chapter of their introductory textbook, Cappelen and Dever, *Bad Language*.

21. Khoo and Sterken, *Handbook of Social and Political Philosophy of Language*, i.

the theory of meaning. There is no good case, for example, that the content-delivery model or the prosocial model of speech is "prior" to the study of other aspects of speech. And there is no good case that anything like the content-delivery model is "ideal," and the use of speech in propaganda is a mere "practical application." This doesn't mean, of course, that the theory of meaning can do without idealizations. But it does perhaps help explain why nonideal approaches have a long and distinguished history in twentieth-century philosophy of language.

PART IV

Oppression and Freedom

CHAPTER TEN

Harmful Speech

*Official language smitheryed to sanction ignorance and preserve privilege
is a suit of armor polished to shocking glitter, a husk from which the
knight departed long ago. Yet there it is: dumb, predatory, sentimental.
Exciting reverence in schoolchildren, providing shelter for despots,
summoning false memories of stability, harmony among the public. . . .
Oppressive language does more than represent violence; it is violence; does
more than represent the limits of knowledge; it limits knowledge.*

—TONI MORRISON[1]

Officialese [Amtssprache] is my only language.

—ADOLF EICHMANN, AS QUOTED BY HANNAH ARENDT[2]

WE BEGAN THIS BOOK by promising that the tools and concepts we develop
would explain how speech can be harmful, as straightforwardly as the ideal
language model explains how speech can be true or false. In this chapter, we
attempt to deliver on this promise.

In chapter 7, we discussed the ideal of neutrality. Whatever oppressive
language is, it is not neutral.[3] The trouble is that the ideal of neutrality has
obscured the nature and indeed the ubiquity of oppressive language. Yet the
centrality of the ideal of neutrality to the dominant ideology of academic philosophy of language and linguistic semantics, what we have called the standard model, has meant that most analysts base their work on the assumption
that all language has a neutral core. That has led to a tendency to ignore much
nonneutrality in language, pushing the study of nonneutrality to pragmatics,
and to some extent exiling it so that many types of nonneutrality, effects of
language other than for conveying factual information about the world, are
only studied in separate academic disciplines altogether, such as communication studies and psychology.

---

1. Morrison, "The Nobel Lecture in Literature," 200.

2. Arendt, *Eichmann in Jerusalem: A Report on the Banality of Evil*, 48.

3. We do not here give an analysis of oppression, but for one with which we are in
sympathy, see Haslanger's *Resisting Reality: Social Construction and Social Critique* (327),
where she defines what it is for an individual x to be oppressed *as an F* by an institution I.
Here, we can think of oppressive language itself, or certain ways of talking, as an institution
that oppresses individuals for their identities.

We return below to the topic of neutrality, specifically how the ideal of neutrality is implicated in masking harm across three categories of speech we discuss in this chapter: slurs, genocidal speech, and bureaucratic speech.

Slurring is one paradigm of nonideal language. With a single word, a speaker can perform an act that is at once noncooperative, centered on an in-group/out-group distinction, indicative of differential power and status, and so emotionally charged that it may foreclose informationally fruitful discussion. To the extent that a slur provides information, what it says is not easily negotiable or debatable. And although slurring is, by its nature, typically a transparent, in-your-face act, it will turn out that a certain amount of hustle is present in all slurring, and that in the case of slurring using words that are not normally regarded as slurs, there is an additional element of hustle connected to the presence of plausible deniability.

We began this book with Cleon's contribution to the Mytilenean debate, where Cleon argues that Athens should massacre the entire population of Mytilene for rebelling. Cleon's speech, the paradigm of demagogic speech in the ancient world, is genocidal speech. We see again today, in Russia's justification for its invasion of Ukraine, these very same tropes, attesting to their permanent power. Cleon explicitly represents democratic values as inimical to his goals. Genocidal speech is the original paradigm of antidemocratic speech, the central example of demagoguery in the ancient world.

Why, however, do we place *bureaucratic language* in the category of oppressive speech? We begin by addressing this question—and the problematic role the ideal of neutrality characteristically plays in masking harm.

10.1. Oppressive Language and the Ideal of Neutrality

In looking at slurs, genocidal language, and bureaucratic language, it is tempting to treat the first two as belonging together, perhaps lumped together under the label "hate speech," and the third as belonging to a distant and unrelated category, similar only insofar as all three are political. It is important to avoid this temptation. First, what is remarkable about much of the language of genocides is its unremarkability. That is, *The Banality of Evil*, to adapt from Arendt's famous title, is reflected in the banality of much of the *language* of evil.[4] As she says,

> None of the various "language rules," carefully contrived to deceive and to camouflage, had a more decisive effect on the mentality of the killers than this first war decree of Hitler, in which the word for "murder" was replaced by the phrase "to grant a mercy death." Eichmann, asked by the police examiner if the directive to avoid "unnecessary hardships"

---

4. Arendt, *Eichmann in Jerusalem: A Report on the Banality of Evil.*

was not a bit ironic, in view of the fact that the destination of these people was certain death anyhow, did not even understand the question, so firmly was it still anchored in his mind that the unforgivable sin was not to kill people but to cause unnecessary pain.[5]

To put it another way, let us borrow instead the title of the historian Christopher Browning's well-known study of the history and psychology of people who became part of the Nazi genocide, as members of a battalion of *Ordnungspolizei* (literally: order police) in occupied Poland. What could be more ordinary than maintaining order according to the rule of law? The problem was that the order they were empowered to maintain implied mass murder. Just as it is remarkable how in a genocide *Ordinary Men* can become twisted into performing the ugliest of atrocities, so too it is remarkable how in a genocide what we might think of as ordinary language can become twisted.[6] Second, bureaucratic language, far from being an unrelated category, is in fact often crucial to genocidal regimes, and to discriminatory ideologies more generally.

We have already argued that language is never neutral. Let us go further: perhaps it is a mistake to ever think of language as ordinary. To say that language is ordinary is to make a claim about what is commonplace in a particular community of practice. But what seems ordinary to those in the midst of a genocide should seem extraordinary to us. So, we must ask ourselves whether the apparent ordinariness of a turn of phrase reflects inherent ordinariness, or whether it in fact reflects our own insensitivity to the role that language plays within ideologies that are so familiar to us as to appear unremarkable.

In *The Language of the Third Reich*, Victor Klemperer states that the first three words that he noticed as being specific to Nazi vocabulary were *Strafexpedition* (punitive expedition), *Staatsakt* (state occasion), and *historisch* (historical).[7] The first, used to describe attacks by groups of brownshirts in the early days of Nazi Germany, is intrinsically violent. This is seen in Klemperer's discussion of what we would term the word's resonances: "For me the word *Strafexpedition* was the embodiment of brutal arrogance and contempt for people who are in any way different, it sounded so colonial, you could see the encircled negro village, you could hear the cracking of the hippopotamus whip."[8] The imagery has visceral power, and perhaps conveys the sense in

---

5. Arendt, *Eichmann in Jerusalem: A Report on the Banality of Evil*, 108–9.

6. Browning, *Ordinary Men: Reserve Police Battalion 101 and the Final Solution in Poland*.

7. Klemperer, *The Language of the Third Reich*, 41–47.

8. The innocent ease with which a convinced young Nazi could use the term *Strafexpedition* is seen in Klemperer's anecdote about a conversation with someone who had been a friend:

> "How are things with you at work?" I asked. "Very good!" he answered. "Yesterday we had a great day. There were a few shameless communists in Okrilla, so we organized a punitive expedition."—"What did you do?"—"You know, we

which the word was not merely violent, but inextricably linked to discriminatory ideology. However, the other two words seem innocuous.

Klemperer describes the propaganda minister, Goebbels, as having staged "an almost incalculably long series" of *Staatsakten*. To use this word was not merely to describe the type of occasion that inevitably happens in a state. It was to imbue it with national significance and to force attention toward it. As Klemperer makes clear, both the word *Staatsakt* and the occasions so described, frequently surrounding the coffin of a war hero, were advertising for the indomitable power of the Nazi state: "The splendour of the banners, parades, garlands, fanfares and choruses, the all-embracing framework of speeches, these all remained constant features and were undoubtedly modelled on the example of Mussolini."[9]

The application of the word *historisch* would appear at first to be up to historians, a group who might be imagined, or who might conceivably imagine themselves, as presenting both a dispassionate view of events that have occurred over large time scales, as well as the logic and significance of those events. Yet it is also a familiar idea that history is intrinsically ideological, so we should not be surprised that the application of the term *historisch* became an important tool of Nazi propaganda. It is the goal of the propagandist to make history. Here is what Klemperer says:

> Which brings us to the word that National Socialism used from beginning to end with inordinate profligacy. It takes itself so seriously, it is so convinced of the permanence of its institutions, or at least is so keen to persuade others of that permanence, that every trifle, however insignificant, and everything that it comes into contact with, has a historical significance. Every speech delivered by the Führer is historical [*historisch*], even if he says the same thing a hundred times over, every meeting the Führer has with the Duce is historical, even if it doesn't make the slightest difference to the existing state of things; the victory of a German racing car is historical, as is the official opening of a new motorway, and every single road, and every single section of every single road, is officially inaugurated; every harvest festival is historical, every Party rally, every feast day of any kind; . . . [the Third Reich] views every single day of its life as historical.[10]

The word *historisch* can be presented as if it is an objective assessment, but it was simply a mask used by those who wished to draw attention to whatever

---

made them run the gauntlet of rubber truncheons, a mild dose of castor-oil, no bloodshed but very effective all the same, a proper punitive expedition in fact."
(Klemperer, *The Language of the Third Reich*, 43)

9. Klemperer, *The Language of the Third Reich*, 43.

10. Klemperer, *The Language of the Third Reich*, 45.

suited their purpose as symbols of the power and success of the Nazi regime. Nazi military defeats were not *historisch*.

A recurring theme of Klemperer's writing is the special language of Nazi bureaucracy, and in particular the use of mechanistic metaphors.[11] As Klemperer describes it, the use of mechanistic language to describe humans emphasized the fact that they were expected to act without thinking. Klemperer describes much of this metaphorical language as already present in abstract descriptions of institutions, but being used in a new way, to apply to individual people. Consider the English word "alignment." It has a purely physical meaning that would be relevant in mechanical and architectural tasks. But people can also be aligned, and they can be forced into line, literally or metaphorically:

> The explicit mechanization of the individual himself is left up to the LTI. Its most characteristic, and probably also earliest, creation in this field is *"gleich-schalten* [to force into line]." You can see and hear the button at work which forces people—not institutions and impersonal authorities—to adopt the same, uniform attitude and movements: teachers in various institutions, various groups of employees in the judiciary and tax authorities, members of the *Stahlhelm* and the SA, and so on, are brought into line almost *ad infinitum*.[12]

The word *gleichschalten* is banal. But the banality of bureaucratic language is precisely what masks its insidious power. It is well established that under the Nazi regime, violence was bureaucratized. Klemperer shows us that the language of violence, too, was bureaucratized.

We now turn to how terms that might be seen as just the ordinary way of referring to a group, and hence supposedly neutral, can mask the way these terms are used as slurs. We approach this indirectly, by first considering how the concept of neutrality has been applied in the case of slurs. Building on recent work in the area, we will suggest that the mistaken assumption that slurs have neutral counterparts is intimately linked to a mistaken view of group-denoting terms more generally. We will offer an analysis of group-denoting terms that depends on the presence of multiple communities of practice in contact with each other, but with differing ideologies. With a toxic

---

11. Klemperer comments in a nuanced way on the importation of mechanistic language, as seen in this passage:

> One of the foremost tensions within the LTI: whilst stressing the organic and natural growth it is at the same time swamped by mechanistic expressions and insensitive to the stylistic incongruities and lack of dignity in such combinations as "a constructed organization [*aufgezogene Organisation*]." (Klemperer, *The Language of the Third Reich*, 48)

12. Klemperer, *The Language of the Third Reich*, 159.

enough background ideology in the context, any group-denoting term can be transformed into a tool for slurring.

We argued in section 7.3 that it was incoherent to treat evaluative words as having neutral counterparts, or for that matter, a neutral core. So it is with slurs. Like other evaluative words (say, "generous"), they lack a neutral core. As for what the neutral counterpart of an act of slurring would be, that is an odd thing to ask for. If you neutralize an insult, the one thing you do not have is an insult. Yet the vast bulk of the prior literature on slurs assumes that slur words have neutral counterparts.

Scholars who take slurs to have a neutral counterpart also commonly assume that the meaning of that counterpart constitutes the neutral core meaning of the slur. Such scholars generally postulate some special add-on to the core, which is variously described as a conventional implicature, a presupposition, or tone. These analyses miss the mark. We agree, rather, with three scholars who have (independently) argued against the neutral-counterpart view: Lauren Ashwell, Heather Burnett, and Jennifer Foster.[13] As we argued in chapter 7, evaluative words like "stupid" or "ugly" cannot possibly have neutral cores. It is implausible that their meaning consists of a sense that lacks evaluativity and a completely independent tone that is evaluative. We see the general argument against evaluative words having neutral cores as applying equally to slurs, as well as to emotively charged expletives. We don't think linguistic theory would be advanced by a claim that an expletive like "Fucking hell!" has a non-emotive, purportedly neutral core, perhaps something like "I am taken aback!" and a patina of tone. In the case of evaluative words, we argued that if there is to be any core, or sense, then it should correspond to a concept that is intrinsically evaluative, that is, an evaluative category. Let us go further in the case of slurs. Slurs do not just have bad tone, or bad presuppositions, or bad conventional implicatures. Their core meaning is a bad category: the category picked out by a slur is inherently negative within the ideology that gives that slur meaning.

We must be careful in naming slurs, but to illustrate, let us consider "fat cat" and "commie."[14] Both have uses in acts of derogatory name-calling, as well

13. Ashwell, "Gendered Slurs"; Burnett, "A Persona-Based Semantics for Slurs"; Foster, "Busting the Ghost of Neutral Counterparts." See also the discussion of the neutral counterpart view in Hess, "Slurs: Semantic and Pragmatic Theories of Meaning," 455–56.

14. We do not in this volume prescribe best practices as regards when slurs might reasonably be mentioned in academic discourse. Nonetheless, our arguments in the next section, and the arguments of scholars we will cite, suggest that some slurs can retain power to harm even when quoted. For this reason, we prefer to take a cautious approach, generally avoiding mention of slurs that we feel is unnecessary for our argument, but occasionally mentioning slurs when it is helpful to use an example or when discussing an example that has been discussed by other scholars, and only doing so for

as within in-group discussion to slur others who are not present. Yet, we take it that at the time of writing neither of them carry such a kick that its mere mention would be deeply upsetting to many people. The phrase "fat cat" exists within an ideology that views some aspects of the prevailing economic system, presumably including wealth inequality, as problematic. The phrase then has as its extension some set of individuals with an inappropriate amount of wealth or power. To predicate the term of one of these individuals is to pass a negative judgment on them for this reason. It is pointless to look for a neutral version of "fat cat." One might claim, for example, that "person" or "person with any amount of wealth and power" was the neutral core, but this would just beg the question of how predication of the term "fat cat" could come to reliably pick out a narrow segment of the population. The reference is clearly to a set of individuals not just with *any* amount of wealth and power, but to a set of individuals with *excessive* wealth and power, and the word "excessive" is normative.

Likewise, to call someone a "commie" is to judge them negatively, to judge them as belonging to a category that is despised within the ideology of the person who passes judgment. Now here one might object that surely "communist" is a neutral counterpart. We disagree, for the simple reason that there is nothing in the least neutral about the term "communist." And in particular, within the communities of practice that use "commie" as a slur, it is clearly the case that both communism and communists are seen as inherently problematic. To be a "commie" or a "communist," according to these ideologies, is just as bad as being a "Marxist," and not much different from being a "looney Marxist" (cf. the Dan Patrick quote in section 3.5). None of these terms neutrally pick out a set of individuals who subscribe to a particular set of political ideals or live within a national system characterized by such ideals.

It can be argued that all of the above terms related to communism are not merely nonneutral, but in fact have racist resonances, and are regularly deployed as a form of racist dog whistling, as we will discuss in the next section. In the ideology within which "commie" is commonly used, it not only categorizes someone negatively, but characterizes them as belonging to a category that is partly defined in terms of race and racial sympathies. Hitler, McCarthy, and many others have tied communism to Jews, and Jews were disproportionately represented as targets of McCarthy's Red Scare. But the racial overtones of communism-related words are more complex. The line "Some

---

slurs that, as best as we can tell, are unlikely to cause grave offense, and for which, as far as we can tell, the mention in an academic context does not in and of itself constitute to marginalization or silencing of others. Here we align with scholars Jyoti Rao (quoted in the coming discussion), and follow a policy close to that suggested by Cassie Herbert, "Exclusionary Speech and Constructions of Community," chapter 5, "Talking about Slurs," 130–60.

say it's a communist plot" from Nina Simone's powerful protest song "Mississippi Goddam" concerns a separate but interwoven racist thread connecting African-Americans, and the goals and successes of the Civil Rights movement, to communist agitation. Martin Luther King Jr. was regularly accused of being a communist. All of this makes sense once one considers the one thing that all these groups, that is, Jews, Blacks, and communists, have in common from the point of view of extreme right-wing discriminatory ideologies: they are all out-groups. Lumping out-groups together into one vast plot is at the heart of conspiracy theorizing. It makes the story about the enemy infinitely simpler than the confounding detail of reality.

There is nothing neutral about the word "communist," or about the concept it picks out, within the discriminatory ideologies that have also offered us "pinko," "lefty," and sneering uses of "comrade." Similar comments apply to the supposedly neutral counterparts of explicitly racial slurs, like the N-word. Neither "Black" nor "African-American" nor any other phrase is a neutral counterpart. The N-word is deployed within ideologies in which none of these words are neutral. In fact, although within the practice the three different terms (the N-word, "Black," and "African-American") are involved in differing categories, all of them may have roughly the same denotation within a particular discriminatory ideology. Within such an ideology, all three terms could pick out a despised out-group category whose extension is understood in essentialist terms, whose members are associated with various stereotypical features and are treated in various oppressive ways. To reprise our comments in chapter 7, while we are not sure that the idea of a neutral concept is even coherent, we certainly doubt that any racial or ethnic categorization could possibly be neutral, since perspective and social location are always relevant to the functioning of communicative acts that involve race and ethnicity.

One of Foster's points is that the supposedly neutral counterparts to slurs can in fact be used to slur. That is, people sometimes use "Black," "Mexican," and "Jew" in an insulting way. Since we don't think they are neutral, let's just call common names for racial, ethnic, and religious groups that are often used without derogation such as these *standard socioethnic group terms*. What, then, is the relationship between standard socioethnic group terms, which are not normally thought of as slurs, and the corresponding terms that are standardly recognized as slurs? We suggest that the difference is that whereas the slurring terms are actively used only within communities of practice with discriminatory ideologies, the parallel standard socioethnic group terms are used within broader communities of practice for which the ideologies are not discriminatory to the same extent, if at all.

As a result of its parallel use within a practice in a salient nondiscriminatory ideology, the use of a standard socioethnic group term does not in and of itself provide evidence as to whether it is being used within a discriminatory ideology. Nonetheless, it will sometimes become apparent that this is the case.

It might become apparent that the speaker is using the term as a slur, perhaps to name the very same role in an ideology that they might otherwise have used the slur term for. That could be because the speaker has signaled their racist ideology through separate means, whether the speaker has adopted a sneering tone or is making an inherently racist claim, or whether the speaker has chosen to refer to a socioethnic group at a point in a conversation where membership of that group would not be relevant outside of a racist ideology. It is, indeed, inevitable that sometimes standard socioethnic group terms will be used to pick out despised roles in discriminatory ideologies, because use of these words allows racists to slur while still maintaining some degree of plausible deniability.

For example, there are antisemitic communities of practice within which slurs are used to refer to Jewish people, and within these communities of practice the word "Jew" might be used coextensively, to label roughly the same people who would be labeled using the slur terms, or might be used to label a slightly different superset of people as would be labeled using the slur term. In either case, the use of "Jew" by people in this community is disdainful, and the disdain may often be manifest among interlocutors. Such an antisemitic community of practice can exist within a much larger broader community of practice, say speakers of American English. Let us assume that the broader community of practice is not, collectively, antisemitic. Then uses of the word "Jew" within this broader community of practice will usually not be acts of slurring, and will not reveal or signal disdain. It is only when a use of "Jew" is a performance of the practices of the antisemitic subcommunity that the use can be a slurring act. The question of when exactly we should take a use of "Jew" to represent the antisemitic practice, and when we should take it to exemplify the practice of the broader community, which by assumption is not intrinsically antisemitic, is always going to be difficult. That is where plausible deniability comes in. The difficulty in establishing which practice a use of the word "Jew" tokens, and hence what resonances are associated with that use, is one reason why an antisemite might on occasion choose to slur people using the term "Jew" rather than using a word that is specialized only for slurring.

The use of standard socioethnic terms by racists can be paralleled to the use of dog whistles. Both depend on the existence of two communities of practice with differing ideologies. A dog whistle has complex resonances, but different audience members are sensitive to different resonances and respond to them in different ways, which allows dog whistling to signal one thing to members of one community, and something else to members of the other community, and yet allow the speaker to maintain plausible deniability. A slurring use of a standard socioethnic term might similarly be described as having resonances that audience members are sensitive to in different ways. It follows that it would be misleading to describe standard socioethnic terms or dog whistles as "ambiguous" between different meanings, for this would suggest that on any occasion of use, one meaning was the correct and intended meaning, and the other was incorrect and not intended.

The true pragmatics of the discursive situation is still more complex. For as with dog whistles, the existence of the two ideologies is often well known to people on both sides of the ideological divide. In our terms, there are strong *second-order* attunements to both ideologies among at least some members of each community. When the racist slurs using a standard socioethnic term, they may intend a double entendre, or indeed succeed in producing it with no such intention. Some see their Janus-faced character, while others fail to see it, or avert their eyes. The metaphor of Janus is apt, for Janus was the Roman god of duality and portals between worlds. It might then be said that disguised slurring practices and dog whistles hang over slightly hidden portals between ideological communities, in which case canonical slurs are highly visible gates to ideological underworlds, opened to some and shut hard in the face of others.

There can be clear strategic value in using the terms "welfare" or "law and order" in ways that speakers know will be recognized as racist by many (if not all) in the less racist community of practice; the same is true when a politician uses a standard socioeconomic term in a racist way. Such uses draw joint attention to inherently divisive issues. These uses will be used strategically when someone in a racist community of practice sees utility in divisiveness. As we saw in chapter 6, such divisiveness is often not just incidental to political movements based around discriminatory ideologies, but is a core strategy. It is a way to form an antagonistic social-identity group, where membership is defined by opposition to another group. As the American far-right strategist Steve Bannon said in 2018, "Let them call you racists, let them call you xenophobes. Let them call you nativists. Wear it as a badge of honor."[15]

The relationship between standard socioethnic group terms and their distinctively slurring counterparts is a complex one. Within the same ideology, they may possibly have very similar meanings, but across ideologies they have at best the status of being something similar to translation equivalents. Since the ideologies are distinct (one being significantly more discriminatory than the other), Quine's problem of radical translation applies. Though certainly a term in one language might be a close counterpart of a term in another language, indicating that the terms play similar roles in the ideologies of their respective communities of practice, something is always, as they say, lost in translation.

The idea of untranslatable words is a familiar one, although it is a curious fact that online lists of untranslatable Yiddish words are typically paired with definitions. In this strange hinterland of borrowed meaning, we note a similarity between borrowings and slurring uses of standard socioethnic group

---

15. Bannon's remarks were made in a speech at a rally of the Front National in France, and reported later that day in Adam Nossiter, "'Let Them Call You Racists': Bannon's Pep Talk to National Front," *New York Times*, March 10, 2018.

terms. Many Yiddish words are borrowed into English, and thence become enmeshed in entirely new communicative practices, so that it is doubtful that they mean the same thing as they did in their original language setting. It is curious that something may be lost when a word is "translated" into itself. How the resonances of a Yiddish borrowing in English are related to the resonances of the original depends on how the history of the practice of using the word is sliced and diced. And there is no fact of the matter. There are just different language users with their own partial awarenesses of different parts of the extension of a practice that has crossed between worlds.

So it is with slurring uses of standard socioethnic group terms, so that racists and nonracists use the same standardized words for races or ethnic groups. Perhaps one should rather describe this situation as being one where it is not well defined whether the word used by racists and nonracists is the same; what is clear is that the usages belong to distinct subpractices in different subcommunities, and that the resonances of these subpractices are distinct. Likewise, left-wing Americans and right-wing Americans have rather different understandings of words like "communist," "liberal," and "fascist," both in the sense that they would understand the terms as applying to different sets of people, and in the sense that members of one group might use them as slurs when the other would not. Different people have different awarenesses of the resonances the words carry. It is a discomforting situation, and that is part of the reason they are so used.

Let us mention one further example that is revealing of the intricacies of words that are not exactly slurs as the term is usually understood: the word "boy." At first blush, at least if we were not writing in a sociopolitical context, the word "boy" might seem as neutral, ordinary, and banal as the word "dog." Yet like "dog," the word "boy" has distinctive resonances. Any use of a diminutive form or reference to someone as if they were a child implies a lack of respect for them. And within certain discriminatory ideologies, this particular word is involved in a very special practice indeed, one interwoven with the awful history of slavery and oppression in the United States. Neither is this practice dead. President Donald Trump's first attorney general, it turns out, repeatedly addressed at least one black assistant US attorney as "boy."[16] To the extent that any word is innocent, in the sense of lacking specifically discriminatory resonance, it may easily be sullied in the mouth of the racist.

16. A CNN news report runs as follows:

> Thomas Figures, a black assistant US attorney who worked for Sessions, testified that Sessions called him "boy" on multiple occasions and joked about the Ku Klux Klan, saying that he thought Klan members were "OK, until he learned that they smoked marijuana." (Scott Zamost, "Sessions Dogged by Old Allegations of Racism," CNN, November 18, 2016, https://www.cnn.com/2016/11/17/politics/jeff-sessions-racism-allegations)

As attorney general, Sessions was active in using legal means to crack down on marijuana use, but not in using legal means to restrict discrimination.

10.2. *Slurring*

The resonances of swearwords and slurs (particularly when used in acts of slurring) impinge themselves on the hearer like an inebriated gatecrasher at a party, drawing attention to themselves, brash, enervating, obdurate, and even violent. Slurs have the power to *wound*, perhaps in a way that demands legal remedies.[17] One slur in particular has been described as "the nuclear bomb of racial epithets."[18] In reaction to the use of this slur by White TV personality Bill Maher, the rapper Ice Cube, who is Black, compared the slur's power to the stab of the knife, observing that it wounds independently of the intentions of the speaker:

> I think there's a lot of guys out there who cross the line because they're a little too familiar, or they think they're too familiar. Or, guys that, you know, might have a black girlfriend or two that made them Kool-Aid every now and then, and then they think they can cross the line. And they can't. You know, it's a word that has been used against us. It's like a knife, man. You can use it as a weapon or you can use it as a tool. It's when you use it as a weapon against us, by white people, and we're not going to let that happened again . . . because it's not cool. . . . That's our word, and you can't have it back. . . .
>
> It's not cool because when I hear my homie say it, it don't feel like venom. When I hear a white person say it, it feel like that knife stabbing you, even if they don't mean to.[19]

Philosophy and law scholar Patricia J. Williams has said of that same slur: "It hits in the gut, catches the eye, knots the stomach, jerks the knee, grabs the arm."[20] Such effects seem almost magical. How do we explain them in terms of conventional properties of words?

---

17. Delgado, "A Tort Action for Racial Insults, Epithets, and Name Calling," which was originally published in 1982 as "Words That Wound: A Tort Action for Racial Insults, Epithets, and Name Calling," *Harvard Civil Rights-Civil Liberties Law Review*, 133–81.

18. Chideya, *The Color of Our Future*, 9.

19. Ice Cube (O'Shea Jackson Sr.) made his remarks on *Real Time with Bill Maher*, June 9, 2017. The quote appears in Kristine Phillips, "'That's Our Word, and You Can't Have It Back': Ice Cube Confronts Bill Maher for Using the N-Word," *Washington Post*, June 10, 2017. The quote is used to make a similar point to ours in Henderson, Klecha, and McCready, "Response to Pullum on Slurs."

20. Patricia J. Williams, "Sensation," *The Nation*, May 6, 2002, 9. Williams is objecting specifically to the extensive discussion of the N-Word in a much-cited book by Randall Kennedy that actually uses the offensive epithet as the first word of its title. Williams, after reporting on an incident in which someone brandished the book in front of her on a bus, is dubious about Kennedy's choice of title. She comments, after describing the emotive power of the word, that "Kennedy milks this phenomenon only to ask with an entirely straight face: 'So what's the big deal?'"

Slurs have been at the center of discussions of harmful speech because of their distinctive power to harm. But slurs have attracted such attention to theorists in philosophy of language and linguistics because they seem to have the surprising property of being able to do such harm *as words*. Given what we have called the standard model, it is not clear how this could be so. The most standard route taken in literature on the meaning of slurs, discussed below, emphasizes the role of the hearer. On this type of view, even someone who utters a slur to the face of a victim in a direct act of name-calling at most expresses or conveys their own negative attitude, thus derogating the victim. That is where the conventional meaning of the slur stops. Any further negative effects on hearers would have to result from pragmatically mediated processes that lead them to take offense.

While we don't doubt that pragmatic reasoning comes into play, as with all human communication, such an account puts the jackboot on the wrong foot, and dangerously so. Although we don't for a moment imagine that this has been the intent of past scholars, it seems to us that this way of looking at the harms of hate speech has much the same abstract structure as victim-blaming rhetoric does in general. Our argument will be that slurs are not merely *offensive* but *injurious*.[21]

We take slurs to be imbued with dangerous power, and yet we do not think them magical. Quite the opposite. As we will suggest below, slurs are about as ordinary as language gets. The properties of slurs, such as their powers to wound, to grab attention, and to reveal ideology, can be analyzed in terms of resonance, but that is not in itself remarkable: it is how we propose to analyze all conventionalized linguistic meaning in this volume. If we are on the right track in proposing our resonance-based framework, then no special grammatical mechanisms are needed for slurs. The job of this section of the chapter is to convince the reader that insofar as slurs are a sound test case we are indeed on the right track.

Before proceeding, let us briefly recap the features of our framework. Words have resonances, all the things that are found in the contexts in which they are used. People and collections of people have attunements, which are ways of behaving, thinking, and feeling about things. When people have attunements to a word, that means not only that they have theoretical knowledge of what the word means and how it fits into the grammar, but also that they have practical knowledge. That means both that they use the word and react to use

---

21. In contrasting *offense* with *injury*, we are inspired by Charles Lawrence's discussion of racist speech: "The word offensive is used as if we were speaking of a difference in taste, as if I should learn to be less sensitive to words that 'offend' me. I cannot help but believe that those people who speak of offense—those who argue that this speech must go unchecked—do not understand the great difference between offense and injury" ("Regulating Racist Speech on Campus," 74).

of the word in ways that are appropriate to the community of practice within which the word is found.

As we have set things up, resonance and attunement are two sides of the same coin. To be attuned to any practice is to have a tendency for change of behavior and state in accord with the resonances of the practice. Our notion of harmony concerns the fact that people feel dissonance when they sense a clash of salient attunements, and consonance when they feel alignment and coherence. An ideology is then a set of collective attunements of a community of practice, a set that the community has harmonized around. Those attunements can include, among other things, ways of using and reacting to words, ways of treating people, ways of looking at the world, and emotional and social attitudes. We introduced a subtype of ideologies, *discriminatory ideologies*, those that include attunements to in-group/out-group distinctions, and in which members of out-groups are valued less than members of in-groups, and hence as inherently deserving of less than equal treatment or resources.

Against these background notions, here are the main points of our account of slurring:

1. *Discriminatory practice*: Slurring labels the target using a negatively evaluative predicate, a slur. The label identifies the target with a disdained, despised, or hated out-group category within a discriminatory ideology, and in this sense, slurring is a *discriminatory practice*.

2. *Presupposed ideology*: Since any communicative action presupposes the ideology within which the action constitutes an exemplar of a practice, so the discriminatory ideology is presupposed by the slurring action.

3. *Attention*: By labeling someone using the slur category, slurring draws attention to whatever properties are stereotypically associated with that category in the discriminatory ideology. Since the discriminatory ideology coexists with an ideology that does not discriminate in the same way, performance of the discriminatory practice also draws attention to broader differences between the ideologies, and thence to the discriminatory ideology more broadly.

4. *Resonances*: The resonances of the slur include these attentional and emotional effects on members of the target group, a range of attunements belonging to the presupposed discriminatory ideology, a demarcation of in-group and out-group, and power differentials between these groups.

5. *In-group attunement*: For an in-group member, attunement to the slurring practice includes feeling such emotions as hatred, superiority, and consonance with the in-group when involved in a slurring interaction as speaker or hearer.

6. *Out-group attunement*: For an out-group member exposed to the slur-ring practice, attunement implies experience of painful loss of face, painful confrontation with the discriminatory ideology to which attention has been drawn, and further dissonance. The dissonance involves a dramatic conflict between desired private face and public face, and in many cases between a desired way of life and life as a member of an oppressed group.[22]

In a nutshell, to slur is to label an individual or group with a despised role within a discriminatory ideology. Within the ideology, the category is associated with distinctive stereotypical features that do not correspond to features that those outside the community of practice assigned to roughly the same set of individuals. The low valuation of these out-group members implies that to a greater or lesser extent, depending on the particular category and the particular ideology, to judge someone as belonging to the category is to judge them as despicable. In acts of slurring, slurs name a category that only exists as such within that ideology.[23] Slurring someone, then, locates them within the ideol-

22. For more extensive discussion of the role of face in slurring, see Croom, "How to Do Things with Slurs."

23. Our analysis of the labeling function of slurs is close to that of Quill Kukla. Kukla adopts terminology from Louis Althusser and later work that includes that of Judith Butler, suggesting that slurs "hail" or "interpellate" the target, positioning them within an ideology:

> Slurs . . . are hails that, like all interpellations, recognize a subject . . . as having a specific identity, and thereby help constitute them as having that identity by calling upon them to recognize themselves as having it and hence as subjected to sets of norms. Specifically, they are interpellations that recognize a subject . . . as having a (1) generic, (2) derogated, and (3) subordinated identity. (Kukla, "Slurs, Interpellation, and Ideology," 19)

Our suggestion that accommodation is a process of harmonization in response to external social stimuli that can be gradual, which we have linked to Klemperer's "tiny doses of arsenic," echoes Kukla's idea that the interpellating impact of hails seems to assume (or presuppose) that someone has a certain identity, and that the effects of this assumption can be gradual:

> In hailing someone, the hail has to recognize that person as already having a certain identity, and, through what often gets called "constitutive misrecognition," the one hailed must in fact come to be (at least incrementally more) the self she is recognized as being, by recognizing herself as properly recognized by the hail. I need not be conscious of an interpellation as an interpellation in order for it to work, but paradigmatically, upon being successfully interpellated, I have an experience of recognizing that it is "really me" who has been recognized as having the identity I have. ("Slurs, Interpellation, and Ideology," 13)

Though we follow Kukla in several respects, our analysis of slurs differs both because we set our account in terms of our own idiosyncratic approach to ideology and speech practice, based on resonance, attunement, and harmonization, but also because we consider

ogy, but it also locates the speaker.[24] Put simply, the slurring practice is performed by in-group members and names members of an out-group category, hence locating representatives of both groups in relationship to the other.

To see how the account works, we'll first consider mild insults, and then move on to stronger slurs. Let's start with the insult "muppet," which is conventionalized in the United Kingdom to suggest something similar to "airhead" in the United States.[25] The resonances of "muppet" build on associations with the soft puppets that came to fame in the television shows *Sesame Street* and *The Muppet Show*, and are suggestive of someone who tends not to act or speak in an incisive, intelligent, or self-directed way. The resonances of "muppet" include not just the features that an individual so-described, the target, might be expected to have, but also emotions, dispositions, and cognitive attitudes.

The emotions, dispositions, and cognitive attitudes on the speaker's side are different than those on the target's side. Emotionally, it is clear that the speaker looks down on the intelligence of the target. The speaker is expected to feel superior, and the target inferior. Dispositionally, the resonances include ways of using "muppet" and ways of reacting to it. A resonance of the term is that it is not simply used to insult people, although it can be, but is also used to upbraid people in a mildly affectionate manner—"You muppet!" To be attuned to the UK "muppet" practice is to use it appropriately and to react to its use appropriately, for example, not feeling cut to the bone when somebody calls you a muppet, but rather feeling a little sheepish about whatever unfortunate thing you have done without thinking properly.

The ideology associated with derogatory use of "muppet" includes various practices of using the word, but also ideas about the type of intelligent and independent behavior that can be expected of people. Insulting uses of the term betray people's values: the slurring use of "muppet" always belittles the target's competence, and a harsher use, although far from being a strong slur ("Get the f- out of my way, you stupid f-ing muppet"), further betrays a strong differential in competence, and possibly power, between speaker and target.

Similar remarks apply to the Southern US use of "precious," in phrases like "Aren't you precious!" except that here being fully attuned to it means reacting to its use in a way that reflects the fact that you are probably not being complimented, but insulted. Southern US "precious" and other expressions that damn with praise ("Bless your heart!") are associated with an ideology in

---

properties of slurs that are not the primary targets of Kukla's work, notably exigence and hyperprojectivity.

24. As Kukla puts it, "The use of a slur, whether targeted directly at its victim or used among insiders, helps generate multiple interrelated subject positions; it does not merely constitute the identity of the one slurred" ("Slurs, Interpellation, and Ideology," 31).

25. For discussion and explanation of the reasons why there is variation in the offensiveness of different slurs, see Jeshion, "Expressivism and the Offensiveness of Slurs."

which a distinction is made between two types of people: those who have got it together and keep things running as they ought, and a second group about whom the best we can say is that they are, for example, cute or deserving of the Good Lord's love, but are functionally less than fully competent.

Let us consider the extent to which "muppet" and "precious" are not merely insults, but slurs. Given our outline account of slurs, this will hold if these terms label people with disdained or despised out-group roles within discriminatory ideologies. Here we come to a point in our account that we have left open: the question of what exactly constitutes a group. One might go further than we have, and require of an out-group that it is viewed as having sufficient social cohesion that the members of the out-group form a distinctive community of practice in their own right, or that the members of the out-group jointly regard membership of the group as part of their identity. In that case, neither "muppet" nor "precious" would be slurs. We have also suggested that, at least in paradigmatic cases of ethnic and gendered slurs, part of the attention-grabbing and revelatory power of the slur comes from contrast, a clash of ideologies that value groups differently. It is far from clear that those using the word "muppet" are beholden to an ideology that is in sharp contrast with an alternative ideology that more fully values people whose actions betray a lack of awareness and control.

While it might be possible to define the technical term *slur* so as to be limited to a small set of words that everybody can agree are clear slurs, let us take a more pragmatic approach, allowing that slurs vary on a scale of strength. We suggest that a slur is *stronger* (a) the more reviled the target group is within the discriminatory ideology, (b) the more the group picked out by the slur itself constitutes a distinct community of practice that is central to the identity of the out-group's members, (c) the greater the extent to which the slur use is associated with a history of oppression of the target group, (d) the greater the power of the in-group over the out-group, and (e) the stronger the contrast is between the discriminatory ideology within which the slurring practice exists and another prevalent ideology that does not devalue those in the out-group.

On this basis, the derogatory terms "muppet" and "precious" are weak slurs, perhaps so weak that some would wish to create a cutoff and say they are not slurs at all but merely members of a broader class of "pejoratives" or "insults." The term "fat cat" is a somewhat stronger slur, because it is clearer that its use involves a clash of ideologies, although here one might say that, definitionally, out-group members are the ones with power, the oppressors rather than the oppressed. We take it that according to the ideology within which some are viewed as "fat cats," at least some of the practices and tenets of free-market capitalism are not supported. On the other hand, we presume that some of those being labeled "fat cats" belong to a community of practice within which the practices that led to their wealth and power are acceptable.

Note that in the "fat cat" case it is perfectly possible that both the ideology of the slurrer and the ideology of the slurred, the fat cats themselves, are discriminatory: the difference is that in only one of these ideologies is the target group itself reviled.

We do not attempt any general taxonomy of slurs here, and leave it to the reader to consider where other slurs might fall in the spectrum. What we hope is clear is that the "nuclear bomb of racial epithets" will on this basis be a paradigmatic example of a strong slur, with (a) a high level of disdain for the target group, (b) the target group itself forming a clear community of practice that is important in shaping the identity of its members, (c) an ugly history of oppression, (d) systemic power differentials operating against the target group, and (e) a decisive clash of ideologies providing highly contrastive valuations for the target group. Such a slur is also paradigmatic in exhibiting the six properties we previously ascribed to slurs in our account: (1) use of the slur is itself a clear discriminatory practice, locating the target within a system in which they have reduced access to rights and resources, (2) the speaker presupposes a racist ideology, (3) the use of the slur draws attention to both stereotypical characteristics of the target group within the discriminatory ideology and to the discriminatory ideology itself, (4) the slur is highly resonant, emotionally, socially, and cognitively, (5) in in-group uses, speakers and hearers feel such emotions as hatred, superiority, and consonance with other racists, and (6) out-group members exposed to the slurring practice, can, if attuned to the practice, experience painful loss of face, painful confrontation with the racist ideology, and further dissonance.

Strong slurs somehow manage not merely to stick a knife into someone, but to open up old wounds, indeed an entire history of wounding behavior. A recent paper by Elin McCready and Chris Davis offers a metaphor that is striking and helpful, even if it does, contra our view, paint a portrait of slurs as somehow magical:

> A sorcerer stands atop a high cliff by the sea. He raises his hands and pronounces a single word; a submerged island rises above the waves, covered with cyclopean masonry and dripping sea plants which make the precise angles of the constructions and their outlines indistinct. . . . The sorcerer has summoned up a city of the past from beneath the sea, where it had heretofore lain invisible. The sorcerer can do so even without knowing every detail of what lies in the city, how it is arranged, or what the consequences of calling it up will be. Utterance of the summoning word is sufficient for the invocation. No one person observing the summoning can see all features of the conjured object. This includes the sorcerer himself.
>
> We suggest that this case is (surprisingly) analogous to the function of slurs. The sorcerer has used a powerful word to call up a hidden,

ruined city; slurs, on our view, also bring a preexisting complex of historical facts and constructed attitudes (stereotypes) about the slurred group to attention, in addition to predicating group membership in the manner of a standard nominal. However, as with the obscured nature of the summoned city, it is hard for any one person to discern exactly what those attitudes are, or what the precise historical facts being deployed are.[26]

How can a single word both wound and reveal an entire ideology? As Lewis Carroll's Humpty Dumpty says (though not of slurs), "When I make a word do a lot of work like that, I always pay it extra."[27] The currency in which slurs are paid (or rather, in which they demand payment) is *attention*.

On the view we have developed, every word is associated with a mass of resonances, essentially everything that is reliably present in contexts of use. These resonances include arbitrary features of the prevailing ideology and its constituent practices within the word's community of practice. In general, no one community member can possibly have access to all those features, since the full set of resonances exists only in the aggregate, that is, as a collective attunement that is not identical to any individual's attunement. For most expressions, the bulk of ideological resonances are not of great salience when the word is used. Relevant aspects of the ideological background of the interlocutors are assumed to be shared to the extent that it matters for the word to perform whatever function it is being used for.

When one uses the word "apple," one is assuming a way of looking at the world that allows categorization according to fruit-type, but one is usually not attempting to draw attention to that background. In exchanges among adult English speakers, interlocutors using the word "apple" are part of the same relevant community of practice, with common understanding of the category. Even though this understanding is at a collective level, individuals can reasonably be expected to have similar personal attunements to the word, to apples, and to practices involving apples. So whatever differences there might be in attunements are not expected to greatly limit the ability of interlocutors to connect with each other. And if there are minor differences in attunement to apples, in most contexts this will not be emotionally or socially significant. In the terminology of chapter 6 (section 6.4), a use of the word "apple" is typically not *meaningful*. That is, using the word "apple" does not draw attention to the background ideology relevant to apples, because that ideology has no personal or social significance. This is where slurs differ from names for fruit. But it is precisely where slurs are similar to brand names, such as "Apple." What makes the brand name powerful, a trademark worth protecting, is its ability to draw

26. McCready and Davis, "An Invocational Theory of Slurs," 2.
27. Carroll, *Alice in Wonderland*, 191.

attention with a mere mention to a powerful array of associations—the brand identity.

What McCready and Davis illustrate is that when a slur is used, an associated ideology becomes powerfully salient, as do categorizations of group membership that are licensed by that ideology. People do not use a slur simply to help identify a particular object in the world, like identifying a piece of fruit one would like with one's packed lunch. Rather, people use a slur to draw attention to a way of thinking about a human being. An important resonance of any slur is a high level of attention paid by interlocutors to the *ideological resonances* of the slur, in the sense of chapter 2 (section 2.6), and to its significance vis-à-vis group membership of the speaker and whoever is being labeled as belonging to the slur category. For a hearer, this change in attention, like the emotional impact of the slur, is largely involuntary. Aspects of the ideology are primed by the use of the slur. In this respect, the hearer cannot help but harmonize with the speaker, in the sense that a result of the slurring act is that the interlocutors share joint attention on an ideology, even if it is an ideology one or both reject.

McCready and Davis provide an insightful way of thinking about the power of slurs. But their quote seems to suggest that slurs are remarkable, almost magical.[28] To repeat, we do not think slurs are magical. Quite the opposite. Analyzing the meaning and function of slurs requires the postulation of no dedicated or extraordinary additional mechanisms within the resonance-based framework.

It might be countered that we have in fact introduced hundreds of pages of machinery. Here we can only aver that we take the machinery we have introduced to be motivated by general considerations of the nature of communication, and political language in particular. The concepts we use in accounting for the meaning of slurs—naming, presupposition, resonance, attention, and ideology—are concepts we take to be needed for the treatment of all political language, and indeed we are far from being the only ones to apply such concepts in this arena.

Slurs are the epitome of political language. They make an emotive in-your-face socially significant us-them distinction that forces people implicitly onto

28. It is unclear to us to what extent McCready and Davis would agree with us that the linguistic mechanisms needed for an analysis of slurs are not unusual. Certainly, there is a mathematical level at which their analysis, worked out in technical detail in their paper, involves only machinery also found in the analysis of other expression types. But they would perhaps accept or even take it as a positive that many aspects of their analysis are far from being standard in formal semantics. It would take us too far afield to attempt a detailed discussion of their formal analysis here. We merely note that we see McCready and Davis's paper as working out a somewhat parallel intuition to that driving our own arguments, and we hope that the relationship between the accounts can be better exposed in future work.

one side or another. In doing so, they attune people to the mores of a discriminatory ideology presupposed by the slur. And yet we claim that slurs are grammatically unexceptional, no more complex than any descriptive name. Slurs are exceptional among descriptive names only for the way their naming depends on ideological distinctions that are themselves divisive.

The linguist Geoff Nunberg can be credited with most clearly centering the importance to understanding slurs of considering the community of practice within which they are used.[29] As he memorably explains, "Here's my thesis in a nutshell: racists don't use slurs because they're derogative; slurs are derogative because they're the words that racists use." [30] Taken as a claim about sufficient and necessary conditions for slurs being derogative, Nunberg's claim doesn't quite hold up. Those subscribing to Nazi ideology in Hitler's Germany can surely be described as racist, and, as Klemperer makes vivid, this community had a range of distinctive language practices. Most of the language practices that Klemperer discussed were not slurs at all. Indeed, many of them were words or phrases that would not have stood out as racist at all, were it not for the careful way in which Klemperer characterized their relationship to broader Nazi ideology. Nonetheless, Nunberg is right to center the derogating power of racist slurs on the properties of the people who use them, racists. At risk of watering down his pithy remark, let us just suggest a friendly addition: racial "slurs are derogative because they're the words that racists use" to label people they take to belong to other races.[31]

Although some slurs are used primarily within an in-group to refer among themselves to out-group members (as in the case of slur terms for rarely seen foreign enemies), most slurs are also used for acts of derogatory name-calling, that is, slurring to someone's face. Slurring to someone's face differs from other

29. The importance of distinguishing communities of practice, and their associated ideologies, is important in much of the work on reclamation, for example, Hess, "Practices of Slur Use"; and Popa-Wyatt, "Reclamation: Taking Back Control of Words." However, the notion of practice plays at most a minor role in most theories of the meaning of slurs in their canonical pejorative uses.

30. Nunberg, "The Social Life of Slurs," 244.

31. Slurs derogate because they are prominent within racist communities of practice and conjure up discriminatory ideologies; this explains why intention is not essential to the power of a slur to harm. A related point is that by explaining the power of the slur in terms of a community rather than in terms of the social position or authority of a speaker, we can explain how slurs used by people lacking high social position or authority can still wound with their words, as in the case of children slurring. Our strategy of locating the power of slurs relative to a larger group than the individual speaker means that our analysis is somewhat parallel to Ishani Maitra's analysis of hate speech (Maitra, "Subordinating Speech"). Her notion of "derived authority" allows the necessary authority for a hateful act to be licensed not by the intrinsic authority of the speaker, but by the authority the speaker inherits from a social group that they are taken to represent. Central to her analysis is the idea that this authority may effectively be given implicitly, as when onlookers to a hateful act are silent and their silence is taken as assent.

acts of addressing in that its primary function is to derogate and hurt the addressee by drawing attention to characteristics listed above:

   a. their membership of the out-group category, and hence the location within the ideology;

   b. their despicability from the perspective of the in-group;

   c. stereotypical features of the out-group, and distinctive oppressive practices toward it.

Note that simply naming an ideology draws attention to the ideology, but is not offensive. We can refer to fascism or racism or sexism without offending anyone, unless someone thinks that by doing so we are also labeling them as having a despised ideology. Using or mentioning these terms is not (re-)enacting a practice within these ideologies, so it does not sustain the ideologies. It also does not necessarily cause anyone to lose public face, because it does not explicitly label anyone. The victim of a name-calling act of slurring loses public face, and will recognize that public loss of face to the extent that they are attuned to the utterance situation. The offensiveness and hurtfulness of a slur depends on its drawing attention to aspects of an ideology that are offensive to a person who is slurred because the ideology debases that person and normalizes oppressive practices against them.

ACCOUNTS OF SLUR MEANING

Here are three views in the literature on slurs that agree with us in the claim that slurs are grammatically unexceptional.[32] The first is the view that the force of a slur derives from is what is known as a *conventional implicature*, meaning an extra component of meaning that is conventionalized, but completely independent of the semantic contribution the word makes to truth conditions. Such a view has been defended in linguistics by Christopher Potts and in philosophy by Timothy Williamson.[33] According to this view, slurs are grammatically unexceptional, since conventional implicature is an already known category of conventional meaning that does not impact assertive content. Asserting a sentence containing a slur predicates something about a group, and conventionally implicates something very negative about that group.

    A second view on which slurs are grammatically unexceptional is due to Christopher Hom. According to Hom, the meaning of a slur incorporates various stereotypically present characteristics, so that "fat cat" would presumably

32 . For broader overviews of the slurs literature, see, for example, Popa-Wyatt, "Slurs, Pejoratives, and Hate Speech"; and Hess, "Slurs: Semantic and Pragmatic Theories of Meaning."

33. Potts, "The Expressive Dimension"; Williamson, "Reference, Inference and the Semantics of Pejoratives."

mean something like "individual who has an inappropriately large amount of money and power." Here is his analysis of a slur word for Chinese people (which we have removed from the quote):

> The epithet [slur word for Chinese people] expresses a complex, socially constructed property like: ought to be subject to higher college admissions standards, and ought to be subject to exclusion from advancement to managerial positions, and . . . , because of being slanty-eyed, and devious, and good-at-laundering, and . . . , all because of being Chinese.[34]

In Hom's view, the meaning of a sentence in which a slur is used to predicate a property of an individual is a gigantic conjunction of all the things that stereotypically hold of people in the slur category according to a racist ideology.[35]

A third view in the literature on slurs is that their special effects result from presuppositions. Phillipe Schlenker is an example of a linguist following this line, and it is seen in work by philosophers such as Bianca Cepollaro and (in single and joint work) Manuel García-Carpintero and Teresa Marques.[36] Again, presupposition is a standard grammatical notion, so this does not in itself

---

34. Hom, "The Semantics of Racial Epithets," 432, ellipses in original.

35. There is much further nuance to Hom's analysis, since, like us, he has an externalist take on meaning. Thus he allows that people using the slur might be no more able to list all the properties of those in the slur category than is someone who uses the term "beech" or "elm" able to list the sufficient and necessary conditions associated with membership of different tree species (to use Putnam's famous motivating example for externalism, once again). However, there is also a disanalogy between Hom's presentation of his account of slurs and a Putnamian account of "elm." Putnam did not propose writing the meaning of "elm" as a conjunction of sufficient and necessary conditions for being an elm, and we presume that if asked to write the first-order meaning of "there is an elm," Putnam would simply have written $\exists x\, elm(x)$, rather than $\exists x\, tree(x) \wedge deciduous(x) \wedge \ldots$, although the question of how an externalist should represent a meaning depends on what the goal of representing a meaning is. To the extent that the representation is supposed to be akin to a mental representation, it seems to us that it would be odd to suppose that mental representations are similar to logical formulae with unspecified conjuncts, which Hom's have. If this is what the representations were for, then Hom's representation of "Fred is a Y" (where Y is a slur) could have simply been "Y(Fred)," rather than a long and largely unspecified conjunction. Hom's point, though, is that individual speakers can use slurs without knowing the truth-conditions of their statements, because the truth conditional meaning is sustained not by individuals alone, but by a community of speakers who share an ideology. Here, we agree with Hom.

36. To be clear, there is no clean division between philosophical and linguistic approaches to these issues, although we hope that the scholars in question would accept our broad-brushed characterizations of their work. The relevant papers are: Marques, "The Expression of Hate in Hate Speech"; García-Carpintero, "Pejoratives, Contexts and Presuppositions"; Marques and García-Carpintero, "Really Expressive Presuppositions"; Schlenker, "Expressive Presuppositions"; Cepollaro, "In Defence of a Presuppositional Account of Slurs." Related to the latter is Cepollaro and Stojanovic, "Hybrid Evaluatives," which

make slurs grammatically exceptional. Let us say that a narrowly presuppositional account of slurs is one in which whatever special powers are associated
with slurs or acts of slurring is claimed to derive from special presuppositions,
whether presuppositions that certain things hold in the world, or, for García-
Carpintero and Marques, special affective presuppositions. In that case, the
account we propose is not narrowly presuppositional, because the effects of
slurs in our account are not merely the results of accommodation (or rejection)
of presuppositions. We take it that many emotive and social resonances of slurs
are *effective* resonances, that is, these resonances are conventionalized effects
of slurring acts that are integral to the practices of using those slurs, and not
merely aspects of the contextual background that may sometimes be accommodated by hearers. On our view, slurring may sometimes trigger accommodation
of ideological background, or indeed trigger divergent accommodation against
that assumed background, but at least some emotional effects are central features of the slurring practice, and not accommodated presuppositions.

There is a more fundamental respect in which not just prior presuppositional
accounts but all three of the types of account distinguished above differ from
ours: they assume that the meaning of a slur has a neutral core, and that there
exists for each slur a neutral counterpart. Prior accounts are typically explicit
about these commitments. Indeed, it might be said that all three types of analysis
follow a long line of philosophical work by adopting divide-and-conquer strategies, aiming to simultaneously explain the phenomena of slurs and yet, as it were,
protect the neutral truth-conditional core of meaning. Thus have these prior
scholars sought to conservatively maintain the important advances in truth-
conditional approaches to meaning made over the last century.

Almost all prior analyses of slurs that provide detail about how the effects
of slurs arise consist of a neutral truth-conditional core plus some other component that is supposed to account for how slurs are used and the emotional
and social effects they have. If the extra component is not a conventional
implicature or a presupposition, then it's often some sort of pragmatic reasoning. This is the case, for example, in Hom's analysis, in which the truth
conditions of the slur are stated relative to the truth conditions of a neutral
counterpart, and the emotional and social effects of the slur are explained in
terms of a hearer's ability to pragmatically infer the speaker's negative attitude
and attachment to a problematic ideology.[37] Another family of approaches

---

generalizes the presuppositional approach to slurs to so-called *thick terms*, i.e., broadly the
sorts of evaluative adjectives we discuss in section 7.3.

37. Other examples of accounts in which the semantics of slurs is identified with a
neutral counterpart and pragmatic mechanisms are evoked to explain further properties
of slurs are Nunberg, "The Social Life of Slurs," and Bollinger, "The Pragmatics of Slurs."
Diana Blakemore offers a pragmatic variant in which the offensiveness of slurs is derived
from "meta-linguistic knowledge that the word is an offensive means of predicating and
referring" ("Slurs and Expletives," 34). She is explicit about the semantic content of slurs

not discussed above (although there are close relationships to both the conventional implicature account of Potts and to the presuppositional account of Marques and García-Carpintero) involves an expressive component of meaning; for example, the accounts of Joseph Hedger, Robin Jeshion, and Leopold Hess are of this type.[38] These accounts again assume that there is a semantic component of meaning which is neutral, and that slur words share this neutral semantic core with neutral counterparts.[39]

While several scholars have argued against slur meanings having neutral counterparts, we know of exactly one detailed semantic analysis of the slur meaning that neither makes a commitment to there being a neutral counterpart, nor defines a slur meaning in terms of a neutral core, namely the analysis of Heather Burnett.[40] It is instructive to consider Burnett's proposal in a little more detail, since her model of meaning, drawing on work of Peter Gärdenfors and others, provides one way of cashing out what a mental space of cognitive and emotional attunements might look like, and suggests a natural path for development of our own model, although not one we seek to follow in this volume.[41]

---

being identical to that of a neutral counterpart, for example stating that the words "dyke" and "lesbian" have identical semantics, these being exactly the cases that, as we will discuss, Heather Burnett convincingly argues cannot be semantically identical.

38. Hedger, "The Semantics of Racial Slurs"; Jeshion, "Expressivism and the Offensiveness of Slurs"; Hess, "Slurs and Expressive Commitments." Note that although Jeshion is committed to slurs having a neutral semantic core, her position on whether there are neutral counterparts is nuanced, first because she thinks that in slurring the extension of a term is sometimes contracted and sometimes extended, and second because she suggests that at least some slurs lack clear counterparts. Although Kent Bach ("Loaded Words: On the Semantics and Pragmatics of Slurs") contrasts his account of slurs with expressivist accounts, terming his view "loaded descriptivism," his view is related, and he explicitly makes the same assumption that slurs share a neutral core semantics with a neutral counterpart. Yet another account that explicitly separates the semantic component of slurs from an expressive component is that of Richards, *When Truth Gives Out*, especially chapter 1, "Epithets and Attitudes," 12–41. Richards offers an account in which slurs have both conventionalized expressive and conventionalized performative components in addition to a semantic component. He does assume there are neutral counterparts, noting, for example, "It is just not open to me to unilaterally detach the affect, hatred, and negative connotations tied to most slurs and use them interchangeably with their neutral counterparts" (41). However, Richards does not assume that the semantic value of slurs is identical to that of the neutral counterpart; rather he denies that sentences containing slur terms are even truth-evaluable.

39. Hess, for example, writes, "The derogatory meaning is not part of the semantic content of a slur (which is identical to its neutral counterpart)" ("Slurs and Expressive Commitments," 280).

40. Burnett, "A Persona-Based Semantics for Slurs."

41. Peter Gärdenfors, *The Geometry of Meaning*. As briefly noted in chapter 3, there is an abstract similarity between his model and ours, both using spatial metaphors. Gärdenfors's account of mental representation is far more technically elaborated than our own,

Burnett focuses on the predicate "dyke" and its supposed neutral counterpart "lesbian." Both can be used to slur, but it's also the case that both have well-established non-slurring and even prideful uses in LGBTQ+ communities that have undoubtedly affected practices and attitudes outside those communities, although this is certainly not to claim that the result of reclamation has been the elimination of slurring usages. Burnett argues that the semantic relationship between the two terms is far more complex than one entailing the other, and furthermore that people with different ideologies may represent the semantic relationship between the two predicates differently.

In Burnett's model, the two predicates express meanings that overlap within a complex multidimensional space, a space that includes evaluative dimensions. Since none of these dimensions are more fundamental to the meanings than any others, and it is the combination of different dimensions that jointly yields an overall affective value, there is no sense in which these meanings have a neutral core. Since neither of the two predicates are defined in terms of the other, and neither conceptual space includes the other, it cannot be said that one is the more basic counterpart of the other, even if it should happen to be the case that for some groups of speakers the words' extensions in the world stand in a subset relation or are even identical. Furthermore, there is no assumption that either word is affectively neutral, so even if there was some sense in which one was the more basic counterpart of the other, it would not be a neutral counterpart. Thus, in this account neither term is intrinsically neutral, neither has a neutral core, and they do not stand in any simple counterpart relation, let alone a neutral counterpart relation.

There are many differences between Burnett's account of slurs and our own, but we suppose that many of these relate to the fact that we set our account within our particular framework for the analysis of political and social aspects of communicative practice. We do not see this broader framework as inherently in tension with the main developments in Burnett's account of slurs. A more fundamental point of contrast is found in our respective analyses of word meaning: Burnett's model of meaning is static whereas ours is dynamic. For Burnett, the meaning of a predicate is a region of a multidimensional conceptual space, a static mental representation of a particular concept. For us, the meaning of any expression is a cluster of resonances that concern the situation prior, during, and after utterance. In this dynamic model there can be conventionalized effects of words and other expressions, for example the effect of making hearers feel good or bad. This is how we explain the exigence of slurs, their power to affect people. For Burnett any such effects must be conversational or perlocutionary effects, not built into the meaning

---

though he does not attempt to model what we term *dispositional attunements*, and he does not apply his model in the political or social sphere.

of a slur, but generated at some point in the process of comprehending that meaning and reacting to it. In this respect, Burnett's model is comparable to prior accounts of slurs that either take the contribution of the slur to be purely truth-conditional, and hence non-emotive, or take there to be some expressive component (perhaps a conventional implicature), but take that component to express the speaker's attitude. In all such analyses, unlike in our own account, the effects of slurs on hearers are taken to be indirect. It might be said that in prior accounts, including even Burnett's, uttering a slur is like showing someone a bullet with the target's name on. We claim that when you utter a slur you shoot the gun.

At a high level, our project in this volume of providing philosophically and linguistically satisfying analyses of political and social aspects of language led to the conclusion that the idealizations of the standard model were getting in the way, idealizations which were spelt out in the last chapter (section 9.2). It might be thought that avoiding standard idealizations would tend to make the analysis of linguistic phenomena harder. Quite to the contrary, our contention is that it is easier to analyze phenomena such as slurring, and oppressive language more generally, in a framework that, like the resonance-based framework of this volume, eschews those idealizations. For example, we think that assumptions such as those associated with the idealizations of *Neutrality* and *Language Homogeneity* and *Social Homogeneity* make it impossible to properly model slurring practices. Slurs cannot be analyzed in terms of neutral cores or neutral counterparts, and an analysis of slurs that assumes by default a fixed ideology among all speakers has to wrestle with nonexistent problems like the question of how it can be that the meaning of a standard socioethnic group term is both the same and different from the meaning of a slur. (Solution: the meaning of the standard socioethnic group term in one ideology cannot possibly be identical with the meaning of a slur in another, since they are completely different practices embedded within different systems of attunement, and for similar reasons we should expect the two predicates to have different resonances even within an ideology, even if both have slurring uses.)

We claim that once slurs are analyzed absent such idealizations, it becomes clear that they are grammatically unexceptional, and that slurring involves a mixture of linguistic practices that are each individually commonplace. This presents us with a challenge: *how can the stark effects of slurs be explained without postulating special mechanisms?* At the very least, a theory of slurs must account for three properties. Slurs are

1. **ideologically revelatory**, bringing a "complex of historical facts and constructed attitudes . . . to attention" even though "it is hard . . . to discern exactly what those attitudes are, or what the precise historical facts being deployed are," as McCready and Davis put it;

2. **exigent**, forcibly impacting hearers' emotional states;
3. **hyperprojective**, blurring the distinction between use and meaning.[42]

The reason slurs have become, rightly, a focus of scholarly interest is that they highlight conventional properties of language that are obscured by standard frameworks. Slurs make salient features of language that the standard model obscures, features that are also present, but less obviously so, with words that are not slurs. Like the pain we feel when kicked, what people experience as they absorb a slur has an immediacy and automaticity. A kick has the effect it has largely because of innate properties of the body. In contrast, attunement to the resonances of a slur is learned, rather than being a natural proclivity. In becoming attuned to a slur, people learn not only what a good dictionary might say the word means, but also ways of reacting to it. The experience of being labeled with a slur, including the emotional reaction and the dispositional reaction (e.g., a tendency to shrink into oneself, a tendency to fight back, or a tendency to attempt to educate) is something that develops over time. We will now show in more detail how the properties of slurs are to be explained within our resonance-based framework.

IDEOLOGICAL REVELATORINESS

The revelatoriness of slurs consists in the fact that the use of a slur draws attention to a nexus of practices, attitudes, and emotions that distinguish between an in-group and an out-group, in short, to a discriminatory ideology. The revelatoriness of slurs is unsurprising in the resonance framework we have set out, since, in a sense, every practice is at least *potentially* revelatory. Every practice presupposes the ideology of the community of practice that uses it.

The revelatoriness of slurs is distinctive for two reasons. First, the role that slurs name, or use to name, does not exist outside of a very specific ideology, an ideology that typically exists in contrast to other ideologies, such as the broader, less discriminatory ideology of a larger community of practice that does not engage actively in the slurring practice. The ideologies differ precisely in the way they discriminate, that is, in the different way they separate out social categories and the different cognitive, emotional, and dispositional attunements associated with those categories. Slurring, as we have said, draws attention to the role of an individual within a discriminatory ideology. As a consequence, slurring also draws attention to whatever features are recognized

---

42. The term *hyperprojective*, used as a description of the special tendency of slurs to have effects even when quoted, is taken from Elizabeth Camp ("A Dual Act Analysis of Slurs"). She says that a perspective (which functions in her theory much like ideologies and perspectives do in ours, with affective as well as cognitive dimensions) is "hyper-projective" in that "it . . . typically projects across indirect attitude and speech reports, which are supposed to be projection 'plugs'" (39).

as distinguishing between ideologies. These features are not merely resonances of the slur, but resonances that become salient when the slur is used. This is what we understand Davis and McCready to mean when they describe a slur as invoking a wealth of ideology, of bringing it into view. Even though every practice has ideological resonances, slurs are special because they bring those ideological resonances into sharp relief due to the salience of other communities of practice that do not share the ideology (presumably usually including communities that are targeted by the slur).

People vary in their individual attunements, so they are individually attuned, or second-order attuned, to various aspects of each of the ideologies to different extents. It is thus no surprise that, as Davis and McCready say, "it is hard . . . to discern exactly what those attitudes are, or what the precise historical facts being deployed are." Individuals are not expected to have full access to the collective attunements of even the community of practice they are part of, since, as we argued in chapter 2 (section 2.4), collective attunement does not imply universal individual or uniform attunement. This is a point where the notion of collective attunement crucially differs from more standard notions of common ground, which typically demand homogeneity of attitude. The expectation of full individual attunement to an ideology is even lower when we are talking about people outside the community of practice that shares that ideology, that is, when we are largely talking about second-order attunements. People who are not part of the actively slurring community of practice cannot be expected to be fully second-order attuned to the ideology of the slurring community.

What follows from these considerations is that an individual outside of the slurring community of practice who encounters a use of the slur can be expected to recognize that there is a mass of ways that the categorization associated with the slur differs from their own categories, and a mass of ways in which the discriminatory practices of the slurring group differ from their own practices, and yet not be able to say for certain exactly which attunements are crucial to the slurring ideology. Thus, the revelatory nature of slurring is paradoxical. The slur has revealed something dramatic, but it is not clear exactly what it consists in. The act conjures an intricate ruined city, and although it is hard to make out many of the individual taverns, steeples, and battlements, what comes suddenly into view is the central square. We see a soldier stamping on a face, a face perhaps like the addressee's. Here lies a type of hustle. It is unclear to the addressee what the details of the oppressive structure are. And indeed, perhaps it is unclear to the speaker, who might be just a child repeating a word they heard their parents use. Slurs are transparently bad acts, but the detailed intention of the speaker, exactly what they mean by saying of someone that they belong to the slur category, is never completely transparent, and may be totally opaque. Yet here we should note that our externalist view of meaning as resonance, whereby the locus of meaning is not the individual speaker but the community of practice, means that this type of hustle is common to all communicative practices: when someone says that a particular tree is a beech rather than an elm, their intentions can only be understood relative to a broader community of practice and the perspective that the community brings on particular practices of tree-labeling. Thus, this type of hustle is not particular to slurs.

More generally, it is not peculiar to slurs that they betray the existence of an "ancient city" of ideological associations. Let us here compare McCready and Davis's use of the ancient city metaphor to Wittgenstein's in the *Investigations*:

> Ask yourself whether our language is complete;—whether it was so before the symbolism of chemistry and the notation of the infinitesimal calculus were incorporated in it; for these are, so to speak, suburbs of our language. (And how many houses or streets does it take before a town begins to be a town?) Our language can be seen as an ancient city: a maze of little streets and squares, of old and new houses, and of houses with additions from various periods; and this surrounded by a multitude of new boroughs with straight regular streets and uniform houses.[43]

The view Wittgenstein expresses is akin to the view Rahel Jaeggi puts in terms of practices existing within a *nexus* of other practices, as discussed in section 2.3. What is missing from this passage of Wittgenstein's is any mention of a sorcerer. For the ideological revelatoriness of slurs is not magical but commonplace. The revelatory act does not involve *conjuring up* a complex nexus of practices, but drawing attention to it. Every language practice exists within and presupposes such a nexus. The practices, along with networks of supporting attunements, are there already, in the discriminatory ideology of a known community of practice. The ideological revelation offered by a slur consists merely in the fact that, due to contrast with an alternative ideology, the slur bathes the "ancient city" in the light of public attention. It turns out it was never submerged beneath the dark waters of a deep ocean to which some might have wished it banished. Indeed, the ancient city is not so distant, and not a complete city at all. It is simply a dangerous neighborhood that many find ugly, just across the tracks.

EXIGENCE

In section 2.6, we made a distinction between the *instrumental power* that communicative practices grant to discourse participants, and the *exigent power* associated with the practice itself, a power intrinsic to the practice and hard to resist, independently of the intention of the speaker. Slurs can serve as instruments of power, and are often wielded with the *intention* of establishing or reinforcing power, but it is the exigent power of slurs we focus on because slurs can harm even when not intended to. We have already seen at least one

---

43. Wittgenstein, *Philosophical Investigations*, 8, proposition 18.

example of this type, involving the comedian Bill Maher. Although Maher is a famously provocative figure, and it might well be said that he knew what he was doing in choosing the slur that he used, what he overtly did was mockingly label himself using the slur, rather than directly slurring anybody else. Despite this being a self-directed use of the slur, and despite (plausibly, at least) no conscious intention to derogate Black people, the result was Ice Cube's "knife stabbing you." Speakers can cause pain "even if they don't mean to."

Prior literature discusses both the immediate harms caused by slurs and other hate speech, and longer-term negative effects. At the longer-term end, Lynne Tirrell writes, "Few ask how language can make us actually sick. The key is to see how speech can generate toxic stress."[44] Mari Matsuda, though commenting on a wider range of hate speech than slurs alone, writes,

> The negative effects of hate messages are real and immediate for the victims. Victims of vicious hate propaganda have experienced physiological symptoms and emotional distress ranging from fear in the gut, rapid pulse rate and difficulty in breathing, nightmares, post-traumatic stress disorder, hypertension, psychosis, and suicide. Professor Patricia Williams has called the blow of racist messages "spirit murder" in recognition of the psychic destruction victims experience.[45]

In a legally oriented discussion of the need to remedy for the harms of hate speech, Charles Lawrence discusses a wide range of victim experiences, including his own as a teenager. He reports on the vivid account of a student of his facing a gay slur on a subway train, and who found "himself in a state of semi-shock, nauseous, dizzy, unable to muster the witty, sarcastic, articulate rejoinder he was accustomed to making," to which Lawrence adds that "it is a nearly impossible burden to bear when one encounters hateful speech face-to-face."[46]

Mihaela Popa-Wyatt and Jeremy Wyatt reference the same passage from Lawrence in arguing that "targets are affected as after a threat of physical assault."[47] While we are sympathetic to the main thrust of their arguments,

---

44. Tirrell, "Discursive Epidemiology," 117. While we take our approach to be compatible with Tirrell's, her focus is on the progressive harm caused by repeated encounters with toxic speech (an important topic for us too), and not so much on the mechanism by which an individual act produces harm, a focus in the current section. As we understand her account, the extreme negative effects that an individual speech act can have should be understood as resulting from an intolerable buildup of toxic stress, like the proverbial straw breaking a camel's back. This way of thinking usefully adds to the account we give here, in terms of attention, presupposed ideology, and emotional attunement.

45. Matsuda, "Public Response to Racist Speech," 2336–37. The Patricia Williams reference is to Williams, "Spirit-Murdering the Messenger."

46. Lawrence, "Regulating Racist Speech on Campus," 70.

47. Popa-Wyatt and Wyatt, "Slurs, Roles and Power," 2897.

let us note in passing that we differ from Popa-Wyatt and Wyatt as regards their analysis of the wounding effects of slurs as perlocutionary, which suggests that they are pragmatically mediated effects of slurring actions rather than being conventionalized as one of the primary functions of the action. We are not sure what sort of argument or evidence would distinguish cleanly between illocutionary and perlocutionary effects, but the distinction is anyway not significant within our resonance-based framework. If an effect is regularly associated with an action of a given type, then it is a resonance of that action. Wounding is regularly present when slurs are used; hence wounding is a resonance of slurring, a part of the practice.

Here is Jyoti Rao, an academic psychotherapist, arguing against academics even mentioning powerful slurs, and placing their use in a clinical context with further supporting citation from the psychoanalytic literature:

> My personal choice to avoid speaking or writing slurs in any context, including this paper, stems in part from my witnessing the intense degree of psychic harm suffered in my patients as a result of these words. The clinical literature, spanning decades, is full of examples of adult and child patients from a wide range of marginalized identities who have sustained psychic lacerations resulting from epithets directed toward them. . . .
>
> Slurs, like guns or whips or grenades, are designed to cause damage. Even when apparently brandished for another purpose, their original function is always nearby.[48]

By focusing on the effects of slurs on hearers, and on a social community more broadly, rather than on the intention of the speaker, we invert the priorities of much of the philosophical and linguistic literature. We do this despite building on many insights in that literature. The theoretical development of the resonance framework in this book built from the very beginning on the idea that language could be expressive. We share with the literature following Kaplan the idea that an important facet of the meaning of slurs is their expressivity.[49] Much of that literature does consider the hearer and is explicit about the offense that slurs cause by virtue of what is expressed. However, we differ from most prior literature in focusing *not on the use of a slur for expression of a speaker's feelings, but on the impression the slur makes on hearers*, for this is equally a resonance of the slur.

Resonances are not the sole province of a speaker, and the exigent power of the slur itself is a power associated with the practice itself. That power is inherited from the community of practice that created the slur and imbued it

---

48. Rao, "Observations on Use of the N-word in Psychoanalytic Conferences," 317–18.

49. Jeshion, "Expressivism and the Offensiveness of Slurs"; Richard, *When Truth Gives Out* (especially chapter 1, 12–42).

with power through use. The slurring act is a manifestation of the power of a discriminatory community of practice. So, an important characteristic of the resonance of a slur is that it replicates power relationships: an act of slurring can induce a local power relationship between the name-caller and the target that, at least in the case of strong slurs, mimics a global power relationship between the oppressive in-group and the oppressed out-group.

To say that a slur has power is not yet to describe the mechanism by which that power has an effect, any more than describing a weapon as powerful would be explaining how it functions. A knife pierces because it is sharp, but how can a slur pierce? The exigent power of slurs derives from the fact that is hard to resist (i) attention-grabbing effects, (ii) awareness of what is depicted by the slur and the ideology that has been brought to attention, (iii) understanding of the speaker's own relationship to that depiction, (iv) awareness of loss of public face, (v) negative self-image and/or tension between self-image and public face, and (vi) a concomitant feeling of dissonance. Thus, the slur *resonates* with the victim in the sense of section 3.9 and is *meaningful* to them in the sense of section 6.4, although, not, unfortunately, in a positive way.

For people who are highly attuned to the slurring practice, typically because they have been regularly exposed to it and understand its history, no reflection is needed to recognize loss of public face and to feel shame, humiliation, or other painful discomfort. They have become attuned not only to the attention-grabbing effect of the slurs, but also to the painful resonances of the practice. Being fully attuned to the practice implies feeling that pain when you are the victim. If you do not feel the pain, it is either because you are not the target of the slur, or because you are not fully, one might say *not bodily*, attuned to the practice.

If you do not feel the pain of a slur, you may have become inured to the practice or learned to resist it emotionally, so that you no longer have the first-order attunement. The exigent power does not imply total irresistibility. It just implies that for those fully (first-order) perceptually attuned to the practice, both attentional and emotional reactions will tend to occur nondeliberatively.

It is possible for the speaker and the victim in a name-calling act of slurring, and for relevant audience members in both the in- and out-groups, to share the same discriminatory ideology. In this case, the victim will see themselves as intrinsically less valued. Colonial power structures are designed to enforce this sense of inferiority through education and subjugation. (We speculate that in such a case the revelatory effects of slurs will be different than in cases where salient ideologies are in clear contrast.) However, a bifurcated community of practice is common. In that case, there are two relevant communities of practice, a larger community of practice (e.g., all English speakers) that contains the smaller slurring community (e.g., racist English speakers).

The larger community is collectively dispositionally attuned to the slurring practice, since nonslurring community members encounter its use. Nonslurring community members may be perceptually attuned to the slurring practice, emotionally attuned to the practice, and have some mixture of first- and second-order attunements to the slurring ideology. In such bifurcated communities of practice, some degree of censure for the slurring practice will tend to arise, as those who are not attuned to the discriminatory ideology attempt to limit it.

Let us also pause to note here that while we emphasize the power of the slur itself, we also accept, with Popa-Wyatt and Wyatt, that part of the function of a slur is to establish a certain power relationship between the speaker and members of the slurred group. They go further, suggesting that the attractiveness of the power thus manifested can act as an advertisement for the discriminatory ideology:

> By slurring the bigot shows others the power they can acquire. On the power theory outlined here, the bigot is not talking about power, they are demonstrating power. The speaker acquires discourse power. We posit that this is emotionally appealing to audience members—who are not members of the target group—who feel less powerful than they would like. They see that they can accrue power to themselves by using a slur. Thus, a perlocutionary effect is to make others desire the power the bigot has grabbed. Increasing desire is different to increasing acceptability. Both are required for audience members to join the side of the bigot.[50]

HYPERPROJECTIVITY

We discussed the notions of projectivity and hyperprojectivity in section 5.4. We take the hyperprojectivity of slurs to consist in the fact that *mere mentions of some slurs*, including quotative uses, can cause offense. Here the N-word is the clearest case.

Here is Jyoti Rao, again, discussing situations in which the N-word is mentioned as an object of study, or quotatively, at academic conferences:

> What happens after the slur is uttered has been equally consistent, and equally notable. Some small part of the group, typically comprising the few people of color and others present who come from marginalized backgrounds, attempt to bring attention to what they have just experienced. Often, they express palpable pain, clearly expressing the destabilizing effect of hearing a word strongly associated with white supremacy

---

50. Popa-Wyatt and Wyatt, "Slurs, Roles and Power," 2897.

spoken at a conference. Aside from occupying a marginalized social identity, those speaking are frequently earlier in their career; hold positions as graduate students, junior faculty, or analytic candidates; are less financially secure; and are speaking to people with greater institutional, organizational, and other forms of power. In response to hearing from these participants, the user of the word, and several other white people in the group, seem mobilized to counter what has been reported about the consequences of the epithet's use. They begin to explain that speaking the n-word is benign, even salutary, and advocate for why the word should be used freely by white people and psychoanalysts. In all the cases I have seen, the person using the word, as well as the people roused in support, have appeared unmoved, unreceptive, and unapologetic, even when it is repeatedly pointed out to them that their speech has caused harm.[51]

Mere mentions of a slur have the potential to do harm. Depending on the slur, mere mentions can help perpetuate marginalization of oppressed groups and solidify oppressive practices. As Judith Butler puts it after describing slurs as "badges of degradation," mentions of slurs "unwittingly recirculate that degradation."[52] Quotation marks play a complex role in discourse and metadiscourse, but whatever quotation marks do, they do not "neutralize." We are not even sure what that could mean. The idea that quoted mentions of slurs are neutral is pernicious.

Note here that the philosophy and linguistics literature is peppered with slurs, though practices of mentioning slurs have evolved in recent decades, as have broader societal norms. Those quoting or mentioning slurs in this literature are not being intentionally vindictive, and many are explicit about their policies on slur mention and the reasons for it. But we think that there is still a great deal of unnecessary explicit mentioning of slurs, and that this might be in part the result of an error centering on more-or-less blind acceptance of a certain interpretation of the use-mention distinction, an idealization at the heart of contemporary analytic study of meaning. According to this idealization, merely mentioned or quoted language is in some sense inert, contributing only its form to the content of what is said, and not directly contributing its meaning. It is as if quotes or italics were a lead-lined box, so the scholar who uses these devices cannot possibly be risking harm with the radioactive material inside. But theoretical prejudice should not interfere with reality. So let us just say this. How can the scholar *know* that their belief that a quoted slur will cause no harm is correct? If some evidence should arise suggesting that someone was harmed by exposure to a mere mention, would that not

---

51. Rao, "Observations on Use of the N-word in Psychoanalytic Conferences," 316–17.
52. Butler, *Excitable Speech*, 100.

suggest that maybe it would be better to treat at least certain slurs a little more carefully, perhaps being very sure that there is no reasonable alternative to mentioning them before doing so?

Let us be clear here. Our analysis of hyperprojectivity does not imply that no slur should ever be mentioned in scholarly work, or indeed that there is any slur at all that should never be mentioned in scholarly work. We recognize that in general there could be many reasons to mention particular slurs, for example legal, lexicographic, or historical, or within a process of reclamation, and we are in no position to legislate the appropriacy of such mentions. It is also important to see that our account does not imply that quoted mentions of slurs will have exactly the same power or effects as other utterances containing slurs, such as simple non-quotational acts of name-calling. The hyperprojectivity of slurs consists in some of the resonances of clear acts of slurring being present to some extent as resonances of communicative acts that involve mentions of slurs, not in the resonances of the two types of speech act being identical. So, while there is danger in the mere mention of a slur, that does not mean that mentioning is the same as slurring.

Let us suppose that X is a strong slur which is in current usage. If someone uses X in a name-calling act, for example saying to someone "You are a <intensifier> X!" then they are canonically instantiating a slurring practice. Likewise, an in-group use like "I blame those <intensifier> Xs!" would be a canonical instantiation of a slurring practice. In such paradigmatic cases, the resonances of the slurring act descend in a clear way from the extension of the slurring practice, that is, the history of prior usages, and hearers who are attuned to the practice will tend to be affected by the utterance in accord with those resonances.

Now let's go to the opposite extreme: an entry in a comprehensive general dictionary for a language in which a slur is simply listed alongside a definition. This is paradigmatic as a lexicographic practice, but not a paradigmatic act of slurring. The lexicographic entry can still succeed in drawing attention to both the despised role described by the slur, and to its ideology, and indeed it would be a poor dictionary if it did not do that. Further, it is possible that some people will be hurt by seeing the entry in the dictionary, since their attention will have been drawn to something painful, and that still others will be offended by the dictionary entry. Certainly, someone could use the dictionary entry in order to perform an act that while not canonical could be readily recognized as a slurring act, for example by mailing the relevant dictionary page to someone who people holding to the slur ideology would take to belong to the target group, perhaps with a ring drawn around the slur, thus making it clear that they took the slur to label the recipient. But that merely shows that a dictionary entry can be abused, can be exploited in an act of slurring, and does not make the production of the dictionary entry itself into a slurring act. To the extent that a lexicographic entry is sufficiently distinct from the extension of the practice of slurring that it is not taken to instantiate that practice, it will not affect people attuned to the practice in the same way as a paradigmatic act of slurring would. The slur will have at most the power to draw attention to something painful, and thereby potentially cause some pain or discomfort, and not the exigent power of a slurring act.

Many cases of slur quotation in the philosophical and linguistic literature on slurs fall in between these two extremes. In such academic contexts, it is clear that the author would deny that they are performing a slurring act, and we will not take issue with this. What we would say is this: first, while one occurrence of a slur (like in a dictionary) will draw a certain amount of attention to the slur category and its attendant ideology, and potentially cause pain, repeated uses will draw a lot of attention to them, and potentially cause significantly more pain. This pain may be magnified if a reader takes some of the repetitions to be gratuitous, which might suggest to them that the writer is repeating them with disregard for the feelings of readers, and hence is also performing something just a little closer to a canonical act of slurring. Second, when scholars report on real or hypothetical contextualized acts of slurring, they may sometimes be demanding of the reader an act of imagination, the imagining of an act of slurring. Suppose that some reader is attuned to the slur, and feels they could plausibly be a target of such a slur. No scholar outside the target group can be relied on to say whether in such a case we should expect the reader to successfully compartmentalize, merely imagining what the pain of encountering the example would be, or whether in such a case a reader might actually feel pain, feel targeted, and perhaps be affected in other ways, like being silenced or having a decreased sense of wanting to be part of that academic milieu.

That slurs are hyperprojective remains a controversial position in philosophy and linguistics. Recently, a special journal issue appeared with the title "The Challenge from Non-Derogatory Uses of Slurs"; the editors write that although "what is peculiar to these expressions is their so-called hyper-projectivity," the collection "focuses on how slurs can be used in non-derogatory ways." They go on to say that "it is disputed whether slurs are derogatory when they occur in reported speech" and that "most scholars agree that quotation marks can seal the derogatory force of slurs."[53] If they are right, then on this issue we find ourselves in sharp disagreement with most scholars.

---

53. Cepollaro and Zeman, "Editors' Introduction: The Challenge from Non-Derogatory Uses of Slurs," 1. Note that for Cepollaro and Zeman, as for Camp, the phenomenon of hyperprojectivity includes both projectivity from direct quotations, but also from indirect quotations, for example of speech reports. Thus it is consistent (although, as we have argued, empirically inadequate) to claim that some effects of slurs are hyperprojective while still maintaining that quotation marks block projection. Note also that the nonderogatory uses of slurs considered in the special issue include reclaimed uses of slurs, which we discuss briefly below, and which we agree are nonderogatory.

Quoted slurs can not only derogate and give offense, but can cause harm.[54] (We will turn to the scholars the editors identify as not agreeing that that quotation marks can seal the derogatory force of slurs, namely Luvell Anderson and Ernie Lepore, below. Unfortunately, we are not in agreement with their account either, though for quite different reasons.)

Theories of slurs set within variants of the standard model generally do not do well at explaining hyperprojectivity of the sort discussed in this section. If the effects of slurs are to be explained as conversational implicatures, then there is a general problem that conversational implicatures typically don't project. If the effects of slurs are to be analyzed by analogy with expressives like "oops" and "ouch," as discussed in chapter 2, then we arrive at the problem that it is completely unclear what is expressed when an expressive is quoted. Presuppositional accounts and conventional implicature accounts, like those discussed earlier in this chapter, make some headway, since there are analyses of projection phenomena for these types of meaning. Presuppositions, as standardly analyzed, are projective but cancellable (as in the well-worn "The King of France is not bald: there is no King of France," in which

54. The extent to which the effects of slurs project from quotation is an empirical issue, so one might look to work in the burgeoning field of experimental semantics and pragmatics for evidence. However, slurs are problematic to work with experimentally, since they might cause harm to experimental subjects, and perhaps for this reason there is a paucity of experimental evidence. There are, to our knowledge, no experimental studies within linguistic semantics and pragmatics directly testing the feelings evoked in the targets of real-world slurs (as opposed to artificial pseudo-slurs), and that is perhaps as it should be. However, there is at least one study that looks at the perceived offensiveness of slurs in direct and indirect quotations, albeit that experiment does not control for whether experimental subjects were in the target group of the slur: Cepollaro et al., "How Bad Is It to Report a Slur? An Empirical Investigation." As we read the results reported in this paper (38), they show (i) that direct quotes of others using various Italian pejorative expressions are approximately as offensive as unquoted occurrences of the same expressions, (ii) that indirect quotations involving the expressions are almost as offensive, and (iii) that both are far more offensive than nonpejorative expressions. However, the authors do not draw any conclusions from the fact that stimuli involving quotations of slurs, in forms like "Y: 'X is a P'" (37), are seen as similarly offensive to slurs that were not within quotation marks, which presumably relates to what they took subjects to be judging (what was quoted vs. the presentation of the quote). As regards indirect quotations, the authors conclude that "utterances featuring slurs or non-slurring insults are perceived as less offensive when they occur in indirect reports, even though the report cannot entirely delete the offensiveness." This formulation suggests that the offensiveness of slurs is very much reduced in indirect quotations, but that it is in tension with the data they report on average levels of offensiveness. If we were to assume for simplicity that the offensiveness scale is linear, and take their mean ratings for "non-slurring labels" as a baseline, we find that indirect reports of slurs are over 70 percent as offensive as direct reports. While it is unclear what numerical conclusions are warranted, it seems to us that a faithful description of the results should perhaps not be that reports *cannot entirely delete the offensiveness*," but rather that reports of slurs *only slightly diminish the offensiveness*.

the presupposed existence of a French King is canceled). Yet it is hard for extant presuppositional accounts to explain why some presuppositions should be more projective than others. The effects of slurs are hyperprojective and not easily cancelable. This requires a kind of special pleading for most presuppositional theories.[55] Even if, like Bianca Cepollaro, one has a theory that treats slurs as presuppositions that are not capable of being contextually cancelled, it remains mysterious why even quoting slurs should be objectionable, or how it could possibly be a source of harm.[56] While it is well established that conventional implicatures tend to be more projective than most presuppositions, neither conventional implicature accounts nor prior presuppositional accounts can directly explain why mere mentions should lead to any projection at all.[57] Again, special pleading would be needed to explain this property, for example a theory of quotation that treated different conventional implicatures differently.

While the details of exactly what effects project depend on the strength of the slur and associated considerations of ideology, the simple fact that some effects of slurs are hyperprojective can be explained straightforwardly in terms of attention. Drawing attention to something does not require use, at least not in the sense of the standard use-mention distinction in philosophy of language. The mere mention of a word suffices to draw attention to its meaning, and often to its reference.

The primary point of names is to draw attention to individuals. Descriptive names like vocative uses of the appellations "Professor" or "Private" simultaneously draw attention both to a person and to a role. The attention that names draw to individuals, one could say, is hyperprojective. Even if one uses a name within quotation marks, the audience's attention is still drawn to its referent. If in a report on an important news event, say concerning revelations

---

55. According to most accounts, presuppositions are conditions that should be met, and are thus propositional. Manuel García-Carpintero and Teresa Marques allow that presuppositions can *also* be affective. Since we have presented in this book a model in which presuppositional resonances have just this property, we obviously agree. García-Carpintero and Marques take the affective nature of slur presuppositions to explain hyperprojectivity, but it is not clear to us exactly how the affective nature of slur presuppositions explains differences in projectivity. Certainly, if the special projectivity of affective presuppositions were to be stipulated, rather than independently explained, then this approach too would amount to special pleading. See Marques, "The Expression of Hate in Hate Speech"; García-Carpintero, "Pejoratives, Contexts and Presuppositions"; Marques and García-Carpintero, "Really Expressive Presuppositions." For a related view, with a similarly structured explanation of hyperprojectivity effects, see also Schlenker, "Expressive Presuppositions."

56. Cepollaro, "In Defence of a Presuppositional Account of Slurs."

57. For experimental data confirming the generally highly projective nature of conventional implicatures, but also the more general variability of projection effects, see Tonhauser, Beaver, and Degen, "Gradience in Projectivity and At-Issueness."

of spying, one paragraph includes a quote from an anonymous official that mentions you by name, you are sure to soon find reporters at your door. By merely mentioning you, the report has drawn attention to you. If someone mentions the combination of a safe in a quote, for example, "I heard Marie muttering the number 1673," they have drawn attention to the named number, which may or may not have security implications.

Perhaps this notion of drawing attention seems mysterious, worthy of special philosophical consideration before being centered in a theory. We don't deny that attention is worth special philosophical attention, but the notion of attention we require is no more mysterious than that evoked, sometimes using the term "salience," in much theorizing about meaning, especially in the context of work on anaphora. Consider this example:

1. My friend said "I met Trump in New Hampshire!" but I don't believe she met him there.

We take it that this constructed example is unobjectionably acceptable English. But note that two of the pronouns in the last clause, "him" and "there," refer anaphorically to entities introduced in the quotation. Entities can only be referred to using pronouns if they are salient. Therefore, something must have drawn attention to them. The names clearly did that. This attention-drawing effect is no more cut off by surrounding quotation marks than light is cut off by clear glass.

Slurs are often said to be epithets, the term "racial epithet" being used almost synonymously with "racial slur," and acts of slurring are often described as name-calling, which is also invariably negative. If a teacher merely refers to Johnny Smith as "Johnny Smith," Johnny can't legitimately say the teacher was "calling him names." It's clear that slurs are commonly thought of as name-like. However, our arguments regarding attention do not depend on slurs being names per se. It is a completely general fact that a use of a predicate inside a quotation draws sufficient attention to the kind or property it denotes that this kind or property has increased availability for later anaphoric reference. Thus in (2) the quoted mention of a pet dodo makes dodos salient, and the later pronouns "they" and "one" refer to dodos at a kind level. Neither quotation marks nor the act of quotation veils the attention drawn to kinds by the quoted material.

2. Johnny is so cute. This morning he said: "Guess what pet I have? A dodo!" I couldn't tell if he doesn't know they're supposed to be extinct, but let's not tell him we know he doesn't have one.

Slurs, then, are both like names and like any other predicate, in drawing attention to whatever individuals, properties, or kinds they make explicit. Making things explicit implies drawing attention to them. The way in which attentional processes are modulated by knowledge of language is undoubtedly complex, but we take it as uncontroversial that once something has become salient, its salience will tend to decay only slowly, presumably as a result of basic psychological processes that are common to humanity, if not to all higher animals. The key to understanding the hyperprojectivity of slurs is recognizing that hyperprojectivity is not in and of itself in the least unusual. What most distinguishes the hyperprojectivity of slurs from the hyperprojectivity associated with most other classes of predicates is simply that people care about it.

Grammatically, slurs are like other predicates, though they are predicates that, like "professor" and "private," have a tendency to be used as epithets, and indeed as vocatives. A practice of slurring, like any other, occurs within a community of practice. Like all predicates that are associated with negative evaluations within an ideology, slurs are used insultingly, to draw attention to despised characteristics of an individual. The crucial way in which slurs differ from other predicates is that the kind they draw attention to is a construct within a distinctive, *discriminatory ideology*, an ideology that makes in-group/out-group distinctions such that "members of out-groups are valued less than members of in-groups, and hence as inherently deserving of less than equal treatment or resources" (cf. section 2.6).

The use-mention distinction has been central to the development of logic and analytic philosophy over the last century, but assuming the distinction to be sharp is an unwarranted idealization, and unhelpful in many cases. Let's consider a few. First, a letter that says "I hereby apologize for saying 'It's the one-year anniversary of my getting the position that you so badly wanted': I shouldn't have reminded you of it." is not a convincing apology. Second, the use-mention distinction is unhelpful for distinguishing between whether an improvisational jazz musician has merely quoted a few bars of a classic or has actually played it. Third, and more pertinently, the use-mention distinction is unhelpful for distinguishing between whether someone reproducing an image of a threatening racist display hanging from a tree in a back yard has merely exhibited someone else's display or has themselves performed a racist act. Finally, we submit that the use-mention distinction is at best a blunt instrument for distinguishing between different occurrences of slurs. That is because both using a predicate and mentioning a predicate can draw attention to whatever kind or property the predicate denotes, and drawing attention to something is one of the main functions of slurs. What makes the hyperprojectivity of slurs significant is that part of the function of a slur is to do just what many quoted or otherwise embedded slurs do, namely draw attention to the disdained or reviled role of a group within a distinctive discriminatory ideology. It follows that a quoted slur can function somewhat like a non-quoted slur.

Let us briefly head off a potential objection to our suggestion that attention is primary. Some might point out that when something is mentioned, the

Gricean maxim of relevance can then explain the communicative significance of the mention. On this view, when a hearer encounters a mention of a term, they must then reconstruct the intention of the speaker in mentioning whatever it is. The reason why a friend keeps mentioning figure-skating news, the hearer might reason, is because he wants people to think about his recent figure-skating success. We completely agree that such reasoning processes occur, and that they can explain aspects of the communicative significance of mentions, including mentions of slurs.

Joe Biden once caricatured former New York City Mayor Rudolph Guiliani by saying, "There's only three things he mentions in a sentence—a noun, a verb, and 9/11."[58] What he was referencing was Giuliani's habit of drawing attention to the terrorist destruction of the World Trade Center, and hence his role in the city's recovery. Although it might be argued that Giuliani was simply obsessed by the event, it seems more plausible that, as Biden was implicitly suggesting, Giuliani was strategically mentioning 9/11. Donald Trump has a habit of beginning sentences with "People say . . ." and related locutions. The discursive logic of this strategy is multifaceted, but at least part of it is that it allows Trump to draw attention to ideas without taking responsibility for them. An authoritarian leader (and perhaps any politician) needs to be a master of attention, and often the strategic point of their utterances is to draw attention to something.

However, as an explanation of the direct emotive and attentional effects of slurs, such a strategic explanation would be backward. Relevance does not explain attentional effects. It's rather the case that a premise of relevance-based argumentation is that the speaker has drawn attention to something. The question the Gricean theorist is then asking is, Why has the speaker drawn attention to it? The question we are asking is, Given that the speaker has drawn attention to something, what effects will that have independently of what the speaker's intention was? We do not dispute that there are effects that should be explained in terms of the speaker's intention, or indeed that such reasoning is important in considering what form of counterspeech is appropriate (e.g., blame and censure vs. education). What we dispute is that considerations of the speaker's motivations are needed to explain the exigent power of the slur, its hyperprojectivity, or its ideological revelatoriness. And our explanation for this hyperprojectivity centers on a claim that we take to be somewhat self-evident: the attention-drawing power of a construction is not plugged by quotation, or, for that matter, by other metalinguistic embeddings.

58. "Democratic Presidential Candidates Debate at Drexel University in Philadelphia, Pennsylvania," October 30, 2007, retrieved February 18, 2023, The American Presidency Project, https://www.presidency.ucsb.edu/documents/democratic-presidential-candidates -debate-drexel-university-philadelphia-pennsylvania.

THE ORDINARINESS OF SLURS

If language is treated primarily as a vehicle for conveying information and information is supposed to consist in neutral and objective facts about the world, then the tools and resources one constructs will be focused in a way that makes expressive and exigent language mysterious. As a result, slurs will be mysterious, as their central function is expressive and exigent, not descriptive. Slurs appear as a puzzle because of the assumptions embedded into the ideal-language model (the predicate calculus, for example, lacks slurs).

We have urged a reorientation of the evidence base of the theory of meaning toward political speech. In so doing, expressive and exigent properties of language use emerge as equally central to descriptive properties. We use language to describe, but also to insult, bond, and emote. In the vocabulary of our picture, words resonate with things, with social identity, with emotions, with practices, with values, and with much else. We do not think of one of these resonances as "primary" and the others as derivative.

From our perspective, slurs are not mysterious, but rather a kind of *paradigm case*. If there is such a thing as ordinary language, then slurs are ordinary. Words belong to speech practices, in most cases, multiple speech practices. But a slur is a *characteristic expression* of a certain kind of speech practice, one that is part of an ideology that negatively stereotypes the targeted group. That does not make slurs special from the point of view of the linguist. It just makes them the right sort of thing to be used in practices of labeling and insulting, as well as further practices of commanding, prohibiting, punishing, or blaming. All of these further practices have linguistic dimensions, but their existence does not need to be explained by a special theory of the linguistic properties of slurs. Slurs are just about as ordinary as language gets. But then again, in line with the discussion of section 10.1, to claim of anything that it is ordinary is perhaps to say as much about your own ideology as about the thing you so describe.

In their introduction to a seminal set of essays on critical race theory in 1993, the editors (Mari Matsuda, Charles Lawrence, Richard Delgado, and Kimberlé Williams Crenshaw) discuss the defacement of a poster of Beethoven in Ujamaa, Stanford's Black-themed house, which two White freshmen had represented as a caricature of a Black man, and upon which they had scrawled the N-word. The editors write,

> The power of the poster's message was derived from its historical and cultural context, from the background of minstrel shows, of racist theories about brain size and gene pools and biblical ancestors that has shaped our conscious and unconscious beliefs about the intellectual capacity of Blacks.[59]

59. Matsuda et al., *Critical Race Theory*, 8.

The defaced poster harmed because it was an endorsement of an ideology of White superiority and Black subordination. It is the connection of the N-word to this ideology, the connection of the caricatured image of a Black man to a past history of minstrel shows, that gave the poster its dangerous power.

In a similar vein, Judith Butler writes,

> Clearly, injurious names have a history, one that is invoked and recon-solidated at the moment of utterance, but not explicitly told. This is not simply a history of how they have been used, in what contexts, and for what purposes; it is the way such histories are installed and arrested in and by the name. The name has, thus, a historicity, what might be understood as the history which has become internal to a name, has come to constitute the contemporary meaning of a name: the sedimen-tation of its usages as they have become part of the very name, a sedi-mentation, a repetition that congeals, that gives the name its force. . . . If we understand the force of the name to be an effect of its historicity, then that force is not the mere causal effect of an inflicted blow, but works in part through an encoded memory or a trauma, one that lives in language and is carried by language.[60]

We agree with Butler's description of both the conventional and the perlocu-tionary facts involved with the use of slur terms, and our apparatus, as it were, cashes her idea out in our own currency. The historicity of a slur is its embed-dedness in a speech practice, which in turn is part of an ideology. When one performs an act of name-calling using a slur, one is making salient an ideology that subordinates them, calling it to their explicit attention, and applying it to them. The reason such name-calling is injurious is because it is the char-acteristic expression of an ideology that places that person in a subordinate role by virtue of their membership in a targeted group. Crucially, the ideology associated with a slur term is conventionally connected to it: it has (as Butler puts it, above) "come to constitute the contemporary meaning of a name." In our terms, a slur is a characteristic expression of such an ideology. Using the slur functions to manifest that ideology. In this sense, the ideology and the slur are interwoven—the slur and its resonances are quite literally part of that ideology.

But it is not just slurs that are connected with ideologies. It is a moral of our book that words generally are connected with ideologies. The word "wife" is connected with an ideology, an ideology about gender. Eric Swanson is right to argue that "slurs cue ideologies"; but it is also true that "wife," "mother," "secretary," and "boss" cue ideologies, albeit that we sometimes miss the cue.[61]

60. Butler, *Excitable Speech*, 36.
61. Swanson, "Slurs and Ideologies," 9–14

Philosophers recognize that there is a kind of overlap in what one wants to say about slurs, and what one wants to say about words that are not slurs. Here is Robin Jeshion, clearly recognizing that the normal word "janitor" also regularly carries with it an ideology, even a subordinating one:

> It is useful to contrast the identifying component of slurs with uses of language that suggest or signal lower status in-a-role. For example, remarks like "He is a janitor," designating someone's occupation may be used as a put-down by signaling lower occupational status by virtue of being a janitor. But such signaling is highly contextual, no part of the semantics of "janitor." This is markedly different from slurs, for which the identifying component is encoded in every context of literal use. Moreover, even in contexts in which "janitor" is used to signal lower status in a role, they fail to negatively evaluate the targets vis-à-vis their humanity, construed along a moral dimension—qua person. "He's a janitor, and the finest person I know" is perfectly acceptable; substitute a slur for "janitor," and it reads as highly problematic.[62]

Here, Jeshion distinguishes between a slur, which signals lower status, according to her, *via its semantics*, and a word like "janitor," which, by her lights, can be *used* to signal lower status, though this is not, according to her, part of its semantics. It's useful to lay out our analysis of the similarities and differences between a slur and a word like "janitor," to compare and contrast them with Jeshion's.

We do not accept Jeshion's claim that the felicity of "He's a janitor, and the finest person I know" removes the imputation of an ideology that ranks janitors as lower status than other professions, any more than "She's a secretary, and the finest person I know" is free of such imputations (it isn't). Low social status is consistent with being a "fine person"—as Kate Manne has emphasized in her work on gender, accepting one's lower social status is in fact often how one comes to be regarded as a fine person (in her analysis, a fine woman).[63] It's probably difficult to rid any use of "janitor" (or "secretary") of its association with an ideology that accords it a lower social status than other professions.

Even if "janitor" only *sometimes* brought with it an imputation of lower social status to those who occupy that role, it would not, in our framework, follow that this imputation was not conventional. Each use of a term manifests a speech practice, and simultaneously presupposes that very speech practice. If there are contexts in which "janitor" does not signal lower status in a role, that could be both because resonances are inherently probabilistic, allowing for a

---

62. Jeshion, "Slurs, Dehumanization, and the Expression of Contempt," 84.

63. In *Down Girl*, Kate Manne argues that women who behave according to patriarchal norms are rewarded in the attitudes taken toward them.

mixture of uses in different types of context, and because "janitor" belongs to several distinct speech practices, only some of which involve ideologies that rank janitors as having a lower status than other professions. When "janitor" is used in a context in which it is part of an ideology that ranks janitors as having a low social status because of their role, the ideology functions in communication exactly as the ideology associated with a slur functions when the slur is used. In both cases, the ideologies are presupposed. Even if "janitor" is not always used to manifest an ideology that ranks janitors as having a lower social status, there is, on our view, no sharp difference in linguistic kind between "janitor" and slurs, beyond the greater tendency for slurs to be used vocatively, and the fact that "janitor" is unlikely to be reclaimed.

In Jeshion's work, we find a rich account of the perlocutionary effects of slurring terms, effects that, for her, are "exclusively pragmatic," and do not obtain "by virtue of conventional linguistic properties of slurring terms, i.e., meanings or conventional rules of use."[64] We find much to agree with in Jeshion's explanation of the perlocutionary effects of slurring uses. For example, Jeshion attributes the difference in force and harmfulness between a use of the N-word and a use of "honky," a slur for White people, to the histories behind the ideologies associated with these words; as she writes, "The former occurs against the background of current widespread racism, history of slavery, and historical civil rights struggles for African-Americans, and nothing comparable for Caucasians."[65] We agree with Jeshion's analysis, which builds on the crucial insights of critical race theory with which we began this section. But, with Judith Butler, we insist that there is a *conventional* tie between standard uses of these words and these different histories.[66]

Jeshion's view about slur terms, which we take to be windows into the conventions associated with them, also explains the fallacy of conflating the distinct notions of *taboo* and *slur*. In German, words associated with Nazi

64. Jeshion, "Expressivism and the Offensiveness of Slurs," 321.

65. Jeshion, "Expressivism and the Offensiveness of Slurs," 322. Note that the difference in strength of the two slurs Jeshion was considering in this passage follows from our definition of slur strength, above.

66. One of Jeshion's arguments (in "Expressivism and the Offensiveness of Slurs") against the conventionality of the link between uses of these slurs and their associated histories of racial domination is that their neutral counterparts, "Black" and "white," when employed with a contemptuous tone, can also have the same perlocutionary effect. We agree with the datum—but the contemptuous tone is a conventional signal that the supposedly neutral word is being used to exemplify a speech practice that is part of the "slurring" ideology. The fact that there is a prominent but sometimes contested practice of capitalizing the first letter of one of these terms but not the other makes it obvious that ideology is tied to the use of either of them: capitalization suggests that the adjective is not merely denoting a property of certain individuals, but marking out a sociopolitically significant classification, by analogy with the capitalization of nationality adjectives and others derived from proper names.

ideology, such as *Lebensraum, Führer,* and *Rasse,* are taboo. They are taboo because of their connections to horrific historical practices. But these words are not slurs. Conversely, there are slurs, like "fat cat," which are not taboo, presumably in part because they are not connected to a history of horrific treatment (in this case, of rich Americans). Some slurs are taboo and some taboo terms are slurs, but the topic of what is a slur and the topic of what is a taboo are entirely distinct subject matters. Words that are connected to particularly horrific histories and practices typically can neither be used nor mentioned without raising those histories and practice to salience.

In a series of papers, Luvell Anderson, Ernie Lepore, and Matthew Stone develop a "prohibitionist" account of slurs, explaining the various properties slurs have, including hyperprojectivity, as resulting from the existence of taboo.[67] Leaving aside for the moment the question of whether this counts as an explanation (one might worry that the "explanation" is that it is offensive to mention slurs because they are unmentionable without causing offense), or whether it can possibly explain which specific resonances project and which don't, there is something right about it. The fact that something is taboo means that mentioning it will immediately catch listeners' attention, and indeed lead to the suspicion that the purpose of mentioning it was to call it to the listeners' attention. Perversely, the social development of taboos around slurs strengthens their effectiveness, by increasing their attention-drawing power. However, the development of these taboos does not so much explain anything about slurs, as add to the complexity of generalizing. For a taboo is itself an idiosyncratic complex of practices. These practices include counterspeech, censorship, and education, all of which are applied in different ways for different slurs, and for which their application varies over time. What have been deemed acceptable mentions of various racial or gender-related slurs has evolved continuously during our own lifetimes.

The non-taboo nature of relatively weak slurs like "fat cat" and pejoratives like "muppet" is illustrative of a problem with using taboo as the basis of an explanation, rather than something that itself needs to be theorized, because the taboos relevant to even the paradigmatic cases of racial slurs are complex. It would be at the very least a gross oversimplification to maintain that in the reconstruction-era South the N-word was taboo, when an officer of the law could openly use it as a term of address. It was a word in general use in a powerful community of practice. And it was a powerful word. How can the power of a word, its exigence as we have termed it, be explained by the illicitness of using it, if those with power feel its use is licit? Similarly, the revelatoriness of slurs, their ability to bring to the fore an ugly discriminatory ideology, is not explained by their taboo nature, but is rather largely responsible for the imposition of societal taboos. Last, the hyperprojectivity of slurs is not explained by their taboo nature. Rather, hyperprojectivity is part of what makes the taboos against using some slurs so sweeping.

Imagine someone explaining why you shouldn't murder by saying "Well, it's illegal." Murdering and many other violent acts are illegal, but that is not satisfying as a general explanation for why you shouldn't perform them, for it merely pushes us back to the question of why there are such prohibitions. Further, in the case of physically violent crimes, nobody would claim that the harmful effects of the acts result from their prohibition. So it is with hurtful methods of social stigmatization more generally: they are hurtful independently of any prohibition against such stigmatization. In particular, slurs are not injurious because they are prohibited; they are prohibited because they are injurious.

Some theories of slurs, like Jeshion's, add an expressive component—for Jeshion, as with other expressivist theories, it is part of the semantics of slurs that they communicate emotion, in this case contempt, for their targets. We agree. And yet, on our way of looking at things, the fact that uses of slurs attune their hearers to the speaker's emotional attitude toward their targets does not make them in any sense distinctive. Affective resonance is a general conventional feature of words, not unique to slurs. Calling someone "a mom" can carry warm resonances of family values, and simultaneously a negative evaluation of their status in industrial society. Talking about something growing in the garden as a "weed" or a "plant" carries emotional resonances that connect with its perceived value.

The supposedly distinctive linguistic behavior of slurs is, for the most part, a straightforward consequence of the fact that they are part of language, embedded in histories, practices, and ideologies, whose nature explains how their capacities to harm have become conventionalized. Because words, generally, carry such histories, we must take care not to treat slurs as special or distinctive in this regard. So doing perpetuates a myth—that "ordinary language" is not linked to ideologies in just the same way. By focusing on slurs, we are led away from thinking critically about the ideological weight of perfectly ordinary terms. Slurs are not distinctive in being the vehicle of ideology. Language generally is a vehicle for ideology.

There are nevertheless important and interesting differences between slurs and other terms. Using words like "wife," "mother," "boss," and "janitor" presupposes ideologies that provide people with social roles. But these ideologies are not normally *highlighted* by the use of these words. When we describe someone with their use, we presuppose these ideologies. When someone says "Mom!" we do not normally expect any relevant clash of attunements between interlocutors as to the role of being a "mom," and while attention is drawn to the role of the addressee, we assume that what the utterance usually does most strongly is draw attention to the person rather than her role. A male politician who calls someone "my wife and the mother of my children" is presupposing a gender ideology. But he is not usually doing so as the explicit and manifest point of his utterance. Using language like this can be a kind of hustle. If a politician intentionally uses this phrase to signal his allegiance to his ideology, but wants his audience to think it was incidental, that is hustle.

In contrast, slurs do not hustle in this way, at least in the mouths of competent language users. Slurs overtly draw attention to a role that is a point of contention; those who do not subscribe to the slur's associated ideology might deny that the role exists at all. Ideologies are constituted by practices, including speech practices. Slurs are characteristic expressions of certain ideologies. Having such an ideology about a group, one can manifest the ideology with that word. Slurs thus present their ideologies (although not the details of those ideologies) explicitly. The *main point* of a use of a slur is to give expression to the ideology for which it is a characteristic expression, and to do so openly. Slurs evoke ideologies by naming despised roles; part of their point is to *draw attention* to those ideologies and to draw attention to the role those labeled by the slur play within that ideology. Because slurs name ideologies, they bring the erasure of ideologies by ideal-theoretic models especially saliently to attention.

According to Jessie Munton, prejudice involves undue attention to certain properties of a group, and it hinders us from gaining important knowledge.[68] The idea that what matters in prejudice is not, or at least not only, what claims are made, but what is drawn attention to is an important one. Although she does not discuss slurs explicitly (at least in recent work with which we are familiar), it's clear that slurring is an expression of prejudice, and thus that her account should apply to slurs. According to Munton, then, a slur could potentially be a vehicle for prejudice not because it falsely describes a group, but because it unduly draws attention primarily to negatively evaluated properties of the group.

While we agree with Munton that attention is highly relevant to the way people conceptualize the groups around them, let us note a tension arising from the fact that Munton focuses on *undue* attention. It might be argued that some terms characteristically express ideologies about an identity group, ideologies that highlight negative properties of that group, but nevertheless may help us think better about social reality. For example, the term "Karen" is used to express something negative about White women. But, arguably, "Karen" may help orient people to features of social reality, and thus may be part of an ideology that better reveals the world, rather than masking it. Is "Karen" still a

68. Munton, "Prejudice as the Misattribution of Salience." Her invocation of attention has been inspirational for us, not only in centering attention in our analysis of slurs, but also as regards the model of harmony in terms of landscapes of attunements in chapter 3. Munton's attentional structures play a similar role to the structuring of attunements in our model, determining when activation of one attunement will tend to lead to activation of another.

slur? The word "prejudice" is negative, implying distorted evaluation or unfair behavior. One might choose to characterize slurs as words that are characteristic expressions of flawed ideologies, or prejudices in Munton's sense, or one might define slurs in such a way that at least some of them focus *appropriately* on negative characteristics of a group, say because those negative characteristics are societally problematic and deserve special attention. Whether one defines slurs so that they always imply prejudice in Munton's sense, or allows that slurs can convey a justifiable bias against a group is a largely terminological question, the answer to which we do not need to legislate here.[69]

So-called *reclaimed* uses of slurs are ones in which members of the targeted group "reclaim" the slur, to perform a different speech act than slurring. As Luvell Anderson discusses, Black Americans typically use the N-word to *address* one another, rather than to slur or insult one another.[70] The reclaimed use of slurs is a mystery for many theories, especially those that make slurs into a special or distinctive category. But from our perspective, there is nothing surprising about slur reclamation. Reclaimed slurs are used as a bonding mechanism between those who are traditionally targeted by the slur. To slur is to label someone with an out-group role, so one thing that is clear is that when someone who appears to be part of that group uses the slur word, they are either denying their membership of the slurred group, or else are not performing an act of slurring. Reclamation concerns a case where someone does not deny their membership of the group, but rather denies the power of others over the nature of the category.

Only if we are close can we talk freely, so the more potentially painful the ideology a term invokes is, the better its invocation is as a means of testing and intensifying our closeness. Reclaiming slurs can also be a way of challenging the very ideologies that the slur has been part of. And here again, there is no contradiction, but rather a confirmation of the slur's power. There are few better ways of manifesting power and stubborn opposition than to hold in your hand your enemy's weapon. The more powerful the weapon, the better: why wave your enemy's toothpicks in front of them, if instead you can fire off an artillery round?

We can focus on "reclaimed uses of slurs" as if these are some baffling linguistic phenomena, but that is a sign of a misunderstanding of the phenomena. Reclaimed slurs are one manifestation of a general tendency, one that we also see when Jewish people make Jewish jokes with one another, or even jokes about the Nazi Holocaust (jokes that do not typically even involve reclaimed slurs). Bonding, group strength, and pride are often gained through

---

69. Thanks to Endure McTier for discussion of "Karen" as a slur.

70. Anderson, "Calling, Addressing, and Appropriation." Further discussion of reappropriation is found in Bianchi, "Slurs and Appropriation"; Jeshion, "Pride and Prejudiced"; Popa-Wyatt, "Reclamation: Taking Back Control of Words"; Quaranto, "How to Win Words and Influence Meanings"; and Ritchie, "Social Identity, Indexicality, and the Appropriation of Slurs."

subversion—waving in the face of a history of oppression by others weapons they fashioned but no longer own. One characteristic reclamatory use of slurs involves embedding the slurs into a new speech practice, a practice of *bonding*, which is a practice one can only engage in as a group member.[71]

Robin Dembroff has argued that the category *gender-queer* is what they call a *critical gender kind*.[72] On their analysis, self-describing as "gender-queer" is a way of undermining the ideology of the Western gender binary. Slur reclamation shares this destabilizing function—it is a method of undermining the problematic ideology behind the slur. Slur reclamation belongs in a category of methods used to attack and undermine ideologies historically associated with terms. Bonding with a slur directed against one's group has the effect of undermining the negative ideology associated with the slur. Not all reclaimed slur uses involve bonding—as Luvell Anderson (p.c.) has pointed out to us, Cornel West's use of "thugs and gangsters" to describe Western Imperialism is not a bonding use of "thugs and gangsters." But it does embody the function of Dembroff's critical gender kinds—it undermines an ideology.

It is not accidental that slurs have attracted so much attention in philosophy and linguistics in recent years. Focusing on slurs brings out the connection between language and ideology, a connection less salient with so-called "ordinary" words. Slurs *highlight* this connection.

When slur terms are used to slur a target directly, in acts of name-calling, they are attempts to fit the audience into an ideology that subordinates them. More generally, slurring, especially openly, and with terms with direct associations with violent ideologies, has characteristic effects on the social context that reinforce hierarchies of value and worth.

In July 2020, US Congresswoman Alexandria Ocasio-Cortez was accosted by her colleague Representative Ted Yoho, who labeled her using, among other things, a highly charged negative gendered slur. Representative Ocasio-Cortez, in a speech on July 23, 2020, addressed the effects of such language directly on the House floor:

> Now what I am here to say is that this harm that Mr. Yoho levied, . . . tried to levy against me, was not just an incident directed at me, but when you do that to any woman, what Mr. Yoho did was give permission to other men to do that to his daughters. In using that language in front of the press, he gave permission to use that language against his wife,

---

71. Famously, in *Excitable Speech*, Butler urges that the reclamation of hurtful speech in this way is the best way forward in the face of hate speech, most clearly in the section "Hate Speech/State Speech" (96–102) where she says, for example, "The possibility of decontextualizing and recontextualizing such terms through radical acts of public misappropriation constitutes the basis of an ironic hopefulness that the conventional relation between word and wound might become tenuous and even broken over time" (100).

72. Dembroff, "Beyond Binary."

his daughters, women in his community, and I am here to stand up to say that is not acceptable. I do not care what your views are. It does not matter how much I disagree or how much it incenses me or how much I feel that people are dehumanizing others. I will not do that myself. I will not allow people to change and create hatred in our hearts.[73]

As Ocasio-Cortez here points out, slurring a woman as she was slurred "gives permission" to a misogynist ideology. Since slurs are the characteristic expression of various toxic ideologies—in this case, a misogynist one—using a slur openly makes it permissible to voice that ideology. It *normalizes* that ideology.

Ocasio-Cortez's speech closely echoes the analysis given by Mary Kate McGowan of oppressive speech. Focusing on a very similar misogynist discourse involving the same slur for women, McGowan writes that such overt misogyny changes the norms in the conversational context, making it subsequently "conversationally permissible to degrade women."[74]

Slur words are a particularly powerful way of normalizing ideologies. Using a slur in a speech act of slurring is an *overt* manifestation of the negative ideology associated with a slur; slurring the target group is a part of a speech practice constitutive of that ideology. And it is the very overtness of a slur in an act of slurring that gives it its ideological power. Eric Swanson has been particularly clear about the attentional function of slurs. As Swanson writes,

> Uses of slurs strengthen ideologies because the use of a slur *makes manifest* the speaker's consent to and endorsement of an ideology, encouraging the speaker and others to feel that their own consent to and endorsement of that ideology would not be out of place.[75]

Slurring using a word that is unambiguously a slur does not covertly smuggle in adherence to a discriminatory ideology, but *manifests* that adherence. Therefore, performances of such acts by competent members of a community of practice may come close to an ideal of straight talk, the intended effects of the act being transparent to hearers. By making manifest what others would prefer remained hidden, slurs give permission to openly endorse the ideology they presuppose. Clearly, much straight talk is far from ideal.

10.3. Genocidal Speech

Genocidal speech is speech that targets a social group and provides justification for its genocide. Genocidal speech is connected to the most extreme formation of an *antagonistic ideological social group* (section 6.6), a community

---

73. "Representative Alexandria Ocasio-Cortez Addresses House on Exchange with Representative Ted Yoho," C-SPAN, July 23, 2020.

74. McGowan, *Just Words*, 110–11.

75. Swanson, "Slurs and Ideologies," 1–2.

of practice whose discriminatory ideology is structured around a strongly negative collective emotional, dispositional, and attitudinal attunement to another group. Genocidal speech builds the strongly negative collective emotional attunement by defining the group as being those whose existence is most directly and existentially threatened by the supposed enemy. A *genocidally antagonistic ideological social group* is a community of practice whose identity is based on being existentially imperiled by the existence of another group.

Genocidal identities are formed by representing the target group as an existential threat. One way the existential threat is posed is as what Susan Benesch and her collaborators in the Dangerous Speech Project call "accusation in a mirror," "attributing to one's enemies the very acts of violence the speaker hopes to commit against them."[76] We began this book with Cleon's speech in the Mytilenean debate, the classical example of demagoguery in Western history. Cleon argues for slaughtering all the Mytilenean citizens, on the grounds that they would slaughter all the Athenians if the tables were turned. Cleon's speech is an exercise in genocidal speech. Its principal narrative structure is accusation in the mirror. Antiquity's paradigm of demagoguery was genocidal speech. It is a central case.

Genocidal speech inherits its power from lengthy histories of conflict, oppression, and revenge, and this is why the presence of such a history is one of the five parameters in our definition of the strength of a slur, in the last section. (It's condition c.) In "Genocidal Language Games," Lynne Tirrell describes the presence of such a history as "social embeddedness":

> Derogatory terms are most effective when they are connected to networks of oppression and discrimination, with the weight of history and social censure behind it. This is what most clearly marks deeply derogatory terms from other sorts of slurs. Let's call this the *social embeddedness condition*. Social context, with embedded practices and conventions, is the major source of the power of derogatory terms that are used to dominate, demean, or dehumanize people.[77]

If, out of the blue, a politician in the United States starts describing Anglo-Saxon men as "vermin," it will not have much effect. Similarly, if, out of the blue, someone on social media describes a *New York Times* columnist as a "bedbug," this too should be expected to have little effect, although predicting the short-term effects of any insult is impossible.[78] To resonate meaningfully, the

---

76. Dangerous Speech Project, *Dangerous Speech: A Practical Guide*, 2022, https://dangerousspeech.org/guide/.

77. Tirrell, "Genocidal Language Games," 192.

78. The effect of calling a *New York Times* columnist turns out to depend substantially on how the target of the insult responds. When in August 2019 an academic, David Karpf, called *New York Times* columnist Bret Stevens a "bedbug" on Twitter, there was little initial

description of the target must take place in an environment in which there is a deep history of conflict with the targeted group, and the term fits in the right way into the context of a historical narrative. The derogatory speech must connect the targeted group in the right way with this richer history of conflict. Here we recall both Deva Woodly's discussion of the importance of history and social context to resonance, discussed in chapter 2, and Rahel Jaeggi's broader analysis of practices as located within a nexus; we might say that the derogatory practice is supported and gains its own strength by virtue of being one thread within a fabric, but the fabric is itself no more than the interweaving formed by the threading of individual practices. Social embeddedness consists in the presence of such a fabric, but the practices in question are oppressive, and the fabric they form is a discriminatory ideology. Given the presence of this ideology and its attendant discriminatory practices and attitudes, the derogatory term produces consonance for oppressors and dissonance for the target group, that is, it resonates positively for the oppressors and negatively for the target, becoming meaningful for both, and developing its own exigent power through the context into which it is woven.

What we observed of slurs in the last section is true of derogatory language more generally, and is true of the speech that attends genocides. Derogatory language is not particularly extraordinary in respect of presupposing ideology, of depending on a network of other practices and attitudes, but neither is genocidal language that is not directly derogatory. The highly charged phrase "Heil Hitler" is an honorific expression, and derogates indirectly by manifesting the power of a social group with a highly genocidal discriminatory ideology. It is an obvious example of a practice that was associated with a genocide, but which, despite its oppressive power, is not what we would usually think of as a slur. But again, the mere fact that it is socially embedded, meaningful in the context of a particular ideology, is not in itself extraordinary. All linguistic practices are like this. The ability of oppressive language to resonate positively or negatively depends on the fact that the term draws attention to particular roles within a discriminatory ideology, and this attentional change is crucial to the development of extreme consonance or dissonance.

In Rwanda, the postcolonial situation created a division between Hutu and Tutsi, riven with jealousy, anger, and competition over favored status with the colonial occupiers. In Rwanda, poisonous snakes are a much-despised threat, and killing them with machetes an honor. Hutus were told that Tutsis were

---

reaction. However, after Stevens sent an email to Karpf (cc-ed to Karpf's provost) suggesting that Karpf call him "bedbug" to his face, and Karpf copied the email in a tweet, the exchange suddenly drew largescale attention, largely at Stevens's expense, leading Stevens to quit Twitter (Luke O'Neil, "NYT Columnist Quits Twitter after Daring Critic to 'Call Me a Bedbug to My Face,'" *Guardian*, August 27, 2019). Despite the story having brief notoriety, we see no evidence of long-term take-up of the practice of labeling newspaper columnists or other center-right political commentators as bedbugs.

enemies as snakes were enemies. This fit into a history of conflict between Hutu and Tutsi and made possible communicating to Hutus that being Hutu meant, in part, to target Tutsis for elimination via a violent practice typically directed toward snakes.

The power of the "super-predator" campaign in the United States in the 1990s, directed against young Black men, derives similarly from social embeddedness. In the United States, there is a long history of demonizing Black men by connecting them to horrendous violent crimes, a process that Khalil Gibran Muhammad has called "writing crime into race."[79] Regularly, US elections take place in a backdrop of panic about "Black crime." Many Americans operate in this social context and use words that are part of speech practices that legitimize the racist ideology that Black American men tend to be criminal by nature. The introduction of a word like "super-predator" must be understood in this long historical context. It was a novel addition to anti-Black racial ideology, and it was effective not primarily because of its isolated shock-value, but because of what it *added* to that ideology. A racist ideology is one that includes attunements to racist practices, attitudes, and affects, one that has a downstream effect on attention to behaviors. The term "super-predator" added a grenade to an already existing racist ideology, which acted like its grenade launcher.

Let's illustrate the central concepts of the study of genocidal speech with a contemporary example of genocidal speech, employed to justify Russia's 2022 unprovoked invasion of Ukraine. On April 3, 2022, the Russian official press agency, RIA Novosti, published an article titled "What Should Russia Do with Ukraine?"[80] The historian Timothy Snyder has aptly described the article as "Russia's genocide handbook," noting "The Russian handbook is one of the most openly genocidal documents I have ever seen."[81] Snyder is a preeminent historian of mass killing. Snyder's assessment means that this document is one of the most openly explicit examples of genocidal speech that has ever been written. From the outset of Russia's invasion of Ukraine, Putin gave as a justification the "denazification" of Ukraine. The document fleshes out this justification.

It begins by describing Ukraine as "the enemy of Russia and a tool of the West used to destroy Russia." It begins, therefore, with an accusation in the

79. Muhammad, *The Condemnation of Blackness*, chapter 2, "Writing Crime into Race: Racial Criminalization and the Dawn of Jim Crow," 35–87.

80. Timofei Sergeitsev, "What Should Russia Do with Ukraine?," *RIA Novosti*, April 5, 2022. See also Mariia Kravchenko, "What Should Russia Do with Ukraine? [translation of a propaganda article by a Russian publication]," *Medium*, August 24, 2022, https://medium.com/@kravchenko_mm/what-should-russia-do-with-ukraine-translation-of-a-propaganda-article-by-a-russian-journalist-a3e92e3cb64.

81. Snyder, "Russia's Genocide Handbook," news page of McGrublian Center for Human Rights, Claremont McKenna, retrieved February 25, 2023, https://human-rights.cmc.edu/2022/04/14/russias-genocide-handbook/.

mirror—the claim that Ukraine will do to Russia what Russia intends to do, via its invasion, to Ukraine. It proceeds to develop the logic behind the accusation. The West has supposedly abandoned its traditional European values in favor of an ideology described as "Western totalitarianism, the imposed programs of civilizational degradation and disintegration, the mechanisms of subjugation under the superpower of the West and the United States." Russia is "the last authority in protecting and preserving those values of historical Europe (the Old World) that deserve to preserve and that the West ultimately abandoned." The supposed Western destruction of Russia by its tool, Ukraine, is an existential threat that requires nothing short of a genocidal response.

In his 1935 speech "Communism with the Mask Off," Nazi propaganda minister Joseph Goebbels describes the threat of Bolshevism in similar terms, though more explicitly antsemitic: "In its final consequences it signifies the destruction of all the commercial, social, political, and cultural achievements of Western Europe, in favour of a deracinated and nomadic international cabal which has found its representation in Judaism."[82] Just as the RIA Novosti article represents Russia as the protector of the West's traditional values in the face of the "Western totalitarianism" that seeks to annihilate them, Goebbels represents Nazism as the protector of the West's traditional values against the existential threat to civilization posed by Judaism.

The "genocide handbook" document outlines a history of grave historical wrongs Russia has supposedly suffered at the hands of the West. "Russia did everything possible to save the West," it proclaims, yet "the West decided to take revenge on Russia for the help that it had selflessly provided." Ukraine is represented as the primary tool of the West's treachery toward Russia. It is a call to do to Ukraine what Ukraine supposedly is doing to Russia and traditional values on behalf of the West: destroy it.

According to the document, "Ukronazism" is the ideology that defines Ukraine as an independent nation. It is a version of Nazism, but far worse: "Ukronazism poses a much bigger threat to the world and Russia than the Hitler version of German Nazism." It defines Ukrainian identity as an "anti-Russian construct that has no civilizational substance of its own"—that is, the central feature of Ukrainian identity is its antagonism to Russia, and it has no other nature. This means that "unlike, for example, Georgia or the Baltic States, history has proved it impossible for Ukraine to exist as a nation-state, and any attempts to 'build' such a nation-state naturally lead to Nazism."

The document describes at length the practices that constitute "denazification" of Ukraine. They include "mass investigations" to uncover personal responsibility for "the spread of Nazi ideology" (Ukrainian democracy) and "support for the Nazi regime" (an independent Ukraine). The punishments are described as forced labor, the death penalty, and imprisonment. The practice of denazification involves "the seizure of educational materials and the pro-hibition of educational programs at all levels that contain Nazi ideological guidelines" (i.e., the prohibition of anything mentioning Ukrainian identity).

The document focuses on the historical role of Russia in fighting the West. It is an attempt to provide a new definition of Russian identity, to transform the meaning of being Russian. It defines Russians as a genocidally antagonis-tic ideological social group. To be Russian is to accept the logic of genocide, the accusation that Russia is existentially threatened by Ukraine, the West's tool of war against Russia. This provides a narrative frame within which pro-Putin nationalist Russians can develop collective harmony. Within this frame, to be Russian is to be motivated by the logic of genocide to engage in the total annihilation of Ukraine. The document represents the practice of "denazifi-cation" of Ukraine as the purest exhibition of Russian identity. According to its logic, Russian identity is most perfectly exemplified by brutal and violent revenge against the treacherous people who willingly allowed themselves to be the West's tool in its mission to destroy Russia.

The propaganda used to motivate Russia's 2014 and 2022 invasions of Ukraine was not created out of whole cloth. It was socially embedded in Russia's long history of justifying colonial brutality in Ukraine.[83] It includes a history of representing Ukrainian identity as a fake anti-Russian construct. It is a campaign that Russian President Vladimir Putin dramatically acceler-ated in the years before the 2022 invasion, starting well before he ordered annexation of Crimea in 2014. It is only with this background that Putin's propaganda of "denazification" of Ukraine had purchase and power to moti-vate genocide.

Ideologies are collective attunements to, among other things, practices of behavior, and this includes verbal behavior. Introducing a word to describe a group without a richer background ideology about that group will have little effect, as a one-word description of a group is hardly rich enough to serve as an ideology, much less a racist one. A discriminatory ideology consists of a web of attunements to practices, attitudes, and affects toward members of the targeted group. To take an earlier example, simply calling members of a group "vermin" out of the blue does not *create* such an ideology. It is an idle naming practice. In contrast, adding to a preexisting racist ideology the prac-tice of calling members of that group "vermin" or "super-predators" will be a mobilizing factor in violent action against them. Similarly, "denazification," far from being created out of whole cloth, is woven tightly into an existing fabric, a nexus of practices.

In the enterprise of genocide, words like "vermin," "snakes," and "traitors" have a certain function—they mark those labeled for violent action, often mass

83. See Snyder, *The Road to Unfreedom*, especially chapter 4, "Novelty or Eternity," 111–58.

death. In order for these words to fulfill this function, they must be connected to violent practices via an ideology. For example, in Rwanda, snakes were associated with the practice of being killed by machetes, including in ceremonial circumstances that granted manhood to boys. Introducing these new labels only will have force if there is an already existing ideology into which they harmonize. Building an ideology that justifies violence against a group takes time—a mere label such as "vermin," without such a background, will be powerless; a one-word speech practice will not harmonize in isolation and is likely simply to be shrugged off by the audience that is meant to absorb it.

One of the key concepts in the study of genocidal speech is that of existential threat. The power of genocidal speech to mobilize depends on local histories of conflict and hatred, which undergird the power of accusations of existential threat. Addressing the legacies of the histories of conflict and hatred that give genocidal speech its power is part of diminishing its effectiveness. Similarly, to undermine the effectiveness of the vocabulary of "super-predators," one must weaken or eliminate the anti-Black racist ideology in the context of which "super-predators" gained the power to eliminate empathy toward Black juveniles. To undermine the genocidal ideology motivating Russia's 2022 invasion of Ukraine, one must make the character of modern Ukraine vivid, showing that it is not an "anti-Russian construct," but an ordinary nation-state in the positive sense, which developed in a way reminiscent of other European nations, with its own language and traditions, not just as a construct defined in political and cultural opposition to Russia. This kind of work, uprooting ideologies that enable genocidal speech to mobilize toward violent goals, is core to critical theory's antifascist practice.

Accusation in a mirror is a way to present a group as an existential threat. *Great Replacement Theory* (GRT) is another way to cast a group as an existential threat. GRT presupposes an ideology of the nation, according to which it is historically ethnically and religiously homogeneous and pure, with a set of fixed traditions, typically including patriarchal ones. In GRT, this ideology, including its traditions and their practitioners, is supposedly existentially imperiled by a target, usually an influx of foreign races, ethnicities, or religions. The foreign elements are sometimes described in the narrative of GRT as vermin or diseases. This influx is presented as an existential threat to the nation, its purity, its traditions, and its values. GRT is employed as a justification for mass violence against these foreign elements, as well as their internal agents.

GRT was central to the official Nazi motivation for the genocide of the Jews of Europe.[84] In *Mein Kampf*, Adolf Hitler discusses the version of GRT

---

84. Our discussion in the rest of this section overlaps and borrows from Jason Stanley and Federico Finchelstein, "White Replacement Theory Is Fascism's New Name," *Los Angeles Times*, March 24, 2022, https://www.latimes.com/opinion/story/2022-05-24/white

that underlies National Socialism, which has as its center Jews, who engineer laws to allow mass non-White immigration. Hitler writes, "The infection of the blood, which hundreds of thousands of our people undertook as though blind, is, . . . promoted by the Jew today. Systematically these black parasites of the nations ravish our innocent young blond-haired girls and thus destroy something that can no longer be replaced in this world."[85] Hitler here suggests that Jews are organizing a mass replacement of the Aryan population of Germany by non-Whites.

Mussolini's rhetoric in the run up to Italy's colonial war against Ethiopia in 1935 harped on racial paranoias about the decline and replacement of the White race. In 1934, Mussolini published a front-page newspaper article "The Death of the White Race?" and in the final paragraph posed as a key political issue: "It is a question of knowing whether in the face of the progress in number and expansion of the yellow and black races, the civilization of the white man is destined to perish."[86] This text laid the ground for the racism and segregation imposed by Italians during the war against Ethiopia in 1935 and later the racist and antisemitic laws of 1938.

In the United States, the fantasy of racial replacement goes back centuries. In 1892, Ida B. Wells, in "Southern Horrors," traces the justification of the racial terror of lynching to the White male horror at the prospect of White women having children as a result of consensual relationships with Black men.

GRT has been central to the mass violence of fascist regimes, such as the National Socialists and the Italian fascists. It has also been central in the United States to racial fascism. GRT is the ideology of the Ku Klux Klan. Federico Finchelstein and Jason Stanley have suggested that the connection between GRT and fascism, both European and American, is not accidental. GRT is central to fascist ideology.[87] This raises the question of whether the ideology of GRT, like fascism, is inconsistent with democracy.

Madison Grant's highly influential 1916 book, *The Passing of the Great Race*, focused on the replacement of Whites in America by intermingling with Black people, as well as with immigrants, such as "Polish Jews."[88] All

-replacement-theory-fascism-europe-history. We are grateful to Finchelstein for the Hitler and Mussolini references.

85. Hitler, *Mein Kampf*, 826–27.

86. Benito Mussolini, "La Razza Bianca Muore?," *La Stampa*, September 5, 1934, retrieved February 25, 2023, https://ia601805.us.archive.org/24/items/lastampa_1934 -09-05/lastampa_1934-09-05.pdf.

87. Jason Stanley and Fredericho Finchelstein, "White Replacement Theory Is Fascism's New Name," *Los Angeles Times*, May 24, 2022, https://www.latimes.com/opinion /story/2022-05-24/white-replacement-theory-fascism-europe-history.

88. Grant, *The Passing of the Great Race*. He writes, "The man of the old stock is being crowded out of many country districts by these foreigners, just as he is to-day being literally driven off the streets of New York City by the swarms of Polish Jews" (81).

of these groups were considered by Grant to be existential threats to Nordic Americans, the most important of America's "native class." (Grant, it should be noted, was fine with the presence of Black people in America, as long as they played a subordinate role.) Grant's book was an exercise in scientific racism, arguing that "Nordic whites" are superior intellectually, culturally, and morally.

Democracy is a system based around two values: freedom and equality. Fascists use GRT to argue that these democratic ideals are existential threats to the nation.[89] The first democratic ideal, equality, brings with it a demand for racial equality, which violates the racial hierarchies presupposed by GRT. The second democratic ideal, freedom, is a threat to fascist purity and tradition. For example, LGBTQ freedom allows violations of traditional patriarchal norms. Freedom threatens the ideology of a pure, patriarchal nation that is presupposed by GRT. The very first chapter of Grant's book is "Race and Democracy," in which he contends that democracy is a threat to Nordic supremacy, because democracy leads inevitably to greater immigration and equality between races.[90]

There is a close connection between fascism and genocide. The connection is not merely historical, that is, due to the prominence of fascist regimes that have committed genocide (Nazi Germany) or racial terror (the Ku Klux Klan). The connection is conceptual. Great replacement theory is both a kind of genocidal speech and a kind of fascist speech. GRT can be used to justify physical genocide, and it can be used as an argument for the necessity of a fascist regime.

GRT also figures in cultural genocide. The ideology presupposed by GRT involves a fixed set of traditions, ones that could be threatened, say, by foreign religions. GRT has been central to the arguments of European far right-wing parties against non-White and non-Christian immigration. It is present in the United States in Christian Nationalist movements, who defend Christian nativism against the threat of non-Christian immigration.

In GRT, equality is taken to be a tool central to the replacement of the dominant ethnic group. In GRT, freedom is regarded as a tool used to destabilize tradition. It is thus of note that GRT is behind two propaganda campaigns sweeping the politics of multiple democratic nations during the writing of this book: the campaign against Critical Race Theory (CRT) and the campaign against gender ideology.

89. The missing third spirit in the French trinity of democracy is of course *fraternité*, a value that tends to be espoused more at the ends of the political spectrum than in the center. "Brotherhood" suggests a fusion of identity whereby harm to one is harm to all, hence "brothers in arms" and its attendant military resonances. On the left, "brother" serves as a variant of "comrade," while the history of the far right is littered with violent political groups labeled, with undisguised sexist intent, "Brotherhood of. . . ."

90. Grant, *The Passing of the Great Race*, 3–10.

CRT, pioneered by academics such as Kimberlé Crenshaw and Derrick Bell, is an approach to understanding persisting gaps in the United States between Black and White Americans, for example, in wealth, housing, incarceration, and education. CRT rests on the fact that America's institutions were designed initially by those who sought to preserve their own status and power, including by maintaining racial hierarchies privileging White Americans.

CRT holds that while attitudes may have changed, the practices and structures they left behind persist (for example, in residential housing segregation). The political will to implement the massive structural change needed to overcome structural inequality of this sort—in education, law, finance, etc.—has not yet emerged. First, as conservative commentator David French has noted, "Time and again, there are non-racist reasons for wanting to maintain the structures racists created."[91] Secondly, the forces that zealously protect these structures as a way of preserving wealth and power remain powerful in American life.

CRT shows that, with a background of stark racial inequality, practices that are on their face neutral or meritocratic can function instead to reinforce disparities. For example, in America, public schools are to a large degree funded by local taxes. Because of racial segregation, many Black Americans are caught in underresourced schools, which leave them at a temporary educational disadvantage, harming them in meritocratic "race-blind" academic competitions.

So much for CRT. What is the campaign against CRT, and upon what is it based? The goal of the campaign is allegedly to ban the teaching of CRT in schools. But if one bans explaining to students that race-blind principles have been behind racist agendas throughout US history, one is in fact banning US history. That is the real goal of this campaign.

The effectiveness of the anti-CRT campaign rests on the discovery that the *expression* "critical race theory" can be used, like "welfare," as a political weapon. The words "critical race theory" tap into a long-standing racist narrative, the version of great replacement theory known as *White replacement theory*. According to White replacement theory, the struggle for Black equality is really an attempt, masterminded by Marxists (historically identified as Jewish) to grab power by *replacing* the culture and political power of White Americans. This narrative is embedded into US history. As a result, it has a certain intuitive familiarity that lends itself to collective harmony within a large segment of the US population.

In other words, the basis of the anti-CRT campaign is a version of great replacement theory. Its power to mobilize is inherited from the embedded narrative power of White replacement theory. The campaign against CRT consists of fomenting panic about the political and cultural power of White Americans

91. David French, "Structural Racism Isn't Wokeness, It's Reality," *Dispatch*, July 25, 2021, https://frenchpress.thedispatch.com/p/structural-racism-isnt-wokeness-its.

being replaced by Black Americans. Just as Russian propaganda represents Ukraine as the vehicle for the West's plan to destroy Russia's traditions and identity, CRT is presented as the Marxists' tool to destroy White traditions and identity. Its effectiveness is aided by the fact that White replacement theory narratives have a deeply ingrained history in the United States.

Great Replacement thinking is also behind another propaganda campaign central to the far right, not just in America but worldwide. This is the propaganda campaign against "gender ideology." The campaign against gender ideology, as Elizabeth Corredor has shown, arose first in the 1990s as a countermovement to the success of the feminist and LGBTQ movements.[92] The feminist and LGBTQ movements had challenged dominant biological understandings of gender, instead understanding gender as a cultural construction. The countermovement, which first started in the Catholic Church but has now spread worldwide, has taken the form of representing these social constructionist views of gender as an existential threat to traditions, particularly patriarchal traditions. In short, the campaign treats feminist and LGBTQ social movements as existential threats to traditional patriarchal values, which they would replace. The campaign against gender ideology is also based on great replacement theory.

Great replacement theory is, in its essence, antidemocratic. The campaigns against CRT and gender ideology inherit their antidemocratic character from their basis in great replacement theory. The basis of the anti-CRT campaign is the desire to preserve White cultural and political dominance. The anti-gender ideology campaign opposes feminist ideals, like female equality, since they threaten the inegalitarian ideology of patriarchy.

Russia's war in Ukraine is, as we have seen in detail, motivated by genocidal speech. In the campaign, all of the elements we have discussed in this section come together. Russian propaganda in support of the invasion represents Ukrainian identity as an existential threat to Russian identity, the Ukrainian language and traditions as threats to replace the Russian language and traditions, and, finally, democracy as an existential threat to Russian nationalism.

10.4. Bureaucratic Speech

Oppressive language does more than represent violence; it is violence; does more than represent the limits of knowledge; it limits knowledge. Whether it is obscuring state language or the faux-language of mindless media; whether it is the proud but calcified language of the academy or the commodity driven language of science; whether it is the malign

---

92. Corredor ("Unpacking 'Gender Ideology' and the Global Right's Antigender Countermovement") gives an excellent description of the history of the propaganda campaign, theorized as a countermovement.

language of law-without-ethics, or language designed for the estrangement
of minorities, hiding its racist plunder in its literary cheek—it must be
rejected, altered and exposed. It is the language that drinks blood, laps
vulnerabilities, tucks its fascist boots under crinolines of respectability
and patriotism as it moves relentlessly toward the bottom line and the
bottomed-out mind. Sexist language, racist language, theistic language—
all are typical of the policing languages of mastery, and cannot, do not
permit new knowledge or encourage the mutual exchange of ideas.

—TONI MORRISON[93]

In her 1993 Nobel Prize address, Toni Morrison calls attention to the oppressive nature of "obscuring state language" and "the commodity driven language of science." Morrison sees in the language of efficiency an ideology that enables mass violence and dehumanization. We are going to call the kinds of speech that are the target of Morrison's address *bureaucratic speech*. According to Morrison, bureaucratic language enables violence by masking it. Specifically, it masks the effect of policies on humanity by speaking of social reality entirely in terms of technocratic ideals. We do not have any kind of detailed theory to offer. Instead, by focusing on some examples in which bureaucratic speech does seem to be causally implicated in violence and harm to communities, we use her insights to unpack it.[94]

Bureaucratic speech certainly does not *always* harm. Much bureaucratic speech is benign, or at the very least not implicated in enabling mass violence. Morrison is calling our attention to the situations in which bureaucratic speech enables mass violence, and in distinctive ways, in virtue of its status as

93. From Morrison's Nobel Prize address, Stockholm, December 7, 1993.

94. We discuss here bureaucratic speech as a state language that is used to control a national population, but we do not mean to suggest that it is the only type of language that fulfills such functions politically. Neither do we mean to imply that those seeking to maintain control in different nation-states and political regions uniformly use the same rhetorical methods. On the contrary, we suppose that the most effective language of control in a given sphere depends heavily on cultural resonance, varying according to local history, social organization, and ways of seeing and talking about the world. Here we think of the work of Lisa Wedeen, who sets detailed ethnographic studies of individual-level discourse in Syria and Yemen in the context of national political situations. An example of a type of discourse we don't discuss in detail in this volume, but that she shows is integral to political discourse in Assad's Syria, is discourse that extends the metaphor of family to a national and political level (*Ambiguities of Domination*, 49–65). Authoritarian regimes commonly use familial metaphors and familial framings, in particular the idea of the leader as father to the nation, but the use of family in Syria is extended: "The official narrative communicates understandings of obedience and community in terms of a chain of filial piety and paternal authority that culminates, and stops, in Asad." Further, while the "invocation of family relationships may be more or less resonant to individual Syrians," it is nonetheless the case that Syrians perforce must partake in the discourse every day: "To be 'Syrian' means, in part, to operate within this rhetorical universe" (65).

bureaucratic. The general challenge bureaucratic speech poses is to explain why speech that is not on the surface harmful is nevertheless almost invariably present as part of the surrounding justification of mass atrocities.

In Golfo Alexopoulos's 2017 book about Stalin's Gulag, she documents how "the Gulag leadership masked the violence of physical exploitation" by the use of bureaucratic terminology.[95] The central concept of Gulag bureaucracy was "labor utilization," which was used as a yardstick of camp function, and was designed to set the Gulag prisoners in a positive light; to do this, four categories were used, which Alexopoulos lists as (i) "labor force, working in industry," (ii) "occupied in the service and maintenance of camps and colonies," (iii) "Sick," and (iv) "Not working for various reasons."[96] Given what we know about the extraordinarily high rates of malnutrition and associated ills in the Gulag, a suspiciously high percentage of prisoners in the Gulag were classified in "labor force, working in industry."[97] The reason here is that in the Gulag bureaucracy, many activities counted as "industry," and even gravely malnourished prisoners too weak to climb out of their beds, could count as participating in some industry, for example knitting. The capacity to participate in some industry or other precluded classification as sick, so prisoners in the Gulag could find themselves denied medical care until they were already well on their way to death from malnourishment and other forms of imposed weaknesses. The word "industry," from the official bureaucratic vocabulary, was defined in a way that masked mass starvation in the Gulag camps. Other official state vocabulary was completely explicit in its purpose, of masking harsh reality. Forced labor for sick patients was called "labor therapy."[98]

These specific Gulag examples are from the language of Gulag bureaucracy, and are also paradigm examples of speech that harms by masking mass violence. In each case, the harm stems from a devious use in the bureaucratic language of some ordinary term ("industry" in one case, and "therapy" in the other). These examples suggest that bureaucracies mask mass violence by the strategic redefinition of ordinary terms, and the strategic aim of the redefinitions is to mask the violence of the state. We should expect that in states whose policies and institutions are implicated in mass violence, some of the language of its bureaucracy was strategically designed to mask it. That is what bureaucracies in such states regularly do.

In May 2022, an investigation by journalist Dean Kirby found that many thousands of Ukrainians from territories occupied by Russia during

---

95. Alexopoulos, *Illness and Inhumanity in Stalin's Gulag*, 208.

96. Alexopoulos, *Illness and Inhumanity in Stalin's Gulag*, 210–11.

97. Alexopoulos (*Illness and Inhumanity in Stalin's Gulag*, 241) writes, "The MVD-Gulag leadership wanted camps to report around 70–80 percent of prisoners in Group A working in industry, so camps were sure to classify this many as 'basically fit for physical labor.'"

98. Alexopoulos, *Illness and Inhumanity in Stalin's Gulag*, 86.

its invasion had been "sent to remote camps up to 5,500 miles from their homes."[99] Analyzing local news reports, Kirby identified up to 66 camps. In language clearly evocative of the Gulag, one activist told Kirby that the "state treats them as a labor force, as objects, moving them around without taking care of what they need." The deep social embeddedness of the ideology of the Gulag forms the background of the Russian genocide in Ukraine today.

Classifying prisoners as "willful work refusers" who, because of starvation, are too weak for work was a very deliberate attempt by the Soviet regime to mask the Gulag's crimes. Alexopoulos's view is that the Gulag labor utilization classification was intentionally designed to mask these crimes. In this case, it was the state bureaucracy that was the source of the intentional masking of mass violence. The reason that state bureaucracies are such effective sources of such masking is, as Toni Morrison argued, because bureaucracies are supposed to be guided by technocratic ideals, which in turn are supposed to be neutral. Institutions that are governed by supposedly neutral ideals, such as bureaucracies, are particularly effective production sites of perniciously ideological state propaganda, because they are supposedly governed by neutral technocratic ideals, which are supposed to be by their nature incompatible with the practice of using vocabulary in the service of strategic masking of injustice. As we saw in chapter 7, claims of neutrality regularly play just this strategic role of masking the presence of problematic ideologies.

Turning to the United States, a Michigan law allowed for "emergency managers" to replace elected officials in cases of "financial emergency." Emergency managers were supposedly experts in "financial efficiency."[100] Mayors, city councils, and school districts supposedly in "financial emergency" across Michigan received emergency managers, including the city of Flint. Under the guise of financial responsibility, the emergency manager regime delivered hazardous waste to Flint's homes, which six thousand or so children bathed in and drank for almost eighteen months.

According to Shawna J. Lee and her University of Michigan School of Social Work based colleagues, African-Americans comprised 14 percent of Michigan's population. Despite their much lower total representation in the Michigan population, 51 percent of African-Americans in Michigan were under an emergency manager at some point from 2008 to 2013. The Hispanic or Latino population comprised just 4.4 percent of the Michigan population, yet it too was also overrepresented, with 16.6 percent of all Michigan Hispanic

99. Dean Kirby, "Putin Sends Mariupol Survivors to Remote Corners of Russia as Investigation Reveals Network of Camps," *inews*, May 7, 2022, https://inews.co.uk/news/putin-mariupol-survivors-remote-corners-russia-investigation-network-camps-1615516.

100. For references and extended discussion of the role of emergency managers in the Flint water crisis, see Stanley, "The Emergency Manager: Strategic Racism, Technocracy, and the Poisoning of Flint's Children."

or Latinos under an emergency manager at some point during 2008–13. In contrast, during the same time period, although non-Hispanic Whites comprised 76.6 percent of Michigan residents, only 2.4 percent of Whites in the state were under an emergency manager.

Michigan's Emergency Manager Law is supposedly guided by neutral metrics of "financial efficiency." Yet in practice, it found 97.6 percent of Michigan White citizens to be capable of democratic self-governance, in contrast to the 51 percent of Black citizens, who were deemed not worthy of elected representation, due to "financial emergency." The language of financial efficiency served to mask anti-Black racism (Morrison's "racist plunder"). The decisions made by the appointed emergency managers, most obviously in Flint, but also in the Detroit public schools, resulted in terrible harm to their populations, largely by favoring attempts to earn or save money over any other goal. The Detroit Public School System was moved into a new statewide system called the Educational Achievement Authority (EAA). In September 2014, investigative journalist Curt Guyette wrote an article titled "The EAA Exposed: An Investigative Report."[101] The article showed that the EAA seemed to function more like a product-testing laboratory for a software company, using its ten thousand children to test its product, "Buzz," and the taxpayer money of their parents to support the company.

In Michigan, the technocratic ideal of financial efficiency masked racism and harmed the populations it was supposed to help. In most cases, the policies passed by appeal to this ideal were not even financially efficient—for example, refusing to allow municipalities under emergency managers to sue banks for fraudulent loans is clearly something done in the interest of banks. Nevertheless, what happened in Michigan under the guise of financial efficiency was not as deliberately bad faith as the Soviet classification of labor utilization. Still, *even if it had resulted in financially efficient outcomes*, the consequences would be unacceptable in a democracy. And yet that very fact is masked by the language.

Bureaucratic speech attunes its audience to a limited set of allegedly neutral metrics. Such metrics by their nature are insensitive to a host of harms to human dignity and human flourishing. The function of the metrics is to direct people's attention away from these harms. Bureaucratic speech pushes attention away from the issues that affect them, and not toward any meaningful a way to think about those issues. As Randal Marlin says (in a discussion of what Jacques Ellul termed "rational propaganda"), "Citations of facts and figures leave the impression of great rationality, but the hearer is unable or unwilling to analyze the figures and is persuaded by the appearance

101. Curt Guyette, "The EAA Exposed: An Investigative Report," *Detroit Metro Times*, September 24, 2014, http://www.metrotimes.com/detroit/the-eaa-exposed-an - investigative-report/Content?oid=2249513.

of rationality rather than by coming to grips with genuine reality."[102] If one designs a school system solely around financial efficiency, one will be led to use the school system as a method to earn money by, for example, exploiting students. Exploiting students to earn money may be financially efficient, and it may lead to an expanded endowment for the school district. But it is an unacceptable outcome in a liberal democracy, as these policies have consequences that diminish human flourishing. Bureaucratic speech is woven into the fabric of an ideology that privileges financial exigency above human rights and equality, and privileges the voices of a technocratic elite in-group who is supposedly in a privileged epistemic position above the majority. An ideology that revolves around practices in which the voices of an in-group have greater weight than those of the out-group is, according to our definition, discriminatory, even if the values expressed by practitioners are superficially democratic.

In May 2022, a US Supreme Court decision revoking *Roe v. Wade*, authored by Supreme Court Justice Samuel Alito, was leaked. One of the arguments Justice Alito gave for his decision involved adoption. In a footnote, Justice Alito cited the Center for Disease Control, commenting that "domestic supply of infants relinquished at birth or within the first month of life and available to be adopted had become virtually non-existent." Justice Alito appealed to this bureaucratic conceptualization of women as "domestic suppliers" of babies to reverse women's access to abortion—if women's function is as "domestic suppliers of babies," they are hardly agents with rights.[103]

Almost definitionally, bureaucratic speech represents itself as neutral and nonideological. This is often given as a selling point. As we saw in chapter 7, this selling point is fictional. Claims to neutrality are invariably ideological. The supposed neutrality that bureaucratic speech typically represents itself as embodying is incoherent. The claim to neutrality is central to the usefulness of bureaucratic speech in masking atrocities of various sorts. Calling attention to such atrocities often requires explicit moral language. As Golfo Alexopoulos notes, "Violent human exploitation constituted the essential purpose of Stalin's Gulag."[104] The purpose was not labor utilization.

Patricia Hill Collins has drawn attention to another venue in which bureaucratic speech can be oppressive, in the academy. In describing the ideology of positivism, Collins writes,

---

102. Marlin, *Propaganda and the Ethics of Persuasion*, 38. Ellul himself writes of the effects of bombarding the public with facts and figures: "What remains with the individual affected by this propaganda is a perfectly irrational picture, a purely emotional feeling, a myth. The facts, the data, the reasoning—all are forgotten, and only the impression remains. . . . Thus propaganda in itself becomes honest, strict, exact, but its effect remains irrational" (*Propaganda: The Formation of Men's Attitudes*, 86).

103. Thanks to Scott Shapiro for calling attention to this on Twitter: @scottjshapiro, Tweet, May 8, 2022, https://twitter.com/scottjshapiro/status/1523309136540098560.

104. Alexopoulos, *Illness and Inhumanity in Stalin's Gulag*, 4.

Positivist approaches aim to create scientific descriptions of reality by producing objective generalizations. Because researchers have widely differing values, experiences, and emotions, genuine science is thought to be unattainable unless all human characteristics except rationality are eliminated from the research process. By following strict methodological rules, scientists aim to distance themselves from the values, vested interests, and emotions generated by their class, race, sex, or unique situation. By decontextualizing themselves, they allegedly become detached observers and manipulators of nature.[105]

As Collins points out, when positivist approaches are the dominant knowledge-validation method, they rule out other sources of knowledge, such as narrative testimony. Positivist ideology masks reality when it blocks legitimate sources of knowledge about it.

Bureaucratic language is openly antidemocratic. The practices of using bureaucratic language signal membership of an exclusive community of practice, which cannot be freely joined because of systemic societal issues and active gatekeeping. The practices have resonances that include the bureaucratic ideology and the practices of wielding power within it. The use of bureaucratic language establishes collective harmony among the controllers, which alleviates individual responsibility, a point familiar from Hannah Arendt.[106] The bureaucrats live in their own echo chamber, like a cult, but a cult with power. A natural analogue is leadership by religious zealots, even if the state religion happens to be technocratic economics. Their ideology is presented as objective and inevitable, but it is in fact discriminatory and arbitrary. The maintenance of bureaucratic practices in the face of a community whose humanity has not been fully recognized involves active resistance to convergent accommodation, which would open the echo chamber to other ways of thinking. Such accommodation would signal common humanity, acceptance of the will of the people as they express that will, and membership of a joint community of practice with common goals. Bureaucratic practices block such accommodation, leaving control in the hands of its exclusive community of practice.

105. Collins, *Black Feminist Thought*, 255.
106. Arendt, *Eichmann in Jerusalem: A Report on the Banality of Evil*.

CHAPTER ELEVEN

Free Speech

The First Amendment was conceived by white men from the point of view of their social position. Some of them owned slaves; most of them owned women. They wrote it to guarantee their freedom to keep something they felt at risk of losing. Namely—and this gets to my next point—speech which they did not want lost through state action. They wrote the First Amendment so their speech would not be threatened by this powerful instrument they were creating, the federal government. You recall that it reads, "Congress shall make no law abridging . . . the freedom of speech." They were creating that body. They were worried that it would abridge something they did have. You can tell that they had speech, because what they said was written down: it became a document, it has been interpreted, it is the law of the state.

—CATHARINE MACKINNON[1]

RUSSIA'S 2013 GAY PROPAGANDA LAW banned the promotion of nontraditional lifestyles to minors. This law had a devastating effect on Russia's society, sending its LGBTQ citizens deeply into the closet for self-protection, and preventing Russian citizens generally from understanding LGBTQ perspectives. Robust free-speech protections would prevent such a law. There is scarcely any question that such principles are vital in protecting freedom. Banning books, restricting history, and suppressing the teaching of minority perspectives— all of these acts are inimical to a free society. And yet, free societies are often *imperiled* by propaganda, which is allowed by robust free-speech protections. Let's call this *the paradox of democracy*. In this chapter, we use our model to sharpen this paradox.

In the bulk of this chapter, we canvass a number of arguments for free-speech principles of various scopes. In each case, we will show that the arguments make problematic idealizations. We conclude by tentatively endorsing a familiar suggestion for refocusing debate about the regulation of speech.

There are a variety of justifications for freedom of speech. These arguments have different *scopes*, in the sense that they are set out to protect different zones for a free-speech principle. For example, Alexander Meiklejohn, emphasizing the point that "the First Amendment . . . is not the guardian of unrestricted talkativeness," aims to protect speech providing relevant viewpoints

1. MacKinnon, *Feminism Unmodified*, 207.

on topics that citizens are deciding upon in joint deliberation of policy, as if in a town meeting.[2] In what follows, we consider various justifications for free-speech principles in the light of our theoretical framework.

Justifications of free speech also differ in the basic moral frameworks upon which they draw. The most salient division is the one between consequentialism and deontology. The largest class of argument for free speech takes the form of a consequentialist argument—having a free-speech ideal will result in society having, collectively, more of a desirable property: knowledge, for instance, or democratically functioning institutions. Other arguments are based not on effects, but on the reasonableness of speech in itself. This is the case for deontological arguments based on autonomy, conceived as something to which we have a right—a right is something we have regardless of its consequences. A consequentialist argument appeals to very different kinds of premises than the autonomy argument. You won't, for example, find premises about rights in consequentialist arguments. And you won't find premises about what maximizes some good property in deontological arguments. If we restrict ourselves either just to consequentialist or autonomy arguments for free speech, we find they too differ in the attendant commitments of their premises. Despite this variety, we will argue that all of them make false idealizing presuppositions about speech.

The view that speech can be inimical to democracy has a long history. In book VIII of Plato's *Republic*, Socrates argues that democracy is the form of government most likely to lead immediately to tyranny. The argument that democracy leads directly to tyranny appeals to the ideal of free speech, which Plato rightly regards as central to the system of democracy. According to Plato, democracy leads to tyranny, because the character of its citizens and its central values enable the rise of a tyrant and virtually guarantee their success:

> [The people's protector's] docile followers grant him so much free rein that he shrinks from nothing, even shedding the blood of his own kin. He resorts to the customary unjust accusations in order to haul the victim into court and then to take his life. So he murders, and with impious tongue and lips consumes his own flesh and blood.[3]

Democracy's liberties enable all character types to vie for power. Using free speech, the would-be tyrant lies and spreads fear, presenting himself as "the people's protector" against a supposedly dangerous group. A tyrant has no barrier against using dangerous propaganda to seize power. Democracy's liberties allow a tyrant to seek this path, using speech that harms democracy.

Plato's concern here is with propaganda and its role in creating what we have termed an *antagonistic ideological social group*. The natural home of political

2. Meiklejohn, *Political Freedom: The Constitutional Powers of the People*, 26.
3. Plato, *The Republic*, 257 (565e).

propaganda is in the drum up to war. The tyrant must ceaselessly promote the people's sense that they "will always be in need of a leader" and thus "undertake[s] an ongoing search for pretexts to make war."[4] Plato is arguing that to stay in power, the tyrant must use language to foment ungrounded fear of others. A system based on liberty as a political ideal must allow those most unsuited to be political leaders to seek that role. And a system based on liberty as a political ideal allows them to use demagogic propaganda to seize it. Plato's argument against liberty as a political ideal depends upon strong assumptions about the power of speech to successfully instill democratically problematic emotions.

Plato is right to warn of speech that threatens freedom. The existence and ubiquity of such speech poses a serious threat to arguments for free-speech principles.

11.1. On the Benefits of Free Speech

The classical philosophical defense of free speech is "Of the Liberty of Thought and Discussion," chapter 2 of John Stuart Mill's *On Liberty*. The guiding principle of Mill's inquiry is the *Harm Principle* laid out in his first chapter:

> The only purpose for which power can be rightfully exercised over any member of a civilized community, against his will, is to prevent harm to others.[5]

In chapter 2, Mill offers a *consequentialist* argument, the goal of achieving the common good being his primary justification in support of free speech. A society with the widest possible freedom of speech will be one that ends up having both better justification for its guiding principles as well as citizens who are more knowledgeable and more able to form correct judgments about policy. These goods must be weighed, of course, against potential harms of having free speech in Mill's broad sense.

Chapter 2 of *On Liberty* concludes with brief consideration of a "more fundamental objection" to freedom of opinion.[6] The objection involves the damage of "intemperate discussion," including "invective, sarcasm, personality." Mill regards these damages as less serious in discussion between equals; for Mill, "whatever mischief arises from their use is greatest when they are employed against the comparatively defenseless." Contrarily, Mill traces the harm ("mischief") of invective and sarcasm to differential power relations— when these tools are directed against the defenseless.

For example, imagine an entrenched religious orthodoxy that has seized the power in the institutions and directs invective against outsiders who raise

---

4. Plato, *The Republic*, 259 (566e).
5. Mill, *On Liberty*, 9.
6. Mill, *On Liberty*, 51.

skepticism against it, or wealthy aristocrats ridiculing impoverished workers who seek better working conditions. A power relation of the one class over the other makes speech harmful, in ways that make the situation harder, rather than easier, for improving the society democratically or otherwise. In short, a concern for Mill's argument for free speech (here, that it does not violate his "harm principle"), is the existence of power differentials in a society. He believes such differentials allow speech to be worrisomely harmful, and in such a way as to impact directly the benefits of free speech.

This suggests that Mill regards authority as necessary to explain harmful speech in these cases. According to Mill, speech is given the power to harm because of large differences in power between people. There is now a large literature devoted to evaluating the question of whether the harm of speech depends on power relations in this way.

The topic of authority and subordinating power has been much discussed in more recent philosophy. Rae Langton's "Pornography's Authority? Response to Leslie Green" begins "Subordinating speech is authoritative speech," continuing a theme from her classic 1993 paper, "Speech Acts and Unspeakable Acts."[7] Using speech act concepts from J. L. Austin, Langton argues that a vital "felicity condition" for subordinating speech is a speaker's authority. Speech is harmful because of the power relations of one group over another. Langton and Mill are no doubt correct that authority can make subordinating speech more harmful. Many of the legal cases involving harmful speech manifest power differentials of the kind that threatens the democratic benefits of speech, for example, employers leveling harmful racist speech at employees who promote adherence to union rules.[8] Other legal cases involve White employees accosting fellow Black employees with racist slurs. However, it is far from obvious that authority of the speaker is necessary for speech to be genuinely harmful.

In Charles Lawrence's paper in the seminal critical race theory volume from 1993, *Words That Wound*, he discusses an incident that affected his family in their home of Wilmington, Delaware. In the school that his nephews attended, four of their peers had drawn racist and antisemitic slogans, pictures of hooded Klansmen, Nazi swastikas, and a burning cross.[9] The slogans and symbols had been drawn by teenagers, with presumably little authority. But Lawrence makes clear that the speech was harmful nonetheless, even on those in greater positions of authority. And there are many such discussions of harmful speech without apparent authority in the critical race theory

---

7. "Pornography's Authority?" is chapter 4 of Langton, *Sexual Solipsism*. The 1993 paper is Langton, "Speech Acts and Unspeakable Acts."

8. Delgado gives, for example, the case of *Alcorn v. Anbro Engineering, Inc.*, in which a White supervisor accosted his Black employee who had confronted him with violating union rules with the N-word (Delgado, "A Tort Action for Racial Insults," 97–98).

9. Lawrence, "Regulating Racist Speech on Campus," 73.

literature. In Mari Matsuda, Charles R. Lawrence III, Richard Delgado, and Kimberlé Williams Crenshaw's introduction to *Words That Wound*, the case of harmful speech they begin by discussing is the Ujamaa incident at Stanford University, in which two White freshmen defaced a Beethoven poster, creating a caricature of a Black man, with racist slurs scrawled across it. This is also not obviously an example in which authority, at least not officially sanctioned authority, is central to the harm.[10]

More recently, Ishani Maitra has argued against the authority claim, on the grounds that a homeless person on a subway with little social authority can yell racist and Islamophobic slogans and still engage in subordinating speech.[11] The case is analogous to one we have considered (section 5.2 and section 10.2), that of a child using a slur that they don't fully understand. We argued that a slur can retain the power to wound independently of the understanding or intention of the speaker, because the ability of the slur to draw attention to a despised categorization rests on the discriminatory ideology of the community of practice within which the slur is used, and so does not depend crucially on the speaker's mental state. In the modern world, we can think of social media, where many random Twitter accounts, none particularly high in authority, combine to create a subordinating speech environment against their target. Again, the mental state of individuals who tweet is not crucial. Indeed, the question of whether some of those producing tweets even have mental states is a vexed one, since they may be bots.

One can easily maintain the view that an imbalance in power relations is necessary for speech to harm, in the face of these examples. It's plausible that power relations are evoked not by the individuals—teenagers drawing on walls, or a homeless person on a subway—but by the ideologies their actions invoke. It is because Black Americans are oppressed that drawing pictures of hooded Klansmen or hanging nooses from trees harms—the White supremacist ideology is powerful. Powerless agents can invoke in their actions and words powerful ideologies.[12] As we suggested in section 10.2, "an important characteristic of the resonance of a slur is that it replicates power relationships," and that characteristic extends to other symbols of discriminatory ideology, rather transparently in the case of the representation of members of a militia or of a standardized mode of oppressive violence.

10. Matsuda et al., *Words That Wound*, 8.

11. Maitra, "Subordinating Speech."

12. To preserve a central role for authority in hate speech, some philosophers have compellingly urged that we need to broaden our conception of authority beyond traditional notions of epistemic or practical authority. For example, Michael Barnes has argued that we need the notion of a *stable informal authority*, which would explain why some propagandists' assertions hold sway over large audiences, despite lack of markers of epistemic or practical authority, that is, no credentials or political office (Barnes, "Presupposition and Propaganda").

Mill's concern is not ultimately with the source of harmful speech, but the fact of harmful speech. Mill regards the power of speech to harm so seriously that he thinks the consequentialist arguments provided in the chapter do not suffice to override them. Did Mill provide a compelling solution to this "more fundamental objection" to the freedom of speech?

Mill's solution to the problem he raises is a "real morality of public discussion."[13] What Mill meant here was that in order for a broad system of free-speech laws to be in place, there must be a system of norms that prevents people in authority from using their power and status to dominate others in conversation. In short, Mill's argument for free speech presupposes what we have called a dialogically healthy environment, one in which joint negotiations of meaning are possible. Perhaps a system of morality of public discussion was robust among the gentlemen in Victorian England in his day—we cannot adjudicate the matter here. But we live in an emotionally, epistemically, and behaviorally polarized society. That is, we live in a society that is not a dialogically healthy environment. It's therefore fair to wonder whether his arguments have contemporary relevance today in our various conflicts about the extent of free-speech principles.

In the presence of a "real morality of public discussion," Mill argues that societies guided by a free-speech ideal are likely to maximize epistemic benefits, without violating the harm principle. Mill's argument depends on robust and controversial claims about extralegal but socially powerful systems of norms. These kinds of systems of norms are manifestly lacking today.

Robert Post has an influential account of how to preserve the epistemic benefits of free speech in the presence of an information space filled with conspiracy theories and other malign speech that threatens the public information space.[14] Post argues for the importance of scientific institutions and universities, maintaining that intelligent self-government requires experts to be shielded from state control, because the democratic competence of participants in public discourse requires their having "access to disciplinary knowledge."[15] Post's thought is that scientific research institutions, by conditioning discourse to rules of scientific debate, when wedded to a raucous public sphere, can lend order and rigor to channel the chaos of open debate in ways that allow the truth to win out. Is this a plausible response to the epistemic threat of oppressive speech?

By securing access to expert knowledge, and thereby securing "democratic competence" of citizens, one might hope to ameliorate the harms of oppressive speech.[16] We are sympathetic to this view, but it creates a tension. As we have

13. Mill, *On Liberty*, 52.

14. Post, *Democracy, Expertise, and Academic Freedom*.

15. Post, *Democracy, Expertise, and Academic Freedom*, 34.

16. The argument for democratic competence is developed in Post, *Democracy, Expertise, and Academic Freedom*, chapter 2, "Democratic Competence and the First Amendment," 27–60.

seen, one kind of oppressive speech is *bureaucratic speech*. When bureaucratic speech oppresses, it does so by masking harmful ideologies and realities. In its positivist version, it is in tension with democracy, since it involves active resistance to accommodating non-experts.

In Frederick Hoffman's 1896 book, *Race Traits and Tendencies of the American Negro*, he argues that Black people have less "vital force" than White people.[17] This is a work of scientific racism, filled with statistics and massive amounts of evidence. Hoffman devotes an entire chapter largely to showing that Black people have "excessive mortality."[18] In another, he argues that Black people have vastly greater propensity toward criminality. In each case, he claims that there is no environmental explanation—for example, he argues that "in Washington, the colored race has had exceptional educational, religious, and social opportunities," in order to show that poor environment cannot explain a lack of "moral progress" or racial differences in arrests.[19] In his discussion of mortality, he argues that the relevant White and Black populations in his studies have the same environmental conditions.

Hoffman's book is presented as the epitome of scientific reason. But these ideals of reason are hijacked by racist ideology. As the historian Khalil Muhammad argues, the vocabulary of crime and disease resonated with anti-Black racist ideology during the end of the nineteenth century (as it does today).[20] The use of this and related vocabulary in this context attuned people to racist ideology, thereby masking social and environmental causes of crime and disease. When Hoffman turns to the topic of White European immigrant populations and their high crime, disease, and divorce rates, these environmental factors suddenly and vividly appear to him as obvious explanations.

In his work, Hoffman argues that White European immigrant populations in Northern cities face terrible social and environmental conditions, and that this explains their high crime rates. What is happening? Recall Jessie Munton's definition of prejudice as a structure that gives undue salience to

---

17. Hoffman, *Race Traits and Tendencies of the American Negro*, 99.

18. Hoffman, *Race Traits and Tendencies of the American Negro*, chapter 2, "Vital Statistics," 33–148.

19. Hoffman, *Race Traits and Tendencies of the American Negro*, 236–37.

20. Muhammad, *The Condemnation of Blackness*. He writes, "Using new data from the 1870, 1880, and 1890 U.S. census reports, the earliest demographic studies to measure the full scale of black life in freedom, these post-emancipation writers helped to create the racial knowledge necessary to shape the future of race relations. Racial knowledge that had been dominated by anecdotal, hereditarian, and pseudo-biological theories of race would gradually be transformed by new social scientific theories of race and society and new tools of analysis, namely racial statistics and social surveys. Out of the new methods and data sources, black criminality would emerge, alongside disease and intelligence, as a fundamental measure of black inferiority" (20).

certain properties (discussed in section 7.6).[21] When crime by Black people is at issue, Hoffman (and anyone with anti-Black racist attitudes) gives their race undue salience. To a racist, even an unconscious one, in the case of crime by Black people, race "leaps out" as an explanation. This has the effect of masking the environment as a cause of crime. But when the topic is high crime rates in White immigrant populations, Hoffman is suddenly able to recognize environmental conditions that explain social problems. Stephen Jay Gould provides similar explanations for other examples of scientific racism. For example, in discussing Samuel George Morton's craniometry studies, he shows that Morton gathered his evidence on the assumption that Black skulls would be smaller, tossing aside large Black skulls as corruptions of the data pool.[22]

The proposal we have been considering is that experts' knowledge, if protected from state control and accessible to citizens, will filter out problematic ideologies that impede rationality. But technocratic and academic discourse can carry along these ideologies, serving as the vehicle of masking.

The long history of scientific racism makes it clear that experts have used their association with institutions of scientific research not to cut through the cacophony of public debate, but to advance biased arguments, whose bias is concealed by scientific vocabulary that is vibrant with resonances that unconsciously affect the scientific community (as in the language of crime, or IQ). As Gould emphasizes, just as in our discussion of bureaucratic speech in the previous chapter, the scientific background of the scientists he discusses— leading figures of their time—served not to pierce racist ideology, but to mask it. Bureaucratic speech is, as we have discussed at length, a particularly powerful vehicle for justifying harmful ideologies. Rather than exposing harmful ideologies, it often conceals them.

In *Epistemic Injustice*, Miranda Fricker defines the central case of what she calls "testimonial injustice" as a credibility excess or deficit due to a social identity or class difference—with characteristic examples being deficits in the credibility given to women due to prejudices about gender, or to people because of their race or class.[23] If a society has traditionally subjugated a group, preventing them from accessing the higher reaches of formal education and limiting the opportunities for the few who make their way through the substantial initial obstacles, equating expertise with institutional power would lead to epistemic injustice against this group, whose lack of access to the elevated status of expert would be read into the flawed stereotype of their group as worthy of less credibility.

In the Black feminist tradition, we find a clear warning about the dangers of giving additional authority in the form of "democratic competence" to experts. Patricia Hill Collins argues that appeal to the special authority of

21. Munton, "Prejudice as the Misattribution of Salience."
22. Gould, *The Mismeasure of Man*, 65.
23. Fricker, *Epistemic Injustice*.

scientific expertise, what she calls "Eurocentric knowledge validation processes," has been used to discount the valid testimony of Black women speaking from their own experiences, who have been denied educational opportunities.[24] Following Collins, Kristie Dotson has singled out a distinctive species of testimonial injustice related to misuses of democratic competence. *Contributory injustice*, in Dotson's terms, occurs when an agent's testimony is discounted or reduced in credence solely because it is not backed up with the proper "official" epistemological resources—in this case, the ones provided by data and statistics.[25] This does not mean, of course, that data and statistics are "White." But restricting public reason to this vocabulary excludes people from discussion who are without access to educational institutions because of structural oppression. As we know, for example, from recent US discussions of the history of policing, this has been a terrible error. As the historian Elizabeth Hinton shows, poor Black communities in the late 1960s living in urban housing projects were vividly clear about the problematic and racist nature of policing practices in their communities, and they suggested changes to policing practices that are now widely regarded as important.[26] Their suggestions were not heeded or taken seriously; they were discredited because of their source.

As we argued in the previous chapter, bureaucratic speech creates a community of practice that is structured by active resistance to accommodating the views of those outside the circle of expertise. In considering the relationship between democratic competence and expert knowledge, we shouldn't abstract away from the kind of bureaucratic speech that serves as a barrier to the deliberative environment that is central to democracy.

There are clear cases in which we do want to rely on scientific expertise in policy making, where oppressive speech is less of an issue—the science of climate change or vaccines are examples. But the science that bears most directly on politics—social science—certainly can and often has functioned to mask harmful ideologies. Social scientific discussions of crime have proven at times shockingly prone to racist bias, suggesting, as Khalil Muhammad argues, that the language of crime resonates with Blackness.[27]

24. Collins, *Black Feminist Thought*, 253–57.

25. Dotson, "A Cautionary Tale."

26. Hinton, *America on Fire*, chapter 2, "The Projects," 46–69. She quotes, for example, Black Unity Conference spokesman Edward Davis: "if the chief can state there have been no problems in the black community, it is obvious that he is unaware of what is going on in his department" (58).

27. The following passage from Muhammad is striking in highlighting a specific change in the way crime was reported so as to focus on Black crime rates: "The nation's most respected and authoritative crime source . . . simplified the racial crime calculus in 1930s America. Blackness now stood as the singular mark of a criminal. 'Negro' became the only statistically significant category in the [Uniform Crime Report] tables upon which to measure 'white' criminality, deviance, and pathology" (*The Condemnation of Blackness*, 270).

In 1996, exactly one hundred years after the publication of Hoffman's influential work predicting the imminent demise of the United States' Black population, the social scientist John DiIulio advanced his influential "Super-Predator Theory," which maintained the United States faced a coming wave of hardened youth criminals, "as many as half" of whom could be "young Black males." DiIulio predicted a massive wave of violent crime in the United States from 1996 to 2010.[28] In fact, by 2010, US violent crimes rates, which had steadily and rapidly decreased since the early 1990s, were at historic lows. In an article thick with statistics, the Princeton professor made bold and confident predictions about a wave in crime despite the fact that crime had been rapidly declining for at least three years, a fact noted at the very beginning of his 1996 article. Essentially, DiIulio's prediction of a crime wave was due to a rising demographic of Black youth—and DiIulio's assumptions that crime rates in populations do not vary with changing socioeconomic circumstances. The bizarre nature of this assumption, embedded in an article that begins by acknowledging that violent crime had been decreasing for several years, was masked by racist resonances of the vocabulary of crime.

The racist resonances of the vocabulary of crime are measurable. We have defined something to be a resonance of a practice to the extent that it has increased likelihood of occurring in the context of that practice. If one looks at occurrences of the crime-related words "crime," "criminal," and "gang member" in books published in the United States, one finds that they are all three to five times as likely to be preceded by "[B/b]lack" than by "[W/w]hite."[29] By comparison, terms associated with non-Black ethnicities or races occur at zero or entirely negligible rates in such contexts. In the context of the word "rapist," the word "[B/b]lack" is nearly ten times as likely to occur as the word "[W/w]hite," and no other word for a race or ethnicity occurs prominently in this context. There is a notable special case of the plural "rapists." From 2015, the frequency of the word "Mexican" suddenly shot up, so that it came to parallel the frequency of "[B/b]lack" before "rapists," with both occurring at well over double "[W/w]hite," and with no other ethnic, racial, or national group being prominent. That spike was created single-handedly by Donald Trump, who in the speech declaring his candidacy for US President in 2015 said of Mexican immigrants "They're rapists" (with the caveat, "And some, I assume, are good people"). Most of the later usages of "Mexican rapists" we see are traceable to Trump's openly racist presentations of a violent stereotype of Mexican immigrants in the United States.

Let us make explicit a comment on this data that otherwise might be uncharitably taken out of context: the changing rate of occurrence of racial,

28. DiIulio, "My Black Crime Problem, and Ours."

29. All frequencies cited were obtained using Google Ngram searches on October 18, 2022, and relate to Google's American English books corpus, with years 1969–2019.

ethnic, and national terms in the context of discussion of crime has nothing to do with changes in actual rates of crime by particular groups, and has everything to do with what people following certain political agendas (whether willfully or not) find it important to talk about. There has been no sudden change in the national origins of rapists during the time we have been writing this book, but there has been a dramatic change in the salience of a particular national origin in talk about rapists.

One thing that follows from the above data on word frequencies is that the resonances of crime talk include the salience of racial, ethnic, and national categories. These resonances are problematic. It is plausible that people who are regularly exposed to terms like "Black crime" have an increased tendency to form the idea that this is an important category in and of itself, and thus that there is an inherent link between being Black and having criminal tendencies. It is inevitable that for some this link will be essentialized, so that there is not only a false overattribution of crime to certain groups, but there is a view that this is an inherent property of people in those groups. Thus, it is plausible, and in line with his writing, that the resonance between crime talk and race led DiIulio to assume that the high rate of crime among Black youth was fixed, rather than fluctuating with social circumstances.

Mill's reliance on the presence of a "real morality of public discussion" represents a serious limitation in his free-speech arguments, since it seems to demand of public speech standards that are not currently met, and for which we are unable to detect any clear positive trend in over 160 years since *On Liberty* was first published.

11.2. On Speaker Autonomy

Let's now consider a radically different argument for free speech than Mill's, to see if it provides a justification for free speech. According to the *speaker-based autonomy argument* for free speech, a free-speech ideal is the direct result of each speaker's individual liberty in a just society.[30] On the face of it, speaker-based autonomy arguments for free speech seem independent of the topic of harmful speech. But they are not.

In *A Theory of Justice*, John Rawls addresses the question of how a just state should go about ensuring liberties. He argues for two principles of justice. The first principle of justice is "each person is to have an equal right to the most extensive basic liberty compatible with a similar liberty to others."[31] If each person has a basic right to free speech, as the speaker-based autonomy

---

30. In "Freedom of Expression," Joshua Cohen argues against this view, on the grounds that it roots the ideal of free expression in a more controversial ethical doctrine, that we have fundamental liberties.

31. Rawls, *A Theory of Justice*, 53.

argument would have it, it is at least limited to cases in which that speech does not restrict similar liberties from others. But some kinds of speech do have the capacity to reduce, impair, or downgrade the capacity of other citizens to act autonomously.

The speaker-based autonomy argument makes the idealization that all speech is straight talk. Hustle can manipulate the hearer, bypassing their rationality. We have, throughout this book, used the much-studied example of the way the word "welfare" in American English resonates with anti-Black racist ideology. When someone with anti-Black racist biases hears a program described as "welfare," they tend to form a negative opinion of that program. It is the word "welfare" doing the work here, as the negative opinion tends to vanish when the program is described with other vocabulary. Typically, "welfare" is used as what Jennifer Saul calls a *covert* dog whistle; it operates by exploiting biases that are unconscious. As we saw in our introductory chapter, politicians exploit the racism of voters strategically by describing various programs they want to defund as "welfare." Code words and dog whistles work in politics by manipulating citizens, often against their obvious material interests. White citizens regularly support defunding programs that materially support them, because politicians describe these programs as "welfare" or with other similarly coded vocabulary (e.g., "public").

In *Dying of Whiteness*, Jonathan Metzl provides a book-length argument that the strategy of using vocabulary that resonates with anti-Black racism leads White voters to support policies that lead to mass death among these very populations of White voters.[32] White voters support these policies because they are described with vocabulary that resonates with anti-Black racism, leading voters who have racial bias to adopt negative attitudes toward the programs.

Recall that covert dog whistles manipulate their audiences by operating on their unconscious biases. When one has been manipulated into a view in this manner, one's adoption of that view is not autonomous. The assumption that all talk is straight talk idealizes away from speech that clearly restricts liberty.

Politicians use covert dog whistles all the time to advance their agendas. Even a perfectly nonracist but cynical politician could in principle use a covert anti-Black dog whistle to attract support from Whites with racial basis for his preferred policy position, by describing with dog whistles the position the politician wants them to oppose. Racist or not, politicians know this, and they use such manipulative tricks all the time (e.g., to get working-class White voters to support cutting taxes for the wealthy).

The American journalist Christopher Rufo has led several successful propaganda campaigns. His first large-scale propaganda campaign was to recognize the dog-whistle power of invoking "critical race theory," which he used to

32. Metzl, *Dying of Whiteness*.

attack an array of targets, but especially public schools. In famous successive tweets, he wrote,

> We have successfully frozen their brand—"critical race theory"—into the public conversation and are steadily driving up negative perceptions. We will eventually turn it toxic, as we put all of the various cultural insanities under that brand category.
>
> The goal is to have the public read something crazy in the newspaper and immediately think "critical race theory." We have decodified the term and will recodify it to annex the entire range of cultural constructions that are unpopular with Americans.[33]

In this propaganda campaign, he directed the charge against federal bureaucracy generally, claiming that critical race theory was something like an official state ideology, and "is now being weaponized against the American people."[34] The goal here was to exploit unconscious racial bias as a weapon against public institutions (Rufo is a libertarian). Calling a program "welfare" will lead those with unconscious racial bias to think negatively of it. What Rufo discovered is that associating an institution with the label "critical race theory" taps into this same mechanism. His campaign was massively successful. Educational gag orders have passed and are pending all across the country, forbidding K–12 schools, universities, and other institutions from teaching "divisive concepts," any material that causes "discomfort, guilt, anguish or any other form of psychological distress." Concepts such as "White supremacy" are banned by such bills, making it difficult to speak accurately about history. Multiple states have passed laws banning the teaching of Nikole Hannah-Jones's *1619 Project*, a multiauthor project documenting the centrality of slavery to all of the nation's institutions. Rufo's propaganda campaign, marshaling racial bias, used speech in the service of passing massive bans on speech.

In 2013, Russia passed its "Gay Propaganda Law," which outlaws "promotion of nontraditional sexual relations to minors"; Russia's attack on the LGBT community was part of its self-presentation as the world's defender of "traditional values."[35] The dog whistle used in country after country to target institutions in this now worldwide movement that Russia represents itself as leading is "gender ideology." Hungarian Prime Minister Viktor Orbán used

---

33. The tweets were for a while unavailable through Twitter. As of October 24, 2022, the tweets are available at https://twitter.com/realchrisrufo/status/1371541044592996352.

34. Rufo is cited in Laura Meckler and Josh Dawsey, "Republicans, Spurred by an Unlikely Figure, See Political Promise in Targeting Critical Race Theory," *Washington Post*, June 21, 2021.

35. Tat Bellamy-Walker, "Russian Court Dissolves Country's Main LGBTQ Rights Organization," NBC News, April 26, 2022, https://www.nbcnews.com/nbc-out/out-news/russian-court-dissolves-countrys-main-lgbtq-rights-organization-rcna25874.

this charge to drive public sentiment against Budapest's Central European University, which was eventually driven out of the country. Orbán also made it illegal for any of Hungary's universities to teach "Gender Ideology." More recently, Rufo has discovered the power of this label, and has launched a campaign against various institutions with its use. A *New York Times* interview profile of him writes,

> Mr. Rufo is convinced that a fight over L.G.B.T.Q. curriculums—which he calls "gender ideology"—has even more potential to spur a political backlash than the debate over how race and American history are taught.
>
> "The reservoir of sentiment on the sexuality issue is deeper and more explosive than the sentiment on the race issues," he said in an interview.[36]

Speech can obviously be used strategically and manipulatively, exploiting unconscious biases. As Plato warned, it is particularly useful for those who have the character of *tyrants*—people whose only value is power. Exploiting unconscious prejudices to one's political advantage strengthens these prejudices. Tyrants are ruthless in their pursuit of power. In the ruthless pursuit of power, strengthening preexisting prejudices is no barrier at all.

In addition to hustle, there is the problem of echo chambers. Recall the definition of an *antagonistic ideological social group* (section 6.6)—a community of practice whose discriminatory ideology is structured around a strongly negative collective emotional, dispositional, and attitudinal attunement to another group.

A feature of antagonistic communities of practice is that they lead to divergent accommodation—reducing attunements to opposed groups. Speech that fosters and maintains antagonistic social groups leads members of those groups to automatically dismiss the claims of opposing groups, to reject them just because of their group affiliation. Speech that fosters antagonistic communities of practice downgrades the capacity of other citizens to be heard.

Antagonistic echo amplification occurs when there are antagonistic communities of practice. In such cases, there is little possibility for joint negotiation of meaning. People are essentially stuck in their echo chambers, as the mistrust that abounds prevents them from considering other attunements. Speech that leads to the formation of echo chambers creates obstacles to autonomy.

There are serious costs to departing from one's antagonistic ideological social group, and in any case the trust required to acquire other attunements is absent in a highly polarized environment. Speech that fosters a necessary connection between one's identity in an antagonistic ideological social group

36. Trip Gabriel, "He Fuels the Right's Cultural Fires (and Spreads Them to Florida)," *New York Times*, April 24, 2022, https://www.nytimes.com/2022/04/24/us/politics/christopher-rufo-crt-lgbtq-florida.html.

and a particular attunement—say, to a conspiracy theory—limits agency, as it places large nonrational pressure on members of that group to accept the conspiracy theory, or risk expulsion.

These facts do not mean that in a highly polarized environment, autonomous rational decisions are impossible. After all, people can and do reject views closely connected to their own social identities. But it's important to bear in mind that the picture of autonomous rational agency is another idealization. It's an idealization that underlies many if not all autonomy arguments for free speech. It is worthwhile to pause and assess its plausibility:

> **Autonomous agent:** "An agent who is sovereign in deciding what to believe and in weighing competing reasons for action."[37]

We suspect this idealization underlies emotional attachment to particularly absolutist conceptions of free speech. Everyone has a *strong urge* to regard themselves as an autonomous agent. When everyone has a strong desire for something to be true, there will be a strong tendency toward wishful thinking.

We have defined autonomous agency, as is standard, with the use of deciding what to believe and what to do, in short, in terms of *accepting propositions*. But in our framework, propositions are not special—attunement is the more general notion, and one can be attuned to propositions (belief), emotions, and practices. This naturally suggests a broader definition of autonomous agency:

> **Broad autonomous agent:** An agent who is sovereign in deciding what attunements to have.

The assumption of autonomous agency functions in autonomy arguments as part of an argument against speech regulation. Typically, one would argue that the proposed regulation of speech would limit agency. Agents, on this assumption, can pick and choose themselves what worldview to form from all the talking around them. So, limiting what options they are offered limits their agency.

However, the effects of speech are far broader than the offering of reasons. Speech can affect emotional state (e.g., producing fear) or social identity (e.g., strengthening some ties and weakening others). We have argued at length that many of the resonances of speech yield nondeliberative uptake, with our emotional reactions to speech being a primary case. The claim here is not that we lack agency over our *reactions* to our emotions—we do have agency here. The claim is rather that we lack agency over the emotions we initially have toward speech we encounter. The vocabulary of autonomy is not apt for expressive resonances. The case for nondeliberative uptake of emotional resonances is particularly strong. It's hard to see how a plausible claim of broad autonomy could be marshaled against the regulation of speech that harms through emotional impact and the intimidating expression of the power of a social group.

37. Scanlon, "A Theory of Freedom of Expression," 15.

But even the narrow idealization of autonomous agency is suspect. According to the idealization, humans can distinguish reasons that are compelling as such, independently from perspective, social identity, and other factors. Recall again the notion of an antagonistic ideological social group. Being in an antagonistic ideological social group places significant nonrational barriers on adopting opposing attunements, including opposing beliefs. In a polarized environment, we make many negative assumptions about people in opposing groups. Some of those assumptions will be falsely taken to be rational, rather than the result of our strongly negative emotional attunement to that group. The idea that people can just put aside their biases in a strongly polarized environment is fantasy. The idea that agents can consider opposing attunements solely on their own rational merits is inconsistent with the very real mechanisms that lead to echo chambers. Even doxastic attunements that fit easily with our background ideology will be updated nondeliberatively.

Once we set the idealization of autonomous rational agency in a broader framework, with attunement, it is problematic—people often do not seem able to choose their emotional reactions to speech. It is only by narrowing the scope of agency to reasons that the idealization can even seem plausible. But even thus restricted, the view that people always freely choose their views sounds more like wishful thinking.

Libel laws and defamation laws recognize other ways in which speech can restrict agency. The scope of the free speech guaranteed by the speaker autonomy argument for free speech depends on an account of speech that provides (to reprise Rawls, above) "the most extensive basic liberty compatible with a similar liberty to others." Insofar as restricting liberties is a matter of making it more difficult to attain them, this category of speech is much more capacious than the category of speech a free society would allow to be banned. It would, for example, clearly include code words and other kinds of hustle.

Similar concerns about subordinating speech practices also raise questions about autonomy-based arguments for free speech more generally, which tend to abstract away from the possibility of speech impairing or downgrading the power of autonomous action. In summarizing her critique of Ronald Dworkin's autonomy-based argument for free speech, Susan Brison writes,

> What Dworkin fails to consider is that others' rights, for example, their rights to free speech or to equality of opportunity, may be undermined by someone's engaging in hate speech. Since he does not consider this case, he does not tell us how invoking the right to autonomy could resolve that conflict of rights. Furthermore, given that his theory of law specifies no procedure for weighing competing rights, this is not an oversight that could be rectified on his account.[38]

---

38. Brison, "The Autonomy Defense of Free Speech," 325.

Let's suppose that hate speech impairs the rights of others. If so, then autonomy-based arguments do not rule out restrictions on hate speech.

In his classic 1972 paper, "A Theory of Freedom of Expression," T. M. Scanlon provides a hearer-based autonomy argument for free speech. Scanlon argues that restrictions on speech cannot be grounded in the potential harm speech has for leading to or encouraging false beliefs, or leading to or encouraging changes in preference. The basis for Scanlon's argument is a claim about autonomy—"To regard himself as autonomous in the sense I have in mind a person must see himself sovereign in deciding what to believe and in weighing competing reasons for action."[39] Scanlon's thought is that speech cannot be significantly curtailed without impinging on autonomy in this sense—the hearer must have the autonomy to decide what to believe and weigh competing reasons for action, and so speech must provide them with all the options.[40]

Scanlon's picture of speech also presupposes the idealization of straight talk. Scanlon describes speech as straight talk, transparently offering the hearer propositions that she can freely accept or reject. But as we have seen, much speech is hustle. For example, simply asking leading questions can affect the actions of hearers, without them realizing it at all. Hustle is speech that can make a decision for its hearers. For example, in sections 4.2 and 4.3, we considered cases of psychologists, in effect, hustling experimental subjects through the presuppositions of frames; the subjects were coerced into making biased decisions or forming biased memories, but did not know they were being hustled. The first problem with Scanlon's argument is that it presupposes the idealization that all speech is straight talk.

Scanlon's argument also presupposes the idealization of an autonomous agent. As we have seen, a polarized environment limits or makes it altogether impossible to be one of Scanlon's sovereign agents. Speech that fosters antagonistic ideological social groups and their attendant echo chambers curtails sovereign agency.

A central function of speech is to attune to social identity. Some social identities, in particular antagonistic ones, function to restrict or even render impossible developing attunements (including attunements to reasons) on their own merits, for example, on the basis of strength of evidence or of

39. Scanlon, "A Theory of Freedom of Expression," 15.

40. John Milton similarly argues that the dangers of free speech, and particularly the possibility of pernicious ideas, do not justify censorship, because encountering pernicious ideas is in fact necessary for developing both our rational faculties and a virtuous character, as well as properly grounded conviction in the truth: "He that can apprehend and consider vice with all her baits and seeming pleasures, and yet abstain, and yet distinguish, and yet prefer that which is truly better, he is the true warfaring Christian. I cannot praise a fugitive and cloistered virtue, unexercised and unbreathed, that never sallies out and sees her adversary, but slinks out of the race where that immortal garland is to be run for, not without dust and heat" (*Areopagitica*, 18).

alignment with the agent's interests. Speech that fosters antagonistic social identities destroys the healthy deliberative environment required for democracy, since negotiation between members of opposing groups becomes impossible. In a very clear sense, then, free speech may pose a threat to democracy.

The autonomy arguments against restricting speech fail because they idealize away from large categories of speech. They idealize away from speech that manipulates hearers (hustle). And they idealize away from the role of speech in creating and maintaining antagonistic social identities and echo chambers. They not only presuppose a healthy deliberative environment, but they also presuppose one in which all talk is straight talk.

In "Free Speech and Its Relation to Self-Government," Alexander Meiklejohn defends free speech on the grounds that a democracy requires its citizens who decide issues to have "acquaintance with information or opinion or doubt or disbelief or criticism which is relevant to that issue."[41] For Meiklejohn, the function of speech in democracy is to *inform*. It is to educate the public about political questions. Jack Balkin summarizes Meiklejohn's view as follows:

> In Meiklejohn's model, free speech has constitutional value because it assures the flow of information that is relevant or potentially relevant to the democratic governance of a state. This formulation explains Meiklejohn's famous comment that it is not important that everyone shall speak, but that everything worth saying be said. The receipt of information to the audience, and not speaker autonomy, is constitutionally valuable, because it allows the people to govern themselves, either directly through public debate and decision making, or indirectly through electing representatives and holding them accountable in elections.[42]

Meiklejohn's free-speech defense has been critiqued for the limited scope of the principle—his defense does not extend to apolitical artistic expression, for example.[43] But the problem is worse. In focusing on the informational function of speech, Meikeljohn's free-speech defense would not protect speech that forms social identities, or speech that attunes to emotion. Yet these are central functions of speech. With our broader perspective, we can see that it is not just artistic expression that it fails to protect. It is *social-identity formation*.

---

41. Meiklejohn, *Free Speech and Its Relation to Self-Government*, 26.

42. Balkin, "Cultural Democracy and the First Amendment," 164.

43. See, e.g., Chafee, review of *Free Speech and Its Relation to Self-Government*; Kalven, "The Metaphysics of the Law of Obscenity." Meiklejohn famously argued in response that one could incorporate art into his conception of free speech, because poetry, movies, and other cultural production ultimately aid political decision-making ("The First Amendment Is an Absolute," 245). This is, however, an unfounded assumption. There is art that can undermine reason in characteristically propagandistic ways.

In "Cultural Democracy and the First Amendment," Jack Balkin bases freedom on *cultural freedom*—the freedom to create meaning in your society with cultural and symbolic forms of production.[44] This is much more promising by our lights. Unlike what Balkin calls "politico-centric" justifications of free speech that focus on its capacity for agential representation in the formation of laws, Balkin's justification of free speech does not guarantee classical democratic equality—equal participation in the formation of laws that govern you.[45] But it appears to guarantee full cultural participation and expression, and accentuates, rather than conceals, the cultural and symbolic force of speech. It clearly is focused on allowing the flourishing of social-identity expression.

A justification for freedom of speech based on cultural democracy faces the same pitfalls as its more "politico-centric" cousins. Social groups share not just views, but also practices and cultural expressions. Speech that creates antagonistic social groups will foster divergent accommodation to alternative cultural expression. Balkin's argument for free speech abstracts away from expression that creates antagonistic social groups and echo chambers. It too presupposes a healthy deliberative environment.

Other defenses of broad free-speech principles have more promise with dealing with the full reality of harmful speech. Judith Butler's defense against hate-speech laws is *premised* on the view that hate speech harms, and that its harms are particularly difficult to overcome.[46]

Butler has several arguments against laws that ban hate speech. First, Butler is distrustful of a legal solution, pointing out that "the legal discourse in which the status of the performativity of hate speech takes place is its own performative exercise. In the current US political climate, the law that decides the question of hate speech tends to be applied inconsistently in order to further reactionary political aims."[47] We agree with Butler's critique of law as a neutral arbiter. Indeed, we have argued for the incoherence of the notion of a neutral arbiter.

Butler's most innovative argument against hate-speech laws appeals to her practice-focused approach to speech. Speech practices evolve and change. Butler argues that laws banning hateful expressions prevent positive linguistic change, freezing the harmful effects in place: "Keeping such terms unsaid and unsayable can also work to lock them in place, preserving their power

44. Balkin, "Cultural Democracy and the First Amendment," 1054.

45. Balkin, "Cultural Democracy and the First Amendment," 1056.

46. Butler, *Excitable Speech*. The book begins "When we claim to have been injured by language, what kind of claim do we make? We ascribe an agency to language, a power to injure, and position ourselves as the objects of its injurious trajectory." (1) Later, she writes, for example: "If we accept that hate speech is illocutionary, we accept as well that words perform injury immediately and automatically, that the social map of power makes it so" (101–2).

47. Butler, *Excitable Speech*, 39.

to injure, and arresting the possibility of a reworking that might shift their context and purpose."[48] Butler argues that the best way to combat hate speech is to *reappropriate* it, as, for example, "Queer" was reappropriated by radical members of that community (so much so that it now figures as the name of a discipline, "Queer Studies"), thereby replacing a harmful practice by a practice that uses the slur to bond, and as an act of protest.

Butler's intervention in the free-speech debate has been criticized on the grounds that reappropriation faces barriers that Butler failed to recognize. The combination of a slur's history, as well as the vicissitudes of its target's identity and social location, can make it more or less difficult to reappropriate slurs directed against them. Reappropriation is one mechanism to bring to bear to change the values and affect associated with a speech practice. As a specific mechanism for a targeted group to bond, it's clearly too thin of a plank upon which to rest a full argument against hate-speech laws. Butler's defense of free speech is then, at the very least, incomplete.

We can see, however, that Butler's defense against speech restrictions appeals to a tradition of rhetorical contestation, one that is embodied by, for example, the battle over the word "freedom" in US politics with which we began this investigation in chapter 1. On the one hand, we have a sense of "freedom" that resonates, as Toni Morrison urged us to recognize, with goods that are possessed in contrast to the state of Black Americans.[49] On the other hand, we have a tradition of Black democratic political thought, from Frederick Douglass's 1852 speech, "What to the Slave Is the Fourth of July?" to the present day, that emphasizes the rhetorical power of the democratic ideals, seeking to cleanse them of these racist associations. Butler's defense of free speech is essentially based on letting these rhetorical power battles over speech practices governing words play out.

What if these power disputes tend to resolve against the interests of oppressed groups? Butler's approach presupposes that groups will have the power to change practices. But who knows if this is plausible? Butler's argument assumes much about the possibility of mutual negotiation of meaning.

The failures of arguments against speech regulation do not yield a positive case for it. Butler is right to emphasize that the state cannot be trusted to be a neutral arbiter. In the United States today, Rufo's campaign against critical race theory has focused on banning speech that causes psychological discomfort to Whites, the dominant group. These laws ban concepts like "White supremacy," making the teaching of US history either vexed or impossible. We can see the consequences of such bans in Russia, where laws forbid the teaching of the Soviet Union's mass atrocities in the 1930s and '40s, including Holodomor, the genocide Stalin caused in Ukraine.

---

48. Butler, *Excitable Speech*, 38.
49. Morrison, *Playing in the Dark*, 64.

It is a material reality, an on the ground fact, that many speech bans erase historical knowledge necessary for society to be self-governing. We see the consequences of such bans vividly, during the writing of this book, in the Russian public's lack of response to Russia's brutal and genocidal invasion of Ukraine. Many of the speech bans we see enacted today, what Timothy Snyder calls "memory laws," target historical knowledge necessary for democracy. We should be against these kinds of bans because they ban knowledge necessary for self-understanding and self-governance. We should promote an information space where mutual negotiation of meaning is possible. This requires knowledge of the history of group relations, including histories of oppression. There can hardly be the trust for mutual negotiation of meaning if there is one-sided ignorance of one group's past history of brutal treatment of another.

A society based on the ideal of liberty is one that allows people to consider a rich variety of attunements, to freely form social identities. Achieving a society based on liberty is incompatible with the demonization of nonhateful alternative social identities. Speech regulation that is aimed at limiting the harm of antidemocratic social identities, or social identities that limit the freedom of others, is tolerable by the lights of our arguments.

Before offering a closing thought on the place of freedom of speech in democracy, let us briefly consider one final argument against speech regulation, already mentioned in our discussion of Butler, the question of "who decides." Although we will not consider it in the same detail, it might be said that this argument is the most challenging of the three for anyone who, like us, would deny that there could possibly be such a thing as a neutral arbiter, someone who can act as a representative of the government and justly apply constraints on speech that are fair and equitable to all parties, without ideological bias toward one group or another. The argument has a pedigree. In his famous address to the English parliament on the value of free speech, the poet John Milton recounted a sorry history of censorship from ancient Greece to the Inquisition and beyond, pointing out its arbitrariness—"so often bad, as good Books were silenc't."[50] Presumably his intention was to cast doubt on the reasonableness of imbuing any particular institution with the right to pass judgment on the value of words, even though he dared not directly question the ability of the august body he was addressing to make sage decisions.

The thought here is that there is no neutral arbiter for social identities. A troubling concomitant is that if we regulate the power of social identities that foment echo chambers and problematic antagonistic ideological social groups (say, genocidal ones), then those who have those social identities, when they take power, will regulate democratically healthy social identities. So no speech regulation of any kind should be permitted.

50. Milton, *Areopagitica*, 28–29.

The problem with this sort of argument is that it assumes those who advance illiberal social agendas will respect liberal norms if they have not themselves been highly regulated. History shows that this is folly. Those advancing harshly antidemocratic programs will regulate speech when they can, no matter what free-speech precedents liberals have established. The rejection of liberal precedent and norms is in fact at the basis of these illiberal identities. It might then be said that the question is not one of who will be a neutral arbiter, but of how we can avoid the very worst kind of arbitration.

11.3. Let Equality Ring

Equality, in the words of Andrea Dworkin, was tacked on to the Constitution with spit and a prayer. And, let me also say, late.

—CATHARINE MACKINNON[51]

Given the failure of so many justifications for free-speech principles, what should we conclude? The paradox of democracy is just that—a paradox. It has been discussed for almost as long as democracy has existed. We will not solve it here. Our aim here has been to sharpen it, not solve it.

The two central values of democracy are *liberty* and *equality*. Justifications of free speech have tended to draw support from the first of these values— liberty. But what if we drew, instead, on the second?

Equality in democratic political philosophy does not mean material equality. It means, rather, political equality. It is standard to take political equality as the capacity to *speak truth to power*. A democracy should ensure that even its most powerless citizens have the capacity to speak truth to power. The capacity for powerful people to be embarrassed by being caught lying, for example, is a mark of a healthy democratic information space.

The goal of free speech in a democracy should be to preserve a healthy democratic discursive space. This implies preservation of the capacity of journalists to operate freely and to have respect given to their findings. It implies preserving social identities that involve accountability and responsiveness to those who lack power, and, while not *banning* antidemocratic social identities, also not rewarding them. An *equality*-based defense of free speech would aim at preserving a democratic discursive space. But an *equality*-based defense of free speech should also accept that unregulated speech can lead to inequality; it can lead to speech harms that systematically wound and partially silence entire segments of society.

Democracy is a system for the development among the people of a nation of collective harmony concerning the government of those people. Healthy democracies maximize the extent to which there is equal participation in this process, so

---

51. MacKinnon, *Feminism Unmodified*, 207.

that as much of the population as possible forms a single community of governmental practice. Political equality, then, is something that varies by degree: there is equality to the extent that a population has uniform access and power in the community of governmental practice, so that collective harmonization of those in the group is not at the expense of dissonance for those left out. Though any ideal of equality must deal with practical questions like how those without a voice (whether children, animals, or the planet itself) are represented, the pragmatic goal here is to support processes that lead to strengthening of the democratic discursive space, a public conversation in which more individuals become more equal participants in the democratic process of collective harmonization, and none become "more equal" than others. Our ambition should not be restricted to free speech, but should reach toward speech that is both free and equal.

As Lynne Tirrell writes, in an article focusing on the interrelated roles of speech regulation and counterspeech in combating misogyny:

> For anyone concerned with justice, the question is not whether something should be done about the misogynist onslaught girls and women encounter; the question is: What should be done, and who should do it? Supreme Court doctrine may favor counterspeech to tort remedies or criminalization, but to justify this we need a robust conception of what sorts of speech might have the power to counter oppressive speech, who can achieve it, and under what circumstances. In setting policy, we cannot assume a speech encounter between equally powerful adults, each fully free to speak their minds and each with the backing of deep and broad social norms. Where inequality reigns, the odds are not in favor of someone who tries to combat . . . bad speech of the powerful with . . . more speech of the vulnerable.[52]

This passage picks out one of many inequalities in contemporary society, inequalities that marginalize significant segments of the population so that their voices are suppressed while other voices are amplified. Democratic action is needed to repair an unhealthy democracy. Perhaps the major democratic force that has led to such repairs in the past century has been mass protest in the context of large civil rights movements.

An unhealthy democracy is one in which discursive access to governmental decision making is restricted to a community of practice that systematically

---

52. Tirrell, "Toxic Misogyny and the Limits of Counterspeech," 2438. Here Tirrell's argument for centering issues of equality in determining how competition between speech interests should be resolved echoes a theme in feminist legal theory that is clear in MacKinnon's work:

> Any system of freedom of expression that does not address a problem where the free speech of men silences the free speech of women, a real conflict between speech interests as well as between people, is not serious about securing freedom of expression in this country. (*Feminism Unmodified*, 193)

omits segments of the population. The higher the barriers to entry into this minority community of practice, the less democratic is the government, and if the minority community of practice that influences government decision making is restricted to a small elite, then there is no democracy at all.

When people are systematically omitted from access to governmental decision making, it is inevitable that the interests of members of the elite community of governmental practice will be better served than the interests of others. In such a situation, the system can only be maintained through coercion. The cheapest way to coerce is verbally, manipulating people through the use of intended hustle, especially undermining propaganda in which messaging presented as in service of an ideal in fact weakens practices that might favor that ideal. Specifically, the elite may simultaneously present itself as the savior of democracy while actively working to destroy it, by convincing the people that inclusive democracy cannot work. Since democracy depends on large-scale collective harmonization, convincing people that democracy cannot work is most easily attained by (i) maximization of antagonism between subgroups, especially by convincing one group that it is existentially imperiled by another, and (ii) efforts to create big differences in discursive practices between groups.

As discussed in chapter 6, a combination of intergroup antagonism and intergroup differences in practice can lead to a runaway process of divergent accommodation, so that groups become less and less compatible with each other, and ultimately echo chambers form. An echo chamber, as we have seen, is a subgroup that has collectively harmonized around discursive practices and ideas that are incompatible with the discursive practices and ideas of other subgroups. Such incompatibility makes collective harmonization of the full population, and hence the possibility of a fully functional democracy centered on a common discourse, impossible. Here we arrive at a conundrum: on the one hand, protest movements play a crucial role in supporting the push for political equality, but on the other hand, a protest movement, which has its own discursive practices, is always in danger of being isolated from the rest of the polity, becoming part of a problem producing antidemocratic fragmentation rather than part of a solution producing prodemocratic integration. Free speech is there to provide protection for such protest movements, so their voices can break through.

Right now, the most powerful forces in society, with the largest capacity to amplify their message, are focused on defending their power to guide public opinion by appeal to the ideal of free speech. Free speech, instead of being the mechanism by which protest movements can be heard, instead seems to be a tool to amplify the voices of the powerful, to protect them against critique. During the writing of this book, in the United States, politicians who present themselves as advocates of free speech are simultaneously passing bans on the teaching of concepts that are at the heart of protest movements for structural change, for example those associated with critical race theory. Banning such concepts ensures that the cases made by such protest movements will not be heard, that they will be consigned to an echo chamber, impossible to be heard outside its walls. An equality-based defense of free speech would not ignore threats to the speech of the powerful. But it would not center them. It would instead refocus attention on what it takes to give everyone a voice—a discursive environment that makes it obviously impermissible to ban concepts that enable the understanding of protests for structural change on behalf of disenfranchised groups. Only then it is possible for both mass protest movements and individuals operating within the electoral system and legislative process to speak truth to power.

GLOSSARY OF TECHNICAL TERMS

Accommodation. Harmonization triggered by the perceived context of communicative interactions. [6.2]

Activation function. A mapping from each of the constituents of a mental state to a number, a level of activation. If a mental state is a system of attunements, it is a function from attunements to a pair consisting of (a) a level of attunement, and (b) a level of activation. [3.4]

Antagonistic ideological social group. A community of practice for which a central feature of the ideology is a strongly negative collective emotional attunement to some other social group. [6.6]

Associative resonance. An action in the extension of a practice is a (positive) resonance of a feature of context to the extent that an occurrence of the action changes the probability of that feature (positively). [1.4]

Associative resonance (formal). p(feature| instantiation of practice) – p(feature) [5.2]

Attunement. An agent is *attuned* to something to the extent that their state and behavior predictably evolve in accordance with its presence in the agent's context. [2.2]

Attunement profile of a practice. The subpart of the presuppositional resonances [of the practice] that involves collective attunements of interactants. [5.2]

Attunement to narrative. To be cognitively attuned to a narrative frame is to have a disposition to see groups of events, actors, and locations as instantiations of that frame; to be dispositionally attuned to a narrative frame is to have a tendency to behave by analogy with characters drawn from it. [3.5]

Attunement to practice. An agent is *attuned* to a practice to the extent that their state and behavior predictably evolve in accordance with its presence in the agent's context. [2.3]

Attunement to practice (in terms of resonance). An agent is *attuned* to a community practice to the extent that their state and behavior tend to evolve in accord with the *resonances* of actions belonging to the extension of that practice in the community. [2.5]

Autonomous agent. "An agent who is sovereign in deciding what to believe and in weighing competing reasons for action." (Scanlon, "A Theory of Freedom of Expression," 15) [11.2]

Black propaganda. A contribution to public discourse that is misrepresented as from a committed group member yet is of a kind that tends to erode that very group. [6.1]

Broad autonomous agent. An agent who is sovereign in deciding what attunements to have. [11.2]

Causal efficacy postulate. Within a speech community, speech practices will not emerge that have as resonances properties that can neither causally affect whether community members perform the practice, nor are causally related to effects of the practice that community members can recognize. [2.5]

Collaborative language accommodation. Collective harmonization around novel language practices, whether primarily implicit or involving overt metalinguistic moves of negotiation. [6.4]

Collective behavioral attunement. A group of agents is behaviorally *attuned* to something to the extent that their collective behaviors predictably accord with its presence in the group's context. [2.4]

Collective effervescence. A state in which behavioral and emotional harmony within a close-knit group dominates the collective attention of that group to the exclusion of anything else. [3.7]

Collective harmony. That which is experienced emotionally by members of a group because of how different group members' attunements relate to each other. This may be an experience of collective consonance, when there is manifest coherence of attunements, which implies a high degree of collective attunement, or collective dissonance, when there is manifest incoherence of attunements. [3.8]

Common ground. The common ground of a group is the collective attunements of that group. [2.4]

Common ground (discrete approximation). The collective common ground is (approximated by) the set of things to which the level of collective attunement of the group is high. [2.4]

Community of practice. A set of individuals with strong collective attunements to a set of practices, such that no larger set of individuals has similarly strong or stronger collective attunements to that set of practices. [2.5]

Consonance. The experience of manifest coherence of systems of attunements. [3.4]

Content-delivery model. Communication consists of conveying meaning inside container-like vessels consisting of symbols, such that the speaker's job is to wrap the meaning up and the hearer's job is to unwrap it. [1.2]

Convergence. Accommodation is *convergent* toward a second party (an individual or group) when it results in a monotonic increase in the level of collective attunement with that party. [6.4]

Cooperation. To *cooperate*, agents must choose to perform actions that enhance the probability that both they and others will reach their goals. [8.2]

Cooperativity (idealization): Speaker and hearer are cooperating in the service of a set of common interests. [9.2]

Coordination. Coordination of activity between entities occurs when their behaviors are correlated in such a way as to make the behavior of one predictable given knowledge of the behavior of the others. [8.2]

Degree to which something resonates for someone. Something resonates (positively) for a group or individual to the extent that it induces increased (positive) harmony for them. [3.9]

Deliberative uptake. A multistage process like that assumed in the content-delivery model, consisting of comprehension, in which the meaning of an utterance is identified, followed by integration, in which a decision is reached deliberatively to accept the message and update one's mental state accordingly, or to reject it. [3.1]

Dialogue (idealization). A talk exchange is between one speaker and one hearer. [9.2]

Discriminatory ideology. An ideology that includes attunements to in-group/out-group distinctions (a.k.a. us-them distinctions), and in which members of out-groups are valued less than members of in-groups, and hence as inherently deserving of less than equal treatment or resources. [2.6]

Dissonance. The experience of manifest incoherence of systems of attunements. [3.4]

Divergence. Accommodation is *divergent* when it results in a monotonic decrease of the level of collective attunement with some party. [6.4]

Effect probability. The probability that a certain feature of the context is an effect of an action instantiating a practice, written as p(instantiation of practice caused feature). [5.2]

Exigence/exigent power. The intrinsic power of a communicative practice to affect participants that is hard to resist, independently of the intention of the speaker (or anyone else). [2.6]

Extent (idealization). The individual utterance is the bearer of significant semantic properties. Properties of larger discourses, or temporally discontinuous exchanges, need to be considered only by extrapolation from the single utterance case.   [9.2]

Force (idealization). The primary level for studying communication is the illocutionary force of the utterance, which is a function of the underlying content.   [9.2]

Fragmentation. In epistemology, splitting representations of knowledge or belief into multiple self-contained segments.   [3.2]

Genocidally antagonistic ideological social group. A community of practice whose identity is based on being existentially imperiled by the existence of another group.   [10.3]

Harmonization. The process by which groups of attunements evolve in order to bring about positive harmony.   [3.4]

Harm Principle. "The only purpose for which power can be rightfully exercised over any member of a civilized community, against his will, is to prevent harm to others." (Mill, *On Liberty*, 9)   [11.1]

Hustle. The *hustle* in an utterance is all the communicative actions performed through that utterance that are not straight talk. (Hustle is what people do with words nontransparently.)   [8.1]

Hyperprojectivity. A construction is a trigger for a hyperprojective resonance if both unembedded uses of the construction and uses of the construction in metalinguistic environments (including indirect speech reports and quotation) tend to carry that resonance to a significant extent.   [5.4]

Ideological resonances. The ideological resonances of a practice consist in the increased tendency for practitioners to have attunements belonging to the ideology.   [2.6]

Ideology. An ideology is the system of collective attunements among members of a community of practice.   [2.6]

Instantiation of a narrative frame. A narrative in which the abstract events, actors, and locations of the narrative frame are identified with particular events, actors, and locations.   [3.5]

Instrumental power of language. The ability language gives people to exercise power over others.   [2.6]

Inter-attunement distance. A mapping from any two attunements to the level of association between the attunements, i.e., the degree to which activation of one attunement is likely to lead to activation of the other.   [3.5]

Internal harmony. What is experienced emotionally when one is aware of how one's attunements relate to one another, a sense of consonance (*positive harmony*, or just *harmony* when this will not cause confusion) or dissonance (*negative harmony*).   [3.4]

Kaplanian meaning of an action. A function mapping features of context to 1 if the conditional probability of the feature given the action is 1, and to 0 otherwise.   [1.7]

Landscape of attunement. The landscape of attunement for a person is the sum of their *neighborhoods of thought*.   [3.4]

Language homogeneity (idealization). Conventional meanings are determined primarily at a level of recognized languages, which may include millions of speakers. Speech practices of individuals or subgroups, registers, styles, differences from one communicative medium to another, and rhetorical frames of particular conversations, are not central   [9.2]

Meaningfulness. Something is inwardly (/outwardly) meaningful for some individual or group to the extent that it resonates for them (/for others) in a way that activates attunements that are distinctive of their identity.   [6.4]

Meaning/signal inequality. What an action means is more than what is signaled.   [1.8]

Mixed Accommodation. Accommodation is mixed when there is a combination of convergence and divergence to the same party. [6.4]

Narrative frame. An abstract template that consists of (i) a set of principle actors that have particular characteristics and relationships with each other, (ii) a set of connected events that involve those actors and locations and lead to particular changes affecting the actors and locations, and (iii) optionally, valuations of some of the actors, behaviors, or events. [3.5]

Narrative harmonization. A change in a system of attunements based on the supposition that real-world characteristics of individuals, relationships, and events match the characteristics found in a narrative, and that behaviors portrayed positively in the narrative are normatively desirable. [3.5]

Neighborhoods of thought. Sets of attunements that tend to be simultaneously activated to some degree because the *inter-attunement distances* are low. [3.4]

Neutrality (idealization). (i) Conventions associated with words assign them a core of neutral and aperspectival meaning; (ii) at least some expressions are completely neutral, in the sense that perspective and attunement to social location are irrelevant to their meaning; and (iii) the neutral core of the meaning of a nonneutral expression is paraphrasable in neutral terms. [9.2]

Neutrality of discussion. Discussion is neutral if perspective and attunement to social location are irrelevant to the understanding and evaluation of each move in the discussion. [7.1]

Nondeliberative uptake. When an idea first enters our minds, it enters as a belief, and only later might we decide to reject it. [3.3]

Non-idiosyncrasy postulate. For a member of a speech community, the resonances of a speech act that follows the practices of that community are not dependent on idiosyncratic features of that individual, be they the speaker or audience member, but only on properties of the context in accord with which the practice is predictably used. [2.5]

Nonveridicality. A linguistic construction that embeds or modifies others is *nonveridical* if the truth of sentences involving that construction does not depend on any proposition expressing material they embed or modify being true. [5.4]

Paradox of democracy. Free societies are often *imperiled* by propaganda, which is allowed by robust free-speech protections. [11]

Perspective. A perspective on a set of features of context is a distinctive system of attunements to those features. [6.4]

Persuasion. What happens when communicative actions cause someone's attunements to shift to conform to some preexisting pattern with which their original attunements would have been in tension, typically through intent to produce that change. [2.6]

Power. An entity exerts *power* to the extent that it changes someone's state, shapes their interests, or causes them to act. An entity has power to the extent that it has the ability to exert power. [2.6]

Priming. Reflexive activation of one attunement by another. [3.6]

Presuppositional resonance. Associative resonance – Effect probability, which equals: p(feature| instantiation of practice) – p(feature) – p(instantiation of practice caused feature). [5.2]

Projection of resonance. A construction is a trigger for a projective resonance if both unembedded uses of the construction and uses of the construction in nonveridical environments tend to carry that resonance. [5.4]

Propositional projection. A construction is a trigger for a projective proposition if both unembedded uses of the construction and uses of the construction in nonveridical environments provide evidence of speaker commitment to the truth of that proposition. [5.4]

Propositionality (idealization). Content is packaged into neat units, one proposition per utterance, and the primary point of communication is to convey these propositions with assertive speech acts. [9.2]

Prosocial communication. Communication that lacks intended hustle. [8.2]

Rationality (idealization). Interlocutors are perfectly rational: they are computationally unlimited, reason scientifically and logically rather than emotionally, and have consistent preferences. [9.2]

Schismogenesis. "A process of differentiation in the norms of individual behaviour resulting from cumulative interaction between individuals." (Bateson, *Naven*, 175) [6.1]

Shared context (idealization). Features of context relevant to interpretation must be mutually known in order that a unique content can be identified. [9.2]

Social alignment hypothesis. Accommodation by an interactional participant promotes confidence in the nature of their attunements to identities or groupings with which coordination is valued. [6.5]

Social homogeneity (idealization). The linguistic community is socially homogeneous, and utterance meaning is computed without reference to social roles, affiliations, power relations, or personalities. [9.2]

Standard socioethnic group term. Common names for racial, ethnic, and religious groups that are often used without derogation. [10.1]

Straight talk. The straight talk in an utterance consists in those communicative acts the speaker performs transparently. Discourse is straight talk if it is composed solely of straight talk. [8.1]

Strength of a slur. A slur is stronger (a) the more reviled the target group is within the discriminatory ideology, (b) the more the group picked out by the slur itself constitutes a distinct community of practice that is central to the identity of the out-group's members, (c) the greater the extent to which the slur use is associated with a history of oppression of the target group, (d) the greater the power of the in-group over the out-group, and (e) the stronger the contrast is between the discriminatory ideology within which the slurring practice exists and another prevalent ideology which does not devalue those in the out-group. [10.2]

Transparency (of a communicative action). A communicative action is *transparent* if the speaker thinks that the hearer will recognize that action. [8.1]

Transparency (idealization). Utterance meaning, including presupposition and implicature, is characterized by a unique set of communicative intentions that are mutually and readily consciously recognizable. [9.2]

Undermining propaganda. "A contribution to public discourse that is presented as an embodiment of certain ideals yet is of a kind that tends to erode those very ideals." (Stanley, *How Propaganda Works*, 69) [6.1]

Weakest-link hypothesis. "The maximum dissonance that can possibly exist between any two elements is equal to the total resistance to change of the less resistant element." (Festinger, *A Theory of Cognitive Dissonance*, 28) [3.2]

BIBLIOGRAPHY

Ajzen, Icek, and Martin Fishbein. *Understanding Attitudes and Predicting Social Behavior.* Englewood Cliffs: Prentice-Hall, 1980.

Alexopoulos, Golfo. *Illness and Inhumanity in Stalin's Gulag.* New Haven, CT: Yale University Press, 2017.

Althusser, Louis. *On the Reproduction of Capitalism: Ideology and Ideological State Apparatuses.* Translated by G. M. Goshgarian. London: Verso Books, 2014.

AnderBois, Scott, Adrian Brasoveanu, and Robert Henderson. "Crossing the Appositive/At-Issue Meaning Boundary." *Semantics and Linguistic Theory,* no. 20 (2010): 328–46.

Anderson, Elizabeth. "Feminist Epistemology and Philosophy of Science." In *Stanford Encyclopedia of Philosophy.* Stanford University, 1997. Article published August 9, 2000; last modified February 13, 2020. https://plato.stanford.edu/entries/feminism-epistemology/.

Anderson, Luvell. "Calling, Addressing, and Appropriation." In *Bad Words: Philosophical Perspectives on Slurs,* edited by David Sosa, 6–28. Oxford: Oxford University Press, 2018.

Anderson, Luvell. "Philosophical Investigations of the Taboo of Insult." In *The Oxford Handbook of Taboo Words and Language,* edited by Keith Allan, 233–47. Oxford: Oxford University Press, 2018.

Anderson, Luvell, and Ernie Lepore. "Slurring Words." *Noûs* 47, no. 1 (2013): 25–48.

Anderson, Luvell, and Ernie Lepore. "What Did You Call Me? Slurs as Prohibited Words." *Analytic Philosophy* 54, no. 3. (2013): 350–63.

Anderson, R. Lanier. "The Wolffian Paradigm and Its Discontent: Kant's Containment Definition of Analyticity in Historical Context." *Archiv für Geschichte der Philosophie* 87, no. 1 (2005): 22–74.

Arendt, Hannah. *Eichmann in Jerusalem: A Report on the Banality of Evil.* 1963. New York: Penguin Books, 2006.

Arendt, Hannah. *On Violence.* London: Allen Lane, 1970.

Arendt, Hannah. *The Origins of Totalitarianism.* 2nd ed. Cleveland: Meridian Books, 1958.

Asher, Nicholas, and Alex Lascarides. "Strategic Conversation." *Semantics and Pragmatics* 6 (2013): 1–58.

Ashwell, Lauren. "Gendered Slurs." *Social Theory and Practice* 42, no. 2 (2016): 228–39.

Augustine of Hippo. *Confessions and Enchiridion.* 397. Translated and edited by Albert C. Outler. Philadelphia: Westminster Press, 1955.

Auster, Paul. *City of Glass.* Vol. 1 of *New York Trilogy.* New York: Penguin, 1985.

Austin, John Langshaw. *How to Do Things with Words: The William James Lectures Delivered at Harvard University in 1955.* Oxford: Clarendon Press, 1962.

Bach, Kent. "Loaded Words: On the Semantics and Pragmatics of Slurs." In *Bad Words: Philosophical Perspectives on Slurs,* edited by David Sosa, 60–76. Oxford: Oxford University Press, 2018.

Bachrach, Peter, and Morton S. Baratz. *Power and Poverty: Theory and Practice.* New York: Oxford University Press, 1970.

Balkin, Jack. "Cultural Democracy and the First Amendment." *Northwest University Law Review* 110, no. 5 (2016): 1053–96.

Balkin, Jack. *Cultural Software: A Theory of Ideology.* New Haven, CT: Yale University Press, 1998.

Bandura, Albert, Dorothea Ross, and Sheila A. Ross. "Transmission of Aggression through Imitation of Aggressive Models." *Journal of Abnormal and Social Psychology* 63, no. 3 (1961): 575–82.

Barnes, Michael. "Presupposition and Propaganda: A Socially Extended Analysis." In *Sbisà on Speech and Action*, edited by Laura Caponetto and Paulo Labinaz. Springer, forthcoming.

Barthes, Roland. "The Discourse of History." In *The Rustle of Language*, edited by Roland Barthes, translated by Richard Howard, 127–40. New York: Hill and Wang, 1984.

Bateson, Gregory. *Naven: A Survey of the Problems Suggested by a Composite Picture of the Culture of a New Guinea Tribe Drawn from Three Points of View*. 1936. Stanford: Stanford University Press, 1958.

Beaver, David. "Have You Noticed That Your Belly Button Lint Colour Is Related to the Colour of Your Clothing?" In *Presuppositions and Discourse: Essays Offered to Hans Kamp*, edited by Rainer Bauerle, Uwe Reyle, and Thomas Zimmermann, 65–100. Bingley, UK: Brill, 2010.

Beaver, David. "When Variables Don't Vary Enough." In *Proceedings of Semantics and Linguistic Theory IV*, edited by Mandy Harvey and Lynn Santelmann, 35–60. Ithaca, NY: Cornell University, 1994.

Beaver, David, and Cleo Condoravdi. "A Uniform Analysis of 'Before' and 'After.'" In *Proceedings of Semantics and Linguistic Theory XIII*, edited by Robert B. Young and Yuping Zhou, 37–54. Ithaca, NY: Cornell University, 2003.

Beaver, David, and Kristie Denlinger. "Linguistic Accommodation." In *Oxford Bibliographies in Linguistics*. Oxford: Oxford University Press, 2022. https://doi.org/10.1093 /OBO/9780199772810-0283.

Beaver, David, and Jason Stanley. "Neutrality." *Philosophical Topics* 49, no. 1 (2021): 165–85.

Beaver, David, and Jason Stanley. "Toward a Non-ideal Philosophy of Language." *Graduate Faculty Philosophy Journal* 39, no. 2 (2018): 503–47.

Beaver, David, and Henk Zeevat. "Towards a General Theory of Presupposition and Accommodation." Unpublished manuscript, 2006. The University of Texas at Austin & University of Amsterdam. Available from the authors on request.

Becker, Howard. "The Nature and Consequences of Black Propaganda." *American Sociological Review* 14, no. 2 (1949): 221–35.

Benford, Robert D. "Master Frame." In *The Wiley-Blackwell Encyclopedia of Social and Political Movements*, edited by David A. Snow, Donatella della Porta, Bert Klandermans, and Doug McAdam, 366–67. Hoboken: Blackwell Publishing, 2013.

Benford, Robert D., and David A. Snow. "Framing Processes and Social Movements: An Overview and Assessment." *Annual Review of Sociology* 26, no. 1 (2000): 611–39.

Bennett, Jonathan. *A Study of Spinoza's "Ethics."* Indianapolis: Hackett Publishing, 1984.

Bernoulli, Daniel. "Exposition of a New Theory on the Measurement of Risk." 1738. Translated by Louise Sommer. *Econometrica* 22, no. 1 (1954): 23–36.

Bianchi, Claudia. "Slurs and Appropriation: An Echoic Account." *Journal of Pragmatics* 66 (2014): 35–44.

Bizer, George Y., and Richard E. Petty. "How We Conceptualize Our Attitudes Matters: The Effects of Valence Framing on the Resistance of Political Attitudes." *Political Psychology* 26, no. 4 (2005): 553–68.

Blakemore, Diane. "Slurs and Expletives: A Case against a General Account of Expressive Meaning." *Language Sciences* 52 (2015): 22–35.

Bolinger, Renée Jorgensen. "The Pragmatics of Slurs." *Noûs* 51, no. 3 (2017): 439–62.

Bonilla-Silva, Eduardo. *Racism without Racists: Color-Blind Racism and the Persistence of Racial Inequality in the United States*. Washington, DC: Rowman & Littlefield, 2006.

Borges, Jorge Luis. *Labyrinths: Selected Stories and Other Writings*. New York: New Directions, 1986.

Borgoni, Cristina, Dirk Kindermann, and Andrea Onofri, eds. *The Fragmented Mind*. Oxford: Oxford University Press, 2021.

Bourdieu, Pierre. *The Logic of Practice*. 1980. Translated by Richard Nice. Stanford: Stanford University Press, 1990.

Bourdieu, Pierre. *Outline of a Theory of Practice*. 1972. Translated by Richard Nice. Cambridge: Cambridge University Press, 1977.

Brewer, Marilynn B. "The Social Self: On Being the Same and Different at the Same Time." *Personality & Social Psychology Bulletin* 17, no. 5 (1991): 475–82.

Brison, Susan. "The Autonomy Defense of Free Speech." *Ethics* 108, no. 2 (1998): 312–39.

Brooks, Daphne. *Bodies in Dissent: Spectacular Performances of Race and Freedom, 1850–1910*. Durham, NC: Duke University Press, 2006.

Brown, Penelope, and Stephen Levinson. *Politeness: Some Universals in Language Usage*. Cambridge: Cambridge University Press, 1987.

Brown, Roger. "How Shall a Thing Be Called?" *Psychological Review* 65, no. 1 (1958): 14–21.

Browning, Christopher. *Ordinary Men: Reserve Police Battalion 101 and the Final Solution in Poland*. New York: Harper Collins, 1992.

Brownstein, Michael, and Jennifer Saul, eds. *Implicit Bias and Philosophy*. Vol. 1, *Metaphysics and Epistemology*. Oxford: Oxford University Press, 2016.

Burke, Peter J. "Identity Control Theory." In *The Blackwell Encyclopedia of Sociology*, edited by George Ritzer, 2202–7. Malden: Blackwell Publishing, 2007.

Burke, Peter J. "Identity Processes and Social Stress." *American Sociological Review* 5, no. 6 (1991): 836–49.

Burnett, Heather. "A Persona-Based Semantics for Slurs." *Grazer Philosophische Studien* 97, no. 1 (2020): 31–62.

Butler, Judith. *Excitable Speech: A Politics of the Performative*. New York: Routledge, 1997.

Butler, Judith. *Gender Trouble: Feminism and the Subversion of Identity*. New York: Routledge, 1990.

Butler, Judith. "Performative Acts and Gender Constitution: An Essay in Phenomenology and Feminist Theory." *Theatre Journal* 40, no. 4 (1988): 519–31.

Buttelmann, David, Norbert Zmyj, Moritz Daum, and Malinda Carpenter. "Selective Imitation of In-Group over Out-Group Members in 14-Month-Old Infants." *Child Development* 84, no. 2 (2013): 422–28.

Cahalan, Margaret Werner, and Lee Anne Parsons. *Historical Corrections Statistics in the United States, 1850–1984*. Washington, DC: U.S. Department of Justice, Bureau of Justice Statistics, 1987.

Camp, Elisabeth. "A Dual Act Analysis of Slurs." In *Bad Words: Philosophical Perspectives on Slurs*, edited by David Sosa, 29–59. Oxford: Oxford University Press, 2018.

Camp, Elisabeth. "Imaginative Frames for Scientific Inquiry: Metaphors, Telling Facts, and Just-So Stories." In *The Scientific Imagination*, edited by Arnon Levy and Peter Godfrey-Smith, 304–36. Oxford: Oxford University Press, 2019.

Camp, Elisabeth. "Insinuation, Common Ground, and the Conversational Record." In *New Work on Speech Acts*, edited by Daniel Fogal, Daniel W. Harris, and Matt Moss, 40–66. Oxford: Oxford University Press, 2018.

Camp, Elisabeth. "Metaphor and That Certain 'Je Ne Sais Quoi.'" *Philosophical Studies* 129 (2006): 1–25.

Camp, Elisabeth. "Slurring Perspectives." *Analytic Philosophy* 54, no. 3 (2013): 330–49.

Camp, Elisabeth. "Two Varieties of Literary Imagination: Metaphor, Fiction, and Thought Experiments." *Midwest Studies in Philosophy* 33 (2009): 107–30.

Cappelen, Herman, and Josh Dever. *Bad Language*. Oxford: Oxford University Press, 2019.

Cappelen, Herman, and Josh Dever. *The Inessential Indexical: On the Philosophical Insignificance of Perspective and the First Person*. Oxford: Oxford University Press, 2014.

Cappelen, Herman, and Josh Dever. "On the Uselessness of the Distinction between Ideal and Non-Ideal Theory (at least in the Philosophy of Language)." In *The Routledge Handbook of Social and Political Philosophy of Language*, edited by Justin Khoo and Rachel Katharine Sterken, 91–105. New York: Routledge, 2021.

Carcasson, Martín. "Ending Welfare as We Know It: President Clinton and the Rhetorical Transformation of the Anti-Welfare Culture." *Rhetoric and Public Affairs* 9, no. 4 (2006): 655–92.

Carrera-Fernández, María Jesús, Joan Guàrdia-Olmos, and Maribel Peró-Cebollero. "Linguistic Style in the Mexican Electoral Process: Language Style Matching Analysis." *Revista Mexicana de Psicología* 31, no. 2 (2014): 138–52.

Carroll, Lewis. *Alice's Adventures in Wonderland & Through the Looking Glass and What Alice Found There*. 1865. London: Penguin Publishing Group, 2015.

Cavell, Stanley. *The Claim of Reason: Wittgenstein, Skepticism, Morality, and Tragedy*. Oxford: Oxford University Press, 1979.

Cepollaro, Bianca. "In Defence of a Presuppositional Account of Slurs." *Language Sciences* 52 (2015): 36–45.

Cepollaro, Bianca, and Isidora Stojanovic. "Hybrid Evaluatives: In Defense of a Presuppositional Account." *Grazer Philosophische Studien* 93, no. 3 (2016): 458–88.

Cepollaro, Bianca, Simone Sulpizio, and Claudia Bianchi. "How Bad Is It to Report a Slur? An Empirical Investigation." *Journal of Pragmatics* 146 (2019): 32–42.

Cepollaro, Bianca, and Dan Zeman. "Editors' Introduction: The Challenge from Non-Derogatory Uses of Slurs." *Grazer Philosophische Studien* 97, no. 1 (2020): 1–10.

Chafee, Zechariah, Jr. Review of *Free Speech and Its Relation to Self-Government*, by Alexander Meiklejohn. *Harvard Law Review* 62, no. 5 (1949): 891–901.

Chaiken, Shelly. "The Heuristic Model of Persuasion." In *Social Influence: The Ontario Symposium*, vol. 5, edited by Mark P. Zanna, James M. Olson, and C. Peter Herman, 3–39. London: Psychology Press, 1987.

Chapman, Graham, John Cleese, Terry Gilliam, Eric Idle, Terry Jones, and Michael Palin. *Monty Python's Flying Circus: Just the Words*. Vol. 1. London: Methuen, 1989.

Charlow, Nate. "Clause-Type, Force, and Normative Judgment in the Semantics of Imperatives." In *New Work on Speech Acts*, edited by Daniel Fogal, Daniel W. Harris, and Matt Moss, 67–98. Oxford: Oxford University Press, 2018.

Chartrand, Tanya L., and John A. Bargh. "The Chameleon Effect: The Perception–Behavior Link and Social Interaction." *Journal of Personality and Social Psychology* 76, no. 6 (1999): 893–910.

Cherniak, Christopher. *Minimal Rationality*. Cambridge, MA: MIT Press, 1986.

Chideya, Farai. *The Color of Our Future: Race in the 21st Century*. New York: Quill, 2000.

Chomsky, Noam. *The Minimalist Program*. Cambridge, MA: MIT Press, 2014.

Chong, Dennis, and James N. Druckman. "Framing Theory." *Annual Review of Political Science* 10, no. 1 (2007): 103–26.

Christensen, David. *Putting Logic in Its Place: Formal Constraints on Rational Belief*. Oxford: Oxford University Press, 2004.

Clark, Herbert H., and Susan E. Brennan. "Grounding in Communication." In *Perspectives on Socially Shared Cognition*, edited by L. Resnick, J. Levine, and S. Teasley, 127–49. Washington, DC: American Psychological Society, 1991.

Clark, Herbert H., and R. J. Gerrig. "Understanding Old Words with New Meanings." *Journal of Verbal Learning and Verbal Behavior* 22 (1983): 591–608.

Clark, Herbert H., and Deanna Wilkes-Gibbs. "Referring as a Collaborative Process." *Cognition* 22, no. 1 (1986): 1–39.

Cohen, Joshua. "Freedom of Expression." *Philosophy & Public Affairs* 22, no. 3 (1993): 207–63.

Collins, Patricia Hill. *Black Feminist Thought: Knowledge, Consciousness, and the Politics of Empowerment*. New York: Routledge, 1990.

Collins, Randall. *Interaction Ritual Chains*. Princeton, NJ: Princeton University Press, 2014.

Collins, Randall. "On the Microfoundations of Macrosociology." *American Journal of Sociology* 86, no. 5 (1981): 984–1014.

Coppock, Elizabeth, and David Beaver. "Definiteness and Determinacy." *Linguistics and Philosophy* 38, no. 5 (2015): 377–435.

Corredor, Elizabeth S. "Unpacking 'Gender Ideology' and the Global Right's Antigender Countermovement." *Signs: Journal of Women in Culture and Society* 44, no. 3 (2019): 613–38.

Cover, Thomas M., and Joy A. Thomas. *Elements of Information Theory*. New York: Wiley, 2006.

Crary, Alice. "The Methodological Is Political: What's the Matter with 'Analytic Feminism'?" *Radical Philosophy* 2, no. 2 (2018): 47–60.

Crary, Alice. "Neutrality, Critique, and Social Visibility: Response to David Beaver and Jason Stanley." *Philosophical Topics* 49, no. 1 (2021): 187–94.

Croom, Adam M. "How to Do Things with Slurs: Studies in the Way of Derogatory Words." *Language & Communication* 33, no. 3 (2013): 177–204.

Csikszentmihalyi, Mihaly. *Flow: The Psychology of Optimal Experience*. New York: Harper & Row, 1990.

Curtiz, Michael, dir. *Casablanca*. Los Angeles: Warner Bros, 1942.

Danto, Arthur C. *Narration and Knowledge*. New York: Columbia University Press, 1985.

Darley, John, and Bibb Latané. "Bystander Intervention in Emergencies: Diffusion of Responsibility." *Journal of Personality and Social Psychology* 8, no. 4 (1968): 377–83.

Davidson, Donald. "Expressing Evaluations." In *Problems of Rationality*, 19–38. Oxford: Oxford University Press, 2004.

Davidson, Donald. "Three Varieties of Knowledge." *Royal Institute of Philosophy Supplement* 30 (1991): 153–66.

Dawkins, Richard. *The Selfish Gene*. Oxford: Oxford University Press, 1976.

Delgado, Richard. "A Tort Action for Racial Insults, Epithets, and Name Calling." In *Words That Wound: Critical Race Theory, Assaultive Speech, and the First Amendment*, edited by Mari Matsuda, Charles R. Lawrence III, Richard Delgado, and Kimberlé Williams Crenshaw, 89–110. New York: Routledge, 1993.

De Marneffe, Marie-Catherine, Mandy Simons, and Judith Tonhauser. "The Commitment-Bank: Investigating Projection in Naturally Occurring Discourse." *Proceedings of Sinn und Bedeutung* 23, no. 2 (2019): 107–24.

Dembroff, Robin. "Beyond Binary: Gender Queer as Critical Gender Kind." *Philosophers' Imprint* 20, no. 9 (April 2020): 1–23.

Dennett, Daniel. *The Intentional Stance*. Cambridge, MA: MIT Press, 1989.

Descartes, René. *Selections from the Principles of Philosophy*. Translated by John Veitch. London: Ezreads Publications LLC, 2009.

Dewey, John. *Art as Experience*. New York: Putnam, 1934.

Dezecache, Guillaume, and Mélissa Berthet. "Working Hypotheses on the Meaning of General Alarm Calls." *Animal Behaviour* 142 (2018): 113–18.

Dickens, Charles. *Hard Times*. London: Bradbury & Evans, 1854.

DiIulio, John, Jr. "My Black Crime Problem, and Ours." *City Journal* 6, no. 2 (1996): 14–28.

Dotson, Kristie. "A Cautionary Tale: On Limiting Epistemic Oppression." *Frontiers: A Journal of Women Studies* 33, no. 1 (2012): 24–47.

Doyle, Gabriel, and Michael C. Frank. "Investigating the Sources of Linguistic Alignment in Conversation." *ACL* 1 (2016): 526–36.

Du Bois, John W. "Towards a Dialogic Syntax." *Cognitive Linguistics* 25, no. 3 (2014): 359–410.

Du Bois, W. E. B. "On the Ruling of Men." In *Darkwater: Voices from Within the Veil*, 78–94. Mineola: Dover, 1999.

Duranti, Alessandro. *The Anthropology of Intentions*. Cambridge: Cambridge University Press, 2015.

Durkheim, Émile. *The Division of Labor in Society*. 1893. Translated by W. D. Halls. New York: Simon and Schuster, 2014.

Durkheim, Émile. *The Elementary Forms of Religious Life*. 1912. Translated by Karen E. Fields. New York: Free Press, 1995.

Durkheim, Émile. *Rules of Sociological Method*. 1901. Translated by W. D. Halls. New York: Free Press, 1982.

Eagleton, Terry. *Ideology: An Introduction*. London: Verso, 1991.

Eckert, Penelope. "Communities of Practice." In *Encyclopedia of Language and Linguistics*, edited by Keith Brown, 683–85. Amsterdam: Elsevier, 2006.

Eckert, Penelope. *Jocks and Burnouts: Social Categories and Identity in the High School*. New York: Teachers College Press, 1989.

Eckert, Penelope, and Sally McConnell-Ginet. "Think Practically and Look Locally: Language and Gender as Community-Based Practice." *Annual Review of Anthropology* 21 (1992): 461–90.

Eckert, Penelope, and Etienne Wenger. "Communities of Practice in Sociolinguistics: What Is the Role of Power in Sociolinguistic Variation?" *Journal of Sociolinguistics* 9, no. 4 (2005): 582–89.

Egan, Andy. "*De se* Pragmatics." *Philosophical Perspectives* 32, no. 1 (2018): 144–64.

Egan, Andy. "Disputing about Taste." In *Disagreement*, edited by Richard Feldman and Ted Warfield, 247–92. Oxford: Oxford University Press, 2010.

Egan, Andy. "Seeing and Believing: Perception, Belief Formation and the Divided Mind." *Philosophical Studies* 140, no. 1 (2008): 47–63.

Eilan, Naomi, Christoph Hoerl, Teresa McCormack, and Johannes Roessler, eds. *Joint Attention: Communication and Other Minds: Issues in Philosophy and Psychology*. Oxford: Oxford University Press, 2005.

Ekman, Paul. "Should We Call It Expression or Communication?" *Innovation: The European Journal of Social Science Research* 10, no. 4 (1997): 333–44.

Elga, Adam, and Augustin Rayo. "Fragmentation and Logical Omniscience." *Noûs* 56 (2022): 716–41.

Ellul, Jacques. *Propaganda: The Formation of Men's Attitudes*. 1962. Translated by Konrad Kellen and Jean Lerneh. New York: Vintage Books, 1965.

Elster, Jon. "When Rationality Fails." In *Solomonic Judgements: Studies in the Limitations of Rationality*, 1–35. Cambridge: Cambridge University Press, 1989.

Evans, Gareth. "Understanding Demonstratives." In *Meaning and Understanding*, edited by Herman Parret and Jacques Bouveresse, 280–303. Berlin and New York: Walter de Gruyter, 1981.

Evans, Jonathan St. B. T. "In Two Minds: Dual-Process Accounts of Reasoning." *Trends in Cognitive Sciences* 7, no. 10 (2003): 454–59.

Evans, Jonathan St. B. T., and Keith E. Stanovich. "Dual-Process Theories of Higher Cognition: Advancing the Debate." *Perspectives on Psychological Science* 8, no. 3 (2013): 223–41.

Executive Office of the President of the United States. "Delivering Government Solutions in the 21st Century: Reform Plan and Reorganization Recommendations." Washington, DC: Executive Office of the President of the United States, 2018.

Executive Office of the President of the United States. Executive Order 13781. "Comprehensive Plan for Reorganizing the Executive Branch." *Federal Register* 82, no. 50 (2017): 13959–60.

Fauconnier, Giles. *Mental Spaces: Aspects of Meaning Construction in Natural Language.* Cambridge: Cambridge University Press, 1994.

Ferrara, Emilio, and Zeyao Yang. "Measuring Emotional Contagion in Social Media." *PloS one* 10, no. 11 (2015): 1–14.

Festinger, Leon. *A Theory of Cognitive Dissonance.* Stanford: Stanford University Press, 1957.

Festinger, Leon, Henry W. Riecken, and Stanley Schachter. *When Prophecy Fails: A Social and Psychological Study of a Modern Group That Predicted the Destruction of the World.* Minneapolis: University of Minnesota Press, 1956.

Fish, Stanley. *There's No Such Thing as Free Speech: And It's a Good Thing, Too.* Oxford: Oxford University Press, 1994.

Fisher, Walter R. *Human Communication as Narration: Toward a Philosophy of Reason, Value, and Action.* Columbia: University of South Carolina Press, 2021.

Fisher, Walter R. "Narrative Rationality and the Logic of Scientific Discourse." *Argumentation* 8 (1994): 21–32.

Fitzhugh, George. *Cannibals All! Or, Slaves without Masters.* 1857. Edited by C. Vann Woodward. Cambridge, MA: Harvard University Press, 1966.

Fitzsimons, Gavan J., and Baba Shiv. "Nonconscious and Contaminative Effects of Hypothetical Questions on Subsequent Decision Making." *Journal of Consumer Research* 28, no. 2 (2001): 224–38.

Fodor, Jerry. *The Language of Thought.* Cambridge, MA: Harvard University Press, 1975.

Foster, Jennifer. "Busting the Ghost of Neutral Counterparts." *Ergo: An Open Access Journal of Philosophy* (forthcoming).

Fraser, Rachel. "Narrative Testimony." *Philosophical Studies* 178, no. 12 (2021): 4025–52.

Frege, Gottlob. "Logic." Translated by Peter Long and Roger White. In *Posthumous Writings,* edited by Hans Hermes, Friedrich Kambartel, and Friedrich Kaulbach, 126–51. Chicago: University of Chicago Press, 1979.

Frege, Gottlob. "On Sense and Reference." 1892. Translated by Max Black. In *Translations from the Philosophical Writings of Gottlob Frege,* 2nd ed., edited by Peter Geach and Max Black, 56–78. Oxford: Basil Blackwell, 1960.

Frege, Gottlob. "The Thought: A Logical Inquiry." 1919. Translated by Marielle Quinton and Anthony M. Quinton. *Mind* 65, no. 259 (1956): 289–311.

Freud, Sigmund. *Jokes and Their Relation to the Unconscious.* 1905. Edited and translated by James Strachey. New York: Norton, 1960.

Freud, Sigmund. "Lecture XXXI, The Dissection of the Psychical Personality." In *The Standard Edition of the Complete Psychological Works of Sigmund Freud, Volume XXII (1932–1936): New Introductory Lectures on Psycho-Analysis and Other Works,* edited by James Strachey, 57–79. London: The Hogarth Press and the Institute of Psychoanalysis, 1933.

Fricker, Elizabeth. "Stating and Insinuating." *Proceedings of the Aristotelian Society* 86, no. 1 (2012): 61–94.

Fricker, Miranda. *Epistemic Injustice: Power and the Ethics of Knowing.* Oxford: Oxford University Press, 2007.

Furman, Brad, dir. *The Lincoln Lawyer.* Santa Monica: Lionsgate, 2011.

Gallagher, Helen L., Anthony I. Jack, Andreas Roepstorff, and Christopher D. Frith. "Imaging the Intentional Stance in a Competitive Game." *Neuroimage* 16, no. 3 (2002): 814–21.

Gallois, Cindy, Tania Ogay, and Howard Giles. "Communication Accommodation Theory: A Look Back and a Look Ahead." In *Theorizing about Intercultural Communication*, edited by William B. Gudykunst, 121–48. Thousand Oaks: Sage, 2005.

Gamson, William. *Talking Politics.* Cambridge: Cambridge University Press, 1992.

García-Carpintero, Manuel. "Pejoratives, Contexts and Presuppositions." In *Modeling and Using Context*, edited by Patrick Brézillon, Ray Turner, and Carlo Penco, 15–24. Berlin: Springer International Publishing, 2017

García Márquez, Gabriel. *One Hundred Years of Solitude.* 1967. Translated by Gregory Rabassa. New York: Harper Collins, 2003.

Gärdenfors, Peter. *The Geometry of Meaning: Semantics Based on Conceptual Spaces.* Cambridge, MA: MIT Press, 2014.

Gawronski, Bertram, and Laura A. Creighton. "Dual Process Theories." In *The Oxford Handbook of Social Cognition*, edited by Donal E. Carlston, 282–312. New York: Oxford University Press, 2013.

Gazdar, Gerald. *Pragmatics, Implicature, Presupposition, and Logical Form.* London: Academic Press, 1979.

Genschow, Oliver, and Simon Schindler. "The Influence of Group Membership on Cross-Contextual Imitation." *Psychonomic Bulletin & Review* 23, no. 4 (2016): 1257–65.

Gerring, John. "Ideology: A Definitional Analysis." *Political Research Quarterly* 50, no. 4 (1997): 957–94.

Geuss, Andrew M., and Benjamin A. Lyons. "Misinformation, Disinformation, and Online Propaganda." In *Social Media and Democracy: The State of the Field, Prospects for Reform*, edited by Nathaniel Persily and Joshua A. Tucker, 10–33. Cambridge: Cambridge University Press, 2020.

Geuss, Raymond. *The Idea of a Critical Theory: Habermas & the Frankfurt School.* Cambridge: Cambridge University Press, 1981.

Gibbard, Allan. *Wise Choices, Apt Feelings.* Cambridge, MA: Harvard University Press, 1990.

Gibson, James J. "The Theory of Affordances." In *The Ecological Approach to Visual Perception*, 127–37. Boston: Houghton Mifflin, 1979.

Gibson, James J. "A Theory of Direct Visual Perception." *Vision and Mind: Selected Readings in the Philosophy of Perception*, edited by Alva Noe and Evan T. Thompson, 77–90. Cambridge, MA: MIT Press, 2002.

Gilbert, Daniel T. "How Mental Systems Believe." *American Psychologist* 46, no. 2 (1991): 107–19.

Gilens, Martin. *Why Americans Hate Welfare: Race, Media, and the Politics of Antipoverty Policy.* Chicago: University of Chicago Press, 1999.

Giles, Howard. "Accent Mobility: A Model and Some Data." *Anthropological Linguistics* 15, no. 2 (1973): 87–105.

Giles, Howard. "Linguistic Differentiation between Ethnic Groups." In *Differentiation between Social Groups: Studies in the Social Psychology of Intergroup Relations*, edited by Henri Tajfel, 361–93. London: Academic Press, 1978.

Giles, Howard. "A Study of Speech Patterns in Social Interaction: Accent Evaluation and Accent Change." PhD diss., University of Bristol, 1971.

Giles, Howard, Justine Coupland, and Nikolas Coupland. "Accommodation Theory: Communication, Context, and Consequence." In *Contexts of Accommodation*, edited by Howard Giles, Justine Coupland, and Nikolas Coupland, 1–68. New York: Cambridge University Press, 1991.

Giles, Howard, Donald M. Taylor, and Richard Bourhis. "Towards a Theory of Interpersonal Accommodation through Language: Some Canadian Data." *Language in Society* 2, no. 2 (1973): 177–92.

Goebbels, Joseph. "Communism with the Mask Off (1935)." In *The Third Reich Sourcebook*, edited by Anson Rabinbach and Sander L. Gilman, 126–34. Berkeley: University of California Press, 2013.

Goffman, Erving. "Presentation of Self in Everyday Life." *American Journal of Sociology* 55 (1949): 6–7.

Gonzales, Amy L., Jeffrey T. Hancock, and James W. Pennebaker. "Language Style Matching as a Predictor of Social Dynamics in Small Groups." *Communication Research* 37, no. 1 (2010): 3–19.

Gould, Stephen Jay. *The Mismeasure of Man*. New York: W. W. Norton, 1981.

Gould, Stephen Jay, and Richard C. Lewontin. *The Spandrels of San Marco and the Panglossian Paradigm: A Critique of the Adaptationist Programme*. New York: Routledge, 2020.

Grant, Madison. *The Passing of the Great Race: Or, The Racial Basis of European History*. New York: C. Scribner's Sons, 1916.

Grice, H. Paul. "Further Notes on Logic and Conversation." In *Studies in the Way of Words*, 41–57. Cambridge, MA: Harvard University Press, 1989.

Grice, H. Paul. "Meaning." *The Philosophical Review* 66, no. 3 (1957): 377–88.

Grice, H. Paul. *Studies in the Way of Words*. Cambridge, MA: Harvard University Press, 1989.

Habermas, Jürgen. *Moral Consciousness and Communicative Action*. Translated by Christian Lenhardt and Shierry Weber Nicholsen. Cambridge: Polity Press, 1990.

Habermas, Jürgen. *Truth and Justification*. Translated by Barbara Fultner. Cambridge, MA: MIT Press, 2003.

Hamming, Richard W. *Coding and Information Theory*. Englewood Cliffs, NJ: Prentice-Hall, 1986.

Haney, Craig, Curtis Banks, and Philip Zimbardo. "Interpersonal Dynamics in a Simulated Prison." In *Sociology of Corrections*, edited by Robert G. Leger and John R. Stratton, 65–92. New York: Wiley, 1977.

Harmon-Jones, Eddie, ed. *Cognitive Dissonance: Reexamining a Pivotal Theory in Psychology*. Washington, DC: American Psychological Association Books, 2019.

Haslanger, Sally. *Resisting Reality: Social Construction and Social Critique*. Oxford: Oxford University Press, 2012.

Haslanger, Sally. "Social Meaning and Philosophical Method." *Proceedings and Addresses of the American Philosophical Association* 88 (2014): 16–37.

Haslanger, Sally. "What Is a Social Practice?" *Royal Institute of Philosophy Supplement* 82 (2018): 231–47.

Hasson, Uri, Joseph P. Simmons, and Alexander Todorov. "Believe It or Not: On the Possibility of Suspending Belief." *Psychological Science* 16, no. 7 (2005): 566–71.

Hatfield, E., J. Cacioppo, and R. L. Rapson. "Emotional Contagion." In *Emotion and Social Behavior*, edited by M. S. Clark, 151–77. Vol. 14 of *Review of Personality and Social Psychology*. Newbury Park: Sage, 1992.

Hawkins, Robert D. "Coordinating on Meaning in Communication." PhD diss., Stanford University, 2019.

Hawthorne, John, and Jason Stanley. "Knowledge and Action." *Journal of Philosophy* 105, no. 10 (2008): 571–90.

Healey, Patrick. "Expertise or Expertese?: The Emergence of Task-Oriented Sub-Languages." In *Proceedings of the 19th Annual Conference of the Cognitive Science Society*, edited by Michael Shafto and Pat Langley, 301–6. Stanford: Stanford University Press, 1997.

Hedger, Joseph A. "The Semantics of Racial Slurs: Using Kaplan's Framework to Provide a Theory of the Meaning of Derogatory Epithets." *Linguistic and Philosophical Investigations* 11 (2012): 74–84.

Heim, Irene. "On the Projection Problem for Presuppositions." In *Second Annual West Coast Conference on Formal Linguistics*, edited by Michael Barlow, Dan Flickinger, and Michael Westcoat, 114–26. Stanford: Stanford University Press, 1983.

Heinamaki, Orvokki. "Semantics of English Temporal Connectives." PhD diss., University of Texas at Austin, 1974.

Hemingway, Ernest. *A Farewell to Arms*. The Hemingway Library Edition. 1929. New York: Scribner, 2014.

Hemingway, Ernest. *The Old Man and the Sea*. New York: Scribner Classics, 1996.

Hemingway, Ernest. "The Short Happy Life of Ernest Macomber." In *The Short Stories of Ernest Hemingway*, edited by Seán Hemingway, 263–300. New York: Scribner, 2017.

Henderson, Robert, Peter Klecha, and Elin McCready. "Response to Pullum on Slurs." LanguageLog, July 20, 2017, accessed March 2, 2023, https://languagelog.ldc.upenn.edu/nll/?p=33784.

Herbert, Cassie. "Exclusionary Speech and Constructions of Community." PhD diss., Georgetown University, 2017.

Herman, Edward S., and Noam Chomsky. *Manufacturing Consent: The Political Economy of the Mass Media*. 1988. New York: Pantheon Books, 2002.

Hesni, Samia. "Normative Discourse and Social Negotiation." PhD diss., Massachusetts Institute of Technology, 2019.

Hess, Leopold. "Practices of Slur Use." *Grazer Philosophische Studien* 97, no. 1 (2020): 86–105.

Hess, Leopold. "Slurs and Expressive Commitments." *Acta Analytica* 36 (2021): 263–90.

Hess, Leopold. "Slurs: Semantic and Pragmatic Theories of Meaning." In *The Cambridge Handbook of the Philosophy of Language*, edited by Peter Stalmaszczyk, 450–66. Cambridge: Cambridge University Press, 2021.

Hill, Jane H. *The Everyday Language of White Racism*. Oxford: Wiley-Blackwell, 2009.

Hinton, Elizabeth. *America on Fire: The Untold History of Police Violence*. New York: Liverwright, 2021.

Hinzen, Wolfram. "Narrow Syntax and the Language of Thought." *Philosophical Psychology* 26, no. 1 (2013): 1–23.

Hitler, Adolf. *Mein Kampf*. 1925/1927. Translated and edited by John Chamberlain, Sidney B. Fay, John Gunther, Carlton J. H. Hayes, Graham Hutton, Alvin Johnson, William L. Langer, Walter Millis, Raoul de Roussy de Sales, and George N. Shuster. New York: Reynal & Hitchcock, 1941.

Hockett, Charles. *Refurbishing Our Foundations: Elementary Linguistics from an Advanced Point of View*. Amsterdam: John Benjamins, 1987.

Hoffman, Frederick Ludwig. *Race Traits and Tendencies of the American Negro*. New York: Published for the American Economic Association by Macmillan, 1896.

Hogg, Michael A., Deborah J. Terry, and Katherine M. White. "A Tale of Two Theories: A Critical Comparison of Identity Theory with Social Identity Theory." *Social Psychology Quarterly* (1995): 255–69.

Hollis, Martin, and Edward Nell. *Rational Economic Man: A Philosophical Critique of Neo-Classical Economics*. London: Cambridge University Press, 1975.

Hom, Christopher. "The Semantics of Racial Epithets." *Journal of Philosophy* 105, no. 8 (2008): 416–40.

Hornsey, Matthew J., and Jolanda Jetten. "The Individual within the Group: Balancing the Need to Belong with the Need to be Different." *Personality and Social Psychology Review* 8, no. 3 (2004): 248–64.

Howard, Lauren H., Annette M. E. Henderson, Cristina Carrazza, and Amanda L. Woodward. "Infants' and Young Children's Imitation of Linguistic In-Group and Out-Group Informants." *Child Development* 86, no. 1 (2015): 259–75.

Humboldt, Wilhelm von. *On Language: The Diversity of Human Language-Structure and Its Influence on the Mental Development of Mankind.* 1836. Translated by Peter Heath. Cambridge: Cambridge University Press, 1988.

Hume, David. *The Natural History of Religion.* In *A Dissertation on the Passions, The Natural History of Religion (1757): A Critical Edition*, edited by Tom L. Beauchhamp, 33–87. New York: Clarendon Press, 2007.

Hume, David. *A Treatise of Human Nature.* Vol. 1. Edited by David Fate Norton and Mary J. Norton. Oxford: Clarendon Press, 2007.

Hyska, Megan. "Against Irrationalism in the Theory of Propaganda." *Journal of the American Philosophical Association* 9, no. 2 (2023): 303–17.

Hyska, Megan. "Propaganda, Irrationality, and Group Agency." In *The Routledge Handbook of Political Epistemology*, edited by Michael Hannon and Jeroen de Ridder, 226–35. New York: Routledge, 2021.

Ireland, Molly E., and Marlone D. Henderson. "Language Style Matching, Engagement, and Impasse in Negotiations." *Negotiation and Conflict Management Research* 7, no. 1 (2014): 1–16.

Ireland, Molly E., and James W. Pennebaker. "Language Style Matching in Writing: Synchrony in Essays, Correspondence, and Poetry." *Journal of Personality and Social Psychology* 99, no. 3 (2010): 549–71.

Ireland, Molly E., Richard B. Slatcher, Paul W. Eastwick, Lauren E. Scissors, Eli J. Finkel, and James W. Pennebaker. "Language Style Matching Predicts Relationship Initiation and Stability." *Psychological Science* 22, no. 1 (2011): 39–44.

Jaeggi, Rahel. *Critique of Forms of Life.* Translated by Ciaran Cronin. Cambridge, MA: The Belknap Press of Harvard University Press, 2018.

James, William. *The Principles of Psychology, in Two Volumes.* New York: Henry Holt and Company, 1890.

James, William. *The Varieties of Religious Experience.* New York: Longmans Green and Co., 1902.

Jayamaha, Buddhika B., and Jahara Matisek. "Social Media Warriors: Leveraging a New Battlespace." *The US Army War College Quarterly: Parameters* 48, no. 4 (2018): 11–23.

Jeshion, Robin. "Expressivism and the Offensiveness of Slurs." *Philosophical Perspectives* 27, no. 1 (2013): 231–59.

Jeshion, Robin. "Pride and Prejudiced: On the Reclamation of Slurs." *Grazer Philosophische Studien* 97 (2020): 106–37.

Jeshion, Robin. "Slurs, Dehumanization, and the Expression of Contempt." In *Bad Words: Philosophical Perspectives on Slurs*, edited by David Sosa, 77–107. Oxford: Oxford University Press, 2018.

Kahan, Dan M. "Ideology, Motivated Reasoning, and Cognitive Reflection." *Judgment and Decision Making* 8, no. 4 (2013): 407–24.

Kahneman, Daniel. *Thinking, Fast and Slow.* New York: Macmillan, 2011.

Kahneman, Daniel, and Amos Tversky. "Choices, Values and Frames." *American Psychologist* 39 (1984): 341–50.

Kalven, Harry, Jr. "The Metaphysics of the Law of Obscenity." *Supreme Court Review* (1960): 1–45.

Kant, Immanuel. *Critique of Pure Reason*. 1781. Translated by J.M.D. Meiklejohn. New York: Wiley Books, 1943.

Kaplan, David. "Demonstratives: An Essay on the Semantics, Logic, Metaphysics, and Epistemology of Demonstratives and Other Indexicals." In *Themes from Kaplan*, edited by Joseph Almog, John Perry, and Howard Wettstein, 481–563. Oxford: Oxford University Press, 1989.

Kaplan, David. "The Meaning of Ouch and Oops." Howison Lecture in Philosophy delivered at UC Berkeley, August 23, 2004, transcribed by Elizabeth Coppock. Available at https://eecoppock.info/PragmaticsSoSe2012/kaplan.pdf.

Karttunen, Lauri. "Presuppositions and Linguistic Context." *Theoretical Linguistics* 1 (1974): 181–94.

Karttunen, Lauri. "Presuppositions of Compound Sentences." *Linguistic Inquiry* 4, no. 2 (1973): 169–93.

Karttunen, Lauri. "Some Observations on Factivity." *Research on Language & Social Interaction* 4, no. 1 (1971): 55–69.

Keiser, Jessica. "Coordinating with Language." *Croatian Journal of Philosophy* 16, no. 2 (2016): 229–45.

Keiser, Jessica. *Non-Ideal Foundations of Language*. Abingdon: Taylor & Francis, 2023.

Kelman, Herbert C., and V. Lee Hamilton. *Crimes of Obedience: Toward a Social Psychology of Authority and Responsibility*. New Haven, CT: Yale University Press, 1989.

Khoo, Justin. "Code Words in Political Discourse." *Philosophical Topics* 45, no. 2 (2017): 33–64.

Khoo, Justin, and Rachel K. Sterken, eds. *The Routledge Handbook of Social and Political Philosophy of Language*. New York & Abingdon: Routledge, 2021.

Klein, Richard A., Kate A. Ratliff, Michelangelo Vianello, Reginald B. Adams Jr, Štěpán Bahník, Michael J. Bernstein, Konrad Bocian, et al. "Investigating Variation in Replicability: A 'Many Labs' Replication Project." *Social Psychology* 45, no. 3 (2014): 142–52.

Klemperer, Victor. *The Language of the Third Reich: LTI–Lingua Tertii Imperii: A Philologist's Notebook*. 1957. Translated by Martin Brady. New York: Bloomsbury, 2013.

Knowles, Eric S., and Christopher A. Condon. "Why People Say 'Yes': A Dual-Process Theory of Acquiescence." *Journal of Personality and Social Psychology* 77, no. 2 (1999): 379–86.

Kramer, Adam D. I., Jamie E. Guillory, and Jeffrey T. Hancock. "Experimental Evidence of Massive-Scale Emotional Contagion through Social Networks." *Proceedings of the National Academy of Sciences* 111, no. 24 (2014): 8788–90.

Kripke, Saul A. *Naming and Necessity*. Cambridge, MA: Harvard University Press, 1980.

Kroch, Anthony S. "Reflexes of Grammar in Patterns of Language Change." *Language Variation and Change* 1, no. 3 (1989): 199–244.

Kühberger, Anton. "The Influence of Framing on Risky Decisions: A Meta-Analysis." *Organizational Behavior and Human Decision Processes* 75, no. 1 (1998): 23–55.

Kukla, Quill R. "Slurs, Interpellation, and Ideology." *Southern Journal of Philosophy* 56 (2018): 7–32.

Lakin, Jessica L., Tanya L. Chartrand, and Robert M. Arkin. "I Am Too Just Like You: Nonconscious Mimicry as an Automatic Behavioral Response to Social Exclusion." *Psychological Science* 19, no. 8 (2008): 816–22.

Lakoff, George. *The All New Don't Think of an Elephant!: Know Your Values and Frame the Debate*. Hartford: Chelsea Green Publishing, 2014.

Lakoff, George, and Mark Johnson. *Metaphors We Live By*. Chicago: University of Chicago Press, 2008.

Langendoen, D. Terence, and Harris Savin. "The Projection Problem for Presuppositions." In *Studies in Linguistic Semantics*, edited by Charles Fillmore and D. Terence Langendoen, 373–88. New York: Holt, Reinhardt and Winston, 1971.

Langton, Rae. "Blocking as Counter-Speech." In *New Work on Speech Acts*, edited by Daniel Fogal, Daniel W. Harris, and Matt Moss, 144–64. Oxford: Oxford University Press, 2018.

Langton, Rae. *Sexual Solipsism: Philosophical Essays on Pornography and Objectification*. Oxford: Oxford University Press, 2009.

Langton, Rae. "Speech Acts and Unspeakable Acts." *Philosophy and Public Affairs* 22, no. 4 (1993): 293–330.

Langton, Rae, and Caroline West. "Scorekeeping in a Pornographic Language Game." *Australasian Journal of Philosophy* 77, no. 3 (1999): 303–19.

Larsson, Staffan. "Coordinating on Ad-hoc Semantic Systems in Dialogue." In *Decalog 2007: Proceedings of the 11th Workshop on the Semantics and Pragmatics of Dialogue*, edited by Ron Artstein and Laure Vieu, 109–16. Rovereto: University of Trento, 2007.

Larsson, Staffan. "Grounding as a Side-Effect of Grounding." *Topics in Cognitive Science* 10, no. 2 (2018): 389–408.

Lasersohn, Peter. "Context-Dependence, Disagreement, and Predicates of Personal Taste." *Linguistics and Philosophy* 28 (2005): 643–86.

Lasersohn, Peter. *Subjectivity and Perspective in Truth-Theoretic Semantics*. Oxford: Oxford University Press, 2017.

Lave, Jean, and Etienne Wenger. *Situated Learning: Legitimate Peripheral Participation*. Cambridge: Cambridge University Press, 1991.

Lawrence, Charles R., III. "If He Hollers Let Him Go: Regulating Racist Speech on Campus." In *Words That Wound: Critical Race Theory, Assaultive Speech, and the First Amendment*, edited by Mari Matsuda, Charles R. Lawrence III, Richard Delgado, and Kimberlé Williams Crenshaw, 53–88. New York: Routledge, 1993.

Le Bon, Gustave. *The Crowd: A Study of the Popular Mind*. New York, Macmillan, 1896.

Leonardelli, Geoffrey J., Cynthia L. Pickett, and Marilynn B. Brewer. "Optimal Distinctiveness Theory: A Framework for Social Identity, Social Cognition, and Intergroup Relations." In *Advances in Experimental Social Psychology* 43, edited by Mark P. Zanna and James Olson, 63–113. Cambridge: Academic Press, 2010.

Lepore, Ernie, and Matthew Stone. "Pejorative Tone." In *Bad Words: Philosophical Perspectives on Slurs*, edited by David Sosa, 134–53. Oxford: Oxford University Press, 2018.

Le Texier, Thibault. "Debunking the Stanford Prison Experiment." *American Psychologist* 74, no. 7 (2019): 823–39.

Levin, Irwin P., Sandra L. Schneider, and Gary J. Gaeth. "All Frames Are Not Created Equal: A Typology and Critical Analysis of Framing Effects." *Organizational Behavior and Human Decision Processes* 76, no. 2 (1998): 149–88.

Lewis, David. "Attitudes *De Dicto* and *De Se*." *The Philosophical Review* 88, no. 4 (1979): 513–43.

Lewis, David. *Convention: A Philosophical Study*. Cambridge, MA: Harvard University Press, 1969.

Lewis, David. "Languages and Language." In *Philosophical Papers*, vol. 1, 163–88. Oxford: Oxford University Press, 1983.

Lewis, David. "Scorekeeping in a Language Game." In *Semantics from Different Points of View*, edited by Rainer Bäuerle, Urs Egli, and Arnim von Stechow, 172–87. Berlin: Springer, 1979.

Lewis, Thomas, Fari Amini, and Richard Lannon. *A General Theory of Love*. New York: Vintage Books, 2000.

Liberman, Alvin M., Katherine Safford Harris, Howard S. Hoffman, and Belver C. Griffith. "The Discrimination of Speech Sounds within and across Phoneme Boundaries." *Journal of Experimental Psychology* 54, no. 5 (1957): 358–68.

Linderholm, Tracy, Sandra Virtue, Yuhtsuen Tzeng, and Paul van den Broek. "Fluctuations in the Availability of Information during Reading: Capturing Cognitive Processes Using the Landscape Model." *Discourse Processes* 37 (2004): 165–86.

Loftus, Elizabeth F. "Leading Questions and the Eyewitness Report." *Cognitive Psychology* 7, no. 4 (1975): 560–72.

Loftus, Elizabeth F., and John C. Palmer. "Reconstruction of Automobile Destruction: An Example of the Interaction between Language and Memory." *Journal of Verbal Learning and Verbal Behavior* 13, no. 5 (1974): 585–89.

Loftus, Elizabeth F., and Guido Zanni. "Eyewitness Testimony: The Influence of the Wording of a Question." *Bulletin of the Psychonomic Society* 5, no. 1 (1975): 86–88.

Lukes, Steven. *Power: A Radical View*. New York: Bloomsbury Publishing, 2021.

MacFarlane, John. *Assessment Sensitivity: Relative Truth and Its Applications*. Oxford: Oxford University Press, 2014.

MacKinnon, Catharine. *Feminism Unmodified: Discourses on Life and Law*. Cambridge, MA: Harvard University Press, 1987.

MacKinnon, Catharine. *Only Words*. Cambridge, MA: Harvard University Press, 1993.

Maitra, Ishani. "Subordinating Speech." In *Speech and Harm: Controversies over Free Speech*, edited by Ishani Maitra and Mary Kate McGowan, 94–121. Oxford: Oxford University Press, 2012.

Malinowski, Bronislaw. "The Problem of Meaning in Primitive Languages." In *The Meaning of Meaning*, edited by C. K. Ogden, & I. A. Richards, 296–336. London: Kegan Paul, Trend, Trubner and Co., 1923.

Mandelbaum, Eric. "The Architecture of Belief: An Essay on the Unbearable Automaticity of Believing." PhD diss., The University of North Carolina at Chapel Hill, 2010.

Manne, Kate. *Down Girl: The Logic of Misogyny*. Oxford: Oxford University Press, 2017.

Marlin, Randal. *Propaganda and the Ethics of Persuasion*. New York: Broadview Press, 2002.

Marques, Teresa. "The Expression of Hate in Hate Speech." *Journal of Applied Philosophy* (2022): 1–19.

Marques, Teresa, and Manuel García-Carpintero. "Really Expressive Presuppositions and How to Block Them." *Grazer Philosophische Studien* 97 (2020): 138–58.

Matsuda, Mari J. "Public Response to Racist Speech: Considering the Victim's Story." *Michigan Law Review* 87, no. 8, "Legal Storytelling" (1989): 2320–81.

Matsuda, Mari J., Charles R. Lawrence III, Richard Delgado, and Kimberlé Williams Crenshaw. *Words That Wound: Critical Race Theory, Assaultive Speech, and the First Amendment*. New York: Westview Press, 1993.

McCready, Elin, and Christopher Davis. "An Invocational Theory of Slurs." Manuscript of talk presented at LENLS 14, 2017. *Semantics Archive*, https://semanticsarchive.net/Archive/TdmNjdiM/mccready-davis-LENLS14.pdf.

McDonnell, Terence E., Christopher A. Bail, and Iddo Tavory. "A Theory of Resonance." *Sociological Theory* 35, no. 1 (2017): 1–14.

McFarland, Daniel A., Dan Jurafsky, and Craig Rawlings. "Making the Connection: Social Bonding in Courtship Situations." *American Journal of Sociology* 118, no. 6 (2013): 1596–649.

McGowan, Mary Kate. *Just Words: On Speech and Hidden Harm*. Oxford: Oxford University Press, 2019.

McNamara, Danielle S., and Joe Magliano. "Toward a Comprehensive Model of Comprehension." *Psychology of Learning and Motivation* 51 (2009): 297–384.

McTiernan, John, dir. *Die Hard*. Los Angeles: Twentieth Century Fox, 1988.

Meiklejohn, Alexander. "The First Amendment Is an Absolute." *Supreme Court Review* (1961): 245–66.

Meiklejohn, Alexander. *Free Speech and Its Relation to Self-Government*. New York: Harper & Brothers, 1948.

Meiklejohn, Alexander. *Political Freedom: The Constitutional Powers of the People*. New York: Oxford University Press, 1965.

Mendelberg, Tali. *The Race Card: Campaign Strategy, Implicit Messages, and the Norm of Equality*. Princeton, NJ: Princeton University Press, 2001.

Metzl, Jonathan M. *Dying of Whiteness: How the Politics of Racial Resentment Is Killing America's Heartland*. Paris: Hachette UK, 2019.

Mill, John Stuart. *On Liberty*. 1859. Indianapolis: Hackett, 1978.

Mills, Charles. "'Ideal Theory' as Ideology." *Hypatia* 20, no. 3 (2005): 165–84.

Mills, Charles. "White Ignorance." In *Race and Epistemologies of Ignorance*, edited by Shannon Sullivan and Nancy Tuana, 13–38. Albany: State University of New York Press, 2007.

Milton, John. *Areopagitica*. 1644. Oxford: Clarendon Press, 1904.

Morrison, Toni. "The Nobel Lecture in Literature." In *What Moves at the Margin: Selected Nonfiction*, 198–207. Jackson: University Press of Mississippi, 2008.

Morrison, Toni. *Paradise*. New York: Alfred A. Knopf, 1997.

Morrison, Toni. *Playing in the Dark: Whiteness and the Literary Imagination*. New York: Vintage Books, 1992.

Moss, Sarah. "Updating as Communication." *Philosophy and Phenomenological Research* 85, no. 2 (2012): 225–48.

Moxey, Linda M., and Gideon Keren. "Mechanisms Underlying Linguistic Framing Effects." In *Perspectives on Framing* (Society for Judgment and Decision Making Series), edited by Gideon Keren, 119–34. New York: Psychology Press, Taylor & Francis Group, 2011.

Muhammad, Khalil Gibran. *The Condemnation of Blackness: Race, Crime, and the Making of Modern Urban America*. Cambridge, MA: Harvard University Press, 2010.

Mullen, Andrew. "The Propaganda Model after 20 Years: Interview with Edward S. Herman and Noam Chomsky." *Westminster Papers in Communication and Culture* 6, no. 2 (2017): 12–22.

Munton, Jessie. "Prejudice as the Misattribution of Salience." *Analytic Philosophy* 64, no. 1 (2023): 1–19.

Murakami, Haruki. "Nausea 1979." In *Blind Willow, Sleeping Woman*, translated by Philip Gabriel and Jay Rubin, 151–62. New York: Random House, 2006.

Murray, Sarah E. "Evidentiality and the Structure of Speech Acts." PhD diss., Rutgers University, New Brunswick, New Jersey, 2010.

Murray, Sarah E. "Varieties of Update." *Semantics and Pragmatics* 7 (2014): 1–53.

Nagel, Jennifer. "Epistemic Territory." *Proceedings and Addresses of the American Philosophical Association* 93 (2019): 67–86.

Nguyen, C. Thi. "Echo Chambers and Epistemic Bubbles." *Episteme* 17, no. 2 (2020): 141–61.

Niederhoffer, Kate G., and James W. Pennebaker. "Linguistic Style Matching in Social Interaction." *Journal of Language and Social Psychology* 21, no. 4 (2002): 337–60.

Nowak, Ethan. "Sociolinguistic Variation, Speech Acts, and Discursive Injustice." *The Philosophical Quarterly* (2022). https://doi.org/10.1093/pq/pqac063.

Nunberg, Geoffrey. "The Social Life of Slurs." In *New Work on Speech Acts*, edited by Daniel Fogal, Daniel W. Harris, and Matt Moss, 237–95. Oxford: Oxford University Press, 2018.

Nye, Robert A. *The Origins of Crowd Psychology: Gustave LeBon and the Crisis of Mass Democracy in the Third Republic*. London: SAGE Publications, 1975.

O'Brien, Edward J., and Jerome L. Myers. "Text Comprehension: A View from the Bottom Up." In *Narrative Comprehension, Causality, and Coherence: Essays in Honor of Tom*

Trabasso, edited by Susan R. Goldman, Arthur C. Graesser, and Paul van den Broek, 41–60. New York: Routledge, 1999.

O'Connor, Flannery. "Everything That Rises Must Converge." In *Everything That Rises Must Converge*, 3–23. New York: Macmillan, 1965.

Ōe, Kenzaburō. "The Day He Himself Shall Wipe My Tears Away." In *Teach Us to Outgrow Our Madness: Four Short Novels*, translated by John Nathan, 1–110. New York: Grove Press, 1977.

O'Neill, Eileen. "Disappearing Ink: Early Modern Women Philosophers and Their Fate in History." In *Philosophy in a Feminist Voice*, edited by Janet Kourany, 17–62. Princeton, NJ: Princeton University Press, 1998.

O'Neill, James. *Prodigal Genius: The Life of Nikola Tesla*. New York: Cosimo Classics, 2006.

Orwell, George. *Nineteen Eighty-Four: A Novel*. London: Secker & Warburg, 1949.

Ottati, Victor, Susan Rhoads, and Arthur C. Graesser. "The Effect of Metaphor on Processing Style in a Persuasion Task: A Motivational Resonance Model." *Journal of Personality and Social Psychology* 77, no. 4 (1999): 688–97.

Parsons, Talcott. *The Social System*. Glencoe: Free Press, 1951.

Paul, Christopher, and Miriam Matthews. "The Russian 'Firehose of Falsehood' Propaganda Model." RAND Corporation, 2016. https://www.rand.org/pubs/perspectives/PE198.html.

Paul, Laurie Ann. *Transformative Experience*. Oxford: Oxford University Press, 2014.

Payne, Rodger A. "Persuasion, Frames and Norm Construction." *European Journal of International Relations* 7, no. 1 (2001): 37–61.

Perry, John. "Frege on Demonstratives." *Philosophical Review* 86, no. 4 (1977): 474–97.

Peters, Mathijs, and Bareez Majid. *Exploring Hartmut Rosa's Concept of Resonance*. Cham, Switzerland: Palgrave Macmillan, 2022.

Petty, Richard E., and John T. Cacioppo. "The Elaboration Likelihood Model of Persuasion." In *Communication and Persuasion*, edited by Richard E. Petty and John T. Cacioppo, 1–24. New York: Springer, 1986.

Petty, Richard E., Rachel Goldman, and John Cacioppo. "Personal Involvement as a Determinant of Argument-Based Persuasion." *Journal of Personality and Social Psychology* 41, no. 5 (1981): 847–55.

Piaget, Jean. *The Construction of Reality in the Child*. Translated by Margaret Cook. New York: Basic Books, 1954.

Piaget, Jean. *The Development of Thought: Equilibration of Cognitive Structures*. Translated by Arnold Rosin. New York: Viking, 1977.

Piaget, Jean. "Problems of Equilibration." In *Topics in Cognitive Development*, edited by M. Appel, 3–13. Boston: Springer, 1977.

Pickering, Martin J., and S. Garrod. "Toward a Mechanistic Psychology of Dialogue." *Behavioral and Brain Sciences* 27, no. 2 (2004): 169–226.

Plato. *Gorgias*. Translated by Terence Irwin. Oxford: Clarendon Press, 1971.

Plato. *The Republic*. Translated by Richard W. Sterling and William C. Scott. New York: Norton, 1996.

Pliny the Younger. "Letter from Pliny to Trajan c.112 CE." Internet History Sourcebooks Project, Fordham University. https://sourcebooks.fordham.edu/ancient/pliny-trajan1.asp.

Plutchik, Robert. *The Emotions*. Lanham, MD: University Press of America, 1991.

Popa-Wyatt, Mihaela. "Reclamation: Taking Back Control of Words." *Grazer Philosophische Studien* 97, no. 1 (2020): 159–76.

Popa-Wyatt, Mihaela. "Slurs, Pejoratives, and Hate Speech." In *Oxford Bibliographies in Philosophy*, edited by Duncan Pritchard. Oxford: Oxford University Press, 2020. https://doi.org/10.1093/OBO/9780195396577-0403.

Popa-Wyatt, Mihaela, and Jeremy L. Wyatt. "Slurs, Roles and Power." *Philosophical Studies* 175, no. 11 (2018): 2879–906.

Portner, Paul. "Imperatives and Modals." *Natural Language Semantics* 15 (2007): 351–83.

Portner, Paul. "The Semantics of Imperatives within a Theory of Clause Types." In *Proceedings of Semantics and Linguistic Theory XIV*, edited by Robert B. Young, 235–52. Ithaca, NY: Cornell University, 2004.

Post, Robert. *Democracy, Expertise, and Academic Freedom: A First Amendment Jurisprudence for the Modern State.* New Haven, CT: Yale University Press, 2012.

Potts, Christopher. "The Expressive Dimension." *Theoretical Linguistics* 33, no. 2 (2007): 165–98.

Powers, Richard. *Galatea 2.2.* New York: Harper Perennial, 1995.

Powers, William T. *Behavior: The Control of Perception.* Chicago: Aldine, 1975.

Purnell, Thomas, Eric Raimy, and Joseph Salmons. "Defining Dialect, Perceiving Dialect, and New Dialect Formation: Sarah Palin's Speech." *Journal of English Linguistics* 37, no. 4 (2009): 331–55.

Putnam, Hilary. "Meaning and Reference." *Journal of Philosophy* 70, no. 19 (1974): 699–711.

Quaranto, Anne. "Dog Whistles, Covertly Coded Speech, and the Practices That Enable Them." *Synthese* 200, article no. 330 (2022).

Quaranto, Anne. "How to Win Words and Influence Meanings: The Subversive Structure of Slur Reclamation." Unpublished manuscript, 2023. University of Texas at Austin.

Quine, Willard V. O. "Translation and Meaning." In *Word and Object*, 26–79. Cambridge, MA: MIT Press, 2013.

Rao, Jyoti M. "Observations on Use of the N-word in Psychoanalytic Conferences." *Journal of the American Psychoanalytic Association* 69, no. 2 (2021): 315–41.

Rawls, John. *A Theory of Justice.* 1971. Cambridge, MA: Belknap Press of Harvard University Press, 1999.

Reboul, Anne. "Why Language Really Is Not a Communication System: A Cognitive View of Language Evolution." *Frontiers in Psychology* 6, article 1434 (2015): 1–12.

Reddy, M. J. "The Conduit Metaphor: A Case of Frame Conflict in Our Language about Language." In *Metaphor and Thought*, edited by Andrew Ortony, 284–310. Cambridge: Cambridge University Press, 1979.

Richard, Mark. *When Truth Gives Out.* Oxford: Oxford University Press, 2008.

Richardson, Beth H., Paul J. Taylor, Brent Snook, Stacey M. Conchie, and Craig Bennell. "Language Style Matching and Police Interrogation Outcomes." *Law and Human Behavior* 38, no. 4 (2014): 357–66.

Ritchie, Katherine. "Social Identity, Indexicality, and the Appropriation of Slurs." *Croatian Journal of Philosophy* 17, no. 50 (2017): 155–80.

Rogers, Melvin. *The Darkened Light of Faith: Race, Democracy, and Freedom in African-American Political Thought.* Princeton, NJ: Princeton University Press, 2023.

Romero, Daniel M., Roderick I. Swaab, Brian Uzzi, and Adam D. Galinsky. "Mimicry Is Presidential: Linguistic Style Matching in Presidential Debates and Improved Polling Numbers." *Personality and Social Psychology Bulletin* 41, no. 10 (2015): 1311–19.

Rosa, Hartmut. *Resonance: A Sociology of Our Relationship to the World.* New York: John Wiley & Sons, 2019.

Ross, W. D. *Aristotle's Prior and Posterior Analytics: A Revised Text with Introduction and Commentary.* Oxford: Oxford University Press, 1957.

Rouse, Joseph. "Practice Theory." In *Philosophy of Anthropology and Sociology*, edited by Stephen Turner and Mark Risjord, 639–81. Amsterdam: North-Holland, 2007.

Sabatini, Rafael. *Scaramouche: A Romance of the French Revolution.* 1921. New York: W. W. Norton & Company, 2002.

Samuels, Richard. "The Magical Number Two, Plus or Minus: Dual-Process Theory as a Theory of Cognitive Kinds." *In Two Minds: Dual Processes and Beyond*, edited by Jonathan Evans and Keith Frankish, 129–46. Oxford: Oxford University Press, 2009.

Saul, Jennifer. "Dogwhistles, Political Manipulation, and Philosophy of Language." In *New Work on Speech Acts*, edited by Daniel Fogal, Daniel W. Harris, and Matt Moss, 360–83. Oxford: Oxford University Press, 2018.

Saul, Jennifer. *Lying, Misleading, and What Is Said: An Exploration in Philosophy of Language and in Ethics*. Oxford: Oxford University Press, 2012.

Saussure, Ferdinand de. *Course in General Linguistics*. 1916. Translated by Wade Baskin. New York: Columbia University Press, 2011.

Sbisà, Marina. "Ideology and the Persuasive Use of Presupposition." In *Language and Ideology: Selected Papers from the 6th International Pragmatics Conference*, vol. 1, edited by Jef Verschueren, 492–509. Antwerp: International Pragmatics Association, 1999.

Scanlon, Thomas M. "A Theory of Freedom of Expression." In *The Difficulty of Tolerance: Essays in Political Philosophy*, 6–25. Cambridge: Cambridge University Press, 2003.

Schmitt, Carl. *The Concept of the Political*. 1932. Translated by George Schwab. Chicago: University of Chicago Press, 1996.

Scheff, Thomas J. *Microsociology: Discourse, Emotion, and Social Structure*. Chicago: University of Chicago Press, 1990.

Schlenker, Philippe. "Expressive Presuppositions." *Theoretical Linguistics* 33 (2007): 237–45.

Schön, Donald. "Generative Metaphor: A Perspective on Problem-Setting in Social Policy." In *Metaphor and Thought*, edited by Andrew Ortony, 137–63. Cambridge: Cambridge University Press, 1979.

Sedivy, Julie, and Greg Carlson. *Sold on Language: How Advertisers Talk to You and What This Says about You*. New York: John Wiley & Sons, 2011.

Seemann, Axel, ed. *Joint Attention: New Developments in Psychology, Philosophy of Mind, and Social Neuroscience*. Cambridge, MA: MIT Press, 2011.

Senate Resolution 68. "To Establish a Select Senate Committee on Technology and the Human Environment." *Hearings Before the Subcommittee on Intergovernmental Relations of the Committee on Government Operations*, United States Senate, 90th Congress, First Session. Hearing of May 14, 1967. 113 *Cong. Rec.* 24,312 (1967).

Sewell, William H., Jr. "A Theory of Structure: Duality, Agency, and Transformation." *American Journal of Sociology* 98, no. 1 (1992): 1–29.

Shakespeare, William. *As You Like It*. Edited by Juliet Dusinberre. London: Bloomsbury Arden Shakespeare, an imprint of Bloomsbury Publishing Plc., 2016.

Sicoli, Mark A. *Saying and Doing in Zapotec: Multimodality, Resonance, and the Language of Joint Actions*. London: Bloomsbury Academic, 2020.

Simon, Herbert. "A Behavioral Model of Rational Choice." *Quarterly Journal of Economics* 69, no. 1 (1955): 99–118.

Simons, Mandy, Judith Tonhauser, David Beaver, and Craige Roberts. "What Projects and Why." In *Proceedings of Semantics and Linguistic Theory* 20, edited by Nan Li and David Lutz, 309–27. Ithaca, NY: Cornell University, 2010.

Singer, Murray, and Jackie Spear. "Validation of Strongly Presupposed Text Concepts in Reading Comprehension: Cleft Constructions." *Canadian Journal of Experimental Psychology/Revue Canadienne de Psychologie Expérimentale* 74, no. 1 (2020): 1–11.

Smith, Adam. *The Theory of Moral Sentiments*. 1759. Text of 6th ed., 1790. MεταLibri Digital Library, 2006.

Snow, David A., and Robert D. Benford. "Clarifying the Relationship between Framing and Ideology." In *Frames of Protest: Social Movements and the Framing Perspective*, edited by Hank Johnston and John A. Noakes, 205–12. Washington, DC: Rowman & Littlefield, 2005.

Snyder, Timothy. *The Road to Unfreedom: Russia, Europe, America*. New York: Crown Publishing, 2018.

Soames, Scott. "How Presuppositions Are Inherited: A Solution to the Projection Problem." *Linguistic Inquiry* 13, no. 3 (1982): 483–545.

Spinoza, Benedictus de. *The Chief Works of Benedict de Spinoza*. Translated by R. H. M. Elwes. London: George Bell and Sons, 1887.

Stalnaker, Robert. "Assertion." In *Pragmatics*, edited by Peter Cole, 315–32. Syntax and Semantics 9. New York: Academic Press, 1978.

Stalnaker, Robert. *Context and Content*. Oxford: Oxford University Press, 1999.

Stalnaker, Robert. "Intellectualism and the Objects of Knowledge." *Philosophy and Phenomenological Research* 85, no. 3 (2012): 754–61.

Stalnaker, Robert. "On the Representation of Context." *Journal of Logic, Language, and Information* 7 (1998): 3–19.

Stalnaker, Robert. *Our Knowledge of the Internal World*. Oxford: Oxford University Press, 2008.

Stanley, Jason. "The Emergency Manager: Strategic Racism, Technocracy, and the Poisoning of Flint's Children." *The Good Society* 25, no. 1 (2016): 1–45.

Stanley, Jason. *How Propaganda Works*. Princeton, NJ: Princeton University Press, 2015.

Stanley, Jason. *Know How*. Oxford: Oxford University Press, 2011.

St. Clair, Robert N. "Cultural Wisdom, Communication Theory, and the Metaphor of Resonance." *Intercultural Communication Studies* 8 (1999): 79–102.

Steiger, Alexander, and Anton Kühberger. "A Meta-analytic Re-appraisal of the Framing Effect." *Zeitschrift für Psychologie* 226, no. 1 (2018): 45–55.

Stenning, Keith, Jo Calder, and Alex Lascarides. *Introduction to Cognition and Communication*. Cambridge, MA: MIT Press, 2006.

Streeck, Jürgen, and Siri Mehus. "Microethnography: The Study of Practices." In *Handbook of Language and Social Interaction*, edited by Kristine L. Fitch and Robert E. Sanders, 381–404. Mahwah, NJ: Laurence Erlbaum Associates, Inc., 2004.

Stroud, Scott R. "Narrative Rationality." In *The International Encyclopedia of Communication Theory and Philosophy*, edited by Klaus Bruhn Jensen and Robert T. Craig, 1303–10. Oxford: Wiley Blackwell, 2016.

Sunstein, Cass R. "Democracy and Filtering." *Communications of the ACM* 47, no. 12 (2004): 57–59.

Swann, William B., Jr., and Michael D. Buhrmester. "Identity Fusion." *Current Directions in Psychological Science* 24, no. 1 (2015): 52–57.

Swann, William B., Jr., Angel Gómez, D. Conor Seyle, J. Morales, and Carmen Huici. "Identity Fusion: The Interplay of Personal and Social Identities in Extreme Group Behavior." *Journal of Personality and Social Psychology* 96, no. 5 (2009): 995–1011.

Swann, William B., Jr., Jolanda Jetten, Ángel Gómez, Harvey Whitehouse, and Brock Bastian. "When Group Membership Gets Personal: A Theory of Identity Fusion." *Psychological Review* 119, no. 3 (2012): 441–56.

Swanson, Eric. "Slurs and Ideologies." In *Analyzing Ideology: Rethinking the Concept*, edited by Robin Celikates, Sally Haslanger, and Jason Stanley. Oxford: Oxford University Press, forthcoming.

Táíwò, Olúfẹmi. "Beware of Schools Bearing Gifts: Miseducation and Trojan Horse Propaganda." *Public Affairs Quarterly* 31, no. 1 (2017): 1–18.

Tajfel, Henri, and John C. Turner. "An Integrative Theory of Intergroup Conflict." In *The Social Psychology of Intergroup Relations*, edited by William G. Austin and Stephen Worchel, 33–53. Belmont: Wadsworth, 1979.

Tajfel, Henri, John C. Turner, William G. Austin, and Stephen Worchel. "An Integrative Theory of Intergroup Conflict." In *Organizational Identity: A Reader*, edited by Mary Jo Hatch and Majken Schultz, 56–65. Oxford: Oxford University Press, 1979.

Tarantino, Quentin, dir. *Pulp Fiction*. Los Angeles: Miramax, 1995.

Tarde, Gabriel. *Laws of Imitation*. 1890. Translated by Elsie Parson. New York: Henry Holt & Co., 1903.

Tarski, Alfred. "The Semantic Conception of Truth and the Foundations of Semantics." *Philosophy and Phenomenological Research* 4, no. 3 (1944): 341–76.

Taylor, Paul J., and Sally Thomas. "Linguistic Style Matching and Negotiation Outcome." *Negotiation and Conflict Management Research* 1, no. 3 (2008): 263–81.

Templeton, Robin. "Superscapegoating: Teen 'Superpredators' Hype Set Stage for Draconian Legislation." *Extra! The Newsletter of FAIR (Fairness and Accuracy in Reporting)* 11, no. 1 (1998). https://fair.org/extra/superscapegoating/.

Thaler, Richard, and Cass Sunstein. *Nudge: Improving Decisions about Health, Wealth, and Happiness*. New Haven, CT: Yale University Press, 2008.

Thomason, Richmond. "Accommodation, Meaning, and Implicature: Interdisciplinary Foundations for Pragmatics." In *Intentions in Communication*, edited by Phillip Cohen, Jerry Morgan, and Martha E. Pollack, 325–64. Cambridge, MA: MIT Press, 1990.

Thucydides. *The Peloponnesian War*. Translated by Martin Hammond. Oxford: Oxford World's Classics, 2009.

Tirrell, Lynne. "Discursive Epidemiology: Two Models." In *Aristotelian Society Supplementary Volume* 95, no. 1 (2021): 115–42.

Tirrell, Lynne. "Genocidal Language Games." In *Speech and Harm: Controversies over Free Speech*, edited by Ishani Maitra and Mary Kate McGowan, 174–221. Oxford: Oxford University Press, 2012.

Tirrell, Lynne. "Toxic Misogyny and the Limits of Counterspeech." *Fordham Law Review* 87 (2018): 2433–52.

Tirrell, Lynne. "Toxic Speech: Inoculations and Antidotes." *Southern Journal of Philosophy* 56 (2018): 116–44.

Tirrell, Lynne. "Toxic Speech: Toward an Epidemiology of Discursive Harm." *Philosophical Topics* 45, no. 2 (2017): 139–62.

Tonhauser, Judith, David Beaver, and Judith Degen. "How Projective Is Projective Content? Gradience in Projectivity and At-Issueness." *Journal of Semantics* 35, no. 3 (2018): 495–542.

Tonhauser, Judith, David Beaver, Craige Roberts, and Mandy Simons. "Toward a Taxonomy of Projective Content." *Language* 89, no. 1 (2013): 66–109.

Tversky, Amos, and Daniel Kahneman. "The Framing of Decisions and the Psychology of Choice." *Science* 211 (1981): 453–58.

Violent Crime Control and Law Enforcement Act, Public Law No. 103–322, 42 USC 13701, 1994.

Vygotsky, Lev. *Mind in Society: The Development of Higher Psychological Processes*. Cambridge, MA: Harvard University Press, 1978.

Walker, Alice. *The Color Purple*. Orlando, FL: Harcourt, 2003.

Watson-Jones, Rachel E., Harvey Whitehouse, and Cristine H. Legare. "In-Group Ostracism Increases High-Fidelity Imitation in Early Childhood." *Psychological Science* 27, no. 1 (2016): 34–42.

Watzl, Sebastian. "The Philosophical Significance of Attention." *Philosophy Compass* 6, no. 10 (2011): 722–33.

Waxman, Sandra R., and Dana B. Markow. "Words as Invitations to Form Categories: Evidence from 12-to 13-Month-Old Infants." *Cognitive Psychology* 29, no. 3 (1995): 257–302.

Wedeen, Lisa. *Ambiguities of Domination: Politics, Rhetoric, and Symbols in Contemporary Syria*. Chicago: University of Chicago Press, 2015.

Wells, Ida B. *Southern Horrors: Lynch Law in All Its Phases*. 1892. Durham, NC: Duke Classics, 2014.

Wenger, Etienne. "Communities of Practice: Learning as a Social System." *Systems Thinker* 9, no. 5 (1998): 2–3.

Westra, Evan, and Jennifer Nagel. "Mindreading in Conversation." *Cognition* 210 (2021): 1–15.

Wetts, Rachel, and Robb Willer. "Privilege on the Precipice: Perceived Racial Status Threats Lead White Americans to Oppose Welfare Programs." *Social Forces* 2 (2018): 793–822.

Whitehouse, Harvey, and Jonathan A. Lanman. "The Ties That Bind Us: Ritual, Fusion, and Identification." *Current Anthropology* 55, no. 6 (2014): 674–95.

Wiesel, Elie. *Night*. Translated by Marion Wiesel. New York: Farrar, Straus and Giroux, 2006.

Wilkes-Gibbs, Deanna, and Herbert H. Clark. "Coordinating Beliefs in Conversation." *Journal of Memory and Language* 31, no. 2 (1992): 183–94.

Williams, Patricia. "Spirit-Murdering the Messenger: The Discourse of Fingerpointing as the Law Response to Racism." *Miami Law Review* 42 (1987): 127–39.

Williamson, Timothy. "Reference, Inference and the Semantics of Pejoratives." In *The Philosophy of David Kaplan*, edited by Joseph Almog and Paolo Leonardi, 137–58. Oxford: Oxford University Press, 2009.

Witten, Kimberly. "Dogwhistle Politics: The New Pitch of an Old Narrative." Unpublished manuscript, available at https://www.academia.edu/42929858/Dogwhistle_Politics_the_New_Pitch_of_an_Old_Narrative.

Wittgenstein, Ludwig. *The Blue and Brown Books*. Translated by G. E. M. Anscombe. Oxford: Blackwell, 1958.

Wittgenstein, Ludwig. *Philosophical Investigations*. 1953. Translated by G. E. M. Anscombe. Oxford: Blackwell, 1958.

Wittgenstein, Ludwig. *Tractatus Logico-Philosophicus*. 1921. Translated by D. F. Pears and B. F. McGuinness. New York: Routledge, 2001.

Woodly, Deva R. *The Politics of Common Sense: How Social Movements Use Public Discourse to Change Politics and Win Acceptance*. Oxford: Oxford University Press, 2015.

Woolf, Virginia. *Orlando: A Biography*. New York: Houghton Mifflin Harcourt, 1928.

Woolley, Samuel, and Philip Howard, eds. *Computational Propaganda: Political Parties, Politicians, and Political Manipulation on Social Media*. Oxford: Oxford University Press, 2019.

Yabar, Yanelia, Lucy Johnston, Lynden Miles, and Victoria Peace. "Implicit Behavioral Mimicry: Investigating the Impact of Group Membership." *Journal of Nonverbal Behavior* 30, no. 3 (2006): 97–113.

Yudkin, Daniel A., Annayah M. B. Prosser, S. Megan Heller, Kateri McRae, Aleksandr Chakroff, and M. J. Crockett. "Prosocial Correlates of Transformative Experiences at Secular Multi-day Mass Gatherings." *Nature Communications* 13 (2022): 1–13.

Zanni, Guido, and John Offermann. "Eyewitness Testimony: An Exploration of Question Wording Upon Recall as a Function of Neuroticism." *Perceptual and Motor Skills* 46, no. 1 (1978): 163–66.

Zwaan, Rolf A., and Lawrence J. Taylor. "Seeing, Acting, Understanding: Motor Resonance in Language Comprehension." *Journal of Experimental Psychology: General* 135, no. 1 (2006): 1–11.